American Government

Power and Purpose

CORE SEVENTH EDITION

American Government

Power and Purpose

CORE
SEVENTH
EDITION

Theodore J. Lowi
Cornell University

Benjamin Ginsberg
The Johns Hopkins University

and

Kenneth A. Shepsle
Harvard University

W • W • NORTON & COMPANY NEW YORK LONDON

The text of this book is composed in Bodoni Book
with the display set in Bawdy.
Composition by TSI Graphics
Manufacturing by R. R. Donnelley & Sons
Book design by Sandra Watanabe
Production manager: Diane O'Connor
Manuscript editor: Jan Hoeper
Project editor: Christine Habernaas

Library of Congress Cataloging-in-Publication Data

Lowi, Theodore J.
   American government : power and purpose.—7th core ed. / Theodore J. Lowi,
   Benjamin Ginsberg, and Kenneth A. Shepsle.
     p. cm.
   Includes bibliographical references and index.
   ISBN 0-393-97824-9 (pbk.)
    1. United States—Politics and government.   I. Ginsberg, Benjamin. II. Shepsle,
Kenneth A. III. Title.

  JK276.L69   2002
  320.473—dc21

                             2001055838

W. W. Norton & Company, Inc.
500 Fifth Avenue, New York, N.Y. 10110

www.wwnorton.com

W. W. Norton & Company Ltd.
Castle House, 75/76 Wells Street, London W1T 3QT

1 2 3 4 5 6 7 8 9 0

Contents

Preface

Someone once asked if it is difficult for scholars to "write down" to introductory students. No. It is difficult to "write up" to them. Introductory students, of whatever age or reading level, need more, require more, and expect more of a book. A good teaching book, like a good novel or play, is written on two levels. One is the level of the narrative, the story line, the characters in action. The second is the level of character development, of the argument of the book or play. We would not be the first to assert that theater is an aspect of politics, but our book may be unusual to the extent that we took that assertion as a guide. We have packed it full of narrative—with characters and with the facts about the complex situations in which they find themselves. We have at the same time been determined not to lose sight of the second level, yet we have tried to avoid making the second level so prominent as to define us as preachers rather than teachers.

Our collective one hundred-plus years of teaching has taught us not to underestimate students. Their raw intelligence is not satisfied until a second level provides a logic linking the disparate parts of what we were asserting was a single system of government. And these linkages had to be made in ordinary language. We hope we brought this to the book.

We hope also that we brought over from our teaching experience a full measure of sympathy for all who teach the introductory course, most particularly those who are obliged to teach the course from departmental necessity rather than voluntarily as a desired part of their career. And we hope our book will help them appreciate the course as we do—as an opportunity to make sense of a whole political system, one's own, and one of the largest, most durable, and most consequential ever. Much can be learned about the system from a re-examination of the innumerable familiar facts, under the still more challenging condition that the facts be somehow interesting, significant, and, above all, linked.

All Americans are to a great extent familiar with the politics and government of their own country. No fact is intrinsically difficult to grasp, and in such an open society, facts abound. In America, many facts are commonplace that are suppressed elsewhere. The ubiquity of political commonplaces is a problem, but it can be turned into a virtue. These very commonplaces give us a vocabulary that is widely shared, and such a vocabulary enables us to communicate effectively at the first level of the book, avoiding abstract concepts and professional language (jargon).

Reaching beyond the commonplaces to the second level also identifies what is to us the single most important task of the teacher of political science—to confront the million commonplaces and to choose from among them the small number of really significant concepts. Students give us proportion; we must in turn give the students priorities. Virtually everything we need to know about the institutions and processes of government and politics is readily at hand. But to choose a few commonplaces from the millions—there's the rub.

We have tried to provide a framework to help teachers make choices among commonplaces and to help students make some of the choices for themselves. This is good political science, and it is good citizenship, which means more than mere obedience and voting; it means participation through constructive criticism, being able to pierce through the periphery of the great information explosion to the core of lasting political reality.

For six editions, our framework was expressed in the subtitle: *Freedom and Power*. But politics and political science as a tool for understanding it is constantly changing and thus it is our responsibility as authors to keep current with both. In addition, our indispensable editor Steve Dunn thought we needed a good intellectual jolt and suggested a means for providing this jolt. For this seventh edition, we have adopted a new framework and subtitle: *Power and Purpose*. And we are pleased to add a coauthor with definite and well-known views about purposive behavior and its problems in politics—our good friend, distinguished colleague, and occasional adversary Kenneth Shepsle.

Having chosen a framework for the book there was also a need for a method. The method must be loyal to the framework; it must facilitate the effort to choose which facts are essential, and it must assist in evaluating those facts in ways that not only enlighten students but enable them to engage in analysis and evaluation for themselves. Although we are not bound exclusively to a single method in any scientific or philosophic sense, the method most consistently employed is one of history, or history as development: First, we present the state of affairs, describing the legislature, the party, the agency, or policy, with as many of the facts as are necessary to tell the story and to enable us to reach the broader question of freedom versus governmental power. Next, we ask how we have gotten to where we are. By what series of steps, and when by choice, and when by accident? To what extent was the history of Congress or of the parties or the presidency a fulfillment of constitutional principle, and when were the developments a series of dogged responses to economic necessity? History is our method because it helps choose which facts are significant. History also helps those who would like to try to explain why we are where we are. But more important even than explanation, history helps us evaluate consequences.

Consequently, for this new edition, we have added questions about the *purpose* for which our power is used. Government is inevitably a choice-making phenomenon; it is composed of the many institutions we have set out to describe, and the function and place of each of those is to make choices that somehow serve the larger political system and the larger society. Individuals in and around each institution—whether they are employed in it or seeking to influence it from the outside—are making choices. Citizens should be familiar with the choices of governments and make individual judgments when exercising their rights to vote and freedom of speech and petition. America is a pragmatic nation, and pragmatism relies on practicality—knowing the facts and being businesslike about judgments. Pragmatism teaches us to restrain from judging people and institutions by some absolute standard and to try as hard as possible to judge people according to their own goals and their own purposes. Is there some reasonable, rational relation between what someone has chosen and the objective toward which that choice was aimed? We try also to be pragmatic about *collective choices:* How reasonable or rational is the relationship between the choices made by electorates or legislatures or agencies or candidates and the objectives they have defined as well as the objectives defined for them by the Constitution or by some rule of law or propriety?

Thus, as a national culture, Americans engage in a kind of "rational choice analysis" before making our personal choices and before judging the choices made by others, individually or collectively. However, in recent years, a rational choice approach to politics has become a much more explicit and systematic method. Drawing inspiration from economics, rational choice has taken its place as a self-conscious subfield of political science and has begun to make significant contributions to introductory as well as advanced professional approaches to politics and government. This has moved an informal, cultural preference for pragmatic judgment toward a more formal method for advancing analysis and assessment. As authors, we also want to move from a more informal pragmatism toward a more explicit employment of rational choice. We want to employ it to the extent that it strengthens pedagogy, and we want to employ it to the extent that it helps teachers of the course to prepare their students for enlightened and constructively critical citizenship.

Rational choice and history are highly complementary methods. Each brings a pragmatic posture toward politics and government, and both are respectful of institutions as ongoing realities that deserve respect precisely because of their longevity. Yet both methods hold institutions to a standard of proper conduct and constructive function in the here and now. The here and now of choice is called contract; drawing from economics, contract is the essence of rational choice. But in politics, rational choice as method must join history as method in recognition that contract itself must be understood in a historical context. And both methods must draw inspiration from the great eighteenth-century conservative Edmund Burke:

> Society is indeed a contract . . . but the state ought not to be considered as nothing better
> than a partnership agreement . . . to be taken out for a little temporary interest, and to be
> dissolved by the fancy of the parties. . . . It is a partnership . . . not only between those
> who are living, but between those who are living, those who are dead, and those who are to
> be born.[1]

---

[1] Edmund Burke, "Reflections on the Revolution in France in a Letter Intended to Have Been Sent to a Gentleman in Paris [1790]," www.knuten.liu.se/~bjoch509/works/burke/reflections/reflections <01January2002>.

In the matter of government, politics, and the maintenance of order with freedom, we are all conservatives and we are all liberals—conservative in our appreciation that rationality takes place in time and is validated by tradition, and liberal in our steadfast commitment to the right of all to make choices based on personal preference and to criticize all institutions and traditions that fall short of living up to the purposes our generation requires.

Evaluation makes political science all the more valuable but all the more difficult. In academia, a distinction is often made between hard science and soft science, with hard science being the only real science, involving laboratories, people in white coats, precision instruments, and hypotheses based on "hard data." Jared Diamond, a medical scientist uncomfortable with that characterization, has observed that this is a recent and narrow view, considering that science derives from the Latin, "to know," based upon the search for knowledge through careful observation. Diamond suggests, and we agree, that a better distinction is between hard science and easy science, with political science and the other social sciences and history fitting into the hard, or difficult, category and physical science fitting into the easy category. Most of the significant phenomena in the world cannot be put in a test tube and measured to several decimal points. The task of the social sciences is made even more difficult by our obligation to evaluate phenomena in terms of their purpose or function, while physicists, chemists, and others in the "easy" sciences "do not assign a purpose or function to a collision of two gas molecules, nor do they seek an ultimate cause for the collision."[2]

THE DESIGN OF THE BOOK

The objective we have taken upon ourselves in writing this book is thus to advance our understanding of power and purpose by exploring in the fullest possible detail the way Americans have tried to balance the two through careful crafting of the rules, through constructing balanced institutions, and by maintaining moderate forms of organized politics. The book is divided into three parts, reflecting the historical process by which Americans have used governmental power. Part 1, "Foundations," comprises the chapters concerned with the bases of political analysis and the writing of the rules of the "game." The founding of 1787–1789 put it all together, but that was actually a second effort after a first failure. The original contract, the Articles of Confederation, did not achieve an acceptable balance—too much freedom, and not enough power. The second founding, the Constitution ratified in 1789, was itself an imperfect effort to establish the rules, and within two years new terms were added—the first ten amendments, called the Bill of Rights. And for the next century and a half following their ratification in 1791, the courts played umpire and translator in the struggle to interpret those terms. Chapter 1

---

[2]Jared Diamond, *Guns, Germs, and Steel: The Fates of Human Societies* (New York: W.W. Norton, 1997), p. 422.

introduces our five analytical principles of politics. Chapter 2 concentrates on the founding itself. Chapters 3 and 4 chronicle the long struggle to establish what was meant by the three great principles of limited government, *federalism, separation of powers,* and *individual liberties and rights.*

Part 2, "Institutions," includes the chapters sometimes referred to as the "nuts and bolts." But none of these particles of government mean anything except in the larger context of the goals governments must meet and the limits, especially of procedure, that have been imposed upon them. Chapter 5 is an introduction to the fundamental problem of *representative government* as this has been institutionalized in Congress. Congress, with all its problems, is the most creative legislative body in the world. But how well does Congress provide a meeting ground between consent and governing? How are society's demands taken into account in debates on the floor of Congress and deliberations by its committees? What interests turn out to be most effectively "represented" in Congress? What is the modern Congress's constituency?

Chapter 6 explores the same questions for the presidency. Although Article II of the Constitution provides that the president should see that the laws made by Congress are "faithfully executed," the presidency was always part of our theory of representative government, and the modern presidency has increasingly become a law *maker* rather than merely a law implementer. What, then, does the strong presidency do to the conduct and the consequences of representative government? Chapter 7 treats the executive branch as an entity separate from the presidency, but ultimately it has to be brought back into the general process of representative government. That, indeed, is the overwhelming problem of what we call "bureaucracy in a democracy." After spelling out the organization and workings of "the bureaucracy" in detail, we then turn to an evaluation of the role of Congress and the president in imposing some political accountability on an executive branch composed of roughly five million civilian and military personnel.

Chapter 8 on the judiciary should not be lost in the shuffle. Referred to by Hamilton as "the least dangerous branch," the judiciary truly has become a co-equal branch, to such an extent that if Hamilton were alive today he would probably eat his words.

Part 3 we entitle simply "Politics" because politics encompasses all the efforts by any and all individuals and groups inside as well as outside the government to determine what government will do and on whose behalf it will be done. Our chapters take the order of our conception of how politics developed since the Age of Revolution and how politics works today: Chapter 9, "Public Opinion"; Chapter 10, "Elections"; Chapter 11, "Political Parties"; Chapter 12, "Groups and Interests"; and Chapter 13, "The Media."

ACKNOWLEDGMENTS

Our students at Cornell, Johns Hopkins, and Harvard have already been identified as an essential factor in the writing of this book. They have been our most immediate intellectual community, a hospitable one indeed. Another part of our community, perhaps a large suburb, is the discipline of political science itself. Our debt to the scholarship of our colleagues is scientifically measurable, probably to several decimal points, in the footnotes of each chapter. Despite many complaints that the field is too scientific or not scientific enough, political science is alive and well in the United States. It is an aspect of democracy itself, and it has grown and changed in response to the developments in government and politics that we have chronicled in our book. If we did a "time line" on the history of political science, as we have done in each chapter of the book, it would show a close association with developments in "the American state." Sometimes the discipline has been out of phase and critical; at other times, it has been in phase and perhaps apologetic. But political science has never been at a loss for relevant literature, and without it, our job would have been impossible.

There have, of course, been individuals on whom we have relied in particular. Of all writers, living and dead, we find ourselves most in debt to the writing of two—James Madison and Alexis de Tocqueville. Many other great authors have shaped us as they have shaped all political scientists. But Madison and Tocqueville have stood for us not only as the bridge to all timeless political problems; they represent the ideal of political science itself—that political science must be steadfastly scientific in the search for what is, yet must keep alive a strong sense of what ought to be, recognizing that democracy is neither natural nor invariably good, and must be fiercely dedicated to constant critical analysis of all political institutions in order to contribute to the maintenance of a favorable balance between individual freedom and public power.

We are pleased to acknowledge our debt to the many colleagues who had a direct and active role in criticism and preparation of the manuscript. The first edition was read and reviewed by Gary Bryner, Brigham Young University; James F. Herndon, Virginia Polytechnic Institute and State University; James W. Riddlesperger, Jr., Texas Christian University; John Schwarz, University of Arizona; Toni-Michelle Travis, George Mason University; and Lois Vietri, University of Maryland. We also want to reiterate our thanks to the four colleagues who allowed us the privilege of testing a trial edition of our book by using it as the major text in their introductory American Government courses. Their reactions, and those of their students, played an important role in our first edition. We are grateful to Gary Bryner, Brigham Young University; Allan J. Cigler, University of Kansas; Burnet V. Davis, Albion College; and Erwin A. Jaffe, California State University-Stanislaus.

For subsequent editions, we relied heavily on the thoughtful manuscript reviews we received from David Canon, University of Wisconsin; Russell Hanson, Indiana University; William Keech, University of North Carolina; Donald Kettl, University of Wisconsin; Anne Khademian, University of Wisconsin; William McLauchlan, Purdue University; J. Roger Baker, Wittenburg University; James Lennertz, Lafayette College; Allan McBride, Grambling State University; Joseph Peek, Jr., Georgia State University; Grant Neeley, Texas Tech University; Mark Graber, University of Maryland; John Gilmour, College of William and Mary; Victoria Farrar-Myers, University of Texas at Arlington; Timothy Boylan, Winthrop

University; Robert Huckfeldt, Indiana University; Mark Joslyn, University of Kansas; Beth Leech, Texas A&M University; and Charles Noble, California State University, Long Beach. Other colleagues who offered helpful comments based upon their own experience with the text include Douglas Costain, University of Colorado; Robert Hoffert, Colorado State University; David Marcum, University of Wyoming; Mark Silverstein, Boston University; and Norman Thomas, University of Cincinnati.

For the seventh edition, we benefited from the thoughtful comments of Scott Adler, University of Colorado–Boulder; John Coleman, University of Wisconsin–Madison; Richard Conley, University of Florida; Keith Dougherty, Florida International University; John Ferejohn, Stanford University; Douglas Harris, University of Texas at Dallas; Brian Humes, University of Nebraska–Lincoln; Jeffrey Jenkins, Michigan State University; Paul Johnson, University of Kansas; Andrew Polsky, Hunter College–CUNY; Mark Richards, Grand Valley State University; Charles Shipan, University of Iowa; Craig Volden, Claremont McKenna; and Garry Young, University of Missouri–Columbia.

We are also extremely grateful to a number of colleagues who were kind enough to loan us their classrooms. During the past six years, we had the opportunity to lecture at a number of colleges and universities around the country and to benefit from discussing our book with those who know it best—colleagues and students who used it. We appreciate the gracious welcome we received at Austin Community College, Cal State–Fullerton, University of Central Oklahoma, Emory University, Gainesville College, Georgia Southern University, Georgia State University, Golden West College, Grambling State, University of Houston–University Park, University of Illinois–Chicago, University of Illinois–Urbana-Champaign, University of Maryland–College Park, University of Massachusetts–Amherst, Morgan State University, University of North Carolina–Chapel Hill, University of North Texas, University of Oklahoma, Oklahoma State University, Pasadena City College, University of Richmond, Sam Houston State, San Bernadino Valley College, Santa Barbara City College, Santa Monica College, University of Southern California, Temple University, University of Texas–Austin, Texas Tech University, Virginia Commonwealth University, and University of Wisconsin–Madison.

We owe a special debt to Greg Wawro of Columbia University, who served as an intellectual bridge between the sixth and seventh editions and helped us set our sights for future editions of the book. We also are grateful for the talents and hard work of several research assistants, whose contribution can never be adequately compensated: Mingus Mapps, Douglas Dow, John Forren, Michael Harvey, Doug Harris, Brenda Holzinger, Steve McGovern, Melody Butler, Nancy Johnson, Noah Silverman, Rebecca Fisher, David Lytell, Dennis Merryfield, Rachel Reiss, Nandini Sathe, Rob Speel, Jennifer Waterston, and Daniel Wirls. For the seventh edition, Israel Waismel-Manor devoted a great deal of time and energy and original ideas.

Jacqueline Discenza not only typed several drafts of the manuscript, but also helped to hold the project together. We thank her for her hard work and dedication.

Theodore Lowi would like to express his gratitude to the French-American Foundation and the Gannett Foundation, whose timely invitations helped him prepare for his part of this enterprise.

Perhaps above all, we wish to thank those who kept the production and all the loose ends of the book coherent and in focus. Steve Dunn has been an extremely talented editor, continuing to offer numerous suggestions for each new edition. Jan Hoeper has been a superb manuscript editor, following in the great tradition of her predecessors. Diane O'Connor has been an efficient production manager. Denise Shanks brought a vision to the Web site and spent countless hours making it a reality. For their work on previous editions of the book, we want to thank Kathy Talalay, Scott McCord, Margaret Farley, Traci Nagle, Margie Brassil, Stephanie Larson, Sarah Caldwell, Nancy Yanchus, Jean Yelovich, Sandra Smith, Sandy Lifland, Amy Cherry, Roby Harrington, and especially Ruth Dworkin.

We are more than happy, however, to absolve all these contributors from any flaws, errors, and misjudgments that will inevitably be discovered. We wish the book could be free of all production errors, grammatical errors, misspellings, misquotes, missed citations, etc. From that standpoint, a book ought to try to be perfect. But substantively we have not tried to write a flawless book; we have not tried to write a book to please everyone. We have again tried to write an effective book, a book that cannot be taken lightly. Our goal was not to make every reader a political scientist. Our goal was to restore politics as a subject matter of vigorous and enjoyable discourse, recapturing it from the bondage of the thirty-second sound bite and the thirty-page technical briefing. Every person can be knowledgeable because everything about politics is accessible. One does not have to be a television anchorperson to profit from political events. One does not have to be a philosopher to argue about the requisites of democracy, a lawyer to dispute constitutional interpretations, an economist to debate a public policy. We would be very proud if our book contributes in a small way to the restoration of the ancient art of political controversy.

Theodore J. Lowi
Benjamin Ginsberg
Kenneth A. Shepsle
December 2001

PART one

Foundations

CHAPTER one

Five Principles of Politics

3

CORE OF THE ANALYSIS

- Government has become a powerful and pervasive force in the United States.

- All political behavior has a purpose.

- Cooperation through bargaining or collective action is difficult, and the difficulty mounts as the number of people grows.

- Rules and procedures matter.

- Political outcomes are the products of individual preferences and institutional procedures.

- History matters.

Americans often complain about "government interference" with their personal affairs and private property. At the same time, however, they have come to expect a great deal of service from every level of government. After September 11, 2001, most Americans forgot their qualms about "big government." They were willing to accept unprecedented levels of government surveillance in their lives in order to stop terrorist activity.

One example of just how much we demand from our government and the dilemmas and complexities these expectations can create is the 1973 Endangered Species Act (ESA). The ESA was enacted to protect wildlife deemed to be at risk of extinction as a result of man-made or natural processes. The act is primarily administered by the U.S. Fish and Wildlife Service (USFWS), which indicates what species are threatened and determines their "critical habitat." Once a species and its critical habitat are properly designated, the act requires that government agencies refrain from undertaking actions that may have an adverse impact upon them. The U.S. Supreme Court later held that the ESA's prohibitions against harming an endangered species also applied to the actions of private persons on private land.[1] In this particular case, a group of landowners, loggers, and families dependent on forest-product industries were prevented from developing private lands because of an alleged threat to the critical habitat of the red-cockaded woodpecker and the northern spotted owl.[2]

The ESA also contains citizen-suit enforcement provisions allowing "any person" to ask a federal court to either enjoin alleged violations of the act or to compel the government to perform duties required by the act. Citizen suits have become one of the chief mechanisms through which ESA is enforced. In practice, "any person" has not meant individuals: The cost of initiating any action in federal court has limited the "persons" seeking injunctions under the act to environmental interest groups (such as the Defenders of Wildlife and the Sierra Club) that are able to raise money from foundations and member dues and, subsequently, to recover legal costs through fee awards if they win the case.

[1]Babbitt v. Sweet Home Chapter of Communities for a Great Oregon, 516 U.S. 687 (1995).
[2]Fiona M. Powell, "Defining Harm Under the Endangered Species Act: Implications of Babbitt v. Sweet Home," 33 *American Business Law Journal* 131 (1995).

Consistent with their environmental goals, these groups invariably argue in favor of the strictest interpretations of the ESA's provisions.

One group of private citizens that ran afoul of the ESA consisted of cattle and sheep ranchers in Idaho, New Mexico, Montana, and Wyoming. In 1995, under pressure from environmental groups to obey the act's mandate to reintroduce endangered species into their historic habitats, the USFWS began releasing populations of wolves imported from Mexico and Canada into several national parks where they had not existed for many decades.[3] The wolves soon began leaving the parks and attacking livestock and dogs on ranches in surrounding areas. Local ranchers, however, discovered they had little or no legal redress. Under federal law, the government is not liable for the actions of wild animals even when the government itself placed the animals in the area.[4]

Thus, ranchers who felt threatened by the wolves began to kill the animals clandestinely and bury the carcasses where they were unlikely to be found by federal authorities. This practice was known as "shoot, shovel, and shut up." A number of wolves were killed in this manner. A Montana rancher named Chad McKittrick, however, was caught and sentenced to six months in federal prison for killing a gray wolf in Red Lodge, Montana, in October 1995. The wolf was part of a pack of Canadian wolves that had been brought to Yellowstone National Park by the USFWS.

By 1997, the Republican-controlled Congress, responding to a militant new interest, the Western-based property-rights movement, began to develop legislative proposals designed to substantially water down ESA restrictions on private development and land use.[5] In July 2000, the USFWS responded to congressional pressure by proposing rules changes that would allow federal agents, but not ranchers, to kill gray wolves that posed a threat to livestock.[6]

In the meantime, the Supreme Court ruled that commercial interests could use the ESA's citizen-suit provisions to claim that their property rights

THE CENTRAL QUESTIONS

WHAT IS GOVERNMENT AND WHY IS IT NECESSARY?

What are the foundations of government?

Why is government necessary?

What forms can a government take?

How can citizens influence what government does?

WHY DO GOVERNMENTS DO WHAT THEY DO?

What are the five principles that serve as the bases for understanding why government does what it does?

[3]Daniel R. Dinger, "Throwing Canis Lupus to the Wolves," 2000 *Brigham Young University Law Review* 377 (2000).

[4]Sickman v. U.S., 184 F. 2nd 616 (7th Cir. 1950).

[5]Stuart Hardy, "The Endangered Species Act: On a Collision Course With Human Needs," 13 *Public Land Law Review* 87 (1992). Also, Craig Baldauf, "Courts, Congress and Common Killers Conspire to Drive Endangered Species Into Extinction," 30 *Wake Forest Law Review* 113 (1995).

[6]Andrew Revkin, "Rules Shielding the Gray Wolf May Soon Ease," *New York Times*, 3 July 2000, p. 1.

were being violated by aggressive enforcement of the ESA. In other words, ranchers concerned about the reintroduction of wolves or developers accused of encroaching on an endangered bird's critical habitat could now bring suit to charge that the act was being overenforced. A number of commentators suggested that by finally giving property owners and other commercial interests access to the courts, the Court may have saved the ESA by relieving it of congressional pressure.[7] Nevertheless, in 2001, prodded by commercial interests, the new Bush administration announced that it would seek legislation limiting the citizen-suit provisions of the ESA in an effort to prevent environmental groups from using the courts to add new species to the ESA list.[8]

The case of the ESA helps to point out four very important facts about American government. The first of these is the sheer scope of government involvement in American life. In 1789, 1889, and even in 1929, America's national government was limited in size, scope, and influence, and most of the important functions of government were provided by the states. By 1933, however, the influence of the government expanded to meet the crises created by the stock market crash of 1929, the Great Depression, and the run on banks of 1933. Congress passed legislation that brought the government into the business of home mortgages, farm mortgages, credit, and relief of personal distress. Whereas in 1933 people tried to withdraw their money from the banks only to find that their savings had been wiped out, almost seventy years later most are confident that although many savings and loan institutions may be insolvent, their money is still safe because it is guaranteed by the government. Today, the national government is an enormous institution with programs and policies reaching into every corner of American life. It oversees the nation's economy; it is the nation's largest employer; it provides citizens with a host of services; it controls a formidable military establishment; and, as discussed above, it supervises the protection of endangered wildlife. America's founders never dreamed the government could take on such obligations; we today can hardly dream of a time when the government was not such a large part of our lives.

The second important point illustrated by the ESA case is that Americans of all political stripes are ready to turn to the government to solve their problems. Environmentalists sought government help for wildlife. Commercial interests not only sought government help against the environmentalists, but relied upon public land, mining, and logging policies for their livelihoods in the first place. Indeed, there seems to be a consensus nowadays in favor of a large and active government. Even self-styled "conservatives" differ more with their "liberal" counterparts over the proper character of government than over its ultimate desirability. In his 1981 inaugural address, Ronald Reagan, our most conservative president in more than half a century, pledged to curb the growth of the federal

---

[7]Deanne M. Barney, "The Supreme Court Gives an Endangered Act New Life," 73 *North Carolina Law Review* 1889 (1998).

[8]Michael Grunwald, "Bush Seeks to Curb Endangered Species Suits," *Washington Post*, 12 April 2001, p. A2.

establishment but at the same time declared, "Now so there will be no misunderstanding, it is not my intention to do away with government. It is, rather, to make it work."[9] Reagan repeated this sentiment in his 1985 inaugural address. In 1992, in his speech accepting the Democratic presidential nomination, Bill Clinton correctly noted that "the Republicans have campaigned against big government for a generation. . . . But have you noticed? They've run this big government for a generation and they haven't changed a thing.[10]

According to the polls, Americans want to keep the political and economic benefits they believe they derive from government. A survey by the *Washington Post*, for example, revealed that nearly 75 percent of all Americans opposed making any cuts in Social Security and Medicare, although, in theory, most also favor the idea of balancing the federal budget.[11] Social Security and Medicare programs are, of course, major components of the federal government's domestic spending. Indeed, many Americans want the government not only to continue its present involvement but actually to do more in a variety of areas. According to another poll, over half of all voters believe that it is important for the government to provide more services, even if it requires more spending and even if the benefits are indirect, such as protection for endangered wildlife.[12]

A third point the ESA case illustrates is that perfection in government, its institutions, and its policies cannot be achieved. Americans are inveterate believers in the perfectability of institutions. We believe there must be one best way that will satisfy all people of good intentions. However, what if those people of good intentions have genuine and legitimate differences of outlook and interest? The environmentalists in our case believed in a noble principle—saving endangered species from extinction. The ranchers, however, were not evil. They simply sought to protect their cattle and means of livelihood from the depredation of the wolves. How do we resolve issues in which both sides have legitimate, but apparently incompatible, claims? As we shall see, the answer to this question is not a simple one. Political life often requires cooperation and compromise between those with conflicting goals. Such trade-offs, in which all of the involved parties are forced to accept something less than their ideal, are a normal part of politics.

Finally, the fourth point brought to the fore by the ESA example is the complexity of government, politics, and policy. The battle over the reintroduction of wolves into national parks involved a federal statute, regulations issued by an administrative agency, decisions of several courts, congressional amendments to the original statute, and presidential intervention. Various governmental agencies, often responding to very different constituencies, pursued competing goals.

---

[9]"President Reagan's Inaugural Address," *New York Times*, 21 January 1981, p. B1.

[10]E. J. Dionne, "Beneath the Rhetoric, an Old Question," *Washington Post*, 31 August 1992, p. 1.

[11]Eric Pianin and Mario Brossard, "Social Security and Medicare: Sacred Cows," *Washington Post National Weekly Edition*, 7 April 1997, p. 35.

[12]1998 American National Election Study conducted by the Center for Political Studies at the University of Michigan. Data is provided by the Inter-University Consortium for Political and Social Research in Ann Arbor, Michigan.

The courts, for example, were friendly to environmentalists while Congress was more responsive to commercial interests. What we blithely call "the government" is actually a complex arrangement of institutions and processes that are frequently disjointed and often work at cross-purposes. We hope that by the time you have completed this book, you will have a healthy respect for the complexity of government and political life as well as a command of some principles that will allow you to bring some order to this chaos.

WHAT IS GOVERNMENT AND WHY IS IT NECESSARY?

government
Institutions and procedures through which a land and its people are ruled.

autocracy A form of government in which a single individual—a king, queen, or dictator—rules.

oligarchy A form of government in which a small group of landowners, military officers, or wealthy merchants controls most of the governing decisions.

democracy A system of rule that permits citizens to play a significant part in the governmental process, usually through the selection of key public officials.

constitutional government
A system of rule in which formal and effective limits are placed on the powers of the government.

authoritarian government
A system of rule in which the government recognizes no formal limits but may nevertheless be restrained by the power of other social institutions.

Government is the term generally used to describe the formal institutions through which a land and its people are ruled. To govern is to rule. *Government is composed of institutions and processes that rulers establish to strengthen and perpetuate their power or control over a land and its inhabitants.* A government may be as simple as a tribal council that meets occasionally to advise the chief, or as complex as our own vast establishment with its forms, rules, and bureaucracies. This more complex government is sometimes referred to as "the state," an abstract concept referring to the source of all public authority.

Forms of Government

Governments vary in their institutional structure, in their size, and in their modes of operation. Two questions are of special importance in determining how governments differ from each other: Who governs? How much government control is permitted?

In some nations, governing is done by a single individual—a king or dictator, for example. This state of affairs is called ***autocracy.*** Where a small group of landowners, military officers, or wealthy merchants controls most of the governing decisions, that government is said to be an ***oligarchy.*** If more people participate, and if the populace is deemed to have some influence over decision making, that government is tending toward ***democracy.***

Governments also vary considerably in terms of how they govern. In the United States and a small number of other nations, governments are severely limited as to *what* they are permitted to control (substantive limits), as well as *how* they go about it (procedural limits). Governments that are so limited are called ***constitutional,*** or liberal governments. In other nations, including many in Europe as well as in South America, Asia, and Africa, though the law imposes few real limits, a government is nevertheless kept in check by other political and social institutions that the government is unable to control but must come to terms with—such as autonomous territories, an organized church, organized business groups, or organized labor unions. Such governments are generally called ***authoritarian.*** In a third group of nations, including the Soviet Union under Joseph Stalin, Nazi Germany, and perhaps pre–World War II Japan and

Italy, governments not only are free of legal limits but in addition seek to eliminate those organized social groupings that might challenge or limit their authority. These governments typically attempt to dominate or control every sphere of political, economic, and social life and, as a result, are called ***totalitarian.***

Foundations of Government

Whatever their makeup, governments historically have included two basic components: a means of coercion, such as an army or police force, and a means of collecting revenue. These two components have been the essential foundations of government—the building blocks that all individuals and groups who ever sought to rule have been compelled to construct if they were to secure and maintain a measure of control over their territory and its people. Groups aspire to govern for a variety of reasons. Some have the most high-minded aims, while others are little more than ambitious robbers. But whatever their motives and character, those who aspire to rule must be able to secure obedience and fend off rivals as well as collect the revenues needed to accomplish these tasks.[13] Some governments, including many of those in the less developed nations today, have consisted of little more than an army and a tax-collecting agency. Other governments, especially those in the developed nations, have attempted to provide services as well as to collect taxes in order to secure popular consent and control. For some, power is an end in itself. For most, power is necessary for the maintenance of public order. For all, power is needed to permit governments to provide the collective goods and services that citizens want and need but cannot provide for themselves.

The Means of Coercion Government must have the power to order people around, to get people to obey its laws, and to punish them if they do not. Coercion takes many different forms, and each year millions of Americans are subject to one form of government coercion or another. Table 1.1 is an outline of the uses of coercion by federal and state governments in America.

One aspect of coercion is ***conscription,*** whereby government requires certain involuntary services of citizens. The best-known example of conscription is military conscription, which is called "the draft." Although there has been no draft since 1974, there were drafts during the Civil War, World War I, World War II, and the wars in Korea and Vietnam. With these drafts, our government compelled millions of men to serve in the armed forces; one-half million of these soldiers made the ultimate contribution by giving their lives in their nation's service. If the need arose, military conscription would undoubtedly be reinstituted. All eighteen-year-old males are required to register today, just in case.

totalitarian government A system of rule in which the government recognizes no formal limits on its power and seeks to absorb or eliminate other social institutions that might challenge it.

conscription Compulsory military service, usually for a prescribed period or for the duration of a war; "the draft."

[13]For an excellent discussion, see Charles Tilly, "Reflections on the History of European State-Making," in *The Formation of National States of Western Europe*, ed. Charles Tilly (Princeton: Princeton University Press, 1975), pp. 3–83. See also Charles Tilly, "War Making and State Making as Organized Crime," in *Bringing the State Back In*, ed. Peter Evans, Dietrich Rueschemeyer, and Theda Skocpol (New York: Cambridge University Press, 1985), pp. 169–91.

TABLE 1.1

The Means of Coercion		
FORMS	**INSTANCES**	**LEVEL OF GOVERNMENT**
Arrests	11,231,000	Federal, state, and local (1998)
Prison inmates	1,194,581	Federal and state (1997)
Jail inmates	605,943	County and municipal (1999)
Executions	98	State (1999)

SOURCE: U.S. Bureau of the Census, *Statistical Abstract of the United States: 2000* (Washington, DC: U.S. Department of Commerce, 2000).

Military conscription, however, is not the only form of involuntary service that government can compel Americans to perform. We can, by law, be compelled to serve on juries, to appear before legal tribunals when summoned, to file a great variety of official reports, including income tax returns, and to attend school or to send our children to school.

The Means of Collecting Revenue   Each year American governments collect enormous sums from their citizens to support their institutions and programs. Taxation has grown steadily over the years. In 2001, the national government alone collected $972 billion in individual income taxes, $195 billion in corporate income taxes, $682 billion in social insurance taxes, $77 billion in excise taxes, $21 billion in custom duties, and another $40 billion in miscellaneous revenue. The grand total amounted to more than $2 trillion, or almost $7,000 from every living soul in the United States. And of course, while some groups receive more in benefits from the government than they pay in taxes, others get less for their tax dollar. One of the perennial issues in American politics is the distribution of tax burdens versus the distribution of program benefits. Every group would like more of the benefits while passing more of the burdens of taxation onto others.

Why Is Government Necessary?

As we have just seen, control is the basis for government. But what forms of government control are justifiable? To answer this question, we begin by examining the ways in which government makes it possible for people to live together in harmony.

To Maintain Order Human beings usually do not venture out of their caves (or the modern counterpart) unless there is a reasonable probability that they can return safely. But in order for people to live together peacefully, law and order are required, the institutionalization of which is called government. From the standpoint of this definition, the primary purpose of government is to maintain order. But order can only come about by controlling a territory and its people. This may sound like a threat to freedom, until you ponder the absence of government, or anarchy—the absence of rule. According to Thomas Hobbes (1588–1679), author of the first great masterpiece of political philosophy in the English language, anarchy is even worse than the potential tyranny of government, because anarchy, or life outside "the state," is one of "continual fear, and danger of violent death [where life is] solitary, poor, nasty, brutish and short."[14] Governmental power can be a threat to freedom, yet at the same time we need government to maintain order so that we can enjoy our freedom.

To Protect Property After safety of persons comes security of a person's labor, which we call property, or private property. Protection of property is almost universally recognized as a justifiable function of government. John Locke (1632–1704), the worthy successor to Thomas Hobbes, was first to assert clearly that whatever we have removed from nature and also mixed our labor with, is considered our property:

> For this "labour" being the unquestionable property of the laborer, no man but [the laborer] can have a right to what that [labour is joined to]. . . .

But even Locke recognized that although the right to the ownership of what we have produced by our own labor is absolute, it means nothing if someone with greater power than ours decides to take it or trespass on it. As Locke puts it,

> If man . . . be absolute Lord of his own person and possessions . . . why will he part with his freedom . . . ? To which, it is obvious to answer, that the enjoyment of it is very uncertain. . . . This makes him willing to quit this condition, which, however free, is full of fears and continual danger; and it is not without reason that he seeks out and is willing to join in society with others . . . for the mutual preservation of their lives, liberties, and estates.[15]

So, something we call our own *is only ours as long as the laws against trespass* improve the probability that we can enjoy it, use it, consume it, trade it, and sell it. In reality, then, property can be defined as *all the laws against trespass* that not only permit us to call something our own but also to make sure that our claim sticks. In other words, property, that is, private property, is virtually meaningless without a government of laws and policies that makes trespass prohibitive.

---

[14]Thomas Hobbes, *Leviathan* (New York: Macmillan, 1947), p. 82.
[15]This quote and the previous one are from John Locke's masterpiece, *Two Treatises of Government* (London: Everyman, 1993), pp. 178 and 180.

To Provide Public Goods David Hume (1711–1776), another worthy successor to Thomas Hobbes, observed that although two neighbors may agree voluntarily to cooperate in draining a swampy meadow, the more neighbors there are, the more difficult it will be to cooperate in order to get the task done. A few neighbors might clear the swamp because they understand the benefits each of them will receive. But as you expand the number of neighbors who benefit from clearing the swamp, many neighbors realize that all of them can get the same benefit if only a few clear the swamp and the rest do nothing. This is an example of *free riding*. A *public* (or collective) *good* is therefore a benefit that neighbors or members of a group cannot be kept from enjoying once any individual or small minority of members have provided the benefit for themselves—the clearing of the swamp, for example, or national defense, for another example. National defense is one of the most important public goods—especially when the nation is threatened by war or terrorism. Without government's coercive powers through a policy (backed by taxation) to build a bridge, produce an army, provide a swamp-free meadow, "legal tender," or uniform standards of weights and measures, there is no incentive, in fact very often there is a *dis*incentive, for even the richest, most concerned members to provide the benefit.[16]

Although public order, the protection of property, and the provision of public goods are justifications for government, they are not justifications for all its actions. A government's actions can only be justified by the people being governed. This is why government would be intolerable without politics. With politics, we have at least a faint hope that a government's actions can be influenced in some way.

Influencing the Government: Politics

In its broadest sense, the term "politics" refers to conflicts over the character, membership, and policies of any organization to which people belong. As Harold Lasswell, a famous political scientist, once put it, politics is the struggle over "who gets what, when, how."[17] Although politics is a phenomenon that can be found in any organization, our concern in this book is more narrow. Here, politics will be used to refer only to conflicts and struggles over the leadership, structure, and policies of *governments*. The goal of politics, as we define it, is to have a share or a say in the composition of the government's leadership, how the government is organized, or what its policies are going to be. Having a share is called *power* or *influence*. Most people are eager to have some "say" in matters affecting them; witness the willingness of so many individuals over the past two centuries to risk

---

free riding
Enjoying the benefits of some good or action and letting others bear the costs.

public good A good that (1) may be enjoyed by anyone if it is provided, and (2) that may not be denied to anyone once it has been provided.

Analyzing American Politics
www.wwnorton.com/lowi7/ch1

Analyze the variety of public goods provided by different levels of government in the United States.

---

[16]The most instructive treatment of the phenomenon of public goods and the "free rider" is Mancur Olson, *The Logic of Collective Action: Public Goods and the Theory of Groups* (Cambridge: Harvard University Press, 1965 and 1971), pp. 33–43, esp. footnote 53.

[17]Harold Lasswell, *Politics: Who Gets What, When, How* (New York: Meridian Books, 1958).

their lives for voting rights and representation. In recent years, of course, Americans have become more skeptical about their actual "say" in government, and many do not bother to vote. This increased skepticism, however, does not mean that Americans no longer want to have a share in the governmental process. Rising levels of skepticism mean, rather, that many Americans doubt the capacity of the political system to provide them with influence.

WHY DO GOVERNMENTS DO WHAT THEY DO?

Choosing between cheese pizza and pepperoni pizza may not seem like a political decision, but American government has made it one. The Food and Drug Administration (FDA) regulates the safety of cheese pizza, while pepperoni pizza is the responsibility of the U.S. Department of Agriculture (USDA).[18] All totaled, the federal government's efforts to maintain a safe food supply—from meat, poultry, and seafood to fresh produce, frozen foods, and the use of pesticides—are guided by more than thirty-five laws and divided among twelve federal government agencies.[19] In the early 1900s, shocking disclosures in the meatpacking industry spurred political actions that quickly brought the federal government into a novel commitment to try to regulate food safety. In the ensuing decades, new federal laws were adopted in response both to new risks and to new efforts to set standards for different foods.[20] Some of the laws were housed in the FDA, but others were housed in new agencies and different departments. There was never a clear blueprint for any of this; politics imposed its influence on government in a haphazard way. Today, the USDA focuses on meat and poultry, employing more than seven thousand inspectors who examine every carcass in the nation's slaughter houses. The USDA is supervised by the House and Senate Agriculture Committees. The FDA, which was once part of the USDA and now (since 1988) is in the Department of Health and Human Services, is responsible for most other food products, including produce and seafood. It is overseen by the House Energy and Commerce Committee and the Senate Health, Education, Labor, and Pensions Committees. Ten other agencies are involved in one aspect or another of food safety.

Many have argued that government regulation of food safety should be handled by just one agency rather than the current twelve. Yet, proposals of this sort, while rational, are considered "dead on arrival" when submitted as bills in the House or Senate. Each of the twelve agencies is linked to different

---

[18]Allan Freedman, "Battles Over Jurisdiction Likely to Keep Congress from Merging Food Agencies," *Congressional Quarterly Weekly*, 30 May 1998.

[19]Allan Freedman, "Unsafe Foods Spark Outbreaks of Concern, Little Action," *Congressional Quarterly Weekly*, 30 May 1998.

[20]"Milestones in U.S. Food and Drug Law History," FDA Backgrounder, FDA Web site (http://www.fda.gov/opacom/backgrounders/miles.html).

congressional committee jurisdictions and each is tied to different interests or interest groups—from dairy farmers to restaurant associations to the meat industry to consumer groups. These groups, and members of Congress with a stake in one or another of these agencies, are reluctant to risk losing influence by moving everything into one new agency; thus, battles over jurisdiction become "turf wars."[21] Consequently, all of the interested groups and members of Congress continue to disagree with each other on a number of things. One thing they do agree about, however, is to prevent the reform.

The multitude of interests, the difficulty in getting people to agree on political goals and to act together to accomplish them, the accumulation of rules, laws, and official bodies, the layering of policies, and the sheer weight of history—these are the aspects of political life on which we draw to understand and explain the complex politics of pizza regulation and other facets of public life. The food-safety example provides a basis for five principles that will help us in our effort to understand why government does what it does:

> Principle 1: All political behavior has a purpose.
> Principle 2: Cooperation through bargaining or collective action is difficult, and the difficulty mounts as the number of people grows.
> Principle 3: Rules and procedures matter.
> Principle 4: Political outcomes are the products of individual preferences and institutional procedures.
> Principle 5: History matters.

Principle 1: All Political Behavior Has a Purpose— or, People Have Goals

One compelling reason why governments do what they do is that all people have goals and they work to achieve those goals through their political behavior. For many citizens, political behavior is as simple as reading a headline or editorial in the newspaper while drinking their morning coffee or discussing the latest local political controversy with a neighbor over the back fence. Though political, these actions are basically routines of everyday life. Beyond these almost perfunctory acts, citizen political behavior broadens out to include still relatively modest activities like watching a political debate on television, arguing about politics with a co-worker, signing a petition, or attending a city council meeting. These are understood to be explicitly political activities that require some forethought and advanced reflection—these are discretionary *choices* rather than mechanical *acts* like accidentally catching a political headline in the newspaper on your way to the sports section, the comics, or the movie listings. Political behavior requiring even more "premeditation"—even

---

[21]Allan Freedman, "Battles Over Jurisdiction Likely to Keep Congress from Merging Food Agencies," *Congressional Quarterly Weekly*, 30 May 1998.

calculation—includes going to the polls and casting a vote in the November election (having first registered in a timely manner), writing one's legislative representatives about a political issue, contributing time or money to a political campaign, or even running for local office.

Some of these acts require effort, time, financial resources, and courage, while others place small, even insignificant, demands on a person. Nevertheless, all of these acts are done for specific reasons. They are not random; they are not entirely automatic or mechanical, even the smallest of them. Sometimes they are engaged in for the sake of entertainment (reading the front page in the morning), or just to be sociable (chatting about politics with a neighbor, co-worker, or family member). At other times, they take on considerable personal importance explicitly because of their political content—because an individual cares about, and wants to influence, an issue, a candidate, a party, or a cause. We will treat all of this political activity as *purposeful*, as having a point. Indeed, our attempts to discern the point of various political activities will help us to understand them better.

We've just noted that many political activities of ordinary citizens are hard to distinguish from conventional everyday behavior—reading newspapers, watching television news, discussing politics, and so on. For the professional politician, on the other hand—legislator, executive, judge, party leader, bureau chief or agency head—nearly everything he or she does is political. The legislator's decision to introduce a particular piece of legislation, to give a speech in the legislative chamber, to move an amendment to a pending bill, to vote for or against that bill, or to accept a contribution from a PAC[22] requires the politician's careful attention. There are pitfalls and dangers, however, and the slightest miscalculation can have huge consequences. Introduce a bill that appears to be too pro-labor in the eyes of your constituents, for example, and before you know it you're charged with being in bed with the unions during the next election campaign. Give a speech against job quotas for minorities, and you set yourself up to have your words turned against you by an electoral opponent, risking your standing with the minority communities in your state or district. Accept campaign contributions from local businesspeople, and environmentalists think you are no friend of the earth. Nearly every move a legislator makes is fraught with risks. And because of these risks, legislators think about their moves before they make them—sometimes carefully, sometimes not; sometimes correctly, sometimes not. But whatever actions they take, or decide against taking, they do so with forethought, with deliberation, with calculation. Their actions are not knee-jerk, but are, in a word, ***instrumental.*** Individuals think through the benefits and the costs of a decision, speculate about future effects, and weigh the risks of their decision. Making decisions is all about weighing probabilities of various events and determining the personal value of various outcomes.

instrumental To do something with purpose, sometimes requiring forethought and even calculation.

---

[22]A PAC (political action committee) is a group established by an interest group, labor union, or some other political organization to collect donations and distribute them as campaign contributions to candidates and political parties.

Principle 2: Cooperation through Bargaining and Collective Action Is Difficult, and the Difficulty Mounts as the Number of People Grows—or, All Politics Is Collective Action

The second factor that helps explain why governments do what they do is that political action is collective, involving the building, combining, mixing, and amalgamating of the individual goals of people. They join together in order to achieve these goals. But, as we shall see, collective action can be very difficult to orchestrate since the individuals involved in the decision-making process often have somewhat different goals and preferences. The result is mixed motives for cooperation. Conflict is inevitable: the question is how it can be resolved. The most typical and widespread means is bargaining, involving a small number of individuals. But when the number of parties involved is too large to engage in face-to-face bargaining, incentives must be provided to get everyone to act collectively.

Informal Bargaining Political bargaining is a process that may be highly formal or entirely informal. Relations among neighbors, for example, are usually based on informal give-and-take. To give a personal example, one of this book's authors has a neighbor with whom he shares a privet hedge on the property line. First one takes responsibility for trimming the hedge, and then the other, alternating from year to year. This arrangement is merely an "understanding," not a legally binding agreement, and it was reached amicably and without much fuss or fanfare after a brief conversation. No organizational effort was required—like hiring lawyers, drafting an agreement, having it signed, witnessed, notarized, filed at the county courthouse, and so on.

Bargaining in politics can also be informal and unstructured. Whether called horse-trading, back-scratching, logrolling, or wheeling-and-dealing, it has much the same flavor as the casual, over-the-fence negotiations among neighbors just described. Deals will be struck depending upon the preferences and beliefs of the participants. If preferences are too incompatible, or beliefs too inconsistent with one another, then a deal simply may not be in the cards. On the other hand, if preferences and beliefs are not too far out of line, then there will be a range of possible bargaining outcomes, some of which slightly advantage one party, others of which advantage other parties. But all deals in this range are at least acceptable to all the parties involved.

In fact, much of politics *is* informal, unstructured bargaining. First, many disputes subjected to bargaining are of sufficiently low impact that it is just not worth establishing elaborate formal machinery for dealing with them. Rules of thumb often develop as a benchmark—such as "split the difference" or "take turns" (the outcome of the hedge-trimming example given earlier). Second, there is repetition. If a small group engages in bargaining today over one matter and tomorrow over another—as neighbors bargain over draining a meadow one day, fixing a fence another, and trimming a hedge on still another occasion—then patterns develop. If one party constantly tries to extract maximal advantage, then the other parties will undoubtedly cease doing business with her. If, on the other hand, each party "gives a little" in order to "get a little," reciprocating kindness at one point with kindness at another, then a pattern of cooperation develops over time. It is the repetition of mixed-motive occasions that allows this pattern to emerge without formal trappings. Many political circumstances are either amenable to rules of thumb like those mentioned above or are repeated with sufficient frequency so as to allow cooperative patterns to emerge.

Formal Bargaining   Formal bargaining entails interactions among bargainers that are governed by rules. The rules describe such things as who gets to make the first offer, how long the recipient parties have to consider it, whether recipient parties must "take it or leave it" or can make counteroffers, the method by which they convey their assent or rejection, what happens when all (or some decisive subset) of the others accept or reject, what transpires next if the proposal is rejected, and so on. One could not imagine two neighbors deciding how to trim their common hedge under procedures as explicit and formal as these. One could, however, imagine a bargaining session over wages and working conditions between labor and management at the local manufacturing plant proceeding in just this manner. This suggests that some parties are more appropriately suited to formal proceedings, whereas others get on well enough without them. The same may be said about situations. A husband and wife are likely to divide household chores by informal bargaining, but this same couple would employ a formal procedure if it were household assets they were dividing (in a divorce settlement).

Formal bargaining is often associated with events that take place in official institutions—legislatures, courts, party conventions, administrative and regulatory agencies. These are settings in which mixed-motive situations arise over and over again. Year in and year out, legislatures pass statutes, approve executive budgets, and oversee the administrative branch of government. Courts administer justice, determine guilt or innocence, impose sentences, resolve differences between disputants, and render interpretive opinions about the meaning of the law. Party conventions nominate candidates and approve the platforms on which they base their campaigns. Administrative and regulatory agencies implement policy and make rulings about their applicability. All of these are instances of mixed-motive circumstances where gains from cooperation are possible, but bargaining failures are also a definite possibility. Consequently, the formal bargaining that takes place under the aegis of institutions is governed by rules that regularize proceedings both to maximize the prospects of reaching agreement and to guarantee that procedural "wheels" don't have to be reinvented each time a similar bargaining problem arises.

Collective Action   The idea of political bargaining suggests an "intimate" kind of politics, involving face-to-face relations, negotiation, compromise, give-and-take, and so on. Such bargaining results from the combination of mixed motives and small numbers. When the numbers become large, bargaining may no longer be practical. If one hundred people own property bordering a swampy meadow, or if a privet hedge runs the length of Main Street in a small town, insulating hundreds of households from the street, then how do these communities solve the swamp's mosquito problem or resolve to trim the hedge to a common height? How do these communities secure the dividends that arise from cooperation?

These are clearly mixed-motive situations. Everyone shares some common values—eliminating the mosquito habitat, or giving the hedge the look of uniformity—but they may disagree on other matters. Some may want to use pesticides in the meadow, while others are concerned about the environmental impact. Some may want the privet hedge cut very short, allowing it to be maintained easily by each household; others may want it kept tall to shield homes from street noise. And in both situations there are bound to be disagreements over how to pay for the project. The collective action problem arises, as in these examples, when there is something to be gained if the group can cooperate and assure group members that some do not get away with bearing less than their fair share of the effort. Face-to-face bargaining, however, is compromised by sheer numbers. The issue, then, is how to accomplish some common objective when explicit bargaining is not an option.

collective action The pooling of resources and coordination of effort and activity by a (often large) group of people to achieve common goals.

Groups of individuals intent upon ***collective action*** will ordinarily establish some decision-making procedures—relatively formal arrangements by which to resolve differences, coordinate the group around a course of action, and sanction slackers, if necessary. Most groups will also require a structure of leadership, which is necessary even if all the members of the group are in agreement about how to proceed. This is due to a phenomenon that we saw in the swamp-draining example above: free riding. Each owner of land bordering the swamp wants the area cleared. But if one or a few owners were to clear the swamp alone, their actions would benefit all the other owners as well, without any efforts on the part of those other owners. Those owners would be free riders. It is this prospect of free riding that risks undermining collective action. A leadership structure will have to be in place to threaten and, if necessary, inflict punishments to discourage individuals from reneging on the individual contributions required to enable the group to pursue its common goals.

by-product theory The idea that groups provide members with private benefits to attract memberships; the possibility for group collective action emerges as a side consequence.

Various solutions to the collective action problem have been proposed. The most famous is Mancur Olson's ***by-product theory.***[23] Briefly, Olson's idea is this: the nub of free riding derives from the fact that most individuals in a large group don't make much difference to the final result, and they know it. This is why they may comfortably abstain from participation—they know that in following their inclination to avoid the costs of participation, they do not damage their prospects (or anyone else's) for receiving benefits. The problem is that while no one person's free riding does much harm, if enough people free ride, then the purpose of the

---

[23]On the general subject of collective action, the interested reader should consult Shepsle and Bonchek, *Analyzing Politics*, Chapter 9, where Olson's work, among others, is taken up.

collective action will be compromised. What if, however, something of value were at stake that would be lost if the person abstained from participation? What if participants were given something special that non-participants were denied? That is, what if some benefits were contingent on contributing to the group effort? Many organizations use this tactic, giving dues-paying or effort-contributing members special insurance or education benefits, reduced-fare travel, free or subsidized subscriptions to magazines and newsletters, bowling and golf tournaments, soccer leagues, access to members-only social events, and so on. Olson argued that if members were prepared to "pay their dues" to join an organization partially (or even mainly) for these special benefits of which they would otherwise be deprived—what Olson called *selective benefits*—then the collective cooperation would end up being provided as well, *as a by-product*, with whatever surplus the dues structure generated. A member's inclination to free ride would be alleviated, not because of feelings of obligation to his or her fellow members, not because of a moral imperative to participate, not even because of a desire for the collective benefit supplied by the group, but rather because of naked self-interest—the desire for selective benefits! Clearly this is an extreme version of the argument; the main point here is that the selective benefits available only to participants and contributors—and denied to nonparticipants and noncontributors—are the key to successful collective action. A group that appeals to its members *only* on the basis of its common collective purposes is a group that will have trouble achieving those purposes.[24]

selective benefits Benefits that do not go to everyone, but rather are distributed selectively—only to those who contribute to the group enterprise.

Individuals try to accomplish things not only as individuals but also as members of larger collectivities—families, friendship groups, clubs and associations, political parties, and in larger categories like economic class, ethnicity, and nationality. Principle 1 covers individual initiative. Principle 2 describes the paradoxes encountered, the obstacles that must be overcome, and the incentives necessary for individuals to combine with like-minded others in order to coordinate their energies, accomplish collective purposes, and secure the dividends of cooperation. Much of politics is about doing this, or failing to do this. The next principle takes this argument to its logical conclusion, focusing on collective activities that are regularized because they are both important and frequently occurring. Institutions do the public's business while relieving communities of having to reinvent collective action each time it is required. Here we provide a rationale for government.

---

[24]Getting such an organizational effort up and running, however, is no mean feat. Olson's argument appreciates what is necessary to keep a group going, but underestimates what it takes to organize collective action in the first place. Put differently, a prior collective action problem needs to be solved—an organizational problem. The solution is leadership, and the individuals imaginative enough to see this need are referred to as *political entrepreneurs*. That is, there must be a selective benefit available to those who bear organizational burdens, thereby facilitating the collective action; the selective benefits of leadership include perquisites of office, financial reward, honor and status, etc.

Principle 3: Rules and Procedures Matter—or, Institutions Are the Forces that Shape Politics

In the last section, we looked at the conditions in which people engage in bargaining, cooperation, and collective action in order to solve some political problem. As people, especially elected leaders and other government officials, repeatedly are required to confront recurring problems, they develop routines and standard ways of dealing with things. In a word, responses to regularly recurring problems are *institutionalized*. Collective action results because standard procedures and rules are established that provide people with appropriate incentives to take the action necessary to solve the problems. Routinized, structured relations are what we call ***institutions.*** What interests students of politics most is how institutions discourage conflict, enable bargaining, and thus facilitate decision making, cooperation, and collective action.

institutions
Rules and procedures that provide incentives for political behavior, thereby shaping politics.

Institutions are part script and part scorecard. As scripts they choreograph political activity. As scorecards, they list the players, their positions, what they want, what they can do, and when they can do it. While the Constitution sets the broad framework, much adaptation and innovation takes place as the institutions themselves are bent to the various political purposes of strategic political actors who want to win for their side and defeat the other side. Our focus here will be on the authority that institutions provide politicians for the pursuit of public policies. The discussion is divided into four broad subjects: jurisdiction, decisiveness, agenda and veto power, and delegation and transaction costs.

Jurisdiction   A critical feature of an institution is the designation of who has the authority to apply the rules or make the decisions; members recognize the jurisdiction of the main players and are quick to impose limits on these players if they feel jurisdictional authority has been exceeded. Political institutions are full of specialized jurisdictions. One of the most unusual features of the U.S. Congress is the existence of the "standing committee," whose jurisdictions are rather carefully defined in law. Some members of Congress are generalists, but most members become specialists in all aspects of the jurisdiction of their committees—and they often seek committee assignments based on the subject in which they want to specialize. Committee members are granted specific authority within their jurisdiction to set the agenda of the larger parent chamber. Thus, the legislative institution in the United States is affected by the way its jurisdiction-specific committees are structured.

Decisiveness   Another crucial feature of an institution is its rules for making decisions. It might sound like a straightforward task to lay out what the rules for deciding are, but it really isn't so easy to do without a raft of conditions and qualifications. Every institutionalized organization has procedural rules, and the more an organization values participation by the broadest range of its members, the more it actually needs these rules: the requirement of participation must be balanced with the need to bring discussion and activity to a close at some point so that an actual decision can be made! This is why one of the most privileged motions that can be made on the floor of a legislature is "to move the previous question," a motion to close the debate and to move immediately to a vote.[25] It is no accident that *Deschler's Procedures*, a book of rules and interpretations about procedure in the House of Representatives, runs to more than six hundred pages! Its companion for the U.S. Senate, *Jefferson's Manual*, is shorter but no less intricate.[26] Institutions are complicated as are descriptions of what constitutes a decision and the conditions under which it can be made.

Even juries have rules for decisiveness; if discussion goes on too long among the members, the judge may in fact declare a *hung jury*, leading to a new trial and another round of discussion. In most organizations, including corporations, the decision to close discussion is left in the hands of the presiding officer, who might simply ask for a motion to vote on the issue in question. But even such a ruling by the chair can be appealed if the participants decide that they have not discussed the matter enough to decide.

Agenda Power and Veto Power   If decisiveness characterizes what it takes to win, then **agenda power** describes who determines what will be taken up for consideration in the first place. Those who exercise some form of agenda power are said to engage in *gate keeping*. They determine what alternatives may pass through the gate onto the agenda, and which ones have the gate slammed in their face. Gate keeping, in other words, consists of the power to make proposals and the power to block proposals from being made. The ability to keep something off an institution's agenda should not be confused with **veto power**. The latter is the ability to defeat something, *even if it does become part of the agenda*. In the legislative process, for example, the president has (limited) veto power. Congress cannot be prevented from taking up a particular bill—the president does not have agenda power in Congress. They cannot be prevented from passing such a measure—the president has no power to block in Congress. But a presidential veto can prevent the measure from becoming the law of the land.[27]

agenda power
Control over what the group will consider for discussion.

veto power   The ability to keep an item or notion off the agenda or to defeat it if it does come up for consideration.

---

[25]For a general discussion of motions to close debate and get on with the decision, see Henry M. Robert, *Robert's Rules of Order* (1876), items III, #21, and VI, #38. *Robert's* has achieved the status of an icon and now exists in an enormous variety of forms and shapes, but the basic principles remain. See, for example, *Robert's Rules of Order*, rev. ed., Darwin Patnod (Uhrichsville, Ohio: Barbour & Company, n.d.).

[26]Lewis Deschler was the long-time Parliamentarian of the House of Representatives who, for many years, kept track of House rules, precedents, and interpretations on little slips of paper stored in his desk in the Capitol. Finally, in the 1970s, he was prevailed upon to codify these. Thomas Jefferson, of course, was the third president of the United States. Before that, while he was vice president under President John Adams, he presided over the U.S. Senate (one of the few duties specified in the Constitution). This, apparently, was not an arduous task for Jefferson, for he had the time to study rules of procedure and write down a body of rules for the Senate that has survived mostly intact for more than two centuries.

[27]Article I, Section 7, of the Constitution specifies that a bill becomes a law in either of two ways: (1) a majority of the House and Senate approve it, and it is signed by the president, or (2) a majority of each chamber approves a measure, the president *vetoes* it, and then, upon Congressional reconsideration, at least two-thirds of each chamber approves the measure.

Delegation and Transaction Costs   Representative democracy is the quintessential instance of ***delegation*** in which citizens, through voting, delegate the authority to make decisions on their behalf to representatives—chiefly legislators and executives—rather than exercising political authority directly.[28] We think of our political representatives as our *agents*, just as we think of professionals and craftsmen whose services we retain—doctors, lawyers, accountants, plumbers, mechanics, and so on—as agents whom we hire to act on our behalf. Now, why would those with authority, whom we will call *principals*, delegate some of their authority to agents? In effect, we are asking about the virtues of decentralization and of a division and specialization of labor. The answer is that both principals and agents benefit from it. Principals benefit because they are able to off-load tasks that they themselves are far less capable of performing to experts and specialists. Ordinary citizens, for example, are not as well versed in the tasks of governance and other forms of collective action as are professional politicians. Thus, by delegating, citizens do not have to be specialists and can focus their energies on other things. This is the rationale for representative democracy.

This same rationale applies to the division and specialization of labor we often observe in specific political institutions. Legislators generally benefit from a decentralized arrangement in which they focus on those aspects of public policy for which they are best equipped—issue areas of special interest to their constituents or on which their prior occupational and life experiences give them familiarity and perspective. In exchange, they are freed from having to be policy generalists, avoiding areas of little interest or relevance to them. The legislative committee system accomplishes this by partitioning policy into different jurisdictions and allowing legislators to gravitate to those committees that most suit their purposes.

The delegation principle, in which a principal delegates authority to an agent, seems almost too good to be true. And it is! Even though both principals and agents benefit, there is a dark side to this relationship too which we generally refer to as ***principal-agent problems.*** As the eighteenth-century economist Adam Smith noted in his classic, *The Wealth of Nations*, economic agents are not motivated by the welfare of their customers to grow vegetables, make shoes, or weave cloth; rather, they do these things out of their own self-interest. Thus, a principal must take care when delegating to agents that these agents are properly motivated to serve the principal's interests, either by sharing the principal's interests or by deriving something of value (reputation, compensation, etc.) for acting to advance those interests. Alternatively, the principal will need to have some instruments by which to monitor and validate what his or her agent is doing and then reward or punish the agent accordingly. Nevertheless, a principal will not bother to eliminate *entirely* the agent's prospective deviations from the

---

delegation
Transmitting authority to some other official or body for the latter's use (though often with the right of review and revision).

principal-agent problems The tension that exists potentially between a principal and his or her agent caused by the fact that each is motivated by self-interest, yet their interests may not be well aligned.

---

[28]A surviving vestige of the direct exercise of political authority is the New England town meeting. This institution still exists in one form or another throughout states in the Northeast. Increasingly, however, town meetings occur only occasionally, with day-to-day governance delegated to an advisory committee and to an elected board of selectmen.

principal's interests. The reason is ***transaction costs.*** The organizational effort necessary to negotiate and then police every aspect of a principal-agent relationship becomes, at some point, more costly than it is worth.

Characterizing institutions in terms of jurisdiction, decisiveness, agenda and veto power, and delegation and transaction cost, covers an immense amount of ground. Our purpose here has been to introduce the reader to the multiplicity of ways collectivities arrange their business, routinize it, and thereby facilitate the recurring political requirements of bargaining and collective action. A second purpose has been to impress upon the reader the potential diversity in institutional arrangements—there are so many ways to do things collectively—for this underscores the amazing sophistication and intelligence of the framers of the U.S. Constitution in the institutional choices they made more than two centuries ago. Finally, we want to make clear that institutions not only comprise rules for governing, but they also describe strategic opportunities for various political interests—opportunities to influence the agenda, to engineer political action, or to block it. As George Washington Plunkitt, the savvy and candid political boss of Tammany Hall, said of the institutional situations in which he found himself, "I seen my opportunities, and I took 'em."[29]

transaction costs
The cost of clarifying each aspect of a principal-agent relationship and monitoring it to make sure arrangements are complied with.

Principle 4: Political Outcomes Are the Products of Individual Preferences and Institutional Procedures—or, Policy Results when Political Goals Meet Institutions

At the end of the day, politics is about policy. It is about the collective decisions that emerge from the political process, and the consequences of these decisions for individuals. A Nebraska farmer is not much interested in the various facets of institutions we've just described, even those concerning the House Agriculture Committee. What he does care about is how public laws and rulings affect his welfare and that of his family, friends, and neighbors. He cares about how export policies affect the prices his crops and livestock products earn in international markets; how monetary policy influences inflation and, as a result, the cost of purchasing fuel, feed, seed, and fertilizer; research and development efforts, both public and private, and their impact on the quality and reliability of scientific information he obtains; the affordability of the state university where he hopes to educate his children; and he cares, eventually, about inheritance laws and their effect on his ability to pass his farm on to his kids without Uncle Sam taking a huge chunk of it in estate taxes. As students of American politics, we need to consider the link between institutional arrangements and policy outcomes. Do the organizational features of institutions leave their marks on policy? What biases, predilections, and tendencies manifest themselves in policies?

[29]Tammany Hall was the club that ran the Democratic Party in New York City as a machine in the nineteenth century and well into the twentieth century.

The linchpin connecting institutions to policy is the motivations of political actors. As we saw earlier in our discussion of Principle 1, their ambitions—ideological, personal, electoral, and institutional—provide politicians with the incentives to craft policies in particular ways. In fact, most policies make sense only as reflections of individual politicians' interests, goals, and beliefs. Examples include:

> Personal interests—Congressman Xcitement is an enthusiastic supporter of subsidizing home heating oil (but opposes regulation to keep its price down) because some of his friends own heating-oil distributorships.[30]

> Electoral ambitions—Senator Yougottabekidding, a well-known political moderate, has lately been introducing very conservative amendments to bills dealing with the economy in order to appeal to more conservative financial donors who might then contribute to her budding presidential campaign.

> Institutional ambitions—Representative Zeal has promised his vote and given a rousing speech on the House floor supporting a particular amendment because he knows it is near and dear to the Speaker's heart. He hopes his support will earn him the Speaker's endorsement next year for an assignment to the prestigious Appropriations Committee.

These examples illustrate how policies are politically crafted according to institutional procedures and individual aspirations. The procedures, as we have seen in a previous discussion, are a series of chutes and ladders that shape, channel, filter, and prune the alternatives from which ultimate policy choices are made. The politicians that populate these institutions, as we have just noted, are driven both by private objectives and public purposes, pursuing their own private interests while working on behalf of their conception of the public interest.

Since the institutional features of the American political system are complex and policy change requires success at every step, change is often impossibly difficult, meaning the status quo usually prevails. A long list of players must be satisfied with the change or it won't happen. Most of these politicians will need some form of "compensation" to provide their endorsement and support.

Majorities are usually built by drafting bills so as to spread the benefits to enough members of the legislature to get the requisite number of votes for that particular bill. Derisively, this is called "pork-barrel" legislation. It can be better understood by remembering that the overwhelming proportion of "pork-barrel" projects that are distributed to build policy majorities are justified to voters as valuable additions to the "public good" of the various districts. What may be "pork" to the critic are actual bridges, roads, and post offices.

Elaborate institutional arrangements, complicated policy processes, and intricate political motivations make for a highly combustible mixture. The policies

---

[30]These friends would benefit from people having the financial means to buy home heating oil, but would not want the price they charge for the oil restricted.

that emerge are inevitably lacking in the neatness that citizens desire. But policies in the United States today are sloppy and slapdash for clear reason—it is the tendency to spread the benefits broadly that results when political ambition comes up against a decentralized political system.

Principle 5: History Matters—or, How Did We Get to Where We Are?

There is one more aspect of our analysis that is important: we must ask how we have gotten to where we are. By what series of steps? When by choice, and when by accident? To what extent was the history of Congress, the parties, and the presidency a fulfillment of constitutional principle, and when were the developments a series of dogged responses to economic necessity? Are the parties a product of democracy, or is democracy a product of the parties? Every question and problem we confront has a history. History will not tell the same story for every institution. Nevertheless, without history, there is neither a sense of causation nor a sense of how institutions are related to each other. In explaining the answer to why governments do what they do, we must turn to history to see what choices were available to political actors at a given time and what consequences resulted from these choices.

At a very elemental level, history matters through the transmission of political memories. Let's take, for example, Senator Strom Thurmond of South Carolina, once a Democrat and now a Republican, who is the longest serving legislator in the Congress at the beginning of the twenty-first century. He overlapped in service with Senator Carl Hayden of Arizona, the very first senator from that state, who began his Senate service in 1909. Hayden's service in Congress, in turn, coincided for a time with that of Joseph Cannon of Illinois, the famous Speaker of the House in early twentieth-century America, who began service in the House in the 1870s. He overlapped with Speaker Reed, who served in the House under Speaker Blaine, who overlapped with a number of Civil War–era legislators. They, in turn, experienced the heady legislative politics of Henry Clay, whose career ran (with brief interruptions) from 1809 to 1852, linking him to a few legislators, like John Randolph of Roanoke, who served in the very first Congress. The political generations since the founding are interconnected and overlapping, and this connectedness serves to transmit shared political experiences from generation to generation.

Institutional actors, by virtue of their connections to their institutional forebears, remember which procedures solved political problems in the past and which are doomed to fail. Politicians remember the precise meaning of terms of discourse; a political "dictionary" need not be reinvented with each new Congress or presidential administration. They remember past deals; generational interconnectedness means that political actors know they can enter into deals today that were affected by past deals and will have a bearing on deals tomorrow. And through the continuity and repetition of institutional practices, institutions develop and become part of the historical context. An understanding of Congress cannot be accomplished by merely studying the voting behavior of current members. All of that, interesting as it is, occurs in a context of more than two centuries of development.[31]

History matters in other ways. It provides an interpretive framework for political conflicts. Memories of rivalry between the legislative and executive branches over the authority to engage the country in warlike activities during the Vietnam era, for example, have conditioned military deployment since that time. The War Powers Act of 1973, which assured Congress full partnership in the foreign deployment of troops, was but the formal manifestation of a broader understanding that presidents could not go off half-cocked on military escapades.[32] President George H. W. Bush, for example, sought formal authority from Congress for sending troops to the Persian Gulf in 1991.

History also provides a context in which to incorporate current information and experiences. It provides, in other words, a basis for updating one's beliefs—about politics in general, about current events, about whom to trust and distrust, and about the way in which the world works. Only a small child takes what he or she sees here and now as the way it is; most of us learn to interpret current experience in light of things that have gone before.

To make our final point about why history matters, we ask the reader to imagine a tree growing from the bottom of the page. Its trunk grows upward from some root-ball at the bottom, dividing into branches that continue to grow upward, further dividing into smaller branches. Imagine a "path" through this tree, from its very roots at the bottom of the page to the end of one of the highest branches at the top of the page. There are many such paths, beginning from the one point at the bottom to many possible points at the top. If instead of a tree, this were a "time diagram," then the root-ball at the bottom would represent some specific beginning point and all of the top-branch endings would represent some terminal time. Each path is now a *history*, the delineation of movement from some specific beginning to some concluding time. Alternative histories, like paths through trees, entail *irreversibilities*. Once one starts down a historical path (or up a tree), one cannot always retrace one's steps.[33] Once things happen, they cannot always "un-happen." One need not subscribe uncompromisingly to historical determinism in order to take the position that some futures are foreclosed by the choices people have already made, or if not literally foreclosed, then made extremely unlikely.

It is in this sense that we explain a current situation at least in part by alluding to the historical path by which we arrived at it. We say that the situation is *path dependent*, that various features of the current situation are what they are

---

[31]The best treatment of Congress as an institution is that of Nelson Polsby, "The Institutionalization of the House of Representatives," *American Political Science Review* 63 (1968), pp. 144–68.

[32]Though possibly apocryphal, it is alleged that President Theodore Roosevelt, after sending a portion of the fleet to the Pacific against the wishes of Congress, is reputed to have said that if Congress didn't like it, they could pay to bring the fleet back!

[33]Clearly with tree climbing this is not literally true, or once we started climbing a tree we would never get down! So the tree analogy is not perfect here.

in part because of the path by which the situation occurred, and, had a different path been taken, the features might well be different, too. Today's events and situations are a storehouse of the historical past. History provides contemporaries with an interpretive framework and a context in which to update beliefs. The principle of ***path dependency*** underscores the contingent nature of things: a particular unfolding of history precludes some things from happening. The historical record combines with the choices of contemporaries and the institutional arrangements they invent to produce final results or outcomes.

Finally, without history we cannot appreciate change. We are not concerned with history for its own sake. But history does allow us the ability to analyze the consequences of institutional change in government, both intended and unintended. For example, the construction of democratic electoral institutions and popular representative bodies in the United States and other Western societies had two historic consequences. First, democratization opened up the possibility that citizens might now use government for their own benefit rather than simply watching government being used for the benefit of others. This consequence is widely understood. But the second is not so well understood: once citizens perceived that governments could operate in response to their demands, citizens *became increasingly willing to support the expansion of government.* The public's belief in its capacity to control the government's actions is only one of the many factors responsible for the growth of government. But at the very least, this linkage of democracy and government set into motion a wave of governmental growth in the West that began in the middle of the nineteenth century and has continued to this day. This, in turn, has influenced how government operates and what it does.

path dependency
The idea that certain possibilities are made more or less likely because of the historical path taken.

SUMMARY

The enormous scope of national programs in the last century has required the construction of a large and elaborate state apparatus and the transfer of considerable decision-making power from political bodies like Congress to administrative agencies. As a consequence, the development and implementation of today's public policies are increasingly dominated by complicated bureaucratic institutions, rules, and procedures that are not so easily affected by the citizen's preferences expressed in the voting booth. Can citizens use the power of the institutions we have created, or are we doomed simply to become their subjects?

In addition, as government has grown in size and power, the need for citizen action has diminished. Unlike their predecessors, many governments today have administrative, military, and police agencies that *can* curb disorder, collect taxes, and keep their foes in check without necessarily depending on popular involvement or approval. Will governments continue to bow to the will of the people even though public opinion may not be as crucial as it once was? Likewise, will citizens participate in the political process when few incentives are provided

Institutional Reform
www.wwnorton.com/
lowi7/ch1
What are some consequences of the growth of government in the United States?

to do so? And by what means will citizens band together to accomplish their shared goals?

Our five principles of politics provide a focus and a means for answering these and other questions. Understanding the complexities of government might seem an overwhelming task, but these basic principles are where we need to begin. Throughout this book, we will refer to the five principles introduced in this chapter. When we do, an icon will appear in the margin to indicate which principle is involved and how that principle applies to the discussion. Try to keep these principles in mind beyond the reading of this book. They are not only the basis of political science as an academic enterprise; they are also important tools for citizens to employ as participants in America's democratic process.

FOR FURTHER READING

Bianco, William T. *American Politics: Strategy and Choice.* New York: W. W. Norton, 2001.

Dahl, Robert A. *Who Governs?* New Haven: Yale University Press, 1961.

Downs, Anthony. *An Economic Theory of Democracy.* New York: Harper & Row, 1957.

Lupia, Arthur and Matthew D. McCubbins. *The Democratic Dilemma: Can Citizens Learn What They Need to Know?* New York: Cambridge University Press, 1998.

Olson, Mancur. *The Logic of Collective Action.* Cambridge: Harvard University Press, 1965.

Putnam, Robert. *Making Democracy Work: Civic Traditions in Modern Italy.* Princeton: Princeton University Press, 1993.

Riker, William H. *Liberalism against Populism: A Confrontation between the Theory of Democracy and the Theory of Social Choice.* San Francisco: W. H. Freeman, 1982.

Skocpol, Theda. *States and Social Revolutions.* New York: Cambridge University Press, 1979.

CHAPTER two

Constructing a Government:
The Founding and the Constitution

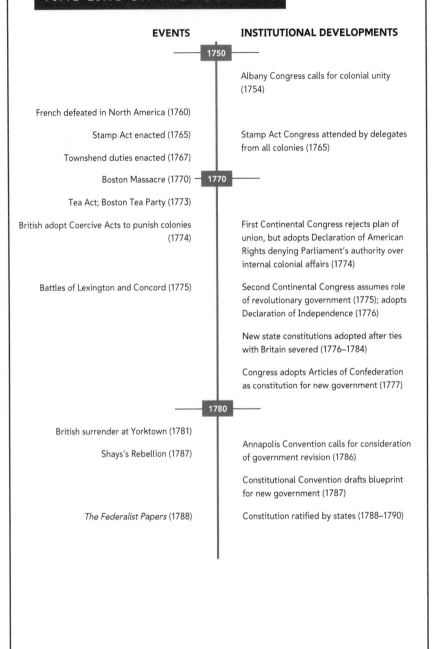

EVENTS	INSTITUTIONAL DEVELOPMENTS
1750	
	Albany Congress calls for colonial unity (1754)
French defeated in North America (1760)	
Stamp Act enacted (1765)	Stamp Act Congress attended by delegates from all colonies (1765)
Townshend duties enacted (1767)	
Boston Massacre (1770) — **1770**	
Tea Act; Boston Tea Party (1773)	
British adopt Coercive Acts to punish colonies (1774)	First Continental Congress rejects plan of union, but adopts Declaration of American Rights denying Parliament's authority over internal colonial affairs (1774)
Battles of Lexington and Concord (1775)	Second Continental Congress assumes role of revolutionary government (1775); adopts Declaration of Independence (1776)
	New state constitutions adopted after ties with Britain severed (1776–1784)
	Congress adopts Articles of Confederation as constitution for new government (1777)
1780	
British surrender at Yorktown (1781)	
Shays's Rebellion (1787)	Annapolis Convention calls for consideration of government revision (1786)
	Constitutional Convention drafts blueprint for new government (1787)
The Federalist Papers (1788)	Constitution ratified by states (1788–1790)

"**N**o taxation without representation" were words that stirred a generation of Americans long before they even dreamed of calling themselves Americans rather than Englishmen. Reacting to new English attempts to extract tax revenues to pay for the troops that were being sent to defend the colonial frontier, protests erupted throughout the colonies against the infamous Stamp Act of 1765. This act required that all printed and legal documents, including newspapers, pamphlets, advertisements, notes and bonds, leases, deeds, and licenses be printed on official paper stamped and sold by English officials. To show their displeasure with the act, the colonists conducted mass meetings, parades, bonfires, and other demonstrations throughout the spring and summer of 1765. In Boston, for example, a stamp agent was hanged and burned in effigy. Later, the home of the lieutenant-governor was sacked, leading to his resignation and that of all of his colonial commission and stamp agents. By November 1765, business proceeded and newspapers were published without the stamp; in March 1766, Parliament repealed the detested law. Through their protest, the nonimportation agreements that the colonists subsequently adopted, and the Stamp Act Congress that met in October 1765, the colonists took the first steps that ultimately would lead to war and a new nation.

The people of every nation tend to glorify their own history and especially their nation's creation. Generally, through such devices as public school texts and national holidays, governments encourage a heroic view of the nation's past as a way of promoting national pride and unity in the present. Great myths are part of the process of nation building and citizenship training in every nation, and America is no exception. To most contemporary Americans, the revolutionary period represents a brave struggle by a determined and united group of colonists against British oppression. The Boston Tea Party, the battles of Lexington and Concord, the winter at Valley Forge—these are the events that we emphasize in our history. Similarly, the American Constitution—the document establishing the system of government that ultimately emerged from this struggle—is often seen as an inspired, if not divine, work, expressing timeless principles of democratic government. These views are by no means false. During the founding era, Americans did struggle against misrule. Moreover, the American

CORE OF THE ANALYSIS

- The American Revolution and the Constitution were expressions of competing interests.

- The framers of the Constitution married interest and principle by creating a government capable of defending national interests, promoting commerce, and protecting property.

- To secure popular consent for the government, the Constitution provides for the direct popular election of representatives and includes the Bill of Rights.

- To prevent the new government from abusing its power, the Constitution incorporates principles such as the separation of powers and federalism.

- The Constitution and its amendments establish a framework within which government and lawmaking can take place.

Constitution did establish the foundations for over two hundred years of democratic government.

To really understand the character of the American founding and the meaning of the American Constitution, however, it is essential to look beyond the myths and rhetoric.

THE CENTRAL QUESTIONS

THE FIRST FOUNDING: INTERESTS AND CONFLICTS

What conflicts were apparent and what interests prevailed during the American Revolution and the drafting of the Articles of Confederation?

THE SECOND FOUNDING: FROM COMPROMISE TO CONSTITUTION

Why were the Articles of Confederation unable to hold the nation together?

In what ways is the Constitution a marriage of interest and principle? How did the framers reconcile their competing interests and principles?

THE CONSTITUTION

What principles does the Constitution embody? Why did the framers establish the legislative, executive, and judicial branches?

What limits on the national government's power are embodied in the Constitution?

THE FIGHT FOR RATIFICATION

What sides did the Federalists and the Antifederalists represent in the fight over ratification?

Over what key principles did the Federalists and Antifederalists disagree?

CHANGING THE INSTITUTIONAL FRAMEWORK: CONSTITUTIONAL AMENDMENT

Why is the Constitution difficult to amend?

What purposes do the amendments to the Constitution serve?

The men and women who became revolutionaries were guided by principles, to be sure, but they also had interests. Most of them were not political theorists, but were hard-headed and pragmatic in their commitments and activities. Although their interests were not identical, they did agree that a relationship of political and economic dependence on a colonial power, one that did not treat them as full-fledged citizens of the empire, was intolerable. In the end, the decision to break away and, over the succeeding decade, to fashion institutions of self-governance was the consequence.

Many of those most active in the initial days of the Revolution felt pushed into a corner, their hands forced. For years, the imperial center in London, preoccupied by a war with France that spread across several continents, had left the colonists to their own devices. These were years in which colonists enjoyed an immense amount of local control and home rule, but suddenly, as the war with France drew to a close in the 1760s, the British presence became more onerous and intrusive. This historical experience incited the initial reactions to taxes. Nearly a century of relatively light-handed colonial administration by London had produced a set of expectations in the colonists that later British actions unmistakably violated.

This is where we begin our story in the present chapter. We will first assess the political backdrop of the American Revolution. Then we will examine the Constitution that ultimately emerged—

after a rather bumpy experience in self-government just after the Revolution—as the basis for America's government. We will conclude with a reflection upon the founding period by emphasizing a lesson to be learned from the founding that continues to be important throughout American history. This lesson is that politics, as James Madison said in *The Federalist*, generally involves struggles among conflicting interests. In 1776, the conflict was between pro- and anti-revolutionary forces. In 1787, the struggle was between the Federalists and the Antifederalists. Today, the struggle is between the Democrats and the Republicans, each representing competing economic, social, and sectional interests. Often, political principles are the weapons developed by competing interests to further their own causes. The New England merchants who cried "no taxation without representation" cared more about lower taxes than expanded representation. Yet, today, representation is one of the foundations of American democracy.

What were the great principles that emerged from the conflicts during the founding period? How do these principles continue to shape our lives long after the Constitution's framers completed their work? These are the important questions that will be addressed in this chapter.

History Principle

The American colonists, used to years of self-governance, believed that the Stamp Act of 1765 threatened their autonomy.

THE FIRST FOUNDING: INTERESTS AND CONFLICTS

Competing ideals and principles often reflect competing interests, and so it was in revolutionary America. The American Revolution and the American Constitution were outgrowths and expressions of a struggle among economic and political forces within the colonies. Five sectors of society had interests that were important in colonial politics: (1) the New England merchants; (2) the Southern planters; (3) the "royalists"—holders of royal lands, offices, and patents (licences to engage in a profession or business activity); (4) shopkeepers, artisans, and laborers; and (5) small farmers. Throughout the eighteenth century, these groups were in conflict over issues of taxation, trade, and commerce. For the most part, however, the Southern planters, the New England merchants, and the royal office and patent holders—groups that together made up the colonial elite—were able to maintain a political alliance that held in check the more radical forces representing shopkeepers, laborers, and small farmers. After 1750, however, by seriously threatening the interests of New England merchants and Southern planters, British tax and trade policies split the colonial elite, permitting radical forces to expand their political influence, and set into motion a chain of events that culminated in the American Revolution.[1]

---

[1] The social makeup of colonial America and some of the social conflicts that divided colonial society are discussed in Jackson Turner Main, *The Social Structure of Revolutionary America* (Princeton: Princeton University Press, 1965).

British Taxes and Colonial Interests

Beginning in the 1750s, the debts and other financial problems faced by the British government forced it to search for new revenue sources. This search rather quickly led to the Crown's North American colonies, which, on the whole, paid remarkably little in taxes to the mother country. The British government reasoned that a sizable fraction of its debt was, in fact, attributable to the expenses it had incurred in defense of the colonies during the recent French and Indian wars, as well as to the continuing protection that British forces were giving the colonists from Indian attacks and that the British navy was providing for colonial shipping. Thus, during the 1760s, England sought to impose new, though relatively modest, taxes upon the colonists.

Like most governments of the period, the British regime had at its disposal only limited ways to collect revenues. The income tax, which in the twentieth century has become the single most important source of governmental revenue, had not yet been developed. For the most part, in the mid-eighteenth century, governments relied on tariffs, duties, and other taxes on commerce, and it was to such taxes, including the Stamp Act, that the British turned during the 1760s.

The Stamp Act and other taxes on commerce, such as the Sugar Act of 1764, which taxed sugar, molasses, and other commodities, most heavily affected the two groups in colonial society whose commercial interests and activities were most extensive—the New England merchants and Southern planters. Under the famous slogan "no taxation without representation," the merchants and planters together sought to organize opposition to the new taxes. In the course of the struggle against British tax measures, the planters and merchants broke with their royalist allies and turned to their former adversaries—the shopkeepers, small farmers, laborers, and artisans—for help. With the assistance of these groups, the merchants and planters organized demonstrations and a boycott of British goods that ultimately forced the Crown to rescind most of its new taxes. It was in the context of this unrest that a confrontation between colonists and British soldiers in front of the Boston customs house on the night of March 5, 1770, resulted in what came to be known as the Boston Massacre. Nervous British soldiers opened fire on the mob surrounding them, killing five colonists and wounding eight others. News of this event quickly spread throughout the colonies and was used by radicals to fan anti-British sentiment.

From the perspective of the merchants and planters, however, the British government's decision to eliminate most of the hated taxes represented a victorious end to their struggle with the mother country. They were anxious to end the unrest they had helped to arouse, and they supported the British government's efforts to restore order. Indeed, most respectable Bostonians supported the actions of the British soldiers involved in the Boston Massacre. In their subsequent trial, the soldiers were defended by John Adams, a pillar of Boston society and a future president of the United States. Adams asserted that the soldiers' actions were entirely justified, provoked by a "motley rabble of saucy boys, negroes and mulattoes, Irish teagues and outlandish Jack tars." All but two of the soldiers were acquitted.[2]

Despite the efforts of the British government and the better-to-do strata of colonial society, it proved difficult to bring an end to the political strife. The more radical forces representing shopkeepers, artisans, laborers, and small farmers, who had been mobilized and energized by the struggle over taxes, continued to agitate for political and social change within the colonies. These radicals, led by individuals like Samuel Adams, cousin of John Adams, asserted that British power supported an unjust political and social structure within the colonies, and they began to advocate an end to British rule.[3]

Organizing resistance to the British authorities, however, required widespread support. Collective action, as we saw in the previous chapter, may emerge *spontaneously* in certain circumstances, but the colonists' campaign against the British imperial power in late-eighteenth-century America was a series of encounters, maneuvers, and ultimately confrontations that required planning, coalition building, bargaining, compromising, and coordinating, all elements of the give-and-take of politics. Conflicts among the colonists had to be solved by bargaining, persuasion, and even by force. Cooperation needed cultivation and encouragement. Leadership was clearly a necessary ingredient.

Collective Action Principle

The colonists required strong leaders to resolve differences and to organize resistance to British authority.

Political Strife and the Radicalizing of the Colonists

The political strife within the colonies was the background for the events of 1773–1774. In 1773, the British government granted the politically powerful East India Company a monopoly on the export of tea from Britain, eliminating a lucrative form of trade for colonial merchants. To add to the injury, the East India Company sought to sell the tea directly in the colonies instead of working through the colonial merchants. Tea was an extremely important commodity in the 1770s, and these British actions posed a mortal threat to the New England merchants. The merchants once again called upon their radical adversaries for support. The most dramatic result was the Boston Tea Party of 1773, led by Samuel Adams.

This event was of decisive importance in American history. The merchants had hoped to force the British government to rescind the Tea Act, but they did not support any demands beyond this one. They certainly did not seek independence from Britain. Samuel Adams and the other radicals, however, hoped to provoke the British government to take actions that would alienate its colonial supporters and pave the way for a rebellion. This was precisely the purpose of the Boston Tea Party, and it succeeded. By dumping the East India

---

[2]George B. Tindall and David E. Shi, *America: A Narrative History*, 5th ed. (New York: W. W. Norton, 1999), p. 218.

[3]For a discussion of events leading up to the Revolution, see Charles M. Andrews, *The Colonial Background of the American Revolution* (New Haven: Yale University Press, 1924).

Company's tea into Boston Harbor, Adams and his followers goaded the British into enacting a number of harsh reprisals. Within five months after the incident in Boston, the House of Commons passed a series of acts that closed the port of Boston to commerce, changed the provincial government of Massachusetts, provided for the removal of accused persons to England for trial, and most important, restricted movement to the West—further alienating the Southern planters who depended upon access to new western lands. These acts of retaliation confirmed the worst criticisms of England and helped radicalize Americans.

The choice of this course of action by English politicians looks puzzling in retrospect, but at the time it appeared reasonable to those who prevailed in Parliament that a show of force was required. The toleration of lawlessness and the making of concessions, they felt, would only egg on the more radical elements in the colonies to take further liberties and demand further concessions. The English, in effect, drew a line in the sand. Their repressive reactions served as a clear point around which dissatisfied colonists could rally. Radicals like Samuel Adams had been agitating for more violent measures to deal with England. But ultimately they needed Britain's political repression to create widespread support for independence.

Thus, the Boston Tea Party set into motion a cycle of provocation and retaliation that in 1774 resulted in the convening of the First Continental Congress—an assembly consisting of delegates from all parts of the country—that called for a total boycott of British goods and, under the prodding of the radicals, began to consider the possibility of independence from British rule. The eventual result was the Declaration of Independence.

The Declaration of Independence

In 1776, the Second Continental Congress appointed a committee consisting of Thomas Jefferson of Virginia, Benjamin Franklin of Pennsylvania, Roger Sherman of Connecticut, John Adams of Massachusetts, and Robert Livingston of New York to draft a statement of American independence from British rule. The Declaration of Independence, written by Jefferson and adopted by the Second Continental Congress, was an extraordinary document both in philosophical and political terms. Philosophically, the Declaration was remarkable for its assertion that certain rights, called "unalienable rights"—including life, liberty, and the pursuit of happiness—could not be abridged by governments. In the world of 1776, a world in which some kings still claimed to rule by divine right, this was a dramatic statement. Politically, the Declaration was remarkable because, despite the differences of interest that divided the colonists along economic, regional, and philosophical lines, the Declaration identified and focused on problems, grievances, aspirations, and principles that might unify the various colonial groups. The Declaration was an attempt to identify and articulate a history and set of principles that might help to forge national unity.[4]

[4]See Carl Becker, *The Declaration of Independence* (New York: Vintage, 1942).

The Articles of Confederation

Having declared their independence, the colonies needed to establish a governmental structure. In November of 1777, the Continental Congress adopted the ***Articles of Confederation and Perpetual Union***—the United States's first written constitution. Although it was not ratified by all the states until 1781, it was the country's operative constitution for almost twelve years, until March 1789.

The Articles of Confederation was a constitution concerned primarily with limiting the powers of the central government. The central government, first of all, was based entirely in Congress. Since it was not intended to be a powerful government, it was given no executive branch. Execution of its laws was to be left to the individual states. Second, Congress had little power. Its members were not much more than delegates or messengers from the state legislatures. They were chosen by the state legislatures, their salaries were paid out of the state treasuries, and they were subject to immediate recall by state authorities. In addition, each state, regardless of its size, had only a single vote.

Congress was given the power to declare war and make peace, to make treaties and alliances, to coin or borrow money, and to regulate trade with the Native Americans. It could also appoint the senior officers of the United States Army. But it could not levy taxes or regulate commerce among the states. Moreover, the army officers it appointed had no army to serve in because the nation's armed forces were composed of the state militias. Probably the most unfortunate part of the Articles of Confederation was that the central government could not prevent one state from discriminating against other states in the quest for foreign commerce.

In brief, the relationship between Congress and the states under the Articles of Confederation was much like the contemporary relationship between the United Nations and its member states, a relationship in which virtually all governmental powers are retained by the states. It was properly called a "confederation" because, as provided under Article II, "each state retains its sovereignty, freedom, and independence, and every power, jurisdiction, and right, which is not by this Confederation expressly delegated to the United States, in Congress assembled." Not only was there no executive, there was also no judicial authority and no other means of enforcing Congress's will. If there was to be any enforcement at all, it would be done for Congress by the states.[5]

Articles of Confederation and Perpetual Union America's first written constitution. Adopted by the Continental Congress in 1777, the Articles of Confederation and Perpetual Union was the formal basis for America's national government until 1789, when it was supplanted by the Constitution.

THE SECOND FOUNDING: FROM COMPROMISE TO CONSTITUTION

The Declaration of Independence and the Articles of Confederation were not sufficient to hold the nation together as an independent and effective nation-state.

[5]See Merrill Jensen, *The Articles of Confederation* (Madison: University of Wisconsin Press, 1963).

From almost the moment of armistice with the British in 1783, moves were afoot to reform and strengthen the Articles of Confederation.

International Standing and Balance of Power

There was a special concern for the country's international position. Competition among the states for foreign commerce allowed the European powers to play the states against each other, which created confusion on both sides of the Atlantic. At one point during the winter of 1786–1787, John Adams of Massachusetts, a leader in the independence struggle, was sent to negotiate a new treaty with the British, one that would cover disputes left over from the war. The British government responded that, since the United States under the Articles of Confederation was unable to enforce existing treaties, it would negotiate with each of the thirteen states separately.

At the same time, well-to-do Americans—in particular the New England merchants and Southern planters—were troubled by the influence that "radical" forces exercised in the Continental Congress and in the governments of several of the states. The colonists' victory in the Revolutionary War had not only meant the end of British rule, but it also significantly changed the balance of political power within the new states. As a result of the Revolution, one key segment of the colonial elite—the royal land, office, and patent holders—was stripped of its economic and political privileges. In fact, many of these individuals, along with tens of thousands of other colonists who considered themselves loyal British subjects, left for Canada after the British surrender. And while the pre-revolutionary elite was weakened, the pre-revolutionary radicals were now better organized than ever before, and were the controlling forces in such states as Pennsylvania and Rhode Island, where they pursued economic and political policies that struck terror into the hearts of the pre-revolutionary political establishment. In Rhode Island, for example, between 1783 and 1785, a legislature dominated by representatives of small farmers, artisans, and shopkeepers had instituted economic policies, including drastic currency inflation, that frightened businessmen and property owners throughout the country. Of course, the central government under the Articles of Confederation was powerless to intervene.

Institution Principle

Institutional arrangements matter, but there is no guarantee that they will be perfect as the Articles of Confederation make apparent.

The Annapolis Convention

The continuation of international weakness and domestic economic turmoil led many Americans to consider whether their newly adopted form of government might not already require revision. Institutional arrangements are experiments in governance, and they don't always work out. Nearly a decade under the Articles had made amply clear the flaws it contained. In the fall of 1786, many state leaders accepted an invitation from the Virginia legislature for a conference of representatives of all the states. Delegates from five states actually attended. This conference, held in Annapolis, Maryland, was the first step toward the second founding. The one positive thing that came out of the Annapolis Convention was a carefully worded resolution calling on Congress to send commissioners to Philadelphia at a later time "to devise such further provisions as shall appear to them necessary to render the Constitution of the Federal Government adequate to the exigencies of the Union."[6] This resolution was drafted by Alexander Hamilton, a thirty-four-year-old New York lawyer who had played a significant role in the Revolution as George Washington's secretary and who would play a still more significant role in framing the Constitution and forming the new government in the 1790s. But the resolution did not necessarily imply any desire to do more than improve and reform the Articles of Confederation.

Shays's Rebellion

It is quite possible that the Constitutional Convention of 1787 in Philadelphia would never have taken place at all except for a single event that occurred during the winter following the Annapolis Convention: Shays's Rebellion. Like the Boston Tea Party, this was a focal event. It concentrated attention, coordinated beliefs, produced widespread fear and apprehension, and thus convinced waverers that "something was broke and needed fixing." In short, it provided politicians who had long been convinced that the Articles were flawed and insufficient with just the ammunition they needed to persuade a much broader public of these facts.[7]

Daniel Shays, a former army captain, led a mob of farmers in a rebellion against the government of Massachusetts. The purpose of the rebellion was to prevent foreclosures on their debt-ridden land by keeping the county courts of western Massachusetts from sitting until after the next election. The state militia dispersed the mob, but for several days, Shays and his followers terrified the state government by attempting to capture the federal arsenal at Springfield, provoking an appeal to Congress to help restore order. Within a few days, the state government regained control and captured fourteen of the rebels (all were eventually pardoned). In 1787, a newly elected Massachusetts legislature granted some of the farmers' demands.

Although the incident ended peacefully, its effects lingered and spread. Washington summed it up: "I am mortified beyond expression that in the moment of our acknowledged independence we should by our conduct verify the predictions of our transatlantic foe, and render ourselves ridiculous and contemptible in the eyes of all Europe."[8]

Congress under the Confederation had been unable to act decisively in a time of crisis. This provided critics of the Articles of Confederation with precisely the evidence they needed to push Hamilton's Annapolis resolution through the

[6]Reported in Samuel E. Morrison, Henry Steele Commager, and William Leuchtenberg, *The Growth of the American Republic*, vol. 1 (New York: Oxford University Press, 1969), p. 244.
[7]For an easy-to-read argument that supports this view, see Keith L. Dougherty, *Collective Action under the Articles of Confederation* (New York: Cambridge University Press, 2001).
[8]Morrison et al., *The Growth of the American Republic*, p. 242.

History Principle

Shays's Rebellion focused attention on the flaws of the Articles of Confederation, leading to the Constitutional Convention.

Congress. Thus, the states were asked to send representatives to Philadelphia to discuss constitutional revision. Delegates were eventually sent by every state except Rhode Island.

The Constitutional Convention

Twenty-nine of a total of 73 delegates selected by the state governments convened in Philadelphia in May 1787, with political strife, international embarrassment, national weakness, and local rebellion fixed in their minds. Recognizing that these issues were symptoms of fundamental flaws in the Articles of Confederation, the delegates soon abandoned the plan to revise the Articles and committed themselves to a second founding—a second, and ultimately successful, attempt to create a legitimate and effective national system. This effort occupied the convention for the next five months.

A Marriage of Interest and Principle   For years, scholars have disagreed about the motives of the founders in Philadelphia. Among the most controversial views of the framers' motives is the "economic" interpretation put forward by historian Charles Beard and his disciples.[9] According to Beard's account, America's founders were a collection of securities speculators and property owners whose only aim was personal enrichment. From this perspective, the Constitution's lofty principles were little more than sophisticated masks behind which the most venal interests sought to enrich themselves.

Contrary to Beard's approach is the view that the framers of the Constitution *were* concerned with philosophical and ethical principles. Indeed, the framers sought to devise a system of government consistent with the dominant philosophical and moral principles of the day. But, in fact, these two views belong together; the founders' interests were reinforced by their principles. The convention that drafted the American Constitution was chiefly organized by the New England merchants and Southern planters. Though the delegates representing these groups did not all hope to profit personally from an increase in the value of their securities, as Beard would have it, they did hope to benefit in the broadest political and economic sense by breaking the power of their radical foes and establishing a system of government more compatible with their long-term economic and political interests. Thus, the framers sought to create a new government capable of promoting commerce and protecting property from radical state legislatures. They also sought to liberate the national government from the power of individual states and their sometimes venal and corrupt local politicians. At the same time, they hoped to fashion a government less susceptible than the existing state and national regimes to populist forces hostile to the interests of the commercial and propertied classes.

[9]Charles A. Beard, *An Economic Interpretation of the Constitution of the United States* (New York: Macmillan, 1913).

It seemed now to be pretty well understood that the real difference of interests lay, not between the large and small but between the northern and southern states. The institution of slavery and its consequences formed the line of discrimination. There were five states on the South, eight on the northern side of this line. Should a proportional representation take place it was true, the northern side would still outnumber the other: but not in the same degree, at this time; and every day would tend towards an equilibrium.[12]

Northerners and Southerners eventually reached agreement through the *Three-fifths Compromise.* The seats in the House of Representatives would be apportioned according to a "population" in which five slaves would count as three persons. The slaves would not be allowed to vote, of course, but the number of representatives would be apportioned accordingly. This arrangement was supported by the slave states, which obviously included some of the biggest and some of the smallest states at that time. It was also accepted by many delegates from nonslave states who strongly supported the principle of property representation, whether that property was expressed in slaves or in land, money, or stocks. The concern exhibited by most delegates was over how much slaves would count toward a state's representation rather than whether the institution of slavery would continue. The Three-fifths Compromise, in the words of political scientist Donald Robinson, "gave Constitutional sanction to the fact that the United States was composed of some persons who were 'free' and others who were not, and it established the principle, new in republican theory, that a man who lives among slaves had a greater share in the election of representatives than the man who did not. Although the Three-fifths Compromise acknowledged slavery and rewarded slave owners, nonetheless, it probably kept the South from unanimously rejecting the Constitution."[13]

The issue of slavery was the most difficult one faced by the framers, and it nearly destroyed the Union. Although some delegates believed slavery to be morally wrong, an evil and oppressive institution that made a mockery of the ideals and values espoused in the Constitution, morality was not the issue that caused the framers to support or oppose the Three-fifths Compromise. Whatever they thought of the institution of slavery, most delegates from the Northern states opposed counting slaves in the distribution of congressional seats. Wilson of Pennsylvania, for example, argued that if slaves were citizens they should be treated and counted like other citizens. If on the other hand, they were property, then why should not other forms of property be counted toward the apportionment of Congress? But Southern delegates made it clear that if the Northerners refused to give in, they would never agree to the new government. William R. Davie of North Carolina heatedly said that it was time "to speak out." He asserted that the people of North Carolina would never enter the Union if slaves

Three-fifths Compromise
Agreement reached at the Constitutional Convention of 1787, which stipulated that for purposes of the apportionment of congressional seats, every slave would be counted as three-fifths of a person.

[12]Ibid., vol. 2, p. 10.
[13]Donald Robinson, *Slavery in the Structure of American Politics, 1765–1820* (New York: Harcourt Brace Jovanovich, 1971), p. 201.

were not counted as part of the basis for representation. Without such agreement, he asserted ominously, "the business was at an end." Even Southerners like Edmund Randolph of Virginia, who conceded that slavery was immoral, insisted upon including slaves in the allocation of congressional seats. This conflict between the Southern and Northern delegates was so divisive that many came to question the possibility of creating and maintaining a union of the two. Pierce Butler of South Carolina declared that the North and South were as different as Russia and Turkey. Eventually, the North and South compromised on the issue of slavery and representation. Indeed, Northerners even agreed to permit a continuation of the odious slave trade to keep the South in the union. But, in due course, Butler proved to be correct, and a bloody war was fought when the disparate interests of the North and South could no longer be reconciled.

THE CONSTITUTION

The political significance of the Great Compromise and Three-fifths Compromise was to reinforce the unity of the mercantile and planter forces that sought to create a new government. The Great Compromise reassured those who feared that the importance of their own local or regional influence would be reduced by the new governmental framework. The Three-fifths Compromise temporarily defused the rivalry between the merchants and planters. Their unity secured, members of the alliance supporting the establishment of a new government moved to fashion a constitutional framework consistent with their economic and political interests.

In particular, the framers sought a new government that, first, would be strong enough to promote commerce and protect property from radical state legislatures such as Rhode Island's. This became the constitutional basis for national control over commerce and finance, as well as the establishment of national judicial supremacy and the effort to construct a strong presidency. Second, the framers sought to prevent what they saw as the threat posed by the "excessive democracy" of the state and national governments under the Articles of Confederation. This led to such constitutional principles as *bicameralism* (division of the Congress into two chambers), checks and balances, staggered terms in office, and indirect election (selection of the president by an electoral college rather than by voters directly). Third, the framers, lacking the power to force the states or the public at large to accept the new form of government, sought to identify principles that would help to secure support. This became the basis of the constitutional provision for direct popular election of representatives and, subsequently, for the addition of the Bill of Rights to the Constitution. Finally, the framers wanted to be certain that the government they created did not use its power to pose even more of a threat to its citizens' liberties and property rights than did the radical state legislatures they feared and despised. To prevent the new government from abusing its power, the framers incorporated principles such as the separation of powers and federalism into the Constitution.

bicameral Having a legislative assembly composed of two chambers or houses.

The framers provided us with a grand lesson in instrumental behavior. They came to Philadelphia united by a common distaste for government under the Articles and animated by the agitation following Shays's Rebellion. They didn't always agree on what it was they disliked about the Articles. They certainly didn't agree on how to proceed—hence the necessity for the historic compromises we have just described. But they did believe that the fostering of commerce and the protection of property could better be served by an alternative set of institutional arrangements than that of the Articles. They agreed that the institutional arrangements of government mattered for their lives and those of their fellow citizens. They believed that both too much democracy and too much governmental power were threats to the common good, and they felt compelled to find instruments and principles that weighed against these. Let us assess the major provisions of the Constitution's seven articles to see how each relates to these objectives.

Rationality Principle

The framers of the Constitution were guided by principles, but they also had interests.

Institution Principle

The constitutional framework promoted commerce, protected property, prevented "excessive democracy," and limited the power of the national government.

The Legislative Branch

The first seven sections of Article I of the Constitution provided for a Congress consisting of two chambers—a House of Representatives and a Senate. Members of the House of Representatives were given two-year terms in office and were to be elected directly by the people. Members of the Senate were to be appointed by the state legislatures (this was changed in 1913 by the Seventeenth Amendment, which instituted direct election of senators) for six-year terms. These terms, moreover, were staggered so that the appointments of one-third of the senators would expire every two years. The Constitution assigned somewhat different tasks to the House and Senate. Though the approval of each body was required for the enactment of a law, the Senate alone was given the power to ratify treaties and approve presidential appointments. The House, on the other hand, was given the sole power to originate revenue bills.

The character of the legislative branch was directly related to the framers' major goals. The House of Representatives was designed to be directly responsible to the people in order to encourage popular consent for the new Constitution and to help enhance the power of the new government. At the same time, to guard against "excessive democracy," the power of the House of Representatives was checked by the Senate, whose members were to be appointed for long terms rather than be elected directly by the people. The purpose of this provision, according to Alexander Hamilton, was to avoid "an unqualified complaisance to every sudden breeze of passion, or to every transient impulse which the people may receive."[14] Staggered terms of service in the Senate, moreover, were intended to make that body even more resistant to popular pressure. Since only one-third of the senators would be selected at any given time, the composition of the institution would be protected from changes in popular preferences transmitted by the state legislatures. This would prevent what James Madison called "mutability in the public councils arising from a rapid succession of new

[14]E. M. Earle, ed., *The Federalist* (New York: Modern Library, 1937), No. 71.

members."[15] Thus, the structure of the legislative branch was designed to contribute to governmental power, to promote popular consent for the new government, and at the same time to place limits on the popular political currents that many of the framers saw as a radical threat to the economic and social order.

The Powers of Congress and the States   The issues of power and consent were important throughout the Constitution. Section 8 of Article I specifically listed the powers of Congress, which include the authority to collect taxes, to borrow money, to regulate commerce, to declare war, and to maintain an army and navy. By granting it these powers, the framers indicated very clearly that they intended the new government to be far more influential than its predecessor. At the same time, by defining the new government's most important powers as belonging to Congress, the framers sought to promote popular acceptance of this critical change by reassuring citizens that their views would be fully represented whenever the government exercised its new powers.

As a further guarantee to the people that the new government would pose no threat to them, the Constitution implied that any powers not listed were not granted at all. This is the doctrine of *expressed power.* The Constitution grants only those powers specifically *expressed* in its text. But the framers intended to create an active and powerful government, and so they included the *necessary and proper clause,* sometimes known as the elastic clause, which signified that the enumerated powers were meant to be a source of strength to the national government, not a limitation on it. Each power could be used with the utmost vigor, but no new powers could be seized upon by the national government without a constitutional amendment. In the absence of such an amendment, any power not enumerated was conceived to be "reserved" to the states (or the people).

The Executive Branch

The Constitution provided for the establishment of the presidency in Article II. As Alexander Hamilton commented, the presidential article aimed toward "energy in the Executive." It did so in an effort to overcome the natural stalemate that was built into the bicameral legislature as well as into the separation of powers among the legislative, executive, and judicial branches. The Constitution afforded the president a measure of independence from the people and from the other branches of government—particularly the Congress.

In line with the framers' goal of increased power to the national government, the president was granted the unconditional power to accept ambassadors from other countries; this amounted to the power to "recognize" other countries. He was also given the power to negotiate treaties, although their acceptance required the approval of the Senate. The president was given the unconditional right to grant reprieves and pardons, except in cases of impeachment. And he was provided with the power to appoint major departmental

expressed power
The notion that the Constitution grants to the federal government only those powers specifically named in its text.

necessary and proper clause
Article I, Section 8, of the Constitution, which enumerates the powers of Congress and provides Congress with the authority to make all laws "necessary and proper" to carry them out; also referred to as the "elastic clause."

[15]Ibid., No. 62.

personnel, to convene Congress in special session, and to veto congressional enactments. (The veto power is formidable, but it is not absolute, since Congress can override it by a two-thirds vote.)

The framers hoped to create a presidency that would make the federal government rather than the states the agency capable of timely and decisive action to deal with public issues and problems. This was the meaning of the "energy" that Hamilton hoped to impart to the executive branch.[16] At the same time, however, the framers sought to help the president withstand (excessively) democratic pressures by making him subject to indirect rather than direct election (through his selection by a separate electoral college). The extent to which the framers' hopes were actually realized will be the topic of Chapter 6.

The Judicial Branch

In establishing the judicial branch in Article III, the Constitution reflected the framers' preoccupations with nationalizing governmental power and checking radical democratic impulses, while guarding against potential interference with liberty and property from the new national government itself.

Under the provisions of Article III, the framers created a court that was to be literally a supreme court of the United States, and not merely the highest court of the national government. The most important expression of this intention was granting the Supreme Court the power to resolve any conflicts that might emerge between federal and state laws. In particular, the Supreme Court was given the right to determine whether a power was exclusive to the federal government, concurrent with the states, or exclusive to the states. The significance of this was noted by Justice Oliver Wendell Holmes, who observed:

> I do not think the United States would come to an end if we lost our power to declare
> an act of Congress void. I do think the union would be imperilled if we could not
> make that declaration as to the laws of the several states.[17]

In addition, the Supreme Court was assigned jurisdiction over controversies between citizens of different states. The long-term significance of this was that as the country developed a national economy, it came to rely increasingly on the federal judiciary, rather than on the state courts, for resolution of disputes.

Judges were given lifetime appointments in order to protect them from popular politics and from interference by the other branches. This, however, did not mean that the judiciary would actually remain totally impartial to political considerations, or to the other branches, for the president was to appoint the judges, and the Senate to approve the appointments. Congress would also have the power to create inferior (lower) courts, to change the jurisdiction of the federal courts, to add or subtract federal judges, even to change the size of the Supreme Court.

---

[16]*The Federalist*, No. 70.

[17]Oliver Wendell Holmes, *Collected Legal Papers* (New York: Harcourt Brace, 1920), pp. 295–96.

judicial review
Power of the courts to declare actions of the legislative and executive branches invalid or unconstitutional. The Supreme Court asserted this power in *Marbury v. Madison*.

No direct mention is made in the Constitution of *judicial review*—the power of the courts to render the final decision when there is a conflict of interpretation of the Constitution or of laws between the courts and Congress, the courts and the executive branch, or the courts and the states. Scholars generally feel that judicial review is implicit in the very existence of a written Constitution and in the power given directly to the federal courts over "all Cases . . . arising under this Constitution, the Laws of the United States, and Treaties made, or which shall be made, under their Authority" (Article III, Section 2). The Supreme Court eventually assumed the power of judicial review. Its assumption of this power, as we shall see in Chapter 8, was not based on the Constitution itself but on the politics of later decades and the membership of the Court.

National Unity and Power

Various provisions in the Constitution addressed the framers' concern with national unity and power, including Article IV's provisions for comity (reciprocity) among states and among citizens of all states.

Each state was prohibited from discriminating against the citizens of other states in favor of its own citizens, with the Supreme Court charged with deciding in each case whether a state had discriminated against goods or people from another state. The Constitution restricted the power of the states in favor of ensuring enough power to the national government to give the country a free-flowing national economy.

supremacy clause
Article VI of the Constitution, which states that all laws passed by the national government and all treaties are the supreme laws of the land and superior to all laws adopted by any state or any subdivision.

The framers' concern with national supremacy was also expressed in Article VI, in the *supremacy clause*, which provided that national laws and treaties "shall be the supreme Law of the Land." This meant that all laws made under the "Authority of the United States" would be superior to all laws adopted by any state or any other subdivision, and the states would be expected to respect all treaties made under that authority. This was a direct effort to keep the states from dealing separately with foreign nations or businesses. The supremacy clause also bound the officials of all state and local as well as federal governments to take an oath of office to support the national Constitution. This meant that every action taken by the United States Congress would have to be applied within each state as though the action were in fact state law.

Amending the Constitution

The Constitution established procedures for its own revision in Article V. Its provisions are so difficult that Americans have availed themselves of the amending process only seventeen times since 1791, when the first ten amendments were adopted. Many other amendments have been proposed in Congress, but fewer than forty of them have even come close to fulfilling the Constitution's requirement of a two-thirds vote in Congress, and only a fraction have gotten anywhere near adoption by three-fourths of the states. The Constitution could also be amended by a constitutional convention. Occasionally, proponents of particular measures, such as a balanced-budget amendment, have called for a constitutional convention to consider their proposals. Whatever the purpose for which it was called, however, such a convention would presumably have the authority to revise America's entire system of government.

It should be noted that any body of rules, including a national constitution, must balance the need to respond flexibly to changes, on the one hand, with the caution not to be too flexible, on the other. An inflexible body of rules is one that cannot accommodate major change. It risks being rebelled against, a circumstance in which the slate is wiped clean and new rules designed, or ignored altogether. Too much flexibility, however, is disastrous. It invites those who lose in normal everyday politics to replay battles at the constitutional level. If institutional change is too easy to accomplish, the stability of the political system becomes threatened.

Ratifying the Constitution

The rules for ratification of the Constitution of 1787 were set forth in Article VII of the Constitution. This provision actually violated the amendment provisions of the Articles of Confederation. For one thing, it adopted a nine-state rule in place of the unanimity required by the Articles of Confederation. For another, it provided that ratification would occur in special state conventions called for that purpose rather than in the state legislatures. All the states except Rhode Island eventually did set up state conventions to ratify the Constitution.

Constitutional Limits on the National Government's Power

As we have indicated, although the framers sought to create a powerful national government, they also wanted to guard against possible misuse of that power. To that end, the framers incorporated two key principles into the Constitution—the *separation of powers* and *federalism* (see Chapter 3). A third set of limitations, in the form of the *Bill of Rights,* was added to the Constitution to help secure its ratification when opponents of the document charged that it paid insufficient attention to citizens' rights.

The Separation of Powers No principle of politics was more widely shared at the time of the 1787 founding than the principle that power must be used to balance power. The French political theorist Baron de Montesquieu (1689–1755) believed that this balance was an indispensable defense against tyranny, and his writings, especially his major work, *The Spirit of the Laws,* "were taken as political gospel" at the Philadelphia Convention.[18] The principle of the separation

separation of powers The division of governmental power among several institutions that must cooperate in decision making.

federalism System of government in which power is divided by a constitution between a central government and regional governments.

Bill of Rights The first ten amendments to the U.S. Constitution, ratified in 1791. They ensure certain rights and liberties to the people.

---

[18]Max Farrand, *The Framing of the Constitution of the United States* (New Haven: Yale University Press, 1962), p. 49.

FIGURE 2.1

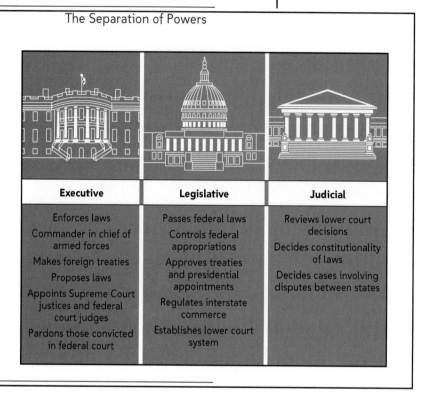

The Separation of Powers

Executive	Legislative	Judicial
Enforces laws	Passes federal laws	Reviews lower court decisions
Commander in chief of armed forces	Controls federal appropriations	Decides constitutionality of laws
Makes foreign treaties	Approves treaties and presidential appointments	Decides cases involving disputes between states
Proposes laws	Regulates interstate commerce	
Appoints Supreme Court justices and federal court judges	Establishes lower court system	
Pardons those convicted in federal court		

checks and balances Mechanisms through which each branch of government is able to participate in and influence the activities of the other branches. Major examples include the presidential veto power over congressional legislation, the power of the Senate to approve presidential appointments, and judicial review of congressional enactments.

of powers is nowhere to be found explicitly in the Constitution, but it is clearly built on Articles I, II, and III, which provide for the following:

1. Three separate and distinct branches of government (see Figure 2.1).
2. Different methods of selecting the top personnel, so that each branch is responsible to a different constituency. This is supposed to produce a "mixed regime," in which the personnel of each department will develop very different interests and outlooks on how to govern, and different groups in society will be assured some access to governmental decision making.
3. *Checks and balances*—a system under which each of the branches is given some power over the others. Familiar examples are the presidential veto power over legislation, the power of the Senate to approve presidential appointments, and judicial review of acts of Congress (see Figure 2.2).

FIGURE 2.2

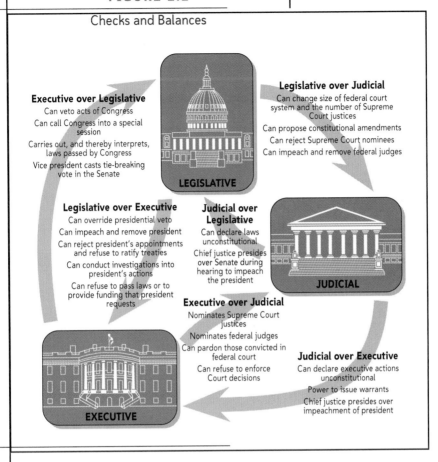

Checks and Balances

Executive over Legislative
Can veto acts of Congress
Can call Congress into a special session
Carries out, and thereby interprets, laws passed by Congress
Vice president casts tie-breaking vote in the Senate

LEGISLATIVE

Legislative over Judicial
Can change size of federal court system and the number of Supreme Court justices
Can propose constitutional amendments
Can reject Supreme Court nominees
Can impeach and remove federal judges

Legislative over Executive
Can override presidential veto
Can impeach and remove president
Can reject president's appointments and refuse to ratify treaties
Can conduct investigations into president's actions
Can refuse to pass laws or to provide funding that president requests

Judicial over Legislative
Can declare laws unconstitutional
Chief justice presides over Senate during hearing to impeach the president

JUDICIAL

Executive over Judicial
Nominates Supreme Court justices
Nominates federal judges
Can pardon those convicted in federal court
Can refuse to enforce Court decisions

Judicial over Executive
Can declare executive actions unconstitutional
Power to issue warrants
Chief justice presides over impeachment of president

EXECUTIVE

One clever formulation of the separation of powers is that of a system not of separated powers but of "separated institutions sharing power,"[19] and thus diminishing the chance that power will be misused.

Federalism   Compared to the confederation principle of the Articles of Confederation, federalism was a step toward greater centralization of power. The delegates agreed that they needed to place more power at the national level,

---

[19]Richard E. Neustadt, *Presidential Power* (New York: Wiley, 1960), p. 33.

without completely undermining the power of the state governments. Thus, they devised a system of two sovereigns—the states and the nation—with the hope that competition between the two would be an effective limitation on the power of both.

The Bill of Rights   Late in the Philadelphia Convention, a motion was made to include a bill of rights in the Constitution. After a brief debate in which hardly a word was said in its favor and only one speech was made against it, the motion to include it was almost unanimously turned down. Most delegates sincerely believed that since the federal government was already limited to its expressed powers, further protection of citizens was not needed. The delegates argued that the states should adopt bills of rights because their greater powers needed greater limitations. But almost immediately after the Constitution was ratified, there was a movement to adopt a national bill of rights. This is why the Bill of Rights, adopted in 1791, comprises the first ten amendments to the Constitution rather than being part of the body of it. We will have a good deal more to say about the Bill of Rights in Chapter 4.

THE FIGHT FOR RATIFICATION

The first hurdle faced by the new Constitution was ratification by state conventions of delegates elected by the people of each state. This struggle for ratification was carried out in thirteen separate campaigns. Each involved different men, moved at a different pace, and was influenced by local as well as national considerations. Two sides faced off throughout all the states, however, calling themselves Federalists and Antifederalists.[20] The Federalists (who more accurately should have called themselves "Nationalists," but who took their name to appear to follow in the revolutionary tradition) supported the Constitution and preferred a strong national government. The Antifederalists opposed the Constitution and preferred a federal system of government that was decentralized; they took on their name by default, in reaction to their better-organized opponents. The Federalists were united in their support of the Constitution, while the Antifederalists were divided as to what they believed the alternative to the Constitution should be.

During the struggle over ratification of the proposed Constitution, Americans argued about great political issues and principles. How much power should the national government be given? What safeguards were most likely to prevent the abuse of power? What institutional arrangements could best ensure adequate

---

[20]An excellent analysis of these ratification campaigns, based on a quantitative assessment of the campaigners' own words as found in campaign documents, pamphlets, tracts, public letters, and the eighteenth-century equivalent of op-ed pieces (like the individual essays that comprise *The Federalist Papers*) is William H. Riker, *The Strategy of Rhetoric: Campaigning for the American Constitution* (New Haven: Yale University Press, 1996).

representation for all Americans? Was tyranny to be feared more from the many or from the few?

In political life, of course, principles—even great principles—are seldom completely divorced from some set of interests. In 1787, Americans were divided along economic, regional, and political lines. These divisions inevitably influenced their attitudes toward the profound political questions of the day. Many well-to-do merchants and planters, as we saw earlier, favored the creation of a stronger central government that would have the capacity to protect property, promote commerce, and keep some of the more radical state legislatures in check. At the same time, many powerful state leaders, like Governor George Clinton of New York, feared that strengthening the national government would reduce their own influence and status. Each of these interests, of course, justified its position with an appeal to principle.

Principles are often important weapons in political warfare, and seeing how and by whom they are wielded can illuminate their otherwise obscure implications. In our own time, dry academic discussions of topics such as "free trade" become easier to grasp once it is noted that free trade and open markets are generally favored by low-cost producers, while protectionism is the goal of firms whose costs of production are higher than the international norm.

Even if a principle is invented and initially brandished to serve an interest, however, once it has been articulated it can take on a life of its own and prove to have implications that transcend the narrow interests it was created to serve. Some opponents of the Constitution, for example, who criticized the absence of a bill of rights in the initial document, did so simply with the hope of blocking the document's ratification. Yet, the Bill of Rights that was later added to the Constitution has proven for two centuries to be a bulwark of civil liberty in the United States.

Similarly, closer to our own time, support for the extension of voting rights and for massive legislative redistricting under the rubric of "one man, one vote" during the 1960s came mainly from liberal Democrats who were hoping to strengthen their own political base, since the groups that would benefit most from these intiatives were overwhelmingly Democratic. The principles of equal access to the ballot and one man, one vote, however, have a moral and political validity that is independent of the political interests that propelled these ideas into the political arena.

These examples show us that truly great political principles surmount the interests that initially set them forth. The first step in understanding a political principle is understanding why and by whom it is espoused. The second step is understanding the full implications of the principle itself—implications that may go far beyond the interests that launched it. Thus, even though the great political principles about which Americans argued in 1787 *did* reflect competing interests, they also represented views of society, government, and politics that surmount interest, and so must be understood in their own terms. Whatever the underlying clash of interests that may have guided

Rationality Principle

The debate over ratification revealed the conflicting interests of the Federalists and Antifederalists.

them, the Federalists and Antifederalists presented important alternative visions of America.

Federalists versus Antifederalists

During the ratification struggle, thousands of essays, speeches, pamphlets, and letters were presented in support of and in opposition to the proposed Constitution. The best-known pieces supporting ratification of the Constitution were the eighty-five essays written, under the name of "Publius," by Alexander Hamilton, James Madison, and John Jay between the fall of 1787 and the spring of 1788. These *Federalist Papers*, as they are collectively known today, defended the principles of the Constitution and sought to dispel fears of a national authority. The Antifederalists published essays of their own, arguing that the new Constitution betrayed the Revolution and was a step toward monarchy. Among the best of the Antifederalist works were the essays, usually attributed to New York Supreme Court justice Robert Yates, that were written under the name of "Brutus" and published in the *New York Journal* at the same time *The Federalist Papers* appeared. The Antifederalist view was also ably presented in the pamphlets and letters written by a former delegate to the Continental Congress and future U.S. senator, Richard Henry Lee of Virginia, using the pen name "The Federal Farmer." These essays highlight the major differences of opinion between Federalists and Antifederalists. Federalists appealed to basic principles of government in support of their nationalist vision. Antifederalists cited equally fundamental precepts to support their vision of a looser confederacy of small republics.

The two sides engaged in what was almost certainly the very first nationwide political campaign in the history of the world. Though each side was itself only loosely organized, a rudimentary form of coordination and cooperation was manifest—especially in the division of labor between Hamilton, Madison, and Jay as they alternately wrote under the "Publius" pseudonym on different aspects of the newly drafted Constitution in an effort to affect its ratification in the state of New York.

Representation   One major area of contention between the two sides was the question of representation. The Antifederalists asserted that representatives must be "a true picture of the people, . . . [possessing] the knowledge of their circumstances and their wants."[21] This could only be achieved, argued the Antifederalists, in small, relatively homogeneous republics such as the existing states. In their view, the size and extent of the entire nation precluded the construction of a truly representative form of government.

The absence of true representation, moreover, would mean that the people would lack confidence in and attachment to the national government and would refuse to voluntarily obey its laws. As a result, according to the Antifederalists,

---

[21]Melancton Smith, quoted in Herbert Storing, *What the Antifederalists Were For: The Political Thought of the Opponents of the Constitution* (Chicago: University of Chicago Press, 1981), p. 17.

the national government described by the Constitution would be compelled to resort to force to secure popular compliance. The Federal Farmer averred that laws of the remote federal government could be "in many cases disregarded, unless a multitude of officers and military force be continually kept in view, and employed to enforce the execution of the laws, and to make the government feared and respected."[22]

Federalists, for their part, did not long for pure democracy and saw no reason that representatives should be precisely like those they represented. In their view, government must be representative *of* the people, but must also have a measure of autonomy *from* the people. Their ideal government was to be so constructed as to be capable of serving the long-term public interest even if this conflicted with the public's current preference.

Federalists also dismissed the Antifederalist claim that the distance between representatives and constituents in the proposed national government would lead to popular disaffection and compel the government to use force to secure obedience. Federalists replied that the system of representation they proposed was more likely to produce effective government. In Hamilton's words, there would be "a probability that the general government will be better administered than the particular governments."[23] Competent government, in turn, should inspire popular trust and confidence more effectively than simple social proximity between rulers and ruled.

The Threats Posed by the Majority   A second important issue dividing Federalists and Antifederalists was the threat of ***tyranny***—unjust rule by the group in power. Both opponents and defenders of the Constitution frequently affirmed their fear of tyrannical rule. Each side, however, had a different view of the most likely source of tyranny and, hence, of the way in which the threat was to be forestalled.

tyranny
Oppressive government that employs the cruel and unjust use of power and authority.

From the Antifederalist perspective, the great danger was the tendency of all governments—including republican governments—to become gradually more and more "aristocratic" in character, where the small number of individuals in positions of authority would use their stations to gain more and more power over the general citizenry. In essence, the few would use their power to tyrannize the many. For this reason, Antifederalists were sharply critical of those features of the Constitution that divorced governmental institutions from direct responsibility to the people—institutions such as the Senate, the executive, and the federal judiciary. The latter, appointed for life, presented a particular threat: "I wonder if the world ever saw . . . a court of justice invested with such immense powers, and yet placed in a situation so little responsible," protested Brutus.[24]

The Federalists, too, recognized the threat of tyranny. They were not naive about the motives and purposes of individuals and took them to be no less

[22]"Letters from the Federal Farmer," No. 2, in Herbert Storing, ed., *The Complete Anti-Federalist* (Chicago: University of Chicago Press, 1981).
[23]*The Federalist*, No. 27.
[24]"Essays of Brutus," No. 15, in Storing (ed.), *The Complete Anti-Federalist*.

opportunistic and self-interested than the Antifederalists did. But the Federalists believed that the danger particularly associated with republican governments was not aristocracy, but instead, majority tyranny. The Federalists were concerned that a popular majority, "united and actuated by some common impulse of passion, or of interest, adverse to the rights of other citizens," would endeavor to "trample on the rules of justice."[25] From the Federalist perspective, it was precisely those features of the Constitution attacked as potential sources of tyranny by the Antifederalists that actually offered the best hope of averting the threat of oppression. The size and extent of the nation, for instance, was for the Federalists a bulwark against tyranny. In Madison's famous formulation,

> The smaller the society, the fewer probably will be the distinct parties and interests . . . the more frequently will a majority be found of the same party; and the smaller the number of individuals composing a majority, and the smaller the compass within which they are placed, the more easily will they concert and execute their plans of oppression. Extend the sphere, and you take in a greater variety of parties and interests; you make it less probable that a majority of the whole will have a common motive to invade the rights of other citizens; or if such a common motive exists, it will be more difficult for all who feel it to discover their own strength, and to act in unison with each other.[26]

The Federalists understood that, in a democracy, temporary majorities could abuse their power (see Box 2.1). The Federalists' misgivings about majority rule were reflected in the constitutional structure. The indirect election of senators, the indirect election of the president, the judicial branch's insulation from the people, the separation of powers, the president's veto power, the bicameral design of Congress, and the federal system were all means to curb majority tyranny. These design features in the Constitution suggest an awareness on the part of the framers of the problems of majority rule and the need for institutional safeguards. Except for the indirect election of senators (which was changed in 1913), these aspects of the constitutional structure remain in place today.[27]

Governmental Power A third major difference between Federalists and Antifederalists, and the one most central to this book, was the issue of governmental power. Both the opponents and proponents of the Constitution agreed on the principle of limited government. They differed, however, on the fundamentally important question of how to place limits on governmental action. Antifederalists favored limiting and enumerating the powers granted to the national government

[25] *The Federalist*, No. 10.
[26] Ibid.
[27] A classic development of this theme is found in James Buchanan and Gordon Tullock, *The Calculus of Consent* (Ann Arbor: University of Michigan Press, 1962). For a review of the voting paradox and a case study of how it applies today, see Kenneth A. Shepsle and Mark S. Bonchek, *Analyzing Politics: Rationality, Behavior, and Institutions* (New York: W. W. Norton, 1997), pp. 49–81.

BOX 2.1

The Instability of Majority Rule

Let's say you and two friends are trying to decide where to go for dinner. You suggest Taco Bell, your friend Joe wants McDonald's, and your other friend Sue wants Pizza Hut. Since you cannot agree on where to go, you decide to take a vote and, through a process of elimination, let the majority decide. The initial step is for each of you to decide what your first, second, and third choices are, as represented below:

	You	Joe	Sue
1st choice	Taco Bell	McDonald's	Pizza Hut
2nd choice	McDonald's	Pizza Hut	Taco Bell
3rd choice	Pizza Hut	Taco Bell	McDonald's

Consider an *agenda*—that is, an order of voting—in which Taco Bell is first pitted against McDonald's and the winner is then pitted against Pizza Hut. In this case Taco Bell wins the first vote (with you and Sue constituting the 2-to-1 majority); then Pizza Hut beats Taco Bell (with Joe and Sue in the majority). Alternatively, suppose the order of voting had Taco Bell pitted against Pizza Hut with the winner against McDonald's. In this first vote, Pizza Hut wins (supported by the Joe-Sue coalition), and then McDonald's wins with the support of you and Joe. Finally, consider the agenda in which McDonald's is paired first with Pizza Hut, and the winner faces Taco Bell. Here McDonald's wins the first vote, and Taco Bell the second. So, with three different agendas we have produced three different winners.

This little example is quite general, and actually quite disturbing. Individuals can have clearly defined preferences and vote in accord with them, yet the final winner depends not only on their preferences, *but also on the order of voting*. Majority-rule outcomes depend on which agenda is employed. He (or she) who controls the agenda controls the final outcome. As different individuals come to control the order of voting, the policy choice changes in turn, introducing a degree of potential instability into policy outcomes.

 Policy Principle

Majority-rule outcomes depend on which agenda is employed. Thus, whoever controls the agenda controls the final outcome.

in relation both to the states and to the people at large. To them, the powers given the national government ought to be "confined to certain defined national objects."[28] Otherwise, the national government would "swallow up all the power of the state governments."[29] Antifederalists bitterly attacked the supremacy clause and the necessary and proper clause of the Constitution as unlimited and dangerous grants of power to the national government.[30]

Antifederalists also demanded that a bill of rights be added to the Constitution to place limits upon the government's exercise of power over the citizenry. "There are certain things," wrote Brutus, "which rulers should be absolutely prohibited from doing, because if they should do them, they would work an injury, not a benefit to the people."[31] Similarly, the Federal Farmer maintained that "there are certain unalienable and fundamental rights, which in forming the social compact . . . ought to be explicitly ascertained and fixed."[32]

Federalists favored the construction of a government with broad powers. They wanted a government that had the capacity to defend the nation against foreign foes, guard against domestic strife and insurrection, promote commerce, and expand the nation's economy. Antifederalists shared some of these goals but still feared governmental power. Hamilton pointed out, however, that these goals could not be achieved without allowing the government to exercise the necessary power. Federalists acknowledged, of course, that every power could be abused but argued that the way to prevent misuse of power was not by depriving the government of the powers needed to achieve national goals. Instead, they argued that the threat of abuse of power would be mitigated by the Constitution's internal checks and controls. As Madison put it, "the power surrendered by the people is first divided between two distinct governments, and then the portion allotted to each subdivided among distinct and separate departments. Hence a double security arises to the rights of the people. The different governments will control each other, at the same time that each will be controlled by itself."[33] The Federalists' concern with avoiding unwarranted limits on governmental power led them to oppose a bill of rights, which they saw as nothing more than a set of unnecessary restrictions on the government.

The Federalists acknowledged that abuse of power remained a possibility, but felt that the risk had to be taken because of the goals to be achieved. "The very idea of power included a possibility of doing harm," said the Federalist John Rutledge during the South Carolina ratification debates. "If the gentleman would show the power that could do no harm," Rutledge continued, "he would at once discover it to be a power that could do no good."[34]

[28]"Essays of Brutus," No. 7.
[29]"Essays of Brutus," No. 6.
[30]Storing, *What the Antifederalists Were For*, p. 28.
[31]"Essays of Brutus," No. 9.
[32]"Letters from the Federal Farmer," No. 2.
[33]*The Federalist*, No. 51.
[34]Quoted in Storing, *What the Antifederalists Were For*, p. 30.

CHANGING THE INSTITUTIONAL FRAMEWORK: CONSTITUTIONAL AMENDMENT

The Constitution has endured for two centuries as the framework of government. But it has not endured without change. Without change, the Constitution might have become merely a sacred relic, stored under glass.

Amendments: Many Are Called, Few Are Chosen

The need for change was recognized by the framers of the Constitution, and the provisions for amendment incorporated into Article V were thought to be "an easy, regular and Constitutional way" to make changes, which would occasionally be necessary because members of Congress "may abuse their power and refuse their consent on the very account . . . to admit to amendments to correct the source of the abuse."[35] Madison made a more balanced defense of the amendment procedure in Article V: "It guards equally against that extreme facility, which would render the Constitution too mutable; and that extreme difficulty, which might perpetuate its discovered faults."[36]

Experience since 1789 raises questions even about Madison's more modest claims. The Constitution has proven to be extremely difficult to amend. In the history of efforts to amend the Constitution, the most appropriate characterization is "many are called, few are chosen." Between 1789 and 1993, 9,746 amendments were formally offered in Congress. Of these, Congress officially proposed only 29, and 27 of these were eventually ratified by the states. But the record is even more severe than that. Since 1791, when the first 10 amendments, the Bill of Rights, were added, only 17 amendments have been adopted. And two of them—Prohibition and its repeal—cancel each other out, so that for all practical purposes, only 15 amendments have been added to the Constitution since 1791. Despite vast changes in American society and its economy, only 12 amendments have been adopted since the Civil War amendments in 1868.

Institution Principle

The procedures for amending the Constitution are difficult. As a result, the amendment route to political change is extremely limited.

Four methods of amendment are provided for in Article V:

1. Passage in House and Senate by two-thirds vote; then ratification by majority vote of the legislatures of three-fourths (thirty-eight) of the states.
2. Passage in House and Senate by two-thirds vote; then ratification by conventions called for the purpose in three-fourths of the states.
3. Passage in a national convention called by Congress in response to petitions by two-thirds of the states; ratification by majority vote of the legislatures of three-fourths of the states.

[35]Observation by Colonel George Mason, delegate from Virginia, early during the convention period. Quoted in Farrand, *The Records of the Federal Convention of 1787*, vol. 1, pp. 202–3.

[36]Clinton Rossiter, ed., *The Federalist Papers* (New York: New American Library, 1961), No. 43, p. 278.

4. Passage in a national convention, as in (3); then ratification by conventions called for the purpose in three-fourths of the states.

Since no amendment has ever been proposed by national convention, however, methods (3) and (4) have never been employed. And method (2) has only been employed once (the Twenty-first Amendment, which repealed the Eighteenth, or Prohibition, Amendment). Thus, method (1) has been used for all the others.

Now we should be better able to explain why it has been so difficult to amend the Constitution. The main reason is the requirement of a two-thirds vote in the House and the Senate, which means that any proposal for an amendment in Congress can be killed by only 34 senators *or* 146 members of the House. What is more, if the necessary two-thirds vote is obtained, the amendment can still be killed by the refusal or inability of only thirteen state legislatures to ratify it. Since each state has an equal vote regardless of its population, the thirteen hold-out states may represent a very small fraction of the total American population.

The Twenty-Seven Amendments

Despite difficulties of the process, the Constitution has been amended twenty-seven times since the framers completed their work. The first ten of these amendments, known as the Bill of Rights, were added to the Constitution shortly after its ratification. As we saw, Federalists feared that a bill of rights would weaken the new government, but they were forced to commit themselves to the principle of an enumeration of rights when the Antifederalists charged that the proposed Constitution was a threat to liberty.

Most of the Constitution's twenty-seven amendments share a common characteristic: all but two are concerned with the structure or composition of government. This is consistent with the dictionary, which defines *constitution* as the makeup or composition of a thing, anything. And it is consistent with the concept of a constitution as "higher law," because the whole point and purpose of a higher law is to establish *a framework within which government and the process of making ordinary law can take place.* Even those who would have preferred more changes in the Constitution would have to agree that there is great wisdom in this principle. A constitution ought to enable legislation and public policies to take place, but it should not determine what that legislation or those public policies ought to be.

The purpose of the ten amendments in the Bill of Rights was basically structural, *to give each of the three branches clearer and more restricted boundaries.* The First Amendment clarified the jurisdiction of Congress. Although the powers of Congress under Article I, Section 8, would not have justified laws regulating religion, speech, and the like, the First Amendment made this limitation explicit: "Congress shall make no law. . . ." The Second, Third, and Fourth Amendments similarly spelled out specific limits on the executive branch. This was seen as a necessity given the abuses of executive power Americans had endured under British rule.

TABLE 2.1

The Bill of Rights: Analysis of Its Provisions

AMENDMENT	PURPOSE
I	*Limits on Congress:* Congress is not to make any law establishing a religion or abridging the freedom of speech, press, assembly, or the right to petition freedoms.
II, III, IV	*Limits on Executive:* The executive branch is not to infringe on the right of people to keep arms (II), is not to arbitrarily take houses for a militia (III), and is not to engage in the search or seizure of evidence without a court warrant swearing to belief in the probable existence of a crime (IV).
V, VI, VII, VIII	*Limits on Courts:* The courts are not to hold trials for serious offenses without provision for a grand jury (V), a petit (trial) jury (VII), a speedy trial (VI), presentation of charges, confrontation of hostile witnesses (VI), immunity from testimony against oneself (V), and immunity from trial more than once for the same offense (V). Neither bail nor punishment can be excessive (VIII), and no property can be taken without just compensation (V).
IX, X	*Limits on National Government:* All rights not enumerated are reserved to the states or the people.

The Fifth, Sixth, Seventh, and Eighth Amendments contain some of the most important safeguards for individual citizens against the arbitrary exercise of government power. And these amendments sought to accomplish their goal by defining the judicial branch more concretely and clearly than had been done in Article III of the Constitution. Table 2.1 analyzes the ten amendments included in the Bill of Rights.

Five of the seventeen amendments adopted since 1791 are directly concerned with expansion of the electorate (see Table 2.2). These occasional efforts to expand the electorate were made necessary by the fact that the founders were unable to establish a national electorate with uniform voting qualifications. Stalemated on that issue, the delegates decided to evade it by providing in the

TABLE 2.2

Amending the Constitution to Expand the Electorate

AMENDMENT	PURPOSE	YEAR PROPOSED	YEAR ADOPTED
XIV	Section I provided national definition of citizenship*	1866	1868
XV	Extended voting rights to all races	1869	1870
XIX	Extended voting rights to women	1919	1920
XXIII	Extended voting rights to residents of the District of Columbia	1960	1961
XXIV	Extended voting rights to all classes by abolition of poll taxes	1962	1964
XXVI	Extended voting rights to citizens aged 18 and over	1971	1971

*In defining *citizenship*, the Fourteenth Amendment actually provided the constitutional basis for expanding the electorate to include all races, women, and residents of the District of Columbia. Only the "eighteen-year-olds' amendment" should have been necessary, since it changed the definition of citizenship. The fact that additional amendments were required following the Fourteenth suggests that voting is not considered an inherent right of U.S. citizenship. Instead it is viewed as a privilege.

final draft of Article I, Section 2, that eligibility to vote in a national election would be the same as "the Qualifications requisite for Electors of the most numerous Branch of the State Legislature." Article I, Section 4, added that Congress could alter state regulations as to the "Times, Places and Manner of holding Elections for Senators and Representatives." Nevertheless, this meant that any important *expansion* of the American electorate would almost certainly require a constitutional amendment.

Six more amendments are also electoral in nature, although not concerned directly with voting rights and the expansion of the electorate (see Table 2.3).

TABLE 2.3

Amending the Constitution to Change the Relationship between Elected Offices and the Electorate

AMENDMENT	PURPOSE	YEAR PROPOSED	YEAR ADOPTED
XII	Provided separate ballot for vice president in the electoral college	1803	1804
XIV	Section 2 eliminated counting of slaves as "three-fifths" citizens for apportionment of House seats	1866	1868
XVII	Provided direct election of senators	1912	1913
XX	Eliminated "lame duck" session of Congress	1932	1933
XXII	Limited presidential term	1947	1951
XXV	Provided presidential succession in case of disability	1965	1967

These six amendments are concerned with the elective offices themselves (the Twentieth, Twenty-second, and Twenty-fifth) or with the relationship between elective offices and the electorate (the Twelfth, Fourteenth, and Seventeenth).

Another five amendments have sought to expand or to delimit the powers of the national and state governments (see Table 2.4).[37] The Eleventh

[37]The Fourteenth Amendment is included in this table as well as in Tables 2.2 and 2.3 because it seeks not only to define citizenship but *seems* to intend also that this definition of citizenship included, along with the right to vote, all the rights of the Bill of Rights, regardless of the state in which the citizen resided. A great deal more will be said about this in Chapter 4.

TABLE 2.4

Amending the Constitution to Expand or Limit the Power of Government

AMENDMENT	PURPOSE	YEAR PROPOSED	YEAR ADOPTED
XI	Limited jurisdiction of federal courts over suits involving the states	1794	1798
XIII	Eliminated slavery and eliminated the rights of states to allow property in persons	1865*	1865
XIV	(Part 2) Applied due process of Bill of Rights to the states	1866	1868
XVI	Established national power to tax incomes	1909	1913
XXVII	Limited Congress's power to raise its own salary	1789	1992

*The Thirteenth Amendment was proposed January 31, 1865, and adopted less than a year later, on December 18, 1865.

Amendment protected the states from suits by private individuals and took away from the federal courts any power to take suits by private individuals of one state (or a foreign country) against another state. The other three amendments in Table 2.4 are obviously designed to reduce state power (Thirteenth), to reduce state power and expand national power (Fourteenth), and to expand national power (Sixteenth). The Twenty-seventh put a limit on Congress's ability to raise its own salary.

The two missing amendments underscore the meaning of the rest: the Eighteenth, or Prohibition, Amendment and the Twenty-first, its repeal. This is the only instance in which the country tried to *legislate* by constitutional amendment. In other words, the Eighteenth is the only amendment that was designed to deal directly with some substantive social problem. And it was the only amendment ever to have been repealed. Two other amendments—the Thirteenth, which abolished slavery, and the Sixteenth, which established the power to levy an income tax—can be said to have had the effect of legislation. But the purpose of the Thirteenth was to restrict the power of the states by forever forbidding them to treat any human being as property. As for the Sixteenth, it is certainly true that income tax legislation followed immediately; nevertheless, the amendment concerns itself strictly with establishing the power of Congress to enact such legislation. The legislation came later; and if down the line a majority in Congress had wanted to abolish the income tax, they could also have done this by legislation rather than through the arduous path of a constitutional amendment repealing the income tax.

For those whose hopes for change center on the Constitution, it must be emphasized that the amendment route to social change is, and always will be, extremely limited. Through a constitution it is possible to establish a working structure of government; and through a constitution it is possible to establish basic rights of citizens by placing limitations and obligations on the powers of that government. Once these things have been accomplished, the real problem is how to extend rights to those people who do not already enjoy them. Of course, the Constitution cannot enforce itself. But it can and does have a real influence on everyday life because a right or an obligation set forth in the Constitution can become a *cause of action* in the hands of an otherwise powerless person.

Private property is an excellent example. Property is one of the most fundamental and well-established rights in the United States; but it is well established not because it is recognized in so many words in the Constitution, but because legislatures and courts have made it a crime for anyone, including the government, to trespass or to take away property without compensation.

Institutional Reform
www.wwnorton.com/
lowi7/ch2
What is the impact of various constitutional amendments on the structure of government?

REFLECTIONS ON THE FOUNDING: PRINCIPLES OR INTERESTS?

The final product of the Constitutional Convention would have to be considered an extraordinary victory for the groups that had most forcefully called for the creation of a new system of government to replace the Articles of Confederation. Antifederalist criticisms forced the Constitution's proponents to accept the addition of a bill of rights designed to limit the powers of the national government. In general, however, it was the Federalist vision of America that triumphed. The Constitution adopted in 1789 created the framework for a powerful national government that for more than two hundred years has defended the nation's interests, promoted its commerce, and maintained national unity. In one notable instance, the national government fought and won a bloody war to prevent the nation from breaking apart.

Though the Constitution was the product of a particular set of political forces, the principles of government it established have a significance that goes far beyond the interests of its authors. As we have observed, political principles often take on lives of their own. The great political principles incorporated into the Constitution continue, more than two centuries later, to shape our political lives in ways that the Constitution's framers may not always have anticipated. For example, when they empowered the Congress of the United States to regulate commerce among the states in Article I, Section 8, of the Constitution, the framers could hardly have anticipated that this would become the basis for many of the federal government's regulatory activities in areas as diverse as the environment and civil rights.

Two great constitutional principles, federalism and civil liberties, will be discussed in Chapters 3 and 4. A third important constitutional principle that has affected America's government for the past two hundred years is the principle of *checks and balances*. As we saw earlier, the framers gave each of the three branches of government a means of intervening in and blocking the actions of the others. Often, checks and balances have seemed to prevent the government from getting much done. During the 1960s, for example, liberals were often infuriated as they watched Congress stall presidential initiatives in the area of civil rights. More recently, conservatives were outraged when President Clinton thwarted congressional efforts to enact legislation promised in the Republican "Contract with America." At various times, all sides have vilified the judiciary for invalidating legislation enacted by Congress and signed by the president.

Over time, checks and balances have acted as brakes on the governmental process. Groups hoping to bring about changes in policy or governmental institutions seldom have been able to bring about decisive and dramatic transformations in a short period of time. Instead, checks and balances have slowed the pace of change and increased the need for compromise and accommodation.

Policy Principle
The constitutional framework, such as the principle of checks and balances, can act as a brake on the policy process.

Groups able to take control of the White House, for example, must bargain with their rivals who remain entrenched on Capitol Hill. New forces in Congress must reckon with the influence of other forces in the executive branch and in the courts. Checks and balances inevitably frustrate those who desire change, but they also function as a safeguard against rash action. During the 1950s, for example, Congress was caught up in a quasi-hysterical effort to unmask subversive activities in the United States, which might have led to a serious erosion of American liberties if not for the checks and balances provided by the executive and the courts. Thus, a governmental principle that serves as a frustrating limitation one day may become a vitally important safeguard the next.

As we close our discussion of the founding, it is also worth reflecting on the Antifederalists. Although they were defeated in 1789, the Antifederalists present us with an important picture of a road not taken and of an America that might have been. Would we have been worse off as a people if we had been governed by a confederacy of small republics linked by a national administration with severely limited powers? Were the Antifederalists correct in predicting that a government given great power in the hope that it might do good would, through "insensible progress," inevitably turn to evil purposes? Two hundred plus years of government under the federal Constitution are not necessarily enough to definitively answer these questions. Only time will tell.

Rationality Principle	Collective Action Principle	Institution Principle	Policy Principle	History Principle
The framers of the Constitution were guided by principles, but they also had interests.	The colonists required strong leaders to resolve differences and to organize resistance to British authority.	Institutional arrangements, such as the Articles of Confederation, can be flawed.	Majority-rule outcomes depend on which agenda is employed. Thus, whoever controls the agenda controls the final outcome.	The American colonists, used to years of self-governance, believed that the Stamp Act of 1765 threatened their autonomy.
The debate over ratification revealed the conflicting interests of the Federalists and Antifederalists.	The framers preferred compromise to the breakup of the union, and thus accepted the Great Compromise and the Three-fifths Compromise.	The constitutional framework promoted commerce, protected property, prevented "excessive democracy," and limited the power of the national government.	The constitutional framework, such as the principle of checks and balances, can act as a brake on the policy process.	Shays's Rebellion focused attention on the flaws of the Articles of Confederation, leading to the Constitutional Convention.
		The procedures for amending the Constitution are difficult. As a result, the amendment route to political change is extremely limited.		

SUMMARY

Political conflicts between the colonies and England, and among competing groups within the colonies, led to the first founding as expressed by the Declaration of Independence. The first constitution, the Articles of Confederation, was adopted one year later (1777). Under this document, the states retained their sovereignty. The central government, composed solely of Congress, had few powers and no means of enforcing its will. The national government's weakness soon led to the Constitution of 1787, the second founding.

In this second founding the framers sought, first, to fashion a new government sufficiently powerful to promote commerce and protect property from radical state legislatures. Second, the framers sought to bring an end to the "excessive democracy" of the state and national governments under the Articles of Confederation. Third, the framers introduced mechanisms that helped secure popular consent for the new government. Finally, the framers made certain that their new government would not itself pose a threat to liberty and property.

The Constitution consists of seven articles. In part, Article I provides for a Congress of two chambers (Sections 1–7), defines the powers of the national government (Section 8), and interprets the national government's powers as a source of strength rather than a limitation (necessary and proper clause). Article II describes the presidency and establishes it as a separate branch of government. Article III is the judiciary article. While there is no direct mention of judicial review in this article, the Supreme Court eventually assumed that power. Article IV addresses reciprocity among states and their citizens. Article V describes the procedures for amending the Constitution. Hundreds of amendments have been offered but only twenty-seven have been adopted. With the exception of the two Prohibition amendments, all amendments were oriented toward some change in the framework or structure of government. Article VI establishes that national laws and treaties are "the supreme Law of the Land." And finally, Article VII specifies the procedure for ratifying the Constitution of 1787.

The struggle for the ratification of the Constitution pitted the Antifederalists against the Federalists. The Antifederalists thought the proposed new government would be too powerful, and they fought against the ratification of the Constitution. The Federalists supported the Constitution and were able to secure its ratification after a nationwide political debate.

FOR FURTHER READING

Anderson, Thornton. *Creating the Constitution: The Convention of 1787 and the First Congress.* University Park: Pennsylvania State University Press, 1993.

Andrews, Charles M. *The Colonial Background of the American Revolution.* New Haven: Yale University Press, 1924.

Bailyn, Bernard. *The Ideological Origins of the American Revolution.* Cambridge: Harvard University Press, 1967.

Beard, Charles. *An Economic Interpretation of the Constitution of the United States.* New York: Macmillan, 1913.

Becker, Carl L. *The Declaration of Independence.* New York: Vintage, 1942.

Cohler, Anne M. *Montesquieu's Politics and the Spirit of American Constitutionalism.* Lawrence: University Press of Kansas, 1988.

Farrand, Max, ed. *The Records of the Federal Convention of 1787.* 4 vols. New Haven: Yale University Press, 1966.

Hamilton, Alexander, James Madison, and John Jay. *The Federalist Papers.* Edited by Isaac Kramnick. New York: Viking Press, 1987.

Jensen, Merrill. *The Articles of Confederation.* Madison: University of Wisconsin Press, 1963.

Lipset, Seymour M. *The First New Nation: The United States in Historical and Comparative Perspective.* New York: Basic Books, 1963.

McDonald, Forrest. *The Formation of the American Republic.* New York: Penguin, 1967.

Main, Jackson Turner. *The Social Structure of Revolutionary America.* Princeton: Princeton University Press, 1965.

Palmer, R. R. *The Age of the Democratic Revolution.* Princeton: Princeton University Press, 1964.

Riker, William H. *The Strategy of Rhetoric: Campaigning for the American Constitution.* New Haven: Yale University Press, 1996.

Rossiter, Clinton, ed. *The Federalist Papers.* New York: New American Library, 1961.

Storing, Herbert, ed. *The Complete Anti-Federalist.* 7 vols. Chicago: University of Chicago Press, 1981.

Wills, Gary. *Explaining America.* New York: Penguin, 1982.

Wood, Gordon S. *The Creation of the American Republic.* New York: W. W. Norton, 1982.

CHAPTER three

The Constitutional Framework:
Federalism and the Separation of Powers

EVENTS	INSTITUTIONAL DEVELOPMENTS
	Congress establishes national economic power, power to tax, power over foreign policy (1791–1795)
	Bill of Rights ratified (1791)
1800	Epoch of dual federalism: Congress promotes commerce; states possess unchallenged police power (1789–1937)
Hartford Convention—New England states threaten secession from Union (1814)	*McCulloch v. Maryland* (1819) and *Gibbons v. Ogden* (1824) reaffirm national supremacy
President Andrew Jackson decisively deals with South Carolina's threat to secede (1833)	
Attempt to use U.S. Bill of Rights to restrict state power (1830s)	*Barron v. Baltimore*—state power not subject to the U.S. Bill of Rights (1833)
Territorial expansion; slaves taken into territories (1800s) **1850**	*Dred Scott v. Sandford*—Congress may not regulate slavery in the territories (1857)
Secession of Southern states (1860–1861); Civil War (1861–1865)	Union destroyed (1860–1861)
	Union restored (1865)
	Constitution amended: XIII (1865), XIV (1868), XV (1870) Amendments
Reconstruction of South (1867–1877) **1870**	
Compromise of 1877—self-government restored to former Confederate states (1877)	Reestablishment of South's full place in the Union (1877)
Consolidation of great national industrial corporations (U.S. Steel, AT&T, Standard Oil) (1880s and 1890s)	Interstate Commerce Act (1887) and Sherman Antitrust Act (1890) provide first national regulation of monopoly practices
1930	
Franklin D. Roosevelt's first New Deal programs for national economic recovery enacted by Congress (1933)	Supreme Court upholds expanded powers of president in *U.S. v. Curtiss-Wright* (1936), and of Congress in *Steward Machine v. Davis* (1937) and *NLRB v. Jones & Laughlin Steel* (1937)

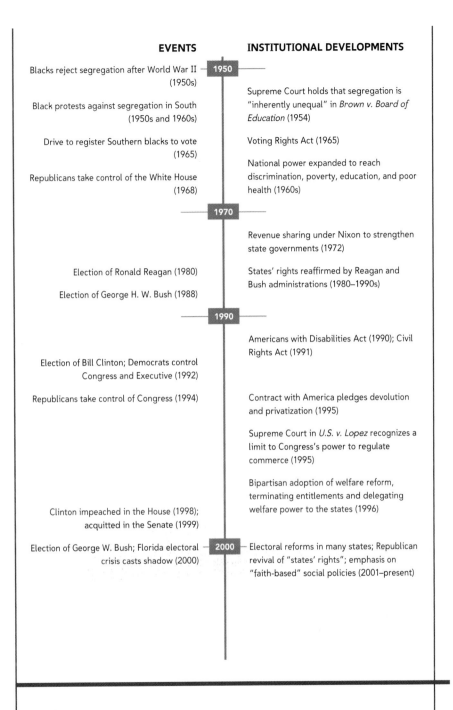

EVENTS	INSTITUTIONAL DEVELOPMENTS
Blacks reject segregation after World War II (1950s)	**1950**
	Supreme Court holds that segregation is "inherently unequal" in *Brown v. Board of Education* (1954)
Black protests against segregation in South (1950s and 1960s)	
Drive to register Southern blacks to vote (1965)	Voting Rights Act (1965)
Republicans take control of the White House (1968)	National power expanded to reach discrimination, poverty, education, and poor health (1960s)
	1970
	Revenue sharing under Nixon to strengthen state governments (1972)
Election of Ronald Reagan (1980)	States' rights reaffirmed by Reagan and Bush administrations (1980–1990s)
Election of George H. W. Bush (1988)	
	1990
	Americans with Disabilities Act (1990); Civil Rights Act (1991)
Election of Bill Clinton; Democrats control Congress and Executive (1992)	
Republicans take control of Congress (1994)	Contract with America pledges devolution and privatization (1995)
	Supreme Court in *U.S. v. Lopez* recognizes a limit to Congress's power to regulate commerce (1995)
	Bipartisan adoption of welfare reform, terminating entitlements and delegating welfare power to the states (1996)
Clinton impeached in the House (1998); acquitted in the Senate (1999)	
Election of George W. Bush; Florida electoral crisis casts shadow (2000)	**2000** — Electoral reforms in many states; Republican revival of "states' rights"; emphasis on "faith-based" social policies (2001–present)

CORE OF THE ANALYSIS

- Federalism limits national power by creating two sovereigns—the national government and the state governments.

- Under "dual federalism," which lasted from 1789–1937, the national government limited itself primarily to promoting commerce, while the state governments directly coerced citizens.

- After 1937, the national government began to expand, yet the states maintained most of their traditional powers.

- Under "cooperative federalism," the national government influences state and local governments through grants-in-aid to encourage the pursuit of national goals.

- Checks and balances ensure the sharing of power among separate institutions of government. Within the system of separated powers, the framers of the Constitution provided for legislative supremacy.

Replacement of the Articles of Confederation by the Constitution is a classic case study of political realism. As an instrument of government, the Articles of Confederation had many virtues. Many considered it the second greatest constitution ever drafted. But as a confederation it left too much power to the states, whose restrictions and boundaries interfered with national and international markets being sought by new economic interests. The Articles of Confederation had to be replaced, and a stronger national power had to be provided for, if the barriers to economic progress were to be lowered.[1]

To a point, political realists are correct. Everything in politics revolves around interests; a constitution must satisfy those interests or it will not last long as a governing instrument. But just as pure force is an inadequate foundation for government, so is pure interest, despite its immediate importance. Interests must be translated into higher principles, and there will be no loyalty or support for any government unless most of the powerful as well as the powerless accept the principles as *legitimate*.

A government can be considered legitimate when its actions appear to be consistent with the highest principles that people already hold. The American approach to legitimacy is based on *contract*. A contract is an exchange, a deal. The contract we call the American Constitution was simply this: *the people would give their consent to a strong national government if that government would in turn accept certain strict limitations on its powers*. In other words, power in return for limits, or ***constitutionalism.***

constitutional government
A system of rule in which formal and effective limits are placed on the powers of the government.

Three fundamental limitations were the principles involved in the contract between the American people and the framers of the Constitution: *federalism*, the *separation of powers*, and *individual rights*. Nowhere in the Constitution were these mentioned by name, but we know from the debates and writings that they were the primary framework of the Constitution. We can call them the

[1]For two important realist interpretations of the rejection of the Articles in favor of the Constitution, see John P. Roche, "The Founding Fathers: A Reform Caucus in Action," *American Political Science Review* 55 (December 1961), pp. 799–816, and the discussion of Charles Beard's economic interpretation in the text.

by the states. The contrast between national and state policies, as shown by the table, demonstrates the difference in the power vested in each. The list of items in column 2 could actually have been made much longer. Moreover, each item on the list is only a category made up of laws that fill many volumes of statutes and court decisions for each state.

This contrast between national and state governments is all the more impressive because it is basically what was intended by the framers of the Constitution. There is probably no better example in world history of consistency between formal intentions and political reality.[5] Since the 1930s, the national government has expanded into local and intrastate matters. But this significant expansion of the national government did not alter the basic framework. The national government has become much larger, but the states have continued to be central to the American system of government.

And here lies probably the most important point of all: the fundamental impact of federalism on the way the United States is governed comes not from any particular provision of the Constitution but from the framework itself, which has determined the flow of government functions and, through that, the political development of the country. By allowing state governments to do most of the fundamental governing, the Constitution saved the national government from many policy decisions that might have proven too divisive for this large but very young country. There is no doubt that if the Constitution had provided for a unitary rather than a federal system, the war over slavery would have come in 1789 or 1809 rather than 1860; and if it had come that early, the South might very well have seceded and established a separate and permanent slaveholding nation. In helping the national government remain small and aloof from the most divisive issues of the day, federalism contributed significantly to the political stability of the nation even as the social, economic, and political systems of many of the states and regions of the country were undergoing tremendous and profound, and sometimes violent, change.[6] As we shall see, some important aspects of federalism have changed, but the federal framework has survived two centuries and a devastating civil war.

Institution Principle

In answering "Who does what?" federalism determines the flow of government functions and, through that, the political development of the country.

The Changing Role of the National Government

Having created the national government, and recognizing the potential for abuse of power, the states sought through federalism to constrain the national government.

---

[5]Alexander Hamilton, the founder most famous for favoring a strong national government, came up with a list of extremely bold proposals for the national government when he was the first secretary of the treasury under President Washington; but when these are examined, they turn out to be nothing more than a detailed set of proposals very like the policies Congress ultimately adopted. Hamilton's proposals are contained in his *Report on Manufactures* (1791), one of the most important state papers ever written.

[6]For a good treatment of the contrast between national political stability and social instability, see Samuel P. Huntington, *Political Order in Changing Societies* (New Haven: Yale University Press, 1968), Chapter 2.

The "traditional system" of weak national government prevailed for over a century despite economic forces favoring its expansion and despite Supreme Court cases giving a pro-national interpretation to Article I, Section 8, of the Constitution.

That article delegates to Congress the power "to regulate commerce with foreign nations, and among the several States and with the Indian tribes." This **commerce clause** was consistently interpreted *in favor* of national power by the Supreme Court for most of the nineteenth century. The first and most important case favoring national power over the economy was *McCulloch v. Maryland*.[7] The case involved the Bank of the United States and the question of whether Congress had the power to charter a bank, since such an explicit grant of power was nowhere to be found in Article I, Section 8. Chief Justice John Marshall answered that the power could be "implied" from other powers that were expressly delegated to Congress, such as the "powers to lay and collect taxes; to borrow money; to regulate commerce; and to declare and conduct a war." The constitutional authority for the implied powers doctrine is a clause in Article I, Section 8, which enables Congress "to make all Laws which shall be necessary and proper for carrying into Execution the foregoing Powers." By allowing Congress to use the "necessary and proper" clause to interpret its delegated powers, the Supreme Court created the potential for an unprecedented increase in national government power.

A second historic question posed by *McCulloch* was whether a state had the power to tax the Baltimore branch of the U.S. Bank, since it was a national agency. Here Marshall again took the side of national supremacy, arguing that an agency created by a legislature representing all the people (Congress) could not be put out of business by a state legislature (Maryland) representing only a small portion of the people (since "the power to tax is the power to destroy"). Marshall concluded that whenever a state law conflicted with a federal law, the state law would be deemed invalid since "the laws of the United States . . . 'shall be the supreme law of the land.'" Both parts of this historic case were "pro-national," yet Congress did not immediately attempt to expand the policies of the national government.

This nationalistic interpretation of the Constitution was reinforced by another major case, that of *Gibbons v. Ogden* in 1824. The important but relatively narrow issue was whether the state of New York could grant a monopoly to Robert Fulton's steamboat company to operate an exclusive service between New York and New Jersey. Ogden had secured his license from Fulton's company, while Gibbons, a former partner, secured a competing license from the U.S. government. Chief Justice Marshall argued that Gibbons could not be kept from competing because the state of New York did not have the power to grant this particular monopoly. In order to reach this decision, it was necessary for Chief Justice Marshall to define what Article I, Section 8, meant by "Commerce . . . among the several States." Marshall insisted that the definition was "comprehensive," extending to "every species of commercial intercourse." He

commerce clause
Article I, Section 8, of the Constitution, which delegates to Congress the power "to regulate Commerce with foreign Nations, and among the several States, and with the Indian Tribes." This clause was interpreted by the Supreme Court in favor of national power over the economy.

---

[7]McCulloch v. Maryland, 4 Wheaton 316 (1819).

did say that this comprehensiveness was limited "to that commerce which concerns more states than one," giving rise to what later came to be called "interstate commerce." *Gibbons* is important because it established the supremacy of the national government in all matters affecting interstate commerce.[8] What would remain uncertain during several decades of constitutional discourse was the precise meaning of interstate commerce, notwithstanding John Marshall's expansive reading of "commerce among the several states."

Article I, Section 8, backed by the "implied powers" decision in *McCulloch* and by the broad definition of "interstate commerce" in *Gibbons*, was a source of power for the national government as long as Congress sought to improve commerce through subsidies, services, and land grants. But later in the nineteenth century, when the national government sought to use those powers to *regulate* the economy rather than merely to promote economic development, federalism and the concept of interstate commerce began to operate as restraints on rather than as sources of national power. Any effort of the federal government to regulate commerce in such areas as fraud, the production of impure goods, the use of child labor, or the existence of dangerous working conditions or long hours was declared unconstitutional by the Supreme Court as a violation of the concept of interstate commerce. Such legislation meant that the federal government was entering the factory and workplace, and these areas were considered inherently local, because the goods produced there had not yet passed into commerce. Any effort to enter these local workplaces was an exercise of police power—the power reserved to the states for the protection of the health, safety, and morals of their citizens. No one questioned the power of the national government to regulate certain kinds of businesses, such as railroads, gas pipelines, and waterway transportation, because they intrinsically involved interstate commerce.[9] But well into the twentieth century, most other efforts by the national government to regulate commerce were blocked by the Supreme Court's interpretation of federalism, which used the concept of interstate commerce as a barrier against most efforts by Congress to regulate local conditions.

This aspect of federalism was alive and well during an epoch of tremendous economic development, the period between the Civil War and the 1930s. It gave the American economy a freedom from federal government control that closely approximated the ideal of "free enterprise." The economy was, of course, never entirely free; in fact, entrepreneurs themselves did not want complete freedom from government. They needed law and order. They needed a stable currency. They needed courts and police to enforce contracts and prevent trespass. They needed roads, canals, and railroads. But federalism, as interpreted by the Supreme Court for seventy years after the Civil War, made it possible for

---

[8] Gibbons v. Ogden, 9 Wheaton 1 (1824).

[9] In Wabash, St. Louis, and Pacific Railway Company v. Illinois, 118 U.S. 557 (1886), the Supreme Court struck down a state law prohibiting rate discrimination by a railroad; in response, Congress passed the Interstate Commerce Act of 1887 creating the Interstate Commerce Commission (ICC), which was the first federal administrative agency.

business to have its cake and eat it, too. Entrepreneurs enjoyed the benefits of national policies facilitating commerce and were protected by the courts from policies regulating commerce.[10]

All this changed after 1937, when the Supreme Court threw out the old distinction between interstate and intrastate commerce, converting the commerce clause from a source of limitations to a source of power. The Court began to refuse to review appeals challenging acts of Congress protecting the rights of employees to organize and engage in collective bargaining, regulating the amount of farmland in cultivation, extending low-interest credit to small businesses and farmers, and restricting the activities of corporations dealing in the stock market, and many other laws that contributed to the construction of the "welfare state."

 Rationality Principle
In 1937, the Supreme Court converted the commerce clause from a source of limitations to a source of power for the national government.

The Role of the States Vis-à-Vis the National Government

As we have seen, the Constitution contained the seeds of a very expansive national government—in the commerce clause. For much of the nineteenth century, federal power remained limited. The Tenth Amendment was used to bolster arguments about *states' rights,* which in their extreme version claimed that the states did not have to submit to national laws when they believed the national government had exceeded its authority. These arguments in favor of states' rights were voiced less often after the Civil War. But the Supreme Court continued to use the Tenth Amendment to strike down laws that it thought exceeded national power, including the Civil Rights Act passed in 1875.

In the early twentieth century, however, the Tenth Amendment appeared to lose its force. Reformers began to press for national regulations to limit the power of large corporations and to preserve the health and welfare of citizens. The Supreme Court approved of some of these laws but it struck others down, including a law combating child labor. The Court stated that the law violated the Tenth Amendment because only states should have the power to regulate conditions of employment. By the late 1930s, however, the Supreme Court had approved such an expansion of federal power that the Tenth Amendment appeared irrelevant. In fact, in 1941, Justice Harlan Fiske Stone declared that the Tenth Amendment was simply a "truism," that it had no real meaning.[11]

Yet the idea that some powers should be reserved to the states did not go away. Indeed, in the 1950s, southern opponents of the civil rights movement revived the idea of states' rights. In 1956, ninety-six southern members of Congress issued a "Southern Manifesto" in which they declared that southern states were not constitutionally bound by Supreme Court decisions outlawing

states' rights
The principle that states should oppose increasing authority of the national government. This view was most popular before the Civil War.

---

[10]The Sherman Antitrust Act, adopted in 1890, for example, was enacted not to restrict commerce but rather to protect it from monopolies, or trusts, so as to prevent unfair trade practices, and to enable the market again to become *self-regulating.* Moreover, the Supreme Court sought to uphold liberty of contract to protect businesses. For example, in Lochner v. New York, 198 U.S. 45 (1905), the Court invalidated a New York law regulating the sanitary conditions and hours of labor of bakers on the grounds that the law interfered with liberty of contract.

[11]U.S. v. Darby Lumber Co., 312 U.S. 100 (1941).

racial segregation. They believed that states' rights should override individual rights to liberty and formal equality. With the triumph of the civil rights movement, the slogan of "states' rights" became tarnished by its association with racial inequality.

Recent years have seen a revival of interest in the Tenth Amendment and important Supreme Court decisions limiting federal power. Much of the interest in the Tenth Amendment stems from conservatives who believe that a strong federal government encroaches on individual liberties. They believe such freedoms are better protected by returning more power to the states through the process of ***devolution.*** In 1996, Republican presidential candidate Bob Dole carried a copy of the Tenth Amendment in his pocket as he campaigned, pulling it out to read at rallies.[12] The Supreme Court's ruling in *United States v. Lopez* in 1995 fueled further interest in the Tenth Amendment. In that case, the Court, stating that Congress had exceeded its authority under the commerce clause, struck down a federal law that barred handguns near schools. This was the first time since the New Deal that the Court had limited congressional powers in this way. The Court further limited the power of the federal government over the states in a 1996 ruling that prevented Native Americans from the Seminole tribe from suing the state of Florida in federal court. A 1988 law had given Indian tribes the right to sue a state in federal court if the state did not negotiate in good faith over issues related to gambling casinos on tribal land. The Supreme Court's ruling appeared to signal a much broader limitation on national power by raising new questions about whether individuals can sue a state if it fails to uphold federal law.[13]

Another significant decision involving the relationship between the federal government and state governments was the 1997 case *Printz v. United States* (joined with *Mack v. United States*), in which the Court struck down a key provision of the Brady Bill, enacted by Congress in 1993 to regulate gun sales. Under the terms of the act, state and local law enforcement officers were required to conduct background checks on prospective gun purchasers. The Court held that the federal government cannot require states to administer or enforce federal regulatory programs. Since the states bear administrative responsibility for a variety of other federal programs, this decision could have far-reaching consequences. Finally, in another major ruling from the 1996–1997 term, in *City of Boerne v. Flores*, the Court ruled that Congress had gone too far in restricting the power of the states to enact regulations they deemed necessary for the protection of public health, safety, or welfare. These rulings signal a move toward a much more restricted federal government.

Federalism returned to a central place in the electoral politics of 2000 as a result of the Supreme Court's consideration of the future of federalism. The first shot came in May 2000 with *United States v. Morrison.*[14] In a 5-to-4 vote, the

devolution A policy to remove a program from one level of government by deregulating it or passing it down to a lower level of government, such as from the national government to the state and local governments.

[12]W. John Moore, "Pleading the 10th," *National Journal*, 29 July 1995, p. 1940.
[13]Seminole Indian Tribe v. Florida, 116 S. Ct. 1114 (1996).
[14]U.S. v. Morrison, 529 U.S. 598 (2000).

Supreme Court invalidated an important provision of the 1994 Violence Against Women Act, which permitted women to bring private damage suits if their victimization was "gender-motivated." Although the 1994 act did not add any new national laws imposing liability or obligations on the states, the Supreme Court still held the act to be "an unconstitutional exercise" of Congress's power. And, although *Morrison* is a quite narrow federalism decision, when it is coupled with *U.S. v. Lopez* (1995)—the first modern holding against national authority to use commerce power to reach into the states—there is a definite trend toward strict scrutiny of the federal intervention aspects of all national civil rights, social, labor, and gender laws.

History Principle

Since the time of the founding, federalism has been shaped strongly by the Supreme Court.

This puts federalism and the Court directly in the line of fire. With an aging and ailing Court, President Bush will have at least one and as many as four Supreme Court justice appointments to make, and these will determine the future of federalism (and many other key issues) for the next quarter century. However, for an appointment to go through, the president must obtain the Senate's "advice and consent"; Senate debate over these appointments promises to be heated, since the makeup of the Supreme Court impacts the future of the federal government's authority to impose on the states national standards in many areas of social policy.[15]

Another important sign of the trend back toward expanding the powers of the states is Congress's own actions, which often go beyond the Supreme Court. In April of 1996, for example, Congress adopted the Antiterrorism and Effective Death Penalty Act, which severely tightened the deadlines for appeals that prisoners can make for review of their capital punishment sentences. In 1996, Congress also killed funding for all nonprofit death-penalty resource centers that provide legal advice for filing capital punishment appeals. And, of course, the best indication of Congress's increasing confidence in the powers of the states is probably the Personal Responsibility and Work Opportunity Reconciliation Act of 1996, popularly known as welfare reform, which devolves to the discretion of the states the lion's share of power over public assistance to the poor. The decision in September 1996 to terminate national poverty entitlements under the most important welfare program, Aid to Families with Dependent Children (AFDC), and to turn over virtually all of the discretion for the implementation of these welfare activities to state governments, is indicative of the present and future of federalism in the United States. There has clearly been a historical ebb and flow to the federal relationship: the national government's authority grew relative to that of the states during the middle decades of the twentieth century but moderated as the century drew to a close.

---

[15]For a superb account of the case United States v. Morrison, see Linda Greenhouse, "Battle on Federalism," *New York Times*, 17 May 2000, p. 18. For an enlightening account of the tremendous commitment of the Democratic side to control of the Senate, see Art Levine, "The Adventures of . . . MONEYMAN!" *The American Prospect*, 24 April 2000, pp. 26–31. See also Cass Sunstein, "The Returns of States' Rights," *The American Prospect*, 20 November 2000, p. 30.

Cooperation and Competition among State Governments   "Horizontal" federalism refers to the cooperative and competitive relations that states have with each other. As we saw earlier, the Constitution sought to discourage destructive competition between the states, such as discriminatory taxes or trade barriers. But today there are many opportunities for competition as well as for cooperation. The most spectacular example of interstate cooperation is probably the Port Authority of New York and New Jersey, a public corporation operating ports, access highways, and other related public works in the vast New York–New Jersey port complex. The corporation was the result of a 1921 "interstate compact," which has become the model for both interstate and intrastate public authorities and public corporations that are set up to engage independently in constructing and operating highways, tunnels, and other public works.[16]

Lines of cooperation may become increasingly important as interstate competition intensifies. Professor Thomas Dye has coined the term "competitive federalism" to describe as well as encourage the rivalries between and among states wanting to attract new industry by offering tax and zoning advantages, improved local public works, and improved education accompanied by a low tax base. But there is a darker side to interstate competition, which many refer to as the "race to the bottom." In their push to compete, governors and mayors may seek to attract new companies by cutting welfare programs, discouraging unions, cracking down on tenement housing, and suppressing rather than expanding public works.

Collective Action Principle
States compete with one another not only for new business, but also in terms of being less attractive to welfare recipients.

State Obligations to One Another   The Constitution also creates obligations among the states. These obligations, spelled out in Article IV, were intended to promote national unity. By requiring the states to recognize actions and decisions taken in other states as legal and proper, the framers aimed to make the states less like independent countries and more like parts of a single nation.

Article IV, Section 1, calls for "Full Faith and Credit" among states, meaning that each state is normally expected to honor the "public Acts, Records, and judicial Proceedings" that take place in any other state. So, for example, if a couple is married in Texas—marriage being regulated by state law—Missouri must also recognize that marriage, even though they were not married under Missouri state law.

This ***full faith and credit clause*** has recently become embroiled in the controversy over gay and lesbian marriage. In 1993, the Hawaii Supreme Court prohibited discrimination against gay and lesbian marriage except in very

full faith and credit clause
Article IV, Section 1, of the Constitution, which provides that each state must accord the same respect to the laws and judicial decisions of other states that it accords to its own.

---

[16]Article I, Section 10, authorizes states to make contracts or compacts with each other, as long as Congress consents. Until 1900, there had been only 24 such interstate compacts. By 1955, there were 121, covering such matters as fisheries, oil extraction, stream pollution, and, especially, water—e.g., equitable access to the Colorado River from the several water-hungry states along its banks. By 1980, 169 interstate compacts were in operation. For a good treatment of this phenomenon, see Nicholas Henry, *Governing at the Grassroots: State and Local Politics* (Englewood Cliffs, NJ: Prentice Hall, 1980).

limited circumstances. Many observers believed that Hawaii would eventually fully legalize gay marriage. In fact, after a long political battle, Hawaii passed a constitutional amendment in 1998 outlawing gay marriage. However, in December 1999, the Vermont Supreme Court ruled that gay and lesbian couples should have the same rights as heterosexuals. The Vermont legislature responded with a new law that allowed gays and lesbians to form "civil unions." Although not legally considered marriages, such unions allow gay and lesbian couples most of the benefits of marriage, such as eligibility for the partner's health insurance, inheritance rights, and the right to transfer property. The Vermont statute could have broad implications for other states. More than thirty states have passed "defense of marriage acts" that define marriage as a union between men and women only; whether these states have to recognize Vermont's civil unions under the full faith and credit clause is still unclear.

Because of this controversy, the extent and meaning of the full faith and credit clause is sure to be considered by the Supreme Court. In fact, it is not clear that the clause requires states to recognize gay marriage because the Court's interpretation of the clause in the past has provided exceptions for "public policy" reasons: if states have strong objections to a law they do not have to honor it. In 1997 the Supreme Court took up a case involving the full faith and credit clause. The case concerns a Michigan court order that prevented a former engineer for General Motors Corporation from testifying against the company. The engineer, who left the company on bad terms, later testified in a Missouri court about a car accident in which a woman died when her Chevrolet Blazer caught fire. General Motors challenged his right to testify, arguing that Missouri should give "full faith and credit" to the Michigan ruling. The Supreme Court ruled that the engineer could testify and that the court system in one state cannot hinder other state courts in their "search for the truth."[17]

privileges and immunities clause Article IV, Section 2, of the Constitution, which provides that the citizens of any one state are guaranteed the "privileges and immunities" of every other state, as though they were citizens of that state.

Article IV, Section 2, known as the "comity clause," also seeks to promote national unity. It provides that citizens enjoying the *privileges and immunities* of one state should be entitled to similar treatment in other states. What this has come to mean is that a state cannot discriminate against someone from another state or give special privileges to its own residents. For example, in the 1970s, when Alaska passed a law that gave residents preference over nonresidents in obtaining work on the state's oil and gas pipelines, the Supreme Court ruled the law illegal because it discriminated against citizens of other states.[18] This clause also regulates criminal justice among the states by requiring states to return fugitives to the states from which they have fled. Thus, in 1952, when an inmate escaped from an Alabama prison and sought to avoid being returned to Alabama on the grounds that he was being subjected to "cruel and unusual punishment" there, the Supreme Court ruled that he must be returned according to

[17]Linda Greenhouse, "Supreme Court Weaves Legal Principles from a Tangle of Legislation," *New York Times*, 30 June 1988, p. A20.
[18]Hicklin v. Orbeck, 437 U.S. 518 (1978).

TABLE 3.2

87,504 Governments in the United States

TYPE	NUMBER
National	1
State	50
County	3,043
Municipal	19,372
Township	16,629
School districts	13,726
Other special districts	34,683
TOTAL	87,504

SOURCE: Department of Commerce, *Statistical Abstract of the United States, 2000* (Washington, DC: Government Printing Office, 2000), Table No. 490.

Article IV, Section 2.[19] This example highlights the difference between the obligations among states and those among different countries. Recently, France refused to return an American fugitive because he might be subject to the death penalty, which does not exist in France.[20] The Constitution clearly forbids states from doing something similar.

Local Government   The continuing vitality of the federal framework and of state government can be seen in still another area: local government. Local government occupies a peculiar but very important place in the American system. In fact, the status of American local government is probably unique in world experience.

   Americans must love local governments because there are so many of them. According to Table 3.2, there were 87,504 governments in the United States as of 2001, and all but 51 of those are local governments. The number of local governments is an important datum in itself, but the role of local government in the nurturing of democracy can be better understood when we add the fact that these 87,453 local governments are comprised of around 500,000 offices that

[19]Sweeny v. Woodall, 344 U.S. 86 (1953).
[20]Marlise Simons, "France Won't Extradite American Convicted of Murder," *New York Times*, 5 December 1997, p. A9.

are filled by election.[21] This makes for an enormous "electoral domain," whose contribution to American democracy can hardly be overestimated. This tremendous electoral domain has first of all provided an extraordinarily broad opportunity for political participation, for voters as well as for the politically ambitious. In addition, this electoral domain provided the spawning ground for political parties. The story of American democracy cannot be told without appreciation of the fact that political parties were a response to electoral opportunity and have little meaning outside this context.[22]

Local governments became administratively important in the early years of the Republic because the states possessed little administrative capability, and they relied on local governments to implement the laws of the state. Local government was an alternative to a statewide bureaucracy. The states created two forms of local government: territorial and corporate. The basic territorial unit is the county; every resident of the state is also a resident of a county (except in Rhode Island and Connecticut, which do not have county governments). Traditionally, counties existed only for handling state obligations, whether these were administrative, legislative, or judicial, whether the job was building roads, or collecting state taxes, or catching bootleggers.

The second, or corporate, unit is the city, town, or village. These are called corporate because each holds an actual corporate charter granted it by the state government; they are formed ("incorporated") by residents of an area as these residents discover that their close proximity and common problems can be more effectively and cheaply dealt with cooperatively. Not everyone lives in a city or town; many rural areas are "unincorporated."

Although cities, especially larger cities, develop their own unique political and government personalities, they are nevertheless like the counties in being units of state administration. We associate police forces, fire fighting companies, and public health and zoning agencies with the very essence of local government. But all of those functions and agencies are operating under state laws. The state legislatures and courts allow cities to adapt state laws to local needs, and out of that discretion cities can develop their own political personalities. But they remain under state authority, applying state laws to local conditions.[23]

[21]Source for the number of elected officials: Department of Commerce, *Statistical Abstract of the United States, 2000* (Washington, DC: Government Printing Office, 2000), Table 490.

[22]The role of local government in the development of democracy is now being recognized in the People's Republic of China. There are about 900,000 villages in China, housing as many as three-quarters of the country's 1.3 billion people. *The Economist* reports that since 1988, over 80 percent of these villages have elected, through universal suffrage and secret ballots, their own chiefs and village committees. By 1997, 95 percent of these villages will have held elections—some their third election in a row. Village democratization has been flowering, despite the return to repressiveness at the national level after Tiananmen in 1989. "China's Grassroots Democracy," *The Economist*, 2 November 1996, pp. 33–35.

[23]A good discussion of the constitutional position of local governments is in York Willbern, *The Withering Away of the City* (Bloomington: Indiana University Press, 1971). For more on the structure and theory of federalism, see Thomas R. Dye, *American Federalism: Competition among the States* (Lexington, MA: Lexington Books, 1990), Chapter 1; and Martha Derthick, "Up-to-Date in Kansas City: Reflections on American Federalism" (the 1992 John Gaus Lecture), *PS: Political Science & Politics* (December 1992), pp. 671–75.

Changes in the traditional place of local governments began to take place in the latter part of the nineteenth century with the adoption of **home rule.** Beginning in Missouri in 1875, the states one after another changed their constitutions to permit cities (and eventually a few counties) of a certain size and urban density to frame and adopt local charters. By the beginning of the twentieth century, home rule was adopted in many of the states, and the provisions were extended until home rule came to mean giving cities the right of ordinary corporations to change their government structures, to hold property, to sue and be sued, and most importantly, to be guaranteed that state legislatures would not pass legislation concerning the "local affairs, property, and government" of cities except by laws of statewide application. This was a guarantee within the state constitution that no city would be subjected to special legislation imposed on that city alone by the state legislature. As part of this movement, many states began to allow cities to make the basic laws for themselves rather than administering laws passed by the state legislature. Cities were given the power to make their own laws *(ordinances)* to regulate slaughterhouses, to regulate and establish public transportation services and facilities, to regulate local markets and trade centers, to set quality and safety standards for the construction of apartments and other private buildings, and to control properties for administering fire prevention.

As local government responsibilities expanded, they often exceeded established government boundaries. Many local programs and services had become too expensive, unless they were carried out on a scale larger than the corporate city, town, or village where the need was first recognized and where the initiative might first have been taken. The way the proponents put it, if they could expand their area of service, they could reduce the "unit cost" of those services. Since all local governments (except the counties, as observed above) are corporate and voluntary and therefore organized for the convenience and efficiency of the residents, it was only natural to organize another unit of local government within a large city, or to create a unit of local government that actually cut across the boundaries of several contiguous towns or cities. This new unit was called the *special district.* If we include school districts as special districts—as we surely should, because they are the most numerous and most prized of all special districts—there were in 2001 just under 48,500 special district governments in the United States, comprising 55 percent of all local governments.[24] The other special districts have been formed to provide, among others, fire protection (the largest type of special district after school districts), water supply, sewerage services, electric power, and air pollution control. Beyond the need to reduce the unit cost of services, another important justification frequently offered in favor of creating a special district is "to take the politics out of government." Wherever there are public services or proposals for public services, there will be politics. But the special district does create its own type of politics, and that, of

home rule Power delegated by the state to a local unit of government to manage its own affairs.

ordinance The legislative act of a local legislature or municipal commission. Puts the force of law under city charter but is a lower order of law than a statute of the national or state legislature.

[24]*Statistical Abstract of the United States, 2000*, Table No. 490.

course, can be a blessing or a curse. In that context it is interesting to offer one particularly significant example of a special district: Walt Disney World. The Reedy Creek Improvement District in Orlando, Florida, was formed in 1967 after lengthy and elaborate negotiations between Walt Disney and the state of Florida. Disney's first legal request was for the creation of the Reedy Creek Drainage District, which would have the power to regulate land use, provide police and fire service, build roads and sewer lines, and construct an airport, as well as carry out the initial plan for flood control and drainage. The deal included an agreement stating that surrounding local governments could not impose any growth control or other fees on highway approaches or other relations to Disney World. What a special district indeed![25]

Finally, there is another kind of local government that has no geographic identity but still looms relatively large in the modern history of local government: government by contract.

Nowadays, many cities, especially in the western states, do not have any public garbage collecting system because it is all done by private companies. As privatization has become more popular over the past twenty years, there has been a parallel expansion of contractual approaches to local government provision for local services, not only an expansion of conventional uses of the contract approach but also less conventional ones—for example, the "charter schools" and private, for-profit prisons. "Charter" is simply another name for contract, one implying closer public regulation and supervision than with a normal contract but still using contracts with private companies to meet compulsory schooling requirements. This movement of charter schooling is slowly but surely taking off nationwide. The contractual, for-profit prison is an even bolder venture in the use of contracts for services, yet it has spread faster and wider than the charter school. Largely done through state contracts, the for-profit prison is an important illustration of the expanding private/contractual approach to local as well as to state government. Thirty states now permit privatized, contract, for-profit prisons, and it is only a matter of time before we see private, for-profit county and city jails as well as state and federal for-profit penitentiaries.[26]

With all of this power already residing in local governments to provide so many services in so many different ways, and with continued expansion of local government responsibilities, it is inevitable that people occasionally come to the conclusion that cities constitute a third level of sovereignty. But such a conclusion is distinctly false. However large some cities become, and however strong

---

[25]For a good treatment of this and other special districts, see Nancy Burns, *The Formation of American Local Governments: Private Values in Public Institutions* (New York: Oxford University Press, 1994), pp. 31–35. See also an important source for her treatment, Richard E. Foglesong, "Do Politics Matter in the Formulation of Local Development Policies? The Orlando–Disney World Relationship," paper presented at 1989 American Political Science Association Annual Meeting, Atlanta, GA, August 31–September 3, 1989. Foglesong has since expanded this story into a book, *Married to the Mouse: Walt Disney World and Orlando* (New Haven: Yale University Press, 2001).

[26]For good treatment of the for-profit prison movement, see Vince Beiser, "Jailing for Dollars: The New Growth Industry," *The New Leader*, 5 May 1997, pp. 10–11.

the support grows for keeping government at the local level, there are still only two levels of sovereignty in the federal system of the United States—the national government and the state governments. Local governments, as important as they have become or may become in this urban nation, remain exactly as they always have been—creatures of state government.

Who Does What? The Changing Federal Framework

Questions about how to divide responsibilities between the states and the national government first arose more than two hundred years ago, when the framers wrote the Constitution to create a stronger union. But they did not solve the issue of who should do what. There is no "right" answer to that question; each generation of Americans has provided its own answer. In recent years, Americans have grown distrustful of the federal government and have supported giving more responsibility to the states.[27] Even so, they still want the federal government to set standards and promote equality.

Political debates about the division of responsibility often take sides: some people argue for a strong federal role to set national standards, while others say the states should do more. These two goals are not necessarily at odds. The key is to find the right balance. During the first 150 years of American history, that balance favored state power. But the balance began to shift toward Washington in the 1930s. In this section, we will look at how this happened, and then we will consider current efforts to shift the balance back toward the states.

Cooperative Federalism and Grants-in-Aid   If the traditional system of two sovereigns performing highly different functions could be called dual federalism, the system since the 1930s could be called *cooperative federalism*—which generally refers to supportive relations, sometimes partnerships, between national government and the state and local governments. It comes in the form of federal subsidization of special state and local activities; these subsidies are called *grants-in-aid.* But make no mistake about it: although many of these state and local programs would not exist without the federal grant-in-aid, the grant-in-aid is also an important form of federal influence. (Another form of federal influence, the mandate, will be covered in the next section.)

A grant-in-aid is really a kind of bribe, or "carrot," whereby Congress appropriates money for state and local governments with the condition that the money be spent for a particular purpose as defined by Congress. Congress uses grants-in-aid because it does not have the political or constitutional power to command cities to do its bidding. When you can't command, a monetary inducement becomes a viable alternative. Grants-in-aid are also mechanisms that help to coordinate the separate activities of all those state and local governments around a common set of standards or policy principles in circumstances when a

Institution Principle

The national-state tug-of-war is an institutional feature of the federal system.

cooperative federalism A type of federalism existing since the New Deal era in which grants-in-aid have been used strategically to encourage states and localities (without commanding them) to pursue nationally defined goals. Also known as intergovernmental cooperation.

grants-in-aid A general term for funds given by Congress to state and local governments.

Collective Action Principle

Grants-in-aid allow the national government to coordinate state and local policies around a common set of national standards.

---

[27]See the poll reported in Guy Gugliotta, "Scaling Down the American Dream," *Washington Post*, 19 April 1995, p. A21.

multiplicity of these things would undermine the purposes of the policy or otherwise be damaging and dysfunctional.

The principle of the grant-in-aid goes back to the nineteenth-century land grants to states for the improvement of agriculture and farm-related education. Since farms were not in "interstate commerce," it was unclear whether the Constitution would permit the national government to provide direct assistance to agriculture. Grants-in-aid to the states, earmarked to go to farmers, presented a way of avoiding the constitutional problem while pursuing what was recognized in Congress as a national goal.

Beginning in the late 1930s, this same approach was applied to cities. Congress set national goals such as public housing and assistance to the unemployed and provided grants-in-aid to meet these goals. World War II temporarily stopped the distribution of these grants. But after the war, Congress resumed providing grants for urban development and lunches in the schools. The value of such *categorical grants-in-aid* increased from $2.3 billion in 1950 to $285 billion in 2000 (see Table 3.3). Sometimes Congress requires the state or local government to match the national contribution dollar for dollar, but for some programs, such as the interstate highway system, the congressional grant-in-aid provides 90 percent of the cost of the program. The nationwide speed limit of 55 mph was not imposed on individual drivers by an act of Congress. Instead, Congress bribed the state legislatures by threatening to withdraw the federal highway grants-in-aid if the states did not set a 55 mph speed limit. In the early 1990s, Congress began to ease up on the states, permitting them, under certain conditions, to go back to the 65 mph speed limit (or higher) without losing their highway grants.

For the most part, the categorical grants created before the 1960s simply helped the states perform their traditional functions such as education and policing.[28] In the 1960s, however, the national role expanded and the number of categorical grants increased dramatically. For example, during the Eighty-ninth Congress (1965–1966) alone, the number of categorical grant-in-aid programs grew from 221 to 379.[29] The grants authorized during the 1960s announced national purposes much more strongly than did earlier grants. Central to that national purpose was the need to provide opportunities to the poor.

Many of the categorical grants enacted during the 1960s were *project grants,* which require state and local governments to submit proposals to federal agencies. In contrast to the older *formula grants,* which used a formula (composed of such elements as need and state and local capacities) to distribute funds, the new project grants made funding available on a competitive basis. Federal agencies would give grants to the proposals they judged to be the best. In this way, the national government acquired substantial control over which state and local governments got money, how much they got, and how they spent it.

categorical grants-in-aid
Funds given by Congress to states and localities, earmarked by law for specific categories such as education or crime prevention.

project grants
Grant programs in which state and local governments submit proposals to federal agencies and for which funding is provided on a competitive basis.

formula grants
Grants-in-aid in which a formula is used to determine the amount of federal funds a state or local government will receive.

---

[28]Kenneth T. Palmer, "The Evolution of Grant Policies," in *The Changing Politics of Federal Grants,* by Lawrence D. Brown, James W. Fossett, and Kenneth T. Palmer (Washington, DC: Brookings Institution, 1984), p. 15.
[29]Ibid., p. 6.

TABLE 3.3

Historical Trend of Federal Grants-in-Aid

		GRANTS-IN-AID AS A PERCENTAGE OF			
FISCAL YEAR	AMOUNT OF GRANTS-IN-AID (IN BILLIONS)	TOTAL FEDERAL OUTLAYS	FEDERAL DOMESTIC PROGRAMS*	STATE AND LOCAL EXPENDITURES	GROSS DOMESTIC PRODUCT
1950	$2.3	5.3	11.6	8.2	0.8
1955	3.2	4.7	17.2	9.7	0.8
1960	7.0	8.0	18.0	19.0	1.0
1965	10.9	9.0	18.0	20.0	2.0
1970	24.1	12.0	23.0	24.0	2.0
1975	49.8	15.0	22.0	27.0	3.0
1980	91.4	15.0	22.0	31.0	3.0
1985	105.9	11.0	18.0	25.0	3.0
1990	135.3	11.0	17.0	21.0	2.0
1995	225.0	15.0	22.0	25.0	3.0
2000	284.7	15.9	22.0	24.7	2.9

*Excludes outlays for national defense, international affairs, and net interest.
SOURCE: Office of Management and Budget, *Budget of the United States Government, Fiscal Year 2002, Analytical Perspectives* (Washington, DC: Government Printing Office, 2001), Table 9-2, p. 202.

On more than one occasion, the number of such specific categorical grants-in-aid and the amount of money involved in them have come under criticism, by Democrats as well as Republicans, ultra-liberals as well as ultra-conservatives. But there is general agreement that grants-in-aid help to reduce disparities of wealth between rich states and poor states. And although some critics have asserted that grants encouraged state and local governments to initiate programs merely because "free money from Washington" was available, the fact is that when federal grants were reduced by the Reagan administration, most states and localities continued funding the same programs with their own revenues. Daniel Elazar, an authority on federalism, has observed that "Despite many protestations to the contrary, only in rare situations have federal grant programs served

FIGURE 3.1

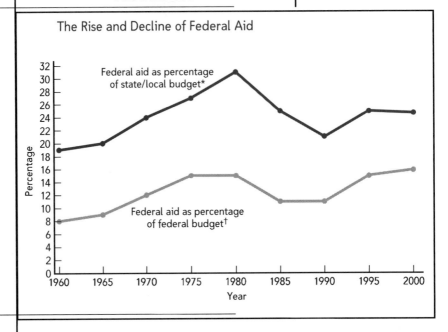

The Rise and Decline of Federal Aid

*Federal aid as a percentage of state/local expenditures after transfers.
†Federal aid as a percentage of federal expenditures from own funds.

SOURCE: Office of Management and Budget, *Budget of the United States Government, Fiscal Year 2002, Analytical Perspectives* (Washington, DC: Government Printing Office, 2001), Table 9-2, p. 202.

to alter state administrative patterns in ways that did not coincide with already established state policies."[30]

Federalism has not stood still. The most important student of the history of federalism, Morton Grodzins, characterized the shift to post–New Deal cooperative federalism as a move from "layer cake federalism" to "marble cake federalism,"[31] in which intergovernmental cooperation and sharing have blurred the distinguishing line, making it difficult to say where the national government ends and the state and local governments begin. Figure 3.1 demonstrates the financial basis of the marble cake idea. At the high point of grant-in-aid policies in the late 1970s federal aid contributed about 25–30 percent of the operating budgets of all the state and

[30]Daniel Elazar, *American Federalism: A View from the States*, 3rd ed. (New York: Harper & Row, 1984), p. 110. For a view from the cities, see Paul Kantor, *The Dependent City: The Changing Political Economy of Urban America* (Glencoe, IL: Scott Foresman, 1988).

[31]Morton Grodzins, "The Federal System," in *Goals for Americans* (Englewood Cliffs, NJ: Prentice-Hall, 1960), p. 265. In a marble cake, the white cake is distinguishable from the chocolate cake, but the two are streaked rather than in distinct layers.

TABLE 3.4

Federal Aid as a Percentage of General Annual Expenditure

CITY	1977	1995	CITY	1977	1995
Chicago	20	8	Houston	13	5
Cleveland	29	10	Indianapolis	21	6
Denver	14	1	Los Angeles	22	12
Detroit	31	12	San Antonio	28	4
Honolulu	30	8	Seattle	23	3

SOURCE: Department of Commerce, *Statistical Abstract of the United States, 1999* (Washington, DC: Government Printing Office, 1999), Tables 504 and 506; *Statistical Abstract, 1998*, Tables 525 and 526.

local governments in the country. The numbers in Table 3.4 present some of the more extreme examples from 1977 and the severe drop since that time.

Regulated Federalism and National Standards Developments in the past twenty-five years have moved well beyond cooperative federalism to what might be called "regulated federalism."[32] In some areas the national government actually regulates the states by threatening to withhold grant money unless state and local governments conform to national standards. The most notable instances of this regulation are in the areas of civil rights, poverty programs, and environmental laws. This reflects a general shift in federal regulation away from the oversight and control of strictly economic activities toward "social regulation"—interventions on behalf of individual rights and liberties, environmental protection, workplace safety, and so on. In these instances, the national government provides grant-in-aid financing but sets conditions the states must meet in order to keep the grants. In other instances, the national government imposes obligations on the states without providing any funding at all. The national government refers to these policies as "setting national standards." Important examples include the Asbestos Hazard Emergency Act of 1986, which requires school districts to inspect for asbestos hazards and to remove them from school buildings when necessary, and the Americans with Disabilities Act of 1990, which requires all state and local governments to promote access for the handicapped to all government buildings. The net effect of these national standards is that state and local policies

---

[32]The concept and the best discussion of this modern phenomenon will be found in Donald F. Kettl, *The Regulation of American Federalism* (Baltimore: Johns Hopkins University Press, 1983 and 1987), especially pp. 33–41.

are more uniform from coast to coast. However, there are a number of other programs in which the national government engages in regulated federalism by imposing obligations on the states *without providing any funding at all.* These have come to be called **unfunded mandates.** States complained that mandates took up so much of their budgets that they were not able to set their own priorities.[33]

These burdens became a major part of the rallying cry that produced the famous Republican Congress elected in 1994, with its Contract with America. One of the first measures adopted by the 104th Republican Congress was an act to limit unfunded mandates—the Unfunded Mandates Reform Act (UMRA). This was considered a triumph of lobbying efforts by state and local governments, and it was "hailed as both symbol and substance of a renewed congressional commitment to federalism."[34] Under this law, any mandate with an uncompensated state and local cost estimated at greater than $50 million a year, as determined by the Congressional Budget Office (CBO), can be stopped by a point of order raised on the House or Senate floor. This was called a "stop, look and listen" requirement, forcing Congress to take positive action to own up to the mandate and its potential costs. During 1996, its first full year of operation, only eleven bills included mandates that exceeded the $50 million threshold—from a total of sixty-nine estimates of actions in which mandates were included. Examples included minimum wage increase, parity for mental health and health insurance, mandated use of Social Security numbers on driver's licenses, and extension of Federal Occupation Safety and Health to state and local employees. Most of them were modified in the House, to reduce their costs. However, as one expert put it, "The primary impact of UMRA came not from the affirmative blockage of [mandate] legislation, but rather from its effect as a deterrent to mandates in the drafting and early consideration of legislation."[35]

As indicated by the first year of its operation, the effect of UMRA will not be revolutionary. UMRA does not prevent congressional members from passing unfunded mandates; it only makes them think twice before they do. Moreover, the act exempts several areas from coverage by UMRA. And states must still enforce antidiscrimination laws and meet other requirements to receive federal assistance. But on the other hand, UMRA does represent a serious effort to move the national/state relationship a bit further toward the state side.

New Federalism and the National-State Tug-of-War   Federalism in the United States can best be understood today as a tug-of-war between those seeking more uniform national standards and those seeking more room for variability from

[33]John DiIulio and Don Kettl report that in 1980 there were thirty-six laws that could be categorized as unfunded mandates. And despite the concerted opposition of the Reagan and Bush administrations, another twenty-seven laws qualifying as unfunded mandates were adopted between 1982 and 1991. See John DiIulio, Jr., and Donald F. Kettl, *Fine Print: The Contract with America, Devolution, and the Administrative Realities of American Federalism* (Washington, DC: Brookings Institution, 1995), p. 41.
[34]Paul Posner, "Unfunded Mandate Reform: How Is It Working?" *Rockefeller Institute Bulletin* (Albany: Nelson A. Rockefeller Institute of Government, 1998), p. 35.
[35]Ibid., p. 36.

state to state. This is a struggle over federalism's script and scorecard—over who does what and how the various activities are structured and sequenced. Presidents Nixon and Reagan called their efforts to reverse this trend toward national standards and reestablish traditional policy making and implementation the "new federalism." They helped to craft national policies whose purpose was to return more discretion to the states. Examples of these policies include Nixon's revenue sharing and Reagan's **block grants,** which consolidated a number of categorical grants into one larger category, leaving the state (or local) government to decide how to use the grant. Presidents Nixon and Reagan, as well as former president Bush, were sincere in wanting to return somewhat to a traditional notion of freedom of action for the states. Although they called it new federalism, their concepts and their goals were really much closer to the older, traditional federalism that predated Franklin Roosevelt.

Although Reagan succeeded in reducing national appropriations for grants-in-aid during his first term, he could not prevent increases during his second term. Both he and Bush were able to hold the line only enough to keep these outlays from increasing faster than the overall increase in the national budget.

Grants-in-aid began to grow slowly toward the end of former president Bush's administration and through Clinton's first term; however, the growth has been modest and almost entirely through block grants that give states and localities considerable flexibility. In effect, President Clinton adopted the "new federalism" of Nixon and Reagan even while expanding federal grant activity: he signed the Unfunded Mandates Reform Act of 1995 as well as the Personal Responsibility and Work Opportunity Reconciliation Act of 1996, which goes farther than any other act of Congress in the past sixty years to relieve the states from national mandates, funded or unfunded. This new law replaces the sixty-one-year-old program of Aid to Families with Dependent Children (AFDC) and its education, work, and training program, with block grants to states for Temporary Assistance to Needy Families (TANF). Although some national standards remain, the place of the states in the national welfare system has been virtually revolutionized through devolution, the strategy of delegating to the states more and more authority over a range of policies that had up until then been under national government authority, plus providing the states with a substantial portion of the cost of these programs. Since the mid-1990s, devolution has been quite consequential for the national-state tug-of-war.

By changing welfare from a combined federal-state program into a block grant to the states, Congress gave the states more responsibility for programs that serve the poor. One argument in favor of devolution is that states can act as "laboratories of democracy," by experimenting with many different approaches to find one that best meets the needs of their citizens.[36] As states have altered their welfare programs in the wake of the new law, they have indeed designed diverse approaches. For example, Minnesota has adopted an incentive-based approach

block grants
Federal funds given to state governments to pay for goods, services, or programs, with relatively few restrictions on how the funds may be spent.

Analyzing American Politics
www.wwnorton.com/lowi7/ch3
Analyze the relationship between poverty and variations in state spending on welfare benefits.

---

[36]The phrase "laboratories of democracy" was coined by Supreme Court Justice Louis Brandeis in his dissenting opinion in New State Ice Co. v. Liebman, 285 U.S. 262 (1932).

that offers extra assistance to families that take low-wage jobs. Other states, such as California, have more "sticks" than "carrots" in their new welfare programs.

Policy Principle
Devolution has had an important influence on policy outcomes, particularly welfare.

As the case of welfare shows, assessments about "the right way" to divide responsibility in the federal system change over time. The case of speed limits provides another example. Speed limits have traditionally been a state and local responsibility. But in 1973, at the height of the oil shortage, Congress passed legislation to withhold federal highway funds from states that did not adopt a maximum speed limit of 55 miles per hour (mph). The lower speed limit, it was argued, would reduce energy consumption by cars. Although Congress had not formally taken over the authority to set speed limits, the power of its purse was so important that every state adopted the new speed limit. As the energy crisis faded, the national speed limit lost much of its support, even though it was found to have reduced the number of traffic deaths. In 1995, Congress repealed the penalties for higher speed limits, and states once again became free to set their own speed limits. Many states with large rural areas raised their maximum to 75 mph; Montana set unlimited speeds in the rural areas during daylight hours. Early research indicates that numbers of highway deaths have indeed risen in the states that increased the limits.[37] As new evidence becomes available, it will surely provide fuel for the ongoing debate about what are properly the states' responsibilities and what the federal government should do.

For the moment, the balance seems to be tipped toward the states, though the tug-of-war between the states and national government will certainly continue. As a result of this ongoing struggle for power, federalism remains a vital part of the American system of government. States and cities may clamor (and lobby) for a larger share of the national budget, and state and local leaders have shown a willingness to cooperate with the national standards embodied in environmental protection laws and civil rights laws. But states continue to hold on jealously to the maximum freedom of action that is embodied in the historic concept of federalism.

THE SEPARATION OF POWERS

In his discussion of the separation of powers, James Madison quotes the originator of the principle, the French political thinker Baron de Montesquieu:

> There can be no liberty where the legislative and executive powers are united in the same person . . . [or] if the power of judging be not separated from the legislative and executive powers.[38]

---

[37]"Motor Vehicle Fatalities in 1996 Were 12 Percent Higher on Interstates, Freeways in 12 States That Raised Speed Limits," press release of the Insurance Institute for Highway Safety, 10 October 1997.

[38]Clinton Rossiter, ed., *The Federalist Papers* (New York: New American Library, 1961), No. 47, p. 302.

Using this same reasoning, many of Madison's contemporaries argued that there was not *enough* separation among the three branches, and Madison had to backtrack to insist that the principle did not require complete separation:

> . . . unless these departments [branches] be so far connected and blended as to give to each a constitutional control over the others, the degree of separation which the maxim requires, as essential to a free government, can never in practice be duly maintained.[39]

This is the secret of how we have made the separation of powers effective: we made the principle self-enforcing by giving each branch of government the means to participate in, and partially or temporarily to obstruct, the workings of the other branches.

Institution Principle

Checks and balances is a system of "separated institutions sharing power."

Checks and Balances

The means by which each branch of government interacts is known informally as **checks and balances.** The best-known examples are the presidential power to veto legislation passed by Congress; the power of Congress to override the veto by a two-thirds majority vote, to impeach the president, and (of the Senate) to approve presidential appointments; the power of the president to appoint the members of the Supreme Court and the other federal judges with Senate approval; and the power of the Supreme Court to engage in judicial review (to be discussed below). These and other examples are shown in Table 3.5. The framers sought to guarantee that the three branches would in fact use the checks and balances as weapons against each other by giving each branch a different political constituency: direct, popular election of the members of the House; indirect election of senators (until the Seventeenth Amendment, adopted in 1913); indirect election of the president (which still exists, at least formally, today); and appointment of federal judges for life. All things considered, the best characterization of the separation of powers principle in action is, as we said in Chapter 2, "separated institutions sharing power."[40]

checks and balances Mechanisms through which each branch of government participates in and influences the activities of the other branches. Major examples include the presidential veto power over congressional legislation, the power of the Senate to approve presidential appointments, and judicial review of congressional enactments.

Legislative Supremacy

Although each branch was to be given adequate means to compete with the other branches, it is also clear that within the system of separated powers the framers provided for **legislative supremacy** by making Congress the preeminent branch. Legislative supremacy made the provision of checks and balances in the other two branches all the more important.

legislative supremacy The preeminent position assigned to the Congress by the Constitution.

[39]Ibid., No. 48, p. 308.
[40]Richard E. Neustadt, *Presidential Power: The Politics of Leadership from Roosevelt to Reagan*, rev. ed. (New York: Free Press, 1990; orig. published 1960), p. 33.

TABLE 3.5

Checks and Balances			
	LEGISLATIVE BRANCH CAN BE CHECKED BY:	**EXECUTIVE BRANCH CAN BE CHECKED BY:**	**JUDICIAL BRANCH CAN BE CHECKED BY:**
Legislative branch can check:	NA	Can overrule veto (two-thirds vote) Controls appropriations Controls by statute Impeachment of president Senate approval of appointments and treaties Committee oversight	Controls appropriations Can create inferior courts Can add new judges Senate approval of appointments Impeachment of judges
Executive branch can check:	Can veto legislation Can convene special session Can adjourn Congress when chambers disagree Vice president presides over Senate and votes to break ties	NA	President appoints judges
Judicial branch can check:	Judicial review of legislation Chief justice presides over Senate during proceedings to impeach president	Judicial review over presidential actions Power to issue warrants Chief justice presides over impeachment of president	NA

NA = Not applicable.

The most important indication of the intention of legislative supremacy was made by the framers when they decided to place the provisions for national powers in Article I, the legislative article, and to treat the powers of the national government as powers of Congress. In a system based on the "rule of law," the power to make the laws is the supreme power. Section 8 provides in part that "*Congress* shall have Power . . . To lay and collect Taxes . . . To borrow Money . . . To regulate Commerce . . ." [emphasis added]. The founders also provided for legislative supremacy in their decision to give Congress the sole power over appropriations and to give the House of Representatives the power to initiate all revenue bills. Madison recognized legislative supremacy as part and parcel of the separation of powers:

Institution Principle

The framers provided for legislative supremacy by making Congress the preeminent branch.

> . . . It is not possible to give to each department an equal power of self-defense. In republican government, the legislative authority necessarily predominates. The remedy for this inconveniency is to divide the legislature into different branches; and to render them, by different modes of election and different principles of action, as little connected with each other as the nature of their common functions and their common dependence on the society will admit.[41]

In other words, Congress was so likely to dominate the other branches that it would have to be divided against itself, into House and Senate. One could say that the Constitution provided for four branches, not three.

Legislative supremacy became a fact soon after the founding decade was over. National politics centered on Congress. Undistinguished presidents followed one another in a dreary succession. Even Madison—so brilliant as a constitutional theorist, so loyal as a constitutional record keeper, and so effective in the struggle for the founding—was a weak president. Jackson and Lincoln are the only two who stand out in the entire nineteenth century, and their successors dropped back out of sight; except for these two, the other presidents operated within the accepted framework of legislative supremacy (see Chapter 6).

The development of political parties, and in particular the emergence in 1832 of the national convention method of nominating presidential candidates (which replaced the congressional "King Caucus" method discussed in Chapter 6), saved the presidency from complete absorption into the orbit of legislative power by giving the presidency a base of power independent of Congress. But although this preserved the presidency and salvaged the separation of powers, it did so only in a negative sense. That is to say, presidents were more likely (after 1832 when the national conventions were established) to veto congressional enactments than before, or to engage in a military action, but they were not more likely to present programs for positive legislation or to attempt to lead Congress

---

[41]*The Federalist Papers*, No. 51, p. 322.

in the enactment of legislation.[42] This fact underscored the significance of the shift to presidential supremacy when it came after 1937 (see also Chapter 6).

The role of the judicial branch in the separation of powers has depended upon the power of judicial review (see also Chapter 8), a power not provided for in the Constitution but asserted by Chief Justice Marshall in 1803:

> If a law be in opposition to the Constitution; if both the law and the Constitution apply to a particular case, so that the Court must either decide that case conformable to the law, disregarding the Constitution, or conformable to the Constitution, disregarding the law; the Court must determine which of these conflicting rules governs the case: This is of the very essence of judicial duty.[43]

The Supreme Court has exercised the power of judicial review with caution, as though to protect its power by using it sparingly.

Review of the constitutionality of acts of the president or Congress is in fact very rare.[44] In the sixty-five years since the rise of big government and strong presidents, only a handful of important congressional enactments have been invalidated on constitutional grounds.[45] During the same time, there have been only three important judicial confrontations with the president. One was the so-called *Steel Seizure* case of 1952. The second case was *U.S. v. Nixon* in 1974, where the Court declared unconstitutional President Nixon's refusal to respond to a subpoena to make available the infamous White House tapes as evidence in a criminal prosecution. The Court argued that although ***executive privilege*** did protect the confidentiality of communications to and from the president, this did not extend to data in presidential files or tapes bearing upon criminal

executive privilege The claim that confidential communications between a president and close advisers should not be revealed without the consent of the president.

---

[42]For a good review of the uses of the veto, see Raymond Tatalovich and Byron Daynes, *Presidential Power in the United States* (Monterey, CA: Brooks/Cole, 1984), pp. 148–51; and Robert Spitzer, *The Presidential Veto: Touchstone of the American Presidency* (Albany: State University of New York Press, 1988).

[43]Marbury v. Madison, 1 Cranch 137 (1803).

[44]In response to New Deal legislation, the Supreme Court struck down eight out of ten New Deal statutes. For example, in Panama Refining Co. v. Ryan, 293 U.S. 388 (1935), the Court ruled that a section of the National Industrial Recovery Act was an invalid delegation of legislative power to the executive branch. And in Schechter Poultry Co. v. U.S., 295 U.S. 495 (1935), the Court found the National Industrial Recovery Act itself to be invalid for the same reason. But since 1935, the Supreme Court has rarely confronted the president or Congress on constitutional questions.

[45]Since 1937, only a handful of cases of any significance whatsoever can be identified where the Court actually invalidated an act of Congress on constitutional grounds. The first of these was INS v. Chadha, 462 U.S. 919 (1983), in which the Supreme Court declared unconstitutional the so-called legislative veto, whereby Congress had required certain regulatory agencies to submit proposed regulations to Congress for approval prior to implementation. The second case, Bowsher v. Synar, 92 L. Ed. 583 (1986), struck down the Gramm-Rudman Act mandating a balanced federal budget. Only one part of the act was declared unconstitutional: the part delegating to the comptroller general the power to direct the president to reduce the budget by a specified amount if the budget deficit provided by Congress exceeded a certain set amount. The Court argued that since the comptroller general could be removed only by Congress, it was unconstitutional for Congress to give the comptroller

prosecutions.[46] And, most recently, the Supreme Court rejected President Clinton's claim that the pressures and obligations of the office were so demanding that "in all but the most exceptional cases the Constitution requires federal courts to defer such litigation until his term end. . . ."[47]

All in all, the separation of powers has had an uneven history. Although "presidential government" seemed to supplant legislative supremacy after 1937, the relative power position of the three branches has not been static. The degree of conflict between the president and Congress has varied with the rise and fall of political parties, and it has been especially tense during periods of ***divided government***, when one party controls the White House and another controls the Congress, as has been the case almost solidly since 1969 (see Table 3.6).

Since Watergate, Congress has tried to get back some of the power it had delegated to the president (see Chapter 6). One of the methods it seized upon was the Ethics in Government Act of 1978, which established a "special prosecutor" (later called ***independent counsel***) with the authority to investigate allegations of wrongdoing by executive branch officials. Independent counsel Kenneth Starr's investigation of President Clinton's affair with Monica Lewinsky and Clinton's subsequent impeachment in the House of Representatives are indications that the give and take between Congress and president is more contested than ever (see also Chapter 5).

The very effort of Congress to provide by law for competition with the executive branch suggests that the separation of powers is still very much alive. And the judiciary is very much a part of the continuing vitality of the separation of powers. Although they rarely question the constitutionality of a statute, the federal courts are constantly involved in judicial review of statutes and administrative orders because agencies have to get court orders to enforce their decisions.

divided government The condition in American government wherein the presidency is controlled by one party while the opposing party controls one or both houses of Congress.

independent counsel An official appointed under the terms of the Ethics in Government Act to investigate criminal misconduct by members of the executive branch.

general "executive" powers. Another case, U.S. v. Lopez, 115 S. Ct. 1624 (1995), validated the Gun-Free School Zones Act of 1990, making it a federal crime to carry firearms within a radius of a thousand feet around a public or private school. This case was followed two years later by judicial review and invalidation of an important provision of the Brady Handgun Violence Prevention Act by imposing unconstitutional "unfunded mandates" to state and local officials to implement the federal law requiring background checks, and the like, on gun customers (Printz v. U.S. and Mack v. U.S., 117 S. Ct. 2365 [1997]). Finally, the case of City of Boerne v. Flores, 117 S. Ct. 73 F. 3d 1352 (1997) struck down the federal Religious Freedom Restoration Act of 1993 (RFRA) on the grounds that Congress had exceeded its constitutional authority by forbidding the local government from obeying the state historic landmark laws. A local Catholic church had been refused a permit to build an expansion of its church because the building had been set aside as a landmark. The church sued the city on the grounds that they had violated First Amendment "free exercise" rights by making them obey the state historic landmark laws. RFRA was invalidated as a consequence. It is thus interesting and probably quite significant that the only cases where congressional enactments were declared unconstitutional by the Supreme Court were cases where the Court was actually defending the principles of federalism and the separation of powers.

[46]Youngstown Sheet & Tube Co. v. Sawyer, 343 U.S. 579 (1952) (the official name of the *Steel Seizure* case); U.S. v. Nixon, 418 U.S. 683 (1974); and Clinton v. Jones, 117 S. Ct. 1636 (1997). See also Raoul Berger, *Executive Privilege: A Constitutional Myth* (Cambridge: Harvard University Press, 1974).

[47]Clinton v. Jones, 117 S. Ct. 1636 (1997).

TABLE 3.6

The Record of Divided Government

DATE	PARTY CONTROLLING: PRESIDENT	CONGRESS	GOVERNMENT: YEARS DIVIDED
1946–48	Truman, Democratic	Republican	Divided 2
1948–52	Truman, Democratic	Democratic	
1952–54	Eisenhower, Republican	Republican	
1954–60	Eisenhower, Republican	Democratic	Divided 6
1960–64	Kennedy/Johnson, Democratic	Democratic	
1964–68	Johnson, Democratic	Democratic	
1968–72	Nixon, Republican	Democratic	Divided 4
1972–76	Nixon/Ford, Republican	Democratic	Divided 4
1976–80	Carter, Democratic	Democratic	
1980–86	Reagan, Republican	Republican Senate Democratic House	Divided/mixed 6
1986–88	Reagan, Republican	Democratic	Divided 2
1988–92	Bush, Republican	Democratic	Divided 4
1992–94	Clinton, Democratic	Democratic	
1994–2000	Clinton, Democratic	Republican	Divided 6
2000–2002	Bush, Republican	Republican House Democratic Senate	Divided 2
	TOTAL YEARS 56	TOTAL YEARS DIVIDED 36	

This gives the judiciary a regular opportunity to influence executive as well as legislative actions, as was shown in Table 3.5 (page 100). In other words, in order to apply a statute, the court has to first interpret it; and to interpret a statute is to have the power to change it (see also Chapter 8). This offers more evidence of the continuing vitality of the separation of powers.

FEDERALISM AND THE SEPARATION OF POWERS AS POLITICAL INSTITUTIONS

The great achievement of American politics is the fashioning of an effective constitutional structure of political institutions. Although it is an imperfect and continuously evolving "work in progress," this structure of law and political practice has served its people well for more than two centuries by managing conflict, providing inducements for bargaining and cooperation, and facilitating collective action. There has been one enormous failure—the cruel practice of slavery, which ended only after a destructive civil war. But the basic configuration of institutions first formulated in Philadelphia in 1787 survived these debacles, though severely scarred by them, and has otherwise stood the test of time.

As we noted earlier, institutional arrangements like federalism and the separation of powers are part *script* and part *scorecard*. As two of the most important features of the constitutional structure, federalism and the separation of powers serve to channel and constrain political agents, first by limiting their jurisdictional authority and second by pitting them against one another as political competitors.

One of the ingenious features of the constitutional design adopted by the framers is the principle of dividing and separating. Leaving political authority unobstructed and undivided, it was thought, would invite intense competition of a winner-take-all variety. The winners would then be in a position to tyrannize, while the losers would either submit, or, with nothing else to lose, be tempted to violent opposition. By adopting the divide-and-separate principle—implemented as federalism and the separation of powers, and consisting of checks and balances—the framers of the Constitution created *jurisdictional arrangements*. The Constitution reflects this in two distinct ways. First, it encourages diversity in the political actors occupying the various institutions of government by requiring that they be selected at different times, from different constituencies, by different modes of selection (chiefly various forms of election and appointment). This, it was believed, would prevent a small clique or narrow slice of the political elite from dominating all the institutions of government at the same time. Second, the Constitution allocates the consideration of different aspects of policy to different institutional arenas. Some explicitly mentioned activities, like the coinage of money or the declaration of war, were assigned to Congress. Matters relating to the execution and implementation of the law were delegated to the president and the executive bureaucracy. Other activities, like adjudicating disputes between states, were made the preserve of the judicial branch. Those activities not explicitly mentioned in the Constitution were reserved to the states. In short, through a jurisdictional arrangement, the Constitution sought a balance in which there was the capacity for action, but in which power was not so concentrated as to make tyranny likely.

Institution Principle

The Constitution created jurisdictional arrangements by encouraging diversity in the elected leaders occupying office and allocating the consideration of different aspects of policy to different institutional arenas.

Rationality Principle

As political institutions, federalism and the separation of powers have adapted to the purposes of various political players.

The amazing thing about these American political institutions is that they are not carved in granite (even if the official buildings that house them are!). While the Constitution initially set a broad framework for the division of authority between the national government and the states and the division of labor among the branches of the national government, much adaptation and innovation took place as these institutions themselves were bent to the purposes of various political players. Politicians, remember, are goal oriented and are constantly exploring the possibilities provided them by their institutional positions and political situations. The "devolution revolution" that followed the 1994 Republican takeover of Congress is one such example. Another political player that has helped shape the current jurisdictional arrangements and sharing of power is worth remembering as well. This is the United States Supreme Court.

Altering the Balance of Power: What Are the Consequences?

Federalism and the separation of powers are two of the three most important constitutional principles upon which the United States' system of limited government is based (the third is the principle of individual rights). As we have seen, federalism limits the power of the national government in numerous ways. By its very existence, federalism recognizes the principle of two sovereigns, the national government and the state government (hence the term "dual federalism"). In addition, the Constitution specifically restrained the power of the national government to regulate the economy. As a result, the states were free to do most of the fundamental governing for the first century and a half of American government. This began to change during and following the New Deal, as the national government began to exert more influence over the states through grants-in-aid and mandates. In the last decade, however, we have noticed a countertrend to the growth of national power as Congress has opted to devolve some of its powers to the states. The most recent notable instance of devolution was the welfare reform plan of 1996.

Institutional Reform

www.wwnorton.com/lowi7/ch3

What is the impact of welfare reform in various states?

But the problem that arises with devolution is that programs that were once uniform across the country (because they were the national government's responsibility) can become highly variable, with some states providing benefits not available in other states. To a point, variation can be considered one of the virtues of federalism. But there are dangers inherent in large variations and inequalities in the provision of services and benefits in a democracy. For example, since the Food and Drug Administration (FDA) has been under attack in recent years, could the problem be solved by devolving its regulatory tasks to the states? Would people care if drugs would require "caution" labels in some states and not in others? Would Americans want each state to set its own air and water pollution control policies without regard to the fact that pollution flows across state boundaries? Devolution, as attractive as it may be, is not an approach that can be applied across the board without analyzing carefully the nature of the program and of the problems it is designed to solve. Even the capacity of states to handle "devolved" programs will vary. According to the Washington research

History Principle

The legacy of cooperative federalism and national standards has raised some doubts about devolution.

organization the Brookings Institution, the level of state and local government employment varies from state to state—from a low of 400 per 10,000 residents in some states to a high of 700 per 10,000 in others. "Such administrative diversity is bound to mediate the course and consequences of any substantial devolution of federal responsibility; no one-size-fits-all devolution [from federal to state and local government] can work."[48]

Moreover, the temptation is ever present for federal politicians to limit state discretion in order to achieve their own policy objectives. Indeed, the "devolution revolution" promised by congressional Republicans created much more rhetoric than action. Despite the complaints of Republican governors, Congress has continued to use its power to preempt state action and impose mandates on states.

The second principle of limited government, separation of powers, is manifested in our system of checks and balances, whereby separate institutions of government share power with each other. Even though the Constitution clearly provided for legislative supremacy, checks and balances have functioned well. Some would say they have worked too well. The last fifty years have witnessed long periods of divided government, when one party has controlled the White House and the other party controlled Congress. During these periods, the level of conflict between the executive and legislative branches has been particularly divisive, resulting in what some analysts derisively call gridlock. Nevertheless, this is a genuine separation of powers, not so far removed from the intent of the framers. With the rise of political parties, Americans developed a parliamentary theory that "responsible party government" requires that the same party control both branches, including both chambers of the legislature. But that kind of parliamentary/party government is a "fusion of powers," not a separation of powers. Although it may not make for good government, having an opposition party in majority control of the legislature reinforces the separation and the competition that was built into the Constitution. We can complain at length about the inability of divided government to make decisions, and we can criticize it as stalemate or gridlock,[49] but even that is in accord with the theory of the framers of the Constitution that public policy is supposed to be difficult to make.

SUMMARY

In this chapter we have traced the development of two of the three basic principles of the U.S. Constitution—federalism and the separation of powers. Federalism involves a division between two layers of government: national and

[48]Eliza Newlin Carney, "Power Grab," *National Journal*, 11 April 1998, p. 798.

[49]Not everybody will agree that divided government is all that less productive than government in which both branches are controlled by the same party. See David Mayhew, *Divided We Govern: Party Control, Law Making and Investigations, 1946–1990* (New Haven: Yale University Press, 1991). For another good evaluation of divided government, see Charles O. Jones, *Separate But Equal Branches—Congress and the Presidency* (Chatham, NJ: Chatham House, 1995).

Rationality Principle	Collective Action Principle	Institution Principle	Policy Principle	History Principle
In 1937, the Supreme Court converted the commerce clause from a source of limitations to a source of power for the national government.	States compete with one another not only for new businesses, but also in terms of being less attractive to welfare recipients.	Federalism and the separation of powers are two of the most important principles on which the U.S. system of limited government is based.	Devolution has had an important influence on policy outcomes, particularly welfare.	Since the time of the founding, federalism has been shaped strongly by the Supreme Court.
As political institutions, federalism and the separation of powers have adapted to the purposes of various political players.	Grants-in-aid allow the national government to coordinate state and local policies around a common set of national standards.	In answering "Who does what?" federalism determines the flow of government functions and, through that, the political development of the country.		The legacy of cooperative federalism and national standards has raised some doubts about devolution.
		The national-state tug-of-war is an institutional feature of the federal system.		
		Checks and balances is a system of "separated institutions sharing power."		
		The framers provided for legislative supremacy by making Congress the preeminent branch.		
		The Constitution created jurisdictional arrangements by encouraging diversity in the elected leaders occupying office and allocating the consideration of different aspects of policy to different institutional arenas.		

state. The separation of powers involves the division of the national government into three branches. These principles are limitations on the powers of government; Americans made these compromises as a condition for giving their consent to be governed. And these principles became the framework within which the government operates. The persistence of local government and the reliance of the national government on grants-in-aid to coerce local governments into following national goals were used as case studies to demonstrate the continuing vitality of the federal framework. Examples were also given of the intense competition between the president, Congress, and the courts to dramatize the continuing vitality of the separation of powers.

The purpose of a constitution is to organize the makeup or the composition of the government, the *framework within which* government and politics, including actual legislation, can take place. A country does not require federalism and the separation of powers to have a real constitutional government. And the country does not have to approach individual rights in the same manner as the American Constitution. But to be a true constitutional government, a government must have a few principles that cannot be manipulated by people in power merely for their own convenience. This is the essence of constitutionalism—principles that are above the reach of everyday legislatures, executives, bureaucrats, and politicians, yet that are not so far above their reach that these principles cannot be adapted to changing times.

FOR FURTHER READING

Anton, Thomas. *American Federalism and Public Policy.* Philadelphia: Temple University Press, 1989.

Bensel, Richard. *Sectionalism and American Political Development: 1880–1980.* Madison: University of Wisconsin Press, 1984.

Bernstein, Richard B., with Jerome Agel. *Amending America—If We Love the Constitution So Much, Why Do We Keep Trying to Change It?* (Lawrence: University Press of Kansas, 1993).

Black, Charles Jr. *Impeachment: A Handbook.* New Haven: Yale University Press, 1974, 1998.

Caraley, Demetrios. "Dismantling the Federal Safety Net: Fictions versus Realities," *Political Science Quarterly,* Summer 1996, Vol. 111, No. 2, pp. 225–58.

Corwin, Edward, and J. W. Peltason. *Corwin & Peltason's Understanding the Constitution,* 13th ed. Fort Worth: Harcourt Brace, 1994.

Crovitz, L. Gordon, and Jeremy Rabkin, eds. *The Fettered Presidency: Legal Constraints on the Executive Branch.* Washington, DC: American Enterprise Institute, 1989.

Elazar, Daniel. *American Federalism: A View from the States,* 3rd ed. New York: Harper & Row, 1984.

Grodzins, Morton. *The American System.* Chicago: Rand McNally, 1974.

Kettl, Donald. *The Regulation of American Federalism.* Baltimore: Johns Hopkins University Press, 1987.

Palley, Marian Lief, and Howard Palley. *Urban America and Public Policies.* Lexington, MA: D. C. Heath, 1981.

Peterson, Paul, Barry Rabe, and Kenneth K. Wong. *When Federalism Works*. Washington, DC: Brookings Institution, 1986.

Smith, Rogers. *Civic Ideals: Conflicting Visions of Citizenship in U.S. History*. New Haven: Yale University Press, 1997.

CHAPTER

four

The Constitutional Framework and the
Individual: Civil Liberties and Civil Rights

EVENTS	INSTITUTIONAL DEVELOPMENTS
Bill of Rights sent to states for ratification (1789)	States ratify U.S. Bill of Rights (1791)
Undeclared naval war with France (1798–1800); passage of Alien and Sedition Acts (1798)	
1800	Alien and Sedition Acts disregarded and not renewed (1801)
	Missouri Compromise regulates expansion of slavery into territories (1820)
Maine admitted to Union as free state (1820); Missouri admitted as slave state (1821)	*Barron v. Baltimore* confirms dual citizenship (1833)
Slaves taken into territories (1800s)	*Dred Scott v. Sandford* invalidates Missouri Compromise, perpetuates slavery (1857)
1860	
Civil War (1861–1865)	Emancipation Proclamation (1863); Thirteenth Amendment prohibits slavery (1865)
Southern blacks now vote but Black Codes in South impose special restraints (1865)	Civil Rights Act (1866)
Reconstruction (1867–1877)	Fourteenth Amendment ratified (1868)
"Jim Crow" laws spread throughout the South (1890s)	*Plessy v. Ferguson* upholds doctrine of "separate but equal" (1896)
World War I (1914–1918)	
Postwar pacifist and anarchist agitation and suppression (1920s and 1930s) **1920**	
	Gitlow v. N.Y. (1925) and *Near v. Minnesota* (1931) apply First Amendment to states
U.S. in World War II (1941–1945); pressures to desegregate in the Army; revelations of Nazi genocide	President's commission on civil rights (1946)
1950	
Civil Rights Movement: Montgomery bus boycott (1955); lunch counter sit-ins (1960); freedom riders (1961)	*Brown v. Board of Education* overturns *Plessy,* invalidates segregation (1954); federal use of troops to enforce court order to integrate schools (1957)
March on Washington—largest civil rights demonstration in American history (1963)	Civil Rights Act outlaws segregation (1964)
	Katzenbach v. McClung upholds use of commerce clause to bar segregation (1964)

EVENTS	INSTITUTIONAL DEVELOPMENTS
Spread of movement politics—students, women, environment, right to life (1970s)	**1970**
	Roe v. Wade prohibits states from outlawing abortion (1973)
Affirmative action plans enacted in universities and corporations (1970s and 1980s)	Court orders to end malapportionment and segregation (1970s and 1980s)
	Bowers v. Hardwick upholds state regulation of homosexual activity (1986)
Challenges to affirmative action plans (1980s–1990s)	Court accepts affirmative action on a limited basis—*Regents of Univ. of Calif. v. Bakke* (1978), *Wards Cove v. Atonio* (1989), *Martin v. Wilks* (1989)
	Missouri law restricting abortion upheld in *Webster v. Reproductive Health Services* (1989)
States adopt restrictive abortion laws (1990–1991)	**1990**
Bush signs civil rights bill favoring suits against employment discrimination (1991)	Court permits school boards to terminate busing (1991)
Right to abortion established in *Roe v. Wade* upheld in *Planned Parenthood of SE Penn. v. Casey* (1992)	Clinton positions on abortion and gay rights revive civil rights activity and controversy (1993)
Clinton appoints Ginsburg (1993) and Breyer (1994) to Supreme Court	President and Congress limit death penalty appeals; quick Court approval in *Felker v. Turpin* (1996) suggests continuing conservative direction on criminal rights; but Court protection of abortion clinics with a "buffer zone" in *Madsen v. Women's Health Center* (1994) suggests a more moderate direction on abortion
Democrats lose Congress; Clinton presides over divided government (1994–2000)	Clinton moves in a conservative direction, claiming civil rights "may have gone too far;" also supports more "states' rights" (1997)
George W. Bush elected; Republicans with narrow majority in Congress (2000); they lose Senate after Jeffords leaves Republican Party (2001)	**2000** Clear rightward turn evident with the appointment of John Ashcroft as attorney general; two federal executions, after 40-year gap, suggest "nationalization of the death penalty" (2001)

Collective Action Principle

The Federalists supported a bill of rights because it would gain the support of the Antifederalists for the Constitution.

Rationality Principle

Madison believed a bill of rights would remove a potential source of opposition to the new government.

W hen the First Congress under the new Constitution met in late April of 1789 (having been delayed since March 4 by lack of a quorum because of bad winter roads), the most important item of business was consideration of a proposal to add a bill of rights to the Constitution. Such a proposal by Virginia delegate George Mason had been turned down with little debate in the waning days of the Philadelphia Constitutional Convention in September 1787, not because the delegates were too tired or too hot or against rights, but because of arguments by Hamilton and other Federalists that a bill of rights was irrelevant in a constitution providing the national government with only delegated powers. How could the national government abuse powers not given to it in the first place? But when the Constitution was submitted to the states for ratification, Antifederalists, most of whom had *not* been delegates in Philadelphia, picked up on the argument of Thomas Jefferson (who also had not been a delegate) that the omission of a bill of rights was a major imperfection of the new Constitution. Whatever the merits of Hamilton's or Jefferson's positions, in order to gain ratification, the Federalists in Massachusetts, South Carolina, New Hampshire, Virginia, and New York made an "unwritten but unequivocal pledge" to add a bill of rights and a promise to confirm (in what became the Tenth Amendment) the understanding that all powers not delegated to the national government or explicitly prohibited to the states were reserved to the states.[1]

James Madison, who had been a delegate at the Philadelphia Convention and later became a member of Congress, may still have agreed privately that a bill of rights was not needed. But in 1789, recognizing the urgency of obtaining the support of the Antifederalists for the Constitution and the new government, he fought for the bill of rights, arguing that the principle it embodied would acquire "the character of fundamental maxims of free Government, and as they become incorporated with the national sentiment, counteract the impulses of interest

[1]Clinton Rossiter, *1787: The Grand Convention*, Norton Library Edition (New York: W. W. Norton, 1987), p. 302.

and passion."[2] Madison and his fellow Virginian delegates were, if nothing else, practical men. While they may have conceded on principle Hamilton's argument against the need for a bill of rights, *principle* was not what the debate was all about. They felt that, as a practical political matter, it was essential to put to rest the arguably unnecessary and exaggerated fears of the less-than-enthusiastic supporters of the new Constitution. It was also thought prudent to take off the table, so to speak, a possible issue—the absence of explicit protections a bill of rights would provide—that could be brandished by opponents of the new regime the first time a crisis occurred. Prudence, foresight, and practicality were behind Madison's support for these changes in the new Constitution.

"After much discussion and manipulation . . . at the delicate prompting of Washington and under the masterful prodding of Madison," the House adopted seventeen amendments; the Senate adopted twelve of these. Ten of the amendments were ratified by the states on December 15, 1791—from the start, these ten were called the Bill of Rights.[3]

The Bill of Rights—its history and the controversy of interpretation surrounding it—can be usefully subdivided into two categories: civil liberties and civil rights. This chapter will be divided accordingly. *Civil liberties* are defined as *protections of citizens from improper government action.* When adopted in 1791, the Bill of Rights was seen as guaranteeing a private sphere of personal liberty free of governmental

THE CENTRAL QUESTIONS

CIVIL LIBERTIES:
NATIONALIZING THE BILL OF RIGHTS

Does the Bill of Rights put limits only on the national government or does it limit state governments as well?

How and when did the Supreme Court nationalize the Bill of Rights?

What is the likelihood that the current Supreme Court will try to reverse the nationalization of the Bill of Rights?

CIVIL RIGHTS

What is the legal basis for civil rights?

How has the equal protection clause historically been enforced?

What is the critical Supreme Court ruling in the battle for equal protection?

In what areas did the civil rights acts seek to provide equal access and protection?

What groups were spurred by the provision of the Civil Rights Act of 1964 outlawing discrimination in employment practices based on race, religion, and gender, to seek broader protection under the law?

What is the basis for affirmative action? What form does it take?

How does affirmative action contribute to the polarization of the politics of civil rights?

---

[2]Quoted in Milton Konvitz, "The Bill of Rights: Amendments I–X," in *An American Primer,* ed. Daniel J. Boorstin (Chicago: University of Chicago Press, 1966), p. 159.

[3]Rossiter, *1787: The Grand Convention,* p. 303, where he also reports that "in 1941 the States of Connecticut, Massachusetts, and Georgia celebrated the sesquicentennial of the Bill of Rights by giving their hitherto withheld and unneeded assent."

civil liberties
Protections of citizens
from improper
government action.

restrictions.[4] As Jefferson had put it, a bill of rights "is what people are entitled to *against every government on earth. . . .*" Note the emphasis—citizen *against* government. In this sense, we could call the Bill of Rights a "bill of liberties" because the amendments focus on what government must *not* do. For example (with emphasis added),

1. "Congress shall make *no* law . . ." (I)
2. "The right . . . to . . . bear Arms, shall *not* be infringed." (II)
3. "*No* Soldier shall . . . be quartered . . ." (III)
4. "*No* Warrants shall issue, but upon probable cause . . ." (IV)
5. "*No* person shall be held to answer . . . unless on a presentment or indictment of a Grand Jury . . ." (V)
6. "Excessive bail shall *not* be required . . . *nor* cruel and unusual punishments inflicted." (VIII)

Thus, the Bill of Rights is a series of "thou shalt nots"—restraints addressed to governments. Some of these restraints are *substantive*, putting limits on *what* the government shall and shall not have power to do—such as establishing a religion, quartering troops in private homes without consent, or seizing private property without just compensation. Other restraints are *procedural*, dealing with *how* the government is supposed to act. For example, even though the government has the substantive power to declare certain acts to be crimes and to arrest and imprison persons who violate its criminal laws, it may not do so except by fairly meticulous observation of procedures designed to protect the accused person. The best-known procedural rule is that "a person is presumed innocent until proven guilty." This rule does not question the government's power to punish someone for committing a crime; it questions only the way the government determines *who* committed the crime. Substantive and procedural restraints together identify the realm of civil liberties.

civil rights Legal
or moral claims that
citizens are entitled
to make upon the
government.

We define ***civil rights*** as obligations imposed on government to guarantee equal citizenship and to protect citizens from discrimination by other private citizens and other government agencies. Civil rights did not become part of the Constitution until 1868 with the adoption of the Fourteenth Amendment, which addressed the issue of who was a citizen and provided for each citizen "the equal protection of the laws." From that point on, we can see more clearly the distinction between civil liberties and civil rights, because civil liberties issues arise under the "due process of law" clause, and civil rights issues arise under the "equal protection of the laws" clause.

We turn first to civil liberties and to the long history of the effort to make personal liberty a reality for every citizen in America. The struggle for freedom against arbitrary and discriminatory actions by governments has continued to this day. And inevitably it is tied to the continuing struggle for civil rights, to

---

[4]Lest there be confusion in our interchangeable use of the words "liberty" and "freedom," treat them as synonyms. "Freedom" is from the German, *Freiheit*. "Liberty" is from the French, *liberté*. Both have to do with the absence of restraints on individual choices of action.

persuade those same governments to take positive actions. We shall deal with that in the second section of this chapter, but we should not lose sight of the connection in the real world between civil liberties and civil rights. We should also not lose sight of the connection between this principle and the constitutional framework established in Chapter 3. Although the principle of individual liberties and rights was identified in Chapter 3 as comprising the third of the three most important principles in the Constitution, the third cannot be understood except in the context of the other two, especially federalism. Americans are forever fearful about losing their individual autonomy, and American history is filled with discourse about how to protect and expand individual freedom. This has given Americans a love/hate relationship with government, because the individual recognizes the need to be protected *from* government and at the same time recognizes that an active government is needed to protect and to advance the individual's opportunity to enjoy liberty.[5] We believe that there is an important lesson to be learned here, and we hope that readers of this book will always keep this important question in mind: "How are Americans protected both from and by the national government?"

CIVIL LIBERTIES: NATIONALIZING THE BILL OF RIGHTS

The First Amendment provides that "Congress shall make no law respecting an establishment of religion . . . or abridging the freedom of speech, or of the press; or the right of [assembly and petition]." But this is the only amendment in the Bill of Rights that addresses itself exclusively to the national government. For example, the Second Amendment provides that "the right of the people to keep and bear Arms, shall not be infringed." The Fifth Amendment says, among other things, that *no person* "shall . . . be twice put in jeopardy of life or limb" for the same crime; that *no person* "shall be compelled in any criminal case to be a witness against himself"; that *no person* shall "be deprived of life, liberty, or property, without due process of law"; and that private property cannot be taken "without just compensation."[6] Since the First Amendment is the only part of the Bill of Rights that is explicit in its intention to put limits on the national government, a fundamental question inevitably arises: *Do the remaining amendments*

[5]For some recent scholarship on the Bill of Rights and its development, see Geoffrey Stone, Richard Epstein, and Cass Sunstein, eds., *The Bill of Rights and the Modern State* (Chicago: University of Chicago Press, 1992); and Michael J. Meyer and William A. Parent, eds., *The Constitution of Rights* (Ithaca, NY: Cornell University Press, 1992).

[6]It would be useful at this point to review all the provisions of the Bill of Rights (in the Appendix) to confirm this distinction between the wording of the First Amendment and the rest. Emphasis in the example quotations was not in the original. For a spirited and enlightening essay on the extent to which the entire Bill of Rights was about equality, see Martha Minow, "Equality and the Bill of Rights," in Meyer and Parent, *The Constitution of Rights*, pp. 118–28.

of the Bill of Rights put limits on state governments or only on the national government?

Dual Citizenship

The question concerning whether the Bill of Rights also limits state governments was settled in 1833 in a way that seems odd to Americans today. The 1833 case was *Barron v. Baltimore*, and the facts were simple. In paving its streets, the city of Baltimore had disposed of so much sand and gravel in the water near Barron's wharf that the value of the wharf for commercial purposes was virtually destroyed. Barron brought the city into court on the grounds that it had, under the Fifth Amendment, unconstitutionally deprived him of his property. Barron had to take his case all the way to the Supreme Court, despite the fact that the argument made by his attorney seemed airtight. The following is Chief Justice Marshall's characterization of Barron's argument:

> The plaintiff [Barron] . . . contends that it comes within that clause in the Fifth Amendment of the Constitution which inhibits the taking of private property for public use without just compensation. He insists that this amendment, being in favor of the liberty of the citizen, ought to be so construed as to restrain the legislative power of a state, as well as that of the United States.[7]

Then Marshall, in one of the most significant Supreme Court decisions ever handed down, disagreed:

> The Constitution was ordained and established by the people of the United States for themselves, for their own government, and not for the government of individual States. Each State established a constitution for itself, and in that constitution provided such limitations and restrictions on the powers of its particular government as its judgment dictated. . . . If these propositions be correct, *the fifth amendment must be understood as restraining the power of the General Government, not as applicable to the States.*[8]

In other words, if an agency of the *national* government had deprived Barron of his property, there would have been little doubt about Barron's winning his case. But if the constitution of the state of Maryland contained no such provision protecting citizens of Maryland from such action, then Barron had no legal leg to stand on against Baltimore, an agency of the state of Maryland.

Barron v. Baltimore confirmed "dual citizenship," that is, that each American was a citizen of the national government and *separately* a citizen of one of the states. This meant that the Bill of Rights did not apply to decisions or to procedures of state (or local) governments. Even slavery could continue, because the

[7]Barron v. Baltimore, 7 Peters 243 (1833).
[8]Ibid. [Emphasis added.]

Bill of Rights could not protect anyone from state laws treating people as property. In fact, the Bill of Rights did not become a vital instrument for the extension of civil liberties for anyone until after a bloody Civil War and a revolutionary Fourteenth Amendment intervened. And even so, as we shall see, nearly another century would pass before the Bill of Rights would truly come into its own.

Institution Principle

Dual citizenship meant that the Bill of Rights did not apply to decisions or to procedures of state governments.

The Fourteenth Amendment

From a constitutional standpoint, the defeat of the South in the Civil War settled one question and raised another. It probably settled forever the question of whether secession was an option for any state. After 1865 there was to be more "united" than "states" to the United States. But this left unanswered just how much the states were obliged to obey the Constitution and, in particular, the Bill of Rights. Just reading the words of the Fourteenth Amendment, anyone might think it was almost perfectly designed to impose the Bill of Rights on the states and thereby to reverse *Barron v. Baltimore.* The very first words of the Fourteenth Amendment point in that direction:

> All persons born or naturalized in the United States, and subject to the jurisdiction thereof, are citizens of the United States and of the State wherein they reside.

This provides for a *single national citizenship*, and at a minimum that means that civil liberties should not vary drastically from state to state. That would seem to be the spirit of the Fourteenth Amendment: *to nationalize the Bill of Rights by nationalizing the definition of citizenship.*

This interpretation of the Fourteenth Amendment is reinforced by the next clause of the Amendment:

> *No State* shall make or enforce any law which shall abridge the privileges or immunities of citizens of the United States; nor shall any State deprive any person of life, liberty, or property, without due process of law. [Emphasis added.]

All of this sounds like an effort to extend the Bill of Rights in its *entirety* to citizens *wherever* they might reside.[9] But this was not to be the Supreme Court's interpretation for nearly a hundred years. Within five years of ratification of the Fourteenth Amendment, the Court was making decisions as though it had never been adopted. The shadow of *Barron* grew longer and longer. In an important 1873 decision known as the *Slaughter-House Cases,* the Supreme

---

[9]The Fourteenth Amendment also seems designed to introduce civil rights. The final clause of the all-important Section 1 provides that no state can "deny to any person within its jurisdiction the equal protection of the laws." It is not unreasonable to conclude that the purpose of this provision was to obligate the state governments as well as the national government to take *positive* actions to protect citizens from arbitrary and discriminatory actions, at least those based on race. This will be explored in the second half of this chapter.

Court determined that the federal government was under no obligation to protect the "privileges and immunities" of citizens of a particular state against arbitrary actions by that state's government. The case had its origins in 1867, when a corrupt Louisiana legislature conferred upon a single corporation a monopoly of all the slaughterhouse business in the city of New Orleans. The other slaughterhouses, facing bankruptcy, all brought suits claiming, like Mr. Barron, that this was a taking of their property in violation of Fifth Amendment rights. But unlike Mr. Barron, they believed that they were protected now because, they argued, the Fourteenth Amendment incorporated the Fifth Amendment, applying it to the states. The suits were all rejected. The Supreme Court argued, first, that the primary purpose of the Fourteenth Amendment was to protect "Negroes as a class." Second, and more to the point here, the Court argued, without trying to prove it, that the framers of the Fourteenth Amendment could not have intended to incorporate the entire Bill of Rights.[10] Yet, when the Civil Rights Act of 1875 attempted to protect blacks from discriminatory treatment by proprietors of hotels, theaters, and other public accommodations, the Supreme Court disregarded its own primary argument in the previous case and held the act unconstitutional, declaring that the Fourteenth Amendment applied only to discriminatory actions by state officials, "operating under cover of law," and not to discrimination against blacks by private individuals, even though these private individuals were companies offering services to the public.[11] Such narrow interpretations raised the inevitable question of whether the Fourteenth Amendment had incorporated *any* of the Bill of Rights. The Fourteenth Amendment remained shadowy until the mid-twentieth century. The shadow was *Barron v. Baltimore* and the Court's unwillingness to "nationalize" civil liberties—that is, to interpret the civil liberties expressed in the Bill of Rights as imposing limitations not only on the federal government but also on the states.

It was not until the very end of the nineteenth century that the Supreme Court began to nationalize the Bill of Rights by incorporating its civil liberties provisions into the Fourteenth Amendment. Table 4.1 outlines the major steps in this process. The only change in civil liberties during the first sixty years following the adoption of the Fourteenth Amendment came in 1897, when the Supreme Court held that the due process clause of the Fourteenth Amendment did in fact prohibit states from taking property for a public use without just compensation.[12] This effectively overruled *Barron*, because it meant that the citizen of Maryland or any state was henceforth protected from a "public taking" of property (eminent domain) even if the state constitution did not provide such protection. However, in a broader sense, *Barron* still cast a shadow, because the Supreme Court had "incorporated" into the Fourteenth Amendment only the property protection provision of the Fifth Amendment and no other

[10]The Slaughter-House Cases, 16 Wallace 36 (1873).
[11]The Civil Rights Cases, 109 U.S. 3 (1883).
[12]Chicago, Burlington, and Quincy Railroad Company v. Chicago, 166 U.S. 226 (1897).

TABLE 4.1

SELECTED PROVISIONS AND AMENDMENTS	NOT "INCORPORATED" UNTIL	KEY CASE
Incorporation of the Bill of Rights into the Fourteenth Amendment		
Eminent domain (V)	1897	Chicago, Burlington, and Quincy R.R. v. Chicago
Freedom of speech (I)	1925	Gitlow v. New York
Freedom of press (I)	1931	Near v. Minnesota
Freedom of assembly (I)	1939	Hague v. CIO
Freedom from warrantless search and seizure (IV) ("exclusionary rule")	1961	Mapp v. Ohio
Right to counsel in any criminal trial (VI)	1963	Gideon v. Wainwright
Right against self-incrimination and forced confessions (V)	1964	Malloy v. Hogan Escobedo v. Illinois
Right to counsel and to remain silent (VI)	1966	Miranda v. Arizona
Right against double jeopardy (V)	1969	Benton v. Maryland
Right to privacy (III, IV, & V)	1973	Roe v. Wade Doe v. Bolton

clause, let alone the other amendments of the Bill of Rights. In other words, although "due process" applied to the taking of life and liberty as well as property, only property was incorporated into the Fourteenth Amendment as a limitation on state power.

No further expansion of civil liberties through incorporation occurred until 1925, when the Supreme Court held that freedom of speech is "among the fundamental personal rights and 'liberties' protected by the due process clause of the Fourteenth Amendment from impairment by the states."[13] In 1931, the

[13]Gitlow v. New York, 268 U.S. 652 (1925).

Court added freedom of the press to that short list of civil rights protected by the Bill of Rights from state action; in 1939, it added freedom of assembly.[14] But that was as far as the Court was willing to go. As late as 1937, the Supreme Court was still loathe to nationalize civil liberties beyond the First Amendment. In fact, the Court in that year took one of its most extreme turns backward toward *Barron v. Baltimore.* The state of Connecticut had indicted a man named Palko for first-degree murder, but a lower court had found him guilty of only second-degree murder and sentenced him to life in prison. Unhappy with the verdict, the state of Connecticut appealed the conviction to its highest court, won the appeal, got a new trial, and then succeeded in getting Palko convicted of first-degree murder. Palko appealed to the Supreme Court on what seemed an open and shut case of ***double jeopardy***—being tried twice for the same crime. Yet, though the majority of the Court agreed that this could indeed be considered a case of double jeopardy, they decided that double jeopardy was *not* one of the provisions of the Bill of Rights incorporated in the Fourteenth Amendment as a restriction on the powers of the states. Justice Benjamin Cardozo, considered one of the most able Supreme Court justices of this century, rejected the argument made by Palko's lawyer that "whatever is forbidden by the Fifth Amendment is forbidden by the Fourteenth also." Cardozo responded tersely, "There is no such general rule." As far as Cardozo and the majority were concerned, the only rights from the Bill of Rights that ought to be incorporated into the Fourteenth Amendment as applying to the states as well as to the national government were those that were "implicit in the concept of ordered liberty." He asked the questions: Does double jeopardy subject Palko to a "hardship so acute and shocking that our polity will not endure it? Does it violate those 'fundamental principles of liberty and justice which lie at the base of all our civil and political institutions?' . . . The answer must surely be 'no.'"[15] Palko was eventually executed for the crime, because he lived in the state of Connecticut rather than in some state whose constitution included a guarantee against double jeopardy.

Cases like *Palko* extended the shadow of *Barron* into its second century, despite adoption of the Fourteenth Amendment. The Constitution, as interpreted by the Supreme Court, left standing the framework in which the states had the power to determine their own law on a number of fundamental issues. It left states with the power to pass laws segregating the races—and thirteen Southern states chose to exercise that power. The constitutional framework also left states with the power to engage in searches and seizures without a warrant, to indict accused persons without benefit of a grand jury, to deprive persons of trial by jury, to force persons to testify against themselves, to deprive accused persons of their right to confront adverse witnesses, and as we have seen, to prosecute accused persons more than once for the same crime.[16] Few states chose the option to use that kind of power, but some states did, and the power to do so was there for any state whose legislative majority so chose.

double jeopardy
Trial more than once for the same crime. The Constitution guarantees that no one shall be subjected to double jeopardy.

[14]Near v. Minnesota, 283 U.S. 697 (1931); Hague v. C.I.O., 307 U.S. 496 (1939).

[15]Palko v. Connecticut, 302 U.S. 319 (1937).

[16]All of these were implicitly identified in the *Palko* case as "not incorporated" into the Fourteenth Amendment as limitations on the powers of the states.

The Constitutional Revolution in Civil Liberties

For nearly thirty years following the *Palko* case,[17] the nineteenth-century framework was sustained, but signs of change came after 1954, in *Brown v. Board of Education*, when the Supreme Court overturned the infamous *Plessy v. Ferguson*.[18] *Plessy* was a civil rights case involving the "equal protection" clause of the Fourteenth Amendment and was not an issue of applying the Bill of Rights to the states. (It will be dealt with in the next section.) Nevertheless, even though *Brown* was not a civil liberties case, it indicated rather clearly that the Supreme Court was going to be expansive about civil liberties, because with *Brown* the Court had effectively promised that it was *actively* going to subject the states and all actions affecting civil rights and civil liberties to *strict scrutiny*. In retrospect, one could say that this constitutional revolution was given a "jump start" by the *Brown* decision,[19] even though the results were not apparent until after 1961, when the number of civil liberties incorporated increased (see Table 4.1).

Nationalizing the Bill of Rights   As with the federalism revolution, the constitutional revolution in civil liberties was a movement toward nationalization. But the two revolutions required opposite motions on the part of the Supreme Court. In the area of commerce (the first revolution), the Court had to decide to assume a *passive* role by not interfering as Congress expanded the meaning of the commerce clause of Article I, Section 8. This expansion has been so extensive that the national government can now constitutionally reach a single farmer growing twenty acres of wheat or a small neighborhood restaurant selling barbecues to local "whites only" without being anywhere near interstate commerce routes. In the second revolution—involving the Bill of Rights through the Fourteenth Amendment rather than the commerce clause—the Court had to assume an *active* role, which required close review not of Congress but of the laws of state legislatures and decisions of state courts, in order to apply a single national Fourteenth Amendment standard to the rights and liberties of all citizens.

Table 4.1 shows that until 1961, only the First Amendment had been fully and clearly incorporated into the Fourteenth Amendment.[20] After 1961, several other important provisions of the Bill of Rights were incorporated. Of the cases

---

[17]*Palko* was explicitly reversed in Benton v. Maryland, 395 U.S. 784 (1969), in which the Court said that double jeopardy was in fact incorporated in the Fourteenth Amendment as a restriction on the states.

[18]Plessy v. Ferguson, 163 U.S. 537 (1896).

[19]The First Constitutional Revolution, beginning with NLRB v. Jones & Laughlin Steel Corp. (1937), was discussed in Chapter 3.

[20]The one exception was the right to public trial (the Sixth Amendment), but the 1948 case did not actually mention the right to public trial as such; it was cited in a 1968 case as a case establishing the right to public trial as part of the Fourteenth Amendment. The 1948 case was in re Oliver, 33 U.S. 257, where the issue was put more generally as "due process" and public trial itself was not actually mentioned. Later opinions, such as Duncan v. Louisiana, 391 U.S. 145 (1968), cited the *Oliver* case as the precedent for incorporating public trials as part of the Fourteenth Amendment.

that expanded the Fourteenth Amendment's reach, the most famous was *Gideon v. Wainwright*, which established the right to counsel in a criminal trial, because it became the subject of a best-selling book and a popular movie.[21] In *Mapp v. Ohio*, the Court held that evidence obtained in violation of the Fourth Amendment ban on unreasonable searches and seizures would be excluded from trial.[22] This "exclusionary rule" was particularly irksome to the police and prosecutors because it meant that patently guilty defendants sometimes go free because the evidence that clearly damned them could not be used. In *Miranda*,[23] the Court's ruling required that arrested persons be informed of the right to remain silent and to have counsel present during interrogation. This is the basis of the ***Miranda rule*** of reading persons their rights, which has been made famous by TV police shows. By 1969, in *Benton v. Maryland*, the Supreme Court had come full circle regarding the rights of the criminally accused, explicitly reversing the *Palko* ruling and thereby incorporating double jeopardy.

During the 1960s and early 1970s, the Court also expanded another important area of civil liberties: rights to privacy. When the Court began to take a more activist role in the mid-1950s and 1960s, the idea of a "right to privacy" was revived. In 1958, the Supreme Court recognized "privacy in one's association" in its decision to prevent the state of Alabama from using the membership list of the National Association for the Advancement of Colored People in the state's investigations.[24]

The sphere of privacy was drawn in earnest in 1965, when the Court ruled that a Connecticut statute forbidding the use of contraceptives violated the right of marital privacy. Estelle Griswold, the executive director of the Planned Parenthood League of Connecticut, was arrested by the state of Connecticut for providing information, instruction, and medical advice about contraception to married couples. She and her associates were found guilty as accessories to the crime and fined $100 each. The Supreme Court reversed the lower court decisions and declared the Connecticut law unconstitutional because it violated "a right of privacy older than the Bill of Rights—older than our political parties, older than our school system."[25] Justice William O. Douglas, author of the majority decision in the *Griswold* case, argued that this right of privacy is also grounded in the Constitution, because it fits into a "zone of privacy" created by a combination of the Third, Fourth, and Fifth Amendments. A concurring opinion, written by Justice Arthur Goldberg, attempted to strengthen Douglas's argument by adding that "the concept of liberty . . . embraces the right of marital privacy though that right is not mentioned explicitly in the Constitution [and] is

Miranda rule
Principles developed by the Supreme Court in the 1966 case of *Miranda v. Arizona* requiring that persons under arrest be informed of their legal rights, including their right to counsel, prior to police interrogation.

 Institution Principle
Most of the important provisions of the Bill of Rights were nationalized by the Supreme Court during the 1960s.

[21]Gideon v. Wainwright, 372 U.S. 335 (1963); Anthony Lewis, *Gideon's Trumpet* (New York: Random House, 1964).

[22]Mapp v. Ohio, 367 U.S. 643 (1961).

[23]Miranda v. Arizona, 384 U.S. 436 (1966).

[24]NAACP v. Alabama ex rel. Patterson, 357 U.S. 449 (1958).

[25]Griswold v. Connecticut, 381 U.S. 479 (1965).

supported by numerous decisions of this Court . . . and *by the language and history of the Ninth Amendment* [emphasis added]."[26]

The right to privacy was confirmed—and extended—in 1973 in the most important of all privacy decisions, and one of the most important Supreme Court decisions in American history: *Roe v. Wade.*[27] This decision established a woman's right to have an abortion and prohibited states from making abortion a criminal act. The basis for the Supreme Court's decision in *Roe* was the evolving right to privacy. But it is important to realize that the preference for privacy rights and for their extension to include the rights of women to control their own bodies was not something invented by the Supreme Court in a political vacuum. Most states did not begin to regulate abortions in any fashion until the 1840s (by 1839 only six of the twenty-six existing states had any regulations governing abortion). In addition, many states began to ease their abortion restrictions well before the 1973 Supreme Court decision. In recent years, however, a number of states have reinstated restrictions on abortion, testing the limits of *Roe.*

History Principle

Roe v. Wade was not decided in a political vacuum. Many states had already eased their restrictions on abortion prior to 1973.

Like any important principle, once privacy was established as an aspect of civil liberties protected by the Bill of Rights through the Fourteenth Amendment, it took on a life all its own. In a number of important decisions, the Supreme Court and the lower federal courts sought to protect rights that could not be found in the text of the Constitution but could be discovered through the study of the philosophic sources of fundamental rights. Through this line of reasoning, the federal courts sought to protect sexual autonomy, lifestyle choices, sexual preferences, procreational choice, and various forms of intimate association.

Criticism mounted with every extension of this line of reasoning. The federal courts were accused of creating an uncontrollable expansion of rights demands. The Supreme Court, the critics argued, had displaced the judgments of legislatures and state courts with its own judgment of what is reasonable, without regard to local popular majorities and without regard to specific constitutional provisions. This is virtually the definition of what came to be called "judicial activism" in the 1980s, and it was the basis for a more strongly critical label, "the imperial judiciary."[28]

Institution Principle

As a political institution, the Bill of Rights has not been carved in stone. Through subsequent amendments, on the one hand, and constant updating of the original ten through judicial review, on the other, the balance between freedom and power has been transformed.

The history of civil liberties in the United States is evidence that, as a political institution, the Bill of Rights has not been carved in stone. Through subsequent amendments, on the one hand, and the interpretations of the Supreme Court, on the other, the balance between freedom and power has been transformed. Indeed, the framers of the Constitution would be unlikely to recognize their original handiwork. But, as we shall see next, what the Supreme Court gives, the Supreme Court can also take away.

[26]Griswold v. Connecticut, concurring opinion. In 1972, the Court extended the privacy right to unmarried women: Eisenstadt v. Baird, 405 U.S. 438 (1972).

[27]Roe v. Wade, 410 U.S. 113 (1973).

[28]A good discussion will be found in Paul Brest and Sanford Levinson, *Processes of Constitutional Decision-Making: Cases and Materials,* 2nd ed. (Boston: Little, Brown, 1983), p. 660. See also Chapter 8.

Rehnquist: A De-Nationalizing Trend?

Rationality Principle

The preferences of individual Supreme Court justices have been consequential for the development of civil liberties.

While constitutional developments may be represented as the history of doctrinal disputes and the general evolution of interpretation—and, as the last few pages have made clear, there is nothing linear and straightforward about these developments—it must be recognized that these events are as much *political* as *philosophical*. Judges and justices are, after all, *politicians*. And courts are *political institutions*. The backdrop, therefore, for debates over legal doctrine and constitutional meaning consists of the preferences of politicians, on the one hand, and the tug and pull of maneuvering between the courts and other (separate) institutions of government, on the other.

The preferences of individual Supreme Court justices have certainly been consequential during the first two centuries of our republic, with John Marshall probably casting the longest shadow. Likewise, conflicts between the judiciary, legislature, and executive have ebbed and flowed. Throughout, controversy over judicial power has not diminished. In fact, it is intensifying under Chief Justice William Rehnquist, an avowed critic of "judicial activism" as it relates to privacy, criminal procedure, and other new liberties, such as the right not to be required to participate in prayers in school.[29] Although it is difficult to determine just how much influence Rehnquist has had as chief justice, the Court has in fact been moving in a less activist and more conservative, de-nationalizing direction.

The best measure of the decline of activism is the decline in the Court's annual case load from 150 to 75, which Court watchers call the "incredible shrinking docket."[30] Eminent Court watchers agree that this is a momentous trend, which must be attributed in large part to Rehnquist's personal influence. Granted, there was a diminishing supply of new statutory activity during the 1980s and early 1990s, and granted also, there was far less civil rights litigation than there had been. As Justice Souter observed in a very frank appraisal of the recent history of the Supreme Court, "There hasn't been an awful lot for us to take."[31] However, this did not "just happen." An activist court can virtually always find cases if it is seeking them. Meanwhile, year by year during the Rehnquist tenure, the case load shrank from the average of 150 cases during the years prior to his appointment in 1986 to 90 cases in 1997–1998.[32]

A good measure of the Court's growing conservatism is the following comparison made by constitutional scholar David M. O'Brien: between 1961 and

---

[29]Engel v. Vitale, 370 U.S. 421 (1962), in which the Court struck down a state-composed prayer for recitation in the schools. Of course, a whole line of cases followed *Engel*, as states and cities tried various ways of getting around the Court's principle that any organized prayer in the public schools violates the First Amendment rights of the individual.

[30]Quoted in David Garrow, "The Rehnquist Reins," *New York Times Magazine*, 6 October 1996, p. 82.

[31]Quoted in ibid., p. 71.

[32]Cited in U.S. Bureau of the Census, *Statistical Abstract of the United States, 2000*, Table 356 (Washington, DC: Government Printing Office, 2001).

1969, more than 76 percent of the Warren Court's rulings from term to term tended to be liberal—that is, tending toward nationalizing the Bill of Rights to protect individuals and minorities mainly against the actions of state government. During the Burger years, 1969–1986, the liberal tendency dropped on the average below 50 percent. During the first four years of the Rehnquist Court (the extent of O'Brien's research), the average liberal "score" dropped to less than 35 percent.[33]

Rationality Principle

The preference of the members of the Rehnquist Court has been to accept fewer cases for review.

The Supreme Court has moved in a conservative direction, for example, regarding the First Amendment's "establishment clause," which established a "wall of separation" between church and state. In the 1995 case of *Rosenberger v. University of Virginia*, the Court seemed to open a new breach in the wall between church and state when it ruled that the university had violated the free speech rights of a Christian student group by refusing to provide student activity funds to the group's magazine, although other student groups had been given funds for their publications. In the 1997 case of *Agostini v. Felton*, the Court again breached the wall between church and state, ruling that states could pay public school teachers to offer remedial courses at religious schools.[34]

The conservative trend has also extended to the burning question of abortion rights. In *Webster v. Reproductive Health Services*, the Court narrowly upheld by a 5-to-4 majority the constitutionality of restrictions on the use of public medical facilities for abortion.[35] And in 1992, in the most recent major decision on abortion, *Planned Parenthood v. Casey*, another 5–to–4 majority of the Court barely upheld *Roe* but narrowed its scope, refusing to invalidate a Pennsylvania law that significantly restricts freedom of choice. The decision defined the right to an abortion as a "limited or qualified" right subject to regulation by the states as long as the regulation does not impose an "undue burden."[36] As one constitutional authority concluded from the decision in *Casey*, "Until there is a Freedom of Choice Act, and/or a U.S. Supreme Court able to wean *Roe* from its respirator, state legislatures will have significant discretion over the access women will have to legalized abortions."[37]

---

[33]David M. O'Brien, *Supreme Court Watch—1991*, Annual Supplement to *Constitutional Law and Politics* (New York: W. W. Norton, 1991), p. 6 and Chapter 4.

[34]Rosenberger v. University of Virginia, 94-329 (1995); Agostini v. Felton, 96-522 (1997).

[35]In Webster v. Reproductive Health Services, 109 S.Ct. 3040 (1989), Chief Justice Rehnquist's decision upheld a Missouri law that restricted the use of public medical facilities for abortion. The decision opened the way for other states to limit the availability of abortion. The first to act was the Pennsylvania legislature, which adopted in late 1989 a law banning all abortions after pregnancy had passed twenty-four weeks, except to save the life of the pregnant woman or to prevent irreversible impairment of her health. In 1990, the pace of state legislative action increased, with new statutes passed in South Carolina, Ohio, Minnesota, and Guam. In 1991, the Louisiana legislature adopted, over the governor's veto, the strictest law yet. The Louisiana law prohibits all abortions except when the mother's life is threatened or when rape or incest victims report these crimes immediately.

[36]Planned Parenthood of Southeastern Pennsylvania v. Casey, 112 S.Ct. 2791 (1992).

[37]Gayle Binion, "Undue Burden? Government Now Has Wide Latitude to Restrict Abortions," *Santa Barbara News-Press*, 5 July 1992, p. A13.

One area in which Chief Justice Rehnquist seems determined to expand rather than shrink the Court's protection of privacy rights is in the constitutional protection of property rights. But this is itself a conservative direction and the Court's conservative justices, led by Chief Justice Rehnquist, have pushed for a broader interpretation of the Fifth Amendment's takings clause to put limits on the degree to which local, state, and federal governments can impose restrictions on land use. In an important case from 1994, the Court overturned a Tigard, Oregon, law that had required any person seeking a building permit to give the city ten percent of his or her property. In a 5-to-4 decision, the Court ruled that such a requirement fell into the Fifth Amendment's prohibition against taking of property "without just compensation." In his opinion, Chief Justice Rehnquist wrote, "We see no reason why the takings clause of the Fifth Amendment, as much a part of the Bill of Rights as the First Amendment or Fourth Amendment, should be relegated to the status of a poor relation in those comparable circumstances."[38]

In recent years, the Court has also expanded the protection of free speech. In the Court's most important recent free speech case, *Reno v. American Civil Liberties Union*, the Communication Decency Act, a federal law restricting indecent material on the Internet, was struck down as a violation of free speech. In another important free speech case, the Court in 1999 ruled that a Colorado statute regulating ballot petitions was a violation of the First Amendment.[39] The state had required that individuals circulating petitions on behalf of ballot initiatives be registered Colorado voters, that they wear name tags, and that their names and occupations be matters of public record. The Court ruled that these requirements constituted an impermissible infringement upon "political conversation and the exchange of ideas."

Still the question remains: Will a Supreme Court, even with a majority of conservatives, reverse the nationalization of the Bill of Rights? Possibly, but not necessarily. First of all, the Rehnquist Court has not actually reversed any of the decisions made during the 1960s by the Warren or Burger Courts nationalizing most of the clauses of the Bill of Rights. As we have seen, the Rehnquist Court has given narrower and more restrictive interpretations of the earlier decisions, but it has not reversed any, not even *Roe v. Wade*. Second, President Clinton's appointments to the Court, Ruth Bader Ginsburg and Stephen Breyer, have helped form a centrist majority that seems unwilling, for the time being at least, to sanction any major steps to turn back the nationalization of the Bill of Rights. But with a new Republican president whose nominations to the Court will have to be approved by a Democrat-controlled Senate, the question of the contraction of the Bill of Rights and the Fourteenth Amendment is certain to be in the forefront of political debate for a long time to come.

Thus we end about where we began. *Barron v. Baltimore* has not been entirely put to rest; its spirit still hovers, casting a shadow over the Bill of Rights.

---

[38]Dolan v. City of Tigard, 93-518 (1994).
[39]Buckley v. American Constitutional Law Foundation, 97-930 (1999).

We hear less of the plea for the Supreme Court to take the final step they didn't quite take in the 1960s, to declare as a matter of constitutional law that the *entire* Bill of Rights is incorporated into the Fourteenth Amendment. If that more liberal Court was not willing to do so, the more conservative Court of today is all the less willing. We are thus still in suspense, because a Court with the power to expand the Bill of Rights also has the power to contract it.[40]

CIVIL RIGHTS

The very simplicity of the "civil rights clause" of the Fourteenth Amendment left it open to interpretation:

> No State shall make or enforce any law which shall . . . deny to any person within its jurisdiction the equal protection of the laws.

But in the very first Fourteenth Amendment case to come before the Supreme Court, the majority gave it a distinct meaning:

> . . . it is not difficult to give meaning to this clause ["the equal protection of the laws"]. The existence of laws in the States . . . which discriminated with gross injustice and hardship against [Negroes] as a class, was the evil to be remedied by this clause, and by it such laws are forbidden.[41]

Beyond that, contemporaries of the Fourteenth Amendment understood well that private persons offering conveyances, accommodations, or places of amusement to the public incurred certain public obligations to offer them to one and all—in other words, these are *public* accommodations, such that arbitrary discrimination in their use would amount to denial of equal protection of the laws—unless a government took action to overcome the discrimination.[42] This puts governments under obligation to take positive actions to equalize the opportunity for each citizen to enjoy his or her freedom. A skeptic once observed that "the law, in its majestic equality, forbids the rich as well as the poor to sleep under bridges, to beg in the streets, and to steal bread."[43] The purpose of civil rights principles and laws is to use government in such a way as to give equality a more substantive meaning than that.

Discrimination refers to the use of any unreasonable and unjust criterion of exclusion. Of course, all laws discriminate, including some people while excluding others; but some discrimination is considered unreasonable. Now, for

---

[40]For a lively and readable treatment of the possibilities of restricting provisions of the Bill of Rights, without actually reversing Warren Court decisions, see David G. Savage, *Turning Right: The Making of the Rehnquist Supreme Court* (New York: Wiley, 1992).

[41]The Slaughter-House Cases, 16 Wallace 36 (1873).

[42]See Civil Rights Cases, 109 U.S. 3 (1883).

[43]Anatole France, *Le lys rouge* (1894), Chapter 7.

example, it is considered reasonable to use age as a criterion for legal drinking, excluding all persons younger than twenty-one. But is age a reasonable distinction when seventy (or sixty-five or sixty) is selected as the age for compulsory retirement? In the mid-1970s, Congress answered this question by making old age a new civil right; compulsory retirement at seventy is now an unlawful, unreasonable, discriminatory use of age.

Plessy v. Ferguson: "Separate but Equal"

Following its initial decisions making "equal protection" a civil rights clause, the Supreme Court turned conservative, no more ready to enforce the civil rights aspects of the Fourteenth Amendment than it was to enforce the civil liberties provisions. As we have seen, the Court declared the Civil Rights Act of 1875 unconstitutional on the ground that the act sought to protect blacks against discrimination by *private* businesses, while the Fourteenth Amendment, according to the Court's interpretation, was intended to protect individuals from discrimination only against actions by *public* officials of state and local governments.

In 1896, the Court went still further, in the infamous case of *Plessy v. Ferguson,* by upholding a Louisiana statute that *required* segregation of the races on trolleys and other public carriers (and by implication in all public facilities, including schools). Homer Plessy, a man defined as "one-eighth black," had violated a Louisiana law that provided for "equal but separate accommodations" on trains and a $25 fine for any white passenger who sat in a car reserved for blacks or any black passenger who sat in a car reserved for whites. The Supreme Court held that the Fourteenth Amendment's "equal protection of the laws" was not violated by racial distinction as long as the facilities were equal. People generally pretended they were equal as long as some accommodation existed. The Court said that although "the object of the [Fourteenth] Amendment was undoubtedly to enforce the absolute equality of the two races before the law, . . . it could not have intended to abolish distinctions based on color, or to enforce social, as distinguished from political, equality, or a commingling of the two races upon terms unsatisfactory to either."[44] What the Court was saying in effect was that the use of race as a criterion of exclusion in public matters was not unreasonable. This was the origin of the *"separate but equal" rule,* which was not reversed until 1954.

separate but equal rule
Doctrine that public accommodations could be segregated by race but still be equal.

Racial Discrimination after World War II

The shame of discrimination against black military personnel during World War II, plus revelation of Nazi racial atrocities, moved President Harry S. Truman finally to bring the problem to national attention, with the appointment in 1946

[44]Plessy v. Ferguson, 163 U.S. 537 (1896).

of a President's Committee on Civil Rights. In 1947, the committee submitted its report, *To Secure These Rights*, which laid bare the extent of the problem of racial discrimination and its consequences. The report also revealed the success of experiments with racial integration in the armed forces during World War II to demonstrate to Southern society that it had nothing to fear. But the committee recognized that the national government had no clear constitutional authority to pass and implement civil rights legislation. The committee proposed tying civil rights legislation to the commerce power, although it was clear that discrimination was not itself part of the flow of interstate commerce.[45] The committee even suggested using the treaty power as a source of constitutional authority for civil rights legislation.[46]

As for the Supreme Court, it had begun to change its position on racial discrimination before World War II by being stricter about the criterion of equal facilities in the "separate but equal" rule. In 1938, the Court rejected Missouri's policy of paying the tuition of qualified blacks to out-of-state law schools rather than admitting them to the University of Missouri Law School.[47]

After the war, modest progress resumed. In 1950, the Court rejected Texas's claim that its new "law school for Negroes" afforded education equal to that of the all-white University of Texas Law School; without confronting the "separate but equal" principle itself, the Court's decision anticipated *Brown v. Board* by opening the question of whether *any* segregated facility could be truly equal.[48]

But the Supreme Court, in ordering the admission of blacks to all-white state law schools, did not directly confront the principle of the "separate but equal" rule of *Plessy* because the Court needed only to recognize the absence of any equal law school for blacks. The same was true in 1944, when the Supreme Court struck down the Southern practice of "white primaries," which legally excluded blacks from participation in the nominating process. Here the Court simply recognized that primaries could no longer be regarded as the private affairs of the parties but were an integral aspect of the electoral process. This made parties "an agency of the State," and therefore any practice of discrimination against blacks was "state action within the meaning of the Fifteenth Amendment."[49] The most important pre-1954 decision was probably *Shelley v.*

---

[45]The prospect of a Fair Employment Practices law tied to the commerce power produced the Dixiecrat break with the Democratic party in 1948. The Democratic party organization of the States of the Old Confederacy seceded from the national party and nominated its own candidate, the then-Democratic governor of South Carolina, Strom Thurmond, who is now a Republican senator. This almost cost President Truman the election.

[46]This was based on the provision in Article VI of the Constitution that "all Treaties made, . . . under the Authority of the United States," shall be the "supreme Law of the Land." The committee recognized that if the U.S. Senate ratified the Human Rights Covenant of the United Nations—a treaty—then that power could be used as the constitutional umbrella for effective civil rights legislation. The Supreme Court had recognized in Missouri v. Holland, 252 U.S. 416 (1920), that a treaty could enlarge federal power at the expense of the states.

[47]Missouri ex rel. Gaines v. Canada, 305 U.S. 337 (1938).

[48]Sweatt v. Painter, 339 U.S. 629 (1950).

[49]Smith v. Allwright, 321 U.S. 649 (1944).

Kraemer,[50] in which the Court ruled against the widespread practice of "restrictive covenants," whereby the seller of a home added a clause to the sales contract requiring the buyers to agree not to sell their home to any non-Caucasian, non-Christian, etc. The Court ruled that although private persons could sign such restrictive covenants, they could not be judicially enforced since the Fourteenth Amendment prohibits any organ of the state, including the courts, from denying equal protection of its laws.

However, none of these pre-1954 cases had yet confronted head-on the principle of "separate but equal" as such and its legal and constitutional support for racial discrimination. Each victory by the Legal Defense Fund of the National Association for the Advancement of Colored People (NAACP) was celebrated for itself and was seen, hopefully, as a trend; but each was still a small victory, not a leading case. After *Shelley v. Kraemer*, Thurgood Marshall, the leading litigator for the Legal Defense Fund, "would no longer try to shoehorn his cases into the often cramped and distorting logic of straight legal precedent."[51] And, all along, both the friends and the foes of segregation were recognizing that

> The bitter fight would be waged on the level of the elementary and secondary schools . . . [and] the segregationists hoped that they would be able to prevent or forestall indefinitely the admission of blacks . . . by moving toward the equalization of Negro schools. . . . Southern states spent funds, almost desparately, on Negro schools . . . to equalize white and black schools as rapidly as possible.[52]

This massive effort by the Southern states to resist direct desegregation, and to prevent further legal actions against it by making a show of equalizing the quality of white and black schools, kept Marshall pessimistic about the readiness of the Supreme Court for a full confrontation with the constitutional principle sustaining segregation. But the 1947 publication of the extraordinary Truman Committee Report on Civil Rights and President Truman's election for a full term in 1948, coupled with the continued unwillingness of Congress after 1948 to consider fair employment legislation, seemed to have convinced Marshall and the NAACP that the courts were their only hope. Thus, by 1951, the NAACP finally decided to attack the principle of segregation itself as unconstitutional and, in 1952, instituted cases in South Carolina, Virginia, Kansas, Delaware, and the District of Columbia. The obvious strategy was that by simultaneously filing suits in different federal districts, inconsistent results between any two states would more quickly lead to Supreme Court acceptance of at least one appeal.[53]

[50]Shelley v. Kraemer, 334 U.S. 1 (1948).

[51]Richard Kluger, *Simple Justice* (New York: Vintage, 1977), p. 254.

[52]John Hope Franklin, *From Slavery to Freedom: A History of Negro Americans*, 4th ed. (New York: Knopf, 1974), pp. 420–21.

[53]The best reviews of strategies, tactics, and goals is found in John Hope Franklin, op cit., Chapter 22; and Kluger, op cit., Chapters 21 and 22.

All through 1951 and 1952, as cases like *Brown v. Board* and *Bolling v. Sharpe* were winding slowly through the lower-court litigation maze, intense discussions and disagreements continued among NAACP lawyers as to whether the full-scale assault on *Plessy* was good strategy.[54] But for lawyers like Marshall, small victories and further delays could amount to defeat. South Carolina, for example, under the leadership of Governor James F. Byrnes, who had left the Supreme Court and Roosevelt's cabinet in order to lead the pro-segregation fight as governor of South Carolina, was making considerable head-way to render moot any further litigation against the principle of separate but equal by making the Negro schools in South Carolina virtually equal in all physical matters to the all-white schools.

In the fall of 1952, the Court had on its docket cases from Kansas, South Carolina, Virginia, Delaware, and the District of Columbia challenging the constitutionality of school segregation. Of these, the Kansas case became the chosen one. It seemed to be ahead of the pack in its district court, and it had the special advantage of being located in a state outside the Deep South.[55]

Oliver Brown, the father of three girls, lived "across the tracks" in a low-income, racially mixed Topeka neighborhood. Every school-day morning, Linda Brown took the school bus to the Monroe School for black children about a mile away. In September 1950, Oliver Brown took Linda to the all-white Sumner School, which was actually closer to home, to enter her into the third grade in defiance of state law and local segregation rules. When they were refused, Brown took his case to the NAACP, and soon thereafter *Brown v. Board of Education* was born. In mid-1953, the Court announced that the several cases on their way up would be re-argued within a set of questions having to do with the intent of the Fourteenth Amendment. Almost exactly a year later, the Court responded to those questions in one of the most important decisions in its history.

In deciding the case, the Court, to the surprise of many, basically rejected as inconclusive all the learned arguments about the intent and the history of the Fourteenth Amendment and committed itself to considering only the consequences of segregation:

> Does segregation of children in public schools solely on the basis of race, even though the physical facilities and other "tangible" factors may be equal, deprive the children of the minority group of equal educational opportunities? We believe that it does. . . . We conclude that, in the field of public education, the doctrine of

[54]Kermit L. Hall, *The Magic Mirror: Law in American History* (New York: Oxford University Press, 1989), pp. 322–24. See also Kluger, op cit., pp. 530–37.

[55]The District of Columbia case came up too, but since the District of Columbia is not a state, this case did not directly involve the Fourteenth Amendment and its "equal protection" clause. It confronted the Court on the same grounds, however—that segregation is inherently unequal. Its victory in effect was "incorporation in reverse," with equal protection moving from the Fourteenth Amendment to become part of the Bill of Rights. See Bolling v. Sharpe, 347 U.S. 497 (1954).

"separate but equal" has no place. Separate educational facilities are inherently unequal.[56]

The *Brown* decision altered the constitutional framework in two fundamental respects. First, after *Brown*, the states would no longer have the power to use race as a criterion of discrimination in law. Second, the national government would from then on have the constitutional basis for extending its power (hitherto in doubt, as we saw earlier) to intervene with strict regulatory policies against the discriminatory actions of state or local governments, school boards, employers, and many others in the private sector.

Simple Justice: The Courts, the Constitution, and Civil Rights after *Brown v. Board of Education*

Although *Brown v. Board of Education* withdrew all constitutional authority to use race as a criterion of exclusion, this historic decision was merely a small opening move.[57] First, the Court ruling "to admit to public schools on a racially nondiscriminatory basis with all deliberate speed," which came a year later,[58] was directly binding only on the five school boards that had been defendants in the cases appealed to the Supreme Court. Rather than fall into line, as most parties do when a new judicial principle is handed down, most states refused to cooperate until sued, and many ingenious schemes were employed to delay obedience (such as paying the tuition for white students to attend newly created "private" academies). Second, even as Southern school boards began to cooperate by eliminating their legally enforced *(de jure)* school segregation, there remained extensive actual *(de facto)* school segregation in the North as well as in the South, as a consequence of racially segregated housing that could not be reached by the 1954–1955 *Brown* principles. Third, discrimination in employment, public accommodations, juries, voting, and other areas of social and economic activity were not directly touched by *Brown*.

A decade of frustration following *Brown* made it fairly obvious to all that adjudication alone would not succeed. The goal of "equal protection" required positive, or affirmative, action by Congress and by administrative agencies. And given massive Southern resistance and a generally negative national public opinion toward racial integration, progress would not be made through courts, Congress, *or* agencies without intense, well-organized support. Table 4.2 shows the increase in civil rights demonstrations for voting rights and public accommodations during the fourteen years following *Brown*.

It shows that there were very few organized civil rights demonstrations prior to *Brown v. Board* and that the frequency of these demonstrations took a

[56]Brown v. Board of Education of Topeka, Kansas, 347 U.S. 483 (1954).

[57]The heading for this section is drawn from the title of Richard Kluger's important book, *Simple Justice.*

[58]Board of Education of Topeka, Kansas, 349 U.S. 294 (1955), often referred to as *Brown II.*

TABLE 4.2

Peaceful Civil Rights Demonstrations, 1954–1968*

YEAR	TOTAL	FOR PUBLIC ACCOMMODATIONS	FOR VOTING
1954	0	0	0
1955	0	0	0
1956	18	6	0
1957	44	9	0
1958	19	8	0
1959	7	11	0
1960	173	127	0
1961	198	122	0
1962	77	44	0
1963	272	140	1
1964	271	93	12
1965	387	21	128
1966	171	15	32
1967	93	3	3
1968	97	2	0

*This table is drawn from a search of the *New York Times Index* for all references to civil rights demonstrations during the years the table covers. The table should be taken simply as indicative, for the data—news stories in a single paper—are very crude. The classification of the incident as peaceful or violent and the subject area of the demonstration are inferred from the entry in the *Index*, usually the headline from the story. The two subcategories reported here—public accommodations and voting—do not sum to the total because demonstrations dealing with a variety of other issues (e.g., education, employment, police brutality) are included in the total.

SOURCE: Jonathan D. Casper, *The Politics of Civil Liberties* (New York: Harper & Row, 1972), p. 90.

sudden jump in 1960 and continued to mount during the 1960s. It is quite evident that this direct-movement action contributed mightily to the congressional majorities that produced a series of historic new civil rights laws in 1964 and 1965. It would appear from the data on Table 4.2 that the constitutional

TABLE 4.3

	Activity of NAACP Legal Defense and Educational Fund (LDF), 1963–1967	
YEAR	INDIVIDUALS DEFENDED BY THE LDF	CASES ON LDF DOCKET
1963	4,200	107
1964	10,400	145
1965	17,000	225
1966	14,000	375
1967	13,000	420

SOURCE: Data from *Report 66*, published in 1967 by the NAACP Legal Defense and Educational Fund. Reprinted from Jonathan D. Casper, *The Politics of Civil Liberties* (New York: Harper & Row, 1972), p. 91. Reprinted by permission of the NAACP Legal Defense and Educational Fund, Inc.

Collective Action Principle

Given the massive resistance to the *Brown* decision, the civil rights movement required large, well-organized protests.

decisions made by the Supreme Court in 1954–1955 had either produced or triggered the civil rights movement, as it came to be known. This was substantially confirmed in a systematic study of all "movement-initiated events" from 1948 through 1970 (see also Process Box 4.1).[59]

Adding Table 4.3 to Table 4.2 brings forth still another insight into the political relationships among the three branches of the national government: just as *political* agitation to expand rights followed the Court's formal recognition of their existence, so did greatly expanded *judicial* action follow the success of political action in Congress. Table 4.3 confirms this with the enormous jump in NAACP-sponsored civil rights cases brought in the federal courts, from 107 in 1963 to 145 in 1964 and 225 in 1965, continuing to move upward thereafter. The number of actual cases brought by the Legal Defense Fund of the NAACP actually continued to go up at a significant rate even as the number of individuals defended by these cases dropped. This suggests how strongly the NAACP was interested in using the cases to advance the principles of civil rights rather than to improve the prospects of individual black litigants.

[59]The data on civil rights movements are from Jonathan D. Casper, *The Politics of Civil Liberties* (New York: Harper & Row, 1972), p. 90; the broader study of social movements providing the confirming data was conducted by Doug McAdam, *Political Process and the Development of Black Insurgency, 1930–1970* (Chicago: University of Chicago Press, 1982), p. 123. For an alternative view, see Gerald N. Rosenberg, *The Hollow Hope* (Chicago: University of Chicago Press, 1991).

Cause and Effect in the Civil Rights Movement:
Which Came First—
Government Action or Political Action?

Judicial and Legal Action	Political Action
1954 *Brown v. Board of Education*	
1955 *Brown* II—Implementation of *Brown* I	**1955** Montgomery Bus Boycott
1956 Federal courts order school integration, especially one ordering Autherine Lucy admitted to University of Alabama, with Governor Wallace officially protesting	
1957 Civil Rights Act creating Civil Rights Commission; President Eisenhower sends paratroops to Little Rock, Arkansas, to enforce integration of Central High School	**1957** Southern Christian Leadership Conference (SCLC) formed, with King as president
1960 First substantive Civil Rights Act, primarily voting rights	**1960** Student Nonviolent Coordinating Committee (SNCC) formed to organize protests, sit-ins, freedom rides
1961 Interstate Commerce Commission orders desegregation on all buses, trains, and in terminals	
1961 JFK favors executive action over civil rights legislation	
1963 JFK shifts, supports strong civil rights law; assassination; LBJ asserts strong support for civil rights	**1963** Nonviolent demonstrations in Birmingham, Alabama, lead to King's arrest and his "Letter from the Birmingham Jail"
	1963 March on Washington
1964 Congress passes historic Civil Rights Act covering voting, employment, public accommodations, education	
1965 Voting Rights Act	**1965** King announces drive to register 3 million blacks in the South
1966 War on Poverty in full swing	**1966** Movement dissipates: part toward litigation, part toward Community Action Programs, part toward war protest, part toward more militant "Black Power" actions

School Desegregation, Phase One Although the District of Columbia and some of the school districts in the border states began to respond almost immediately to court-ordered desegregation, the states of the Deep South responded with a carefully planned delaying tactic commonly called "massive resistance" by the more demagogic Southern leaders and "nullification" and "interposition" by the centrists. Either way, Southern politicians stood shoulder to shoulder to declare that the Supreme Court's decisions and orders were without effect. The legislatures in these states enacted statutes ordering school districts to maintain segregated schools and state superintendents to terminate state funding wherever there was racial mixing in the classroom. Some Southern states violated their own long traditions of local school autonomy by centralizing public school authority under the governor or the state board of education and by giving states the power to close the schools and to provide alternative private schooling wherever local school boards might be tending to obey the Supreme Court.

Most of these plans of "massive resistance" were tested in the federal courts and were struck down as unconstitutional.[60] But Southern resistance was not confined to legislation. For example, in Arkansas in 1957, Governor Orval Faubus mobilized the National Guard to intercede against enforcement of a federal court order to integrate Little Rock's Central High School, and President Eisenhower was forced to deploy U.S. troops and literally place the city under martial law. The Supreme Court considered the Little Rock confrontation so historically important that the opinion it rendered in that case was not only agreed to unanimously but was, unprecedentedly, signed personally by each and every one of the justices.[61] The end of massive resistance, however, became simply the beginning of still another Southern strategy, "pupil placement" laws, which authorized school districts to place each pupil in a school according to a whole variety of academic, personal, and psychological considerations, never mentioning race at all. This put the burden of transferring to an all-white school on the nonwhite children and their parents, making it almost impossible for a single court order to cover a whole district, let alone a whole state. This delayed desegregation a while longer.[62]

As new devices were invented by the Southern states to avoid desegregation, the federal courts followed with cases and decisions quashing them. Ten years

[60]The two most important cases were Cooper v. Aaron, 358 U.S. 1 (1958), which required Little Rock, Arkansas, to desegregate; and Griffin v. Prince Edward County School Board, 377 U.S. 218 (1964), which forced all the schools of that Virginia county to reopen after five years of closing to avoid desegregation.

[61]In *Cooper*, the Supreme Court ordered immediate compliance with the lower court's desegregation order and went beyond that with a stern warning that it is "emphatically the province and duty of the judicial department to say what the law is."

[62]Shuttlesworth v. Birmingham Board of Education, 358 U.S. 101 (1958), upheld a "pupil placement" plan purporting to assign pupils on various bases, with no mention of race. This case interpreted *Brown* to mean that school districts must stop explicit racial discrimination but were under no obligation to take positive steps to desegregate. For a while black parents were doomed to case-by-case approaches.

after *Brown*, less than 1 percent of black school-age children in the Deep South were attending schools with whites.[63] It had become unmistakably clear well before that time that the federal courts could not do the job alone. The first modern effort to legislate in the field of civil rights was made in 1957, but the law contained only a federal guarantee of voting rights, without any powers of enforcement, although it did create the Civil Rights Commission to study abuses. Much more important legislation for civil rights followed, especially the Civil Rights Act of 1964. It is important to observe here the mutual dependence of the courts and legislatures—not only do the legislatures need constitutional authority to act, but the courts need legislative and political assistance, through the power of the purse and the power to organize administrative agencies to implement court orders, and through the focusing of political support. Consequently, even as the U.S. Congress finally moved into the field of school desegregation (and other areas of "equal protection"), the courts continued to exercise their powers, not only by placing court orders against recalcitrant school districts, but also by extending and reinterpreting aspects of the "equal protection" clause to support legislative and administrative actions.

Collective Action Principle
Enforcement of civil rights law required that courts and legislatures work together.

School Desegregation: Busing and Beyond   The most important judicial extension of civil rights in education after 1954 was probably the *Swann* decision (1971), which held that state-imposed desegregation could be brought about by busing children across school districts even where relatively long distances were involved:

> If school authorities fail in their affirmative obligations under these holdings, judicial authority may be invoked. Once a right and a violation have been shown, the scope of a district court's equitable powers to remedy past wrongs is broad. . . . *Bus transportation [is] a normal and accepted tool of educational policy.*[64]

But the decision went beyond that, adding that under certain limited circumstances even racial quotas could be used as the "starting point in shaping a remedy to correct past constitutional violations," and that pairing or grouping of schools and reorganizing school attendance zones would also be acceptable.

Three years later, however, the *Swann* case was severely restricted when the Supreme Court determined that only cities found guilty of deliberate and *de jure* racial segregation (segregation in law) would have to desegregate their schools.[65] This decision was handed down in the 1974 case of *Milliken v. Bradley* involving the city of Detroit and its suburbs. The *Milliken* ruling had the effect of exempting most Northern states and cities from busing because school

---

[63]For good treatments of that long stretch of the struggle of the federal courts to integrate the schools, see Brest and Levinson, *Process of Constitutional Decision-Making*, pp. 471–80; and Kelly et al., *The American Constitution*, pp. 610–16.
[64]Swann v. Charlotte-Mecklenburg Board of Education, 402 U.S. 1 (1971). [Emphasis added.]
[65]Milliken v. Bradley, 418 U.S. 717 (1974).

segregation in Northern cities is generally *de facto* segregation (segregation in fact) that follows from segregated housing and from thousands of acts of private discrimination against blacks and other minorities.

Detroit and Boston provide the best illustrations of the agonizing problem of making further progress in civil rights in the schools under the constitutional framework established by the *Swann* and *Milliken* cases. Following *Swann*, the federal district court and the court of appeals had found that Detroit had engaged in deliberate segregation and that, since Detroit schools were overwhelmingly black, the only way to provide a remedy was to bus students between Detroit and the white suburbs beyond the Detroit city boundaries. The Supreme Court in *Swann* had approved a similar "interdistrict" integration plan for Charlotte, North Carolina, but in *Milliken* it refused to do so for Detroit. Although Detroit's segregation had been deliberate, the city and suburban boundary lines had not been drawn deliberately to separate the races. Therefore, the remedy had to take place within Detroit. That same year, and no doubt influenced by the Detroit decision as well as by President Nixon, Congress amended Title VI of the 1964 Civil Rights Act, reducing the authority of the federal government to withhold monetary assistance only in instances of proven *de jure*, state-government-imposed segregation. This action was extremely significant in taking the heat off most Northern school districts.

In Boston, school authorities were found guilty of deliberately building school facilities and drawing school districts "to increase racial segregation." After vain efforts by Boston school authorities to draw up an acceptable plan, federal Judge W. Arthur Garrity ordered an elaborate desegregation plan of his own involving busing between the all-black ghetto of Roxbury and the nearby white, working-class community of South Boston. Opponents of this plan were organized and eventually took the case to the Supreme Court, where *certiorari* (the Court's device for accepting appeals) was denied; this had the effect of approving Judge Garrity's order. The facts were that the city's schools were so segregated and uncooperative that even the conservative Nixon administration had already initiated a punitive cutoff of funds. But many liberals also criticized Judge Garrity's plan as being badly conceived, because it involved two neighboring communities with a history of tension and mutual resentment. The plan worked well at the elementary school level but proved so explosive at the high school level that it generated a continuing crisis for the city of Boston and for the whole nation over court-ordered, federally directed desegregation in the North.[66]

Additional progress in the desegregation of schools is likely to be extremely slow unless the Supreme Court decides to permit federal action against *de facto* segregation and against the varieties of private schools and academies that have sprung up for the purpose of avoiding integration. The prospects for further school integration diminished with the Supreme Court decision handed down on

[66]For a good evaluation of the Boston effort, see Gary Orfield, *Must We Bus? Segregated Schools and National Policy* (Washington: Brookings Institution, 1978), pp. 144–46. See also Bob Woodward and Scott Armstrong, *The Brethren: Inside the Supreme Court* (New York: Simon and Schuster, 1979), pp. 426–27; and J. Anthony Lukas, *Common Ground* (New York: Random House, 1986).

January 15, 1991. The opinion, written for the Court by Chief Justice Rehnquist, held that lower federal courts could end supervision of local school boards if those boards could show compliance "in good faith" with court orders to desegregate and could show that "vestiges of past discrimination" had been eliminated "to the extent practicable." It is not necessarily easy for a school board to prove that the new standard has been met, but this is the first time since *Brown* and the 1964 Civil Rights Act that the Court opened the door at all to retreat.[67] This door was opened wider in *Freeman v. Pitts* (1992) when the Court gave lower courts still greater leeway to withdraw judicial supervision of desegregation efforts; this cast a very deep and dark shadow over the historic ruling in *Brown v. Board of Education* of 1954.[68] And if there was any doubt that the door might close, this was put to rest in 1995 in *Missouri v. Jenkins*, in which the Court signaled to the lower courts that they should "disengage from desegregation efforts."[69] This is a direct and explicit threat to the main basis of the holding in the original 1954 *Brown v. Board*.

The Rise of the Politics of Rights

Outlawing Discrimination in Employment   Despite the agonizingly slow progress of school desegregation, there was some progress in other areas of civil rights during the 1960s and 1970s. Voting rights were established and fairly quickly began to revolutionize Southern politics. Service on juries was no longer denied to minorities. But progress in the right to participate in politics and government dramatized the relative lack of progress in the economic domain, and it was in this area that battles over civil rights were increasingly fought.

The federal courts and the Justice Department entered this area through Title VII of the Civil Rights Act of 1964, which outlawed job discrimination by all private and public employers, including governmental agencies (such as fire and police departments), that employed more than fifteen workers. We have already seen that the Supreme Court gave "interstate commerce" such a broad definition that Congress had the constitutional authority to cover discrimination by virtually any local employers.[70] Title VII makes it unlawful to discriminate in

---

[67]Board of Education of Oklahoma City Public Schools v. Dowell, 111 S.Ct. 630 (1991).

[68]Freeman v. Pitts, 503 U.S. 467 (1992).

[69]Missouri v. Jenkins, 115 S.Ct. 2038 (1995). The quote is from O'Brien, *Supreme Court Watch 1996*, op cit., p. 220.

[70]See especially Katzenbach v. McClung, 379 U.S. 294 (1964). Almost immediately after passage of the Civil Rights Act of 1964, a case challenged the validity of Title II, which covered discrimination in public accommodations. Ollie's Barbecue was a neighborhood restaurant in Birmingham, Alabama. It was located eleven blocks from an interstate highway and even farther from railroad and bus stations. Its table service was for whites only; there was only a take-out service for blacks. The Supreme Court agreed that Ollie's was strictly an intrastate restaurant, but since a substantial proportion of its food and other supplies were bought from companies outside Alabama, there was a sufficient connection to interstate commerce; therefore, racial discrimination at such restaurants would "impose commercial burdens of national magnitude upon interstate commerce." Although this case involved Title II, it had direct bearing on the constitutionality of Title VII.

employment on the basis of color, religion, sex, or national origin, as well as race.

The first problem with Title VII was that the complaining party had to show that deliberate discrimination was the cause of the failure to get a job or a training opportunity. Rarely does an employer explicitly admit discrimination on the basis of race, sex, or any other illegal reason. Recognizing the rarity of such an admission, the courts have allowed aggrieved parties (the plaintiffs) to make their case if they can show that an employer's hiring practices had the *effect* of exclusion. A leading case in 1971 involved a "class action" by several black employees in North Carolina attempting to show with statistical evidence that blacks had been relegated to only one department in the Duke Power Company, which involved the least desirable, manual-labor jobs, and that they had been kept out of contention for the better jobs because the employer had added high school education and the passing of specially prepared aptitude tests as qualifications for higher jobs. The Supreme Court held that although the statistical evidence did not prove intentional discrimination, and although the requirements were race-neutral in appearance, their effects were sufficient to shift the burden of justification to the employer to show that the requirements were a "business necessity" that bore "a demonstrable relationship to successful performance."[71] The ruling in this case was subsequently applied to other hiring, promotion, and training programs.[72]

Gender Discrimination   Even before equal employment laws began to have a positive effect on the economic situation of blacks, something far more dramatic began happening—the universalization of civil rights. The right not to be discriminated against was being successfully claimed by the other groups listed in Title VII—those defined by sex, religion, or national origin—and eventually by still other groups defined by age or sexual preference. This universalization of civil rights has become the new frontier of the civil rights struggle, and women have emerged with the greatest prominence in this new struggle. The effort to define and end gender discrimination in employment has led to the historic joining of women's rights to the civil rights cause.

Despite its interest in fighting discrimination, the Supreme Court during the 1950s and 1960s paid little attention to gender discrimination. Ironically, it was left to the more conservative Burger Court (1969–1986) to establish gender discrimination as a major and highly visible civil rights issue. Although the Burger Court refused to treat gender discrimination as the equivalent of racial discrimination,[73] it did make it easier for plaintiffs to file and win suits on the basis of gender discrimination by applying an

[71]Griggs v. Duke Power Company, 401 U.S. 24 (1971). See also Allan Sindler, *Bakke, DeFunis, and Minority Admissions* (New York: Longman, 1978), pp. 180–89.

[72]For a good treatment of these issues, see Charles O. Gregory and Harold A. Katz, *Labor and the Law* (New York: W. W. Norton, 1979), Chapter 17.

[73]See Frontiero v. Richardson, 411 U.S. 677 (1973).

"intermediate" level of review to these cases.[74] This intermediate level of scrutiny is midway between traditional rules of evidence, which put the burden of proof on the plaintiff, and the doctrine of "strict scrutiny," which requires the defendant to show not only that a particular classification is reasonable but also that there is a need or compelling interest for it. "Intermediate" scrutiny, therefore, shifts the burden of proof partially onto the defendant, rather than leaving it entirely on the plaintiff.

One major step was taken in 1992, when the Court decided in *Franklin v. Gwinnett County Public Schools* that violations of Title IX of the 1972 Education Act could be remedied with monetary damages.[75] Title IX forbade gender discrimination in education, but it initially sparked little litigation because of its weak enforcement provisions. The Court's 1992 ruling that monetary damages could be awarded for gender discrimination opened the door for more legal action in the area of education. The greatest impact has been in the areas of sexual harassment—the subject of the *Franklin* case—and in equal treatment of women's athletic programs. The potential for monetary damages has made universities and public schools take the problem of sexual harassment more seriously. Colleges and universities have also started to pay more attention to women's athletic programs. In the two years after the *Franklin* case, complaints to the Education Department's Office for Civil Rights about unequal treatment of women's athletic programs nearly tripled. In several high-profile legal cases, some prominent universities have been ordered to create more women's sports programs; many other colleges and universities have begun to add more women's programs in order to avoid potential litigation.[76] In 1997, the Supreme Court refused to hear a petition by Brown University challenging a lower court ruling that the university establish strict sex equity in its athletic programs. The Court's decision meant that in colleges and universities across the country, varsity athletic positions for men and women must now reflect their overall enrollment numbers.[77]

In 1996, the Supreme Court made another important decision about gender and education by putting an end to all-male schools supported by public funds. It ruled that the policy of the Virginia Military Institute not to admit women was unconstitutional.[78] Along with the Citadel, another all-male military college in South Carolina, VMI had never admitted women in its 157-year history. VMI argued that the unique educational experience it offered—including intense physical training and the harsh treatment of freshmen—would be destroyed if women students were admitted. The Court, however, ruled that the male-only policy denied "substantial equality" to women. Two days after the Court's ruling, the Citadel announced that it would accept women. VMI considered becoming a

[74]See Craig v. Boren, 423 U.S. 1047 (1976).

[75]*Franklin v. Gwinnett County Public Schools*, 503 U.S. 60 (1992).

[76]Jennifer Halperin, "Women Step Up to Bat," *Illinois Issues* 21 (September 1995), pp. 11–14.

[77]Joan Biskupic and David Nakamura, "Court Won't Review Sports Equity Ruling," *Washington Post*, April 22, 1997, p. A1.

[78]*U.S. v. Virginia*, 116 S.Ct. 2264 (1996).

private institution in order to remain all-male, but in September 1996, the school board finally voted to admit women. The legal decisions may have removed formal barriers to entry, but the experience of the new female cadets at these schools has not been easy. The first female cadet at the Citadel, Shannon Faulkner, won admission in 1995 under a federal court order but quit after four days. Although four women were admitted to the Citadel after the Supreme Court decision, two of the four quit several months later. They charged harassment from male students, including attempts to set the female cadets on fire.[79]

Ever since sexual harassment was first declared a form of employment discrimination, employers and many employees have worried about the ambiguity of the issue. When can an employee bring charges and when is the employer liable? In 1998, the Court clarified these questions in an important ruling. It said that if a company has an effective antiharassment policy in place, which the employee fails to use, the company cannot be held liable for sexual harassment. If no policy is in place, the company may be held legally responsible for harassment. In addition, the Court ruled that to pursue a suit on the grounds of sexual harassment, the employee does not have to show that she or he suffered a tangible loss, such as loss of promotion. Most important is whether an effective policy is in place and available to employees.[80]

The development of gender discrimination as an important part of the civil rights struggle has coincided with the rise of women's politics as a discrete movement in American politics. As with the struggle for racial equality, the relationship between changes in government policies and political action suggests a two-way pattern of causation, where changes in government policies can produce political action and vice versa. Today, the existence of a powerful women's movement derives in large measure from the enactment of Title VII of the Civil Rights Act of 1964 and from the Burger Court's vital steps in applying that law to protect women. The recognition of women's civil rights has become an issue that in many ways transcends the usual distinctions of American political debate. In the heavily partisan debate over the federal crime bill enacted in 1994, for instance, the section of the bill that enjoyed the widest support was the Violence Against Women Act, whose most important feature was that it defined gender-biased violent crimes as a matter of civil rights, and created a civil rights remedy for women who had been the victims of such crimes. But since the act was ruled unconstitutional by the Supreme Court in 2000, the struggle for women's rights will likely remain part of the political debate.

History Principle

The civil rights and women's rights movements both suggest that changes in government policies can produce political action and vice versa.

Discrimination against Other Groups   As gender discrimination began to be seen as an important civil rights issue, other groups arose demanding recognition and active protection of their civil rights. Under Title VII of the 1964 Civil Rights

[79]Judith Havemann, "Two Women Quit Citadel over Alleged Harassment," *Washington Post*, January 13, 1997, p. A1.
[80]*Burlington Industries v. Ellerth*, 118 S.Ct. 2257 (1998); *Faragher v. City of Boca Raton*, 118 S.Ct. 2275 (1998).

Act, any group or individual can try, and in fact is encouraged to try, to convert goals and grievances into questions of rights and the deprivation of those rights. A plaintiff must only establish that his or her membership in a group is an unreasonable basis for discrimination unless it can be proven to be a "job-related" or otherwise clearly reasonable and relevant decision. In America today, the list of individuals and groups claiming illegal discrimination is lengthy. The disabled, for instance, increasingly press their claim to equal treatment as a civil rights matter, a stance encouraged by the Americans with Disabilities Act of 1990.[81] Deaf Americans increasingly demand social and legal recognition of deafness as a separate culture, not simply as a disability.[82] One of the most familiar of these groups has been the gay and lesbian movement, which in less than thirty years has emerged from invisibility to become one of the largest civil rights movements in contemporary America. The place of gays and lesbians in American society is now the subject of a highly charged debate, but it is a debate that was not even heard before the rise of the politics of rights in the last thirty years. The debate is out of the closet and the movement's progress is also producing equal and opposite reactions, to say the least. What appeared at first to be a most important breakthrough was the promise made by President Clinton, during the 1992 campaign, to end discrimination against gays in the military. But soon after his inauguration in 1993, President Clinton was unable to handle the heat of opposition, and he settled for a compromise that could only have been treated as a dismal disappointment by the gay and lesbian movement: "Don't ask, don't tell," meaning that a gay or lesbian member of the armed forces would be protected against discrimination only as long as they remain silent and inactive with regard to the observances of their own lifestyle. But despite their disappointment, homosexuals can claim some progress along legal lines, especially in *Romer v. Evans* (1996). In November 1992, a Colorado referendum approved an amendment to the state constitution forbidding localities from enacting any ordinance that outlaws discrimination against homosexuals. The amendment denied to any municipality the power to adopt a law that gives homosexuals "minority status" that protects them from discrimination. In a 6-to-3 decision, the Court held that the Colorado amendment actually classifies homosexuality not as a status equal to everyone else but as a status that "make[s] them unequal to everyone else. This Colorado cannot do. A State cannot so deem a class of persons a stranger to its laws. Amendment 2 violated the Equal Protection Clause. . . ."[83]

---

[81]In 1994, for instance, after pressure from the Justice Department under the terms of the Americans with Disabilities Act, one of the nation's largest rental-car companies agreed to make special hand-controls available to any customer requesting them. See "Avis Agrees to Equip Cars for Disabled," *Los Angeles Times*, 2 September 1994, p. D1.

[82]Thus a distinction has come to be made between "deaf," the pathology, and "Deaf," the culture. See Andrew Solomon, "Defiantly Deaf," *New York Times Magazine*, 28 August 1994, pp. 40ff.

[83]Romer v. Evans, 116 S.Ct. 1620 (1996).

Affirmative Action

The politics of rights not only spread to increasing numbers of groups in the society, it also expanded its goal. The relatively narrow goal of equalizing opportunity by eliminating discriminatory barriers had been developing toward the far broader goal of *affirmative action*—compensatory action to overcome the consequences of past discrimination and to encourage greater diversity. An affirmative action policy tends to involve two novel approaches: (1) positive or benign discrimination in which race or some other status is actually taken into account, but for compensatory action rather than mistreatment; and (2) compensatory action to favor members of the disadvantaged group who themselves may never have been the victims of discrimination. Quotas may be, but are not necessarily, involved in affirmative action policies.

In 1965, President Johnson attempted to inaugurate affirmative action by executive orders directing agency heads and personnel officers to pursue vigorously a policy of minority employment in the federal civil service and in companies doing business with the national government. But affirmative action did not become a prominent goal until the 1970s.

The Supreme Court and the Burden of Proof As this movement spread, it also began to divide civil rights activists and their supporters. The whole issue of qualification versus minority preference was addressed in the case of Allan Bakke. Bakke, a white male with no minority affiliation, brought suit against the University of California at Davis Medical School on the grounds that in denying him admission the school had discriminated against him on the basis of his race (that year the school had reserved 16 of 100 available slots for minority applicants). He argued that his grades and test scores had ranked him well above many students who had been accepted at the school and that the only possible explanation for his rejection was that those others accepted were black or Hispanic while he was white. In 1978, Bakke won his case before the Supreme Court and was admitted to the medical school, but he did not succeed in getting affirmative action declared unconstitutional. The Court rejected the procedures at the University of California because its medical school had used both a quota *and* a separate admissions system for minorities. The Court agreed with Bakke's argument that racial categorizations are suspect categories that place a severe burden of proof on those using them to show a "compelling public purpose." The Court went on to say that achieving "a diverse student body" was such a public purpose, but the method of a rigid quota of student slots assigned on the basis of race was incompatible with the equal protection clause. Thus, the Court permitted universities (and other schools, training programs, and hiring authorities) to continue to take minority status into consideration, but limited severely the use of quotas to situations in which (1) previous discrimination had been shown, and (2) in which quotas were used more as a *guideline* for social diversity than as a mathematically defined ratio.[84]

[84]Regents of the University of California v. Bakke, 438 U.S. 265 (1978).

affirmative action A policy or program designed to redress historic injustices committed against specific groups by making special efforts to provide members of these groups with access to educational and employment opportunities.

Analyzing American Politics

www.wwnorton.com/ lowi7/ch4

Analyze the impact of affirmative action policies on the workplace and the educational system.

For nearly a decade after *Bakke*, the Supreme Court was tentative and permissive about efforts by corporations and governments to experiment with affirmative action programs in employment.[85] But in 1989, the Court returned to the *Bakke* position that any "rigid numerical quota" is suspect. In *Wards Cove v. Atonio*, the Court further weakened affirmative action by easing the way for employers to prefer white males, holding that the burden of proof of unlawful discrimination should be shifted from the defendant (the employer) to the plaintiff (the person claiming to be the victim of discrimination).[86] This decision virtually overruled the Court's prior holding.[87] That same year, the Court ruled that any affirmative action program already approved by federal courts could be subsequently challenged by white males who alleged that the program discriminated against them.[88]

In 1991, after a lengthy battle with the White House, Congress enacted a piece of legislation designed to undo the effects of these decisions. Under the terms of the Civil Rights Acts of 1991, the burden of proof in employment discrimination cases was shifted back to employers, overturning the *Wards Cove* decision. In addition, the act made it more difficult to mount later challenges to consent decrees in affirmative action cases, reversing the *Martin v. Wilks* decision. Despite Congress's actions, however, the federal judiciary will have the last word when cases under the new law reach the courts. In a 5-to-4 decision in 1993, the Court ruled that employees had to prove their employers intended discrimination, thus again placing the burden of proof on employees.[89]

In 1995, the Supreme Court's ruling in *Adarand Constructors v. Pena* further weakened affirmative action. This decision stated that race-based policies, such as preferences given by the government to minority contractors, must survive strict scrutiny, placing the burden on the government to show that such affirmative action programs serve a compelling government interest and are narrowly tailored to address identifiable past discrimination.[90] President Clinton responded to the *Adarand* decision by ordering a review of all government affirmative action policies and practices. Although many observers suspected that the president would use the review as an opportunity to back away from affirmative action, the conclusions of the task force largely defended existing policies. Reflecting the influence of the Supreme Court's decision in

---

[85]United Steelworkers v. Weber, 443 U.S. 193 (1979); and Fullilove v. Klutznick, 100 S.Ct. 2758 (1980).

[86]Wards Cove v. Atonio, 109 S.Ct. 2115 (1989).

[87]Griggs v. Duke Power Company, 401 U.S. 24 (1971).

[88]Martin v. Wilks, 109 S.Ct. 2180 (1989). In this case, some white firefighters in Birmingham challenged a consent decree mandating goals for hiring and promoting blacks. This was an affirmative action plan that had been worked out between the employer and aggrieved black employees and had been accepted by a federal court. Such agreements become "consent decrees" and are subject to enforcement. Chief Justice Rehnquist held that the white firefighters could challenge the legality of such programs, even though they had not been parties to the original litigation.

[89]St. Mary's Honor Center v. Hicks, 113 S.Ct. 2742 (1993).

[90]Adarand Constructors, Inc. v. Pena, 115 S.Ct. 2097 (1995).

Adarand, President Clinton acknowledged that some government policies would need to change. But on the whole, the review found that most affirmative action policies were fair and did not "unduly burden nonbeneficiaries."[91]

Although Clinton sought to "mend, not end" affirmative action, developments in the courts and the states continued to restrict affirmative action in important ways. One of the most significant was the *Hopwood* case, in which white students challenged admissions practices in the University of Texas Law School, charging that the school's affirmative action program discriminated against whites. In 1996, a federal court (the U.S. Court of Appeals for the Fifth Circuit) ruling on the case stated that race could never be considered in granting admissions and scholarships at state colleges and universities.[92] This decision effectively rolled back the use of affirmative action permitted by the 1978 *Bakke* case. In *Bakke*, as discussed earlier, the Supreme Court had outlawed quotas but said that race could be used as one factor among many in admissions decisions. Many universities and colleges have since justified affirmative action as a way of promoting racial diversity among their student bodies. What was new in the *Hopwood* decision was the ruling that race could *never* be used as a factor in admissions decisions, even to promote diversity.

In 1996, the Supreme Court refused to hear a challenge to the *Hopwood* case. This meant that its ruling remains in effect in the states covered by the Fifth Circuit—Texas, Louisiana, and Mississippi—but does not apply to the rest of the country. The impact of the *Hopwood* ruling is greatest in Texas because Louisiana and Mississippi are under conflicting court orders to desegregate their universities. In Texas, in the year after the *Hopwood* case, minority applications to Texas universities declined. Concerned about the ability of Texas public universities to serve the state's minority students, the Texas legislature quickly passed a new law granting students who graduate in the top 10 percent of their classes automatic admission to the state's public universities. It is hoped that this measure will ensure a racially diverse student body.[93]

The weakening of affirmative action in the courts was underscored in a case the Supreme Court agreed to hear in 1998. A white schoolteacher in New Jersey who had lost her job had sued her school district, charging that her layoff was racially motivated: a black colleague hired on the same day was not laid off. Under President George Bush, the Justice Department had filed a brief on her behalf in 1989, but in 1994 the Clinton administration formally reversed course in a new brief supporting the school district's right to make distinctions based on race as long as it did not involve the use of quotas. Three years later, the administration, worried that the case was weak and could result in a broad decision against affirmative action, reversed course again. It filed a brief with the Court

[91]Ann Devroy, "Clinton Study Backs Affirmative Action," *Washington Post*, 19 July 1995, p. A1.
[92]Hopwood v. State of Texas, 78 F3d 932 (Fifth Circuit, 1996).
[93]See Lydia Lum, "Applications by Minorities Down Sharply," *Houston Chronicle*, 8 April 1997, p. A1; R. G. Ratcliffe, "Senate Approves Bill Designed to Boost Minority Enrollments," *Houston Chronicle*, 8 May 1997, p. A1.

urging a narrow ruling in favor of the dismissed worker. Because the school board had justified its actions on the grounds of preserving diversity, the administration feared that a broad ruling by the Supreme Court could totally prohibit the use of race in employment decisions, even as one factor among many designed to achieve diversity. But before the Court could issue a ruling, a coalition of civil rights groups brokered and arranged to pay for a settlement. This unusual move reflected the widespread fear of a sweeping negative decision. Cases involving dismissals, as the New Jersey case did, are generally viewed as much more difficult to defend than cases that concern hiring. In addition, the particular facts of the New Jersey case—two equally qualified teachers hired on the same day—were seen as unusual and unfavorable to affirmative action.[94]

Referendums on Affirmative Action   The courts have not been the only center of action: challenges to affirmative action have also emerged in state and local politics. One of the most significant state actions was the passage of the California Civil Rights Initiative, also known as Proposition 209, in 1996. Proposition 209 outlawed affirmative action programs in the state and local governments of California, thus prohibiting state and local governments from using race or gender preferences in their decisions about hiring, contracting, or university admissions. The political battle over Proposition 209 was heated, and supporters and defenders took to the streets as well as the airwaves to make their cases. When the referendum was held, the measure passed with 54 percent of the vote, including 27 percent of the black vote, 30 percent of the Latino vote, and 45 percent of the Asian American vote.[95] In 1997, the Supreme Court refused to hear a challenge to the new law.

Many observers predicted that the success of California's ban on affirmative action would provoke similar movements in states and localities across the country. But the political factors that contributed to the success of Proposition 209 in California may not exist in many other states. Winning a controversial state referendum takes leadership and lots of money. Popular California Republican governor Pete Wilson led with a strong anti–affirmative action stand (favoring Proposition 209) and his campaign had a lot of money for advertising. But those conditions did not exist elsewhere. Few prominent Republican leaders in other states were willing to come forward to lead the anti–affirmative action campaign. Moreover, the outcome of any referendum, especially a complicated and controversial one, depends greatly on how the issue is drafted and placed on the ballot for the voters. California's Proposition 209 was framed as a civil rights initiative: "the state shall not discriminate against, or grant preferential treatment to, any individual or group on the basis of race, sex, color, ethnicity, or national origin." Different wording can produce quite different outcomes, as a

Institutional Reform
www.wwnorton.com/
lowi7/ch4
How have the Supreme Court's decisions in affirmative action cases affected the polarization of politics in the United States?

Policy Principle
Individual challenges in the courts as well as several state and local referenda have weakened affirmative action.

---

[94]Linda Greenhouse, "Settlement Ends High Court Case on Preferences," *New York Times*, 22 November 1997, p. A1; Barry Bearak, "Rights Groups Ducked a Fight, Opponents Say," *New York Times*, 22 November 1997, p. A1.

[95]Michael A. Fletcher, "Opponents of Affirmative Action Heartened by Court Decision," *Washington Post*, 13 April 1997, p. A21.

1997 vote on affirmative action in Houston revealed. There, the ballot initiative asked voters whether they wanted to ban affirmative action in city contracting and hiring, not whether they wanted to end preferential treatment. Fifty-five percent of Houston voters decided in favor of affirmative action.[96]

Affirmative action will continue to be a focus of controversy in coming years, as several other cases challenging affirmative action reach the Supreme Court. There are now several suits similar to the *Hopwood* case working their way through the lower courts, including one against the University of Michigan's affirmative action program. If the Supreme Court decides to hear these cases, the future of affirmative action in universities and colleges will be on the line. Affirmative action is also sure to remain prominent in state and local politics across the country. Efforts to ban affirmative action are under way in a number of states, including Washington, Colorado, Michigan, Massachusetts, Arizona, Arkansas, Ohio, North Dakota, and Oregon.

Affirmative Action and American Political Values   One consequence, perhaps unforeseen, of affirmative action is that it contributed to the polarization of the politics of civil rights. At the risk of grievous oversimplification, we can divide the sides by two labels: liberals and conservatives.[97] The conservatives' argument against affirmative action can be reduced to two major points. The first is that rights in the American tradition are innately individual, and affirmative action violates this concept by concerning itself with "group rights," an idea said to be alien to the American tradition. The second point has to do with quotas. Conservatives would argue that the Constitution is "color blind," and that any discrimination, even if it is called positive or benign discrimination, ultimately violates the equal protection clause and the American way.

The liberal side agrees that rights ultimately come down to individuals but argues that, since the essence of discrimination is the use of unreasonable and unjust criteria of exclusion to deprive *an entire group* of access to something valuable the society has to offer, then the phenomenon of discrimination itself has to be attacked on a group basis. Liberals can also use Court history to support their side, because the first definitive interpretation of the Fourteenth Amendment by the Supreme Court in 1873 gave a "color conscious" argument:

> The existence of laws in the States where the newly emancipated negroes resided, which discriminated with gross injustice and hardship against them *as a class*, was the evil to be remedied by this clause.[98]

---

[96]See Sam Howe Verhovek, "Houston Vote Underlined Complexity of Rights Issue," *New York Times*, 6 November 1997, p. A1.

[97]There are still many genuine racists in America, but with the exception of a lunatic fringe, made up of neo-Nazis and members of the Ku Klux Klan, most racists are too ashamed or embarrassed to take part in normal political discourse. They are not included in either category here.

[98]Slaughter-House Cases, 16 Wallace 36 (1873). [Emphasis added.]

TABLE 4.4

Opinions on Affirmative Action Programs

Responses to the question "All in all, do you favor or oppose affirmative action programs for blacks and other minority groups?"

	WHITES	BLACKS
Favor	36%	76%
Oppose	50	16
Not sure	14	8

SOURCE: NBC/Wall Street Journal Poll, October 1995, reported in *The Public Perspective*, February/March 1996, p. 26.

Although the problems of rights in America are agonizing, they can be looked at optimistically. The United States has a long way to go before it constructs a truly just, "equally protected" society. But it also has come very far in a relatively short time. All explicit *de jure* barriers to minorities have been dismantled. Many *de facto* barriers have also been dismantled, and thousands upon thousands of new opportunities have been opened. Perhaps the greatest promise, however, is in fact the rise of the "politics of rights." The American people are now accustomed to interest groups—conservative and liberal—who call themselves "public interest groups" and accept the efforts of such groups to translate their goals in vigorous and eloquent statements about their rights to their goals. Few people now fear that such a politics of rights will produce violence. Deep and fundamental differences have polarized many groups (see Table 4.4), but political and governmental institutions have proven themselves capable of maintaining balances between them. This kind of balancing can be done without violence so long as everyone recognizes that policy choices, even about rights, cannot be absolute.

Finally, the most important contribution to be made by the politics of rights is probably to the American conscience. Whatever compromises have to be made in order to govern without violence, Americans cannot afford to be satisfied. Injustices do exist. We cannot eliminate them all, but we must maintain our sense of shame for the injustices that persist. This is precisely why the constitutional framework is so important in the real world and not just in theory. It establishes a context of rights, defined both as limits on the power of the government (civil liberties) and as rightful claims to particular opportunities or benefits (civil rights). Without that framework, rights would remain in the world of abstract philosophy; with that framework, in the United States, they remain now as they did two hundred years ago, as real *causes of action.*

BOX 4.1

Collective Action and
the Civil Rights Movement

In the past several decades, a new approach to studying politics—the *rational-choice* approach—has emerged and taken its place among other ways of studying politics. One of the key differences between the rational-choice approach and other approaches is that the former assumes that individuals are self-interested, rational actors.

People often object to the rational-choice approach because the words "self-interested" and "rational" are too loaded. How can one claim that a prominent political actor such as Martin Luther King, Jr., was self-interested? Is it reasonable to assume that in the realm of politics, where fundamental questions over heated topics such as racism, freedom of speech, and abortion are debated and resolved, that people behave rationally—at least in the traditional sense of the word? However, those who adopt the rational-choice approach to politics actually have a very broad and inclusive definition for the terms "self-interested" and "rational." By "self-interested," they mean that individuals have goals. Thus, Martin Luther King's behavior was motivated by self-interest, not in the sense that he was out for material gain, but in that he had personal goals for protecting and guaranteeing the civil rights of African Americans. He entertained personal political ambitions as well, not for political office but rather for political leadership of the civil rights movement. The term "rational" means that for a given set of choices, individuals will opt for the alternative that they think will offer them the best terms for achieving their goals.

Although this approach has become widely accepted in the study of political science, it still remains controversial.[1] One of the tenets of our five principles of politics from Chapter 1 is that individuals have little incentive to participate in mass action politics. After all, what possible difference could one person make by taking part in a civil rights protest? Participation was costly in terms of time and, in the case of civil rights marchers, even health or one's life were endangered. The risks outweighed the potential benefits, yet hundreds of thousands of people *did* participate. Why?

Collective Action Principle

People participated in the civil rights movement for experiential as well as instrumental purposes.

Though little scholarly attention has been paid by those who apply this perspective to the civil rights movements,[2] a general answer is available. Most rational analysis takes behavior to be *instrumental*—to be motivated by and directed toward some purpose or objective. But behavior may also be *experiential*. People do things, on this account, because they like doing them—they feel good inside, they feel free of guilt, they take pleasure in the activity for its own sake. We maintain that this second view of behavior is entirely compatible with rational accounts. Instrumental behavior may be thought of as *investment activity,* whereas experiential behavior may be thought of as *consumption activity*. It is the behavior itself that generates utility, rather than the consequences produced by the behavior. To take a specific illustration of collective action, many people certainly attended the 1964 march on Washington because they cared about civil rights. But it is unlikely that many deluded themselves into thinking their individual participation made a large difference to the fate of the civil rights legislation in support of which the march was organized. Rather, they attended because they wanted to be a part of a social movement, to hear Martin Luther King speak, and to identify with the hundreds of thousands of others who felt the same way. Also, and this should not be minimized, they participated because they anticipated that the march would be fun—an adventure of sorts.

So, experiential behavior is consumption-oriented activity predicated on the belief that the activity in question is fulfilling apart from its consequences. Individuals, complicated things that they are, are bound to be animated both by the consumption value of a particular behavior that we just described *and* its instrumental value, the rational (investment) explanation that we have used throughout this book. To insist on only one of these complementary forms of rationality, and to exclude the other, is to provide but a partial explanation.

[1] Theodore Lowi, "The State in Political Science: How We Become What We Study," *American Political Science Review* 86 (March 1992), pp. 1–7; Donald P. Green and Ian Shapiro, *Pathologies of Rational Choice Theory* (New Haven: Yale University Press, 1994).

[2] One notable exception is Dennis Chong, *Collective Action and the Civil Rights Movement* (Chicago: University of Chicago Press, 1991).

SUMMARY

Although freedom and power are inextricably intertwined, they had to be separated for the purpose of analysis. *Civil liberties* and *civil rights* are two quite different phenomena and have to be treated legally and constitutionally in two quite different ways. We have defined *civil liberties* as that sphere of individual freedom of choice created by restraints on governmental power. When the Constitution was ratified, it was already seen as inadequate in the provision of protections of individual freedom and required the addition of the Bill of Rights. The Bill of Rights explicitly placed a whole series of restraints on government. Some of these were *substantive*, regarding *what* government could do; and some of these restraints were *procedural*, regarding *how* the government was permitted to act. We call the rights in the Bill of Rights civil liberties because they are rights to be free from arbitrary government interference.

But *which* government? This was settled in the *Barron* case in 1833 when the Supreme Court held that the restraints in the Bill of Rights were applicable only to the national government, and not to the states. The Court was recognizing "dual citizenship." At the time of its adoption in 1868, the Fourteenth Amendment was considered by many as a deliberate effort to reverse *Barron*, to put an end to dual citizenship, and to nationalize the Bill of Rights, applying its restrictions to state governments as well as to the national government. But the post–Civil War Supreme Court interpreted the Fourteenth Amendment otherwise. Dual citizenship remained almost as it had been before the Civil War, and

Rationality Principle	Collective Action Principle	Institution Principle	Policy Principle	History Principle
Madison believed that passage of a bill of rights was a practical political matter, because it would remove a potential source of opposition to the new government.	The Federalists supported the addition of a bill of rights because it would help gain the support of the Antifederalists for the Constitution as a whole.	Dual citizenship meant that the Bill of Rights did not apply to decisions or to procedures of state governments.	The civil liberties decisions of the Rehnquist Court during the 1990s reveal the conservative preferences of a majority of its justices.	Dual citizenship was upheld by the Supreme Court for nearly one hundred years after *Barron v. Baltimore* (1833).
The preferences of individual Supreme Court justices have been consequential for the development of civil liberties.	Given the massive resistance to the *Brown* decision, the civil rights movement required large, well-organized protests.	Most of the important provisions of the Bill of Rights were nationalized by the Supreme Court during the 1960s.	Individual challenges in the courts as well as several state and local referenda have weakened affirmative action.	*Roe v. Wade* was not decided in a political vacuum. Many states had already eased their restrictions on abortion prior to 1973.
The preference of the members of the Rehnquist Court has been to accept fewer cases for review.	Enforcement of civil rights law required that courts and legislatures work together.	As a political institution, the Bill of Rights has not been carved in stone. Through subsequent amendments, on the one hand, and constant updating of the original ten through judicial review, on the other, the balance between freedom and power has been transformed.		The *Brown* decision was the basis of the modern civil rights movement.
	People participated in the civil rights movement for experiential as well as instrumental purposes.	The *Brown* decision altered the constitutional framework by giving the national government the power to intervene against the discriminatory actions of state and local governments and some aspects of the private sector.		The civil rights and women's rights movements both suggest that changes in government policies can produce political action and vice versa.

the shadow of *Barron* extended across the rest of the nineteenth century and well into the twentieth century. The slow process of nationalizing the Bill of Rights began in the 1920s, when the Supreme Court recognized that at least the restraints of the First Amendment had been "incorporated" into the Fourteenth Amendment as restraints on the state governments. But it was not until the 1960s that most of the civil liberties in the Bill of Rights were incorporated into the Fourteenth Amendment. Almost exactly a century after the adoption of the Fourteenth Amendment, the Bill of Rights was nationalized. Citizens now enjoy close to the same civil liberties regardless of the state in which they reside.

As for the second aspect of protection of the individual, *civil rights*, stress has been put upon the expansion of governmental power rather than restraints upon it. If the constitutional base of civil liberties is the "due process" clause of the Fourteenth Amendment, the constitutional base of civil rights is the "equal protection" clause. This clause imposes a positive obligation on government to advance civil rights, and its original motivation seems to have been to eliminate the gross injustices suffered by "the newly emancipated negroes . . . as a class." But as with civil liberties, there was little advancement in the interpretation or application of the "equal protection" clause until after World War II. The major breakthrough came in 1954 with *Brown v. Board of Education*, and advancements came in fits and starts during the succeeding ten years.

After 1964, Congress finally supported the federal courts with effective civil rights legislation that outlawed a number of discriminatory practices in the private sector and provided for the withholding of federal grants-in-aid to any local government, school, or private employer as a sanction to help enforce the civil rights laws. From that point, civil rights developed in two ways. First, the definition of civil rights was expanded to include victims of discrimination other than African Americans. Second, the definition of civil rights became increasingly positive; affirmative action has become an official term. Judicial decisions, congressional statutes, and administrative agency actions all have moved beyond the original goal of eliminating discrimination toward creating new opportunities for minorities and, in some areas, compensating today's minorities for the consequences of discriminatory actions not directly against them but against members of their group in the past. Because compensatory civil rights action has sometimes relied upon quotas, there has been intense debate over the constitutionality as well as the desirability of affirmative action.

The story has not ended and is not likely to end. The politics of rights will remain an important part of American political discourse.

FOR FURTHER READING

Abraham, Henry. *Freedom and the Court: Civil Rights and Liberties in the United States.* 5th ed. New York: Oxford University Press, 1994.

Baer, Judith A. *Equality under the Constitution: Reclaiming the Fourteenth Amendment.* Ithaca, NY: Cornell University Press, 1983.

Drake, W. Avon, and Robert D. Holsworth. *Affirmative Action and the Stalled Quest for Black Progress.* Urbana: University of Illinois Press, 1996.

Eisenstein, Zillah. *The Female Body and the Law.* Berkeley: University of California Press, 1988.

Friendly, Fred W. *Minnesota Rag: The Dramatic Story of the Landmark Supreme Court Case that Gave New Meaning to Freedom of the Press.* New York: Vintage, 1982.

Garrow, David J. *Bearing the Cross: Martin Luther King and the Southern Christian Leadership Conference: A Personal Portrait.* New York: William Morrow, 1986.

Glendon, Mary Ann. *Rights Talk: The Impoverishment of Political Discourse.* New York: Free Press, 1991.

Greenberg, Jack. *Crusaders in the Courts: How a Dedicated Band of Lawyers Fought for the Civil Rights Revolution.* New York: Basic Books, 1994.

Hentoff, Nat. *The First Freedom: The Tumultuous History of Free Speech in America.* New York: Delacorte, 1980.

Kelly, Alfred, Winfred A. Harbison, and Herman Beltz. *The American Constitution: Its Origins and Development.* 7th ed. New York: W. W. Norton, 1991.

Levy, Leonard. *Freedom of Speech and Press in Early America: Legacy of Suppression.* New York: Harper, 1963.

Lewis, Anthony. *Gideon's Trumpet.* New York: Random House, 1964.

Minow, Martha. *Making All the Difference—Inclusion, Exclusion, and American Law.* Ithaca, NY: Cornell University Press, 1990.

Nava, Michael. *Created Equal: Why Gay Rights Matter to America.* New York: St. Martin's Press, 1994.

Rosenberg, Gerald N. *The Hollow Hope: Can Courts Bring About Social Change?* Chicago: University of Chicago Press, 1991.

Silberman, Charles. *Criminal Violence, Criminal Justice.* New York: Random House, 1978.

Silverstein, Mark. *Constitutional Faiths.* Ithaca, NY: Cornell University Press, 1984.

Thernstrom, Abigail M. *Whose Votes Count? Affirmative Action and Minority Voting Rights.* Cambridge: Harvard University Press, 1987.

PART

two

Institutions

EVENTS	INSTITUTIONAL DEVELOPMENTS
New Congress of U.S. meets for first time (1789)	Creation of House Ways and Means Committee (1789)
Jeffersonian party born in Congress (1792)	House committees develop. First procedural rules adopted—Jefferson's Rules (1790s)

1800

	Congressional party caucuses control presidential nominations (1804–1828)
	Congressional committees take control of legislative process. Rise of congressional government (1820s)
Andrew Jackson renominated for president by Democratic party convention (1832)	Presidential nominating conventions replace caucuses (1831–1832)

Abraham Lincoln elected president (1860) — **1860**

South secedes. Its delegation leaves Washington (1860–1861); period of Republican leadership (1860s)	No longer blocked by Southerners, Congress adopts protective tariff, transcontinental railroad, Homestead Act, National Banking Act, Contract Labor Act (1861–1864)
Congress impeaches but does not convict Andrew Johnson (1868)	Filibuster developed as a tactic in the Senate (1880s)
Era of Republican ascendancy begins (1897)	

1900

Theodore Roosevelt makes U.S. a world power (1901–1909)	House revolt against power of Speaker; rise of seniority system in House (1910)
Democratic interlude with election of Woodrow Wilson (1912)	Seventeenth Amendment ratified; authorizes direct election of senators (1913)
	Senate cloture rule (1917)
	Budget and Accounting Act—development of presidential budget (1921)

1930

	Rise of presidential government as Congress passes FDR's New Deal legislation (1930s)
Democrats take charge; Franklin Delano Roosevelt elected president (1932)	Legislative Reorganization Act (1946)
	Regulation of lobbyists (1949)
	Democratic Congresses expand Social Security and federal expenditures for public health (1954–1959)

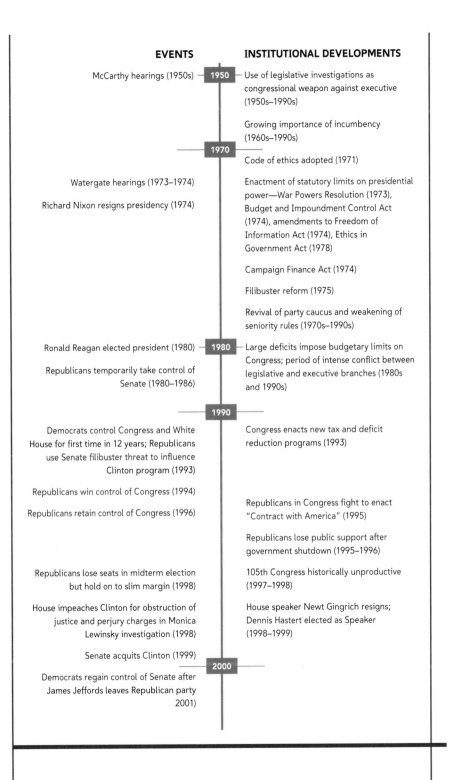

EVENTS

INSTITUTIONAL DEVELOPMENTS

McCarthy hearings (1950s) — **1950** — Use of legislative investigations as congressional weapon against executive (1950s–1990s)

Growing importance of incumbency (1960s–1990s)

1970

Code of ethics adopted (1971)

Watergate hearings (1973–1974)

Richard Nixon resigns presidency (1974)

Enactment of statutory limits on presidential power—War Powers Resolution (1973), Budget and Impoundment Control Act (1974), amendments to Freedom of Information Act (1974), Ethics in Government Act (1978)

Campaign Finance Act (1974)

Filibuster reform (1975)

Revival of party caucus and weakening of seniority rules (1970s–1990s)

Ronald Reagan elected president (1980) — **1980** — Large deficits impose budgetary limits on Congress; period of intense conflict between legislative and executive branches (1980s and 1990s)

Republicans temporarily take control of Senate (1980–1986)

1990

Democrats control Congress and White House for first time in 12 years; Republicans use Senate filibuster threat to influence Clinton program (1993)

Congress enacts new tax and deficit reduction programs (1993)

Republicans win control of Congress (1994)

Republicans retain control of Congress (1996)

Republicans in Congress fight to enact "Contract with America" (1995)

Republicans lose public support after government shutdown (1995–1996)

Republicans lose seats in midterm election but hold on to slim margin (1998)

105th Congress historically unproductive (1997–1998)

House impeaches Clinton for obstruction of justice and perjury charges in Monica Lewinsky investigation (1998)

House speaker Newt Gingrich resigns; Dennis Hastert elected as Speaker (1998–1999)

Senate acquits Clinton (1999)

2000

Democrats regain control of Senate after James Jeffords leaves Republican party 2001)

CORE OF THE ANALYSIS

- The struggle for power between Congress and the president results from the Constitution's system of checks and balances.

- Many of the institutional practices in Congress help to facilitate cooperation.

- By institutionalizing the division and specialization of labor, the committee system makes Congress more effective.

- Before a bill can become a law, it must pass through the legislative process, a complex set of organizations and procedures in Congress.

- The legislative process is driven by six sets of political forces: political parties, committees, staffs, caucuses, rules of lawmaking, and the president.

- During the first hundred years of American government, Congress was the dominant institution; with the beginning of the New Deal, the presidency became the more accessible and dominant branch of American government.

T he U.S. Congress is the "first branch" of government under Article I of our Constitution and is also among the world's most important representative bodies.

Congress is also the only national representative assembly that can actually be said to govern. Many of the world's representative bodies only represent, that is, their governmental functions consist mainly of affirming and legitimating the national leadership's decisions, tying local activists more firmly to the central government by allowing them to take part in national political affairs, and giving all citizens the impression that popular views actually play a role in the decision-making process. For example, before the collapse of the U.S.S.R., its national representative body, the Supreme Soviet, included deputies representing every locality, as well as every ethnic, religious, and occupational group in Soviet society. The Supreme Soviet, however, possessed only the power to say "yes" to leadership proposals. Its visible approval of policies and programs was seen by the Communist party hierarchy as a useful way of convincing citizens that their interests were taken into account at some point in the national decision-making process.

Although many of the world's representative bodies possess only the right to say "yes," a second, smaller group of representative institutions—most notably West European parliaments—also have the power to say "no" to the proposals of executive agencies. Such institutions as the British Parliament have the power to reject programs and laws sought by the government, although the use of this power is constrained by the fact that the rejection of an important governmental proposal can lead to Parliament's dissolution and the need for new elections. While they can and sometimes do say "no," West European parliaments generally do not have the power to modify governmental proposals or, more important, to initiate major programs. The only national representative body that actually possesses such powers is the U.S. Congress. For example, while the U.S. Congress never accedes to the president's budget proposals without making major changes, both the British House of Commons and the Japanese Diet always accept the budget exactly as proposed by the government.

In this chapter, we shall try to understand how the U.S. Congress is able to serve simultaneously as a representative assembly and a powerful agency of government. Unlike most of its counterparts around the world, Congress controls a formidable battery of powers that it uses to shape policies and, when necessary, defend its prerogatives against the executive branch. We shall examine each of these powers in its turn.

As we shall see, however, congressional power cannot be separated from congressional representation. Indeed, there is a reciprocal relationship between the two. Without its important governmental powers, Congress would be a very different sort of representative body. Americans might feel some sense of symbolic representation if they found that Congress contained members of their own race, religion, ethnic background, or social class. They might feel some sense of gratification if members of Congress tried to help them with their problems. But without its array of powers, Congress could do little to represent effectively the views and interests of its constituents. Power is necessary for effective congressional representation. At the same time, the power of Congress is ultimately a function of its capacity to effectively represent important groups and forces in American society.

Questions of power and representation are also closely tied to the issue of congressional reform. Critics of Congress want it to be both more representative and more effective. On the one hand, Congress is frequently criticized for falling victim to "gridlock" and failing to reach decisions on important issues like Social Security reform. This was one reason why, in 1995, the Republican House leadership reduced the number of committees and subcommittees in the lower chamber. Having fewer committees and subcommittees generally means greater centralization of power and more expeditious decision

THE CENTRAL QUESTIONS

REPRESENTATION

How does Congress represent the United States as a whole?

In what ways does the electoral system determine who is elected to Congress?

THE ORGANIZATION OF CONGRESS

What are the underlying problems in organizing a legislative assembly?

What are the basic building blocks of congressional organization and how does each help institutionalize cooperation?

RULES OF LAWMAKING: HOW A BILL BECOMES A LAW

How do the rules of congressional procedure influence the fate of legislation as well as determine the distribution of power in Congress?

HOW CONGRESS DECIDES

What sorts of influences inside and outside of government determine how members of Congress vote on legislation? How do these influences vary according to type of issue?

BEYOND LEGISLATION: ADDITIONAL CONGRESSIONAL POWERS

Besides the power to pass legislation, what other powers allow Congress to influence the process of government?

POWER AND REPRESENTATION

Can Congress be both effective and representative?

making. On the other hand, critics demand that Congress become more representative of the changing makeup and values of the American populace. In recent years, for example, some reformers have demanded limits on the number of terms that any member of Congress can serve. Term limits are seen as a device for producing a more rapid turnover of members and, hence, a better chance for new political and social forces to be represented in Congress. The problem, however, is that while reforms such as term limits and greater internal diffusion of power may make Congress more representative, they may also make it less efficient and effective. By the same token, reforms that may make Congress better able to act, such as strong central leadership, reduction of the number of committees and subcommittees, and retention of members with seniority and experience, may make Congress less representative.

As we shall see, congressional power cannot be separated either from the bases of congressional representation or from the precise form taken by its decision-making institutions. We begin our discussion with a brief consideration of representation. Then we examine the institutional structure of the contemporary Congress, and the manner in which congressional powers are organized and employed. Throughout, we will point out the connections between these two aspects—the ways in which representation affects congressional operations (especially through "the electoral connection") and the ways in which congressional institutions enhance or diminish representation (especially Congress's division- and specialization-of-labor committee system).

REPRESENTATION

constituency
The district comprising the area from which an official is elected.

Congress is the most important representative institution in American government. Each member's primary responsibility is to the district, to his or her ***constituency***; not to the congressional leadership, a party, or even Congress itself. Yet the task of representation is not a simple one. Views about what constitutes fair and effective representation differ, and constituents can make very different kinds of demands on their representatives. Members of Congress must consider these diverse views and demands as they represent their districts (see Process Box 5.1). A representative claims to act or speak for some other person or group. But how can one person be trusted to speak for another? How do we know that those who call themselves our representatives are actually speaking on our behalf, rather than simply pursuing their own interests?

delegate
Representative who votes according to the preferences of his or her constituency.

trustee
Representative who votes based on what he or she thinks is best for his or her constituency.

Legislators generally vary in the weight given to personal priorities and the things desired by campaign contributors and past supporters. Some see themselves as perfect agents of others; they have been elected to do the bidding of those that sent them to the legislature, and act as ***delegates.*** Other legislators see themselves as being selected by their fellow citizens to do what the legislator thinks is "right," and act as ***trustees.*** Most legislators are mixes of these two types.

As we discussed in Chapter 1, one person might be trusted to speak for another if the two are formally bound together so that the representative is in some

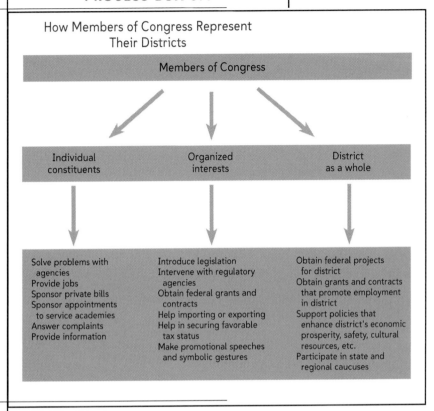

How Members of Congress Represent Their Districts

Members of Congress

Individual constituents	Organized interests	District as a whole
Solve problems with agencies Provide jobs Sponsor private bills Sponsor appointments to service academies Answer complaints Provide information	Introduce legislation Intervene with regulatory agencies Obtain federal grants and contracts Help importing or exporting Help in securing favorable tax status Make promotional speeches and symbolic gestures	Obtain federal projects for district Obtain grants and contracts that promote employment in district Support policies that enhance district's economic prosperity, safety, cultural resources, etc. Participate in state and regional caucuses

agency representation
The type of representation by which representatives are held accountable to their constituents if they fail to represent them properly; that is, constituents have the power to hire and fire their representatives. This is the incentive for good representation when the personal backgrounds, views, and interests of the representatives differ from their constituents'.

way accountable to those he or she purports to represent. If representatives can somehow be punished or held to account for failing to speak properly for their constituents, then we know they have an incentive to provide good representation even if their own personal backgrounds, views, and interests differ from those they represent. This principle is called *agency representation*—the sort of representation that takes place when constituents have the power to hire and fire their representatives. The idea of representative as agent is similar to the relationship of lawyer and client. True, the relationship between the member of Congress and as many as 600,000 "clients" in the district, or the senator and millions of clients in the state, is very different from that of the lawyer and client. But the criteria of performance are comparable.

One expects at the very least that each representative will constantly be seeking to discover the interests of the constituency and will be speaking for those

Institution Principle

According to the principle of agency representation, elections induce a member of Congress to act according to the preferences of his or her constituency.

interests in Congress and in other centers of government.[1] We expect this because we believe that members of Congress, like politicians everywhere, are ambitious. For many, this ambition is satisfied simply by maintaining a hold on their present office and advancing up the rungs of power in that legislative body. Some may be looking ahead to the next level—to higher legislative office, as when a representative seeks a Senate seat, or to an executive office, as when a legislator returns home to run for his or her state's governorship, or, at the highest level, when a legislator seeks the presidency.[2] We will return to this topic shortly in a discussion of elections. But we can say here that in each of these cases, the legislator is eager to serve the interests of constituents, either to enhance his or her prospects of contract renewal at the next election or to improve the chances of moving to another level. In short, the agency conception of representation works in proportion to the ambition of politicians (as "agents") and the capacity of constituents (as "principals") to reward or punish on the basis of their legislator's performance and reputation. This latter capacity depends on, among other things, the quality of political competition, which, in turn, is a product of the electoral and campaign finance systems.

House and Senate: Differences in Representation

The framers of the Constitution provided for a *bicameral legislature*—that is, a legislative body consisting of two chambers. As we saw in Chapter 2, the framers intended each of these chambers, the House and Senate, to represent a different constituency. Members of the Senate, appointed by state legislatures for six-year terms, were to represent the elite members of society and to be more attuned to the interests of property than of population. Today, members of the House and Senate are elected directly by the people. The 435 members of the House are elected from districts apportioned according to population; the 100 members of the Senate are elected by state, with two senators from each. Senators continue to have much longer terms in office and usually represent much larger and more diverse constituencies than do their counterparts in the House of Representatives (see Table 5.1).

The House and Senate play different roles in the legislative process. In essence, the Senate is the more deliberative of the two bodies—the forum in which any and all ideas can receive a thorough public airing. The House is the more centralized and organized of the two bodies—better equipped to play a routine role in the governmental process. In part, this difference stems from the different rules governing the two bodies. These rules give House leaders more control over the legislative process and provide for House members to specialize

---

[1]For some interesting empirical evidence, see Angus Campbell, Philip Converse, Warren Miller, and Donald Stokes, *Elections and the Political Order* (New York: Wiley, 1966), Chapter 11. See also Richard Fenno, *Home Style: House Members in Their Districts* (Boston: Little, Brown, 1978).

[2]For more on "progressive ambition," see Joseph Schlesinger, *Ambition and Politics* (Chicago: Rand McNally, 1966).

TABLE 5.1

Differences between the House and the Senate		
	HOUSE	**SENATE**
Minimum age of member	25 years	30 years
U.S. citizenship	at least 7 years	at least 9 years
Length of term	2 years	6 years
Number per state	Depends on population: 1 per 30,000 in 1789; now 1 per 600,000	2 per state
Constituency	Tends to be local	Both local and national

in certain legislative areas. The rules of the much-smaller Senate give its leadership relatively little power and discourage specialization.

Both formal and informal factors contribute to differences between the two chambers of Congress. Differences in the length of terms and requirements for holding office specified by the Constitution in turn generate differences in how members of each body develop their constituencies and exercise their powers of office. The result is that members of the House most effectively and frequently serve as the agents of well-organized local interests with specific legislative agendas—for instance, used-car dealers seeking relief from regulation, labor unions seeking more favorable legislation, or farmers looking for higher subsidies. The small size and relative homogeneity of their constituencies and the frequency with which they must seek re-election make House members more attuned to the legislative needs of local interest groups.

Senators, on the other hand, serve larger and more heterogeneous constituencies. As a result, they are somewhat better able than members of the House to serve as the agents for groups and interests organized on a statewide or national basis. Moreover, with longer terms in office, senators have the luxury of considering "new ideas" or seeking to bring together new coalitions of interests, rather than simply serving existing ones.

In recent years, the House has exhibited considerably more intense partisanship and ideological division than the Senate. Because of their diverse constituencies, senators are more inclined to seek compromise positions that will offend as few voters and interest groups as possible. Members of the House, in contrast, typically represent more homogeneous districts in which their own party is dominant. This situation has tended to make House members less inclined to seek compromises and more willing to stick to their partisan and ideological guns than their counterparts in the Senate during the past several decades. For instance, the House divided almost exactly along partisan lines on the 1998 vote to impeach President Clinton. In the Senate, by contrast, ten Republicans joined Democrats to acquit Clinton of obstruction of justice charges and, in a separate vote, five Republicans joined Democrats to acquit Clinton of perjury.[3] Also, in October 2001, the Senate passed an airport security bill unanimously. The House, however, divided votes along partisan lines over whether new security personnel should be federal employees or private contractors.

The Electoral System

In light of their role as agents for various constituencies in their states and districts, and the importance of elections as a mechanism by which principals (constituents) reward and punish their agents, representatives are very much influenced by electoral considerations. Three factors related to the U.S. electoral system affect who gets elected and what they do once in office. The first set of issues concerns who decides to run for office and which candidates have an edge over others. The second issue is that of incumbency advantage. Finally, the way congressional district lines are drawn can greatly affect the outcome of an election. Let us examine more closely the impact that these considerations have on who serves in Congress.

Running for Office   Voters' choices are restricted from the start by who decides to run for office. In the past, decisions about who would run for a particular elected office were made by local party officials. A person who had a record of service to the party, or who was owed a favor, or whose "turn" had come up might be nominated by party leaders for an office. Today, few party organizations have the power to slate candidates in that way. Instead, the decision to run for Congress is a more personal choice. One of the most important factors determining who runs for office is a candidate's individual ambition.[4] A potential candidate may also assess whether he or she can attract enough money to mount a credible campaign. The ability to raise money depends on connections with other politicians, interest groups, and national party organizations. Wealthy individuals may finance their own races. In 2000, for example, New Jersey Democrat and former investment banker Jon Corzine spent more than $60 million of his own money to win a U.S. Senate seat.

 Rationality Principle
One of the most important factors determining who runs for office is each candidate's individual ambition.

---

[3] Eric Pianin and Guy Gugliotta, "The Bipartisan Challenge: Senate's Search for Accord Marks Contrast to House," *Washington Post*, 8 January 1999, p. 1.

[4] See Linda Fowler and Robert McClure, *Political Ambition: Who Decides to Run for Congress* (New Haven: Yale University Press, 1989); and Alan Ehrenhalt, *The United States of Ambition* (New York: Times Books, 1991).

In the past, the difficulty of raising campaign funds posed a disadvantage to female candidates. Since the 1980s, however, a number of political action committees (PACs) and other organizations have emerged to recruit women and fund their campaigns. The largest of them, EMILY's List, has become one of the most powerful fundraisers in the nation. Recent research shows that money is no longer the barrier it once was to women running for office.[5]

Features distinctive to each congressional district also affect the field of candidates. Among them are the range of other political opportunities that may lure potential candidates away. In addition, the way the congressional district overlaps with state legislative boundaries may affect a candidate's decision to run. A state-level representative or senator who is considering running for the U.S. Congress is more likely to assess his or her prospects favorably if his or her state district coincides with the congressional district (because the voters will already know him or her). For similar reasons, U.S. representatives from small states, whose congressional districts overlap with a large portion of their state, are far more likely to run for statewide office than members of Congress from large states. And for any candidate, decisions about running must be made early, because once money has been committed to already-declared candidates, it is harder for new candidates to break into a race. Thus, the outcome of a November election is partially determined many months earlier, when decisions to run are finalized.

Incumbency *Incumbency* plays a very important role in the American electoral system and in the kind of representation citizens get in Washington. Once in office, members of Congress possess an array of tools that they can use to stack the deck in favor of their re-election. Through effective use of this arsenal of weapons, an incumbent establishes a reputation for competence, imagination, and responsiveness—the attributes most principals look for in an agent. Particularly important is the incumbent's reputation for constituency service: taking care of the problems and requests of individual voters. Through such services and their advertisement by word of mouth, the incumbent seeks to establish an attractive political reputation and a "personal" relationship with his or her constituents. Well over a quarter of the representatives' time and nearly two-thirds of the time of their staff members is devoted to constituency service (termed "casework"). This service is not merely a matter of writing and mailing letters. It includes talking to constituents, providing them with minor services, presenting special bills for them, and attempting to influence decisions by regulatory commissions on their behalf. Indeed, one might think of the member's

incumbency
Holding a political office for which one is running.

[5]See Barbara C. Burrell, *A Woman's Place Is in the House: Campaigning for Congress in the Feminist Era* (Ann Arbor: University of Michigan Press, 1994), Chapter 6; and the essays in Elizabeth Adell Cook, Sue Thomas, and Clyde Wilcox, eds., *The Year of the Woman: Myths and Realities* (Boulder, CO: Westview, 1994).

legislative staff and office operation as a "congressional enterprise," much like a firm, with the member him- or herself as the CEO.[6]

One very direct way in which incumbent members of Congress serve as the agents of their constituencies is through the venerable institution of *patronage.* Patronage refers to a variety of forms of direct services and benefits that members provide for their districts. One of the most important forms of patronage is *pork-barrel legislation.* Through pork-barrel legislation, representatives seek to capture federal projects and federal funds for their own districts (or states in the case of senators), and thus to "bring home the pork" for their constituents. Many observers of Congress argue that pork-barrel bills are the only ones that some members are serious about moving toward actual passage because they are seen as so important to members' re-election bids.

A common form of pork barreling is the "earmark," the practice through which members of Congress insert into otherwise pork-free bills language that provides special benefits for their own constituents.[7] For instance, the massive transportation bill enacted in 1998 contained billions of dollars in earmarks. One senator, Ted Kennedy (D-Mass.), claimed that he was able to obtain nearly $200 million in earmarks. In addition to $100 million for highway construction in Boston, these included a myriad of small items such as $1.6 million for the Longfellow National Historic Site and $3.17 million for the Silvio Conte National Fish and Wildlife Refuge.[8]

The pork-barrel tradition in Congress is so strong that some members insist on providing their districts with special benefits whether their constituents want them or not. In 1994, for example, members of the House Public Works Committee managed to channel millions of dollars in federal highway funds to their own states and districts. California, which has eight representatives on the Public Works Committee, received fifty-one special federal highway projects worth nearly $300 million. The problem is that under federal law, these special funds are charged against the state's annual grant from the Highway Trust Fund. States rely heavily upon their Highway Trust Fund grants to fund high-priority road work. One exasperated state official declared, "For years our members have tried to explain that to the members of Congress . . . 'No, you did not bring me any new money. All you did was reprogram money from here to there.'"[9]

So, why do legislators continue this exasperating practice? One answer is that each individual legislator can credibly and visibly claim personal responsibility, and thus take personal credit, for earmarked programs and special

patronage The resources available to higher officials, usually opportunities to make partisan appointments to offices and to confer grants, licenses, or special favors to supporters.

pork-barrel legislation Appropriations made by legislative bodies for local projects that are often not needed but that are created so that local representatives can carry their home district in the next election.

---

[6]For more on the congressional office as an "enterprise" that processes the casework demands of constituents, see Robert H. Salisbury and Kenneth A. Shepsle, "Congressman as Enterprise," *Legislative Studies Quarterly* 6 (1981): 559–76.

[7]For an excellent study of academic earmarking, see James Savage, *Funding Science in America* (New York: Cambridge University Press, 1999).

[8]*Congressional Quarterly Weekly Report*, 17 October 1998, p. 2792.

[9]Jon Healey, "The Unspoken Expense of the Highway Bill," *Congressional Quarterly Weekly Report*, 28 May 1994, p. 1375.

highway projects. This enhances the legislator's reputation back home as a Washington mover and shaker, and thus also enhances his or her re-election prospects. If the same money came to the states or districts through an existing program, like the Highway Trust Fund, the individual legislator would get little credit for being personally responsible.

A limited amount of other direct patronage also exists. One important form of this constituency service is intervention with federal administrative agencies on behalf of constituents. Members of the House and Senate and their staff members spend a great deal of time on the telephone and in administrative offices seeking to secure favorable treatment for constituents and supporters. A small but related form of patronage is getting an appointment to one of the military academies for the child of a constituent. Traditionally, these appointments are allocated one to a district.

A different form of patronage is the ***private bill***—a proposal to grant some kind of relief, special privilege, or exemption to the person named in the bill. The private bill is a type of legislation, but it is distinguished from a public bill, which is supposed to deal with general rules and categories of behavior, people, and institutions. As many as 75 percent of all private bills introduced (and one-third of the ones that pass) are concerned with providing relief for foreign nationals who cannot get permanent visas to the United States because the immigration quota for their country is filled or because of something unusual about their particular situation.[10]

Private legislation is a congressional privilege that is often abused, but it is impossible to imagine members of Congress giving it up completely. It is one of the easiest, cheapest, and most effective forms of patronage available to each member. It can be defended as an indispensable part of the process by which members of Congress seek to fulfill their role as representatives. And obviously they like the privilege because it helps them win re-election.

The incumbency advantage is evident in the high rates of re-election for congressional incumbents: over 95 percent for House members and nearly 90 percent for members of the Senate in recent years (see Figure 5.1).[11] It is also evident in what is called sophomore surge—the tendency for candidates to win a higher percentage of the vote when seeking future terms in office. In the 2000 national elections, incumbency had a powerful effect with nearly 98 percent of House incumbents re-elected and 83 percent of incumbent candidates re-elected to the Senate.

> **Policy Principle**
>
> Pork-barrel legislation exists because it allows members of Congress to claim credit for federally granted resources, thus improving their chances for re-election.

> **private bill** A proposal in Congress to provide a specific person with some kind of relief, such as a special exemption from immigration quotas.

[10]Congressional Quarterly, *Guide to the Congress of the United States*, pp. 229–310.

[11]Norman J. Ornstein, Thomas E. Mann, and Michael J. Malbin, *Vital Statistics on Congress, 1995–1996* (Washington, DC: Congressional Quarterly Press, 1996), pp. 60–61; Robert S. Erickson and Gerald C. Wright, "Voters, Candidates, and Issues in Congressional Elections," in *Congress Reconsidered*, 5th ed., ed. Lawrence C. Dodd and Bruce I. Oppenheimer (Washington, DC: Congressional Quarterly Press, 1993), p. 99; John R. Alford and David W. Brady, "Personal and Partisan Advantage in U.S. Congressional Elections, 1846–1990," in *Congress Reconsidered*, pp. 141–57.

FIGURE 5.1

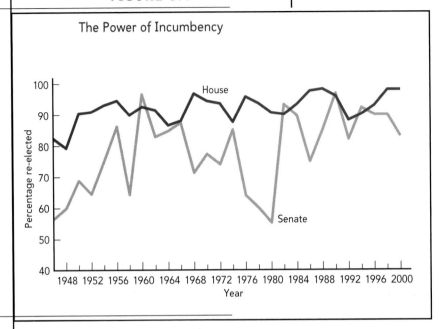

The Power of Incumbency

SOURCE: Norman J. Ornstein et al., eds., *Vital Statistics on Congress, 1995–1996* (Washington, DC: Congressional Quarterly Press, 1996), pp. 60–61, and authors' update.

Incumbency can help a candidate by scaring off potential challengers. In many races, potential candidates may decide not to run because they fear that the incumbent simply has too much money or is too well liked or too well known.[12] Potentially strong challengers may also decide that a district's partisan leanings are too unfavorable. The experience of Republican representative Dan Miller in Florida is instructive. When Miller first ran in 1992, he faced five opponents in the Republican primary and a bruising campaign against his Democratic opponent in the general election. In the 1994 election, by contrast, Miller faced only nominal opposition in the Republican primary, winning 81 percent of the vote. In the general election, the strongest potential challenger from the Democratic party decided not to run; the combination of the incumbency advantage coupled with the strongly Republican leanings of the district

[12]See Sara Fritz and Dwight Morris, *Gold-Plated Politics* (Washington, DC: Congressional Quarterly Press, 1992).

gave the Democrats little chance of winning. Miller was re-elected without a challenge.[13]

The advantage of incumbency thus tends to preserve the status quo in Congress by discouraging potentially strong challengers from running. When incumbents do face strong challengers, they are often defeated.[14] For example, in 1998, New York Republican senator Al D'Amato was trounced by former representative Charles Schumer, a strong candidate who was able to raise nearly as much money as D'Amato. The role of incumbency has implications for the social composition of Congress. For example, incumbency advantage makes it harder for women to increase their numbers in Congress because most incumbents are men. Women who run for open seats (for which there are no incumbents) are just as likely to win as male candidates.[15] Supporters of term limits argue that such limits are the only way to get new faces into Congress. They believe that incumbency advantage and the tendency of many legislators to view politics as a career mean that very little turnover will occur in Congress unless limits are imposed on the number of terms a legislator can serve.

But the tendency toward the status quo is not absolute. In recent years, political observers have suggested that the incumbency advantage may be declining. In the 1992 and 1994 elections, for example, voters expressed considerable anger and dissatisfaction with incumbents, producing a 25 percent turnover in the House in 1992 and a 20 percent turnover in 1994. Yet the defeat of incumbents was not the main factor at work in either of these elections: 88.3 percent of House incumbents were re-elected in 1992, and 90.2 percent won re-election in 1994. In 1992, an exceptionally high retirement rate (20 percent, as opposed to the norm of 10 percent) among members of Congress created more open seats, which brought new faces into Congress. In 1994, a large number of open seats combined with an unprecedented mobilization of Republican voters to shift control of Congress to the Republican party. Incumbents fared better in 1996 and 1998, when approximately 95 percent of House and Senate incumbents were re-elected.[16]

Congressional Districts   The final factor that affects who wins a seat in Congress is the way congressional districts are drawn. Every ten years, state legislatures must redraw congressional districts to reflect population changes. This is a highly political process: districts are shaped to create an advantage for the majority party in the state legislature, which controls the redistricting process. In this complex process, those charged with drawing districts use sophisticated

---

[13]Kevin Merida, "The 2nd Time Is Easy; Many House Freshmen Have Secured Seats," *Washington Post*, 18 October 1994, p. A1.

[14]Gary Jacobson, *The Politics of Congressional Elections* (Reading, MA: Addison-Wesley, 1996).

[15]See Burrell, *A Woman's Place Is in the House;* and David Broder, "Key to Women's Political Parity: Running," *Washington Post*, 8 September 1994, p. A17.

[16]Based on authors' tabulations.

computer technologies to come up with the most favorable district boundaries. Redistricting can create open seats and may pit incumbents of the same party against one another, ensuring that one of them will lose. Redistricting can also give an advantage to one party by clustering voters with some ideological or sociological characteristics in a single district, or by separating those voters into two or more districts. *Gerrymandering* can have a major impact upon the outcomes of congressional elections. For example, prior to 1980, California House seats had been almost evenly divided between the two parties. After the 1980 census, a redistricting effort controlled by the Democrats, who held both houses of the state legislature as well as the governorship, resulted in Democrats taking control of two-thirds of the state's seats in the U.S. House of Representatives.[17] Examples like this explain why the two parties invest substantial resources in state legislative and gubernatorial contests during the electoral cycle prior to the year that congressional district boundaries will be redrawn. This also helps to explain why the two parties clashed bitterly over the 2000 census. Democrats charged that the census undercounted America's minority population by as many as 3.5 million persons, and they demanded the use of statistical sampling measures to correct the alleged error. Republicans, in turn, accused the Democrats of seeking to manipulate the census in order to increase the number of congressional districts in Democratic states in the Northeast and for other political purposes as well. Once the GOP won control of the executive branch in the 2000 elections, Republican commerce secretary Don Evans blocked Democrat efforts to alter census numbers through sampling methods.

As we shall see in Chapter 10, since the passage of the 1982 amendments to the 1964 Civil Rights Act, race has become a major—and controversial—consideration in drawing voting districts. These amendments, which encouraged the creation of districts in which members of racial minorities have decisive majorities, have greatly increased the number of minority representatives in Congress. After the 1991–1992 redistricting, the number of predominantly minority districts doubled, rising from twenty-six to fifty-two. Among the most fervent supporters of the new minority districts were white Republicans, who used the opportunity to create more districts dominated by white Republican voters. These developments raise thorny questions about representation. Some analysts argue that the system may grant minorities greater sociological representation, but it has made it more difficult for minorities to win substantive policy goals.[18]

In 1995, the Supreme Court limited racial redistricting in *Miller v. Johnson*, in which the Court stated that race could not be the predominant factor in creating electoral districts. Yet concerns about redistricting and representation have not disappeared. The distinction between race being a "predominant" factor and its being one factor among many is very hazy. Because the drawing of

gerrymandering
Apportionment of voters in districts in such a way as to give unfair advantage to one political party.

Analyzing American Politics

www.wwnorton.com/
lowi7/ch5

Analyze the impact of redistricting on minority representation.

---

[17]David Butler and Bruce Cain, *Congressional Redistricting* (New York: Macmillan, 1992).

[18]Lani Guinier, *The Tyranny of the Majority: Fundamental Fairness in Representative Democracy* (New York: Free Press, 1995).

district boundaries affects incumbents as well as the field of candidates who decide to run for office, it continues to be a key battleground on which political parties fight about the meaning of representation.

THE ORGANIZATION OF CONGRESS

The United States Congress is not only a representative assembly. It is also a legislative body. For Americans, representation and legislation go hand in hand. As we saw earlier, however, many parliamentary bodies are representative without the power to legislate. It is no small achievement that the U.S. Congress both represents *and* governs.

It is extraordinarily difficult for a large, representative assembly to formulate, enact, and implement laws. The internal complexities of conducting business within Congress—the legislative process—alone are daunting. In addition, there are many individuals and institutions that have the capacity to influence the legislative process. Since successful legislation requires the confluence of so many distinct factors, it is little wonder that most of the thousands of bills considered by Congress each year are defeated long before they reach the president.

Before an idea or proposal can become a law, it must pass through a complex set of organizations and procedures in Congress. Collectively, these are called the policy-making process, or the legislative process. Understanding this process is central to understanding why some ideas and proposals eventually become law while most do not. Although the supporters of legislative proposals often feel that the formal rules of the congressional process are deliberately designed to prevent their own deserving proposals from ever seeing the light of day, these rules allow Congress to play an important role in lawmaking. If it wants to be more than simply a rubber stamp for the executive branch, like so many other representative assemblies around the world, a national legislature like the Congress must develop a division of labor, set an agenda, maintain order through rules and procedures, and place limits on discussion. If it wants to accomplish these things in a representative setting in which a veritable diversity of political preferences exists, then it must find the ways and means to enable cooperation despite the variety of interests and coalitions, and compromises despite conflicts. We will first take up the general issues that face any legislature or decision-making group possessing diverse preferences—the problems of cooperation, coalitions, and compromises.

Cooperation in Congress

A popularly elected legislative assembly—the Boston city council, the Massachusetts legislature, the U.S. Congress, the French National Assembly, or the European Parliament—consists of politicians who harbor a variety of political objectives. Since they got where they are by winning an election, and many hope to stay where they are or possibly advance their political careers, these politicians are intimately aware of whom they must please to do so:

- Because campaigns are expensive propositions, most politicians are eager to please those who can supply resources for the next campaign—financial "fat cats," political action committees, important endorsers, small contributors, party officials, volunteer activists.
- The most recent campaign—one that the politician won—provides her with information about just why the victory was secured. It is sometimes quite difficult to sort out the myriad of factors, but at the very least the politician has a good sense of what categories of voters supported her and may be prepared to support her again if performance is adequate.
- Many politicians aim to please not only campaign contributors and voters; they also have an agenda of their own. Whether for virtuous reasons or evil ones, for private gain or public good, politicians come to the legislature with policy goals of personal importance.

Congress therefore consists of a motley crew of legislators, each motivated by a combination of desires—wanting to please those who control his or her political future and wanting to achieve personal policy goals.

 Rationality Principle
The political opinions and policy goals of members of Congress are many and varied.

In a representative democracy the specific public policies that representatives want to pursue are many and varied. We mean this in two respects. First, owing to their different constituencies, legislators will give priority to different realms of public policy. A Cape Cod congressman will be interested in shipping, fishing, coastal preservation, harbor development, tourism, and shipbuilding. A Philadelphia congresswoman may not care much at all about any of those issues, focusing her attention instead on welfare reform, civil rights policy, aid to inner-city school systems, and job retraining programs. Montana's sole member of Congress is probably not interested in coastal preservation, nor in inner city schools, but rather in issues of ranching, agriculture, mining, and public land use. Congress contains a mélange of legislative priorities.

Congress is also varied in the opinions its members hold on any given issue. While some may care passionately about the issue in question, and others not a whit, there is bound to be conflict, both at the broad philosophical or ideological level and at the practical level, on how to proceed. Thus, while interest in environmental protection ranges from high priority among those who count many Sierra Club members among their constituents to low priority among those who have other fish to fry, once environmental protection is on the agenda there is a broad range of preferences over specific environmental initiatives. Some want pollution discharges carefully monitored and regulated by a relatively powerful environmental watchdog agency. Others believe that more decentralized and less intrusive means, such as marketable pollution permits, are the way to go. Still others think the entire issue is overblown, that any proposed cure is worse than the disease, and that the republic would best be served by leaving well enough alone. The distribution of individual preferences reflects a range of ideal policies.

As a result, diversity in priorities and preferences among legislators is sufficiently abundant that the view of no group of legislators predominates. Legislative consensus must be built—this is what legislative politics is all about. Each legislator clamors to get her priority issue the attention she believes it deserves, or to make sure that her position on a given issue prevails. But neither effort is likely to succeed on its own merits. Support must be assembled, deals consummated, and promises and threats utilized. In short, legislators intent upon achieving their objectives must cooperate, coalesce, and compromise.

Cooperation may be assembled separately on each occasion. But one-shot efforts at cooperating often run into insurmountable difficulties. Cooperating parties are often suspicious, for one thing, and thus guard against being taken advantage of. At the very same time, they contemplate the pros and cons of taking advantage of others. Finally, they loathe having to waste resources on securing compliance each and every time.

Cooperation, especially on recurring matters like congressional votes, is facilitated by *institutionalization*. Indeed, we shall claim that many institutional practices in Congress reflect the requirements of facilitating cooperation. This leads to work being divided and specialized, procedures regularized, specific forms of agenda power and other distinctive advantages delegated, and the interactions fostered by these arrangements monitored to assure compliance with cooperative objectives. All of these organizational features of Congress arise as part of a cooperative governance structure.

Collective Action Principle
Cooperation on recurring matters like congressional votes is facilitated by the institutionalization of legislative structures and procedures.

Other Underlying Problems

Before we can understand why Congress selects particular ways to institutionalize its practices, we need a finer appreciation of other underlying problems with which legislators must grapple.

Matching Influence and Interest   Legislatures are highly egalitarian institutions. Each legislator has one vote on any issue coming before the body. Unlike a consumer, who has a cash budget that she may allocate in any way she wishes over categories of consumer goods, a legislator is not given a vote budget in quite the same sense. Instead, his budget of votes is "earmarked"—one vote for each motion before the assembly. He is a bit like a consumer who is given a series of $1 bills, each designated for a different consumer good category; he cannot aggregate the votes in his possession and cast them all, or some large fraction of them, for a motion on a subject near and dear to his heart (or those of his constituents). This is a source of frustration since, as we have noted, the premise of instrumental behavior means that legislators would, if they could, concentrate whatever resources they commanded on those subjects of highest priority to them.

Information   The refrain of many urban legislators in the early twenty-first century, like our Philadelphia congresswoman above, is "more jobs at a living wage." This is a response both to the disappearance of many jobs from most

American cities (they gravitate to lower-wage regions of the country or out of the country altogether to lower-wage regions of the world) and to the often unattractive wages, benefits, and career prospects attached to those jobs that remain. Many legislative solutions to this serious problem have been proposed. Some urge a higher minimum wage; some mandate better fringe benefits—health care coverage, day care subsidies, pension benefits, parental leave policies, and so on; some underwrite training programs to improve the productivity of workers; some advocate all these things and more. What works? These are very complicated matters; even those legislators for whom the problems are most pressing are often quite unsure how to answer this question.

If legislators voted directly for social outcomes, then this wouldn't be a problem at all. The Philadelphia legislator could simply offer a bill "mandating" more jobs at a better wage in urban areas and, if it passed, then—*abracadabra!*—the mandated effects would become a reality. Alas, legislators do not vote for outcomes directly, but rather for *instruments* (or policies) whose effects produce outcomes. Thus legislators, in order to vote intelligently, must know the connection between the instruments they vote for and the effects they desire. In short, they must have information and knowledge about how the world works.

Few legislators—indeed few people in general—know how the world works in very many policy domains except in the most superficial of ways. Nearly everyone in the legislature would benefit from the production of valuable information—at the very least information that would allow legislators to eliminate policy instruments that make very little difference in solving social problems, or even make matters worse. Producing such information, however, is not a trivial matter. Simply to digest the knowledge that is being produced outside the legislature by knowledge-industry specialists (academics, scientists, journalists, interest groups) is a taxing task. Clearly, institutional arrangements that provide incentives to some legislators to produce, evaluate, and disseminate this knowledge for others will permit public resources to be utilized more effectively.

Compliance   The legislature is not the only game in town. The promulgation of public policies is a joint undertaking in which courts, executives, bureaucrats, and others participate alongside legislators. If the legislature develops no means to monitor what happens after a bill becomes law, then it risks public policies implemented in ways other than those intended when the law was passed. Cooperation does not end with the successful passage of a law. If legislators wish to have an impact on the world around them, especially on those matters to which their constituents give priority, then it is necessary to attend to policy *implementation* as well as policy *formulation*. But it is just not practical for all 435 representatives and all 100 senators to march down to this or that agency at the other end of Pennsylvania Avenue to insure appropriate implementation by the executive bureaucracy. Compliance will not "just happen" and, like the production and dissemination of reliable information at the policy formulation stage, the need for oversight of the executive bureaucracy is but an extension of the cooperation that produced legislation in the first place. It, too, must be institutionalized.

What we have tried to suggest in this rather abstract discussion about legislative institutions and practices is that, first and foremost, Congress is a place in which very different kinds of representatives congregate and try to accomplish things so that they may reap the support of their respective constituents back home. This very diversity is problematic—it requires cooperation, coalitions, and compromise. In addition, there is a mismatch between influence and interest (owing to one person/one vote), information about the effectiveness of alternative policies is in short supply, and the legislature must worry about how its product—public laws—gets treated by other branches of government. These are the problems for which legislatures, of which the U.S. Congress is the preeminent example, devise institutional arrangements to mitigate, if not solve altogether.

We will now examine the organization of Congress and the legislative process, particularly the basic building blocks of congressional organization: political parties, the committee system, congressional staff, the caucuses, and the parliamentary rules of the House and Senate. Each of these factors plays a key role in the organization of Congress and in the process through which Congress formulates and enacts laws. We will also look at other powers Congress has in addition to lawmaking and explore the future role of Congress in relation to the powers of the executive.

Party Leadership in the House and the Senate

One significant aspect of legislative life is not part of the *official* organization at all: political parties. The legislative parties—Democratic and Republican in modern times, but numerous others over the course of American history—are exemplars of organizations that foster cooperation, coalitions, and compromise. They are the vehicles of collective action, both for legislators sharing common policy objectives inside the legislature and for those very same legislators as candidates in periodic election contests back home.[19] In short, political parties in Congress are the fundamental building blocks from which policy coalitions are fashioned to pass legislation and monitor its implementation, thereby providing a track record on which members build electoral support back home.

Every two years, at the beginning of a new Congress, the members of each party gather to elect their House leaders. This gathering is traditionally called the *caucus,* or conference (by the Republicans). The elected leader of the majority party is later proposed to the whole House and is automatically elected to

caucus A normally closed meeting of a political or legislative group to select candidates, plan strategy, or make decisions regarding legislative matters.

[19]For a historically grounded analysis of the development of political parties, as well as a treatment of their general contemporary significance, see John Aldrich, *Why Parties?* (Chicago: University of Chicago Press, 1995). For an analysis of the parties in the legislative process, see Gary Cox and Mathew McCubbins, *Legislative Leviathan* (Berkeley, CA: University of California Press, 1993).

Speaker of the House The chief presiding officer of the House of Representatives. The Speaker is elected at the beginning of every Congress on a straight party vote. The Speaker is the most important party and House leader, and can influence the legislative agenda, the fate of individual pieces of legislation, and members' positions within the House.

majority leader The elected leader of the party holding a majority of the seats in the House of Representatives or in the Senate. In the House, the majority leader is subordinate in the party hierarchy to the Speaker.

minority leader The elected leader of the party holding less than a majority of the seats in the House or Senate.

 Rationality Principle

Generally, members of Congress seek committee assignments that allow them to acquire more influence in areas important to their constituents.

the position of **Speaker of the House,** with voting along straight party lines. The House majority caucus (or conference) then also elects a **majority leader.** The minority party goes through the same process and selects the **minority leader.** Both parties also elect whips to line up party members on important votes and relay voting information to the leaders.

In December 2000, prior to the opening of the 107th Congress, Democrats and Republicans chose their leaders. In both houses, the two parties retained their established leadership groups. House Republicans, who hung on to a slim majority, re-elected Dennis Hastert of Illinois as Speaker. Dick Armey of Texas was re-elected majority leader, and Tom DeLay, also of Texas, we re-elected majority whip. On the Democratic side, Dick Gephardt of Missouri won re-election as minority leader, and David Bonior of Michigan was renamed minority whip.

Next in order of importance come the caucus (Democrats) or conference (Republicans) chairs, followed by the Committee on Committees (called the Steering and Policy Committee by the Democrats), whose tasks are to assign new legislators to committees and to deal with the requests of incumbent members for transfers from one committee to another. The Speaker serves as chair of the Republican Committee on Committees, while the minority leader chairs the Democratic Steering and Policy Committee. (The Republicans have a separate Policy Committee.) At one time, party leaders strictly controlled committee assignments, using them to enforce party discipline. Today, representatives expect to receive the assignments they want and resent leadership efforts to control committee assignments. For example, during the 104th Congress (1995–1996) the then-Chairman of the powerful Appropriations Committee, Robert Livingston (R-La.), sought to remove freshman Mark Neumann (R-Wisc.) from the committee because of his lack of party loyalty. The entire Republican freshman class angrily opposed this move and forced the leadership to back down. Not only did Neumann keep his seat on the Appropriations Committee, but he was given a seat on the Budget Committee as well, to placate the freshmen.[20] The leadership's best opportunities to use committee assignments as rewards and punishments come when a seat on the same committee is sought by more than one member.

Generally, representatives seek assignments that will allow them to influence decisions of special importance to their districts. Representatives from farm districts, for example, may request seats on the Agriculture Committee.[21] This is one method by which the egalitarian allocation of power in the legislature is overcome. Even though each legislator has just one vote in the full chamber on each and every issue, he or she, by serving on the right committees, is nevertheless able to acquire more influence in areas important to constituents. Seats on

---

[20]Linda Killian, *The Freshman: What Happened to the Republican Revolution* (Boulder, CO: Westview, 1998).

[21]Fenno, Jr., *Home Style: House Members in Their Districts.* For an extensive discussion of the committee assignment process in the U.S. House, see Kenneth A. Shepsle, *The Giant Jigsaw Puzzle: Democratic Committee Assignments in the Modern House* (Chicago: University of Chicago Press, 1978).

FIGURE 5.2

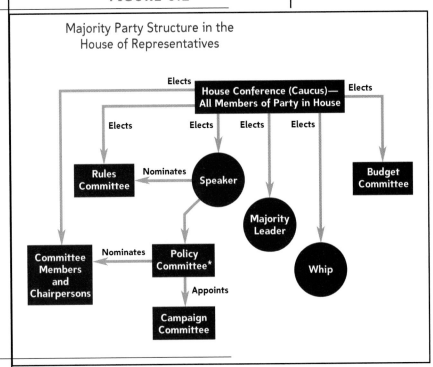

Majority Party Structure in the
House of Representatives

*Includes Speaker (chair), majority leader, chief and deputy whips, caucus chair, four mem-
bers appointed by the Speaker, and twelve members elected by regional caucuses.

powerful committees such as Ways and Means, which is responsible for tax legislation, and Appropriations are especially popular.

Within the Senate, the president pro tempore exercises mainly ceremonial
leadership. Usually, the majority party designates the member with the greatest
seniority to serve in this capacity. Real power is in the hands of the majority
leader and minority leader, each elected by party caucus. The majority and minority leaders, together, control the Senate's calendar, or agenda for legislation. In
addition, the senators from each party elect a whip. Each party also selects a
Policy Committee, which advises the leadership on legislative priorities. The structure of majority party leadership in the House and Senate is shown in Figures 5.2
and 5.3.

The structure of power and responsibility in the Senate became somewhat
muddled as a result of the 2000 elections which produced an evenly divided
Senate—fifty Republicans and fifty Democrats. With Republican vice president
Dick Cheney casting tie-breaking votes, the GOP would just barely control the

FIGURE 5.3

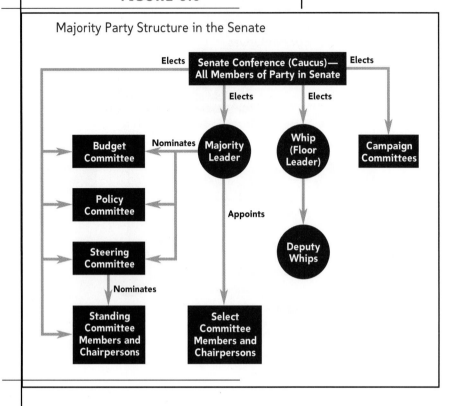

Majority Party Structure in the Senate

upper chamber. Republican majority leader Trent Lott of Mississippi was re-elected along with his counterpart, Democratic minority leader Tom Daschle of South Dakota.

In May 2001, nearly six months after the November elections seemed to have determined which party would control the Senate, the GOP suddenly lost its narrow hold on power in the upper chamber. Moderate Republican senator James Jeffords of Vermont unexpectedly announced that he was leaving the Republican party to become an independent. Jeffords, who had been unhappy with President Bush's tax program and other Republican initiatives, expressed displeasure with the GOP's conservative leadership and said he could no longer maintain his Republican allegiance. Jeffords's decision meant that the Democrats would now hold a one-vote Senate majority, giving them control of the chamber and its committees and subcommittees. In June 2001, Tom Daschle was elected Senate majority leader while senior Democrats succeeded to the chairmanships of all Senate committees.

In recent years, party leaders have sought to augment their formal powers by reaching outside Congress for resources that might enhance their influence within Congress. One aspect of this external strategy is the increased use of national communications media, including televised speeches and talk show appearances by party leaders. Former Republican House Speaker Newt Gingrich, for example, used television extensively to generate support for his programs among Republican loyalists.[22] As long as it lasted, Gingrich's support among the Republican rank-and-file gave him an added measure of influence over Republican members of Congress.

A second external strategy involves fund-raising. In recent years, congressional leaders have frequently established their own political action committees. Interest groups are usually eager to contribute to these "leadership PACs" to curry favor with powerful members of Congress. The leaders, in turn, use these funds to support the various campaigns of their party's candidates in order to create a sense of obligation. For example, in the 1998 congressional election, House majority leader Dick Armey, who was running unopposed, raised more than $6 million, which he distributed to less well-heeled Republican candidates. Armey's generosity served him well in the leadership struggle that erupted after the election.

In addition to the tasks of organizing Congress, congressional party leaders may also seek to set the legislative agenda. Since the New Deal, presidents have taken the lead in creating legislative agendas (this trend will be discussed in the next chapter). But in recent years congressional leaders, especially when facing a White House controlled by the opposing party, have attempted to devise their own agendas. Democratic leaders of Congress sought to create a common Democratic perspective in 1981 when Ronald Reagan became president. The Republican Congress elected in 1994 expanded on this idea with its "Contract with America." In both cases, the majority party leadership has sought to create a consensus among its congressional members around an overall vision to guide legislative activity and to make individual pieces of legislation part of a bigger picture that is distinct from the agenda of the president. Not only do party leaders have considerable sway over Congress's agenda "in the large," but also they regulate the fine-grained deliberation over specific items on the agenda. This aspect of agenda setting is multifaceted. For example, at the outset, when a bill is initially "dropped in the hopper" as a legislative proposal, the Speaker of the House determines which committee has jurisdiction over the proposal. Indeed, since the mid-1970s, the Speaker has been given additional bill-assignment powers, known as *multiple referral*, permitting him to assign different parts of a bill to different committees, or to assign the same parts sequentially or simultaneously to several committees. We have hinted at the steering and agenda setting by party leaders. They work, however, within an institutional framework

Institution Principle
Party leaders have considerable agenda-setting powers.

---

[22]Douglas Harris, *The Public Speaker* (Ph.D. diss., Johns Hopkins University, 1998).

consisting of structures and procedures. Let's now turn to this "backbone" of Congress, the committee system, and the party leadership's role in guiding it.

The Committee System: The Core of Congress

If the system of leadership in each party and chamber constitutes the first set of organizational arrangements in the U.S. Congress, then the committee system provides it with a second set of organizational structures. But these are more a division- and specialization-of-labor system rather than the hierarchy-of-power system that determines leadership arrangements.

Congress began as a relatively unspecialized assembly, with each legislator participating equally in each and every step of the legislative process in all realms of policy. By the time of the War of 1812, if not earlier, Congress began employing a system of specialists, the committee system, as members with different interests and talents wished to play disproportionate roles in some areas of policy making while ceding influence in other areas in which they were less interested.[23]

The congressional committee system consists of a set of standing committees, each with its own jurisdiction, membership, and authority to act. Each **standing committee** is given a permanent status by the official rules, with a fixed membership, officers, rules, staff, offices, and, above all, a jurisdiction that is recognized by all other committees and usually the leadership as well (see Table 5.2). The jurisdiction of each standing committee is defined by the subject matter of legislation. Except for the House Rules Committee, all the important committees receive proposals for legislation and process them into official bills. The House Rules Committee decides the order in which bills come up for a vote and determines the specific rules that govern the length of debate and opportunity for amendments. Standing committees' jurisdictions usually parallel those of the major departments or agencies in the executive branch. There are important exceptions—Appropriations (House and Senate) and Rules (House), for example—but by and large, the division of labor is self-consciously designed to parallel executive branch organization.

standing committee
A permanent legislative committee that considers legislation within its designated subject area; the basic unit of deliberation in the House and Senate.

Institution Principle

The committee system is a means of dividing labor and allowing members of Congress to specialize in certain policy areas.

Jurisdiction   Congress is organized into specialized jurisdictions. The world of policy is partitioned into policy jurisdictions which become the responsibility of committees. The members of the Committee on Armed Services, for example, become specialists in all aspects of military affairs, the subject matter defining their committee's jurisdiction. Committee members tend to have disproportionate influence in their respective jurisdictions, not only because they have become the most knowledgeable members of the legislature in that area of policy, but

---

[23]The story of the evolution of the standing committee system in the House and Senate in the early part of the nineteenth century is told in Gerald Gamm and Kenneth A. Shepsle, "Emergence of Legislative Institutions: Standing Committees in the House and Senate, 1810–1825," *Legislative Studies Quarterly* 14 (1989): 39–66.

TABLE 5.2

Permanent Committees of Congress

HOUSE COMMITTEES

Agriculture	Judiciary
Appropriations	Resources
Armed Services	Rules
Budget	Science
Education and the Workforce	Small Business
Energy and Commerce	Standards of Official Conduct
Financial Services	Transportation and Infrastructure
Government Reform	Veterans Affairs
House Administration	Ways and Means
International Relations	

SENATE COMMITTEES

Agriculture, Nutrition, and Forestry	Finance
Appropriations	Foreign Relations
Armed Services	Governmental Affairs
Banking, Housing, and Urban Affairs	Health, Education, Labor, and Pensions
Budget	Judiciary
Commerce, Science, and Transportation	Rules and Administration
Energy and Natural Resources	Small Business and Entrepreneurship
Environment and Public Works	Veterans Affairs

also because they are given the opportunity to exercise various forms of agenda power—a subject we will develop further in the next section.

Dividing up institutional activities among jurisdictions, thus encouraging participants to specialize, has its advantages. But it has costs, too. If the Armed Services Committee of the House of Representatives had no restraints, its members would undoubtedly shower their own districts with military facilities and contracts. In short, the delegation of authority and resources to specialist subunits exploits the advantages of the division and specialization of labor, but risks jeopardizing collective objectives of the group as a whole.

The monitoring of subunit activities, thus, goes hand in hand with delegation. A political majority either of the full chamber, or of the majority party in a chamber, can control the assignment of members to committees, the assignment of policy areas to a committee's jurisdiction, and the final disposition of any legislation the committee approves, thereby keeping committees from pursuing a private agenda at the expense of the larger institution.

Sometimes, however, new issues arise that often fit neatly into no jurisdiction. Some, like the issue of energy supplies that emerged during the 1970s, are so multifaceted that bits and pieces of them are spread across many committee jurisdictions. Thus, the Energy and Commerce Committee of the U.S. House of Representatives had jurisdiction over the regulation of energy prices, the Armed Services Committee dealt with military implications, the Ways and Means Committee dealt with tax-related energy aspects, the Science and Technology Committee claimed jurisdiction over energy research, the Agriculture Committee dealt with grain-to-energy conversion matters, and several other committees picked off still other pieces of this hydra-headed issue. Other issues, like that of regulating tobacco products, fall in the gray area claimed by several different committees—in this case the Energy and Commerce Committee, with its traditional claim over health-related issues, fought with the Agriculture Committee, whose traditional domain includes crops like tobacco, for jurisdiction over this issue. Turf battles between committees of the U.S. Congress are notorious.[24] These battles, often extending over many years, involve committee chairs, the Parliamentarian's Office, the political leadership of the chamber, and, from time to time, select committees appointed to realign committee jurisdictions. All in all, jurisdictional conflict is the raw stuff of politics since, as we shall see, committees with jurisdiction over issues have significant leverage over their resolution.

Authority Committees may be thought of as *agents* of the parent body to whom jurisdiction-specific authority is provisionally delegated. Of what does this delegation consist? In this section, we describe committee authority in terms of gatekeeping and after-the-fact authority.

Normally, any member of the legislature can submit a bill calling for changes in some policy area. Almost automatically, this bill is assigned to the committee of jurisdiction and, very nearly always, there it languishes. In a typical year in the House of Representatives, nearly 15,000 bills are submitted, fewer than 1,000 of which are acted on by the appropriate committee of jurisdiction. In effect, then, while any member is entitled to make proposals, committees get to

[24]An outstanding description and analysis of these battle is found in David C. King, "The Nature of Congressional Committee Jurisdictions," *American Political Science Review* 88 (1994): 48-63. See also his *Turf Wars: How Congressional Committees Claim Jurisdiction* (Chicago: University of Chicago Press, 1997).

decide whether or not to open the gates and allow the bill to be voted on by the full chamber. Related to **gatekeeping authority** is a committee's **proposal power.** After a bill is referred to a committee, the committee may amend the legislation in any way or even write its own legislation before bringing the bill to a vote on the floor. Committees, then, are lords of their jurisdictional domains, setting the table, so to speak, for their parent chamber.[25]

A committee also has responsibilities for bargaining with the other chamber and for conducting oversight or **after-the-fact authority.** Because many legislatures are bicameral—the U.S. Congress, for instance, has a House and a Senate—once one chamber passes a bill, it must be transmitted for consideration to the other chamber. If the other chamber passes a bill different from the one passed in the first chamber, and the first chamber refuses to accept the changes made, then the two chambers ordinarily meet in a **conference committee** in which representatives from each chamber hammer out a compromise. In the wide majority of cases, conferees are drawn from the committees that had original jurisdiction over the bill. For example, in a sample of Congresses in the 1980s, of the 1,388 House members who served as conferees for various bills during a three-year period, only 7 were not on the committee of original jurisdiction; similarly, in the Senate on only 7 of 1,180 occasions were conferees not drawn from the "right" committee.[26] The committee's effective authority to represent its chamber in conference committee proceedings constitutes after-the-fact power that complements its before-the-fact gatekeeping and proposal powers.

A second manifestation of after-the-fact committee authority consists of the committee's primacy in legislative **oversight** of policy implementation by the executive bureaucracy. Even after a bill becomes a law, it is not always (indeed, it is rarely) self-implementing. Executive agents—bureaucrats in the career civil service, commissioners in regulatory agencies, political appointees in the executive branch—march to their own drummers. Unless legislative actors hold their feet to the fire, they may not do precisely what the law requires (especially in light of the fact that statutes are often vague and ambiguous). Given this possibility, the Legislative Reorganization Act of 1946, a law that reformed and redefined how the House and Senate have conducted their business through most of the postwar period, instructed congressional committees to be "continuously watchful" of the manner in which legislation is implemented and administered. Committees of jurisdiction play this after-the-fact

gatekeeping authority The right and power to decide if a change in policy will be considered.

proposal power The capacity to bring a proposal to the full legislature.

after-the-fact authority Authority to follow up on the fate of a proposal once it has been approved by the full chamber.

 Institution Principle

Among the powers delegated to committees are gatekeeping authority, bargaining with the other chamber, and oversight.

conference committee A joint committee created to work out a compromise for House and Senate versions of a piece of legislation.

oversight The effort by Congress, through hearings, investigations, and other techniques, to exercise control over the activities of executive agencies.

[25]This clearly gives committee members extraordinary power in their respective jurisdictions, allowing them to push policy into line with their own preferences. But only up to a point. If the abuse of their agenda power becomes excessive, the parent body has structural and procedural remedies available to counteract this—like stacking the committee with more compliant members, deposing a particularly obstreperous committee chair, or removing policies from a committee's jurisdiction. These are the "clubs behind the door" that only rarely have to be employed; their mere presence suffices to keep committees from the more outrageous forms of advantage-taking.

[26]See Kenneth A. Shepsle and Barry R. Weingast, "The Institutional Foundations of Committee Power," *American Political Science Review* 81 (1987), pp. 85–104.

role by allocating committee staff and resources to keep track of what the executive branch is doing and, from time to time, holding oversight hearings in which particular policies and programs are given intense scrutiny. Anticipating this surveillance, and knowing what grief a congressional committee can cause an executive branch agent found deviating from what legislators want, these officials are very keen to keep their congressional "masters" content. This, in turn, gives congressional committees an additional source of leverage over policy in their jurisdictions.

Subcommittees   Committees, in effect, are legislatures writ small; they have the corresponding motive to divide business and specialize labor. Thus, the roughly twenty standing committees of the U.S. House are, in turn, divided into about a hundred, even more specialized *subcommittees*. With so many of the Montana congressman's constituents involved in growing wheat, for example, he could best serve them—and best position himself to secure their votes in the next election—if he were not only a member of the Agriculture Committee, but also on its Subcommittee on Feedgrains. These subcommittees serve their full committees in precisely the same manner the full committees serve the parent chamber. Thus, in their narrow jurisdictions, they have gatekeeping, proposal, interchamber bargaining, and oversight powers. In order for a bill on wheat to be taken up by the full Agriculture Committee, it first has to clear the Feedgrains Subcommittee. All of the issues involving assignments, jurisdictions, amendment control, and monitoring that we discussed earlier regarding full committees apply at the subcommittee level as well.

Hierarchy   At the committee level, the mantle of leadership falls on the committee chair. He or she determines, together with party leaders, the committee's agenda and then orchestrates the proceedings of the committee's staff, investigatory resources, and subcommittee structure.[27] This includes scheduling hearings, marking up bills—that is, transforming legislative drafts into final versions—and scripting the process by which a bill goes from introduction to final passage. For many years, the Congress followed a rigid *seniority* rule for the selection of these chairs. Accordingly, a person was elevated to the chair if he or she had the longest continuous service on the committee. The benefits of this rule are twofold. First, the chair will be occupied by someone knowledgeable in the committee's jurisdiction, familiar with interest group and executive branch players, and politically experienced. Second, the larger institution will be spared divisive leadership contests that often reduce the legislative process to efforts in vote-grubbing by contenders. There are costs, however. Senior individuals may well be knowledgeable, familiar, and experienced, as suggested above; but they also may be unenergetic, out of touch, even senile. Even when these liabilities do not appear, senior members may nevertheless be out of step with their

seniority Priority or status ranking given to an individual on the basis of length of continuous sevice on a congressional committee.

---

[27]Subcommittee chairs do essentially the same things in their narrower jurisdictions, so we won't provide a separate discussion of them.

committee and the parent chamber. Despite the fact that, from the time of the 1965 Voting Rights Act to the Republican Revolution of 1994, old-fashioned southern conservatives have been a declining force within the Democratic party, those that remained benefited from a seniority system that elevated them to chairmanships. It was thus not at all unusual for a committee consisting chiefly of northern and "New South" Democrats to be run by a southerner who had been around for thirty years.

Different legislatures make the trade-off differently between seniority-rule automatic elevation, with its profile of benefits and costs, and leadership election, the main alternative to seniority. The U.S. House operated according to a strict seniority principle from about 1910 until the mid-1970s, when most members felt the burdens of this arrangement were beginning to outweigh its advantages.[28] Committee chairs are now elected by the majority-party members of the full legislature, though there remains a presumption (which may be rebutted of course) that the most senior committee member will normally assume the chair.

Monitoring Committees If unchecked, committees could easily take advantage of their authority. Indeed, what prevents committees from exploiting their before-the-fact proposal power and their after-the-fact bargaining and oversight authority? As we saw in Chapter 1 in our discussion of the principal-agent problem, principals must be certain that agents are *properly motivated* to serve the principal's interests, either by actually sharing the principal's interest themselves, or by deriving something of value (reputation, compensation, etc.) for acting to advance that interest. Alternatively, the principal will need to have some instruments by which to monitor and validate what his or her agent is doing, and rewarding or punishing the agent accordingly.

Consider again the example of congressional committees. The House or Senate delegates responsibility to its Committee on Agriculture to recommend legislative policy in the field of agriculture. Not surprisingly, legislators from farm districts are most eager to get onto this committee and, for the most part, their wishes are accommodated. The Committee on Agriculture, consequently, is composed mainly of these farm legislators. And non-farm legislators are relieved at not having to spend their time on issues of little material interest to themselves or their constituents. In effecting this delegation, however, the parent legislature is putting itself in the hands of its farm colleagues, benefiting from their expertise on farm-related matters, to be sure, but laying itself open to the danger of planting the fox squarely in the henhouse. The Committee on Agriculture will have become not only a collection of specialists but also a collection of *advocates* for farm interests. How can the parent body know for certain that a recommendation from that committee is not more a reflection of its

[28]In 1972, the Democratic Caucus approved caucus-wide election of committee chairs, though it was assumed at the time that no incumbent, previously elevated to a chair because of seniority, would lose his or her chairmanship. This in fact occurred though John McMillan (D-S.C.), chair of the District of Columbia Committee, attracted considerable opposition. After the 1974 elections, on the other hand, three committee chairs were defeated (and a fourth resigned to avoid defeat).

advocacy than of its expertise? This is the risk inherent in principal-agent relationships.

And it is for this reason that the parent legislature maintains a variety of tools and instruments to protect itself from being exploited by its agents. First, it does not allow committees to make final decisions on agriculture policy, but only *recommendations*, which the parent legislature retains the authority to accept, amend, or reject. A committee has agenda power, but it is not by itself decisive. Second, the parent body relies on the committee's concern for its own reputation. Making a recommendation on a piece of legislation is not a one-shot action; the committee knows it will return to the parent body time and time again with legislative recommendations, and it will not want to tarnish its reputation for expertise by too much advocacy. Third, the parent body relies on *competing* agents—interest groups, expert members not on the committee, legislative specialists in the other chamber of the legislature, executive branch specialists, and even academics—to keep its own agents honest. In sum, a principal—in this case the House or Senate—will balance the benefits of delegation against the risks, utilizing specialized agents and delegating authority to them, but doing so prudently.

Institution Principle

The House and Senate have methods of keeping committees in check.

agency loss The difference between what a principal would like an agent to do and the agent's actual performance.

Nevertheless, a principal will not bother to eliminate *entirely* these prospective deviations from his or her interests by agents who have interests of their own. A principal will suffer some ***agency loss*** from having delegated authority to a "hired hand"; therefore, nearly all principal-agent relationships will be imperfect in some respects from the principal's perspective. Agents will be in a position to extract some advantage from the privileged relationship they have with their principal—not too much or it will undermine the relationship altogether, but enough to diminish the benefits of the relationship a bit from the principal's point of view. The Committee on Agriculture, for example, cannot get away with spending huge proportions of the federal budget on agricultural subsidies to farmers. But they can insert small things into agriculture bills from time to time—an experimental grain-to-fuel conversion project in an important legislator's state or district, for example, or special funds to the U.S. trade representative to give priority to agriculture trade issues.

While the parent body, as we suggested, will find it worth its while to keep an eye on the Agriculture Committee in order to guard against egregious behavior, it won't be worth its while to take action on every single instance of indulgence by the Committee. The reason is *transaction costs* (see Chapter 1). If the cure for agency loss is worse than the disease, then some agency loss will be tolerated. The great advantage to legislators of delegating authority for making recommendations on agriculture policy to specialist legislators interested in this subject is the freedom the delegating legislators win to pursue their own interests. They certainly don't want to spend much of their newly found time and freed-up resources watching over the shoulders of their experts. The cost of doing that—the transaction cost of monitoring and oversight—gets excessive if perfection is the objective. Imperfect principal-agent relationships survive and prosper from a pragmatic willingness that "the best not be the enemy of the good."

Committee Reform Over the years, Congress has reformed its organizational structure and operating procedures. Most changes have been made to improve efficiency, but some reforms have also represented a response to political considerations. In the 1970s, for example, a series of reforms substantially altered the organization of power in Congress. Among the most important changes put into place at that time were an increase in the number of subcommittees; greater autonomy for subcommittee chairs; the opening of most committee deliberations to the public; and a system of multiple referral of bills, which allowed several committees to consider one bill at the same time. One of the driving impulses behind these reforms was an effort to reduce the power of committee chairs. In the past, committee chairs exercised considerable power; they determined hearing schedules, selected subcommittee members, and appointed committee staff. Some chairs used their power to block consideration of bills they opposed. Because of the seniority system, many of the key committees, as we saw earlier, were chaired by conservative southern Democrats who stymied liberal legislation throughout the 1960s and early 1970s. By enhancing subcommittee power and allowing more members to chair subcommittees and appoint subcommittee staff, the reforms undercut the power of committee chairs.

Yet the reforms of the 1970s created unintended consequences for Congress. One of these reforms, the opening of most committee hearings to the public—sometimes called a "sunshine" rule—is frequently criticized by members of Congress. Most members believe that "sunshine" makes deliberation difficult—because members "grandstand" for the TV camera—and renders compromise impossible because rival constituency groups often view any compromise as a betrayal of principle.[29] As a consequence of the reforms, power became more fragmented, making it harder to reach agreement on legislation. With power dissipated over a large number of committees and subcommittees, members spent more time in unproductive "turf battles."[30] In addition, as committees expanded in size, members found they had so many committee meetings that they had to run from meeting to meeting. Thus their ability to specialize in a particular policy area diminished as their responsibilities increased.[31] The Republican leadership of the 104th Congress sought to reverse the fragmentation of congressional power and concentrate more authority in the party leadership. One of the ways the House achieved this was by abandoning the principle of seniority in the selection of a number of committee chairs, appointing them instead according to their loyalty to the party. This move tied committee chairs more closely to the leadership. In addition, the Republican leadership eliminated 25 of the House's

[29]See, for example, Dale Bumpers, "How the Sunshine Harmed Congress," *New York Times*, 3 January 1999, p. 9.

[30]See David C. King, *Turf Wars.*

[31]See Thomas E. Mann and Norman J. Ornstein, *Renewing Congress: A First Report of the Renewing Congress Project* (Washington, DC: American Enterprise Institute and Brookings Institution, 1992). See also the essays in Roger H. Davidson, ed., *The Postreform Congress* (New York: St. Martin's, 1992).

115 subcommittees and gave committee chairs more power over their subcommittees. The result was an unusually cohesive congressional majority, which pushed forward a common agenda. In 1995, House Republicans also agreed to impose a three-term limit on committee and subcommittee heads. As a result, all the chairmen were replaced in 2001 when the 107th Congress convened. In many instances, chairmen were replaced by the most senior Republican committee member, but the net result was some redistribution of power in the House of Representatives.

The Staff System: Staffers and Agencies

A congressional institution second in importance only to the committee system is the staff system. Every member of Congress employs a large number of staff members, whose tasks include handling constituency requests and, to a large and growing extent, dealing with legislative details and the activities of administrative agencies. Increasingly, staffers bear the primary responsibility for formulating and drafting proposals, organizing hearings, dealing with administrative agencies, and negotiating with lobbyists. Indeed, legislators typically deal with one another through staff, rather than through direct, personal contact. Representatives and senators together employ nearly eleven thousand staffers in their Washington and home offices. Today, staffers even develop policy ideas, draft legislation, and in some instances, have a good deal of influence over the legislative process.

In addition to the personal staffs of individual senators and representatives, Congress also employs roughly two thousand committee staffers. These individuals comprise the permanent staff, who stay regardless of turnover in Congress and are attached to every House and Senate committee. They are responsible for organizing and administering the committee's work, including research, scheduling, organizing hearings, and drafting legislation. Congressional staffers can come to play key roles in the legislative process. One example of the importance of congressional staffers is the so-called Gephardt health care reform bill, named for the then-House majority leader Richard Gephardt of Missouri, and introduced in August 1994. Though the bill bore Gephardt's name, it was actually crafted by a small group of staff members of the House Ways and Means Committee. These aides, under the direction of David Abernathy, the staff's leading health care specialist, debated methods of cost control, service delivery, the role of the insurance industry, and the needs of patients, and listened to hundreds of lobbyists before drafting the complex Gephardt bill.[32]

The number of congressional staff members grew rapidly during the 1960s and 1970s, leveled off in the 1980s, and decreased dramatically in 1995. This sudden drop fulfilled the Republican congressional candidates' 1994 campaign promise to reduce the size of committee staffs.

[32]Robert Pear, "With Long Hours and Little Fanfare, Staff Members Crafted a Health Bill," *New York Times*, 6 August 1994, p. 7.

Not only does Congress employ personal and committee staff, but it has also established three ***staff agencies*** designed to provide the legislative branch with resources and expertise independent of the executive branch. These agencies enhance Congress's capacity to oversee administrative agencies and to evaluate presidential programs and proposals. They are the Congressional Research Service, which performs research for legislators who wish to know the facts and competing arguments relevant to policy proposals or other legislative business; the General Accounting Office, through which Congress can investigate the financial and administrative affairs of any government agency or program; and the Congressional Budget Office, which assesses the economic implications and likely costs of proposed federal programs, such as health care reform proposals.

staff agency An agency responsible for providing Congress with independent expertise, administration, and oversight capability.

Informal Organization: The Caucuses

In addition to the official organization of Congress, there also exists an unofficial organizational structure—the caucuses, formally known as legislative service organizations (LSOs). ***Caucuses*** are groups of senators or representatives who share certain opinions, interests, or social characteristics. They include ideological caucuses such as the liberal Democratic Study Group, the conservative Democratic Forum (popularly known as the "boll weevils"), and the moderate Republican Wednesday Group. At the same time, there are a large number of caucuses composed of legislators representing particular economic or policy interests, such as the Travel and Tourism Caucus, the Steel Caucus, the Mushroom Caucus, and the Concerned Senators for the Arts. Legislators who share common backgrounds or social characteristics have organized caucuses such as the Congressional Black Caucus, the Congressional Caucus for Women's Issues, and the Hispanic Caucus. All these caucuses seek to advance the interests of the groups they represent by promoting legislation, encouraging Congress to hold hearings, and pressing administrative agencies for favorable treatment. The Congressional Black Caucus, for example, which included forty representatives and one senator in 1996, has played an active role in Congress since 1970.

caucus An association of members of Congress based on party, interest, or social group such as gender or race.

Before 1995, many of the largest and most effective caucuses were registered as Legislative Service Organizations (LSOs). LSOs were allotted office space in congressional buildings and congressional members were allowed to transfer some of their own budgets to the LSO. Several of the most effective LSOs, including the Black Caucus, the Hispanic Caucus, and the Women's Caucus, were closely tied to the Democratic party. One LSO, the Democratic Study Group, once employed eighteen full-time analysts to help congressional Democrats evaluate proposed and pending legislation. The Republican leadership of the 104th Congress (1995–1996) took away the budgets, staff, and offices of all LSOs, in part because of these large LSOs' links to the Democrats.[33] But most caucuses continued their activities, and new ones were created after this change. Of

[33]Kenneth Cooper, "GOP Moves to Restrict Office Funds," *Washington Post*, 7 December 1994, p. 1.

course, some of the larger caucuses found it harder to coordinate their activities and provide information to their members after they lost their status as LSOs, but caucuses continue to be an important part of congressional organization.[34]

RULES OF LAWMAKING: HOW A BILL BECOMES A LAW

The institutional structure of Congress is one key factor that helps to shape the legislative process. A second and equally important set of factors are the rules of congressional procedures. These rules govern everything from the introduction of a bill through its submission to the president for signing. Not only do these regulations influence the fate of each and every bill, they also help to determine the distribution of power in the Congress.

Committee Deliberation

Even if a member of Congress, the White House, or a federal agency has spent months developing and drafting a piece of legislation, it does not become a bill until it is submitted officially by a senator or representative to the clerk of the House or Senate and referred to the appropriate committee for deliberation. No floor action on any bill can take place until the committee with jurisdiction over it has taken all the time it needs to deliberate. During the course of its deliberations, the committee typically refers the bill to one of its subcommittees, which may hold hearings, listen to expert testimony, and amend the proposed legislation before referring it to the full committee for its consideration. The full committee may accept the recommendation of the subcommittee or hold its own hearings and prepare its own amendments. Or, even more frequently, the committee and subcommittee may do little or nothing with a bill that has been submitted to them. Many bills are simply allowed to "die in committee" with little or no serious consideration given to them. Often, members of Congress introduce legislation that they neither expect nor desire to see enacted into law, merely to please a constituency group. This is what the political scientist David Mayhew refers to as "position taking."[35] These bills die a quick and painless death. Other pieces of legislation have ardent supporters and die in committee only after a long battle. But, in either case, most bills are never reported out of the committees to which they are assigned. In a typical congressional session, 95 percent of the roughly eight thousand bills introduced die in committee—an indication of the power of the congressional committee system.

---

[34]Susan Webb Hammond, "Congressional Caucuses in the 104th Congress," in *Congress Reconsidered*, 6th ed., ed. Lawrence C. Dodd and Bruce I. Oppenheimer (Washington, DC: Congressional Quarterly Press, 1997).

[35]David R. Mayhew, *Congress: The Electoral Connection* (New Haven: Yale University Press, 1974).

Once the bill's assigned committee or committees in the House of Representatives have acted affirmatively, the whole bill or various parts of it are transmitted to the Rules Committee, which determines the specific rules under which the legislation will be considered by the full House. Here the Speaker influences when debate will be scheduled, for how long, what amendments will be in order, and in what order they will be considered. The Speaker also rules on all procedural points of order and points of information raised during the debate. A bill's supporters generally prefer what is called a ***closed rule,*** which puts severe limits on floor debate and amendments. Opponents of a bill usually prefer an "open rule," which permits potentially damaging floor debate and makes it easier to add amendments that may cripple the bill or weaken its chances for passage. Thus, the outcome of the Rules Committee's deliberations can be extremely important, and the committee's hearings can be an occasion for sharp conflicts.

closed rule Provision by the House Rules Committee prohibiting the introduction of amendments during debate.

Debate

Party control of the agenda is reinforced by the rule giving the Speaker of the House and the majority leader of the Senate the power of recognition during debate on a bill. Usually the chair knows the purpose for which a member intends to speak well in advance of the occasion. Spontaneous efforts to gain recognition are often foiled. For example, the Speaker may ask, "For what purpose does the member rise?" before deciding whether to grant recognition. In general, the party leadership in the House has total control over debate. In the Senate, each member has substantial power to block the close of debate. A House majority can override opposition, while it takes an *extraordinary* majority (a three-fifths vote) to close debate in the Senate; thus, the Senate tends to be far more tolerant in debate, far more accommodating of various views, and far less partisan.

In the House, virtually all of the time allotted by the Rules Committee for debate on a given bill is controlled by the bill's sponsor and by its leading opponent. In almost every case, these two people are the committee chair and the ranking minority member of the committee that processed the bill—or those they designate. These two participants are, by rule and tradition, granted the power to allocate most of the debate time in small amounts to members who are seeking to speak for or against the measure. Preference in the allocation of time goes to the members of the committee whose jurisdiction covers the bill.

In the Senate, other than the power of recognition, the leadership has much less control over floor debate. Indeed, the Senate is unique among the world's legislative bodies for its commitment to unlimited debate. Once given the floor, a senator may speak as long as he or she wishes. On a number of memorable occasions, senators have used this right to prevent action on legislation that they opposed. Through this tactic, called the ***filibuster,*** small minorities or even one individual in the Senate can force the majority to give in to their demands.

filibuster A tactic used by members of the Senate to prevent action on legislation they oppose by continuously holding the floor and speaking until the majority backs down. Once given the floor, senators have unlimited time to speak, and it requires a cloture vote of three-fifths of the Senate to end the filibuster.

During the 1950s and 1960s, for example, opponents of civil rights legislation often sought to block its passage by adopting the tactic of filibuster. The votes of three-fifths of the Senate, or sixty votes, are needed to end a filibuster. This procedure is called **cloture.**

Whereas the filibuster was once an extraordinary tactic used only on rare occasions, in recent years it has been used increasingly often. In 1994, the filibuster was used by Republicans and some Democrats to defeat legislation that would have prohibited employers from permanently replacing striking workers. Later, Republicans threatened to filibuster health care reform legislation. Some Democrats argued that Senate Republicans had begun to use the filibuster as a routine instrument of legislative obstructionism to make up for their minority status in Congress, and proposed rule changes that would make filibustering more difficult. One of the most senior Democrats in the Senate, however, former majority leader Robert Byrd of West Virginia, warned against limiting the filibuster, saying, "The minority can be right, and on many occasions in this country's history, the minority was right."[36] After the GOP won control of the Senate in 1994, many Democrats began to agree with Senator Byrd. Democrats employed the filibuster to block Republican initiatives on environmental and social policy. Similarly, a Republican-led filibuster in 1998 killed campaign finance reform legislation.

Although it is the best known, the filibuster is not the only technique used to block Senate debate. Under Senate rules, members have a virtually unlimited ability to propose amendments to a pending bill. Each amendment must be voted on before the bill can come to a final vote. The introduction of new amendments can only be stopped by unanimous consent. This, in effect, can permit a determined minority to filibuster-by-amendment, indefinitely delaying the passage of a bill.

In 1996, for example, an anti-stalking bill sponsored by Senator Kay Bailey Hutchison (R-Tex.) was delayed by Senator Frank Lautenberg's (D-N.J.) effort to attach an amendment prohibiting individuals convicted of domestic violence from purchasing or possessing a handgun. Lautenberg's proposal had been opposed by the powerful National Rifle Association and had little chance of reaching the floor on its own. By offering his proposal as an amendment, Lautenberg was effectively holding the popular anti-stalking bill hostage to obtain a vote on his proposal.[37]

Senators can also place "holds," or stalling devices, on bills to delay debate. Senators place holds on bills when they fear that openly opposing them will be unpopular. Because holds are kept secret, the senators placing the holds do not have to take public responsibility for their actions. For example, Senator John Chafee (R-R.I.) was widely believed to be responsible for a 1996 hold on a bill

---

[36]Richard Sammon, "Panel Backs Senate Changes, But Fights Loom for Floor," *Congressional Quarterly Weekly Report*, 18 June 1994, pp. 1575–76.

[37]Stephen Green, "Anti-Stalking Bill Falls Victim to Gun Control Politics," *San Diego Union-Tribune*, 24 July 1996, p. A2.

imposing sanctions against foreign companies that engaged in business with Iran and Libya. Chafee's office refused to confirm or deny the speculation.[38] In 1997, opponents of this practice introduced a proposal to require publicizing the name of any senator putting a bill on hold. A majority of senators, however, favored retaining the practice, and the effort was defeated.

Once a bill is debated on the floor of the House and the Senate, the leaders schedule it for a vote on the floor of each chamber. By this time, congressional leaders know what the vote will be; leaders do not bring legislation to the floor unless they are fairly certain it is going to pass. As a consequence, it is unusual for the leadership to lose a bill on the floor. On rare occasions, the last moments of the floor vote can be very dramatic, as each party's leadership puts its whip organization into action to make sure that wavering members vote with the party.

Conference Committee: Reconciling House and Senate Versions of a Bill

Getting a bill out of committee and through one of the houses of Congress is no guarantee that a bill will be enacted into law. Frequently, bills that began with similar provisions in both chambers emerge with little resemblance to each other. Alternatively, a bill may be passed by one chamber but undergo substantial revision in the other chamber. In such cases, a conference committee composed of the senior members of the committees or subcommittees that initiated the bills may be required to iron out differences between the two pieces of legislation. Sometimes members or leaders will let objectionable provisions pass on the floor with the idea that they will get the change they want in conference. Usually, conference committees meet behind closed doors. Agreement requires a majority of each of the two delegations. Legislation that emerges successfully from a conference committee is more often a compromise than a clear victory of one set of forces over another.

Collective Action Principle
If a bill passes both the House and Senate, the differences need to be ironed out in a conference committee.

When a bill comes out of conference, it faces one more hurdle. Before a bill can be sent to the president for signing, the House-Senate conference report must be approved on the floor of each chamber. Usually such approval is given quickly. Occasionally, however, a bill's opponents use the conference report as one last opportunity to defeat a piece of legislation.

Presidential Action

Once adopted by the House and Senate, a bill goes to the president, who may choose to sign the bill into law or *veto* it (see Process Box 5.2). The veto is the president's constitutional power to reject a piece of legislation. To veto a bill, the president returns it within ten days to the house of Congress in which it

veto The president's constitutional power to turn down acts of Congress. A presidential veto may be overridden by a two-thirds vote of each house of Congress.

---

[38]Kimberley Music, "Iran/Libya Bill Remains Stalled in Senate," *Oil Daily*, vol. 46, no. 131, 12 July 1996, p. 1.

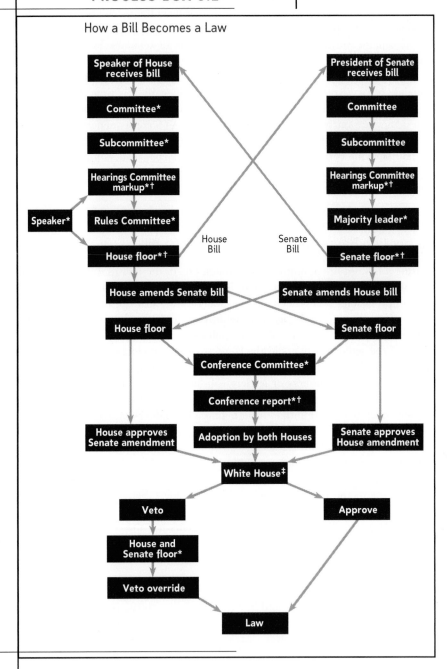

How a Bill Becomes a Law

*Points at which bill can be amended.

†Points at which bill can die.

‡If the president neither signs nor vetoes the bill within ten days, it automatically becomes law.

originated, along with his objections to the bill. If Congress adjourns during the ten-day period, and the president has taken no action, the bill is also considered to be vetoed. This latter method is known as the ***pocket veto.*** The possibility of a presidential veto affects how willing members of Congress are to push for different pieces of legislation at different times. If they think a proposal is likely to be vetoed they might shelve it for a later time. Alternatively, the sponsors of a popular bill opposed by the president might push for passage in order to force the president to pay the political costs of vetoing it.[39] For example, in 1996 and 1997, Republicans passed bills outlawing partial-birth abortions though they knew President Clinton would veto them. The GOP calculated that Clinton would be hurt politically by vetoing legislation that most Americans favored.

A presidential veto may be overridden by a two-thirds vote in both the House and Senate. A veto override says much about the support that a president can expect from Congress, and it can deliver a stinging blow to the executive branch. President George H. W. Bush used his veto power on forty-six occasions during his four years in office and, in all but one instance, was able to defeat or avoid a congressional override of his action. Bush's frequent resort to the veto power was one indicator of the struggle between the White House and the Congress over domestic and foreign policy that took place during his term. Similarly, President Clinton used the veto to block Republican programs in 1995 and 1996. For example, in May 1996, President Clinton vetoed a Republican bill that would have placed limits on the punitive damages that could be awarded in product liability suits. The bill was supported by business groups and opposed by consumer groups and trial lawyers. Republicans charged that Clinton's veto was a pay-off to the trial lawyers, who are major contributors to the Democratic party.

The president's veto power is provided in Article I, Section 7, of the Constitution. In 1996, as part of the Republicans' "Contract with America," Congress granted the president a line-item veto, which allows the president to eliminate such earmarks from bills presented to the White House for signature. Republican leaders were willing to risk giving such a powerful tool to a Democratic president because they calculated that, over the decades of Democratic congresses, the GOP had learned to live without much pork, while Democrats had become dependent upon pork to solidify their electoral support. Republican leaders also hoped that a future Republican president, wielding the line-item veto, would be able to further undermine Democratic political strength. President Clinton used the line-item veto eleven times, eliminating eighty-two individual spending items. But in 1998, the Supreme Court struck down the line-item veto on the grounds that the Constitution does not give the president the power to amend or repeal parts of statutes.[40]

pocket veto
Method by which the president vetoes a bill by taking no action on it when Congress has adjourned.

[39]John Gilmour, *Strategic Disagreement* (Pittsburgh: University of Pittsburgh Press, 1995).
[40]Clinton v. City of New York, 118 S.Ct. 2091 (1998).

The Distributive Tendency in Congress

In order to pass a policy, it is necessary to *authorize* the policy—that is, to provide statutory authority to a government agency to implement the legislation—and then to provide *appropriations* to fund the implementation. It is not too much of an exaggeration to suggest the following list of political actors whose support is necessary in order to get a measure through Congress and signed into law:

- a majority of the authorizing subcommittees in House and Senate (probably including the subcommittee chairs)
- a majority of the full authorizing committees in House and Senate (probably including committee chairs)
- a majority of the appropriations subcommittees in House and Senate (probably including the subcommittee chairs)
- a majority of the full appropriations committees in House and Senate (probably including committee chairs)
- a majority of the House Rules Committee (including its chair)
- a majority of the full House
- a majority—possibly as many as sixty votes, if needed to shut off a filibuster—of the Senate
- the Speaker and majority leader in the House
- the majority leader in the Senate
- the president

This list constitutes an extraordinarily large number of public officials. Some of them may go along without requiring much for their states or districts in the bill on the assumption that their turn will come on another bill. But most of these politicians will need some form of "compensation" to provide their endorsement and support.

With so many hurdles to clear for a legislative initiative to become a public law, the benefits must be spread quite broadly. It is as though a bill must travel on a toll road past a number of tollbooths, each one containing a collector with his or her hand out for payment. On rare occasions, the required toll is in the form of a personal bribe—a contract to a firm run by a congressman's brother, a job for a senator's son, a boondoggle "military inspection" trip to some exotic Pacific isle for a legislator and spouse. Occasionally, there is a "wink and a nod" understanding, usually given by the majority leader or committee chair, that support from a legislator today will result in reciprocal support for legislation of interest to him or her down the road. Most frequently, features of the bill are drafted initially or revised so as to be more inclusive, spreading the benefits widely among beneficiaries. This is the ***distributive tendency.***

**distributive
tendency**
Tendency of
Congress to spread
the benefits of a pol-
icy to a wide range of
members' districts.

The distributive tendency is part of the American system of representative democracy. It is as American as apple pie! Legislators, in advocating the interests of their constituents, are eager to advertise their ability to deliver for their state or district. They maneuver to put themselves in a position to claim credit for good things that happen there and to duck blame for bad things. This is the way they earn trust back home, deter strong challengers in upcoming elections, and defeat those who do run against them. This means that legislators must take advantage of every opportunity that presents itself. This system, which is practiced in Washington and most state capitals, means that political pork gets spread around; it is not controlled by a small clique of politicians or concentrated in a small number of states or districts. But it also means that public authority and appropriations are not targeted where they are most needed. The most impoverished cities do not get as much money as is appropriate, because some of the money must be diverted elsewhere to buy political support. The most needy individuals often do not get tax relief, health care, or occupational subsidies for reasons quite unrelated to philosophy or policy grounds. It is the distributive tendency at work. It is one of the unintended consequences of the separation of powers and the multiple veto.

Policy Principle

The distributive tendency in Congress results from the need for a broad base of support in order for a bill to be passed.

HOW CONGRESS DECIDES

What determines the kinds of legislation that Congress ultimately produces? According to the simplest theories of representation, members of Congress respond to the views of their constituents. In fact, the process of creating a legislative agenda, drawing up a list of possible measures, and deciding among them is a very complex process, in which a variety of influences from inside and outside government play important roles. External influences include a legislator's constituency and various interest groups. Influences from inside government include party leadership, congressional colleagues, and the president. Let us examine each of these influences individually and then consider how they interact to produce congressional policy decisions.

Policy Principle

Multiple factors influence how a member of Congress votes on legislation. These include constituency, interest groups, party leaders, congressional colleagues, and the president.

Constituency

Because members of Congress, for the most part, want to be re-elected, we would expect the views of their constituents to have a key influence on the decisions that legislators make. Yet constituency influence is not so straightforward as we might think. In fact, most constituents do not even know what policies their representatives support. The number of citizens who *do* pay attention to such matters—the attentive public—is usually very small. Nonetheless, members of Congress spend a lot of time worrying about what their constituents think, because these representatives realize that the choices they make may be scrutinized in a future election and used as ammunition by an opposing candidate. Because of this possibility, members of Congress will try to anticipate their constituents' policy views.[41] Legislators are more likely to act in accordance

[41]See John W. Kingdon, *Congressmen's Voting Decisions* (New York: Harper Row, 1973), Chapter 3; and R. Douglas Arnold, *The Logic of Congressional Action* (New Haven: Yale University Press, 1990).

with those views if they think that voters will take them into account during elections. In this way, constituents may affect congressional policy choices even when there is little direct evidence of their influence.

Interest Groups

Interest groups are another important external influence on the policies that Congress produces. When members of Congress are making voting decisions, those interest groups that have some connection to constituents in particular members' districts are most likely to be influential. For this reason, interest groups with the ability to mobilize followers in many congressional districts may be especially influential in Congress. The small-business lobby, for example, played an important role in defeating President Clinton's proposal for comprehensive health care reform in 1993–1994. The mobilization of networks of small businesses across the country meant that virtually every member of Congress had to take their views into account. In recent years, Washington-based interest groups with little grass-roots strength have recognized the importance of such locally generated activity. They have, accordingly, sought to simulate grassroots pressure, using a strategy that has been nicknamed "Astroturf lobbying." Such campaigns encourage constituents to sign form letters or postcards, which are then sent to congressional representatives. Sophisticated "grassroots" campaigns set up toll-free telephone numbers for a system in which simply reporting your name and address to the listening computer will generate a letter to your congressional representative. One Senate office estimated that such organized campaigns to demonstrate "grassroots" support account for two-thirds of the mail the office received. As such campaigns increase, however, they may become less influential, because members of Congress are aware of how rare actual constituent interest actually is.[42]

Interest groups also have substantial influence in setting the legislative agenda and in helping to craft specific language in legislation. Today, sophisticated lobbyists win influence by providing information about policies to busy members of Congress. As one lobbyist noted, "You can't get access without knowledge. . . . I can go in to see [former Energy and Commerce Committee chair] John Dingell, but if I have nothing to offer or nothing to say, he's not going to want to see me."[43] In recent years, interest groups have also begun to build broader coalitions and comprehensive campaigns around particular policy issues. These coalitions do not rise from the grassroots, but instead are put together by Washington lobbyists who launch comprehensive lobbying campaigns that combine stimulated grassroots activity with information and campaign funding for members of Congress. In recent years, the Republican leadership worked so closely with lobbyists that critics

Collective Action Principle
Interest groups with the ability to mobilize followers in many congressional districts are especially influential in Congress.

---

[42]Jane Fritsch, "The Grass Roots, Just a Free Phone Call Away," *New York Times*, 23 June 1995, p. A1.

[43]Daniel Franklin, "Tommy Boggs and the Death of Health Care Reform," *Washington Monthly*, April 1995, p. 36.

charged that the boundaries between lobbyists and legislators had been erased, and that lobbyists had become "adjunct staff to the Republican leadership."[44]

In the 2000 electoral cycle, many millions of dollars in campaign contributions were given by interest groups and political action committees (PACs) to incumbent legislators and challengers. What does this money buy? A popular conception is that campaign contributions buy votes. In this view, legislators vote for whichever proposal favors the bulk of their contributors. Although the vote-buying hypothesis makes for good campaign rhetoric, it has little factual support. Empirical studies by political scientists show little evidence that contributions from large PACs influence legislative voting patterns.[45]

If contributions don't buy votes, then what do they buy? Our claim is that campaign contributions influence legislative behavior in ways that are difficult for the public to observe and for political scientists to measure. The institutional structure of Congress provides opportunities for interest groups to influence legislation outside the public eye.

Committee proposal power enables legislators, if they are on the relevant committee, to introduce legislation that favors contributing groups. Gatekeeping power enables committee members to block legislation that harms contributing groups. The fact that certain provisions are *excluded* from a bill is as much an indicator of PAC influence as the fact that certain provisions are *included*. The difference is that it is hard to measure what you don't see. Committee oversight powers enable members to intervene in bureaucratic decision making on behalf of contributing groups. In the infamous case of Charles Keating, Jr., for example, five senators on the Senate Banking Committee used their oversight authority to induce bank regulators to ease up on their supervision of Keating's savings and loan (which ultimately failed).

The point here is that voting on the floor, the alleged object of campaign contributions according to the vote-buying hypothesis, is a highly visible, highly public act, one that could get a legislator in trouble with his or her broader electoral constituency. The committee system, on the other hand, provides loads of opportunities for legislators to deliver "services" to PAC contributors and other donors that are more subtle and disguised from broader public view. Thus, we suggest that the most appropriate places to look for traces of campaign contribution influence on the legislative process are in the manner in which committees deliberate, mark up proposals, and block legislation from the floor: outside public view, these are the primary arenas for interest group influence.

Party Discipline

In both the House and Senate, party leaders have a good deal of influence over the behavior of their party members. This influence, sometimes called "party

---

[44]Peter H. Stone, "Follow the Leaders," *National Journal*, 24 June 1995, p. 1641.

[45]See Janet M. Grenke, "PACs and the Congressional Supermarket: The Currency is Complex," *American Journal of Political Science* 33 (1989): 1–24.

party vote A
roll-call vote in the
House or Senate in
which at least 50 per-
cent of the members
of one party take a
particular position
and are opposed by
at least 50 percent of
the members of the
other party. Party
votes are rare today,
although they were
fairly common in the
nineteenth century.

roll-call vote
Vote in which each
legislator's yes or no
vote is recorded.

discipline," was once so powerful that it dominated the lawmaking process. At the turn of the century, party leaders could often command the allegiance of more than 90 percent of their members. A vote on which 50 percent or more of the members of one party take one position while at least 50 percent of the members of the other party take the opposing position is called a *party vote.* At the beginning of the twentieth century, most *roll-call votes* in the House of Representatives were party votes. Today, this type of party-line voting is less common in Congress. In the fifteen Congresses between 1887 and 1917, there were twelve Congresses in which over one in five votes had 90 percent of Republicans voting against 90 percent of Democrats. In only one Congress from 1917 to 1969 has this level of partisanship been met—the first two years of Franklin Roosevelt's New Deal. Indeed, after 1950, the level of 90 percent versus 90 percent party voting never reached 10 percent.[46]

Typically, party unity is greater in the House than in the Senate. House rules grant greater procedural control to the majority party leaders, which gives them more influence over House members. In the Senate, however, the leadership has few sanctions over its members. Senate Majority Leader Tom Daschle once observed that a Senate leader seeking to influence other senators has as incentives "a bushel full of carrots and a few twigs."[47]

Party unity increased somewhat in recent decades as a result of the intense partisan struggles that began during the Reagan and Bush years (see Figure 5.4). Straight party-line voting was seen briefly in the 103rd Congress (1993–1994) following Bill Clinton's election in 1992. The situation, however, soon gave way to the many long-term factors working against party discipline in Congress (see Figure 5.4).[48]

In 2001, newly elected president George W. Bush called for an end to partisan squabbling in Congress. During the 2000 campaign, Bush claimed that as governor of Texas he had been able to build effective bipartisan coalitions, which, he said, should serve as a model for the conduct of the nation's business, as well. September 11, 2001, prompted almost every member of Congress to rally behind President Bush's military response. But, as we read earlier, Democrats and Republicans in the House divided sharply over the issue of airport security.

To some extent, party divisions are based on ideology and background. Republican members of Congress are more likely than Democrats to be drawn from rural or suburban areas. Democrats are likely to be more liberal on economic and social questions than their Republican colleagues. These differences certainly help to explain roll-call divisions between the two parties. Ideology and background, however, are only part of the explanation of party unity. The other part has to do with party organization and leadership. Although party organization has

---

[46]See Joseph Cooper, David W. Brady, and Patricia Hurley, "The Electoral Basis of Party Voting: Patterns and Trends in the U.S. House of Representatives, 1887–1969," in *The Impact of the Electoral Process,* ed. Louis Maisel and Joseph Cooper (Beverly Hills, CA: Sage, 1977), pp. 133–65.

[47]Holly Idelson, "Signs Point to Greater Loyalty on Both Sides of the Aisle," *Congressional Quarterly Weekly Report,* 19 December 1992, p. 3849.

[48]David Broder, "Hill Democrats Vote as One: New Era of Unity or Short-term Honeymoon?" *Washington Post,* 14 March 1993, p. A1. See also Adam Clymer, "All Aboard: Clinton's Plan Gets Moving," *New York Times,* 21 March 1993, sec. 4, p. 1.

FIGURE 5.4

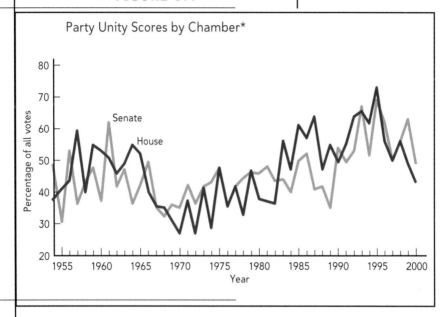

Party Unity Scores by Chamber*

*The percentage of times that members voted with the majority of their party, based on recorded votes on which a majority of one party voted against the majority of the other party.

SOURCE: Congressional Quarterly Weekly Report, 6 January 2001.

weakened since the turn of the century, today's party leaders still have some resources at their disposal: (1) committee assignments, (2) access to the floor, (3) the whip system, (4) logrolling, and (5) the presidency. These resources are regularly used and are often effective in securing the support of party members. [49]

[49]Legislative leaders may behave in ways that embellish their reputation for being willing to punish party members who stray from the party line. The problem for leaders of developing such credible reputations is analyzed in Randall Calvert, "Reputation and Legislative Leadership," *Public Choice* 55 (1987), pp. 81–120, and is summarized in Kenneth Shepsle and Mark Boncheck, *Analyzing Politics*, pp. 397–403. The classic example of such punishment occurred after the 1964 election in which two prominent House Democrats, John Bell Williams of Mississippi and Albert Watson of South Carolina, were disciplined for having supported the Republican presidential nominee, Barry Goldwater. The party leaders pushed for, and the Democratic Caucus supported, a punishment in which each was demoted to the bottom of the seniority roster on the committees of which they were members. In Williams's case, the punishment was serious, as he was the second highest ranking Democrat on the House Commerce Committee. Each resigned from the House in the wake of this punishment, and ran for elective office (both successfully) as Republicans. The message was clear: there are some partisan lines that party members cross at their peril! Put slightly differently, the famous mid-twentieth-century House Speaker, Sam Rayburn (D-Tex.), is known to have believed that deviation from the party position would be tolerated for "reasons of conscience or constituency." Of one wayward Democrat he is alleged to have said that the departure from the party line "better be a matter of conscience, because it damn sight isn't because of his constituency." In short, there would be hell to pay!

Committee Assignments Leaders can create debts among members by helping them get favorable committee assignments. These assignments are made early in the congressional careers of most members and cannot be taken from them if they later balk at party discipline. Nevertheless, if the leadership goes out of its way to get the right assignment for a member, this effort is likely to create a bond of obligation that can be called upon without any other payments or favors.

Access to the Floor The most important everyday resource available to the parties is control over access to the floor. With thousands of bills awaiting passage and most members clamoring for access in order to influence a bill or to publicize themselves, floor time is precious. In the Senate, the leadership allows ranking committee members to influence the allocation of floor time—who will speak for how long; in the House, the Speaker, as head of the majority party (in consultation with the minority leader), allocates large blocks of floor time. Thus, floor time is allocated in both houses of Congress by the majority and minority leaders. More importantly, the Speaker of the House and the majority leader in the Senate possess the power of recognition. Although this power may not appear to be substantial, it is a formidable authority and can be used to stymie a piece of legislation completely or to frustrate a member's attempts to speak on a particular issue. Because the power is significant, members of Congress usually attempt to stay on good terms with the Speaker and the majority leader in order to ensure that they will continue to be recognized.

whip system
Primarily a communications network in each house of Congress, whips take polls of the membership in order to learn their intentions on specific legislative issues and to assist the majority and minority leaders in various tasks.

 Collective Action Principle
The whip system helps maintain party unity in Congress.

The Whip System Some influence accrues to party leaders through the ***whip system***, which is primarily a communications network. Between twelve and twenty assistant and regional whips are selected by zones to operate at the direction of the majority or minority leader and the whip. They take polls of all the members in order to learn their intentions on specific bills. This enables the leaders to know if they have enough support to allow a vote, as well as whether the vote is so close that they need to put pressure on a few swing votes. Leaders also use the whip system to convey their wishes and plans to the members, but only in very close votes do they actually exert pressure on a member. In those instances, the Speaker or a lieutenant will go to a few party members who have indicated they will switch if their vote is essential. The whip system helps the leaders limit pressuring members to a few times per session.

The whip system helps maintain party unity in both houses of Congress, but it is particularly critical in the House of Representatives because of the large number of legislators whose positions and votes must always be accounted for. The majority and minority whips and their assistants must be adept at inducing compromise among legislators who hold widely differing viewpoints. The whips' personal styles and their perception of their function significantly affect the development of legislative coalitions and influence the compromises that emerge.

Logrolling An agreement between two or more members of Congress who have nothing in common except the need for support is called *logrolling.* The agreement states, in effect, "You support me on bill X and I'll support you on another bill of your choice." Since party leaders are the center of the communications networks in the two chambers, they can help members create large logrolling coalitions. Hundreds of logrolling deals are made each year, and while there are no official record-keeping books, it would be a poor party leader whose whips did not know who owed what to whom.[50] In some instances, logrolling produces strange alliances. A seemingly unlikely alliance emerged in Congress in June 1994, when 119 mainly conservative senators and representatives from oil-producing states met with President Clinton to suggest that they might be willing to support the president's health care proposals in exchange for his support for a number of tax breaks for the oil industry. Senator J. Bennett Johnson of Louisiana, a leader of the oil-state representatives, contended that the issues of health care and oil production were closely related since both "affected the longterm economic security of the nation." Ironically, the oil-producing groups that promoted this alliance are generally among the most conservative forces in the nation. When asked what he personally thought of the president's health care proposal, George Alcorn, a leading industry lobbyist involved in the logrolling effort, dismissed Clinton's plan as "socialized medicine." Another logrolling alliance of strange bedfellows was the 1994 "corn for porn" logroll, in which liberal urbanites supported farm programs in exchange for rural support for National Endowment for the Arts funding. Good logrolling, it would seem, is not hampered by minor ideological concerns.[51]

logrolling A legislative practice wherein reciprocal agreements are made between legislators, usually in voting for or against a bill. In contrast to bargaining, logrolling unites parties that have nothing in common but their desire to exchange support.

Collective Action Principle
Logrolling is an informal means of facilitating cooperation in Congress.

The Presidency Of all the influences that maintain the clarity of party lines in Congress, the influence of the presidency is probably the most important. Indeed, it is a touchstone of party discipline in Congress. Since the late 1940s, under President Truman, presidents each year have identified a number of bills to be considered part of their administration's program. By the mid-1950s, both parties in Congress began to look to the president for these proposals, which became the most significant part of Congress's agenda. The president's support is a criterion for party loyalty, and party leaders are able to use it to rally some members.

[50]For an analysis of the formal problems that logrolling (or vote trading) both solves and creates, see Shepsle and Bonchek, *Analyzing Politics*, pp. 317–19. They argue that logrolling cannot be the entire solution to the problem of assembling majority coalitions out of the diverse preferences found in any political party. The reason is that, while party leaders can try to keep track of who owes what to whom, this is imperfect and highly complex bookkeeping, at best. Nevertheless, if anyone is positioned to orchestrate a system of logrolls, it is the party leaders. And, of all those who have tried to facilitate such "cooperation," Robert Byrd of West Virginia, who served both as majority whip and majority leader in the Senate, has been the acknowledged master.

[51]Allen R. Meyerson, "Oil-Patch Congressmen Seek Deal With Clinton," *New York Times*, 14 June 1994, p. D2.

Weighing Diverse Influences

Clearly, many different factors affect congressional decisions. But at various points in the decision-making process, some factors are likely to be more influential than others. For example, interest groups may be more effective at the committee stage, when their expertise is especially valued and their visibility is less obvious. Because committees play a key role in deciding what legislation actually reaches the floor of the House or Senate, interest groups can often put a halt to bills they dislike, or they can ensure that the options that do reach the floor are those that the group's members support.

Once legislation reaches the floor, and members of Congress are deciding among alternatives, constituent opinion will become more important. Legislators are also influenced very much by other legislators: many of their assessments about the substance and politics of legislation come from fellow members of Congress.

The influence of the external and internal forces described in the preceding section also varies according to the kind of issue being considered. On policies of great importance to powerful interest groups—farm subsidies, for example—those groups are likely to have considerable influence. On other issues, members of Congress may be less attentive to narrow interest groups and more willing to consider what they see as the general interest.

Finally, the mix of influences varies according to the historical moment. The 1994 electoral victory of Republicans allowed their party to control both houses of Congress for the first time in forty years. The fact, combined with an unusually assertive Republican leadership, meant that party leaders became especially important in decision making. The willingness of moderate Republicans to support measures they had once opposed indicated the unusual importance of party leadership in this period. As House Minority Leader Richard Gephardt put it, "When you've been in the desert forty years, your instinct is to help Moses."[52]

BEYOND LEGISLATION: ADDITIONAL CONGRESSIONAL POWERS

In addition to the power to make the law, Congress has at its disposal an array of other instruments through which to influence the process of government.

Advice and Consent: Special Senate Powers

The Constitution has given the Senate a special power, one that is not based on lawmaking. The president has the power to make treaties and to appoint top

---

[52]David Broder, "At 6 Months, House GOP Juggernaut Still Cohesive," *Washington Post*, 17 July 1995, p. A1.

executive officers, ambassadors, and federal judges—but only "with the Advice and Consent of the Senate" (Article II, Section 2). For treaties, two-thirds of those present must concur; for appointments, a majority is required.

The power to approve or reject presidential requests also involves the power to set conditions. The Senate only occasionally exercises its power to reject treaties and appointments, and usually that is when opposite parties control the Senate and the White House. During the final two years of President Reagan's term, Senate Democrats rejected Judge Robert Bork's Supreme Court nomination and gave clear indications that they would reject a second Reagan nominee, Judge Douglas Ginsburg, who withdrew his nomination before the Senate could act. These instances, however, actually underscore the restraint with which the Senate usually uses its power to reject presidential requests. For example, only nine judicial nominees have been rejected by the Senate during the past century, while hundreds have been approved.

More common than Senate rejection of presidential appointees is a senatorial "hold" on an appointment. By Senate tradition, any member may place an indefinite hold on the confirmation of a mid- or lower-level presidential appointment. The hold is typically used by senators trying to wring concessions from the White House on matters having nothing to do with the appointment in question. In 1994, for example, Senator Max Baucus (D-Mont.) placed a hold on the confirmation of Mary Shapiro, President Clinton's choice to head the Commodity Futures Trading Commission, as well as those of four other Clinton nominees for federal regulatory posts. His aim was to win concessions from the administration for farmers in his state.

Most presidents make every effort to take potential Senate opposition into account in treaty negotiations and will frequently resort to *executive agreements* with foreign powers instead of treaties. The Supreme Court has held that such agreements are equivalent to treaties, but they do not need Senate approval.[53] In the past, presidents sometimes concluded secret agreements without informing Congress of the agreements' contents, or even their existence. For example, American involvement in the Vietnam War grew in part out of a series of secret arrangements made between American presidents and the South Vietnamese during the 1950s and 1960s. Congress did not even learn of the existence of these agreements until 1969. In 1972, Congress passed the Case Act, which requires that the president inform Congress of any executive agreement within sixty days of its having been reached. This provides Congress with the opportunity to cancel agreements that it opposes. In addition, Congress can limit the president's ability to conduct foreign policy through executive agreement by refusing to appropriate the funds needed to implement an agreement. In this way, for example, executive agreements to provide American economic or military assistance to foreign governments can be modified or even canceled by Congress.

executive agreement An agreement between the president and another country which has the force of a treaty but does not require the Senate's "advice and consent."

[53]U.S. v. Pink, 315 U.S. 203 (1942). For a good discussion of the problem, see James W. Davis, *The American Presidency* (New York: Harper & Row, 1987), Chapter 8.

Impeachment

impeachment
To charge a governmental official (president or otherwise) with "Treason, Bribery, or other high Crimes and Misdemeanors" and bring him or her before Congress to determine guilt.

The Constitution also grants Congress the power of ***impeachment*** over the president, vice president, and other executive officials. Impeachment means to charge a government official (president or otherwise) with "Treason, Bribery, or other high Crimes and Misdemeanors" and bring him or her before Congress to determine guilt. Impeachment is thus like a criminal indictment in which the House of Representatives acts like a grand jury, voting (by simple majority) on whether the accused ought to be impeached. If a majority of the House votes to impeach, the impeachment trial moves to the Senate, which acts like a trial jury by voting whether to convict and forcibly remove the person from office (this vote requires a two-thirds majority of the Senate).

Controversy over Congress's impeachment power has arisen over the grounds for impeachment, especially the meaning of "high Crimes and Misdemeanors." A strict reading of the Constitution suggests that the only impeachable offense is an actual crime. But a more commonly agreed upon definition is that "an impeachable offense is whatever the majority of the House of Representatives considers it to be at a given moment in history."[54] In other words, impeachment, especially impeachment of a president, is a political decision.

The closest that the United States has come to impeaching and convicting a president came in 1867. President Andrew Johnson, a southern Democrat who had battled a congressional Republican majority over Reconstruction, was impeached by the House but saved from conviction by one vote in the Senate. At the height of the Watergate scandal in 1974, the House started impeachment proceedings against President Richard M. Nixon, but Nixon resigned before the House could proceed. The possibility of impeachment arose again in 1998 when President Clinton was accused of lying under oath and obstructing justice in the investigation into his sexual affair with White House intern Monica Lewinsky. In October 1998, the House voted to open an impeachment inquiry against President Clinton. At the conclusion of the Senate trial in 1999, Democrats, joined by a handful of Republicans, acquitted the president of both charges.

The impeachment power is a considerable one; its very existence in the hands of Congress is a highly effective safeguard against the executive tyranny so greatly feared by the framers of the Constitution.

POWER AND REPRESENTATION

Because they feared both executive and legislative tyranny, the framers of the Constitution pitted Congress and the president against one another. But for more than one hundred years, the contest was unequal. During the first

---

[54]Carroll J. Doherty, "Impeachment: How It Would Work," *Congressional Quarterly Weekly Report*, 31 January 1998, p. 222.

century of American government, Congress was the dominant institution. American foreign and domestic policy was formulated and implemented by Congress and generally, the most powerful figures in American government were the Speaker of the House and the leaders of the Senate—not the president. During the nineteenth century, Congress—not the president—dominated press coverage on "the affairs of government."[55] The War of 1812 was planned and fought by Congress. The great sectional compromises prior to the Civil War were formulated in Congress, without much intervention from the executive branch. Even during the Civil War, a period of extraordinary presidential leadership, a joint congressional committee on the conduct of the war played a role in formulating war plans and campaign tactics, and even had a hand in the promotion of officers. After the Civil War, when President Andrew Johnson sought to interfere with congressional plans for Reconstruction, he was summarily impeached, saved from conviction by only one vote. Subsequent presidents understood the moral and did not attempt to thwart Congress.

This congressional preeminence began to diminish after the turn of the century, so that by the 1960s, the executive had become, at least temporarily, the dominant branch of American government. The major domestic policy initiatives of the twentieth century—Franklin Roosevelt's "New Deal," Harry Truman's "Fair Deal," John F. Kennedy's "New Frontier," and Lyndon Johnson's "Great Society"—all included some congressional involvement but were essentially developed, introduced, and implemented by the executive. In the area of foreign policy, although Congress continued to be influential during the twentieth century, the focus of decision-making power clearly moved into the executive branch. The War of 1812 may have been a congressional war, but in the twentieth century, American entry into World War I, World War II, Korea, Vietnam, and a host of lesser conflicts was essentially a presidential—not a congressional—decision. In the last thirty years, there has been a good deal of resurgence of congressional power vis-à-vis the executive. This has occurred mainly because Congress has sought to represent many important political forces, such as the civil rights, feminist, environmental, consumer, and peace movements, which in turn became constituencies for congressional power. During the mid-1990s, Congress became more receptive to a variety of new conservative political forces, including groups on the social and religious right as well as more traditional economic conservatives. After Republicans won control of both houses in the 1994 elections, Congress took the lead in developing programs and policies supported by these groups. These efforts won Congress the support of conservative forces in its battles for power against a Democratic White House.

To herald the new accessibility of Congress, Republican leaders instituted a number of reforms designed to eliminate many of the practices they had

History Principle

During the first century of American government, Congress was the dominant institution. In recent decades, members of Congress have sought to restore that dominance.

[55]Samuel Kernell and Gary C. Jacobson, "Congress and the Presidency as News in the Nineteenth Century," *Journal of Politics* 49 (1987), pp. 1016–35.

criticized as examples of Democratic arrogance during their long years in opposition. Republican leaders reduced the number of committees and subcommittees, eliminated funding of the various unofficial caucuses, imposed term limits on committee chairmen, eliminated the practice of proxy voting, reduced committee staffs by one-third, ended Congress's exemption from the labor health and civil rights laws it imposed on the rest of the nation, and prohibited members from receiving most gifts. With these reforms, Republicans hoped to make Congress both more effective and more representative. Term limits and gift bans were seen as increasing the responsiveness of Congress to new political forces and to the American people more generally. Simplification of the committee structure was seen as making Congress more efficient and, thus, potentially more effective and powerful. To some extent, unfortunately, the various reforms worked at cross-purposes. Simplification of the committee structure and elimination of funding for the caucuses increased the power of the leadership but reduced the representation of a variety of groups in the legislative process. For example, the Congressional Black Caucus, one of the major groups to lose its funding, had come to play an important role in representing African Americans. For their part, when term limits for committee and subcommittee chairmen were finally imposed in 2001, the result was confusion as experienced chairmen were forced to step down. This is the dilemma of congressional reform. Efficiency and representation are often competing principles in our system of government, and we must be wary of gaining one at the expense of the other.

At the same time, the constant struggle between Congress and the president can hinder stable, effective governance. Over the past quarter-century, in particular, presidents and Congresses have often seemed to be more interested in undermining one another than in promoting the larger public interest. On issues of social policy, economic policy, and foreign policy, Congress and the president have been at each other's throats while the nation suffered.

For example, during its first months in session, the 105th Congress (1997–1998) was able to pass a number of important pieces of legislation, including a major budget bill and legislation designed to protect taxpayers from abuse by the Internal Revenue Service. As the session continued, however, Congress became fully involved in its battle with President Clinton, culminating in the president's impeachment in December 1998. As a result, the Congress failed to act on most of the major pieces of legislation on its agenda. An even more striking example of the disruptive consequences of all-out struggle between the Congress and the president came in December 1998. While American forces were involved in military action against Iraq, Congress was so engrossed in the conflict over Republican efforts to impeach President Clinton that lawmakers regarded the Iraqi crisis as a diversion from the "real" political issue. Some even suggested that Clinton had manufactured the crisis to save his presidency.

Thus, we face a fundamental dilemma: a representative system that can undermine the government's power. Indeed, it can undermine the government's

Institutional Reform
www.wwnorton.com/
lowi7/ch5
Do term limits make Congress more representative?

very capacity to govern. In the next chapter, we will turn to the second branch of American government, the presidency, to view this dilemma from a somewhat different angle.

SUMMARY

The U.S. Congress is one of the few national representative assemblies that actually governs. Members of Congress take their representative function seriously. They devote a significant portion of their time to constituent contact and service. Representation and power go hand in hand in congressional history.

The legislative process must provide the order necessary for legislation to take place amid competing interests. It is dependent on a hierarchical organizational structure within Congress. Six basic dimensions of Congress affect the legislative process: (1) the parties, (2) the committees, (3) the staff, (4) the caucuses (or conferences), (5) the rules, and (6) the presidency.

Since the Constitution provides only for a presiding officer in each house, some method had to be devised for conducting business. Parties quickly assumed the responsibility for this. In the House, the majority party elects a leader every two years. This individual becomes Speaker. In addition, a majority leader and a minority leader (from the minority party) and party whips are elected. Each party has a committee whose job it is to make committee assignments.

The committee system surpasses the party system in its importance in Congress. In the early nineteenth century, standing committees became a fundamental aspect of Congress. They have, for the most part, evolved to correspond to executive branch departments or programs and thus reflect and maintain the separation of powers.

The Senate has a tradition of unlimited debate, on which the various cloture rules it has passed have had little effect. Filibusters still occur. The rules of the House, on the other hand, restrict talk and support committees; deliberation is recognized as committee business. The House Rules Committee has the power to control debate and floor amendments. The rules prescribe the formal procedure through which bills become law. Generally, the parties control scheduling and agenda, but the committees determine action on the floor. Committees, seniority, and rules all limit the ability of members to represent their constituents. Yet, these factors enable Congress to maintain its role as a major participant in government.

While voting along party lines remains strong, party discipline has declined. Still, parties do have several means of maintaining discipline:

1. Favorable committee assignments create obligations;
2. Floor time in the debate on one bill can be allocated in exchange for a specific vote on another;
3. The whip system allows party leaders to assess support for a bill and convey their wishes to members;

Rationality Principle	Collective Action Principle	Institution Principle	Policy Principle	History Principle
Members of Congress, like all politicians, are ambitious and thus eager to serve the interests of constituents in order to improve their own chances of re-election.	Cooperation on recurring matters like congressional votes is facilitated by the institutionalization of legislative structures and procedures.	According to the principle of agency representation, elections induce a member of Congress to act according to the preferences of his or her constituency.	Pork-barrel legislation exists because it allows members of Congress to claim credit for federally granted resources, thus improving their chances for re-election.	During the first century of American government, Congress was the dominant institution. In recent decades, members of Congress have sought to restore that dominance.
One of the most important factors determining who runs for office is each candidate's individual ambition.	If a bill passes both the House and Senate, the differences need to be ironed out in a conference committee.	Party leaders have considerable agenda-setting powers.	The distributive tendency in Congress results from the need for a broad base of support in order for a bill to be passed.	
The political opinions and policy goals of members of Congress are many and varied.	Interest groups with the ability to mobilize followers in many congressional districts are especially influential in Congress.	The committee system is a means of dividing labor and allowing members of Congress to specialize in certain policy areas.	Multiple factors influence how a member of Congress votes on legislation. These include constituency, interest groups, party leaders, congressional colleagues, and the president.	
Generally, members of Congress seek committee assignments that allow them to acquire more influence in areas important to their constituents.	The whip system helps maintain party unity in Congress.	Among the powers delegated to committees are gatekeeping authority, bargaining with the other chamber, and oversight.		
	Logrolling is an informal means of facilitating cooperation in Congress.	The House and Senate have methods of keeping committees in check.		
		The Rules Committee's decision about whether to adopt a closed or open rule for floor debate greatly influences a bill's chances for passage.		

4. Party leaders can help members create large logrolling coalitions; and
5. The president, by identifying pieces of legislation as his own, can muster support along party lines.

In most cases, party leaders accept constituency obligations as a valid reason for voting against the party position.

The power of the post–New Deal presidency does not necessarily signify the decline of Congress and representative government. During the 1970s, Congress again became the "first branch" of government. During the early years of the Reagan administration, some of the congressional gains of the previous decade were diminished, but in the last two years of Reagan's second term, and in former president Bush's term, Congress reasserted its role. At the start of the Clinton administration, congressional leaders promised to cooperate with the White House rather than confront it. But only two years later, confrontation was once again the order of the day.

FOR FURTHER READING

Arnold, R. Douglas. *The Logic of Congressional Action.* New Haven: Yale University Press, 1990.

Baker, Ross K. *House and Senate*, 3rd ed. New York: W. W. Norton, 2001.

Dodd, Lawrence, and Bruce I. Oppenheimer, eds. *Congress Reconsidered*, 7th ed. Washington, DC: Congressional Quarterly Press, 2000.

Fenno, Richard F. *Homestyle: House Members in Their Districts.* Boston: Little, Brown, 1978.

Fiorina, Morris. *Congress: Keystone of the Washington Establishment*, 2nd ed. New Haven: Yale University Press, 1989.

Fowler, Linda, and Robert McClure. *Political Ambition: Who Decides to Run for Congress?* New Haven: Yale University Press, 1989.

Mayhew, David R. *Congress: The Electoral Connection.* New Haven: Yale University Press, 1974.

Rieselbach, Leroy. *Congressional Reform.* Washington, DC: Congressional Quarterly Press, 1986.

Rohde, David W. *Parties and Leaders in the Postreform House.* Chicago: University of Chicago Press, 1991.

Sinclair, Barbara. *The Transformation of the U.S. Senate.* Baltimore: Johns Hopkins University Press, 1989.

Smith, Steven S., and Christopher Deering. *Committees in Congress*, 2nd ed. Washington, DC: Congressional Quarterly Press, 1990.

Sundquist, James L. *The Decline and Resurgence of Congress.* Washington, DC: Brookings Institution, 1981.

EVENTS	INSTITUTIONAL DEVELOPMENTS
George Washington elected first president (1789)	President establishes powers in relation to Congress (1789)
Thomas Jefferson elected president (1800) — **1800**	
	Orderly transfer of power from Federalists to Jeffersonian Republicans (1801)
	Marbury v. Madison holds that Congress and the president are subject to judicial review (1803)
Republican caucus nominates James Madison, who is elected president (1808)	Congress dominates presidential nominations through "King Caucus" (1804–1831)
Andrew Jackson elected president (1828)	
Period of weak presidents (Martin Van Buren, William Harrison, James Polk, Zachary Taylor, Franklin Pierce, James Buchanan) (1836–1860)	Strengthening of presidency; nominating conventions introduced, broaden president's base of support (1830s)
Abraham Lincoln elected president (1860) — **1860**	
	"Constitutional dictatorship" during Civil War and after (1861–1865)
Impeachment of President Andrew Johnson (1868)	Congress takes back initiative for action (1868–1933)
Industrialization, big railroads, big corporations (1860s–1890s)	*In re Neagle*—Court holds to expansive inference from Constitution on rights, duties, and obligations of president (1890)
World War I (1914–1918)	
1920	
	Budget and Accounting Act; Congress provides for an executive budget (1921)
	Congress adopts first New Deal programs; epoch of presidential government (1930s)
FDR proposes New Deal programs to achieve economic recovery from the Depression (1933)	
U.S. in World War II (1941–1945)	*U.S. v. Pink*—Court confirms legality of executive agreements in foreign relations (1942)
1950	
Korean War without declaration (1950–1953)	
	Steel Seizure case holds that president's power must be authorized by statute and is not inherent in the presidency (1952)

	EVENTS	INSTITUTIONAL DEVELOPMENTS
	Gulf of Tonkin Resolution (1964); U.S. troop buildup begins in Vietnam (1965)	Great Society program enacted; president sends troops to Vietnam without consulting Congress (1965)
1970		
	Watergate affair (1972); Watergate cover-up revealed (1973–1974)	Congressional resurgence begins—War Powers Act (1973); Budget and Impoundment Act (1974)
	Nixon becomes first president to resign; Gerald Ford succeeds after Nixon's resignation (1974)	
	Reagan's election begins new Republican era (1980–1988)	INS v. Chadha—Court holds legislative veto to be unconstitutional (1983)
		Gramm-Rudman Act seeks to contain deficit spending (1985)
		End of cold war puts new emphasis on foreign policy (1989)
1990		
		Desert Storm defines post–cold war conduct of foreign policy (1991)
	Clinton election ends "divided government" (1992)	
	Republican takeover of both houses of Congress renews "divided government" (1994)	
	Clinton re-elected, but divided government continues (1996)	Congress gives president limited line-item veto power over appropriations (1997)
		Court refuses to give president immunity from civil suit in *Clinton v. Jones* (1997)
	Democrats reverse midterm precedent and gain seats in House (1998)	Supreme Court rules that limited line-item veto power is unconstitutional (1998)
	Impeachment proceeds, despite election and high job ratings for Clinton (1998–1999)	
2000		
	Narrow Bush electoral margin imperils "presidential power" (2001)	Early triumph with tax cut; major initiatives on strategic missile defense and reorientation from Europe to Asia (2001)

CORE OF THE ANALYSIS

- In the twentieth century, the president has been transformed from "chief clerk," the executor of Congress's wishes, into "chief executive," the leader and shaper of the national government.

- The institutional growth of the presidency since the 1930s has vastly increased its power, but the constitutional basis for presidential action means that the president is constantly vulnerable to congressional or judicial challenges.

- The critical resource of the modern presidency is mass public opinion.

- Because of their ultimate reliance on mass support rather than other resources such as party, patronage, or the cabinet, presidents tend to govern using the resource they control most firmly—the White House staff.

Throughout 1998, the presidency appeared to be in crisis. In January of that year, President Bill Clinton had just been cleared of accusations that he was involved with illegal fundraising during the 1996 campaign, but he was still defending himself against two sets of charges. The first involved a sexual harassment suit by Paula Jones, a former employee of the state of Arkansas (of which Clinton was governor before his election to the presidency). The second charge, being investigated by independent counsel Kenneth Starr, focused on Clinton's alleged involvement with illegal real-estate speculation as part of the Whitewater Development Corporation. In seeking to prove that Clinton made a practice of seeking sexual favors from employees, Paula Jones's lawyers issued a subpoena to a former White House intern, Monica Lewinsky. It was alleged that Clinton and Lewinsky had had a sexual affair and that Clinton had urged Lewinsky to perjure herself by denying the accusation in a sworn deposition. Although sexual misconduct of this kind has no legal significance, the charges against Clinton involved serious criminal charges of obstruction of justice. In December 1998, he was impeached by the House of Representatives on two articles—perjury and obstruction of justice—and was put before the Senate for possible conviction and removal from office, the first such action since President Andrew Johnson's impeachment in 1868. President Clinton was in trouble. What about the office of the presidency?

Public opinion about the President's affair with Lewinsky sheds light on the nature of the presidency today. When asked if they thought Clinton was engaged in a cover-up, 51 percent of respondents said yes. When asked if Clinton should be removed from office if he lied under oath about the affair, 55 percent said yes. When asked if he should be removed from office if he had encouraged Lewinsky to lie while under oath, 63 percent said yes. But when asked whether they approved or disapproved of the way President Clinton was handling his job, a whopping 68 percent said they approved, giving Clinton his highest approval rating up to that time.[1] Although the results of these polls may appear confusing at first glance, they confirm one important fact: the presidency has a dual

[1]CNN/*Times* polls, 23 and 30 January 1998.

nature, which Americans sense and act upon. The power that President Clinton exercised and the approval he seemed to gain following this setback are based more in the institution of the presidency than in the person of the president. In other words, Americans respect the presidency as an institution and all of its capabilities for governance, even if they don't approve of the individual in the office. It's the office that wields great power, not necessarily the person.

As we shall see, the power of the office has gradually developed over time. The framers, wanting "energy in the Executive," provided for a single-headed office with an electoral base independent of Congress. But by giving the presidency no explicit powers independent of Congress, each president would have to provide that energy by asserting the inherent powers of the office.

A tug-of-war between formal constitutional provisions for a president who is little more than chief clerk and a theory of necessity favoring a real chief executive has persisted for over two centuries. President Jefferson's acquisition of the Louisiana Territory in virtual defiance of the Constitution seemed to establish the chief executive presidency; yet he was followed by three chief clerks, James Madison, James Monroe, and John Quincy Adams. Presidents Andrew Jackson and Abraham Lincoln believed in and acted on the theory of the strong president with power transcending the formal Constitution, but neither of them institutionalized the role, and both were followed by a series of chief clerks. Theodore Roosevelt and Woodrow Wilson were also considered genuine chief executives. But it was not until Franklin Roosevelt's election in 1932 that the tug-of-war seems to have been won for the chief executive presidency, because after FDR, as we shall see, every president has been strong, whether he was committed to the strong presidency or not.

Thus, a strong executive, a genuine chief executive, was institutionalized in the twentieth century. But it continues to operate in a schizoid environment: as the power of the presidency has increased, popular expectations of presidential performance have increased at

THE CENTRAL QUESTIONS

THE CONSTITUTIONAL BASIS OF THE PRESIDENCY

What conflicting views of presidential power were held by the framers of the Constitution?

What powers does the Constitution provide to the president?

THE RISE OF PRESIDENTIAL GOVERNMENT

What accounts for a president's success in exercising power?

What events led to the growth of a more powerful presidency?

PRESIDENTIAL GOVERNMENT

What formal resources does the president use to manage the executive branch? Which of these resources have presidents increasingly relied on?

What informal resources can the president draw on in exercising the powers of the presidency? Which of these resources is a potential liability? Why?

IS A PARLIAMENTARY SYSTEM BETTER?

Would a parliamentary system cure the problems of divided government? Why or why not?

an even faster rate, requiring more leadership than was ever exercised by any but the greatest presidents in the past.

Our focus in this chapter will be on the development of the institutional character of the presidency, the power of the presidency, and the relationship between the two. The chapter is divided into four sections. First, we shall review the constitutional origins of the presidency. In particular, this will involve an examination of the constitutional basis for the president's foreign and domestic roles. Second, we shall review the history of the American presidency to see how the office has evolved from its original status under the Constitution. We will look particularly at the ways in which Congress has augmented the president's constitutional powers by deliberately delegating to the presidency many of Congress's own responsibilities. Third, we shall assess both the formal and informal means by which presidents can enhance their own ability to govern. We will conclude by analyzing an alternative to the U.S. presidential system: parliamentary democracy.

THE CONSTITUTIONAL BASIS OF THE PRESIDENCY

expressed powers The notion that the Constitution grants to the federal government only those powers specifically named in its text.

delegated powers Constitutional powers assigned to one governmental agency that are exercised by another agency with the express permission of the first.

 Institution Principle

The Constitution established the presidency as an office of delegated powers.

Article II of the Constitution, which establishes the presidency and defines a small number of *expressed powers* of the office, is the basis for the dual nature of the presidency. Although Article II has been called "the most loosely drawn chapter of the Constitution,"[2] the framers were neither indecisive nor confused. They held profoundly conflicting views of the executive branch, and Article II was probably the best compromise they could make. The formulation the framers agreed upon is magnificent in its ambiguity: "The executive Power shall be vested in a President of the United States of America" (Article II, Section 1, first sentence). The meaning of "executive power," however, is not defined except indirectly in the very last sentence of Section 3, which provides that the president "shall take Care that the Laws be faithfully executed."[3]

One very important conclusion can be drawn from these two provisions: the office of the president was to be an office of *delegated powers.* Since, as we have already seen, all of the powers of the national government are defined as powers of Congress and are incorporated into Article I, Section 8, then the "executive Power" of Article II, Section 3, must be understood to be defined as the power to execute faithfully the laws *as they are adopted* by Congress. This does not doom the presidency to weakness. Presumably, Congress can pass laws delegating almost any of its powers to the president. But presidents are not free to discover sources of executive power completely independent of the laws as passed by Congress. In the 1890 case of *In re Neagle*, the Supreme Court did hold that the

---

[2]E. S. Corwin, *The President: Office and Powers*, 3rd rev. ed. (New York: New York University Press, 1957), p. 2.

[3]Article II, Section 3. There is a Section 4, but all it does is define impeachment.

president could be bold and expansive in the inferences he drew from the Constitution as to "the rights, duties and obligations" of the presidency; but the ***inherent powers*** of the president would have to be inferred from that Constitution and laws, not from some independent or absolute idea of executive power.[4]

Immediately following the first sentence of Section 1, Article II defines the manner in which the president is to be chosen. This is a very odd sequence, but it does say something about the struggle the delegates were having over how to provide great power of action or energy to the executive and at the same time to balance that power with limitations. The struggle was between those delegates who wanted the president to be selected by, and thus responsible to, Congress and those delegates who preferred that the president be elected directly by the people. Direct popular election would create a more independent and more powerful presidency. With the adoption of a scheme of indirect election through an electoral college in which the electors would be selected by the state legislatures (and close elections would be resolved in the House of Representatives), the framers hoped to achieve a "republican" solution: a strong president responsible to state and national legislators rather than directly to the electorate.

The heart of presidential power as defined by the Constitution, however, is found in Sections 2 and 3, where the several clauses define the presidency in two dimensions: the president as head of state and the president as head of government. Although these will be given separate treatment here, the presidency can be understood only by the combination of the two.

The President As Head of State: Some Imperial Qualities

The constitutional position of the president as head of state is defined by three constitutional provisions, which are the source of some of the most important powers on which presidents can draw. The areas can be classified as follows:

1. *Military.* Article II, Section 2, provides for the power as "Commander in Chief of the Army and Navy of the United States, and of the Militia of the several States, when called in to the actual Service of the United States."
2. *Judicial.* Article II, Section 2, also provides the power to "grant Reprieves and Pardons for Offences against the United States, except in Cases of Impeachment."
3. *Diplomatic.* Article II, Section 3, provides the power to "receive Ambassadors and other public Ministers."

inherent powers
Powers claimed by a president that are not expressed in the Constitution, but are inferred from it.

---

[4]In re Neagle, 135 U.S. 1 (1890). Neagle, a deputy U.S. marshal, had been authorized by the president to protect a Supreme Court justice whose life had been threatened by an angry litigant. When the litigant attempted to carry out his threat, Neagle shot and killed him. Neagle was then arrested by the local authorities and tried for murder. His defense was that his act was "done in pursuance of a law of the United States." Although the law was not an act of Congress, the Supreme Court declared that it was an executive order of the president, and the protection of a federal judge was a reasonable extension of the president's power to "take Care that the Laws be faithfully executed."

Military First, the position of commander in chief makes the president the highest military authority in the United States, with control of the entire defense establishment. No American president, however, would dare put on a military uniform for a state function—not even a former general like Eisenhower—even though the president is the highest military officer in war and in peace. The president is also the head of the secret intelligence hierarchy, which includes not only the Central Intelligence Agency (CIA) but also the National Security Council (NSC), the National Security Agency (NSA), the Federal Bureau of Investigation (FBI), and a host of less well-known but very powerful international and domestic security agencies. But of course, care must be taken not to conclude too much from this—as some presidents have done. Although Article II, Section 1, does state that all the executive power is vested in the president, and Section 2 does provide that the president shall be commander in chief of all armed forces, including state militias, these impressive provisions must be read in the context of Article I, wherein seven of the eighteen clauses of Section 8 provide particular military and foreign policy powers to Congress, including the power to declare wars that presidents are responsible for. Presidents have tried to evade this at their peril. In full awareness of the woe visited upon President Lyndon Johnson for evading and misleading Congress at the outset of the Vietnam War, former president Bush sought congressional authorization for the Gulf War in January 1991.

Judicial The presidential power to grant reprieves, pardons, and amnesties involves the power of life and death over all individuals who may be a threat to the security of the United States. Presidents may use this power on behalf of a particular individual, as did Gerald Ford when he pardoned Richard Nixon in 1974 "for all offenses against the United States which he . . . has committed or may have committed." Or they may use it on a large scale, as did President Andrew Johnson in 1868, when he gave full amnesty to all Southerners who had participated in the "Late Rebellion," and President Carter in 1977, when he declared an amnesty for all the draft evaders of the Vietnam War. This power of life and death over others helped elevate the president to the level of earlier conquerors and kings by establishing him as the person before whom supplicants might come to make their pleas for mercy.

Diplomatic When President Washington received Edmond Genêt ("Citizen Genêt") as the formal emissary of the revolutionary government of France in 1793 and had his cabinet officers and Congress back his decision, he established a greatly expanded interpretation of the power to "receive Ambassadors and other public Ministers," extending it to the power to "recognize" other countries. That power gives the president the almost unconditional authority to review the claims of any new ruling groups to determine if they indeed control the territory and population of their country, so that they can commit it to treaties and other agreements. Critics questioned the wisdom of President Nixon's recognition of the People's Republic of China and of President Carter's recognition of the Sandinista government in Nicaragua. But they did not question the president's authority to make such decisions. Because the breakup of the Soviet bloc was generally perceived as a positive event, no one criticized former president Bush for his quick recognition of the several former Soviet and Yugoslav republics as soon as they declared themselves independent states.

The Imperial Presidency? Have presidents used these three constitutional powers—military, judicial, and diplomatic—to make the presidency more powerful, indeed "imperial?"[5] Debate over the answer to this question has produced an unusual lineup, with presidents and the Supreme Court on one side and Congress on the other. The Supreme Court supported the expansive view of the presidency in three historically significant cases. The first was *In re Neagle*, discussed above. The second was the 1936 *Curtiss-Wright* case, in which the Court held that Congress may delegate a degree of discretion to the president in foreign affairs that might violate the separation of powers if it were in a domestic arena.[6] In the third case, *U.S. v. Pink*, the Supreme Court upheld the president's power to use executive agreements to conduct foreign policy.[7] An *executive agreement* is exactly like a treaty because it is a contract between two countries; but an executive agreement does not require a two-thirds vote of approval by the Senate. Ordinarily, executive agreements are used to carry out commitments already made in treaties, or to arrange for matters well below the level of policy. But when presidents have found it expedient to use an executive agreement in place of a treaty, the Court has gone along. This verges on an imperial power.

Many recent presidents have even gone beyond formal executive agreements to engage in what amounts to unilateral action. They may seek formal congressional authorization, as in 1965 when President Lyndon Johnson convinced Congress to adopt the Gulf of Tonkin Resolution authorizing him to expand the American military presence in Vietnam. Johnson interpreted

> **Rationality Principle**
> Presidents can and have advanced their own priorities, and those of their office, by claiming inherent powers through the faithful execution of the law.

> **executive agreement** An agreement between the president and another country, which has the force of a treaty but does not require the Senate's "advice and consent."

---

[5]Arthur Schlesinger, Jr., *The Imperial Presidency* (Boston: Houghton Mifflin, 1973).

[6]U.S. v. Curtiss-Wright Corp., 299 U.S. 304 (1936). In 1934, Congress passed a joint resolution authorizing the president to prohibit the sale of military supplies to Bolivia and Paraguay, who were at war, if the president determined that the prohibition would contribute to peace between the two countries. When prosecuted for violating the embargo order by President Roosevelt, the defendants argued that Congress could not constitutionally delegate such broad discretion to the president. The Supreme Court disagreed. Previously, however, the Court had rejected the National Industrial Recovery Act precisely because Congress had delegated too much discretion to the president in a domestic policy. See Schechter Poultry Corp. v. U.S., 295 U.S. 495 (1935).

[7]In United States v. Pink, 315 U.S. 203 (1942), the Supreme Court confirmed that an executive agreement is the legal equivalent of a treaty, despite the absence of Senate approval. This case approved the executive agreement that was used to establish diplomatic relations with the Soviet Union in 1933. An executive agreement, not a treaty, was used in 1940 to exchange "fifty over-age destroyers" for ninety-nine-year leases on some important military bases.

the resolution as a delegation of discretion to use any and all national resources according to his own judgment. Others may not even bother with the authorization but merely assume it, as President Nixon did when he claimed to need no congressional authorization at all to continue or to expand the Vietnam War.

These presidential claims and actions led to a congressional reaction, however. In 1973, Congress passed the War Powers Resolution over President Nixon's veto. This resolution asserted that the president could send American troops into action abroad only in the event of a declaration of war or other statutory authorization by Congress, or if American troops were attacked or directly endangered. This was an obvious effort to revive the principle that the presidency is an office of *delegated* powers—that is, powers granted by Congress—and that there is no blanket prerogative—that is, no inherent presidential power.

Nevertheless, this resolution has not prevented presidents from using force when they deemed it necessary. President Reagan took at least four military actions that could be seen as violations of the War Powers Resolution. Former president Bush disregarded Congress in the 1989 invasion of Panama but was fortunate in bringing the affair to a successful conclusion quite quickly. In contrast, once he saw that the situation in Kuwait was tending toward protracted military involvement, he submitted the issue to Congress.

President George W. Bush followed in his father's footsteps by seeking congressional authorization for the war against the Taliban regime in Afghanistan; it was granted in a joint resolution adopted in the Senate by a vote of 98 to 0 and in the House by a vote of 420 to 1. Some criticism was voiced in the week following the resolution when Attorney General John Ashcroft set up a process of military tribunals for suspected terrorists and authorized electronic surveillance without search warrants. But no criticism was voiced against the president's air and ground campaign against Afghanistan or the offer of a $25 million reward for the apprehension of Osama bin Laden and other Al Qaeda members. Congress did attach a two-year "sunset provision" to the authorization resolution and planned for congressional oversight during and after the war.

The Domestic Presidency: The President As Head of Government

The constitutional basis of the domestic presidency also has three parts. And here again, although real power grows out of the combination of the parts, the analysis is greatly aided by examining the parts separately:

1. *Executive.* The "executive Power" is vested in the president by Article II, Section 1, to see that all the laws are faithfully executed (Section 3), and to appoint, remove, and supervise all executive officers and to appoint all federal judges (Article II, Section 2).

2. *Military.* This power is derived from Article IV, Section 4, which stipulates that the president has the power to protect every state "against Invasion; and . . . against domestic Violence."

3. *Legislative.* The president is given the power under various provisions to participate effectively and authoritatively in the legislative process.

Executive Power   The most important basis of the president's power as chief executive is to be found in Article II, Section 3, which stipulates that the president must see that all the laws are faithfully executed, and Section 2, which provides that the president will appoint, remove, and supervise all executive officers, and appoint all federal judges. The *Neagle* case has already demonstrated the degree to which Article II, Section 1, is a source of executive power. Further powers do indeed come from this appointing power, although at first this may not seem to be very impressive. But the power to appoint the "principal executive officers" and to require each of them to report to the president on subjects relating to the duties of their departments makes the president the true chief executive officer (CEO) of the nation. In this manner, the Constitution focuses executive power and legal responsibility upon the president. The famous sign on President Truman's desk, "The buck stops here," was not merely an assertion of Truman's personal sense of responsibility but was in fact recognition by him of the legal and constitutional responsibility of the president. The president is subject to some limitations, because the appointment of all such officers, including ambassadors, ministers, and federal judges, is subject to a majority approval by the Senate. But these appointments are at the discretion of the president, and the loyalty and the responsibility of each appointment are presumed to be directed toward the president. Although the Constitution is silent on the power of the president to remove such officers, the federal courts have filled this silence with a series of decisions that grant the president this power.[8] Although the United States has no cabinet in the parliamentary sense of a collective decision-making body or board of directors with collective responsibilities (discussed later in this chapter), the Constitution nevertheless recognizes departments with department heads, and that recognition establishes the lines

---

[8]The Supreme Court defined the president's removal power very broadly in Myers v. U.S., 272 U.S. 52 (1926). Later, in Humphrey's Executor v. U.S., 295 U.S. 62 (1935), the Court accepted Congress's effort to restrict presidential removal powers as they applied to heads of independent regulatory commissions. In those instances, the president can remove officers only "for cause." Two later cases restricted presidential power a bit further by providing that he could not remove at his pleasure certain other officers whose tasks require independence from the executive. See Wiener v. U.S., 357 U.S. 349 (1958); and Bowsher v. Synar, 478 U.S. 714 (1986). In another, more tricky case, the Court held that the attorney general, not the president, could remove a special prosecutor because of the power and obligation of the prosecutor to investigate the president. See Morrison v. Olson, 108 S.Ct. 2597 (1988).

of legal responsibility up and down the executive hierarchy, culminating in the presidency (see Figure 6.1).

Military Sources of Domestic Presidential Power   Although Article IV, Section 4, provides that the "United States shall [protect] every State . . . against Invasion . . . and . . . domestic Violence," Congress has made this an explicit presidential power through statutes directing the president as commander in chief to discharge these obligations.[9] The Constitution restrains the president's use of domestic force by providing that a state legislature (or governor when the legislature is not in session) must request federal troops before the president can send them into the state to provide public order. Yet, this proviso is not absolute. First, presidents are not obligated to deploy national troops merely because the state legislature or governor makes such a request. And more important, the president may deploy troops in a state or city without a specific request from the state legislature or governor if he considers it necessary in order to maintain an essential national service, in order to enforce a federal judicial order, or in order to protect federally guaranteed civil rights.

One historic example of the unilateral use of presidential power to protect the states against domestic disorder, even when the states don't request it, was the decision by President Eisenhower in 1957 to send troops into Little Rock, Arkansas, literally against the wishes of the state of Arkansas, to enforce court orders to integrate Little Rock's Central High School (see Chapter 4). Arkansas Governor Orval Faubus had actually posted the Arkansas National Guard at the entrance of the Central High School to prevent the court-ordered admission of nine black students. After an effort to negotiate with Governor Faubus failed, President Eisenhower reluctantly sent a thousand paratroopers to Little Rock, who stood watch while the black students took their places in the all-white classrooms. These cases make quite clear that the president does not have to wait for a request by a state legislature or governor before acting as a domestic commander in chief.[10]

However, in most instances of domestic disorder—whether from human or from natural causes—presidents tend to exercise unilateral power by declaring a "state of emergency," thereby making available federal grants, insurance, and direct assistance. In 1992, in the aftermath of the devastating riots in Los Angeles and the hurricanes in Florida, American troops were very much in evidence, sent in by the president, but in the role more of good Samaritans than of military police.

The President's Legislative Power   The president plays a role not only in the administration of government but also in the legislative process. Two constitutional provisions are the primary sources of the president's power in the legislative

---

[9]These statutes are contained mainly in Title 10 of the United States Code, Sections 331, 332, and 333.

[10]The best study covering all aspects of the domestic use of the military is that of Adam Yarmolinsky, *The Military Establishment* (New York: Harper & Row, 1971).

FIGURE 6.1

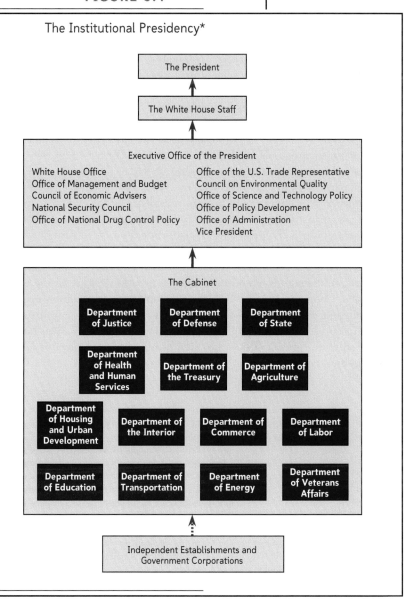

The Institutional Presidency*

The President

The White House Staff

Executive Office of the President

White House Office
Office of Management and Budget
Council of Economic Advisers
National Security Council
Office of National Drug Control Policy

Office of the U.S. Trade Representative
Council on Environmental Quality
Office of Science and Technology Policy
Office of Policy Development
Office of Administration
Vice President

The Cabinet

Department of Justice | Department of Defense | Department of State

Department of Health and Human Services | Department of the Treasury | Department of Agriculture

Department of Housing and Urban Development | Department of the Interior | Department of Commerce | Department of Labor

Department of Education | Department of Transportation | Department of Energy | Department of Veterans Affairs

Independent Establishments and Government Corporations

*NOTE: Arrows are used to indicate lines of legal responsibility.

SOURCE: Office of the Federal Register, National Archive and Records Administration, *The United States Government Manual*, 1995–1996 (Washington, DC: Government Printing Office, 1995), p. 22.

arena. The first of these is the provision in Article II, Section 3, providing that the president "shall from time to time give to the Congress Information of the State of the Union, and recommend to their Consideration such Measures as he shall judge necessary and expedient." The second of the president's legislative powers is of course the "veto power" assigned by Article I, Section 7.[11]

The first of these powers does not at first appear to be of any great import. It is a mere obligation on the part of the president to make recommendations for Congress's consideration. But as political and social conditions began to favor an increasingly prominent role for presidents, each president, especially since Franklin Delano Roosevelt, began to rely upon this provision to become the primary initiator of proposals for legislative action in Congress and the principal source for public awareness of national issues, as well as the most important single individual participant in legislative decisions. This is an instance of agenda power (see Chapter 1). Few today doubt that the president and the executive branch together are the primary agenda setters for many important congressional actions.[12]

The **veto** power is the president's constitutional power to turn down acts of Congress. This power alone makes the president the most important single legislative leader.[13] No bill vetoed by the president can become law unless both the House and Senate override the veto by a two-thirds vote. In the case of a **pocket veto**, Congress does not even have the option of overriding the veto, but must reintroduce the bill in the next session. A pocket veto can occur when the president is presented with a bill during the last ten days of a legislative session. Usually, if a president does not sign a bill within ten days, it automatically becomes law. But this is true only while Congress is in session. If a

Institution Principle

The president can be an important agenda setter for congressional action.

veto The president's constitutional power to turn down acts of Congress. A presidential veto may be overridden by a two-thirds vote of each house of Congress.

pocket veto Method by which the president vetoes a bill by taking no action on it when Congress has adjourned.

[11]There is a third source of presidential power implied from the provision for faithful execution of the laws. This is the president's power to impound funds—that is, to refuse to spend money Congress has appropriated for certain purposes. One author referred to this as a "retroactive veto power" (Robert E. Goosetree, "The Power of the President to Impound Appropriated Funds," *American University Law Review*, January 1962). This impoundment power was used freely and to considerable effect by many modern presidents, and Congress occasionally delegated such power to the president by statute. But in reaction to the Watergate scandal, Congress adopted the Budget and Impoundment Control Act of 1974 and designed this act to circumscribe the president's ability to impound funds by requiring that the president must spend all appropriated funds unless both houses of Congress consent to an impoundment within forty-five days of a presidential request. Therefore, since 1974, the use of impoundment has declined significantly. Presidents have either had to bite their tongues and accept unwanted appropriations or had to revert to the older and more dependable but politically limited method of vetoing the entire bill.

[12]For a different perspective, see William F. Grover, *The President as Prisoner: A Structural Critique of the Carter and Reagan Years* (Albany: State University of New York Press, 1989).

[13]Although the veto power is the most important legislative resource in the hands of the president, it can often end in frustration, especially when the presidency and Congress are held by opposing parties. George H. W. Bush vetoed forty-six congressional enactments during his four years, and only one was overridden. Ronald Reagan vetoed thirty-nine in his eight years, and nine were overridden. This compares to thirty-one during Jimmy Carter's four years, with two overridden. In 1994, Bill Clinton did not veto a single bill, a record unmatched since the days of President Millard Fillmore in 1853; both, of course, were working with Congresses controlled by their own political party. For more on the veto, see Chapter 5 and Robert J. Spitzer, *The Presidential Veto—Touchstone of the American Presidency* (Albany: State University of New York Press, 1988).

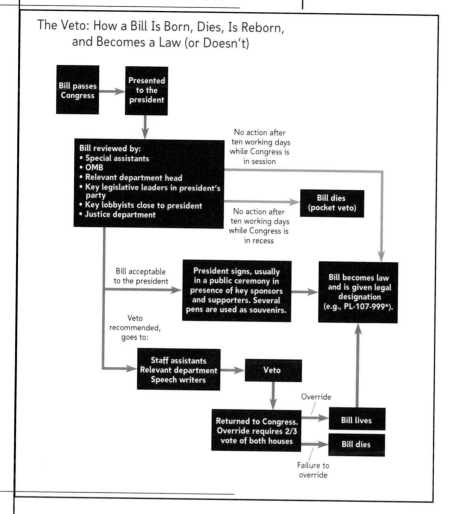

The Veto: How a Bill Is Born, Dies, Is Reborn, and Becomes a Law (or Doesn't)

*PL = Public Law, 107 = number of Congress (107th is 2000–2001); 999 = the number of the actual law.

president chooses not to sign a bill within the last ten days that Congress is in session, then the ten-day limit does not expire until Congress is out of session, and instead of becoming law, the bill is vetoed. Process Box 6.1 illustrates the president's veto options. In 1996, a new power was added—the line-item veto—giving the president power to strike specific spending items from appropriations bills passed by Congress, unless re-enacted by a two-thirds vote of both House and Senate. In 1997, President Clinton used this power eleven times to strike eighty-two items from the federal budget. But, as we saw in Chapter 5, in 1998, the Supreme Court ruled that the Constitution does not authorize the line-item veto power. Only a constitutional amendment would restore this power to the president.

The Games Presidents Play: The Veto   Use of the veto varies according to the political situation that each president confronts. During Bill Clinton's first two years in office, when Democrats controlled both houses of Congress, he vetoed no bills. Following the congressional elections of 1994, however, Clinton confronted a Republican-controlled Congress with a definite agenda, and he began to use his veto power more vigorously. In general, presidents have used the veto to equalize or perhaps upset the balance of power with Congress. While the simple power to reject or accept legislation in its entirety might seem like a crude tool for making sure that legislation adheres to a president's preferences, the politics surrounding the veto are quite complicated, and it is rare that vetoes are used simply as bullets to kill legislation dead. Instead, vetoes are usually part of an intricate bargaining process between the president and Congress, involving threats of vetoes, vetoes, repassing legislation, and re-vetoes.[14]

Although presidents rarely veto legislation, this does not mean vetoes and veto bargaining have an insignificant influence over the policy process. The fact that presidents vetoed only 434 of the 17,000 public bills that Congress sent to them between 1945 and 1992 belies the centrality of the veto to presidential power. Many of these bills were insignificant and not worth the veto effort. Thus, it is important to separate "significant" legislation, for which vetoes frequently occur, from insignificant legislation.[15] Vetoes can also be effective—even though they are rarely employed—because of a concept known as "the second face of power," that is, individuals will condition their actions based on how they think others will respond.[16] With respect to vetoes, this means that members of Congress will alter the content of a bill to make it more to a president's liking in order to preempt a veto. Thus the veto power can be influential even when the veto pen rests in its inkwell. The concept of "the second face of power" works to influence the content of legislation.

Rhetoric and reputation take on particular importance when vetoes become part of a bargaining process. The key to veto bargaining is uncertainty. Members of Congress are often unsure about the president's policy preferences and therefore don't know which bills the president would be willing to sign. When the policy preferences of the president and Congress diverge, as they typically do under divided government, the president tries to convince Congress that his preferences are more extreme than they really are in order to get Congress to enact something that is closer to what he really wants. If members of Congress knew the president's preferences ahead of time, they would pass a bill that was closest to what *they* wanted, minimally satisfying the president. Through strategic use of the veto

Institution Principle

The veto power makes the president the most important single legislative leader.

Collective Action Principle

Vetoes are usually part of an intricate bargaining process between the president and Congress.

Policy Principle

Because of the president's veto power, Congress will alter the content of a bill to make it more to a president's liking.

Analyzing American Politics

www.wwnorton.com/ lowi7/ch6

Analyze the impact of a veto threat on legislation.

[14]Charles Cameron, *Veto Bargaining: Presidents and the Politics of Negative Power* (Cambridge: Cambridge University Press, 2000).
[15]David R. Mayhew, *Divided We Govern: Party Control, Lawmaking, and Investigations, 1946–1990* (New Haven: Yale University Press, 1991).
[16]Jack H. Nagel, *The Descriptive Analysis of Power* (New Haven: Yale University Press, 1975).

and veto threats, a president tries to shape Congress's beliefs about his policy preferences to gain greater concessions from Congress. Reputation is central to presidential effectiveness.[17] By influencing congressional beliefs, the president is building a policy reputation that will affect future congressional behavior.

What about the relationship between mass public support for the president and the use of the veto? At least for the modern presidency, a crucial resource for the president in negotiating with Congress has been his public approval as measured by opinion polls.[18] In some situations, members of Congress pass a bill, not because they want to change policy but because they want to force the president to veto a popular bill that he disagrees with in order to hurt his approval ratings.[19] The key is that the public, uncertain of the president's policy preferences, uses information conveyed by vetoes to reassess what they know about his preferences. As a result, vetoes may come at a price to the president. A president must weigh the advantages of vetoing or threatening to do so—to gain concessions from Congress—against the hit he may take in his popularity. The president may be reluctant to use the veto or the threat of a veto to gain concessions from Congress if such vetoes will hurt them in the polls. But in some cases, the president will take a hit in his approval ratings if the bill is drastically inconsistent with his policies.

Rationality Principle

A president must weigh the advantages of vetoing legislation against the possible drop in his public approval.

Legislative Initiative Clinton recaptured some of his leadership by finding the path of legislative initiative that he had lost with the Republican takeover of the House and Senate after the 1994 congressional elections. Although not explicitly stated, the Constitution provides the president with the power of legislative initiative. To "initiate" means to originate, and in government that can mean power. The framers of the Constitution clearly saw legislative initiative as one of the keys to executive power. Initiative obviously implies the ability to formulate proposals for important policies, and the president, as an individual with a great deal of staff assistance, is able to initiate decisive action more frequently than Congress, with its large assemblies that have to deliberate and debate before taking action. With some important exceptions, Congress banks on the president to set the agenda of public policy. And quite clearly, there is power in initiative; there is power in being able to set the terms of discourse in the making of public policy.

During Clinton's time in office, the terms of discourse were largely set by the president, and he tended to get the credit even on many of the occasions where the groundwork had been done by the Republicans. Important crime legislation, drug-control legislation, gun-control legislation, and the all-important welfare reform laws of 1996 were all presidential initiatives, even though the two most important of these—crime and welfare—contain many features first advanced

[17]Richard E. Neustadt, *Presidential Power* (New York: Wiley, 1960).

[18]Theodore J. Lowi, *The Personal President: Power Invested, Promise Unfulfilled* (Ithaca, NY: Cornell University Press, 1985).

[19]Timothy Groseclose and Nolan McCarty, "Presidential Vetoes: Bargaining, Blame-Game, and Gridlock," *American Journal of Political Science*, 45 (2001): 100–19.

by the Republicans in Congress. The same seems to have been true of budget and fiscal matters. For example, it was Clinton, not the tax-cutting Republicans, who established the principle that the Social Security surplus should not be any longer drawn upon to pay for other programs or for tax cuts.

Regarding areas of foreign policy, it was also largely Clinton who set the agenda. Let's look at what happened in 1999. First of all, it was Clinton who led a multilateral effort to save Kosovo from the aggressive advances made by Serbia. Clinton also resumed negotiations with the Russians and maintained multilateral discussion on arms control. Clinton managed to maintain discussion of America's $1 billion delinquency in UN dues until Congress finally included authorization for those payments in the budget.

The president's initiative does not end with policy making involving Congress and the making of laws in the ordinary sense of the term. The president has still another legislative role (in all but name) within the executive branch. This is designated as the power to issue *executive orders.* The executive order is first and foremost simply a normal tool of management, a power possessed by virtually any CEO to make "company policy" rules setting procedures, etiquette, chains of command, functional responsibilities, etc. But evolving out of this normal management practice is a recognized presidential power to promulgate rules that have the effect and the formal status of legislation. Most of the executive orders of the president provide for the reorganization of structures and procedures or otherwise direct the affairs of the executive branch—either to be applied across the board to all agencies or applied in some important respect to a single agency or department. One of the most important examples is Executive Order No. 8248, September 8, 1939, establishing the divisions of the Executive Office of the President. Another one of equal importance is President Nixon's executive order establishing the Environmental Protection Agency in 1970–1971, which included establishment of the Environmental Impact Statement. President Reagan's Executive Order No. 12291 of 1981 provided for a regulatory reform process that was responsible for more genuine deregulation in the past twenty years than was accomplished by any acts of congressional legislation. President Clinton's most important policy toward gays and gay rights in the military took the form of an executive order referred to as "Don't ask, don't tell."

In sum, President Clinton's ability to regain the policy initiative after the Republican triumph in Congress in 1994 and to keep the policy initiative during and after his impeachment crisis confirms the proposition that the presidency and presidential power includes legislative leadership. This legislative or policy leadership role of the presidency is an institutionalized feature of the office that exists independent of the occupant of the office.

When these two sources of power—agenda power from the president's constitutional duty to address Congress on the state of the union and the president's power to veto legislation—are taken together, it is remarkable that it took so long—well over a century—for these constitutional powers to be fully realized. Let us see how this happened as well as why it took so long.

executive order
A rule or regulation issued by the president that has the effect and formal status of legislation.

THE RISE OF PRESIDENTIAL GOVERNMENT

Most of the real influence of the modern presidency derives from the powers granted by the Constitution and the laws made by Congress. Thus, any person properly elected and sworn in as president will possess almost all of the power held by the strongest presidents in American history. Even when they are "lame ducks," presidents still possess all the power of the office. For example, in the weeks following the election of 2000, lame-duck President Clinton took the opportunity to become the first U.S. president to visit a united Vietnam and to continue major diplomatic efforts to bring peace to the Middle East.

This case illustrates an extremely important fact about the presidency: *the popular base of the presidency is important less because it gives the president power than because it gives him consent to use all the powers already vested by the Constitution in the office.* Anyone installed in the office could exercise most of its powers. But what variables account for a president's success in exercising these powers? Why are some presidents considered to be great successes and others colossal failures? This relates broadly to the very concept of presidential power. Is it a reflection of the attributes of the person or is it more characteristic of the political situations that a president encounters? The personal view of presidential power dominated political scientists' view for several decades,[20] but recent scholars have argued that presidential power should be analyzed in terms of the strategic interactions that a president has with other political actors. The veto, which we reviewed in the last section, is one example of this sort of strategic interaction, but there are many other "games" that presidents play: the Supreme Court nomination and treaty ratification games with the Senate, the executive order game, the agency supervision and management game with the executive branch. As the political scientist Charles M. Cameron has argued, *"Understanding the presidency means understanding these games."*[21] Success in these "games" translates into presidential power.

We must not forget, however, the tremendous resources that a president can rely on in his strategic interactions with others. Remember that the presidency is a democratic institution with a national constituency. Its broad popular base is a strategic presidential resource that can be deployed in the various bargaining games just discussed; a president's success depends on the qualities of the person in office and the situations that arise. For example, political scientist Sam Kernell suggests that presidents may rally public opinion and put pressure on Congress by "going public."[22] With the occasional exception, however, it took more than a century, perhaps as much as a century and a half, before presidents

> **Collective Action Principle**
> Presidential power should be analyzed in terms of the strategic interactions that a president has with other political actors.

> **Collective Action Principle**
> The president can use public approval as a strategic resource.

---

[20]Neustadt, *Presidential Power.*

[21]Charles M. Cameron, "Bargaining and Presidential Power," in Robert Y. Shapiro, Martha Joynt Kumar, and Lawrence R. Jacobs, eds., *Presidential Power: Forging the Presidency for the Twenty-First Century* (New York: Columbia University Press, 2000), p. 47. [Emphasis in original.]

[22]Samuel Kernell, *Going Public*, 3rd ed. (Washington, DC: Congressional Quarterly Press, 1998).

came to be seen as consequential players in these strategic encounters. A bit of historical review will be helpful in understanding how the presidency has risen to its current level of influence.

The Legislative Epoch, 1800–1933

In 1885, a then-obscure political science professor named Woodrow Wilson entitled his general textbook *Congressional Government* because American government was just that, "congressional government." There is ample evidence that Wilson's description of the national government was not only consistent with nineteenth-century reality but also with the intentions of the framers. Within the system of three separate and competing powers, the clear intent of the Constitution was for *legislative supremacy*.

The strongest evidence of original intent is the fact that the powers of the national government were not placed in a separate article of the Constitution, but were instead listed in Article I, the legislative article. Madison had laid it out explicitly in *The Federalist* No. 51: "In republican government, the legislative authority necessarily predominates." President Washington echoed this in his first inaugural address in 1789:

> By the article establishing the Executive Department, it is made the duty of the President "to recommend to your consideration, such measures as he shall judge necessary and expedient." The circumstances under which I now meet you, will acquit me from entering into that subject, farther than to refer to the Great Constitutional Charter . . . which, in defining your powers, designates the objects to which your attention is to be given. It will be more consistent with those circumstances . . . to substitute, in place of a recommendation of particular measures, the tribute that is due . . . the characters selected to devise and adopt them.

The first decade was of course unique precisely because it was first; everything was precedent making, and nothing was secure. It was a state-building decade in which relations between the president and Congress were more cooperative than they would be at any time thereafter. The First Congress of 1789–1791 accomplished an incredible amount. In seven short months following Washington's inauguration, Congress provided for the organization of the executive and judicial branches, established a system of national revenue, and worked through the first seventeen amendments proposed to the Constitution, ten of which were to be ratified to become the Bill of Rights.[23]

One of the last actions of the First Congress, First Session, was to authorize the secretary of the treasury, Alexander Hamilton, to develop a policy to establish a system for national credit. In January 1790, during the Second Session, Hamilton submitted to Congress such a proposal; his *Report on Public Credit* is

---

[23]See Richard Buel, Jr., *Securing the Revolution: Ideology in American Politics, 1789–1815* (Ithaca, NY: Cornell University Press, 1972), Part I.

one of the great state papers in the history of American public policy. In 1791, Hamilton presented the second of the reports ordered by Congress, the *Report on Manufactures*, probably of even greater significance than the first, because its proposals for internal improvements and industrial policies influenced Congress's agenda for years to come. Thus, it was Congress that ordered that a policy agenda be prepared by the president or his agent. In creating the executive departments, however, Congress (in particular the House) was so fearful of the powers to be lodged in the Treasury Department that it came close to adopting a three-man board, which many Antifederalists favored. The compromise tried to make the Treasury Department an agent of Congress rather than simply a member of the independent executive branch.[24] This kind of cooperation resembles the British parliamentary system, but it was not to last.

Before the Republic was a decade old, Congress began to develop a strong organization, including its own elected leadership, the first standing committees, and the party hierarchies. By President Jefferson's second term (1805), the executive branch was beginning to play the secondary role anticipated by the Constitution. The quality of presidential performance and then of presidential personality and character declined accordingly. The president during this era was seen by some observers as little more than America's "chief clerk." It was said of President James Madison, who had been principal author of the Constitution, that he knew everything about government except how to govern. Indeed, after Jefferson and until the beginning of this century, most historians agree that Presidents Jackson and Lincoln were the only exceptions to what had been a dreary succession of weak presidents. And those two exceptions can be explained. Jackson was a war hero and founder of the Democratic party. Lincoln was also a founder of his party, the Republican party, and although not a war hero, he was a wartime president who exercised the extraordinary powers that are available to any president during war, because during war the Constitution is put on hold. Both Jackson and Lincoln are considered great presidents because they used their great power wisely. But it is important in the history of the presidency that neither of these great presidents left their own powers as a new institutional legacy to their successors. That is to say, once Jackson and Lincoln left office, the presidency went back to the subordinate role it played during the nineteenth century.

One of the reasons that so few great men became presidents in the nineteenth century is that there was only occasional room for greatness in such a weak office.[25] As Chapter 3 indicated, the national government of that period was not a

---

[24]See, for example, Forrest McDonald, *The Presidency of George Washington* (Lawrence: University Press of Kansas, 1974), pp. 36–42.

[25]For related appraisals, see Jeffrey Tulis, *The Rhetorical Presidency* (Princeton: Princeton University Press, 1987); Stephen Skowronek, *The Politics Presidents Make: Leadership from John Adams to George Bush* (Cambridge: Harvard University Press, 1993); and Robert Spitzer, *President and Congress: Executive Hegemony at the Crossroads of American Government* (New York: McGraw-Hill, 1993).

particularly powerful entity. Moreover, most of the policies adopted by the national government were designed mainly to promote the expansion of commerce. These could be directed and administered by the congressional committees and political parties without much reliance on an executive bureaucracy.

Another reason for the weak presidency of the nineteenth century is that during this period the presidency was not closely linked to major national political and social forces. Indeed, there were few important *national* political or social forces to which presidents could have linked themselves even if they had wanted to. Federalism had taken very good care of this by fragmenting political interests and diverting the energies of interest groups toward the state and local levels of government, where most key decisions were being made.

The presidency was strengthened somewhat in the 1830s with the introduction of the national convention system of nominating presidential candidates. Until then, presidential candidates had been nominated by their party's congressional delegates. This was the *caucus* system of nominating candidates, and it was derisively called "King Caucus" because any candidate for president had to be beholden to the party's leaders in Congress in order to get the party's nomination and the support of the party's congressional delegation in the election. The national nominating convention arose outside Congress in order to provide some representation for a party's voters who lived in districts where they weren't numerous enough to elect a member of Congress. The political party in each state made its own provisions for selecting delegates to attend the presidential nominating convention, and in virtually all states the selection was dominated by the party leaders (called "bosses" by the opposition party). It is only in recent decades that state laws have intervened to regularize the selection process and to provide (in all but a few instances) for open election of delegates. The convention system quickly became the most popular method of nominating candidates for all elective offices and remained so until well into the twentieth century, when it succumbed to the criticism that it was a nondemocratic method dominated by a few leaders in a "smoke-filled room." But in the nineteenth century, it was seen as a victory for democracy against the congressional elite. And the national convention gave the presidency a base of power independent of Congress.

History Principle
The presidency was strengthened somewhat in the 1830s with the introduction of a national convention system of nominating presidential candidates.

This additional independence did not immediately transform the presidency into the office we recognize today because the parties disappeared back into their states and Congress once the national election was over. But the national convention did begin to open the presidency to larger social forces and newly organized interests in society. In other words, it gave the presidency a constituency base that would eventually support and demand increased presidential power. Improvements in telephone, telegraph, and other forms of mass communication allowed individuals to share their complaints and allowed national leaders—especially presidents and presidential candidates—to reach out directly to people to ally themselves with, and even sometimes to create, popular groups and forces. Eventually, though more slowly, the presidential selection process began to be further democratized, with the adoption of primary elections through which millions of ordinary citizens were given an opportunity to take part in the presidential nominating process by popular selection of convention delegates.

Despite political and social conditions favoring the enhancement of presidential power, however, the development of presidential government as we know it today did not mature until the middle of our own century. For a long period, even as the national government began to grow, Congress was careful to keep tight rein on the president's power. For example, when Congress began to make its first efforts to exert power over the economy (beginning in 1887 with the adoption of the Interstate Commerce Act and in 1890 with the adoption of the Sherman Antitrust Act), it sought to keep this power away from the president and the executive branch by placing these new regulatory policies in "independent regulatory commissions" responsible to Congress rather than to the president (see also Chapter 7).

The real turning point in the history of American national government came during the administration of Franklin Delano Roosevelt. The New Deal was a response to political forces that had been gathering national strength and focus for fifty years. What is remarkable is not that they gathered but that they were so long gaining influence in Washington—and even then it took the Great Depression, a popular new president, and substantial working majorities for his party in both chambers of Congress to bring about a new shape to the national government. The New Deal combined the personal brilliance and persuasiveness of a new president, economic conditions that generated an agenda of political action and unified partisan government, and a bargaining circumstance that put a premium on coordination among kindred spirits in the Capitol and White House. Roosevelt seized the opportunity, and the shape of American government has never been the same since.

The New Deal and the Presidency

The "First Hundred Days" of the Roosevelt administration in 1933 had no parallel in U.S. history. But this period was only the beginning. The policies proposed by President Roosevelt and adopted by Congress during the first thousand days of his administration so changed the size and character of the national government that they constitute a moment in American history equivalent to the founding or to the Civil War. The president's constitutional obligation to see "that the laws be faithfully executed" became, during Roosevelt's presidency, virtually a responsibility to shape the laws before executing them.

New Programs Expand the Role of National Government   Many of the New Deal programs were extensions of the traditional national government approach, which was described already in Chapter 3 (see especially Table 3.1). But the New Deal went well beyond the traditional approach, adopting types of policies never before tried on a large scale by the national government; it began intervening into economic life in ways that had hitherto been reserved to the states. In other words, the national government discovered that it, too, had "police power" and could directly regulate individuals as well as provide roads and other services.

The new programs were such dramatic departures from the traditional policies of the national government that their constitutionality was in doubt. The Supreme Court in fact declared several of them unconstitutional, mainly on the grounds that in regulating the conduct of individuals or their employers, the national government was reaching beyond "*inter*state" into "*intra*state," essentially local, matters. Most of the New Deal remained in constitutional limbo until 1937, five years after Roosevelt was first elected and one year after his landslide 1936 re-election.

The turning point came with *National Labor Relations Board v. Jones & Laughlin Steel Corporation.* At issue was the National Labor Relations Act, or Wagner Act, which prohibited corporations from interfering with the efforts of employees to organize into unions, to bargain collectively over wages and working conditions, and under certain conditions, to go on strike and engage in picketing. The newly formed National Labor Relations Board (NLRB) had ordered Jones & Laughlin to reinstate workers fired because of their union activities. The appeal reached the Supreme Court because Jones & Laughlin had made a constitutional issue over the fact that its manufacturing activities were local and therefore beyond the national government's reach. The Supreme Court rejected this argument with the response that a big company with subsidiaries and suppliers in many states was innately in interstate commerce:

> When industries organize themselves on a national scale, making their relation to interstate commerce the dominant factor in their activities, how can it be maintained that their industrial labor relations constitute a forbidden field into which Congress may not enter when it is necessary to protect interstate commerce from the paralyzing consequences of industrial war?[26]

Since the end of the New Deal, the Supreme Court has never again seriously questioned the constitutionality of an important act of Congress broadly authorizing the executive branch to intervene into the economy or society.[27]

[26]NLRB v. Jones & Laughlin Steel Corporation, 301 U.S. 1 (1937). Congress had attempted to regulate the economy before 1933, as with the Interstate Commerce Act and Sherman Antitrust Act of the late nineteenth century and with the Federal Trade Act and the Federal Reserve in the Wilson period. But these were rare attempts, and each was restricted very carefully to a narrow and acceptable definition of "interstate commerce." The big break did not come until after 1933.

[27]Some will argue that there are some exceptions to this statement. One was the 1976 case declaring unconstitutional Congress's effort to supply national minimum wage standards to state and local government employees (National League of Cities v. Usery, 426 U.S. 833 [1976]). But the Court reversed itself on this nine years later, in 1985 (Garcia v. San Antonio Metropolitan Transit Authority, 469 U.S. 528 [1985]). Another was the 1986 case declaring unconstitutional the part of the Gramm-Rudman law authorizing the comptroller general to make "across the board" budget cuts when total appropriations exceeded legally established ceilings (Bowsher v. Synar, 478 U.S. 714 [1986]). In 1999, executive authority was compromised somewhat by the Court's decision to question the Federal Communication Commission's authority to supervise telephone deregulation under the Telecommunications Act of 1996. But cases such as these are few and far between, and they only touch on part of a law, not the constitutionality of an entire program.

Delegation of Power The most important constitutional effect of Congress's actions and the Supreme Court's approval of those actions during the New Deal was the enhancement of *presidential power.* Most major acts of Congress in this period involved significant exercises of control over the economy. But few programs specified the actual controls to be used. Instead, Congress authorized the president or, in some cases, a new agency to determine what the controls would be. Some of the new agencies were independent commissions responsible to Congress. But most of the new agencies and programs of the New Deal were placed in the executive branch directly under presidential authority.

Technically, this form of congressional act is called the "delegation of power." In theory, the delegation of power works as follows: (1) Congress recognizes a problem; (2) Congress acknowledges that it has neither the time nor expertise to deal with the problem; and (3) Congress therefore sets the basic policies and then delegates to an agency the power to "fill in the details." But in practice, Congress was delegating not merely the power to "fill in the details," but actual and real *policy-making powers,* that is, real legislative powers, to the executive branch. For example, the president through the secretary of agriculture was authorized by the 1938 Agricultural Adjustment Act to determine the amount of acreage each and every farmer could devote to crops that had been determined to be surplus commodities, in order to keep prices up and surpluses down. This new authority extended from growers of thousands of acres of wheat for market to farmers cultivating twenty-five acres of feed for their own livestock.[28]

This authority continues today in virtually the same form, covering many commodities and millions of acres. Lest this is thought to be a power delegated to the president only during emergencies like the 1930s, take the example of environmental protection laws passed by Congress in the 1960s and 1970s. Under the president, the Environmental Protection Agency was given the authority to "monitor the conditions of the environment," "establish quantitative base lines for pollution levels," and "set and enforce standards of air and water quality and for individual pollutants."[29]

No modern government can avoid the delegation of significant legislative powers to the executive branch. But the fact remains that this delegation produced a fundamental shift in the American constitutional framework. During the 1930s, the growth of the national government through acts delegating legislative power tilted the American national structure away from a Congress-centered

History Principle
The New Deal's expanded role for the national government enhanced presidential power.

---

[28]See Wickard v. Filburn, 317 U.S. 111 (1942).

[29]Environmental Reorganization Plan of 9 July 1970, reprinted in *Congressional Quarterly Almanac,* 1970, pp. 119a–120a. Other examples of broad delegations of power to the president will be found in Theodore J. Lowi, *The End of Liberalism* (New York: W. W. Norton, 1979), Chapter 5. See also Sotirios Barber, *The Constitution and the Delegation of Congressional Power* (Chicago: University of Chicago Press, 1975).

government toward a president-centered government.[30] Make no mistake, Congress continues to be the constitutional source of policy. Legislative supremacy remains a constitutional fact of life, even at the beginning of the twenty-first century, because delegations are *contingent*. And not all delegations are the same. A Democratic Congress, for example, is unwilling to empower a Republican president and vice versa; unified governments are more likely to engage in broad delegation than divided governments.[31] In short, Congress can rescind these delegations of power, restrict them with later amendments, and oversee the exercise of delegated power through congressional hearings, oversight agencies, budget controls, and other administrative tools. However, it is fair to say that presidential government has become an administrative fact of life as government-by-delegation has expanded greatly over the past hundred years. The world of Woodrow Wilson's *Congressional Government* (1885) is forever changed. But Congress has many "clubs behind its door" with which to influence the manner in which the executive branch exercises its newly won power to delegate authority.

PRESIDENTIAL GOVERNMENT

Rationality Principle

Congress delegates more power to the president as more demands are made on its agenda.

Institution Principle

Congress delegates authority to the president but also maintains the means to influence how the executive branch exercises this power.

The locus of policy decision making shifted to the executive branch because, as we just noted, Congress made delegations of authority to the president. But this should not be construed as Congress having abdicated its constitutional position in policy making. Delegation is not abdication, and Congress retained many strings by which to oversee and regulate the executive's use of delegated authority.[32] Congress delegated to the executive for instrumental reasons, much as a principal delegates to an agent. An expanded agenda of political demands, necessitated first by economic crisis—the Great Depression—but also by an accumulation of the effects of nearly a century's worth of industrialization, urbanization, and greater integration into the world economy, confronted the national government, forcing Congress's hand. The legislature itself was limited in its ability to expand its own capacity to undertake these growing responsibilities, so delegation proved a natural administrative strategy. If you can't do it yourself, then hire agents to do it! The president, executive branch bureaus, and the independent regulatory commissions constituted precisely

---

[30]The Supreme Court did in fact *dis*approve broad delegations of legislative power by declaring the National Industrial Recovery Act of 1933 unconstitutional on the grounds that Congress did not accompany the broad delegations with sufficient standards or guidelines for presidential discretion (Panama Refining Co. v. Ryan, 293 U.S. 388 [1935], and Schechter Poultry Corp. v. United States, 295 U.S. 495 [1935]). The Supreme Court has never reversed those two decisions, but it has also never really followed them. Thus, broad delegations of legislative power from Congress to the executive branch can be presumed to be constitutional.

[31]David Epstein and Sharyn O'Halloran, *Delegating Powers: A Transaction Cost Politics Approach to Policy Making Under Separate Powers* (New York: Cambridge University Press, 1999).

[32]D. Roderick Kiewiet and Mathew D. McCubbins, *The Logic of Delegation* (Chicago: University of Chicago Press, 1991).

this army of agents. They were (at least in part) *congressional* agents, however, since it was delegation with a catch—oversight, regulation, amendment, budgetary control, etc., from the legislative branch. Nevertheless, these delegations certainly gave a far greater role to the president, empowering this "agent" to initiate in his own right.

In the case of Franklin D. Roosevelt, it is especially appropriate to refer to his New Deal as launching an era of "presidential government." Congress certainly retained many "clubs behind its door" with which to threaten, cajole, encourage, and persuade its executive agent to do its bidding. But presidents in general, and Roosevelt in particular, are not *only* agents of the Congress, and not *only* dependent upon Congress for resources and authority. They are also agents of national constituencies before whom they are eager to demonstrate their capacity for leadership in executing constituency policy agendas.[33] Likewise, congressional delegations of power are not the only resources available to a president.

Presidents have at their disposal a variety of other formal and informal resources that have important implications for their ability to govern. Indeed, without these other resources, presidents would lack the ability—the tools of management and public mobilization—to make much use of the power and responsibility given to them by Congress. Let us first consider the president's formal or official resources and then, in the section following, turn to the more informal resources that affect a president's capacity to govern, in particular the president's base of popular support.

Formal Resources of Presidential Power

Patronage As a Tool of Management   The first tool of management available to most presidents is a form of ***patronage***—the choice of high-level political appointees. Political appointments should be thought of as *strategic* resources for presidents—as productive factors or instruments that may be deployed to achieve presidential objectives. These appointments allow the president to fill top management positions with individuals who will attempt to carry out his agenda. But he must appoint individuals who have experience and interest in the programs that they are to administer and who share the president's goals with respect to these programs. At the same time, presidents use the appointment process to build links to powerful political and economic constituencies by giving representation to important state political party organizations, the business community, organized labor, the scientific and university communities, organized agriculture, and certain large and well-organized religious groups. Of course, most high-level

patronage The resources available to higher officials, usually opportunities to make partisan appointments to offices and to confer grants, licenses, or special favors to supporters.

 Rationality Principle

Presidential appointments are strategic resources that help a president achieve political objectives.

---

[33]As the political scientist Terry Moe writes, "This is the rational basis for the institutional presidency. Throughout [the twentieth] century, presidents have struggled to provide themselves with a structural capacity for leadership by building institutions of their own." See Terry Moe, "Presidents, Institutions, and Theory," in George C. Edwards III, John H. Kessel, and Bert A. Rockman, eds., *Researching the Presidency: Vital Questions, New Approaches* (Pittsburgh: University of Pittsburgh Press, 1993), p. 367.

appointments to the bureaucracy and the courts must be confirmed by the Senate. This means that appointees must be acceptable to a Senate majority, but such appointments also constitute opportunities for a president to repay senators for previous favors or to obligate senators for favors down the road.

cabinet The secretaries, or chief administrators, of the major departments of the federal government. Cabinet secretaries are appointed by the president with the consent of the Senate.

The Cabinet   In the American system of government, the ***cabinet*** is the traditional but informal designation for the heads of all the major federal government departments. The cabinet has no constitutional status. Unlike in England and many other parliamentary countries, where the cabinet *is* the government, the American cabinet is not a collective body. It meets but makes no decisions as a group. Each appointment must be approved by the Senate but cabinet members are not responsible to the Senate or to Congress at large. Cabinet appointments help build party and popular support, but the cabinet is not a party organ. The cabinet is made up of directors, but is not a board of directors.

Aware of this fact, the president tends to develop a burning impatience with and a mild distrust of cabinet members; to make the cabinet a rubber stamp for actions already decided on; and to demand results, or the appearance of results, more immediately and more frequently than most department heads can provide. Since cabinet appointees generally have not shared political careers with the president or with each other, and since they may meet literally for the first time after their selection, the formation of an effective governing group out of this motley collection of appointments is unlikely.

Some presidents have relied more heavily on an "inner cabinet," the National Security Council (NSC). The NSC, established by law in 1947, is composed of the president, the vice president, the secretaries of state, defense, and the treasury, the attorney general, and other officials invited by the president. It has its own staff of foreign-policy specialists run by the special assistant to the president for national security affairs. For these highest appointments, presidents turn to people from outside Washington, usually long-time associates. A counterpart, the Domestic Council, was created by law in 1970, but no specific members were designated for it. President Clinton hit upon his own version of the Domestic Council, called the National Economic Council, which shares competing functions with the Council of Economic Advisers.

Presidents have obviously been uneven and unpredictable in their reliance on the NSC and other subcabinet bodies, because executive management is inherently a personal matter. Despite all the personal variations, however, one generalization can be made: presidents have increasingly preferred the White House staff instead of the cabinet as their means of managing the gigantic executive branch.

The White House Staff[34]   The White House staff is composed mainly of analysts and advisers. Although many of the top White House staffers are given the title

---

[34]A substantial portion of this section is taken from Lowi, *The Personal President*, pp. 141–50.

"special assistant" for a particular task or sector, the types of judgments they are expected to make and the kinds of advice they are supposed to give are a good deal broader and more generally political than those which come from the Executive Office of the President or from the cabinet departments.

From an informal group of fewer than a dozen people (at one time popularly called the **Kitchen Cabinet**), and no more than four dozen at the height of the domestic Roosevelt presidency in 1937, the White House staff has grown substantially (see Table 6.1).[35] President Clinton promised during the 1992 campaign to reduce the White House staff by 25 percent, and by 1996 had trimmed it by about 15 percent. Nevertheless, a large White House staff has become essential.

The biggest variation among presidential management practices lies not in the size of the White House staff but in its organization. President Reagan went to the extreme in delegating important management powers to his chief of staff, and he elevated his budget director to an unprecedented level of power in *policy* making rather than merely *budget* making. Former president Bush centralized his staff even more under Chief of Staff John Sununu. At the same time, Bush continued to deal directly with his cabinet heads, the press, and key members of Congress. President Clinton showed a definite preference for competition among equals in his cabinet and among senior White House officials, obviously liking competition and conflict among staff members, for which FDR's staff was also famous. But the troubles Clinton had in turning this conflict and competition into coherent policies and well-articulated messages suggest that he might have done better to emulate his immediate predecessors in their preference for hierarchy and centralization.[36]

Kitchen Cabinet
An informal group of advisers to whom the president turns for counsel and guidance. Members of the official cabinet may or may not also be members of the Kitchen Cabinet.

The Executive Office of the President   The development of the White House staff can be appreciated only in its relation to the still larger Executive Office of the President (EOP). Created in 1939, the EOP is what is often called the "institutional presidency"—the permanent agencies that perform defined management tasks for the president. The most important and the largest EOP agency is the Office of Management and Budget (OMB). Its roles in preparing the national budget, designing the president's program, reporting on agency activities, and overseeing regulatory proposals make OMB personnel part of virtually every conceivable presidential responsibility. The status and power of the OMB has grown in importance with each successive president. The process of budgeting at one time was a "bottom-up" procedure, with expenditure and program requests passing from the lowest bureaus through the departments to "clearance" in OMB and hence to Congress, where each agency could be called in to reveal what its

---

[35]All the figures since 1967, and probably 1957, are understated, because additional White House staff members were on "detailed" service from the military and other departments (some secretly assigned) and are not counted here because they were not on the White House payroll.

[36]See Donna K. H. Walter, "The Disarray at the White House Proves Clinton Wouldn't Last as a Fortune 500 CEO," *The Plain Dealer*, 10 July 1994, p. JC; and Paul Richeter, "The Battle for Washington: Leon Panetta's Burden," *Los Angeles Times Sunday Magazine*, 8 January 1995, p. 16.

TABLE 6.1

The Expanding White House Staff

YEAR	PRESIDENT	FULL-TIME EMPLOYEES*
1937	Franklin D. Roosevelt	45
1947	Harry S. Truman	190
1957	Dwight D. Eisenhower	364
1967	Lyndon B. Johnson	251
1972	Richard M. Nixon	550
1975	Gerald R. Ford	533
1980	Jimmy Carter	488
1984	Ronald Reagan	575
1992	George Bush	605**
1996	Bill Clinton	511**

*The vice president employs over 20 staffers, and there are at least 100 on the staff of the National Security Council. These people work in and around the White House and Executive Office but are not included in the above totals.

**These figures include the staffs of the Office of the President, the Executive Residence, and the Office of the Vice President. None of the figures include the employees temporarily detailed to the White House from outside agencies (approximately 50 to 75 in 1992 and 1996). While not precisely comparable, these figures convey a sense of scale.

SOURCE: Thomas E. Cronin, "The Swelling of the Presidency: Can Anyone Reverse the Tide?" in *American Government: Readings and Cases*, 8th ed., ed. Peter Woll (Boston: Little Brown, 1984), p. 347. Copyright © 1984 by Thomas E. Cronin. Reproduced with the permission of the author. Figures for 1992 and 1996 provided by the Office of Management and Budget and the White House.

"original request" had been before OMB revised it. Now the budgeting process is "top-down"; OMB sets the terms of discourse for agencies as well as for Congress. The director of OMB is now one of the most powerful officials in Washington. The staff of the Council of Economic Advisers (CEA) constantly analyzes the economy and economic trends and attempts to give the president the ability to anticipate events rather than to wait and react to events. The Council on Environmental Quality was designed to do the same for environmental issues as the CEA does for economic issues. The National Security Council (NSC) is composed of designated cabinet officials who meet regularly with the president to advise him on the large national security picture. The staff of the NSC both

FIGURE 6.2

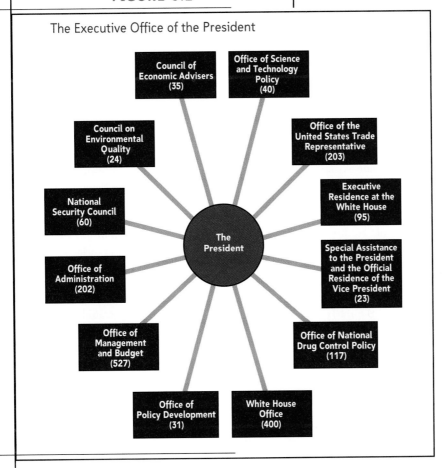

The Executive Office of the President

- Council of Economic Advisers (35)
- Office of Science and Technology Policy (40)
- Council on Environmental Quality (24)
- Office of the United States Trade Representative (203)
- National Security Council (60)
- Executive Residence at the White House (95)
- Office of Administration (202)
- The President
- Special Assistance to the President and the Official Residence of the Vice President (23)
- Office of Management and Budget (527)
- Office of National Drug Control Policy (117)
- Office of Policy Development (31)
- White House Office (400)

NOTE: Figures in parentheses refer to number of staff. Figures are estimates for 2001.

SOURCE: Office of Management and Budget, *Budget of the United States Government, Fiscal Year 2002* (Washington, DC: Government Printing Office, 2001), pp. 957–67.

assimilates and analyzes data from all intelligence-gathering agencies (CIA, etc.). Other EOP agencies perform more specialized tasks for the president.

Somewhere between fifteen hundred and two thousand highly specialized people work for the EOP agencies.[37] Figure 6.2 shows the official numbers of employees in each agency of the EOP. However, these numbers do not include a substantial but variable number of key specialists detailed to EOP agencies from

[37]The actual number is difficult to estimate because, as with White House staff, some EOP personnel, especially in national security work, are detailed to the EOP from outside agencies.

outside agencies, especially from the Pentagon to the staff of the NSC. The importance of each agency in the EOP varies according to the personal orientations of each president. For example, the NSC staff was of immense importance under President Nixon, especially because it served essentially as the personal staff of presidential assistant Henry Kissinger. But it was of less importance to former president Bush, who looked outside the EOP altogether for military policy matters, much more to the Joint Chiefs of Staff and its chair at the time, General Colin Powell.

The Vice Presidency The vice presidency is a constitutional anomaly even though the office was created along with the presidency by the Constitution. The vice president exists for two purposes only: to succeed the president in case of death, resignation, or incapacitation and to preside over the Senate casting the tie-breaking vote when necessary.[38]

The main value of the vice presidency as a political resource for the president is electoral. Traditionally, a presidential candidate's most important rule for the choice of a running mate is that he or she bring the support of at least one state (preferably a large one) not otherwise likely to support the ticket. Another rule holds that the vice presidential nominee should provide some regional balance and, wherever possible, some balance among various ideological or ethnic subsections of the party. It is very doubtful that John Kennedy would have won in 1960 without his vice presidential candidate, Lyndon Johnson, and the contribution Johnson made to carrying Texas. The emphasis, however, has recently shifted away from geographical to ideological balance. In 1992, Bill Clinton combined considerations of region and ideology in his selection of a vice presidential running mate. The choice of Al Gore signaled that Bill Clinton was solidly in the right wing of the Democratic party and would also remain steadfastly a Southerner. Democratic strategists had become convinced that Clinton could not win without carrying a substantial number of Southern states.

George W. Bush and Al Gore continued this shift in emphasis in the 2000 election. Bush certainly didn't select Dick Cheney primarily to bring his home state of Wyoming (with its three electoral votes) into the fold! Rather, it was to add some political experience (especially in military and foreign affairs) and gravitas to the ticket. Gore selected Joe Lieberman of Connecticut as his running mate, making Lieberman the first Jewish-American to serve on a national ticket. The Jewish vote, though small, is distributed in the urban areas of pivotal states. Campaign finance considerations also may have figured in this choice given the Democratic dependence on contributions from the heavily Jewish Hollywood film industry. Geographically, it was not Connecticut, Lieberman's home state, that made him attractive—it was never really in doubt as a Democratic state—but rather his prospective appeal in Florida, home to a large population of Jewish-Americans. Presidents have constantly

[38]Article I, Section 3, provides that "The Vice President . . . shall be President of the Senate, but shall have no Vote, unless they be equally divided." This is the only vote the vice president is allowed.

promised to give their vice presidents more responsibility, but they almost always break their promise, indicating that they are unable to utilize the vice presidency as a management or political resource after the election. No one can explain exactly why. Perhaps it is just too much trouble to share responsibility. Perhaps the president as head of state feels unable to share any part of that status. Perhaps, like many adult Americans who do not draw up their wills, presidents may simply dread contemplating their own death. But management style is certainly a factor. President Clinton relied greatly on his vice president, Al Gore. Gore emerged as one of the most effective figures in the White House and earned a place as arguably the most plugged-in, strategically located vice president in history.

However, Gore did not hold the record long without some significant competition from his successor, Dick Cheney. Even before inauguration, Cheney was being referred to as the prime minister for a young president with little experience and even less electoral credibility. Cheney's resume was extraordinary; he served as a member of and a leader in Congress, White House chief of staff, secretary of defense under the president's father, successful CEO of a major international oil company, and senior adviser to George W. for selection of a vice presidential running mate, until Bush decided Cheney was his choice. Unquestioned chieftain of the transition team under unusually difficult conditions, Cheney came into the office with an unprecedented stature.

Informal Resources of Presidential Power

Elections As a Resource   What do we mean by the "democratization" of the presidency? We have already observed that an ordinary citizen placed legitimately in the presidency would be very powerful, regardless of any other consideration, because the Constitution and Congress have delegated to that office the legal powers and resources—in money and personnel—to carry out the duties of that office. But as we also saw, presidential power comes from resources other than the formal, legal ones: success often results from strategic interactions with others and reliance on the democratic base of the presidency. Obviously, presidents vary in their real power according to the size of their electoral victory. With a landslide (decisive) national electoral victory, a president may claim a "mandate," which is interpreted to mean that the electorate approved the victorious candidate's promised programs, and Congress must therefore go along. But even short of a mandate, a decisive election does increase the effectiveness of presidential leadership in Congress. Presidents Johnson and Reagan were much more effective in Congress during the "honeymoon" year following their landslide elections of 1964 and 1980, respectively, than were Kennedy after 1960, Nixon after 1968, and Carter after 1976. All three were hampered by their narrow victory margins.

President Clinton, an action-oriented president, was nevertheless seriously hampered by having been elected in 1992 by a minority of the popular vote, a mere 43 percent. Clinton was re-elected in 1996 with 49 percent of the vote, a larger percentage of the electorate, but still a minority. His appeals to bipartisanship in 1997 reflected his lack of a mandate from the electorate.

The outcome of the 2000 presidential election indicated a popular-vote deadlock of 48 percent to 48 percent, reflecting a difference of a mere 500,000 votes out of approximately 103 million cast. Given the closeness of the election—as well as the close partisan balance in Congress—it mattered little who won, since any president possessing such a narrow margin of victory would have little claim to mandate. In this context, the United States can look forward to a long siege of stalemate between the president and Congress until, at the earliest, the 2002 congressional elections and perhaps beyond, i.e., if those elections do not produce a significant shift in the number of House and Senate seats held by the president's party.

But the electoral base of presidential power goes deeper than the size of the margin during an election. Presidential power also comes from the selection process prior to the election. In the United States this is called the nominating process. Nomination means to name, and naming is what each party does when its members select the person they want to support as their candidate for a particular elective office. We will deal with this in detail in Chapter 11, but it is important to place the nominating process in the context of the presidency.

As we mentioned earlier, the original method for nominating presidential candidates was called "King Caucus"—the selection of a party's candidate for president by members of Congress who were declared affiliates of that party. But King Caucus was actually undermining both the independence of the presidency and the viability of the separation of powers by making all candidates for president, including the one eventually elected, beholden to Congress. America was becoming a parliamentary, "fusion-of-powers" system. The rise of the national presidential nominating convention in the 1830s gave the presidency a popular power base, which allowed enough independence from Congress to restore the separation of powers. Although the national convention method fell into disrepute during the twentieth century for being too much under the control of party bosses in "smoke-filled rooms," it was, relative to King Caucus, an extremely significant democratizing force in the nineteenth century: the method broadened the base of the parties by permitting all districts in the country to send delegates to a national convention for president, even if that district was not represented in Congress by a member of its party. Thus the national convention provided a channel for popular loyalty to the president that was separate from any loyalty that individuals might hold for their member of Congress.

Nomination by primary elections has become the more popular method, but primaries did not destroy the national convention system, because primaries *elect* the delegates who go to the national conventions (rather than letting the state bosses appoint their own personal choices). It has now become an absolute prerequisite that presidential candidates prove themselves by having a significant number of delegates pledge their support in the primaries. This has made presidential candidacies much more expensive, but has also given the victor a far wider public base. The evolution of presidential selection, from caucus to convention to primary, is an example of what we mean by "democratization" of the presidency.

Initiative as a Presidential Resource   "To initiate" means to originate, and in government that can mean power. The framers of the Constitution clearly saw this as one of the keys to executive power. The president as an individual is able to initiate decisive action, while Congress as a relatively large assembly must deliberate and debate before it can act. Initiative also means the ability to formulate proposals for important policies. There is power in this too.

Presidents often send proposals to Congress. Congress, in turn, takes these proposals up by referring them to the relevant committee of jurisdiction. Sometimes these proposals are said to be "dead on arrival," an indication that presidential preferences are at loggerheads with those in the House or Senate. This is especially common during periods of divided government in which the president and at least one chamber majority are loyal to different parties. In such circumstances, presidents and legislators engage in *bargaining*, although at the end of the day the status quo may prevail. Presidents are typically in a weak position in this circumstance, especially if they have grand plans to change the status quo.[39] During periods of unified government, the president has fellow copartisans in charge of each chamber; in these cases, the president may, indeed, seize the initiative, seeking to *coordinate* policy initiatives from the White House. Political scientist Charles Cameron suggests that the distinction between unified and divided government is quite consequential for presidential "style": it makes the chief executive either bargainer in chief or coordinator in chief.[40]

Over the years, Congress has sometimes deliberately and sometimes inadvertently enhanced the president's power to seize the initiative. Curiously, the most important congressional gift to the president seems the most mundane, namely, the Office of Management and Budget, known until 1974 as the Bureau of the Budget.

In 1921, Congress provided for an "executive budget," and turned over to a new Bureau of the Budget in the executive branch the responsibility for maintaining the nation's accounts. In 1939, this bureau was moved from the Treasury Department to the newly created Executive Office of the President. The purpose of this move was to permit the president to make use of the budgeting process as a management tool. Through the new budgeting process, the president could keep better track of what was going on among all of the executive branch's hundreds of agencies and hundreds of thousands of civil servants. In this respect, the budget is simply a good investigative and informational tool for management. But in addition to that, Congress provided for a process called *legislative clearance,* defined as the power given to the president to require all agencies of the executive branch to submit through the budget director all requests for new legislation along with estimates of their budgetary needs. Thus, heads of agencies must submit budget requests to the White House so that the requests of all the competing agencies can be balanced. Although there are many violations of this rule, it is usually observed.

Collective Action Principle
Whether government is divided or unified has a big influence on whether a president is a bargainer or a coordinator.

legislative clearance   The power given to the president to require all agencies of the executive branch to submit through the budget director all requests for new legislation along with estimates of their budgetary needs.

[39] Kiewiet and McCubbins, *The Logic of Delegation.*
[40] Cameron, "Bargaining and Presidential Power."

At first, legislative clearance was a defensive weapon, used mainly to allow the president to avoid the embarrassment of having to oppose or veto legislation originating in his own administration. But eventually, legislative clearance became far more important. It became the starting point for the development of comprehensive presidential programs.[41] As noted earlier, recent presidents have also used the budget process as a method of gaining tighter "top down" management control.

Presidential proposals fill the congressional agenda and tend to dominate congressional hearings and floor debates, not to speak of the newspapers. Everyone recognizes this, but few appreciate how much of this ability to maintain the initiative is directly and formally attributable to legislative clearance. Through this seemingly routine process, the president is able to review the activities of his administrators, to obtain a comprehensive view of all legislative proposals, and to identify those that are in accord with his own preferences and priorities. This is why the whole process of choice has come to be called "planning the president's program." Professed anti-government Republicans, such as Reagan and Bush, as well as allegedly pro-government Democrats, such as Clinton, are alike in their commitment to central management, control, and program planning. This is precisely why all three presidents have given the budget director cabinet status.

Presidential Use of the Media   The president is able to take full advantage of access to the communications media mainly because of the legal and constitutional bases of initiative. In the media, reporting on what is new sells newspapers. The president has at his command the thousands of policy proposals that come up to him through the administrative agencies; he can feed these to the media as being newsworthy initiatives. Consequently, virtually all newspapers and television networks habitually look to the White House as the chief source of news about public policy. They tend to assign one of their most skillful reporters to the White House "beat." And since news is money, they need the president as much as he needs them in order to meet their mutual need to make news. In this manner, the formal and the informal aspects of initiative tend to reinforce each other: the formal resources put the president at the center of policy formulation; this becomes the center of gravity for all buyers and sellers of news, which in turn requires the president to provide easy access to this news. Members of Congress, especially senators, are also key sources of news. But Congress is an anarchy of sources. The White House has more control over what and when. That's what initiative is all about.

Different presidents have used the media in quite different ways. For example, the press conference as an institution probably got its start in the 1930s, when Franklin Roosevelt gave several a month. But his press conferences were not recorded or broadcast "live"; direct quotes were not permitted. The model

---

[41]Although dated in some respects, the best description and evaluations of budgeting as a management tool and as a tool of program planning is still found in Richard E. Neustadt's two classic articles, "Presidency and Legislation: Planning the President's Program," and "Presidency and Legislation: The Growth of Central Clearance," in *American Political Science Review*, September 1954 and December 1955.

we know today got its start with Eisenhower and was put into final form by Kennedy. Since 1961, the presidential press conference has been a distinctive institution, available whenever the president wants to dominate the news. Between three hundred and four hundred certified reporters attend and file their accounts within minutes of the concluding words, "Thank you, Mr. President." But despite the importance of the press conference, its value to each president has varied. Although the average from Kennedy through Carter was about two press conferences a month, Johnson dropped virtually out of sight for almost half of 1965 when Vietnam was warming up, and so did Nixon for over five months in 1973 during the Watergate hearings. Moreover, Johnson and Ford preferred to call impromptu press conferences with only a few minutes' notice. President Reagan single-handedly brought the average down by holding only seven press conferences during his entire first year in office and only sporadically thereafter. In great contrast, former president Bush held more conferences during his first seventeen months than Reagan held in eight years. Bush also shifted them from elaborate prime-time affairs in the ornate East Room to less formal gatherings in the White House briefing room. Fewer reporters and more time for follow-up questions permitted media representatives to "concentrate on information for their stories, rather than getting attention for themselves."[42] President Clinton tended to take both the Reagan and Bush approaches, combining Reagan's high profile—elaborate press conferences and prime-time broadcasts—with the more personal one-on-one approach generally preferred by Bush.

Of course, in addition to the presidential press conference there are other routes from the White House to news prominence.[43] For example, President Nixon preferred direct television addresses, and President Carter tried to make the initiatives more homey with a television adaptation of President Roosevelt's "fireside chats." President Reagan made unusually good use of primetime television addresses and also instituted more informal but regular Saturday afternoon radio broadcasts, a tradition that President Clinton continued. Clinton also added various kinds of impromptu press conferences and town meetings.

Walter Mondale, while vice president in 1980, may have summed up the entire media matter with his observation that if he had to choose between the power to get on the nightly news and veto power, he would keep the former and jettison the latter.[44] Of course, substance also counts. If you aren't good in front of reporters, or if you say inane or inappropriate things, getting media coverage can be a disaster. As a result, presidents (and all other important public figures) go to great lengths to prepare well in advance in order to *appear* spontaneous.

[42]David Broder, "Some Newsworthy Presidential CPR," *Washington Post National Weekly Edition*, 4–10 June 1990, p. 4.

[43]See George Edwards III, *At the Margins—Presidential Leadership of Congress* (New Haven: Yale University Press, 1989), Chapter 7; and Robert Locander, "The President and the News Media," in *Dimensions of the Modern Presidency*, ed. Edward Kearney (St. Louis: Forum Press, 1981), pp. 49–52.

[44]Reported in Timothy E. Cook, *Governing with the News—The News Media as a Political Institution* (Chicago: University of Chicago Press, 1998), p. 133.

FIGURE 6.3

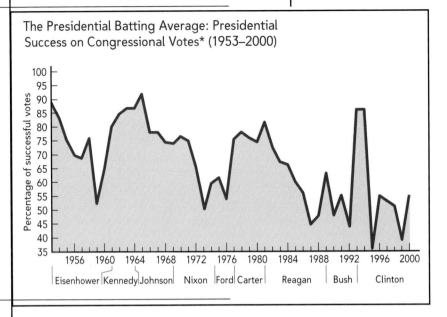

The Presidential Batting Average: Presidential Success on Congressional Votes* (1953–2000)

*Percentages based on votes on which presidents took a position.

SOURCE: *Congressional Quarterly Weekly Report*, 6 January 2001, p. 52.

This is why one of the greatest technological advances for presidents in the past fifty years is the "see-through" lectern, a transparent monitor that the speaker can see through and the audience can see back through as if it weren't there, but on the speaker's side is the text of the speech, which is scrolled. The speaker reads the text word for word while the unsuspecting audience sees an exceptionally well-prepared public figure.

Party as a Presidential Resource   Although on the decline, the president's party is far from insignificant as a political resource (see also Chapter 11). Figure 6.3 dramatically demonstrates the point with a forty-three-year history of the "presidential batting average" in Congress—the percentage of winning roll-call votes in Congress on bills publicly supported by the president.

Bill Clinton, in his first two years in office, enjoyed very high legislative success rates—86 percent in both 1993 and 1994. But these dropped drastically to 35.1 percent in 1995 and hovered around 50 percent in the years after (except for 1999, when success rates dropped to 39 percent). Clinton's pattern of congressional success demonstrates the *importance of the political party as a presidential resource*. Democratic control of Congress was a regular pattern between 1954 and 1994, and therefore presidential batting averages were very high, with a Democratic president and a Democratic House and Senate. President Eisenhower's averages were also very high for his first two years, when his own party controlled Congress; but they quickly dropped when Republicans lost control of Congress, as did President Clinton's success rate when Republicans took over Congress in 1995 following the 1994 election.

At the same time, party has its limitations as a resource. The more unified the president's party is behind his legislative requests, the more unified the opposition party is also likely to be. Unless the president's party majority is very large, he must also appeal to the opposition to make up for the inevitable defectors within the ranks of his own party. Consequently, the president often poses as being above partisanship in order to win "bipartisan" support in Congress. But to the extent he pursues a bipartisan strategy, he cannot throw himself fully into building the party loyalty and party discipline that would maximize the value of his own party's support in Congress. This is a dilemma for every president, particularly those faced with an opposition-controlled Congress.

Collective Action Principle

The more unified the president's party is in Congress, the more unified the opposition is likely to be.

The role of the filibuster in the Senate should not be underestimated in this context. Even a president with a large House majority and a good working Senate majority may not have the 60 votes needed to shut down debate in the Senate. Put differently, those in a position to threaten filibuster, though often constituting only a minority, can nevertheless extract concessions from a president who "thinks" he has the initiative! This is especially apparent in the case of presidential appointments, where individual senators can place a "hold" on the nomination, putting everyone on notice that if the president pursues this particular candidate, it will trigger a filibuster.[45]

Partisan opposition in Congress proved so strong that President Clinton was unable even to bring the centerpieces of his legislative agenda—health care and welfare reform—to votes during the years in which he enjoyed majorities in Congress. This helps explain the paradox of Clinton's legislative scorecard: high batting averages but failures on key issues. Clinton had a different kind of problem in 1997, one indicative of the vital role of the parties, even though in this case he was opposed by his own party. Clinton made a concerted effort throughout 1997 to restore "fast-track" authority to negotiate trade agreements that would get expedited review and yes-or-no votes in Congress, without the usual amendments that could substantially alter the agreement. Clinton feared he would lose in the House because of opposition by a large faction of his own party. So he turned to the Senate, even though the Constitution requires that such bills must originate in the House because they raise or lower revenues (in this case tariffs). He figured that a strong show of support in the Senate would influence the House. He even got the cooperation of Republican majority leader Senator Trent Lott in this flanking attack. The Senate action was not enough, however. The House leadership tabled the presidentially supported bill because of continued opposition by House Democrats, and the bill never even came to a

[45]A powerful argument that invokes this logic is that of Keith Krehbiel in *Pivotal Politics* (Chicago: University of Chicago Press, 1998).

vote. Clinton's difficulties in maintaining Democratic support in Congress were also evident from the October 1998 House vote in favor of investigating Clinton's possible impeachment. In the days leading up to the vote, Clinton and his staff lobbied House Democrats behind the scenes. Nonetheless, thirty-one Democrats broke ranks and voted in favor of the investigation. House Republicans, for their part, were united in favor of the impeachment inquiry. Fortunately for Clinton, Republicans failed to convince any Senate Democrats to convict him in his impeachment trial in early 1999.

Groups As a Presidential Resource   The classic case in modern times of groups as a resource for the presidency is the Roosevelt or New Deal coalition.[46] The New Deal coalition was composed of an inconsistent, indeed contradictory, set of interests. Some of these interests were not organized interest groups, but were regional interests, such as Southern whites, or residents of large cities in the industrial Northeast and Midwest, or blacks who later succeeded in organizing as an interest group. In addition to these sectional interests that were drawn to the New Deal, there were several large, self-consciously organized interest groups. The most important in the New Deal coalition were organized labor, agriculture, and the financial community.[47] All of the parts were held together by a judicious use of patronage—not merely patronage in jobs but patronage in policies. Many of the groups were permitted virtually to write their own legislation. In exchange, the groups supported President Roosevelt and his successors in their battles with opposing politicians.

Policy Principle

Public policy is used by presidents as a means to build and maintain political support.

Republican presidents have had their group coalition base also. The most important segments of organized business, especially the large, "labor intensive" industries that deal with unions affiliated with the CIO, have tended to support Republican presidents. Organized business has been joined by upper-income interests, not set up as a single upper-class group but usually organized around their respective areas of wealth. Republicans also have their share of ethnic groups, including staunch Republican organizations whose members hail from Eastern European countries. An important and recent sectionally based ethnic group is the white South. Once a solid-Democratic South, whites in most of the Southern states have become virtually a solid-Republican group; and not far behind in importance within the Republican coalition is the so-called Sun Belt.

---

[46]A wider range of group phenomena will be covered in Chapter 12. In that chapter the focus is on the influence of groups *upon* the government and its policy-making processes. Here our concern is more with the relationship of groups to the presidency and the extent to which groups and coalitions of groups become a dependable resource for presidential government.

[47]For a more detailed review of the New Deal coalition in comparison with later coalitions, see Thomas Ferguson and Joel Rogers, *Right Turn: The Decline of the Democrats and the Future of American Politics* (New York: Hill & Wang, 1986), Chapter 2. For updates on the group basis of presidential politics, see Thomas Ferguson, "Money and Politics," in *Handbooks to the Modern World—The United States*, vol. 2, ed. Godfrey Hodgson (New York: Facts on File, 1992), pp. 1060–84; and Lucius J. Barker, ed., "Black Electoral Politics," *National Political Science Review*, vol. 2 (New Brunswick, NJ: Transaction Publishers, 1990).

Except for the white South, most of these groups have been Republicans for a long time. A newer presence within the white South is the Christian Right; although heavily Southern, its membership extends far beyond the South. The two best organized groups within the Christian Right—the Christian Coalition and the Focus on the Family—have a strong and effective presence in many states in the West, the Northwest, and the border states.

In 2000, Al Gore's campaign strategy was to mobilize the mass base of the Democratic Party with a populist appeal to working families, African Americans, the poor, and the elderly. He was able to win the endorsement of all the major trade unions, despite some of their misgivings about his views on international trade. In a sense, Gore sought to return to the class politics of the New Deal coalition, but without the support of Southern whites.

In contrast, George W. Bush attempted to rebuild the GOP base that had been shattered during the 1998 fall of former House speaker Newt Gingrich. In July 1999, at a meeting of Republican governors in St. Louis, twenty-three of twenty-nine governors, along with nineteen Republican senators and 136 Republican House members, endorsed Bush for president. They did so because Bush appeared to them to be the only Republican candidate who could pull the party together and win the presidency. Consequently, Bush's strategy was not to challenge Gore head-on, but instead, to consolidate the GOP base. To do so, Bush promised a massive tax cut to appeal to upper-income groups and espoused family values to appeal to rural and small-town conservatives.

The interest bases of the two parties have remained largely unchanged since 1980, when the GOP completed its absorption of most white Southerners and religious conservatives. But whether these coalitions will last remains to be seen.

Public Opinion and Mass Popularity: Resource or Liability?   As presidential government grew, a presidency developed whose power is directly linked to the people. Successful presidents have to be able to mobilize mass opinion. But presidents tend to follow public opinion rather than lead it.

Presidents who devote too much of their time to the vicissitudes of public opinion polls often discover that they are several steps behind shifts in opinion, for polls tell politicians what the public wanted yesterday, not what it will think tomorrow. This was certainly President Clinton's experience in 1993–1994 with the issue of health care reform. Administration polls continually showed public support for the president's policy initiatives—until opponents of his efforts began getting their own message through. Using several highly effective media campaigns, Clinton's opponents convinced millions of Americans that the president's program was too complex and that it would reduce access to health care. The president was left promoting an unpopular program.

Bill Clinton relied heavily on public opinion in formulating and presenting many of his administration's programs. Several members of his staff were hired specifically to shape and influence public opinion. For example, Dick Morris had a reputation as an uncanny diviner of the polls. One of the most fateful reliances on public opinion in the history of modern polling was its role in Clinton's decision following the exposure of Monica Lewinsky's taped admission of their affair in January 1998. When confronted with data demonstrating that public opinion was intensely negative on sexual misconduct, Clinton decided to "tough it out" and to try to win by asserting that he "did not have sexual relations with that woman. . . ." By the time Clinton could no longer deny the affair, after eight months of mounting testimony against him, in August 1998, public opinion had actually turned in his favor.

Politicians are generally better off if they try to do what they believe is best and then hope that the public will come to agree with them. Most politicians, however, are afraid to use such a simple approach.

In addition to utilizing the media and public opinion polls, recent presidents, particularly Bill Clinton, have "gone public" by reaching out directly to the American public to gain its approval. If successful, presidents can use this approval as a weapon against Congress.[48] President Clinton's high public profile, as is indicated by the number of public appearances he made (see Figure 6.4), was a dramatic expression of the presidency as a permanent campaign for re-election. A study by political scientist Charles O. Jones shows that President Clinton engaged in campaignlike activity throughout his presidency and proved to be the most-traveled American president in history. In his first twenty months in office, he made 203 appearances outside of Washington, compared with 178 for George H. W. Bush and 58 for Ronald Reagan. Clinton's tendency to go around rather than through party organizations is reflected in the fact that while Presidents Bush and Reagan devoted about 25 percent of their appearances to party functions, Clinton's comparable figure was only 8 percent.[49] Throughout the controversy over campaign-finance abuses during 1997, President Clinton attended numerous fund-raising events to raise enough money to pay off the $30 million or more of debt from the 1996 presidential campaign. In fact, during the Monica Lewinsky scandal of early 1998, Clinton continued his fund-raising, and the Democratic National Committee added staff to answer all the telephone calls and mail that responded positively to President Clinton's appeals. President George W. Bush, in only his first one-hundred days in office, made public appearances in twenty-six states. This is the essence of the permanent campaign.

Even with the help of all other institutional and political resources, successful presidents have to be able to mobilize mass opinion in their favor in order to keep Congress in line. But as we shall see, each president tends to *use up* mass resources. Virtually everyone is aware that presidents are constantly making appeals to the public over the heads of Congress and the Washington community. But the mass public is not made up of fools. The American people react to presidential actions rather than to mere speeches or other image-making devices.

Collective Action Principle

Presidents now engage in a permanent campaign for public support.

---

[48]Kernell, *Going Public*, 3rd ed.

[49]Study cited in Ann Devroy, "Despite Panetta Pep Talk, White House Aides See Daunting Task," *Washington Post*, 8 January 1995, p. A4.

FIGURE 6.4

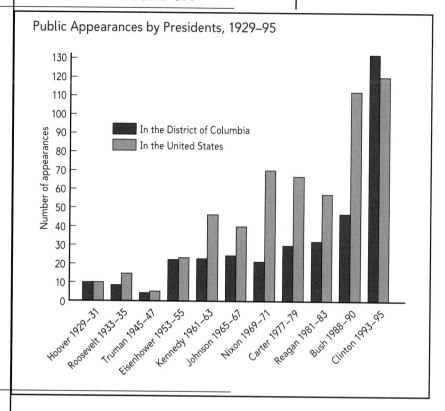

Public Appearances by Presidents, 1929–95

SOURCE: Samuel Kernell, *Going Public*, 3rd ed. (Washington, DC: Congressional Quarterly Press, 1998), p. 118.

The public's sensitivity to presidential actions can be seen in the tendency of all presidents to lose popular support. As shown in Figure 6.5, the percentage of positive responses to "Do you approve of the way the president is handling his job?" starts out at a level significantly higher than the percentage of votes the president got in the previous national election and then declines over the next four years. Though the shape of the line differs, the destination is the same. This downward tendency is to be expected if American voters are rational, inasmuch as almost any action taken by the president can be divisive. Public disapproval of specific actions has a cumulative effect on the president's overall performance rating. Thus, all presidents face the problem of boosting their approval ratings. And the public generally reacts favorably to presidential actions in foreign policy or, more precisely, to international events associated with the president. For example, President George W. Bush's approval ratings surpassed the 90-percent level as the Taliban fell from power in Afghanistan. Analysts call this the ***rallying effect.***

rallying effect
The generally favorable reaction of the public to presidential actions taken in foreign policy, or more precisely, to decisions made during international crises.

FIGURE 6.5

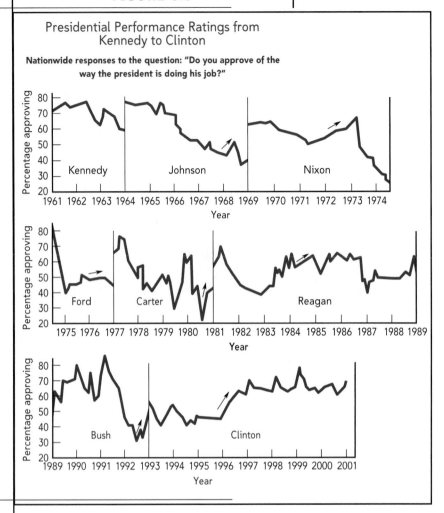

Presidential Performance Ratings from
Kennedy to Clinton

Nationwide responses to the question: "Do you approve of the
way the president is doing his job?"

*NOTE: Arrows indicate pre-election upswings.

SOURCE: Courtesy of the Gallup Organization and Louis Harris & Associates.

Nevertheless, the rallying effect is only a momentary reversal of the more general tendency of presidents to lose popular support. As a result, Bush's public approval will likely follow the same downward trajectory his father's ratings took from spring 1991 to summer 1992.

Looking again at Figure 6.5, the one notable exception to this general downward trend of presidential approval was during Clinton's second term. As expected, Clinton's approval rating surged before and after his re-election and then dropped over the course of 1997. But Clinton experienced two important upward blips, one early in 1998 and the other early in 1999, that were both related to the impeachment controversy, not to an international crisis. In both of these cases, the American people, while disapproving of Clinton's behavior in the Lewinsky scandal, were nonetheless rallying behind the institution of the presidency. In fact, it is probable that this rallying effect around the presidency kept Clinton in office. The rise and fall of presidential performance ratings is evidence that *with power goes vulnerability*. Since the president cannot possibly fulfill his oath of office by meeting all the mandates from Congress, he must turn to the next best strategy, *to control appearances*. In other words, to deceive. Ever since Teddy Roosevelt, the presidency has been called a "bully pulpit." And so it is. On many occasions this pulpit has been used magnificently to rally Americans to a good cause, to comfort Americans in their grief, to mobilize Americans for a worthy public policy goal, to inspire Americans to set aside their private interests for the greater good. But that same pulpit is subject to abuse, and many feel that the abuses have become the norm.

President Clinton was criticized for subjecting every planned public appearance, every vacation, and virtually every phrase in his speeches to test marketing, tracking polls, and focus groups. These criticisms are appropriate, but what makes them more damning is that President Clinton was simply extending the practices of his predecessors. The distinction between campaigning and governing has been getting fuzzier and fuzzier. Many people are getting accustomed to referring to presidential conduct as "the permanent campaign."

IS A PARLIAMENTARY SYSTEM BETTER?

Americans often get depressed over the phenomenon referred to as *divided government*. It is alleged by inside-the-beltway pundits that this is a formula for gridlock as partisan majorities in the different branches of government prevent anything from happening. Such pundits often cast a wistful look across the Atlantic, touting the advantages of parliamentary government. Parliamentary democracy is organized according to a principle that emphasizes the coordination and concentration of power. The textbooks refer to this as a "fusion of powers" in contrast to the American-style "separation of powers." The centerpieces of this arrangement are the supremacy of parliament and the accountability of the political executive to it.

Institution Principle

A parliamentary system is a fusion of powers, rather than a separation of powers.

Governmental Arrangements

In parliamentary regimes, there is a division and specialization of labor. The House of Commons does not run British politics. Nor does the Dutch *Tweede Kamer*, the German *Bundestag*, the Japanese *Diet*, or the Norwegian *Storting* run the politics of the Netherlands, Germany, Japan, or Norway, respectively. Rather, each parliament "elects" a *government* to serve as the executive arm of the regime. We thus need to describe exactly what a "government" is, on the one hand, and how a country's parliament "elects" one, on the other.

The political executive in a parliamentary democracy is, with a few exceptions that we won't stop to consider here, chosen by parliament. This executive is called the *government*; it is also known as the *cabinet* or *council of ministers.* It is a collection of senior politicians, each of whom is the head of a department or ministry of state. In nearly every parliamentary regime, there is a finance minister, foreign minister, interior minister, defense minister, justice minister, education minister, environment minister, and so on.

Thus, there is a division and specialization of labor at two different levels. The first distinguishes between legislature and executive. The legislature selects the executive in the first place; keeps it in place or replaces it with a different one; and considers various pieces of legislation, the most important of which is the annual budget.[50] We will discuss these features momentarily. The second level of division and specialization of labor is in the government itself. In a manner quite parallel to the arrangements involving committees in the U.S. Congress, each ministry of state has jurisdiction over specified dimensions of public policy, called a *ministerial portfolio.* In this domain, the minister and his or her senior civil servants have considerable discretion to interpret statutory authority and implement public policy.

Another way to think about this arrangement is as a chain of principal-agent relationships. Parliament, as principal, delegates executive authority to a collective agent, the cabinet. The cabinet, as principal, in turn, delegates discretionary authority in various policy jurisdictions to its agents, namely particular cabinet ministers. To control its agents and coordinate their activities, the cabinet employs various before-the-fact and after-the-fact mechanisms; usually one member of the cabinet plays the role of policeman and maestro—the *prime minister.* Likewise, to control *its* agent, parliament, too, exercises before-the-fact and after-the-fact authority. We refer to this authority as that of "making and breaking governments," since parliament votes a cabinet into office in the first place, and, if it is unhappy with cabinet performance after the fact, may vote it out of office and replace it with an alternative cabinet.[51]

The Government Formation Process

A typical sequence of events in one cycle of parliamentary democracy begins with a triggering event like an election. When the new parliament convenes, a number of parties may be represented, no one of which commands a majority

---

[50]It should be noted that legislatures in parliamentary regimes are not the hyperactive lawmaking engines we encounter in the American setting. Typically, parliaments vote a few broad delegations of statutory authority which are then implemented by the government. In America, on the other hand, Congress and the various state legislatures legislate with much greater frequency and in a much more fine-grained fashion.

[51]These details are developed in Michael Laver and Kenneth A. Shepsle, *Making and Breaking Governments: Cabinets and Legislatures in Parliamentary Democracies* (New York: Cambridge University Press, 1996).

TABLE 6.2

Government Parties in Parliament*

		MAJORITY	MINORITY
EXECUTIVE	**SINGLE PARTY**	Unified (.134)	Single-party minority (.238)
	COALITION	Multiparty majority (.500)	Multiparty minority (.128)

*Cell entries give the proportion of each type as determined by Strom for a sample of Western parliamentary democracies, 1945–1982.

SOURCE: Kaare Strom, *Minority Government and Majority Rule* (New York: Cambridge University Press, 1990), p. 61.

of votes on its own. Each party has an *endowment* of a certain number of seats under its control and a set of policy priorities and positions on which it has just conducted its electoral campaign. Also at this time there will be a government in place—the cabinet that was running the country just before the election. The first order of business facing the new parliament is whether to retain the status quo cabinet or replace it with a new cabinet. If the political fortunes of the various parties have changed as a result of the election, it is highly likely that a new cabinet will be selected to better reflect the balance of political forces in the new parliament. But since no one party is a majority in its own right, the new government will have to reflect the preferences of a *coalition* of political parties. Government formation requires coalition building. This process produces governments of quite a variety of sizes and shapes (Table 6.2).

The number of parties represented at the cabinet table can be one or many—in which case the executive is a single party or a coalition, respectively. The number of seats in parliament controlled by the government parties can constitute either a majority or a minority. Thus, there are four different types of government. Their relative frequencies in Europe since 1945 are given parenthetically in Table 6.2.

Unified governments, which arise in slightly more than one of every eight governments in the period of study, are formed by parties that win outright parliamentary majorities. This is a relatively rare event, which occurs frequently in Great Britain but only occasionally anywhere else in Europe. In this case the majority party votes itself all the cabinet portfolios. The only serious threat to these "juggernauts" is intraparty factionalism. One faction of the majority party, if sufficiently numerous, can bring the government down by deserting it on a key vote.

Much more common, occurring about half the time in the postwar era, is a cabinet composed of several parties that jointly control a parliamentary majority. These *multiparty majority* governments need to control their rank-and-file in order to continue in office, but the ordinary tools of party discipline are typically sufficient for this task. A member of parliament that threatens to break ranks with the majority may find that his or her parliamentary career prospects suddenly become bleak, not to speak of the fact that the party organization will refuse to back him or her at the next election.

A more serious threat to these governments is that, during their incumbency, one or more of the governing parties will become dissatisfied and resign, essentially uniting with the opposition to bring down the government. Short of pulling out of a sitting government in order to defeat it, a governing party may insist on a reallocation of portfolios. If, for example, recent poll results suggested that one of the minor government parties were rising in popularity at the expense of one of the major government parties, the former could insist on a *cabinet reshuffle* in which it received more portfolios, or more important portfolios.

A *single-party minority* government sounds pretty strange to American ears (although we shall suggest shortly that the reader has more familiarity with it than he or she realizes). It is a government in which one party receives all cabinet portfolios, but that party has less than a majority of parliamentary seats. It governs at the sufferance of an opposition that, in combination, controls a majority of parliamentary seats. How can this be? It is able to retain office, as we shall shortly demonstrate, because the opposition, even though a majority, cannot agree on an alternative that it prefers. Imagine a large social democratic party—slightly left of center—controlling, say, 40 percent of parliamentary seats, that faces a radical left-wing party, an extremist right-wing party, and a religious party, controlling roughly 20 percent of the seats each. It is quite likely that anything preferred to a social democratic minority government by the left-wingers is strongly opposed by the right-wingers and religious partisans, whereas anything preferred to the social democrats by the two more conservative parties is opposed by the left-wingers. The opposition majority simply cannot get its act together, allowing the social democrats to survive in office even though they comprise but a minority of the whole parliament. This is not at all an unusual scenario and, as the evidence reported in Table 6.2 suggests, something like it occurs nearly one-quarter of the time in western parliamentary democracies.

To complete the picture, about one in every eight governments in the postwar western experience is a coalition government whose partners control less than a parliamentary majority. Typically they will be center-left or center-right coalitions that, like the single-party minority governments described in the previous paragraph, split the opposition.

So while some might wish that an alternative institutional arrangement might solve the alleged problems of divided government, the data of Table 6.2

Institutional Reform
www.wwnorton.com/
lowi7/ch6

Is a parliamentary system a cure for divided government?

suggest that parliamentary regimes are also highly prone to divided government. Multiparty majority coalition governments are those that control a parliamentary majority, but divided government occurs *within* the executive. Single-party minority governments have a unified executive but, lacking a majority in parliament, are divided in exactly the same way American governments often are—an executive whose party lacks a legislative majority. (Thus, despite sounding pretty strange to American ears, single-party minority governments are structurally identical to the divided governments with which Americans have had frequent experience.) Minority coalition governments are divided both within the executive and between executive and legislature. Indeed, European parliamentary experience suggests that governments are divided about seven-eighths of the time, a proportion roughly equal to the postwar American experience. Parliamentary government, in short, is no cure for divided government.

SUMMARY

The foundations for presidential government were laid in the Constitution by providing for a unitary executive who is head of state as well as head of government. The first section of the chapter reviewed the powers of each: the head of state with its military, judicial, and diplomatic powers; and the head of government with its executive, military, and legislative powers. But this section noted that the presidency was subordinated to congressional government during the nineteenth century and part of the twentieth, when the national government was relatively uninvolved in domestic functions and inactive or sporadic in foreign affairs.

The second section of the chapter traced out the rise of modern presidential government after the much longer period of congressional dominance. There is no mystery in the shift to government centered on the presidency. Congress built the modern presidency by delegating to it not only the power to implement the vast new programs of the 1930s but also by delegating its own legislative power to make the policies themselves. The cabinet, the other top appointments, the White House staff, and the Executive Office of the President are some of the impressive formal resources of presidential power.

The chapter then focused on the president's informal resources, in particular his political party, the supportive group coalitions, and his access to the media and, through that, his access to the millions of Americans who make up the general public. But it was noted that these resources are not cost- or risk-free. The president's direct relation with the mass public is his most potent modern resource, but also the most problematic. The chapter concluded with a description of the parliamentary system, a common form of government in many of today's powerful democracies; while the parliamentary and presidential systems differ in set-up, they both often end up in gridlock.

Rationality Principle	Collective Action Principle	Institution Principle	Policy Principle	History Principle
Presidents can and have advanced their own priorities, and those of their office, by claiming inherent powers through the faithful execution of the law.	Vetoes are usually part of an intricate bargaining process between the president and Congress.	The Constitution established the presidency as an office of delegated powers.	Because of the president's veto power, Congress will alter the content of a bill to make it more to a president's liking.	The presidency was strengthened somewhat in the 1830s with the introduction of a national convention system of nominating presidential candidates.
A president must weigh the advantages of vetoing legislation against the possible drop in his public approval.	Presidential power should be analyzed in terms of the strategic interactions that a president has with other political actors.	The president can be an important agenda setter for congressional action.	Public policy is used by presidents as a means to build and maintain political support.	The New Deal's expanded role for the national government enhanced presidential power.
Congress delegates more power to the president as more demands are made on its agenda.	The president can use public approval as a strategic resource.	The veto power makes the president the most important single legislative leader.	A parliamentary system is no cure for divided government.	
Presidential appointments are strategic resources that help a president achieve political objectives.	Whether government is divided or unified has a big influence on whether a president is a bargainer or a coordinator.	Congress delegates authority to the president but also maintains the means to influence how the executive branch exercises this power.		
	The more unified the president's party is in Congress, the more unified the opposition is likely to be.			
	Presidents now engage in a permanent campaign for public support.	A parliamentary system is a fusion of powers, rather than a separation of powers.		

FOR FURTHER READING

Cameron, Charles. *Veto Bargaining: Presidents and the Politics of Negative Power.* New York: Cambridge University Press, 2000.

Drew, Elizabeth. *On the Edge: The Clinton Presidency.* New York: Simon and Schuster, 1994.

Hinckley, Barbara, and Paul Brace. *Follow the Leader: Opinion Polls and Modern Presidents.* New York: Basic Books, 1992.

Kernell, Samuel. *Going Public: New Strategies of Presidential Leadership,* 3rd ed. Washington, DC: Congressional Quarterly Press, 1998.

Lowi, Theodore J. *The Personal President: Power Invested, Promise Unfulfilled.* Ithaca, NY: Cornell University Press, 1985.

Milkis, Sidney M. *The President and the Parties: The Transformation of the American Party System Since the New Deal.* New York: Oxford University Press, 1993.

Nelson, Michael, ed. *The Presidency and the Political System,* 4th ed. Washington, DC: Congressional Quarterly Press, 1994.

Neustadt, Richard E. *Presidential Power: The Politics of Leadership from Roosevelt to Reagan,* rev. ed. New York: Free Press, 1990.

Pfiffner, James P. *The Modern Presidency.* New York: St. Martin's Press, 1994.

Polsby, Nelson, and Aaron Wildavsky. *Presidential Elections: Contemporary Strategies of American Electoral Politics,* 8th ed. New York: Free Press, 1991.

Skowronek, Stephen. *The Politics Presidents Make: Leadership from John Adams to George Bush.* Cambridge: Harvard University Press, 1993.

Spitzer, Robert. *The Presidential Veto: Touchstone of the American Presidency.* Albany: State University of New York Press, 1988.

Tulis, Jeffrey. *The Rhetorical Presidency.* Princeton: Princeton University Press, 1987.

seven

The Executive Branch: Bureaucracy in a Democracy

TIME LINE ON THE BUREAUCRACY

EVENTS	INSTITUTIONAL DEVELOPMENTS
Washington appoints Jefferson (State), Knox (War), Hamilton (Treasury) to the first cabinet (1789)	**1789** — Congress creates first executive departments (State, War, Treasury) (1789)
Jackson elected president; "rule of the common man" (1828)	Jackson supports "party rotation in office" and "spoils system" (1829–1836)
	1880
President Garfield assassinated by disappointed office-seeker; President Arthur allies himself with civil service reformers (1881)	Pendleton Act sets up Civil Service Commission and merit system for filling "classified services" jobs (1883)
Conflict between railroads and farmers over freight rates (1880s)	Interstate Commerce Commission (ICC) created to regulate railroads; first independent regulatory commission (1887)
	1900
Progressives attack parties and advance civil service reforms (1901–1908)	Department of Commerce and Labor created (1903)
World War I (1914–1918)	Federal Reserve Board (1913); Federal Trade Commission (1914)
Postwar labor unrest, race riots, Red Scare (1919–1920)	General Accounting Office and Budget Bureau created; Congress turns over budget to the executive branch (1921)
Teapot Dome scandal (1924)	Classification Act (1923); Corrupt Practices Act (1925)
Franklin Roosevelt and the New Deal (1930s)	**1930** — New Deal "alphabetocracy" created (1930s)
	Administrative Reorganization Act creates Executive Office of the President (EOP) (1939)
	Hatch Act restricts political activity of executive-branch employees (1939)
U.S. in World War II (1941–1945)	Veterans' preference begun for civil service jobs (1944)
Cold war (1945–1989)	National Security Act creates Department of Defense, National Security Council (NSC), Central Intelligence Agency (1947); Truman and Eisenhower loyalty programs (1947–1954)
Red Scare (late 1940s–mid-1950s)	

EVENTS	INSTITUTIONAL DEVELOPMENTS

1950

Civil rights movement (1950s and 1960s)

Growth of government (1962–1974)

Equal Employment Opportunity Commission (EEOC) created (1964)

New welfare and social regulatory agencies (1965); Department of Housing and Urban Development, Dept. of Transportation (1966)

President Nixon enlarges the managerial presidency (1969–1974)

1970

Watergate cover-up revealed (1973–1974)

EOP reorganized; Office of Management and Budget (OMB) created (1970)

President Carter attempts to make bureaucracy more accountable (1977–1980)

Civil Service Reform Act (1978); creation of new departments: Energy (1977); Education (1980); Health and Human Services (1980)

President Reagan fires over 10,000 air traffic controllers; centralizes presidential management (1981–1988)

OMB given power to review all proposed agency rules and regulations (1984)

Reagan and Bush tighten presidential control of all top political appointees (1982–1992)

Federal civilian employment up from 2.8 million (1982) to 3.1 million (1992)

1990

Supreme Court declares political patronage unconstitutional except for top political positions (1990)

Clinton decentralizes somewhat by appointing cabinet first and giving them share of subcabinet selection (1993)

National Performance Review, headed by Vice President Gore, streamlines procurement, rules, and procedures; job reduction occurs (1993–1996)

"Reinventing government" plan launched by Clinton to overhaul the federal government and reduce number of federal employees by more than 200,000 (1993)

Clinton campaign continues to tackle bureaucracy with promises of more cuts of employees and pages of regulations (1996)

Clinton signs GOP welfare law replacing six decades of federal programs with devolution to state agencies (1996)

Divided government reduces policy output; Clinton emphasizes administrative reform through National Performance Review (NPR) (1996–2000)

Significant reductions in the number of federal employees contribute to a historic reversal from budget deficits to surpluses (1999–)

Gore credited with success of NPR, but loses to Bush in the 2000 presidential election

2000

Terrorist attacks on New York City and Washington, D. C. (2001)

Creation of Office of Homeland Security to coordinate bureaucratic agencies overseeing internal security (2001)

CORE OF THE ANALYSIS

- Despite its problems, the bureaucracy is necessary for the maintenance of order in a large society.

- The size of the federal bureaucracy is large, but it has not been growing any faster than the economy or the population as a whole.

- Government agencies vary in their levels of responsiveness to the president and his political appointees, congressional members and committees, and commercial and private interests.

- Responsible bureaucracy requires more than presidential power and management control.

- Congress has delegated much of its legislative power to the president and the bureaucracy; congressional committees use oversight to make the bureaucracy accountable.

During his 1980 campaign, Ronald Reagan promised to dismantle the Departments of Energy and Education as part of the "Reagan Revolution" commitment to "get the government off our backs." Reagan claimed that abolishing the Department of Energy not only would save $250 million over a three-year period, but also would permit the free market to develop a much better system of energy production and distribution. At the same time, Republicans criticized President Carter for having created the Department of Education mainly to repay a debt he owed the powerful National Education Association for its political support. After his election, in keeping with his campaign promises, President Reagan appointed as the new heads of these two departments individuals publicly committed to eliminating their departments and therefore their own jobs.

Even though the Departments of Energy and Education had only been established in 1977 and 1980 respectively, they had powerful allies. Strong support for both agencies developed in Congress, including support from some members who were otherwise supportive of the Reagan program of tax cuts, domestic budget cuts, and defense budget increases. By 1984, President Reagan seemed to have changed his mind, indicating he had "no intention of recommending abolition of the Department of Education at this time." Plans for abolishing the Energy Department and turning over its functions to other departments were relegated to the dead end of "further discussion." President Reagan actually did cut some employees after his inauguration and tried strenuously to continue cutting, but despite his commitment to this, the number of federal employees actually grew by about 18,000 during his first year in office. Although he continued to denounce "big government," by 1984, President Reagan had retreated from this arena in defeat. Eleven years later, in January 1995, one of the first commitments of the Republican 104th Congress was to abolish these same two departments along with a third, the Department of Commerce. Yet by 1997, all three departments were still very much alive. The Energy budget was cut barely, from the 1995 authorization of $15 billion to the 1997 authorization of $14.2 billion, while the Education budget was cut a bit more, from $32.3 billion to $30.2 billion. The authorization for the Department of Commerce fell from $4 billion to

History Principle

Once a government agency is established, it is difficult to abolish.

$3.7 billion. The campaign to abolish the three departments had virtually disappeared.[1]

What is this bureaucratic phenomenon that seems to expand despite policies to keep it in check? What is this structure that is the frustration of every president? Why does it seem to have a life of its own despite every presidential effort to make it respond to voters and public opinion? How is it possible for agencies that are composed of highly dependent employees to resist pointed efforts to reorganize or abolish their positions?

In this chapter, we will focus on the federal bureaucracy—the administrative structure that on a day-to-day basis *is* the American government. We will first seek to answer these questions by defining and describing bureaucracy as a social and political phenomenon. Second, we will look in detail at American bureaucracy in action by examining the government's major administrative agencies, their role in the governmental process, and their political behavior. These details of administration are the very heart and soul of modern government.

In asking these questions, we mean for the reader to keep an open mind about bureaucracy. It is often portrayed as "runaway" and "out of control." It is often thought of pejoratively as self-serving, bloated, and highly inefficient. In short, bureaucracy has a very serious public relations problem! But bureaucracy is created by legislation—that is, an agency's existence (both initial and continued) is approved by both houses of Congress and the president. A bureau's authority can be expanded or trimmed by legislative authorization, its budgets increased or decreased via the normal appropriations process, and

THE CENTRAL QUESTIONS

THE BUREAUCRATIC PHENOMENON

Why do bureaucracies exist? Why are they needed?

How large is the federal bureaucracy?

What roles do government bureaucrats perform? What motivates bureaucratic behavior?

AGENCIES AND THEIR POLITICS

What are the agencies that make up the executive branch?

How can these agencies be classified according to their purpose and politics?

CONTROLLING THE BUREAUCRACY

How do the president and Congress manage and oversee the bureaucracy?

What means can be used to make the bureaucracy accountable?

DOWNSIZING GOVERNMENT

What methods have been used to reduce the size and the role of the federal bureaucracy? How effective are these efforts to reduce the bureaucracy?

---

[1]For a very good case study on the politics (and the problems) of terminating agencies, see "Pressure to Curtail EPA Boomeranged . . . But GOP Can Claim Some Influence," *Congressional Quarterly*, 7 September 1996, pp. 2518–19.

its actions subjected to scrutiny by legislative oversight committees and executive watchdog agencies. In short, bureaus and agencies of the federal government are the *creatures* of Congress and the president. We should wonder, before castigating bureaus and agencies, whether our elected officials are as much to blame as are appointees and civil servants for the excesses laid at the door of the federal bureaucracy.

THE BUREAUCRATIC PHENOMENON

Despite widespread and consistent complaints about "bureaucracy," most Americans recognize that maintaining order in a large society is impossible without a large governmental apparatus of some sort. When we approve of what a government agency is doing, we give the phenomenon a positive name, *administration*; when we disapprove, we call the phenomenon *bureaucracy*.[2]

Although the terms "administration" and "bureaucracy" are often used interchangeably, it is useful to distinguish between the two. Administration is the more general of the two terms; it refers to all the ways human beings might rationally coordinate their efforts to achieve a common goal. This applies to private as well as public organizations. ***Bureaucracy*** refers to the actual offices, tasks, and principles of organization that are employed in the most formal and sustained administration. Table 7.1 defines bureaucracy by identifying its basic characteristics.

bureaucracy The complex structure of offices, tasks, rules, and principles of organization that are employed by all large-scale institutions to coordinate the work of their personnel.

Bureaucratic Organization

The core of bureaucracy is the *division of labor*. The key to bureaucratic effectiveness is the coordination of experts performing complex tasks. If each job is specialized in order to gain efficiencies, then each worker must depend upon the output of other workers, and that requires careful *allocation* of jobs and resources. Inevitably, bureaucracies become hierarchical, often approximating a pyramid in form. At the base of the organization are workers with the fewest skills and specializations; one supervisor can deal with a relatively large number of these workers. At the next level of the organization, where there are more highly specialized workers, the supervision and coordination of work involves fewer workers per supervisor. Toward the top of the organization, a very small number of high-level executives engages in the "management" of the organization, meaning the organization and reorganization of all the tasks and functions, plus the allocation of the appropriate supplies, and the distribution of the outputs of the organization to the market (if it is a "private sector" organization) or to the public.

[2]The title of this section is drawn from an important sociological work by Michel Crozier, *The Bureaucratic Phenomenon* (Chicago: University of Chicago Press, 1964).

TABLE 7.1

The Six Primary Characteristics of Bureaucracy

CHARACTERISTIC	EXPLANATION
Division of labor	Workers are specialized. Each worker develops a skill in a particular job and performs the job routinely and repetitively, thereby increasing productivity.
Allocation of functions	Each task is assigned. No one makes a whole product; each worker depends on the output of other workers.
Allocation of responsibility	Each task becomes a personal responsibility—a contractual obligation. No task can be changed without permission.
Supervision	Some workers are assigned the special task of watching over other workers rather than contributing directly to the creation of the product. Each supervisor watches over a few workers (a situation known as span of control), and communications between workers or between levels move in a prescribed fashion (known as chain of command).
Purchase of full-time employment	The organization controls all the time the worker is on the job, so each worker can be assigned and held to a task. Some part-time and contracted work is tolerated, but it is held to a minimum.
Identification of career within the organization	Workers come to identify with the organization as a way of life. Seniority, pension rights, and promotions are geared to this relationship.

The Size of the Federal Service

Americans like to complain about bureaucracy. Americans don't like Big Government because Big Government means Big Bureaucracy, and bureaucracy means *the federal service*—about 2.78 million civilian and 1.47 million military employees.[3] Promises to cut the bureaucracy are popular campaign appeals; "cutting out the fat" with big reductions in the number of federal employees is held out as a sure-fire way of cutting the deficit. President Bill Clinton made it a priority, even though the Democratic party has traditionally been the pro-growth party. One of President Clinton's most successful efforts was his National Performance Review, which cut more than a quarter of a million jobs from the federal labor force (the total force reductions for most of his first term amounted actually to 293,000, although only 163,000 of those were from the civilian agencies that were subject to the NPR)[4]—although most Americans, according to polls, believed that the federal bureaucracy under Clinton was bigger than ever.

Despite fears of bureaucratic growth getting out of hand, however, the federal service has hardly grown at all during the past thirty years; it reached its peak postwar level in 1968 with 2.9 million civilian employees plus an additional 3.6 million military personnel (a figure swollen by Vietnam). The number of civilian federal employees has since remained close to that figure. (In 2000, it was about 2,645,000.[5]) The growth of the federal service is even less imposing when placed in the context of the total workforce and when compared to the size of state and local public employment. Figure 7.1 indicates that, since 1950, the ratio of federal service employment to the total workforce has been steady and in fact has declined slightly in the past twenty-five years. Another useful comparison is to be found in Figure 7.2. Although the dollar increase in federal spending shown by the bars looks very impressive, the horizontal line indicates that even here the national government has simply kept pace with the growth of the economy.

In 1950, there were 4.3 million state and local civil service employees (about 6.5 percent of the country's workforce). In 1978, there were 12.7 million (nearly 15 percent of the workforce), and the ratio remained about the same for the ensuing two decades. By 2000, state and local governments employed around 17.8 million workers, or about 12 percent of the workforce. Federal employment, in contrast, exceeded 5 percent of the workforce only during World War II (not shown), and almost all of that momentary growth was military. After the demobilization, which continued until 1950 (as shown in Figure 7.1), the federal service has tended to grow at a rate that keeps pace with the economy and society. That is demonstrated by the lower line on Figure 7.1, which shows a constant relation between federal civilian employment and the size of the workforce. Variations in federal employment since 1946 have been in the military and directly related to war and the cold war (as shown by the top line on Figure 7.1). The same has been roughly true of state and local government personnel, but that may be changing because state and local government employment

---

[3]This is just under 99 percent of all national government employees. About 1.4 percent work for the legislative branch and for the federal judiciary. See Office of Management and Budget, *Historical Tables, Budget of the United States Government, Fiscal Year 1999* (Washington, DC: Government Printing Office, 1998), p. 279.

[4]Data source, *Historical Tables, Budget of the United States Government, Fiscal Year 1997* (Washington, DC: Government Printing Office, 1996), pp. 263–64.

[5]*Historical Tables, Budget of the United States Government, Fiscal Year 2000*, Table 17.5, p. 304.

FIGURE 7.1

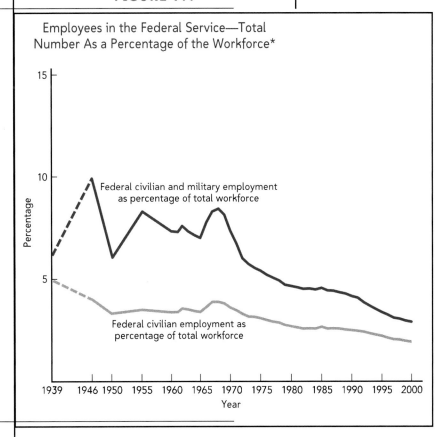

Employees in the Federal Service—Total
Number As a Percentage of the Workforce*

Federal civilian and military employment
as percentage of total workforce

Federal civilian employment as
percentage of total workforce

Percentage

1939   1946 1950   1955   1960   1965   1970   1975   1980   1985   1990   1995   2000
Year

*Workforce includes unemployed persons.
SOURCE: Tax Foundation, *Facts & Figures on Government Finance* (Baltimore: Johns Hopkins
University Press, 1990), pp. 22, 44; Office of Management and Budget, *Historical Tables,
Budget of the United States Government, Fiscal Year 2002* (Washington, DC: Government
Printing Office, 2001), p. 304; and U.S. Department of Labor, Bureau of Labor Statistics,
Table A-1 at stats.bls.gov/webapps/legacy/cpsatab1.htm. Lines between 1939 and 1946 are
broken because they connect the last prewar year with the first postwar year, disregarding the
temporary ballooning of federal employees, especially military, during war years.

continued to grow while federal civil service personnel actually shrank. Thanks
in part to the vigor of many contemporary governors and in part to the bipartisan support in Washington for devolving more and more federal programs to the
state and local governments, the number of civil service employees of state government, local government, county government, and special district government
had grown to 17.8 million by 2000, and was still growing.[6] In sum, the national

[6]Ibid.

FIGURE 7.2

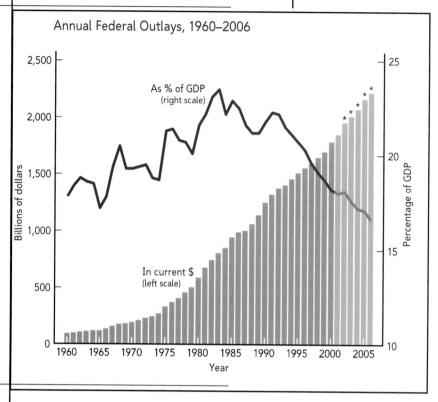

Annual Federal Outlays, 1960–2006

*Data from 2001–2006 are estimated.

SOURCE: Office of Management and Budget, *Historical Tables, Budget of the United States Government, Fiscal Year 2002* (Washington, DC: Government Printing Office, 2001), pp. 25–26.

History Principle

The size of the federal bureaucracy has kept pace with the growth of the economy and the needs of society.

government is indeed "very large," but the federal service has not been growing any faster than the economy or the society. The same is roughly true of the growth pattern of state and local public personnel. Bureaucracy keeps pace with our society, despite our seeming dislike for it, because we can't operate the control towers, the prisons, the Social Security system, and other essential elements without bureaucracy. And we certainly could not have conducted a successful war in the Persian Gulf without a gigantic military bureaucracy.

Although the federal executive branch is large and complex, everything about it is commonplace. Bureaucracies are commonplace because they touch so many aspects of daily life. Government bureaucracies implement the decisions made by the political process. Bureaucracies are full of routine because that assures the regular delivery of the services and ensures that each agency fulfills its mandate. Public bureaucracies are powerful because legislatures and chief executives, and indeed the people, delegate to them vast power to make sure a particular job is done—enabling the rest of us to be more free to pursue our private ends. And for the same reason, bureaucracies are a threat to freedom, because their size, their momentum, and the interests of the civil servants themselves in keeping their jobs impel bureaucracies to resist any change of direction.

Bureaucrats

"Government by offices and desks" conveys to most people a picture of hundreds of office workers shuffling millions of pieces of paper. There is a lot of truth in that image, but we have to look more closely at what papers are being shuffled and why. More than fifty years ago, an astute observer defined bureaucracy as "continuous routine business."[7] Almost any organization succeeds by reducing its work to routines, with each routine being given to a different specialist. But specialization separates people from each other; one worker's output becomes another worker's input. The timing of such relationships is essential, requiring these workers to stay in communication with each other. In fact, bureaucracy was the first information network. Voluminous routine came as bureaucracies grew and specialized. As bureaucracies have grown, the term "bureaucrat" now connotes sluggishness and inefficiency.

Motivational Considerations
The popular view of bureaucrats as failing to live up to the expectation that they will serve the public interest is judgmental and emotionally laden, not analytical. In a now-classic treatment, the economist William Niskanen rejected this misbegotten view entirely.[8] Instead, he proposed that we consider a bureau or department of government as analogous to a division of a private firm, and conceive of the bureaucrat just as we would the manager who runs that division. In particular, Niskanen stipulates for the purposes of modeling bureaucratic behavior that a bureau chief or department head be thought of as a maximizer of his or her budget (just as the private-sector counterpart is a maximizer of his or her division's profits).

Rationality Principle
One view of bureaucratic behavior is that bureaucrats are motivated to maximize their budgets.

There are quite a number of different motivational bases on which bureaucratic budget-maximizing might be justified. A cynical (though some would say realistic) basis for budget-maximizing is that the bureaucrat's own compensation is often tied to the size of his or her budget. Not only might bureaus with large budgets have higher-salaried executives with more elaborate fringe benefits, but also there may be enhanced opportunities for career advancement, travel, a poshly appointed office, possibly even a chauffeur-driven limousine.

A second, related motivation for large budgets is nonmaterial personal gratification. An individual quite understandably enjoys the prestige and respect that comes from running a major enterprise. You can't take these things to the bank, or put them on your family's dinner table, but your sense of esteem and stature are surely buoyed by the conspicuous fact that your bureau or division has a large budget. That you are also boss to a large number of subordinates, made possible by a large bureau budget, is another aspect of this sort of ego gratification.

[7]Arnold Brecht and Comstock Glaser, *The Art and Techniques of Administration in German Ministries* (Cambridge: Harvard University Press, 1940), p. 6.
[8]William Niskanen, *Bureaucracy and Representative Government* (Chicago: Aldine, 1971).

But personal salary, "on-the-job consumption," and power-tripping are not the only forces driving a bureaucrat toward gaining as large a budget as possible. Some bureaucrats, perhaps most, actually *care* about their missions. They initially choose to go into public safety, or the military, or health care, or social work, or education—as police officers, soldiers, hospital managers, social workers, and teachers, respectively—because they believe in the importance of helping people in their communities. As they rise through the ranks of a public bureaucracy into management responsibilities, they take this mission orientation with them. Thus, as chief of detectives in a big-city police department, as head of procurement in the air force, as director of nursing services in a public hospital, as supervisor of the social work division in a county welfare department, or as assistant superintendent of a town school system, individuals try to secure as large a budget as they can in order to succeed in achieving the missions to which they have devoted their professional lives.

Whether from cynical, self-serving motives, or for the noblest of public purposes, it is entirely plausible that individual bureaucrats seek to persuade others (typically legislators or taxpayers) to provide them with as many resources as possible. Indeed, it is sometimes difficult to distinguish the saint from the sinner since each sincerely argues that he or she needs more in order to do more. This is one of the nice features of Niskanen's assumption of budget-maximizing: it doesn't really matter *why* a bureaucrat is interested in a big budget; what matters is simply that she wants more resources rather than less.

Critics of the budget-maximizing theory call into question its assumption about the passivity of the legislature. The legislature, the only customer of the bureau's product, in essence tells the bureau how much it is willing to pay for various production levels. The critics suggest that this is akin to a customer walking onto a used-car lot and telling the salesman precisely how much she is willing to spend for each of the vehicles.[9]

In a representative democracy, it may be difficult for the legislature to keep silent about its own willingness to pay. The bureau, at any rate, can do some research in order to judge the preferences of various legislators based on who their constituents are. But legislators can do research, too. Indeed, we suggested in Chapter 5 that the collection, evaluation, and dissemination of information—in this case information about the production costs of bureaucratic supply—are precisely the things in which specialized legislative committees engage. Committees hold hearings, request documentation on production, assign investigatory staff to various research tasks, and query bureau personnel on the veracity of their data and on whether they employ lowest-cost technologies (making it more difficult for the bureau to disguise on-the-job consumption). After the fact, the committees engage in oversight, making sure that what the legislature was told at the time authorization and appropriations were voted actually holds in practice. In short, the legislature can be much more proactive than the Niskanen

Analyzing American Politics

www.wwnorton.com/ lowi7/ch7

Test the theory that all bureaucrats attempt to maximize their budgets.

[9]This and other related points are drawn from Gary J. Miller and Terry M. Moe, "Bureaucrats, Legislators, and the Size of Government," *American Political Science Review*, 77 (1983): 297–323.

budget-maximizing theory gives them credit for. And, in the real world, it is, as we shall see later in the chapter.

What Do Bureaucrats Do?

Bureaucrats, whether in public or in private organizations, communicate with each other in order to coordinate all the specializations within their organization. This coordination is necessary to carry out the primary task of bureaucracy, which is ***implementation,*** that is, implementing the objectives of the organization as laid down by its board of directors (if a private company) or by law (if a public agency). In government, the "bosses" are ultimately the legislature and the elected chief executive. As we saw in Chapter 1, in a principal-agent relationship, it is the principal who stipulates what he wants done, relying upon the agent's concern for her reputation, appropriate incentives, and other control mechanisms to secure compliance with his wishes. Thus, it may be argued that legislative principals establish bureaucratic agents—in departments, bureaus, agencies, institutes, and commissions of the federal government—to implement the policies promulgated by Congress and the president.

When the bosses—Congress, in particular, when it is making the law—are clear in their instructions to bureaucrats, implementation is a fairly straightforward process. Bureaucrats translate the law into specific routines for each of the employees of an agency. But what happens to routine administrative implementation when there are several bosses who disagree as to what the instructions ought to be? The agent of multiple principals who disagree often finds him- or herself in a real bind. The agent must chart a delicate course, seeking to do the best he or she can and trying not to offend any of the bosses too much. This requires yet another job for bureaucrats: interpretation. Interpretation is a form of implementation, in that the bureaucrats still have to carry out what they believe to be the intentions of their superiors. But when bureaucrats have to interpret a law before implementing it, they are in effect engaging in *lawmaking.*[10] Congress often deliberately delegates to an administrative agency the responsibility of lawmaking. Members of Congress often conclude that some area of industry needs regulating or some area of the environment needs protection, but they are unwilling or unable to specify just how that should be done. In such situations, Congress delegates to the appropriate agency a broad authority within which the bureaucrats have to make law, through the procedures of ***rulemaking*** and ***administrative adjudication.***

Rulemaking is exactly the same as legislation; in fact, it is often referred to as "quasi-legislation." The rules issued by government agencies provide more

Collective Action Principle

Coordination among bureaucrats is necessary to carry out the primary task of bureaucracy—implementation.

implementation
The efforts of departments and agencies to translate laws into specific bureaucratic routines.

Institution Principle

Legislative principals establish bureaucratic agents to implement policies.

rulemaking A quasi-legislative administrative process that produces regulations by government agencies.

administrative adjudication
Applying rules and precedents to specific cases to settle disputes with regulated parties.

---

[10] When bureaucrats engage in interpretation, the result is what political scientists call bureaucratic drift. Bureaucratic drift occurs because, as we've suggested, the "bosses" (in Congress) and the agents (within the bureaucracy) don't always share the same purposes. Bureaucrats also have their own agendas to fulfill. There exists a vast body of political science literature on the relationship between Congress and the bureaucracy. For a review, see Shepsle and Bonchek, *Analyzing Politics,* pp. 355–68. We'll also return to this point at the end of this chapter.

detailed and specific indications of what the policy actually will mean. For example, the Occupational Health and Safety Administration is charged with ensuring that our workplaces are safe. OSHA has regulated the use of chemicals and other well-known health hazards. In recent years, the widespread use of computers in the workplace has been associated with a growing number of cases of repetitive stress injury, which hurts the hands, arms, and neck. To respond to this new threat to workplace health, OSHA issued a new set of ergonomic rules in November 1999 that tell employers what they must do to prevent and address such injuries among their workers. Such rules only take force after a period of public comment. Reaction from the people or businesses that will be subject to the rules may cause an agency to modify the rules they first issue. The rules about ergonomic safety in the workplace, for example, are sure to be contested by many businesses, which view them as too costly. The rulemaking process is thus a highly political one. Once rules are approved, they are published in the *Federal Register* and have the force of law.

🏛️ **Institution Principle**

Congress also delegates authority to bureaucrats to make law, through the procedures of rulemaking and administrative adjudication.

Administrative adjudication is very similar to what the judiciary ordinarily does: applying rules and precedents to specific cases in order to settle disputes. In administrative adjudication, the agency charges the person or business suspected of violating the law. The ruling in an adjudication dispute applies only to the specific case being considered. Many regulatory agencies use administrative adjudication to make decisions about specific products or practices. For example, in December 1999, the Consumer Product Safety Commission held hearings on the safety of bleachers, sparked by concern over the death of children after falls from bleachers. It will issue guidelines about bleacher construction designed to prevent falls. These guidelines have the force of law. Likewise, product recalls are often the result of adjudication.

A good case study of the role agencies can play is the story of how ordinary federal bureaucrats created the Internet. Yes, it's true: what became the Internet was developed largely by the U.S. Department of Defense, and defense considerations still shape the basic structure of the Internet. In 1957, immediately following the profound American embarrassment over the Soviet Union's launching of *Sputnik*, Congress authorized the establishment of the Advanced Research Projects Agency (ARPA) to develop, among other things, a means of maintaining communications in the event the existing telecommunications network (the telephone system) was disabled by a strategic attack. Since the telephone network was highly centralized and therefore could have been completely disabled by a single attack, ARPA developed a decentralized, highly redundant network. Redundancy in this case improved the probability of functioning after an attack. The full design, called by the pet name of ARPANET, took almost a decade to create. By 1971, around twenty universities were connected to ARPANET. The forerunner to the Internet was born.[11]

[11]Alan Stone, *How America Got On-Line: Politics, Markets, and the Revolution in Telecommunication* (Armonk, NY: M. E. Sharpe, 1997).

In sum, government bureaucrats do essentially the same things that bureaucrats in large private organizations do, and neither type deserves the disrespect embodied in the term "bureaucrat." But because of the authoritative, coercive nature of government, far more constraints are imposed on public bureaucrats than on private bureaucrats, even when their jobs are the same. Public bureaucrats are required to maintain a far more thorough paper trail. Public bureaucrats are also subject to a great deal more access from the public. Newspaper reporters, for example, have access to public bureaucrats. Public access has been vastly facilitated in the past thirty years; the adoption of the Freedom of Information Act (FOIA) in 1966 gave ordinary citizens the right of access to agency files and agency data to determine whether derogatory information exists in the file about citizens themselves and to learn about what the agency is doing in general.

And finally, citizens are given far more opportunities to participate in the decision-making processes of public agencies. There are limits of time, money, and expertise to this kind of access, but it does exist, and it occupies a great deal of the time of mid-level and senior public bureaucrats. This public exposure and access serves a purpose, but it also cuts down significantly on the efficiency of public bureaucrats. Thus, much of the lower efficiency of public agencies can be attributed to the political, judicial, legal, and publicity restraints put on public bureaucrats.

AGENCIES AND THEIR POLITICS

Cabinet departments, agencies, and bureaus are the operating parts of the bureaucratic whole. These parts can be separated into four general types: (1) cabinet departments, (2) independent agencies, (3) government corporations, and (4) independent regulatory commissions.

Although Figure 7.3 is an "organizational chart" of the Department of Agriculture, any other department could have been used as an illustration. At the top is the head of the department, who in the United States is called the "secretary" of the department. Below the department head are several top administrators, such as the general counsel and the judicial officer, whose responsibilities cut across the various departmental functions and provide the secretary with the ability to manage the entire organization. Of equal status are the assistant and under secretaries, each of whom has management responsibilities for a group of operating agencies, which are arranged vertically below each of the assistant secretaries.

The next tier, generally called the "bureau level," is the highest level of responsibility for specialized programs. The names of these "bureau-level agencies" are often very well known to the public: the Forest Service and the Food Safety and Inspection Service are two examples. Sometimes they are officially called bureaus, as in the Federal Bureau of Investigation (FBI), which is a bureau in the Department of Justice. Nevertheless, "bureau" is also the generic

FIGURE 7.3

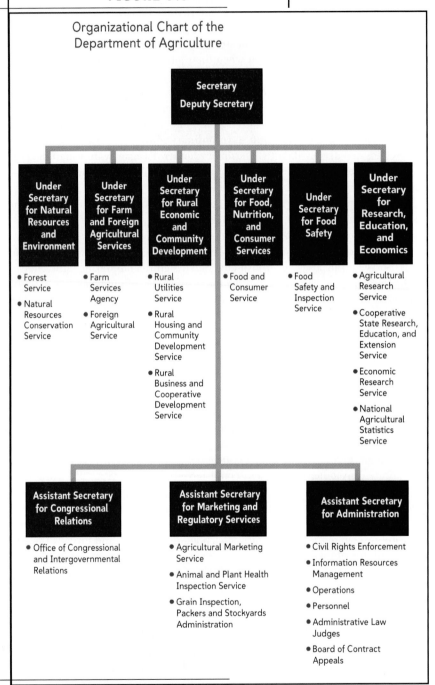

Organizational Chart of the Department of Agriculture

Secretary
Deputy Secretary

Under Secretary for Natural Resources and Environment
- Forest Service
- Natural Resources Conservation Service

Under Secretary for Farm and Foreign Agricultural Services
- Farm Services Agency
- Foreign Agricultural Service

Under Secretary for Rural Economic and Community Development
- Rural Utilities Service
- Rural Housing and Community Development Service
- Rural Business and Cooperative Development Service

Under Secretary for Food, Nutrition, and Consumer Services
- Food and Consumer Service

Under Secretary for Food Safety
- Food Safety and Inspection Service

Under Secretary for Research, Education, and Economics
- Agricultural Research Service
- Cooperative State Research, Education, and Extension Service
- Economic Research Service
- National Agricultural Statistics Service

Assistant Secretary for Congressional Relations
- Office of Congressional and Intergovernmental Relations

Assistant Secretary for Marketing and Regulatory Services
- Agricultural Marketing Service
- Animal and Plant Health Inspection Service
- Grain Inspection, Packers and Stockyards Administration

Assistant Secretary for Administration
- Civil Rights Enforcement
- Information Resources Management
- Operations
- Personnel
- Administrative Law Judges
- Board of Contract Appeals

SOURCE: U.S. Department of Agriculture, www.usda.gov/agencies/agchart.htm.

term for this level of administrative agency. Within the bureaus, there are divisions, offices, services, and units—sometimes designating agencies of the same status, sometimes designating agencies of lesser status.

Not all government agencies are part of cabinet departments. A second type of agency, independent agencies, are set up by Congress outside the departmental structure altogether, even though the president appoints and directs the heads of these agencies. Independent agencies usually have broad powers to provide public services that are either too expensive or too important to be left to private initiatives. Some examples of independent agencies are the National Aeronautics and Space Administration (NASA), the Central Intelligence Agency (CIA), and the Environmental Protection Agency (EPA). Government corporations are a third type of government agency, but are more like private businesses performing and charging for a market service, such as delivering the mail (the United States Postal Service) or transporting railroad passengers (Amtrak).

Yet a fourth type of agency is the independent regulatory commission, given broad discretion to make rules. The first regulatory agencies established by Congress, beginning with the Interstate Commerce Commission in 1887, were set up as independent regulatory commissions because Congress recognized that regulatory agencies are "minilegislatures," whose rules are exactly the same as legislation but require the kind of expertise and full-time attention that is beyond the capacity of Congress. Until the 1960s, most of the regulatory agencies that were set up by Congress, such as the Federal Trade Commission (1914) and the Federal Communications Commission (1934), were independent regulatory commissions. But beginning in the late 1960s and the early 1970s, all new regulatory programs, with two or three exceptions (such as the Federal Election Commission), were placed within existing departments and made directly responsible to the president. Since the 1970s, no major new regulatory programs have been established, independent or otherwise.

There are too many agencies in the executive branch to identify, much less to describe, so a simple classification of agencies will be helpful. Instead of dividing the bureaucracy into four general types, as we did above, this classification is organized by the mission of each agency, as defined by its jurisdiction: clientele agencies, agencies for maintenance of the Union, regulatory agencies, and redistributive agencies. We shall examine each of these types of agencies, focusing on both their formal structure and their place in the political process.

The Clientele Agencies: Structures and Politics

The entire Department of Agriculture is an example of a *clientele agency*. So are the Departments of Interior, Labor, and Commerce. Although all administrative agencies have clientele, certain agencies are singled out and called by that name because they are directed by law to foster and promote the interests of their clientele. For example, the Department of Commerce and Labor was founded in 1903 as a single department "to foster, promote, and develop the foreign and domestic commerce, the mining, the manufacturing, the shipping, and fishing

clientele agencies Departments or bureaus of government whose mission is to promote, serve, or represent a particular interest.

industries, and the transportation facilities of the United States."[12] It remained a single department until 1913, when the law created the two separate departments of Commerce and Labor, with each statute providing for the same obligation—to support and foster their respective clienteles.[13] The Department of Agriculture serves the many farming interests that, taken together, are the United States's largest economic sector (agriculture accounts for one-fifth of the U.S. total domestic output).

Most clientele agencies locate a relatively large proportion of their total personnel in field offices dealing directly with the clientele. The Extension Service of the Department of Agriculture is among the most familiar, with its numerous local "extension agents" who consult with farmers on farm productivity. These same agencies also seek to foster the interests of their clientele by providing "functional representation"; that is, they try to learn what their clients' interests and needs are and then operate almost as a lobby in Washington on their behalf. In addition to the Department of Agriculture, other clientele agencies include the Department of Interior and the five newest cabinet departments: Housing and Urban Development (HUD), created in 1966; Transportation (DOT), created in 1966; Energy (DOE), created in 1977; and Education (ED) and Health and Human Services (HHS), both created in 1979.[14]

Since clientele agencies exist to foster the interests of clients, it is no wonder that clients support the agency when it is in jeopardy of being abolished, reorganized, or cut back. Thus, it is not surprising to learn that client-supported agency resistance finally wore down President Reagan's resolve to abolish the Department of Energy, an entire clientele department. When created by President Carter, the Department of Energy had 18,000 employees and a $10 billion budget. The agencies in the new department were mainly pre-existing agencies drawn from other departments on the theory that agencies with related programs can be better managed within a common department. But each brought its own supportive clientele along. Imagine the resistance to abolition that arose from all the universities and corporations whose research labs depended on a piece of the DOE's multi-billion-dollar energy research budget.

The Department of Education is another case in point. Although President Reagan failed in his effort to abolish the department, he did manage to cut its budget. Yet, by 1987, the Office of Education and the entire Department of Education was back up to its pre-Reagan size. As reported earlier, the 1997 budget authorization for the Department of Education was barely cut, despite the strenuous efforts of the Republican 104th Congress. President Clinton's Goals 2000 renewed support for education with a $34 billion package for the

---

[12]32 Stat. 825; 15 USC 1501.

[13]For a detailed account of the creation of the Department of Commerce and Labor and its split into two separate departments, see Theodore J. Lowi, *The End of Liberalism* (New York: W. W. Norton, 1979), pp. 78–84.

[14]The Departments of Education and of Health and Human Services until 1979 were joined in a single department, the Department of Health, Education, and Welfare (HEW), which had been established by Congress in 1953.

Department of Education in the fiscal 1999 budget and $35 billion in the fiscal 2000 budget, giving the department a 46-percent appropriations' increase since fiscal 1996. And the boldest proposal was yet to come. Secretary of Education Riley presented a major proposal that the Department of Education regulate national teacher quality with a system of national testing and licensing. This would involve a quantum leap in the size of his department. Even conservative Elizabeth Dole jumped in with support for a larger education budget in her first speech on the 2000 presidential circuit.[15] The prime reason for the recovery of the Department of Education goes back to the nature of clientele agencies: Unless a president wants to drop everything else and concentrate on a single department, its constituency is just too much for a president to handle on a part-time basis. For example, the constituency of the Department of Education includes the departments of education in all the fifty states, and all the boards and school systems in thousands of counties and cities; there are also the teachers' colleges, and the major unions of secondary school teachers. One of the most formidable lobbies in the United States is the National Education Association (NEA), and there is a chapter of the NEA in every state in the country. It was the NEA's access to Carter that led to the creation of the Department of Education, and it is their continuing support of the department that frustrates efforts to change it, much less to abolish it.

These examples and those shown in Figure 7.4 point to what is known as an *iron triangle*, a pattern of stable relationships between an agency in the executive branch, a congressional committee or subcommittee, and one or more organized groups of agency clientele. Other configurations are of course possible. One of those might be called an iron rectangle or a network, because in recent years the federal courts have entered the process, sometimes on the side of clientele groups against an agency. But even so, the result reinforces the program against drastic change or abolition by a hostile president.[16]

These iron triangles, rectangles, and complexes make the clientele agencies the most difficult to change or to coordinate. Generally, these agencies are able to resist external demands or pressures for change and vigorously defend their own prerogatives and institutional integrity. Congress, in fact, felt compelled to adopt the Whistleblower Act in 1989, to encourage civil servants to report abuses of trust and to protect them from retaliations from within their own agencies. Because of their power of resistance, Congress and the president have frequently discovered that it is far easier to create new clientele agencies than to compel an existing agency to implement programs that it opposes. This has produced a strong tendency in the United States toward duplication, waste, and collusion.

iron triangle
Name for the stable and cooperative relationships that often develop between a congressional committee or subcommittee, an administrative agency, and one or more supportive interest groups.

Collective Action Principle
Iron triangles, rectangles, and complexes make clientele agencies the most difficult to change or to coordinate.

[15]For details on President Clinton's Department of Education Program, see *Congressional Quarterly Weekly*, 6 February 1999, pp. 308–9.
[16]Martin Shapiro, "The Presidency and the Federal Courts," in *Politics and the Oval Office*, ed. Arnold Meltsner (San Francisco: Institute for Contemporary Studies, 1981), Chapter 8; and Hugh Heclo, "Issue Networks and the Executive Establishment," in *The New American Political System*, ed. A. King (Washington, DC: American Enterprise Institute, 1978), Chapter 3.

FIGURE 7.4

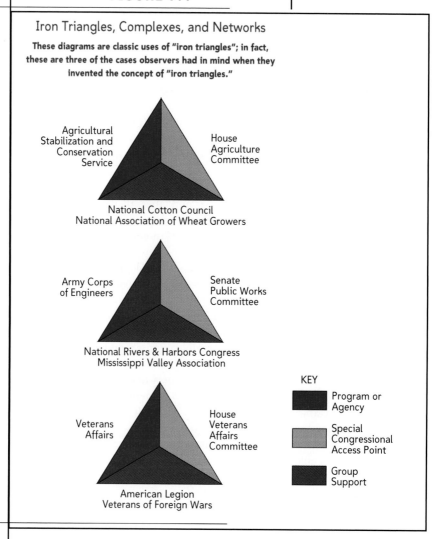

Iron Triangles, Complexes, and Networks

These diagrams are classic uses of "iron triangles"; in fact,
these are three of the cases observers had in mind when they
invented the concept of "iron triangles."

Agricultural Stabilization and Conservation Service

House Agriculture Committee

National Cotton Council
National Association of Wheat Growers

Army Corps of Engineers

Senate Public Works Committee

National Rivers & Harbors Congress
Mississippi Valley Association

Veterans Affairs

House Veterans Affairs Committee

American Legion
Veterans of Foreign Wars

KEY

Program or Agency

Special Congressional Access Point

Group Support

SOURCE: Adapted from U.S. Congress, House of Representatives, *Report of the Subcommittee for Special Investigations of the Committee on Armed Services*, 86th Congress, 1st session (Washington, DC: Government Printing Office, 1960), p. 7. Reprinted from Theodore J. Lowi, *Incomplete Conquest: Governing America*, 2nd ed. (New York: Holt, Rinehart and Winston. 1981), p. 139.

Agencies for Maintenance of the Union

These agencies could be called public order agencies were it not for the fact that the Constitution entrusts so many of the vital functions of public order, such as the police, to the state governments. This is indeed a remarkable feature of the

American system, the more so because it is taken for granted that the United States has no national police force and little national criminal law. But some agencies vital to maintaining *national* bonds do exist in the national government, and they can be grouped for convenience into three categories: (1) agencies for control of the sources of government revenue, (2) agencies for control of conduct defined as a threat to internal national security, and (3) agencies for control of conduct threatening to external security. Most revenue control is housed in the Treasury Department. Agencies for defending internal national security are housed mainly in the Department of Justice. Some such agencies are also found in the Departments of Defense and State, but the law is careful to limit their jurisdictions to external threats to security.

Revenue Agencies   The Internal Revenue Service (IRS) is the most important revenue agency. The IRS is also one of the federal government's largest bureaucracies. Its 102,000 employees are spread through four regions, sixty-three districts, ten service centers, and hundreds of local offices. In 1996, the IRS processed over 200 million tax returns and supplemental documents, with total collections amounting to $1,486,546,674. (It costs the IRS 49 cents to collect every $100 in taxes; this figure has risen from 45 cents in 1970). Nearly 19,000 IRS tax auditors and revenue agents are engaged in auditing tax returns, and in 1996 they recommended additional taxes and penalties on 1,941,546 individual returns, a total of $7.6 billion in additional revenues.[17]

One experience with the IRS is enough to remind anyone of the very close relationship between taxation and control. Control is justified on the grounds of necessity, but there is a thin line between necessary control and abusing the rights guaranteed to all citizens since, for example, a citizen's privacy can be invaded if there is a suspicion of fraud or nonreporting. Indeed, persons accused in tax cases bear the burden of proving their own innocence—the reverse of the normal rule that a person accused of a crime is presumed innocent until proven guilty. Al Capone, the infamous gangland figure, was convicted in 1931 of federal income tax evasion and sentenced to eleven years in prison, served eight years, and was released in 1939 because he was dying. Although Capone was universally recognized as a leading crime figure, all other efforts to convict Capone had failed, and the tax approach was utilized because it was the only way to apprehend him. Although Capone was a disreputable person, his case is an example of the conflict between freedom and power. The power to tax is very close to the **police power,** since governments must rely on police power to collect taxes. But to use personal income tax records to imprison someone like Capone because the government lacked the evidence to convict him of his more serious crimes comes close to an improper linkage of the power to tax and the power to police. It can undermine the legitimacy of the tax system and instill fear in ordinary citizens that their privacy, if not their freedom, could be in danger.

police power
Power reserved to the state to regulate the health, safety, and morals of its citizens.

[17]These figures are from the *1998 Information Please Almanac* (Boston and New York: Houghton Mifflin, 1997), pp. 1000–1.

The IRS is not unresponsive to political influences, given its close working relationship with Congress through the staffs as well as the members of the House Ways and Means Committee and Senate Finance Committee. But the political patterns of the IRS are virtually opposite to those of a clientele agency; as one expert puts it, "probably no organization in the country, public or private, creates as much clientele *dis*favor as the Internal Revenue Service. The very nature of its work brings it into an adversary relationship with vast numbers of Americans every year."[18]

Back in the 1980s and early 1990s, when deficits were growing higher every year, Congress voted to stiffen penalties and to enforce the tax laws more stringently in order to collect a greater proportion of estimated tax revenues. But in the mid-1990s, as deficit pressures subsided and the budget began to balance and even show a surplus, Congress relented and began drawing up what came to be called a "taxpayer's bill of rights," which even included a reversal of the "burden of proof." Under the new provisions, the taxpayer would still have to cooperate, but proof of guilt would have to be provided by the IRS agents. This and other reforms would make tax collection a lot more difficult, but the hope was that the new bill would reduce animosities and improve voluntary cooperation in the payment of taxes. Whatever comes of the taxpayer bill of rights, it must be said that, despite many complaints, the IRS has maintained a reputation for being professional and evenhanded in its administration of the tax code; surprisingly few scandals have soiled its record.[19]

Most complaints against the IRS are against its needless complexity, its lack of sensitivity and responsiveness to individual taxpayers, and its overall lack of efficiency. As one of its critics put it, "Imagine a company that's owed $216 billion plus interest, a company with a 22-percent error rate. A company that spent $4 billion to update a computer system—with little success. It all describes the Internal Revenue Service."[20] Again, leaving aside the issue of the income tax itself, all the other complaints amount to just one big complaint: the IRS is not bureaucratic enough. It needs to succeed with its new computer processing system; it needs vast improvement in its "customer services"; it needs long-term budgeting and other management control; and it needs to borrow more management and technology expertise from the private sector.

Agencies for Internal Security   As long as the country is not in a state of insurrection, most of the task of maintaining the Union takes the form of legal work, and the main responsibility for that lies in the Department of Justice. It is indeed a luxury, and rare in the world, when national unity can be maintained by routines of civil law instead of imposed by a real army with guns.

[18]George E. Berkley, *The Craft of Public Administration* (Boston: Allyn & Bacon, 1975), p. 417.
[19]Good accounts of the efforts at reform of the IRS will be found in *Congressional Quarterly Weekly*, 9 May 1998, pp. 1224–27 and 6 June 1998, pp. 1505–6.
[20]Correspondent Kelli Arena,"Overhauling the IRS," CNN Financial Network, 7 March 1997.

A strong connection exists between the Justice and Treasury Departments, because a major share of the responsibility for protecting national revenue sources is held by the Tax Division of the Justice Department. This agency handles the litigation arising out of actions taken by the IRS against delinquency, fraud, and disputes over interpretation of the Internal Revenue Code—the source of the tax laws and court interpretations.

In tax cases and in most other legal matters coming before agencies in the Justice Department, the United States itself is the sole party, as it is considered the legal representative of the American people as a whole and thus a legal individual (a legal fiction) that can sue and be sued. The Civil Division of the Justice Department (a bureau) deals with all litigation in which the United States is the defendant being sued by plaintiffs for injury and damage allegedly inflicted by the government or one of its officials. The agency also handles the occasional admiralty cases involving all disputes as to navigable waters or those concerning shippers and shipworkers. The work of several other agencies in the Justice Department involves cases where the United States is the plaintiff. The largest and most important of these is the Criminal Division, which is responsible for enforcing all the federal criminal laws, except for a few specifically assigned to other divisions. Criminal litigation is actually done by the U.S. Attorneys. There is a presidentially appointed U.S. Attorney assigned to each federal judicial district, and he or she supervises the work of assistant U.S. Attorneys. The work or jurisdiction of the Antitrust, Civil Rights, and Internal Security divisions is described by their official names.

Although it looms so very large in American folklore, the Federal Bureau of Investigation (FBI) is simply another bureau of the Department of Justice. The FBI handles no litigation, but instead serves as the information-gathering agency for all the other divisions. Established in 1908, the FBI expanded and advanced in stature during the 1920s and 1930s under the early direction of J. Edgar Hoover. Although it is only one of the fifteen bureaus and divisions in the department, and although it officially has no higher legal status than any of the others, its political importance is greater than that of the others. It is also the largest, taking over 40 percent of the appropriations allocated to the Department of Justice.

Despite its professionalism and its fierce pride in its autonomy, the FBI has not been unresponsive to the partisan commitments of Democratic and Republican administrations. Although the FBI has always achieved its best publicity from the spectacular apprehension of famous criminals, such as John Dillinger, George "Machine Gun" Kelly, and Bonnie and Clyde,[21] it has followed the president's direction in focusing on particular crime problems. Thus it has infiltrated Nazi and Mafia organizations; it operates the vast loyalty and security investigation programs covering all federal employees since the Truman presidency; it monitored and infiltrated the Ku Klux Klan and the civil rights

[21]See William Keller, *The Liberals and J. Edgar Hoover* (Princeton: Princeton University Press, 1989). See also Victor Navasky, *Kennedy Justice* (New York: Atheneum, 1971), Chapter 2 and p. 8.

movement in the 1950s and 1960s; and it has infiltrated radical political groups and extreme religious cults and survivalist militias in the 1980s and 1990s.

Agencies for External National Security Two departments occupy center stage here, State and Defense. There are a few key agencies outside State and Defense that have external national security functions. They will be treated in this chapter only as bureaucratic phenomena and as examples of the political problems relevant to administration.

Although diplomacy is generally considered the primary task of the State Department, diplomatic missions are only one of its organizational dimensions. The State Department is also comprised of geographic or regional bureaus concerned with all problems within a defined region of the world, "functional" bureaus, handling such things as economic and business affairs, intelligence and research, and international organizations and bureaus of internal affairs, which handle such areas as security, finance and management, and legal issues.

These bureaus support the responsibilities of the elite of foreign affairs, the foreign service officers (FSOs), who staff U.S. embassies around the world and who hold almost all of the most powerful positions in the department below the rank of ambassador.[22] The ambassadorial positions, especially the plum positions in the major capitals of the world, are filled by presidential appointees, many of whom get their positions by having been important donors to the victorious political campaign.

Despite the importance of the State Department in foreign affairs, fewer than 20 percent of all U.S. government employees working abroad are directly under its authority. By far the largest number of career government professionals working abroad are under the authority of the Defense Department.

The creation of the Department of Defense by legislation from 1947 to 1949 was an effort to unify the two historic military departments, the War Department and the Navy Department, and to integrate with them a new department, the Air Force Department. Real unification, however, did not occur. Instead, the Defense Department adds more pluralism to national security.

The American military, following worldwide military tradition, is organized according to "chain of command," a tight hierarchy of clear responsibility and rank, made clearer by uniforms, special insignia, and detailed organizational charts and rules of order and etiquette (see Figure 7.5). The line agencies are the military commands, distributed geographically by divisions and fleets. *Staff agencies*, serving each military region, are logistics, intelligence, personnel, research and development (R&D), quartermaster, and engineering. At the top of the military chain of command is a chief of staff (called chief of naval operations in the navy, and commandant in the marines) of four-star rank. These chiefs of

staff agency An agency responsible for maintaining the bureaucracy, with responsibilities such as purchasing, budgeting, personnel management, planning.

---

[22]For more detail, consult John E. Harr, *The Professional Diplomat* (Princeton: Princeton University Press, 1972), p. 11; and Nicholas Horrock, "The CIA Has Neighbors in the 'Intelligence Community,'" *New York Times*, 29 June 1975, sec. 4, p. 2. See also Roger Hilsman, *The Politics of Policy Making in Defense and Foreign Affairs*, 3rd ed. (Englewood Cliffs, NJ: Prentice Hall, 1993).

FIGURE 7.5

The Chain of Command in the Department of Defense

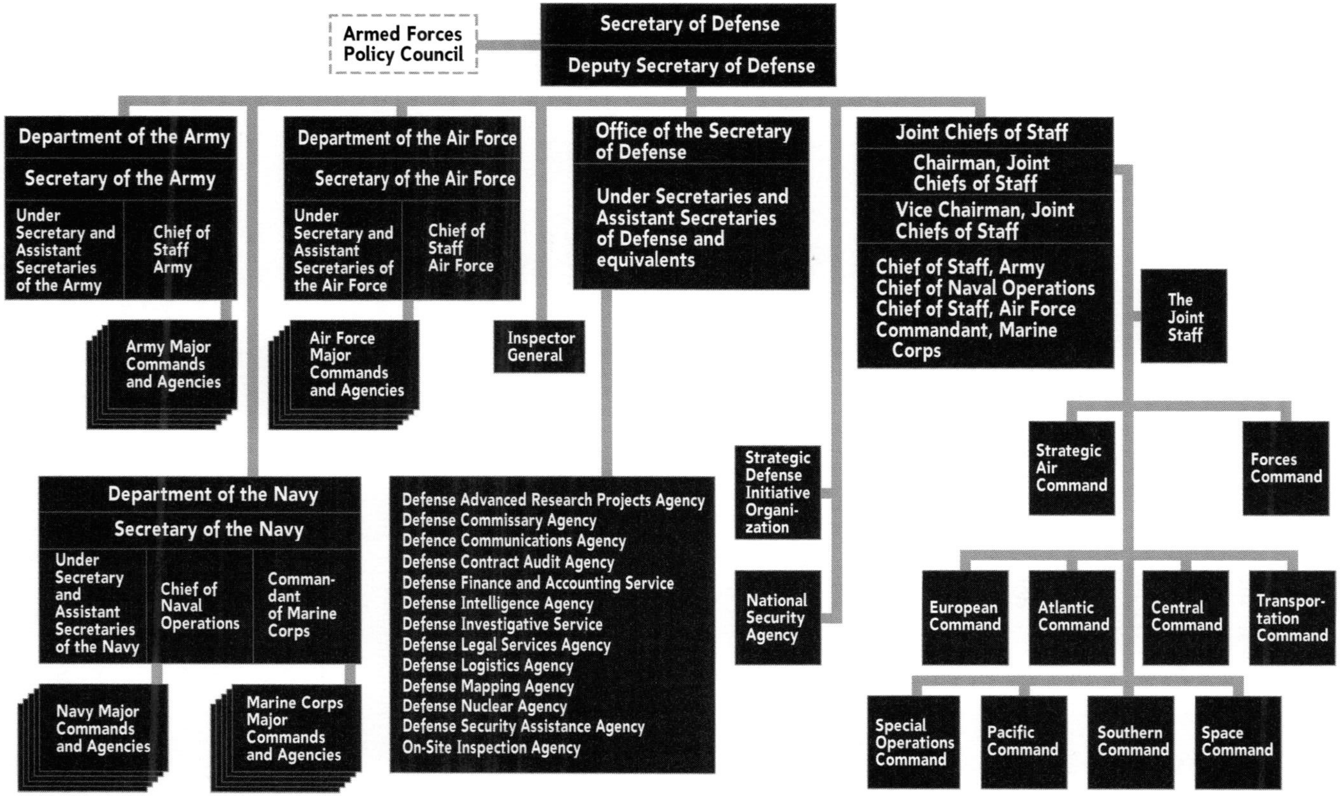

SOURCE: Office of the Federal Register, *U. S. Government Manual, 1992–1993* (Washington. DC: Government Printing Office, 1992). p. 184.

staff serve as *ex officio* ("by virtue of their office") members of the Joint Chiefs of Staff—the center of military policy and management.

America's primary political problem with its military has not been the historic one of how to keep the military out of the politics of governing—a problem that has plagued so many countries in Europe and Latin America. The American military problem is one of the lower politics of the "pork barrel." President Clinton's long list of proposed military base closings, a major part of his budget-cutting drive for 1993, caused a firestorm of opposition even within his own party, including a number of members of Congress who were otherwise prominently in favor of significant reductions in the Pentagon budget. Emphasis on jobs rather than strategy and policy means pork-barrel use of the military for political purposes. This is a classic way for a bureaucracy to defend itself politically in a democracy. It is the distributive tendency, in which the bureaucracy assures political support among elected officials by making sure to distribute things—military bases, contracts, facilities, and jobs—to the states and districts from which the legislators were elected. As is commonly known, it is hard to bite the hand that feeds you! Thus, the best way to understand the military in American politics is to study it within the same bureaucratic framework used to explain the domestic agencies.

President Clinton's willingness to cooperate in increases by having proposed a $25 billion supplemental increase in the Pentagon budget for 1995, even in the face of tremendous fiscal pressures, had more to do with the domestic pressures of employment in defense and defense-related industries than with military necessity in a post–cold war era. This is why Congress had to create a Base Closing Commission in the late 1980s with authority independent of Congress and the president to decide which military bases could be closed and whether and how to compensate communities for job losses and other sacrifices.

President Bush and Secretary of Defense Donald Rumsfeld changed, at least temporarily, the terms of discourse by demanding of Congress a significant increase in the defense budget for revival of strategic missile defense ("Star Wars"), despite the fact that it could break through the budget ceiling imposed by the $1.35 trillion tax cut. It also put Secretary Rumsfeld at odds with the commitment of almost all his military leaders to maintenance of the existing "force structure"—army divisions, naval battle groups, fighter wings, etc. Ultimately, the military will keep their status quo—and with congressional complicity—because the status quo exists locally, in congressional districts.

The Regulatory Agencies

As we saw in Chapter 3, our national government did not even begin to get involved in the regulation of economic and social affairs until the late nineteenth century. Until then, regulation was strictly a state and local affair. The federal *regulatory agencies* are, as a result, relatively new, most dating from the 1930s. But they have come to be extensive and important. In this section, we will look at these regulatory agencies as an administrative phenomenon, with its attendant politics.

The United States has no Department of Regulation but has many regulatory agencies. Some of these are bureaus within departments, such as the Food and Drug Administration (FDA) in the Department of Health and Human Services, the Occupational Safety and Health Administration (OSHA) in the Department of Labor, and the Animal and Plant Health and Inspection Service (APHIS) in the Department of Agriculture. Other regulatory agencies are independent regulatory commissions. An example is the Federal Trade Commission (FTC). But whether departmental or independent, an agency or commission is regulatory if Congress delegates to it relatively broad powers over a sector of the economy or a type of commercial activity and authorizes it to make rules governing the conduct of people and businesses within that jurisdiction. Rules made by regulatory agencies have the force and effect of legislation; indeed, the rules they make are referred to as ***administrative legislation.*** And when these agencies make decisions or orders settling disputes between parties or between the government and a party, they are really acting like courts.

administrative legislation
Rules made by regulatory agencies and commissions.

Since regulatory agencies exercise a tremendous amount of influence over the economy, and since their rules are a form of legislation, Congress was at first loath to turn them over to the executive branch as ordinary agencies under the control of the president. Consequently, most of the important regulatory programs were delegated to independent commissions with direct responsibility to Congress rather than to the White House. This is the basis of the 1930s reference to them as the "headless fourth branch."[23] With the rise of presidential government, most recent presidents have supported more regulatory programs but have successfully opposed the expansion of regulatory independence. The 1960s and 1970s witnessed adoption of an unprecedented number of new regulatory programs but only four new independent commissions.

The political patterns of these agencies arise from their ability to play the president against the Congress. But this tends to throw the agencies into a more direct struggle with the interests they are regulating. And even though many of the regulatory programs were enacted over the opposition of the regulated groups, these groups often have succeeded in turning the programs to their advantage. Thus, for example, during the years when the airlines were being regulated by the Civil Aeronautics Board (CAB), they were able to protect themselves from competition from each other and to prevent new and more competitive transportation companies from entering the airlines market. Even organized labor found security within the CAB regulatory umbrella; regulation permitted the companies not only to charge exorbitant fares but to yield to pressure from airline unions for wage escalation far out of line with the rest of the work force. Consequently, in 1978, both airlines and organized labor within the airlines industry strongly opposed congressional efforts to deregulate the airlines by eliminating the CAB.[24]

[23]*Final Report of the President's Committee on Administrative Management* (Washington, DC: Government Printing Office, 1937). The term "headless fourth branch" was invented by a member of the committee staff, Cornell University government professor Robert Cushman.
[24]See Walter Adams and James Brock, *The Business Complex—Industry, Labor, and Government in the American Economy* (New York: Pantheon Books, 1986), pp. 229–31 and 322–23.

Three factors in particular have enabled regulated companies to turn the programs to their advantage. First, the top agency personnel are often drawn from the regulated industries themselves or from related law firms. Second, throughout its life, the regulatory agency has to depend on the regulated industries for important data about whether the industry is complying with the laws and rules. Third, regulated industries and their trade associations provide a preponderance of expert witnesses at agency hearings where new regulations are formulated. These factors encourage not only interdependence but interpenetration between regulators and regulated.[25]

During the 1970s there were two reactions. First, many citizens and members of Congress began to learn that regulatory agencies weren't necessarily regulating on behalf of what they considered to be the public interest. These people formed "public interest groups" or "public interest lobbies" and began to agitate to get regulatory agencies to maintain a more adversarial relation with the regulated companies. These groups even brought hundreds of lawsuits in federal courts to try to force agencies to be more zealous in regulating their part of the economy or society. The second reaction was from many of the regulated interests themselves, who became convinced that they could do better without the safety of protective regulation; deregulation and the resulting more competitive market would, after a period of adjustment, be better for their entire industry. Moreover, the globalization of the economy provided new and vigorous international sources of competition in many industries, making the need for domestic regulation of these industries less compelling than when they had enjoyed virtual monopoly power within their domestic borders.[26]

deregulation A policy of reducing or eliminating regulatory restraints on the conduct of individuals or private institutions.

Thus, the "new politics" movement and the ***deregulation*** movement started at about the same time, the first coming mainly from the liberal side of the political spectrum, and the second coming from some liberals as well as libertarians and conservatives. Nevertheless, all this pressure for both deregulation and for more regulation neither invigorated regulatory programs nor terminated them.

Redistributive Administration: Fiscal/Monetary and Welfare Agencies

Welfare agencies and fiscal/monetary agencies seem at first to be too far apart to belong to the same category, but they are related in a very special way. They are responsible for the transfer of literally hundreds of billions of dollars annually between the public and the private spheres, and through such transfers these agencies influence how people and corporations spend and invest trillions of dollars annually. We call them agencies of redistribution because they influence the amount of money in the economy and because they directly influence who has

[25]Lowi, *The End of Liberalism*, especially Chapters 5 and 11.
[26]Alfred C. Aman, Jr., *Administrative Law in a Global Era* (Ithaca, NY: Cornell University Press, 1992).

money, who has credit, and whether people will want to invest or save their money rather than spend it.

Fiscal and Monetary Agencies   The best generic term for government activity affecting or relating to money is "fiscal" policy. The *fisc* was the Roman imperial treasury; fiscal can refer to anything and everything having to do with public finance. However, we in the United States choose to make a further distinction, reserving *fiscal* for taxing and spending policies and using *monetary* for policies having to do with banks, credit, and currency. And the third, *welfare*, deserves to be treated as an equal member of this redistributive category.

Administration of fiscal policy is primarily performed in the Treasury Department. It is no contradiction to include the Treasury here as well as with the agencies for maintenance of the Union. This indicates (1) that the Treasury is a complex department performing more than one function of government, and (2) that traditional controls have had to be adapted to modern economic conditions and new technologies.

Today, in addition to administering and policing income tax and other tax collections, the Treasury is also responsible for managing the enormous federal debt, which was close to $6 trillion in 1997. In 1998, interest payments on the debt amounted to 15 percent of the annual budget. This item alone is the fifth largest item in the entire annual budget, coming after Medicare and Medicaid (18 percent), Social Security (22 percent), national defense (16 percent), and all other domestic expenditures (16 percent). But debt is not something the country *has;* it is something a country has to *manage* and *administer.* Those thousands of billions of dollars of debt exist in the form of bonds, bank deposits, and obligations spelled out in contracts to purchase goods and services and research from the private sector. Even after we managed to balance the budget—a goal accomplished in 1998—and begin paying off the national debt, we still have to manage and administer the debt as one of the major functions of the national government. This requires a large and expert bureaucracy under any conditions.

The Treasury Department is also responsible for printing the currency that we use, but of course currency represents only a tiny proportion of the entire money economy. Most of the trillions of dollars used in the transactions that comprise the private and public sectors of the U.S. economy exist on printed accounts and computers, not in currency.

Another important fiscal agency (although for technical reasons it is called an agency of monetary policy) is the **Federal Reserve System**, headed by the Federal Reserve Board. The Federal Reserve System (the Fed) has authority over the credit rates and lending activities of the nation's most important banks. Established by Congress in 1913, the Fed is responsible for adjusting the supply of money to the needs of banks in the different regions and of the commerce and industry in each. The Fed helps shift money from where there is too much to where it is needed. It also ensures that the banks do not overextend themselves by too-liberal lending policies, out of fear that if there is a sudden economic scare, a run on a few banks might be contagious and cause another terrible crash

Federal Reserve System (Fed) Consisting of twelve Federal Reserve Banks, the Fed facilitates exchanges of cash, checks, and credit; it regulates member banks; and it uses monetary policies to fight inflation and deflation.

like the one in 1929. The Federal Reserve Board sits at the top of the pyramid of twelve district Federal Reserve Banks, which are "bankers' banks," serving the monetary needs of the hundreds of member banks in the national bank system.

Welfare Agencies   Welfare agencies seem at first glance to be just another set of clientele agencies. But there is a big difference between the two categories. Access to clientele agencies is open to almost anyone who puts forward a claim. It may cost something to make one's way to a clientele agency or to write a proposal or to spend some time getting the agency's attention. But access is open to almost anyone. In contrast, welfare agencies operate under laws that discriminate between rich and poor, old and young, employed and unemployed. In other words, access to welfare agencies is restricted to those individuals who fall within some legally defined category. Those who fall outside the legal standards of that category would not be entitled to access even if they sought it.

The most important and expensive of the welfare programs are the Social Security programs. These are, roughly speaking, insurance programs, to which all employed persons contribute during their working years and from which those persons receive specified benefits as a matter of right when in need.[27] But there is an entirely separate category of programs that are popularly known as "welfare." The two most familiar examples are Temporary Assistance to Needy Families (TANF) and Supplemental Security Income (SSI)—both of which provide *cash benefits.* Eligible individuals receive actual cash payments. There is another category of public assistance or welfare called *in-kind benefits*, which include food stamps and Medicaid. In-kind benefits do involve expenditures of money, but not directly to the beneficiaries. For example, cash is involved in the Medicaid program, but the government acts as the "third party," guaranteeing payment to the doctor or hospital for the services rendered to the beneficiary.

No single government agency is responsible for all the programs comprising the "welfare state." The largest agency in this field is the Social Security Administration (SSA), which manages the social insurance aspects of Social Security and SSI. Other agencies in the Department of Health and Human Services administer TANF and Medicaid, and the Department of Agriculture is responsible for the food stamp program. With the exception of Social Security, these are *means-tested* programs, requiring applicants to demonstrate that their total annual cash earnings fall below an officially defined poverty line. These public assistance programs comprise a large administrative burden.

In August 1996, virtually all of the means-tested public assistance programs were legally abolished as national programs and were "devolved" to the states (see also Chapter 3). However, for the five years between fiscal 1996 and 2001, there was still a great deal of national administrative responsibility, because

---

[27]These are called insurance because people pay premiums; however, the programs are not fully self-sustaining, and people do not receive benefits in proportion to the size of their premiums.

federal funding of these programs continued through large, discretionary block grants to each state. Other aspects of state welfare activity were policed by federal agencies, and all of that required about the same size of administrative capacity in welfare as existed before. Those who expected some kind of revolution following adoption of the Personal Responsibility and Work Opportunity Reconciliation Act of 1996 were in for something of a disappointment.

Our concern in the first two sections of this chapter has been to present a picture of bureaucracy, its necessity as well as its scale, and the particular uses to which the bureaucracies are being put by the national government. But it is clearly impossible to present these bureaucracies merely as organizations when in fact they exist to implement actual public policies. What remains for this chapter is to explore how the American system of government has tried to accommodate this vast apparatus to the requirements of representative democracy. The title of the chapter, "Bureaucracy in a Democracy,"[28] was intended to convey the sense that the two are contradictory. We cannot live without bureaucracy, because it is the most efficient way to organize people and technology to get a large collective job done. But we can't live comfortably with bureaucracy either. Bureaucracy requires hierarchy, appointed authority, and professional expertise. Those requirements make bureaucracy the natural enemy of representation, which requires discussion among equals, reciprocity among equals, and a high degree of individualism. Yet, the task is not to retreat from bureaucracy but to try to take advantage of its strengths while trying to make it more *accountable* to the demands made upon it by democratic politics and representative government. That is the focus of the remainder of this chapter.

CONTROLLING THE BUREAUCRACY

Two hundred years, millions of employees, and trillions of dollars after the founding, we must return to James Madison's observation that "You must first enable the government to control the governed; and in the next place oblige it to control itself."[29] Today the problem is the same, but the form has changed. Our problem today is bureaucracy and our inability to keep it accountable to elected political authorities. We conclude this chapter with a review of the presidency and Congress as institutions for keeping the bureaucracy accountable. Some of the facts from this and the preceding two chapters are repeated, but in this important context. We will then look at the special role of the federal courts in Chapter 8.

---

[28]The title was inspired by an important book by Charles Hyneman, *Bureaucracy in a Democracy* (New York: Harper, 1950). For a more recent effort to describe the federal bureaucracy and to provide some guidelines for improvement, see Patricia W. Ingraham and Donald F. Kettl, *Agenda for Excellence: Public Service in America* (Chatham, NJ: Chatham House, 1992).

[29]Clinton Rossiter, ed., *The Federalist Papers* (New York: New American Library, 1961), No. 51.

President as Chief Executive

Making the Managerial Presidency[30]   The rise of "presidential government" means above all that our system depends upon the president to establish and maintain a connection between popular aspirations and day-to-day administration. Congress and the American people have shown a consistent willingness to delegate to the president almost any powers he seeks, to enable him to meet this primary obligation. But there is no guarantee that the powers granted, no matter how many, will be sufficient. In 1937, President Roosevelt, through his President's Committee on Administrative Management, made the plea that "the president needs help." Each president since that time has found it necessary to make the same plea, because *presidents have great power to commit but much less power to guide.* In other words, the president can summon up popular opinion and congressional support to impose a new program and a new agency on the bureaucracy—even to impose an unwanted new responsibility on the FBI. But since the president can never have enough time and staff to watch over more than a few high-priority agencies, all the others can take advantage of their obscurity and go their merry way—until some scandal or dissatisfied client turns on the light.

History Principle

Each expansion of the national government is accompanied by a parallel expansion of presidential management authority.

The story of the modern presidency can be told largely as a series of responses to the rise of big government. *Each expansion of the national government in the twentieth century was accompanied by a parallel expansion of presidential management authority;* that is, the expansion of the presidency as a real chief executive office. The first sustained expansion of the national government in the twentieth century, the Wilson period, was followed by one of the most important executive innovations in U.S. history, the Budget and Accounting Act of 1921. By this act, Congress turned over this prime legislative power, the budget, to the executive branch. Moving on to FDR, expansions of government during the 1930s were so large and were sustained over such a long period of time that reactions to control government growth occurred under the same president, producing some of the most important innovations in executive-branch management.

After World War II, the "managerial presidency" was an established fact, but its expansion continued, with each president trying to keep pace with the continually growing bureaucracy. And the purpose of the struggle remained the same: to react to every expansion with another mechanism of popular control. For example, the two presidents most supportive of big government since Roosevelt were Kennedy and Johnson, but they were also equally committed to expanding the executive branch's managerial and oversight powers to control the expanded government. Management reform had become a regular and frequent activity.

---

[30]Title inspired by Peri Arnold, *Making the Managerial Presidency* (Princeton: Princeton University Press, 1986).

President Nixon also greatly enlarged the managerial presidency. Nixon's approach to presidential reorganization can be attributed in part to his own boldness and confidence as president and in part to the great need of the Republicans at that time to impose their own brand of control on an executive branch that had been tremendously enlarged by the "pro-government" Democrats who had controlled the White House for twenty-eight of the previous thirty-six years.[31]

President Carter was probably more preoccupied with administrative reorganization than any other Democratic president in this century. Responding to Watergate, his 1976 campaign was filled with plans to make the bureaucracy more accountable as well as more efficient. His reorganization of the civil service will long be recognized as one of his more significant contributions. The Civil Service Reform Act of 1978 was the first major revamping of the civil service since its inception in 1883.

Although President Reagan gave the impression of being a "laid-back" president, he actually centralized management to an unprecedented degree. Reagan adopted a "top-down" approach whereby a White House budgetary decision would be made first and the agencies would be required to fit within it. The effect of this process was to convert OMB into an agency of policy determination and presidential management. As one expert put it, the Reagan management strategy was "centralization in the service of decentralization."[32] President Reagan brought the director of OMB into the cabinet and centralized the budget process as well as the process of regulatory review, as discussed earlier. Former president Bush went even further than President Reagan in using the White House staff instead of cabinet secretaries in management.

President Clinton engaged in the most systematic and probably the most successful effort to "change the way the government does business," to borrow a phrase he often used to describe the goal of his National Performance Review (NPR). The NPR is one of the more important administrative reforms of the twentieth century. All recent American presidents have decried the size and unmanageability of the federal bureaucracy, but Clinton actually managed to turn proposals for change into real reform. In September 1993, Clinton launched the

---

[31]For the story of Nixon's effort to transform the cabinet as a means of improving the management capacities of the chief executive, see Richard Nathan, *The Plot That Failed: Nixon and the Administrative Presidency* (New York: Wiley, 1975), pp. 68–76. To the secretary of state, there would be added three super secretaries, who were also to be appointed "counsellors to the president" and also to serve in the chair of each of three Domestic Council Committees, enabling them to supervise not only their own department but one or two other departments in their area. The secretary of agriculture would head a group called Natural Resources; the secretary of the then-Department of Health, Education, and Welfare would head a committee supervising other departments in the area of Human Resources, and the secretary of housing and urban development would head other departments in a general area called Community Development. This would have been a much more hierarchical approach to executive management, but it was a perfectly logical effort that failed largely because of the mounting distrust during the Watergate turmoil.

[32]Lester Salamon and Alan Abramson, "Governance: The Politics of Retrenchment," in *The Reagan Record*, ed. John Palmer and Isabel Sawhill (Cambridge, MA: Ballinger, 1984), p. 40.

NPR, based on a set of 384 proposals drafted by a panel headed by Vice President Gore. The goal of the NPR was to "reinvent government"—to make the federal bureaucracy more efficient, accountable, and effective. Its goals included saving more than $100 billion over five years, in large part by cutting the federal workforce by 12 percent, or more than 270,000 jobs, by the end of fiscal year 1999. The NPR focused on cutting red tape, streamlining how the government purchases goods and services, improving the coordination of federal management, and simplifying federal rules. Virtually all observers agreed that the NPR made substantial progress. For instance, the government's Office of Personnel Management abolished the notorious 10,000-page Federal Personnel Manual and Standard Form 171, the government's arduous job application. Another example illustrates the nature of the NPR's work: the Defense Department's method for reimbursing its employees' travel expenses used to take seventeen steps and two months; an employee-designed reform encouraged by the NPR streamlined this to a four-step, computer-based procedure that takes less than fifteen minutes, with anticipated savings of $1 billion over five years.

"Reinventing government" was a great trumpet call summoning the movement for administrative reform. And Gore can be proud of NPR as a legacy. But as respected reform advocate Donald Kettl warns, "Virtually no reform that really matters can be achieved without at least implicit congressional support."[33] For example, in 1994, just as NPR began to pick up support (and while the Democrats still controlled Congress), Congress voted to exempt the Department of Veterans Affairs from the personnel reductions specified by the NPR.

Another fact about administrative reform is that no reform movement will survive a change of president. Thus, although Republicans have an equal or better record than Democrats in the history of administrative form, one of the first things that happened as President Bush took the oath of office was termination of NPR. Vice President Gore's National Partnership for Reinventing Government was officially closed on January 19, 2001. Nine months later, on September 11, Bush faced his own managerial crisis, when the need for coordinating the actions of the United States's many security agencies became apparent. Bush responded with an executive order that created the new cabinet-level Office of Homeland Security. This office has the authority to centralize and coordinate over forty departments and agencies, including the more than $11 billion these departments and agencies spend each year on counterterrorism. Bush also established the Homeland Security Council, which is comprised of the Attorney General; the Secretaries of Defense, Treasury, Transportation, Agriculture, and Health and Human Services; and the directors of the FBI, CIA, and the Federal Emergency Management Agency (FEMA). The Homeland Security Council will advise the president on policy that the Office of Homeland Security will implement.

Institutional Reform

www.wwnorton.com/lowi7/ch7

What are the problems and consequences of reinventing government?

History Principle

Administrative reforms such as NPR tend not to have an effect on a president's chances for re-election.

[33]Quoted in Stephen Bar, "Midterm Exam for 'Reinvention': Study Cites 'Impressive Results' but Calls for Strategy to Win Congressional Support," *Washington Post*, 19 August 1994, p. A25.

The Problem of Management Control by the White House Staff   The cabinet's historic failure to perform as a board of directors, and the inability of any other agency to perform that function, has left a vacuum. OMB has met part of the need, and the management power of the director seems to go up with each president. But the need for executive management control goes far beyond what even the boldest of OMB directors can do. The White House staff has filled the vacuum to a certain extent precisely because in the past thirty years, the "special assistants to the president" have been given relatively specialized jurisdictions over one or more departments or strategic issues. These staffers have additional power and credibility beyond their access to the president because they also have access to confidential information. Since information is the most important bureaucratic resource, White House staff members gain management power by having access to the CIA for international intelligence and the FBI and the Treasury for knowledge about agencies, not only beyond what the agencies report but on matters that are likely to make agency personnel fearful and respectful. The FBI has exclusive knowledge about the personal life of every bureaucrat, since each one has to go through a rigorous FBI security clearance procedure prior to being appointed and promoted.

Responsible bureaucracy, however, is not going to come simply from more presidential power, more administrative staff, and more management control. All this was inadequate to the task of keeping the National Security Staff from seizing the initiative to run its own policies toward Iran and Nicaragua for at least two years (1985–1986) after Congress had restricted activities on Nicaragua and the president had forbidden negotiations with Iran. The Tower Commission, appointed to investigate the Iran-Contra affair, concluded that although there was nothing fundamentally wrong with the institutions involved in foreign policy making—State, Defense, the White House, and their relation to Congress—there had been a "flawed process" and "a failure of responsibility," and a thinness of the president's personal engagement in the issues. The Tower Commission found that "at no time did [President Reagan] insist upon accountability of performance review."[34]

No particular management style is guaranteed to work. Each White House management innovation, from one president to the next, shows only the inadequacy of the approaches of previous presidents. And as the White House and the EOP grow, the management bureaucracy itself becomes a management problem. Something more and different is obviously needed.

Congress and Responsible Bureaucracy

Congress is constitutionally essential to responsible bureaucracy because the key to government responsibility is legislation. When a law is passed and its intent is

---

[34]Quoted in I. M. Destler, "Reagan and the World: An 'Awesome Stubbornness,'" in *The Reagan Legacy—Promise and Performance*, ed. Charles O. Jones (Chatham, NJ: Chatham House, 1988), pp. 244, 257. The source of the quote is *Report of the President's Special Review Board*, 26 February 1987.

clear, then the president knows what to "faithfully execute" and the responsible agency understands what is expected of it. In our modern age, legislatures rarely make laws directly for citizens; most laws are really instructions to bureaucrats and their agencies. But when Congress enacts vague legislation, agencies are thrown back upon their own interpretations. The president and the federal courts step in to tell them what the legislation intended. And so do the intensely interested groups. But when everybody, from president to courts to interest groups, gets involved in the actual interpretation of legislative intent, to whom is the agency responsible? Even when it has the most sincere desire to behave responsibly, how shall this be accomplished?

oversight The effort by Congress, through hearings, investigations and other techniques, to exercise control over the activities of executive agencies.

The answer is *oversight.* The more legislative power Congress has delegated to the executive, the more it has sought to get back into the game through committee and subcommittee oversight of the agencies. The standing committee system in Congress is well-suited for oversight, inasmuch as most of the congressional committees and subcommittees are organized with jurisdictions roughly parallel to one or more executive departments or agencies. Appropriations committees as well as authorization committees have oversight powers—as do their respective subcommittees. In addition to these, there is a committee on government operations both in the House and in the Senate, each with oversight powers not limited by departmental jurisdiction.

The best indication of Congress's oversight efforts is the use of public hearings, before which bureaucrats and other witnesses are summoned to discuss and defend agency budgets and past decisions. The data drawn from systematic studies of congressional committee and subcommittee hearings and meetings show quite dramatically that Congress has tried through oversight to keep pace with the expansion of the executive branch. Between 1950 and 1980, the annual number of committee and subcommittee meetings in the House of Representatives rose steadily from 3,210 to 7,022 and in the Senate from 2,607 to 4,265 (in 1975–1976). Beginning in 1980 in the House and 1978 in the Senate, the number of committee and subcommittee hearings and meetings slowly began to decline, reaching 4,222 in the House and 2,597 in the Senate by the mid-1980s. This pattern of rise and decline in committee and subcommittee oversight activity strongly suggests that congressional vigilance toward the executive branch is responsive to long-term growth in government rather than to yearly activity or to partisan considerations.[35]

Oversight can also be carried out by individual members of Congress. Such inquiries addressed to bureaucrats are considered standard congressional "case

[35]Data from Norman Ornstein et al., *Vital Statistics on Congress, 1987–1988* (Washington, DC: Congressional Quarterly Press, 1987), pp. 161–62. Lawrence Dodd and Richard Schott, counting only hearings and not all meetings, report the same pattern for a shorter period. Between 1950 and 1970, the annual number of public hearings grew from about 300 in the Senate and 350 in the House to 700 in the Senate and 750 in the House. See *Congress and the Administrative State* (New York: Wiley, 1979), p. 169. For a valuable and skeptical assessment of legislative oversight of administrations, see James W. Fesler and Donald F. Kettl, *The Politics of the Administrative Process* (Chatham, NJ: Chatham House, 1991), Chapter 11.

work" and can turn up significant questions of public responsibility even when the motivation is only to meet the demand of an individual constituent. Oversight also takes place very often through communications between congressional staff and agency staff. Congressional staff has been enlarged tremendously since the Legislative Reorganization Act of 1946, and the legislative staff, especially the staff of the committees, is just as professionalized and specialized as the staff of an executive agency. In addition, Congress has created for itself three quite large agencies whose obligations are to engage in constant research on problems taking place in the executive branch: the General Accounting Office, the Congressional Research Service, and the Congressional Budget Office. Each is designed to give Congress information independent of the information it can get through hearings and other communications directly from the executive branch.[36]

Control of the Bureaucracy As a Principal-Agent Problem

Two broad categories of control mechanisms enable a principal to guard against opportunistic or incompetent agent behavior. They may be illustrated by a homeowner (the principal) who seeks out a contractor (the agent) to remodel a kitchen. The first category is employed before-the-fact and depends upon the *reputation* an agent possesses. One guards against selecting an incompetent or corrupt agent by relying on various methods for authenticating the promises made by the agent. These include advice from people you trust (your neighbor who just had his kitchen remodeled); certification by various official boards (association of kitchen contractors); letters of recommendation and other testimonials; credentials (specialized training programs); and interviews. Before-the-fact protection relies upon the assumption that an agent's reputation is a valuable asset which he or she does not want to depreciate.

The second class of control mechanisms operates after the fact. Payment may be made contingent on completion of various tasks by specific dates, so that it may be withheld for nonperformance. Alternatively, financial incentives (for example, bonuses) for early or on-time completion may be part of the arrangement. The agent may be required to post a bond that is forfeited for lack of performance. An inspection process, after the work is completed, may lead to financial penalties, bonuses, or possibly even legal action. Of course, the principal can always seek legal relief for breach of contract, either in the form of an injunction that the agent comply or an order that the agent pay damages.

---

[36]Until 1983, there was still another official tool of legislative oversight, the legislative veto. Each executive agency was obliged to submit to Congress proposed decisions or rules. These were to lie before both houses for thirty to sixty days; then if Congress took no action by one-house or two-house resolution explicitly to veto a proposed measure, it became law. The legislative veto was declared unconstitutional by the Supreme Court in 1983 on the grounds that it violated the separation of powers because the resolutions Congress passed to exercise its veto were not subject to presidential veto, as required by the Constitution. See Immigration and Naturalization Service v. Chadha, 462 U.S. 919 (1983).

How does the principal-agent problem apply to the president's and Congress's control of the bureaucracy?

Suppose the legislation that created the Environmental Protection Agency (EPA) required that new legislation be passed after ten years renewing its existence and mandate. The issue facing the House, the Senate, and the president in their consideration of renewal revolves around how much authority to give this agency and how much money to permit it to spend. The House, quite conservative on environmental issues, prefers limited authority and a limited budget. The Senate wants the agency to have wide-ranging authority, but is prepared to give it only slightly more resources than the House (because of its concern with the budget deficit). The president is happy to split the difference between House and Senate on the matter of authority, but feels beholden to environmental types and thus is prepared to shower the EPA with resources. Bureaucrats in the EPA want more authority than even the Senate is prepared to condone, and more resources than even the president is willing to grant. Eventually relevant majorities in the House and Senate (including the support of relevant committees) and the president agrees on a policy reflecting a compromise among their various points of view.

The bureaucrats are not particularly pleased with this compromise, since it gives them considerably less authority and funding than they had hoped for. If they flout the wishes of their principals and implement a policy exactly to their liking, they risk the unified wrath of the House, Senate, and president. Undoubtedly, the politicians would react with new legislation (and also presumably would find other political appointees and career bureaucrats at the EPA to replace the current bureaucratic leadership). If, however, the EPA implemented some policy located between their own preferences and the preferences of their principals, they might be able to get away with it.

Thus, we have a principal-agent relationship in which a political principal formulates policy and creates an implementation agent to execute its details. The agent, however, has policy preferences of its own and, unless subjected to further controls, inevitably will implement a policy that drifts towards its ideal.

A variety of controls might conceivably restrict this ***bureaucratic drift***. Indeed, legislative scholars often point to congressional hearings in which bureaucrats may be publicly humiliated; annual appropriations decisions which may be used to punish "out-of-control" bureaus; and the use of watchdog agents, like the Government Accounting Office, to monitor and scrutinize the bureau's performance. But these all come after the fact and aren't really credible threats to the agency.

Before-the-fact Controls   The most powerful before-the-fact political weapon is the *appointment process*. The adroit control of the political stance of a given bureau by the president and Congress, through their joint powers of nomination and confirmation (especially if they can arrange for appointees who more nearly share the political consensus on policy) is a self-enforcing mechanism for assuring reliable agent performance.

bureaucratic drift   The oft-observed phenomenon of bureaucratic implementation that produces policy more to the liking of the bureaucracy than originally legislated, but not so much so to trigger a political reaction from elected officials.

 Rationality Principle

Bureaucratic drift occurs because bureaucratic agents have different policy preferences from those of members of Congress or the president.

A second powerful before-the-fact weapon is *procedural controls*. The general rules and regulations that direct the manner in which federal agencies conduct their affairs are contained in the Administrative Procedures Act. This act is almost always the boilerplate that enables legislation creating and renewing every federal agency. It is not uncommon, however, for an agency's procedures to be tailored to suit particular circumstances.

Institution Principle

The appointment process and procedural controls allow the president and Congress some before-the-fact control over bureaucratic agents.

Congressional Oversight: Abdication or Strategic Delegation?   Congress often grants the executive-branch bureaucracies discretion in determining certain features of a policy during the implementation phase. Although the complexities of governing a modern industrialized democracy make the granting of discretion necessary, there are some who argue that Congress not only gives unelected bureaucrats too much discretion but also delegates too much policy-making authority to them. Congress, they say, has transferred so much power that it has created a "runaway bureaucracy" in which unelected officials accountable neither to the electorate nor to Congress make important policy decisions.[37] By enacting vague statutes that give bureaucrats broad discretion, members of Congress have effectively abdicated their constitutionally designated roles and effectively removed themselves from the policy-making process. The ultimate impact of this extreme delegation has left the legislative branch weak and ineffectual and has dire consequences for the health of our democracy.

Others claim that even though Congress may possess the tools to engage in effective oversight, it fails to do so, simply because we do not see Congress actively engaging in much oversight activity.[38] However, Mathew McCubbins and Thomas Schwartz argue that these critics have focused on the wrong type of oversight and have missed a type of oversight that benefits members of Congress in their bids for re-election.[39] McCubbins and Schwartz distinguish between two types of oversight: *police patrol* and *fire alarm*. Under the police patrol variety, Congress systematically initiates investigation into the activity of agencies. Under the fire alarm variety, members of Congress do not initiate investigations but wait for adversely affected citizens or interest groups to bring bureaucratic perversions of legislative intent to the attention of the relevant congressional committee. To make sure that individuals and groups will bring these violations to members' attention, Congress passes laws that help individuals and groups make claims against the bureaucracy, including granting them legal standing before administrative agencies and federal courts.

McCubbins and Schwartz argue that this type of oversight is more efficient than the police patrol variety, given costs and the electoral incentives of members

[37]Lowi, *The End of Liberalism*; Lawrence C. Dodd and Richard L. Schott, *Congress and the Administrative State* (New York: Wiley, 1979).

[38]Morris Ogul, *Congress Oversees the Bureaucracy* (Pittsburgh: University of Pittsburgh Press, 1976); Peter Woll, *American Bureaucracy* (New York: W. W. Norton, 1977).

[39]Mathew D. McCubbins and Thomas Schwartz, "Congressional Oversight Overlooked: Police Patrols versus Fire Alarms," *American Journal of Political Science* 28 (1984), pp. 165–79.

of Congress. Why should members spend their scarce resources (mainly time) to initiate investigations without having any evidence that they will reap electoral rewards? Police patrol oversight can waste taxpayer dollars, too, since many investigations will not turn up any evidence on violations of legislative intent. It is much more cost-effective for members to conserve their resources and then claim credit for fixing the problem (and saving the day) after the fire alarms are pulled. McCubbins and Schwartz argue that given the incentives of elected officials, it makes sense that we would see Congress engaging more in fire alarm oversight than police patrol oversight.

On the other hand, bureaucratic drift might be contained if Congress spent more of its time clarifying its legislative intent and less of its time on oversight activity. If its original intent in the law were clearer, Congress could then afford to defer to presidential management in order to maintain bureaucratic responsibility. Bureaucrats are more responsive to clear legislative guidance than to anything else. But when Congress and the president are at odds (or coalitions within Congress are at odds), bureaucrats have an opportunity to evade responsibility by playing one branch off against the other.

Coalitional Drift As a Collective Action Problem   Politicians not only want the legislative deals they strike to be faithfully implemented, they also want those deals to endure. This is especially problematic in American political life with its shifting alignments and absence of permanent political cleavages. Today's coalition transforms itself overnight. Opponents today are partners tomorrow and vice versa. A victory today, even one implemented in a favorable manner by the bureaucracy, may be undone tomorrow. What is to be done?

To some extent, legislative structure leans against undoing legislation. If such a coalition votes for handsome subsidies to grain farmers, say, it is very hard to reverse this policy without the gatekeeping and agenda-setting resources of members on the House and Senate Agriculture Committees; yet their members undoubtedly participated in the initial deal and are unlikely to turn against it. But even these structural units are unstable, old politicians departing and new ones enlisted.

In short, legislatively formulated and bureaucratically implemented output is subject to ***coalitional drift.***[40] To prevent shifting coalitional patterns among politicians to endanger carefully fashioned policies, one thing the legislature might do is *insulate* the bureaucracy and its implementation activities from legislative interventions. If an enacting coalition makes it difficult for its *own* members to intervene in implementation, then it also makes it difficult for enemies of the policy to disrupt the flow of bureau output. This political insulation can be provided by giving bureaucratic agencies long lives; their political heads long

---

Collective Action Principle

When Congress and the president are at odds (or coalitions within Congress are at odds), bureaucrats have an opportunity to evade responsibility.

coalitional drift

The prospect that enacted policy will change because the composition of the enacting coalition is so temporary and provisional.

Collective Action Principle

Coalitional drift makes the long-term implementation of policy more difficult.

---

[40]This idea, offered as a supplement to the analysis of bureaucratic drift, is found in Murray J. Horn and Kenneth A. Shepsle, "Administrative Process and Organizational Form as Legislative Responses to Agency Costs," *Virginia Law Review* 75 (1989): 499–509. It is further elaborated in Kenneth A. Shepsle, "Bureaucratic Drift, Coalitional Drift, and Time Consistency," *Journal of Law, Economics, and Organization* 8 (1992): 111–18.

terms of office and wide-ranging administrative authority; and other political appointees overlapping terms of office and secure sources of revenue. This insulation comes at a price, however. The civil servants and political appointees of bureaus insulated from political overseers are thereby empowered to pursue independent courses of action. Protection from coalitional drift comes at the price of an increased potential for bureaucratic drift. It is one of the great trade-offs in the field of intergovernmental relations.

Policy Principle

Bureaucratic drift and coalitional drift are contrary tendencies. Fixing them often involves a tradeoff.

DOWNSIZING GOVERNMENT

Some Americans would argue that bureaucracy is always too big and that it always should be reduced. In the 1990s Americans seemed particularly enthusiastic about reducing (or to use the popular contemporary word, "downsizing") the federal bureaucracy.

The only *certain* way to reduce the size of the bureaucracy is to eliminate programs. Variations in the levels of federal personnel and expenditures demonstrate the futility of trying to make permanent cuts in existing agencies. Furthermore, most agencies have a supportive constituency that will fight to reinstate any cuts that are made. Termination is the only way to ensure an agency's reduction, and it is a rare occurrence.

The Republican-led 104th Congress (1995–1996) was committed to the termination of programs. Newt Gingrich, Speaker of the House, took Congress by storm with his promises of a virtual revolution in government. But when the dust had settled at the end of the first session of the first Gingrich-led Congress, no significant progress had been made toward downsizing through termination of agencies and programs.[41] This lack of success is a reflection of Americans' love/hate relationship with the national government. As antagonistic as Americans may be toward bureaucracy in general, they grow attached to the services being rendered and protections being offered by particular bureaucratic agencies; that is, they fiercely defend their favorite agencies while perceiving no inconsistency between that defense and their antagonistic attitude toward the bureaucracy in general. A good case in point is the agonizing problem of closing military bases in the wake of the end of the cold war with the former Soviet Union, when the United States no longer needs so many bases. Since every base is in some congressional member's district, it proved impossible for Congress to decide to close any of them. Consequently, between 1988 and 1990, Congress established a Defense Base Closure and Realignment Commission to decide on base closings, taking the matter out of Congress's hands altogether.[42] And even so, the process has been slow and agonizing.

History Principle

Americans have grown attached to the programs implemented by government agencies and thus are reluctant to cut back on their size and scope.

[41]A thorough review of the first session of the 104th Congress will be found in "Republican's Hopes for 1996 Lie in Unfinished Business," *Congressional Quarterly Weekly Report*, 6 January 1996, pp. 6–18.

[42]Public Law 101-510, Title XXIX, Sections 2,901 and 2,902 of Part A (Defense Base Closure and Realignment Commission).

Elected leaders have come to rely on a more incremental approach to downsizing the bureaucracy. Much has been done by budgetary means, reducing the budgets of all agencies across the board by small percentages, and cutting some less-supported agencies by larger amounts. Yet these changes are still incremental, leaving the existence of agencies unaddressed.

An additional approach has been taken to thwart the highly unpopular regulatory agencies, which are so small (relatively) that cutting their budgets contributes virtually nothing to reducing the deficit. This approach is called *deregulation*, simply defined as a reduction in the number of rules promulgated by regulatory agencies. But deregulation by rule reduction is still incremental and has certainly not satisfied the hunger of the American public in general and Washington representatives in particular for a genuine reduction of bureaucracy.

Privatization, another downsizing option, seems like a synonym for termination, but that is true only at the extreme. Most of what is called "privatization" is not termination at all but the provision of government goods and services by private contractors under direct government supervision. Except for top-secret strategic materials, virtually all of the production of military hardware, from boats to bullets, is done on a privatized basis by private contractors. Billions of dollars of research services are bought under contract by governments; these private contractors are universities as well as ordinary industrial corporations and private "think tanks." *Privatization* simply means that a formerly public activity is picked up under contract by a private company or companies. But such programs are still very much government programs; they are paid for by government and supervised by government. Privatization downsizes the government only in that the workers providing the service are no longer counted as part of the government bureaucracy.

Bureaucracy is here to stay. The administration of a myriad of government functions and responsibilities in a large, complex society will always require "rule by desks and offices" (the literal meaning of "bureaucracy"). No "reinvention" of government, however well conceived or executed, can alter that basic fact. President Clinton's National Performance Review accomplished some impressive things: the national bureaucracy became somewhat smaller. But these efforts are no guarantee that the bureaucracy itself will become more malleable. Congress will not suddenly change its practice of loose and vague legislative draftsmanship. Presidents will not suddenly discover new reserves of power or vision to draw more tightly the reins of responsible management. No deep solution can be found in quick fixes. As with all complex social and political problems, the solution to the problem of bureaucracy in a democracy lies mainly in a sober awareness of the nature of the problem. This awareness enables people to avoid fantasies about the abilities of a democratized presidency—or the potential of a reform effort, or the magical powers of the computer, or the populist rhetoric of a new Congress—to change the nature of governance by bureaucracy.

Rationality Principle	Collective Action Principle	Institution Principle	Policy Principle	History Principle
One view of bureaucratic behavior is that bureaucrats are motivated to maximize their budgets.	Coordination among bureaucrats is necessary to carry out the primary task of bureaucracy—implementation.	Legislative principals establish bureaucratic agents to implement policies.	The policies of clientele agencies promote the interests of their clientele.	Once a government agency is established, it is difficult to abolish.
Bureaucratic drift occurs because bureaucratic agents have different policy preferences from those of members of Congress or the president.	Iron triangles, rectangles, and complexes make clientele agencies the most difficult to change or to coordinate.	Congress also delegates authority to bureaucrats to make law, through the procedures of rulemaking and administrative adjudication.	The military pork barrel is an example of the distributive tendency in Congress.	The size of the federal bureaucracy has kept pace with the growth of the economy and the needs of society.
	When Congress and the president are at odds (or coalitions within Congress are at odds), bureaucrats have an opportunity to evade responsibility.	The appointment process and procedural controls allow the president and Congress some before-the-fact control over bureaucratic agents.	Bureaucratic drift and coalitional drift are contrary tendencies. Fixing them often involves a tradeoff.	Each expansion of the national government is accompanied by a parallel expansion of presidential management authority.
	Coalition drift makes the long-term implementation of policy more difficult.			Administrative reforms such as NPR tend not to have an effect on a president's chances for re-election.
				Americans have grown attached to the programs implemented by government agencies and thus are reluctant to cut back on their size and scope.

SUMMARY

Most American citizens possess less information and more misinformation about bureaucracy than about any other feature of government. We therefore began the chapter with an elementary definition of bureaucracy, identifying its key characteristics and demonstrating the extent to which bureaucracy is not only a phenomenon but an American phenomenon. In the second section of the chapter we showed how all essential government services and controls are carried out by bureaucracies—or to be more objective, administrative agencies. Following a very general description of the different types of bureaucratic agencies in the executive branch we divided up the agencies of the executive branch into four categories according to mission: clientele agencies, agencies for maintaining the Union, regulatory agencies, and redistributive agencies. These illustrate the varieties of administrative experience in American government. Although the bureaucratic phenomenon is universal, not all the bureaucracies are the same in the way they are organized, in the degree of their responsiveness, or in the way they participate in the political process.

Finally, the chapter concluded with a review of all three of the chapters on "representative government" (Chapters 5, 6, and 7) in order to assess how well the two political branches (the legislative and the executive) do the toughest job any government has to do: making the bureaucracy accountable to the people it serves and controls. "Bureaucracy in a Democracy" was the subtitle and theme of the chapter not because we have succeeded in democratizing bureaucracies but because it is the never-ending challenge of politics in a democracy.

FOR FURTHER READING

Arnold, Peri E. *Making the Managerial Presidency: Comprehensive Organization Planning.* Princeton: Princeton University Press, 1986.

Downs, Anthony. *Inside Bureaucracy.* Boston: Little, Brown, 1966.

Fesler, James W., and Donald F. Kettl. *The Politics of the Administrative Process*, 2nd ed. Chatham, NJ: Chatham House, 1996.

Heclo, Hugh. *A Government of Strangers.* Washington, DC: Brookings Institution, 1977.

Skowronek, Stephen. *Building a New American State: The Expansion of National Administrative Capacities, 1877–1920.* New York: Cambridge University Press, 1982.

Wildavsky, Aaron, and Naomi Caiden. *The New Politics of the Budget Process*, 4th ed. New York: Longman, 2001.

Wilson, James Q. *Bureaucracy: What Government Agencies Do and Why They Do It.* New York: Basic Books, 1989.

Wood, Dan B. *Bureaucratic Dynamics: The Role of Bureaucracy in a Democracy.* Boulder, CO: Westview, 1994.

CHAPTER eight

The Federal Courts: Least Dangerous Branch or Imperial Judiciary?

EVENTS	INSTITUTIONAL DEVELOPMENTS
George Washington appoints John Jay chief justice (1789–1795)	Judiciary Act creates federal court system (1789)

1800

John Marshall appointed chief justice (1801)	
	Marbury v. Madison provides for judicial review (1803)
States attempt to tax the Second Bank of the U.S. (1818)	*McCulloch v. Maryland*—Court upholds supremacy clause, broad construction of necessary and proper clause; denies right of states to tax federal agencies (1819)
Andrew Jackson appoints Roger Taney chief justice; Taney Court expands power of states (1835)	*Barron v. Baltimore*—Court rules that only the federal government and not the states are limited by the U.S. Bill of Rights (1833)

1850

Period of westward expansion; continuing conflict and congressional compromises over slavery in the territories (1830s–1850s)	*Dred Scott v. Sanford*—Court rules that federal government cannot exclude slavery from the territories (1857)
Civil War (1861–1865)	*Slaughter-House Cases*—Court limits scope of Fourteenth Amendment to newly freed slaves; states retain right to regulate state businesses (1873)
Reconstruction (1867–1877)	
Self-government restored to former Confederate states (1877)	
"Jim Crow" laws spread throughout Southern states (1890s)	**1890**
	Plessy v. Ferguson—Court upholds doctrine of "separate but equal" (1896)
World War I; wartime pacifist agitation in U.S. (1914–1919)	*Abrams v. U.S.* (1919) and *Gitlow v. N.Y.* (1925) apply First Amendment to states and limit free speech by "clear and present danger" test
Red Scare; postwar anarchist agitation (1919–1920)	
FDR's New Deal (1930s)	**1930**
	Court invalidates many New Deal laws, e.g., *Schechter Poultry Co. v. U.S.* (1935)
Court-packing crisis—proposal to increase the number of Supreme Court justices defeated by Congress (1937)	Court reverses position, upholds most of New Deal, e.g., *NLRB v. Jones & Laughlin Steel* (1937)
U.S. enters World War II (1941–1945)	*Korematsu v. U.S.*—Court approves sending Japanese-Americans to internment camps (1944)

	EVENTS		**INSTITUTIONAL DEVELOPMENTS**

Korean War (1950–1953) — **1950**

Youngstown Sheet & Tube Co. v. Sawyer—
Court rules that president's steel seizure
must be authorized by statute (1952)

Earl Warren appointed chief justice (1953)

Civil rights movement (1950s and 1960s)

Brown v. Board of Education—Court holds
that school segregation is unconstitutional
(1954)

Court begins nationalization of the Bill of
Rights—*Gideon v. Wainwright* (1963);
Escobedo v. Illinois (1964); *Miranda v.
Arizona* (1966), etc.

Flast v. Cohen—Court permits class action
suits (1968)

Warren Burger appointed chief justice
(1969)

Right-to-life movement (1970s–2000) — **1970**

Roe v. Wade—Court strikes down state laws
making abortion illegal (1973)

Affirmative action programs (1970s–2000)

Univ. of Calif. v. Bakke—Court holds that
race may be taken into account but limits
use of quotas (1978)

Court arbitrates conflicts between Congress
and president (1970s and 1980s)

U.S. v. Nixon—Court limits executive
privilege (1974); *Bowsher v. Synar*—Court
invalidates portion of Gramm-Rudman Act
(1986); *Morrison v. Olson*—Court upholds
constitutionality of special prosecutor (1988)

William Rehnquist appointed chief justice
(1986)

Webster v. Reproductive Health Services—
Court nearly overturns *Roe* (1989)

Bush appoints David Souter (1990), Clarence — **1990**
Thomas (1991) to the Supreme Court

Lucas v. South Carolina Coastal Council—
Court supports property owners against
state land seizures (1992)

Clinton appoints Ruth Bader Ginsburg
(1993), Stephen Breyer (1994) to the
Supreme Court

Court limits use of redistricting to help
minorities—*Shaw v. Reno* (1993); *Holder v.
Hall* and *Johnson v. DeGrandy* (1994)

Supreme Court decision effectively gives — **2000**
George W. Bush Florida's 25 disputed
electoral votes, handing him the presidential
victory (2000)

Board of Trustees v. Garrett continues trend
of cases expanding states' immunity from
federal power (2001)

CORE OF THE ANALYSIS

- By engaging in rule interpretation, courts act as political institutions.

- The Supreme Court's power of judicial review makes the Court a lawmaking body.

- The dominant influences shaping Supreme Court decisions are the philosophies, attitudes, and policy preferences of the members of the Court, as well as the influence of other political actors.

- The role and power of the federal courts, particularly the Supreme Court, have been significantly strengthened and expanded in the last fifty years.

Georgew W. Bush won the 2000 national presidential election. The final battle in the race, however, was not decided in the electoral arena and did not involve the participation of ordinary Americans. Instead, the battle was fought in the courts, in the Florida state legislature, and in the executive institutions of the Florida state government, by small groups of attorneys and political activists. During the course of the dispute, some forty lawsuits were filed in the Florida circuit and supreme courts, the U.S. District Court, the U.S. Court of Appeals, and the U.S. Supreme Court.[1] Together, the two campaigns amassed nearly $10 million in legal fees during the month of litigation. In most of the courtroom battles, the Bush campaign prevailed. Despite two setbacks before the all-Democratic Florida supreme court, Bush attorneys won most of the circuit court cases and the ultimate clash before the U.S. Supreme Court in a narrow 5-4 vote.

During the arguments before the Supreme Court, it became clear that the conservative majority seemed determined to prevent a Gore victory. Conservative justices were sharply critical of the arguments presented by Vice President Al Gore's lawyers, while openly sympathetic to the arguments made by Bush's lawyers. Conservative justice Antonin Scalia went so far as to intervene when Bush attorney Theodore Olson responded to a question from Justices Souter and Ginsburg. Scalia evidently sought to ensure that Olson did not concede too much to the Gore argument. "It's part of your submission, I think," Scalia said, "that there is no wrong when a machine does not count those ballots that it's not supposed to count?" Scalia was seeking to remind Olson that when voter error rendered a ballot unreadable by a tabulating machine, it was not appropriate for a court to order them counted by hand. "The voters are instructed to detach the chads entirely," Scalia said, "and if the machine does not count those chads where those instructions are not followed, there isn't any wrong." Olson was happy to accept Scalia's reminder.[2]

Liberal justice John Paul Stevens said the majority opinion smacked of partisan politics. The opinion, he said, "can only lend credence to the most cynical appraisal of the work of judges throughout the land." He concluded, "Although

---

[1] "In the Courts," *San Diego Union-Tribune*, 7 December 2000, p. A14.
[2] Linda Greenhouse, "U.S. Supreme Court Justices Grill Bush, Gore Lawyer in Effort to Close the Book on Presidential Race," *New Orleans Times-Picayune*, 12 December 2000, p. 1.

we may never know with complete certainty the identity of the winner of this year's presidential election, the identity of the loser is perfectly clear. It is the nation's confidence in the judge as an impartial guardian of the rule of law." Justice Stevens's eloquent dissent did not change the outcome. Throughout the nation, Democrats saw the Supreme Court majority's opinion as a blatantly partisan decision. Nevertheless, the contest was over. The next day, Al Gore made a speech conceding the election, and on December 18, 2000, 271 presidential electors—the constitutionally prescribed majority—cast their votes for George W. Bush.

What does the court battle over Florida's twenty-five electoral votes reveal about the power of courts and judges in the American political system? First of all, this battle shows that judges are similar to other politicians in that they have political goals and policy preferences and they act accordingly so that those goals are realized. While thinking of judges as "legislators in robes" is antithetical to the view that judges rule according to a well-thought-out judicial philosophy based on constitutional law, there is evidence that strategic thinking on the part of judges is also a factor in their decision-making process. Second, this battle illustrates the political power that the courts now exercise. Over the past fifty years, the prominence of the courts has been heightened by the sharp increase in the number of major policy issues that have been fought and decided in the judicial realm. But since judges are not elected and accountable to the people, what does this shift in power mean for American democracy?

In this chapter, we will first examine the judicial process, including the types of cases that the federal courts consider

THE CENTRAL QUESTIONS

THE JUDICIAL PROCESS

Within what broad categories of law do cases arise?

THE ORGANIZATION OF THE COURT SYSTEM

How is the U.S. court system structured? What is the importance of the federal court system?

What factors play a role in the appointment of federal judges?

COURTS AS POLITICAL INSTITUTIONS

What general roles do the courts play in the political system? How do these roles help explain judicial behavior?

THE POWER OF JUDICIAL REVIEW

What is the basis for the Supreme Court's power of judicial review?

How does the power of judicial review make the Supreme Court a lawmaking body?

THE SUPREME COURT IN ACTION

How does a case reach the Supreme Court? What shapes the flow of cases through the Supreme Court? Once accepted, how does a case proceed?

JUDICIAL DECISION MAKING

What factors influence the judicial decision-making process of the Supreme Court?

JUDICIAL POWER AND POLITICS

How has the power of the federal courts been limited throughout much of American history?

How have the role and power of the federal courts been transformed over the last fifty years?

How has the increase in the Supreme Court's power changed its role in the political process?

Rationality Principle

Judges have political goals and policy preferences and act to achieve them.

Policy Principle

A number of major policy issues have been fought and decided in the courts.

criminal law The branch of law that deals with disputes or actions involving criminal penalties (as opposed to civil law). It regulates the conduct of individuals, defines crimes, and provides punishment for criminal acts.

plaintiff The individual or organization who brings a complaint in court.

defendant The individual or organization charged with a complaint in court.

and the types of law with which they deal. Second, we will assess the organization and structure of the federal court system as well as how judges are appointed to the courts. Third, we will analyze courts as political institutions and consider their roles in the political system. Fourth, we will consider judicial review and how it makes the Supreme Court a "lawmaking body." Fifth, we will examine the flow of cases through the courts and various influences on the Supreme Court's decisions. Finally, we will analyze the power of the federal courts in the American political process, looking in particular at the growth of judicial power in the United States.

The framers of the American Constitution called the Court the "least dangerous branch" of American government. Today, it is not unusual to hear friends and foes of the Court alike refer to it as the "imperial judiciary."[3] However, we must look in some detail at America's judicial process before we can understand this transformation and its consequences, and answer the question: "Is the Supreme Court the 'least dangerous branch' or an 'imperial judiciary'?"

THE JUDICIAL PROCESS

Originally, a "court" was the place where a sovereign ruled—where the king and his entourage governed. Settling disputes between citizens was part of governing. According to the Bible, King Solomon had to settle the dispute between two women over which of them was the mother of the child both claimed. Judging is the settling of disputes, a function that was slowly separated from the king and the king's court and made into a separate institution of government. Courts have taken over from kings the power to settle controversies by hearing the facts on both sides and deciding which side possesses the greater merit. But since judges are not kings, they must have a basis for their authority. That basis in the United States is the Constitution and the law. Courts decide cases by applying the relevant law or principle to the facts.

Cases and the Law

Court cases in the United States proceed under two broad categories of law: criminal law and civil law. One form of civil law, public law, is so important that we will consider it as a separate category. (See Table 8.1.)

Cases of *criminal law* are those in which the government charges an individual with violating a statute that has been enacted to protect the public health, safety, morals, or welfare. In criminal cases, the government is always the *plaintiff* (the party that brings charges) and alleges that a criminal violation has been committed by a named *defendant.* Most criminal cases arise in state and municipal courts and involve matters ranging from traffic offenses to robbery and murder. However, a large and growing body of federal criminal law deals with

[3]See Richard Neely, *How Courts Govern America* (New Haven: Yale University Press, 1981).

TABLE 8.1

Types of Laws and Disputes

TYPE OF LAW	TYPE OF CASE OR DISPUTE	FORM OF CASE
Criminal law	Cases arising out of actions that violate laws protecting the health, safety, and morals of the community. The government is always the plaintiff.	*U.S. (or state) v. Jones* *Jones v. U.S. (or state)*, if Jones lost and is appealing
Civil law	Law involving disputes between citizens or between government and citizen where no crime is alleged. Two general types are contract and tort. *Contract cases* are disputes that arise over voluntary actions. *Tort cases* are disputes that arise out of obligations inherent in social life. Negligence and slander are examples of torts.	*Smith v. Jones* *New York v. Jones* *U.S. v. Jones* *Jones v. New York*
Public law	All cases where the powers of government or the rights of citizens are involved. The government is the defendant. *Constitutional law* involves judicial review of the basis of a government's action in relation to specific clauses of the Constitution as interpreted in Supreme Court cases. *Administrative law* involves disputes over the statutory authority, jurisdiction, or procedures of administrative agencies.	*Jones v. U.S. (or state)* *In re Jones* *Smith v. Jones*, if a license or statute is at issue in their private dispute

such matters as tax evasion, mail fraud, and the sale of narcotics. Defendants found guilty of criminal violations may be fined or sent to prison.

Cases of *civil law* involve disputes among individuals or between individuals and the government where no criminal violation is charged. Unlike criminal cases, the losers in civil cases cannot be fined or sent to prison, although they may be required to pay monetary damages for their actions. In a civil case, the one who brings a complaint is the plaintiff and the one against whom the complaint is brought is the defendant. The two most common types of civil cases involve contracts and torts. In a typical contract case, an individual or corporation charges

civil law A system of jurisprudence, including private law and governmental actions, to settle disputes that do not involve criminal penalties.

that it has suffered because of another's violation of a specific agreement between the two. For example, the Smith Manufacturing Corporation may charge that Jones Distributors failed to honor an agreement to deliver raw materials at a specified time, causing Smith to lose business. Smith asks the court to order Jones to compensate it for the damage allegedly suffered. In a typical tort case, one individual charges that he or she has been injured by another's negligence or malfeasance. Medical malpractice suits are one example of tort cases.

precedents Prior cases whose principles are used by judges as the bases for their decisions in present cases.

In deciding civil cases, courts apply statutes (laws) and legal ***precedents*** (prior decisions). State and federal statutes often govern the conditions under which contracts are and are not legally binding. Jones Distributors might argue that it was not obliged to fulfill its contract with the Smith Corporation because actions by Smith—the failure to make promised payments—constituted fraud under state law. Attorneys for a physician being sued for malpractice, on the other hand, may search for prior instances in which courts ruled that actions similar to those of their client did not constitute negligence. Such precedents are applied under the doctrine of ***stare decisis,*** a Latin phrase meaning "let the decision stand."

stare decisis Literally "let the decision stand." A previous decision by a court applies as a precedent in similar cases until that decision is overruled.

A case becomes a matter of the third category, ***public law,*** when a plaintiff or defendant in a civil or criminal case seeks to show that their case involves the powers of government or rights of citizens as defined under the Constitution or by statute. One major form of public law is constitutional law, under which a court will examine the government's actions to see if they conform to the Constitution as it has been interpreted by the judiciary. Thus, what began as an ordinary criminal case may enter the realm of public law if a defendant claims that his or her constitutional rights were violated by the police. Another important arena of public law is administrative law, which involves disputes over the jurisdiction, procedures, or authority of administrative agencies. Under this type of law, civil litigation between an individual and the government may become a matter of public law if the individual asserts that the government is violating a statute or abusing its power under the Constitution. For example, land owners have asserted that federal and state restrictions on land use constitute violations of the Fifth Amendment's restrictions on the government's ability to confiscate private property. Recently, the Supreme Court has been very sympathetic to such claims, which effectively transform an ordinary civil dispute into a major issue of public law.

public law Cases in private law, civil law, or criminal law in which one party to the dispute argues that a license is unfair, a law is inequitable or unconstitutional, or an agency has acted unfairly, violated a procedure, or gone beyond its jurisdiction.

Most of the Supreme Court cases we will examine in this chapter involve judgments concerning the constitutional or statutory basis of the actions of government agencies. As we shall see, it is in this arena of public law that Court decisions can have significant consequences for American politics and society.

THE ORGANIZATION OF THE COURT SYSTEM

Types of Courts

In the United States, systems of courts have been established both by the federal government and by the governments of the individual states. Both systems have

FIGURE 8.1

The U.S. Court System

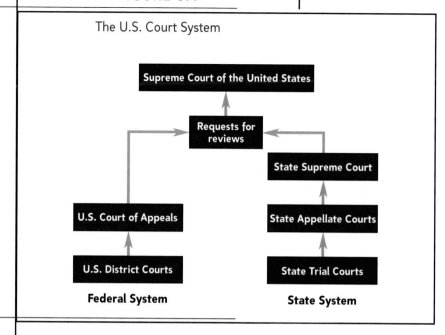

Supreme Court of the United States

Requests for reviews

State Supreme Court

U.S. Court of Appeals

State Appellate Courts

U.S. District Courts

State Trial Courts

Federal System

State System

trial court The first court to hear a criminal or civil case.

appellate court A court that hears the appeals of trial court decisions.

supreme court The highest court in a particular state or in the United States. This court primarily serves an appellate function.

plea bargains Negotiated agreements in criminal cases in which a defendant agrees to plead guilty in return for the state's agreement to reduce the severity of the criminal charge the defendant is facing.

several levels, as shown in Figure 8.1. Nearly 99 percent of all court cases in the United States are heard in state courts. The overwhelming majority of criminal cases, for example, involve violations of state laws prohibiting such actions as murder, robbery, fraud, theft, and assault. If such a case is brought to trial, it will be heard in a state *trial court,* in front of a judge and sometimes a jury, who will determine whether the defendant violated state law. If the defendant is convicted, he or she may appeal the conviction to a higher court, such as a state *appellate court,* and from there to a state's *supreme court.* Similarly, in civil cases, most litigation is brought in the courts established by the state in which the activity in question took place. For example, a patient bringing suit against a physician for malpractice would file the suit in the appropriate court in the state where the alleged malpractice occurred. The judge hearing the case would apply state law and state precedent to the matter at hand. (It should be noted that in both criminal and civil matters, most cases are settled before trial through negotiated agreements between the parties. In criminal cases, these agreements are called *plea bargains.*)

In addition, the U.S. military operates its own court system under the Uniform Code of Military Justice, which governs the behavior of men and women in the armed services. On rare occasions, the government has constituted special military tribunals to hear cases deemed inappropriate for the civil courts. Such tribunals tried Nazi saboteurs apprehended in the United States during World War II. More recently, President Bush ordered the creation of military tribunals to try foreigners suspected of acts of terrorism against the United States.

Federal Jurisdiction

jurisdiction The sphere of a court's power and authority.

Cases are heard in the federal courts if they involve federal laws, treaties with other nations, or the U.S. Constitution; these areas are the official *jurisdiction* of the federal courts. In addition, any case in which the U.S. government is a party is heard in the federal courts. If, for example, an individual is charged with violating a federal criminal statute, such as evading the payment of income taxes, charges would be brought before a federal judge by a federal prosecutor. Civil cases involving the citizens of more than one state and in which more than fifty thousand dollars are at stake may be heard in either the federal or the state courts, usually depending upon the preference of the plaintiff.

due process The right of every citizen against arbitrary action by national or state governments.

Federal courts serve another purpose in addition to trying cases within their jurisdiction: that of hearing appeals from state-level courts. Individuals found guilty of breaking a state criminal law, for example, can appeal their convictions to a federal court by raising a constitutional issue and asking a federal court to determine whether the state's actions were consistent with the requirements of the U.S. Constitution. An appellant might assert, for example, that the state court denied him or her the right to counsel, imposed excessive bail, or otherwise denied the appellant *due process.* Under such circumstances, an appellant can ask the federal court to overturn his or her conviction. Federal courts are not obligated to accept such appeals and will do so only if they feel that the issues raised have considerable merit and if the appellant has exhausted all possible remedies within the state courts. (This procedure is discussed in more detail later in this chapter.) The decisions of state supreme courts may also be appealed to the U.S. Supreme Court if the state court's decision has conflicted with prior U.S. Supreme Court rulings or has raised some important question of federal law. Such appeals are accepted by the U.S. Supreme Court at its discretion.

Of all the cases heard in the United States in 1998, federal district courts (the lowest federal level) received 269,119. Although this number is up substantially from the 87,000 cases heard in 1961, it still constitutes under 1 percent of the judiciary's business. A major reason that the caseload of the federal courts has increased in recent years is that Congress has greatly expanded the number of federal crimes, particularly in the realm of drug possession and sale. Behavior that once was exclusively a state criminal question is now covered by federal law. Recently, Chief Justice Rehnquist criticized Congress for federalizing too many offenses and intruding unnecessarily into areas that should be handled by the states.[4] The federal courts of appeal listened to

[4]Roberto Suro, "Rehnquist: Too Many Offenses are Becoming Federal Crimes," *Washington Post*, 1 January 1999, p. A2.

53,328 cases in 1998, and the U.S. Supreme Court reviewed 4,951 in its 1998–1999 term. Only 90 cases were given full-dress Supreme Court review (the nine justices actually sitting *en banc*—in full court—and hearing the lawyers argue the case).[5]

Although the federal courts hear only a small fraction of all the civil and criminal cases decided each year in the United States, their decisions are extremely important. It is in the federal courts that the Constitution and federal laws that govern all Americans are interpreted and their meaning and significance established. Moreover, it is in the federal courts that the powers and limitations of the increasingly powerful national government are tested. Finally, through their power to review the decisions of the state courts, it is ultimately the federal courts that dominate the American judicial system.

The Lower Federal Courts

Most of the cases of original federal jurisdiction are handled by the federal district courts. The federal district courts are trial courts of general jurisdiction and their cases are, in form, indistinguishable from cases in the state trial courts.

There are eighty-nine district courts in the fifty states, plus one in the District of Columbia and one in Puerto Rico, and three territorial courts. In 1978, Congress increased the number of district judgeships from 400 to 517 in an effort to deal with the greatly increased court workload. District judges are assigned to district courts according to the workload; the busiest of these courts may have as many as twenty-eight judges. Only one judge is assigned to each case, except where statutes provide for three-judge courts to deal with special issues. The routines and procedures of the federal district courts are essentially the same as those of the lower state courts, except that federal procedural requirements tend to be stricter. States, for example, do not have to provide a grand jury, a twelve-member trial jury, or a unanimous jury verdict. Federal courts must provide all these things. In addition to the district courts, cases are handled by several specialized courts including the U.S. Tax Court, the Court of Claims, the Customs Court, and the federal regulatory agencies.

The Appellate Courts

Roughly 10 percent of all lower court and agency cases are accepted for review by the federal appeals courts and by the Supreme Court in its capacity as an appellate court. The country is divided into twelve judicial circuits, each of which has a U.S. Court of Appeals. Every state and the District of

---

[5]U.S. Bureau of the Census, *Statistical Abstract of the United States, 2000* (Washington, DC: Government Printing Office, 2000).

Columbia is assigned to the circuit in the continental United States that is closest to it.

Except for cases selected for review by the Supreme Court, decisions made by the appeals courts are final. Because of this finality, certain safeguards have been built into the system. The most important is the provision of more than one judge for every appeals case. Each court of appeals has from three to fifteen permanent judgeships, depending on the workload of the circuit. Although normally three judges hear appealed cases, in some instances a larger number of judges sit together *en banc.*

Another safeguard is provided by the assignment of a Supreme Court justice as the circuit justice for each of the twelve circuits. Since the creation of the appeals court in 1891, the circuit justice's primary duty has been to review appeals arising in the circuit in order to expedite Supreme Court action. The most frequent and best-known action of circuit justices is that of reviewing requests for stays of execution when the full Court is unable to do so—mainly during the summer, when the Court is in recess.

The Supreme Court

chief justice
Justice on the Supreme Court who presides over the Court's public sessions.

The Supreme Court is America's highest court. Article III of the Constitution vests "the judicial Power of the United States" in the Supreme Court, and this court is supreme in fact as well as form. The Supreme Court is made up of a chief justice and eight associate justices. The ***chief justice*** presides over the Court's public sessions and conferences. In the Court's actual deliberations and decisions, however, the chief justice has no more authority than his or her colleagues. Each justice casts one vote. To some extent, the influence of the chief justice is a function of his or her own leadership ability. Some chief justices, such as the late Earl Warren, have been able to lead the court in a new direction. In other instances, a forceful associate justice, such as the late Felix Frankfurter, is the dominant figure on the Court.

The Constitution does not specify the number of justices that should sit on the Supreme Court; Congress has the authority to change the Court's size. In the early nineteenth century, there were six Supreme Court justices; later there were seven. Congress set the number of justices at nine in 1869, and the Court has remained that size ever since. In 1937, President Franklin D. Roosevelt, infuriated by several Supreme Court decisions that struck down New Deal programs, asked Congress to enlarge the court so that he could add a few sympathetic justices to the bench. Although Congress balked at Roosevelt's "court packing" plan, the Court gave in to FDR's pressure and began to take a more favorable view of his policy initiatives. The president, in turn, dropped his efforts to enlarge the Court. The Court's surrender to FDR came to be known as "the switch in time that saved nine."

JUDGES

How Judges Are Appointed

Federal judges are appointed by the president and are generally selected from among the more prominent or politically active members of the legal profession. Many federal judges previously served as state court judges or state or local prosecutors. In an informal nominating process, candidates for vacancies on the U.S. District Court are generally suggested to the president by a senator from the president's own party who represents the state in which the vacancy has occurred. Senators often see such a nomination as a way to reward important allies and contributors in their states. If the state has no senator from the president's party, the governor or members of the state's House delegation may make suggestions. In general, presidents endeavor to appoint judges who possess legal experience and good character and whose partisan and ideological views are similar to the president's own. During the presidencies of Ronald Reagan and George H. W. Bush, most federal judicial appointees were conservative Republicans. Bush established an advisory committee to screen judicial nominees in order to make certain that their legal and political philosophies were sufficiently conservative. Bill Clinton's appointees to the federal bench, on the other hand, tended to be liberal Democrats. Clinton also made a major effort to appoint women and African Americans to the federal courts. Nearly half of his nominees were drawn from these groups.

Once the president has formally nominated an individual, the nominee must be considered by the Senate Judiciary Committee and confirmed by a majority vote in the full Senate. Before the president makes a formal nomination, however, the senators from the candidate's own state must indicate that they support the nominee. This is an informal but seldom violated practice called *senatorial courtesy*. Because the Senate will rarely approve a nominee opposed by a senator from his or her own state, the president will usually not bother to present such a nomination to the Senate. Through this arrangement, senators are able to exercise veto power over appointments to the federal bench in their own states. In recent years, the Senate Judiciary Committee has also sought to signal the president when it has had qualms about a judicial nomination. After the Republicans won control of the Senate in 1994, for example, Judiciary Committee chair Orrin Hatch of Utah let President Clinton know that he considered two of Clinton's nominees to be too liberal. The president withdrew the nominations.

Federal appeals court nominations follow much the same pattern. Since appeals court judges preside over jurisdictions that include several states, however, senators do not have as strong a role in proposing potential candidates. Instead, potential appeals court candidates are generally suggested to the president by the Justice Department or by important members of the administration. The senators from the nominee's own state are still consulted before the president will formally act.

Collective Action Principle
Appointments to the federal bench involve informal bargaining (senatorial courtesy) as well as formal bargaining (Senate confirmation).

senatorial courtesy The practice whereby the president, before nominating a person formally for a federal judgeship, checks on whether senator's from the candidate's state support the nomination.

If political factors play an important role in the selection of district and appellate court judges, they are decisive when it comes to Supreme Court appointments. Because the high court has so much influence over American law and politics, virtually all presidents have made an effort to select justices who share their own political philosophies. Presidents Ronald Reagan and George H. W. Bush, for example, appointed five justices whom they believed to have conservative perspectives: Justices Sandra Day O'Connor, Antonin Scalia, Anthony Kennedy, David Souter, and Clarence Thomas. Reagan also elevated William Rehnquist to the position of chief justice. Reagan and Bush sought appointees who believed in reducing government intervention in the economy and who supported the moral positions taken by the Republican Party in recent years, particularly opposition to abortion. However, not all the Reagan and Bush appointees have fulfilled their sponsors' expectations. Bush appointee David Souter, for example, has been attacked by conservatives as a turncoat for his decisions on school prayer and abortion rights. Nevertheless, through their appointments, Reagan and Bush were able to create a far more conservative Supreme Court. For his part, President Bill Clinton endeavored to appoint liberal justices. Clinton named Ruth Bader Ginsburg and Stephen Breyer to the Court, hoping to counteract the influence of the Reagan and Bush appointees. President George W. Bush hopes to appoint conservatives to the Court but must take into account the views of the Democratic-controlled Senate. (Table 8.2 shows information about the current Supreme Court justices.)

In recent years, Supreme Court nominations have come to involve intense partisan struggle. Typically, after the president has named a nominee, interest groups opposed to the nomination have mobilized opposition in the media, the public, and the Senate. When former president Bush proposed conservative judge Clarence Thomas for the Court, for example, liberal groups launched a campaign to discredit Thomas. After extensive research into his background, opponents of the nomination were able to produce evidence suggesting that Thomas had sexually harassed a former subordinate, Anita Hill. Thomas denied the charge. After contentious Senate Judiciary Committee hearings, highlighted by testimony from both Thomas and Hill, Thomas narrowly won confirmation.

Likewise, conservative interest groups carefully scrutinized Bill Clinton's liberal nominees, hoping to find information about them that would sabotage their appointments. During his two opportunities to name Supreme Court justices, Clinton was compelled to drop several potential appointees because of information unearthed by political opponents.

These struggles over judicial appointments indicate the growing intensity of partisan struggle in the United States today. They also indicate how much importance competing political forces attach to Supreme Court appointments. Because these contending forces see the outcome as critical, they are willing to engage in a fierce struggle when Supreme Court appointments are at stake.

The matter of judicial appointments became an important issue in the 2000 election. Democrats charged that, if he was elected, George W. Bush would appoint conservative judges who might, among other things, reverse the *Roe v.*

TABLE 8.2

Supreme Court Justices, 2001 (In Order of Seniority)				
NAME	**YEAR OF BIRTH**	**PRIOR EXPERIENCE**	**APPOINTED BY**	**YEAR OF APPOINTMENT**
William H. Rehnquist* *Chief Justice*	1924	Assistant attorney general	Nixon	1972
John Paul Stevens	1920	Federal judge	Ford	1975
Sandra Day O'Connor	1930	State judge	Reagan	1981
Antonin Scalia	1936	Law professor, federal judge	Reagan	1986
Anthony Kennedy	1936	Federal judge	Reagan	1988
David Souter	1939	Federal judge	Bush	1990
Clarence Thomas	1948	Federal judge	Bush	1991
Ruth Bader Ginsburg	1933	Federal judge	Clinton	1993
Stephen Breyer	1938	Federal judge	Clinton	1994

*Appointed chief justice by Reagan in 1986.

Wade decision and curb abortion rights. Bush would say only that he would seek judges who would uphold the Constitution without reading their own political biases into the document.

From the liberal perspective, the danger of a conservative judiciary was underlined by the Supreme Court's decision in the Florida election case, *Bush v. Gore.* The Court's conservative bloc, in recent years, has argued that the states deserve considerable deference from the federal courts. In this instance, however, the Supreme Court overturned a decision of the Florida supreme court regarding Florida election law. The Court ruled that its Florida counterpart had ignored the U.S. Constitution's equal protection doctrine when it mandated recounts in some, but not all, Florida counties. Defenders of the decision argued that it was doctrinally sound and that it averted the chaos that might have ensued if a recount gave Gore the victory and the Florida legislature carried out its threat to appoint Bush electors. Two competing slates of electors might then have sought congressional certification. Critics of the decision, however, asserted that the Court was merely searching for a rubric under which it could ensure

Bush's victory. As a result of the Florida contest, there can be little doubt that the next Supreme Court vacancy will generate sharp fighting in Washington.

COURTS AS POLITICAL INSTITUTIONS

Judges are central players in important political institutions and this makes them politicians. In order to understand what animates judicial behavior, we thus need to place the judge or justice in context by briefly considering the role of the courts in the political system more generally. In doing so we emphasize the role of courts as *dispute resolvers*, as *coordinators*, and as *interpreters of rules*.

Dispute Resolution

So much of the productive activity that occurs within families, among friends and associates, even between absolute strangers takes place because the participants do not have to devote substantial resources to protecting themselves and their property or monitoring compliance with agreements.[6] For any potential violation of person or property, or defection from an agreement, all parties know in advance that an aggrieved party may take an alleged violator to court. The court, in turn, serves as a venue in which the facts of a case are established, punishment is meted out to violators, and compensation awarded to victims. The court, therefore, is an institution that engages in fact-finding and judgment.

In disputes between private parties, the court serves principally to determine whether claims of violation can be substantiated. An employee, for example, may sue her employer for allegedly violating the terms of a privately negotiated employment contract. Or a consumer may sue a producer for violating the terms of a product warranty. Or a tenant may sue a landlord for violating provisions of a lease. In all of these cases, some issue between private parties is in dispute. The court system provides the service of dispute resolution.

The examples in the preceding paragraph involve civil law. An entirely separate category of dispute, one in which the courts also have a role to play, involves criminal law. In these cases "the public" is a party to the dispute because the alleged violation concerns not (only) something involving private parties, but (also) a public law. This brings the public agencies of justice into play as parties to a dispute. When an individual embezzles funds from his partner, he not only violates a privately negotiated agreement between them (namely, a promise of honest dealings), he also violates a public law prohibiting embezzlement gener-

---

[6]Naturally, some resources are devoted to protection and monitoring. However, if extraordinary resources had to be devoted, then their rising cost would cause the frequency of the productive activities alluded to in the text to decline, according to elementary economic theory. Indeed, since the costs of negotiating, monitoring, and enforcing agreements (what political economists call *transaction costs*) can be very high, they are a serious impediment to social interaction and productive activities of all sorts. Economizing on them—by providing the services of courts and judges, for example—is one of the great contributions of the modern state to social welfare.

ally. A court proceeding, in this case, determines not only whether a violation of a private arrangement has occurred but also whether the alleged perpetrator is innocent or guilty of violating a public law.

In all of these instances, the judge is responsible for managing the fact-finding and judgment phases of dispute resolution (sometimes in collaboration with a jury). Thus, a large part of the daily life of a judge involves making an independent, experienced assessment of the facts, determining whether the dispute involves a violation of a private agreement or a public law (or both), and finally rendering a judgment—a determination of which party (if either) is liable, and what compensation is in order (to the private party victimized and, if judged a criminal activity, to the larger public). Judging is a sophisticated blend of reading a mystery novel, solving a crossword puzzle, and providing wise counsel.

Coordination

Dispute resolution occurs after the fact—that is, after a dispute has already occurred. In a manner of speaking, it represents a failure of the legal system, since one function of law and its judicial institutions is to discourage such disputes in the first place. We may also think of courts and judges as before-the-fact *coordination mechanisms* inasmuch as the anticipation of what happens once their services are called upon allows private parties to form rational expectations and thereby coordinate their actions in advance of possible disputes. A prospective embezzler, estimating the odds of getting caught, prosecuted, and subsequently punished, may think twice about cheating his partner. Surely, *some* prospective embezzlers are deterred from their crimes by these prospects. Conversely, the legal system can work as an incentive: two acquaintances, for example, may confidently entertain the possibility of going into business together, knowing that the sword of justice hangs over their collaboration.

Collective Action Principle
The legal system coordinates private behavior by providing incentives and disincentives for specific actions.

In this sense, the court system is as important for what it doesn't do as for what it does. The system of courts and law coordinates private behavior by providing incentives and disincentives for specific actions. To the extent that these work, there are fewer disputes to resolve and thus less after-the-fact dispute resolution for courts and judges to engage in. What makes the incentives and disincentives work is their power (are the rewards and penalties big or small?), their clarity, and the consistency with which judges administer them. Clear incentives, consistently employed, provide powerful motivations for private parties to resolve disputes ahead of time. This sort of advanced coordination, encouraged by a properly functioning legal system, economizes on the transaction costs that would diminish the frequency of, and otherwise discourage, socially desirable activity.

Rule Interpretation

Dispute resolution and coordination affect private behavior and the daily lives of ordinary citizens tremendously. Judges, however, are not entirely free agents (despite the fact that some of them are tyrants in their courtrooms). In matching the facts of a specific case to judicial principles and statutory guidelines, judges must engage in *interpretive* activity. They must determine what particular statutes or judicial principles mean, which of them fit the facts of a particular case, and then, having determined all this, they must ascertain the disposition of the case at hand. Does the statute of 1927 regulating the electronic transmission of radio waves apply to television, cellular phones, ship-to-shore radios, fax machines, and E-mail? Does the law governing the transportation of dangerous substances, passed in 1937, apply to nuclear fuels, infected animals, and artificially created biological hazards? Often, the enacting legislative body has not been crystal clear about the scope of the legislation it passes. Indeed, a legislature acting in 1927 or 1937 could not have anticipated technological developments to come. Nevertheless, cases such as these come up on a regular basis, and judges must make judgment calls, so to speak, on highly complex issues.

Interpreting the rules is probably the single most important activity in which higher courts engage. This is because the court system is *hierarchical* in the sense that judgments by higher courts constrain the discretion of judges in lower courts. If the Supreme Court rules that nuclear fuels are covered by the 1937 law on transporting dangerous substances, then lower courts must render subsequent judgments in a manner consistent with this ruling. The judge in a civil or criminal trial concerning the shipment of nuclear isotopes from a laboratory to a commercial user, for example, must make sure his or her ruling complies with the legal interpretations passed down by the higher courts. Also, because of the federal principle by which the American polity is organized, federal law and interpretations thereof often trump state and local laws.

As we shall see in the following section, courts and judges engage not only in *statutory interpretation* but in *constitutional interpretation* as well. Here they interpret the provisions of the U.S. Constitution, determining their scope and content. In determining, for example, whether the act of Congress regulating the transportation of dangerous substances from one state to another is constitutional, the justices of the Supreme Court might appeal to the commerce clause of the Constitution (allowing the federal government to regulate interstate commerce) to justify the constitutionality of that act. On the other hand, a Supreme Court majority might also rule that a shipment of spent fuel rods from a nuclear reactor in Kansas City to a nuclear waste facility outside of St. Louis is *not* covered by this law since the shipment took place entirely within the boundaries of a single state and thus did not constitute interstate commerce.

In short, judges and justices are continually engaged in elaborating, embellishing, even rewriting the rules by which private and public life are organized. In these interpretive acts they are conscious of the fact that their rulings will affect not only the participants in a specific case before them, but also will carry interpretive weight in all similar cases that percolate down to the lower courts. Thus, statutory and constitutional interpretations have authority over subsequent deliberations (and, in turn, are themselves influenced by earlier interpretations according to *stare decisis*).

However, judicial interpretation—elaboration, embellishment, and "redrafting"—of statutes is naturally subject to review. Statutory interpretation, even if it is conducted by the highest court in the land, is exposed to legislative review. If Congress is unhappy with a specific statutory interpretation—for example, suppose the current Congress does not like the idea of federal regulation of E-mail that a federal court claimed to be permissible under the 1927 act on electronic transmission—then it may amend the legislation so as explicitly to reverse the court ruling. Of course, if the court makes a *constitutional* ruling, Congress cannot then abrogate that ruling through new legislation. But Congress can commence the process of constitutional amendment, thereby effectively reversing constitutional interpretations with which it disagrees.

THE POWER OF JUDICIAL REVIEW

Courts have the power of ***judicial review***—the authority and the obligation to review any lower court decision where a substantial issue of public law is involved. The disputes can be over the constitutionality of federal or state laws, over the propriety or constitutionality of the court procedures followed, or over whether public officers are exceeding their authority. The Supreme Court's power of judicial review has come to mean review not only of lower court decisions but also of state legislation and acts of Congress. For this reason, if for no other, the Supreme Court is more than a judicial agency—it is also a major lawmaking body.

judicial review
Power of the courts to declare actions of the legislative and executive branches invalid or unconstitutional. The Supreme Court asserted this power in *Marbury v. Madison*.

The Supreme Court's power of judicial review over lower court decisions has never been at issue. Nor has there been any serious quibble over the power of the federal courts to review administrative agencies in order to determine whether their actions and decisions are within the powers delegated to them by Congress. There has, however, been a great deal of controversy occasioned by the Supreme Court's efforts to review acts of Congress and the decisions of state courts and legislatures.

Judicial Review of Acts of Congress

Since the Constitution does not give the Supreme Court the power of judicial review of congressional enactments, the Court's exercise of it is something of a usurpation. Various proposals were debated at the Constitutional Convention. Among them was the proposal to create a council composed of the president and the judiciary that would share the veto power over legislation. Another proposal would have routed all legislation through the Court as well as through the president; a veto by either one would have required an overruling by a two-thirds vote of the House and Senate. Each proposal was rejected by the delegates, and no further effort was made to give the Supreme Court review power over the other branches.

BOX 8.1

Marbury v. Madison

The 1803 Supreme Court decision handed down in *Marbury v. Madison* established the power of the Court to review acts of Congress. The case arose over a suit filed by William Marbury and seven other people against Secretary of State James Madison to require him to approve their appointments as justices of the peace. These had been last-minute ("midnight judges") appointments of outgoing President John Adams. Chief Justice John Marshall held that although Marbury and the others were entitled to their appointments, the Supreme Court had no power to order Madison to deliver them, because the relevant section of the first Judiciary Act of 1789 was unconstitutional—giving the Courts powers not intended by Article III of the Constitution.

Marshall reasoned that constitutions are framed to serve as the "fundamental and paramount law of the nation." Thus, he argued, with respect to the legislative action of Congress, the Constitution is a "superior . . . law, unchangeable by ordinary means." He concluded that an act of Congress that contradicts the Constitution must be judged void.

As to the question of whether the Court was empowered to rule on the constitutionality of legislative action, Marshall responded emphatically that it is "the province and duty of the judicial department to say what the law is." Since the Constitution is the supreme law of the land, he reasoned, it is clearly within the realm of the Court's responsibility to rule on the constitutionality of legislative acts and treaties. This principle has held sway ever since.

SOURCES: Gerald Gunther, *Constitutional Law* (Mineola, NY: Fountain Press, 1980), pp. 9–11; and Marbury v. Madison, 1 Cr. 137 (1803).

History Principle

Since *Marbury v. Madison* (1803), the power of judicial review has not been in question.

This does not prove that the framers of the Constitution opposed judicial review, but it does indicate that "if they intended to provide for it in the Constitution, they did so in a most obscure fashion."[7] Disputes over the intentions of the framers were settled in 1803 in the case of *Marbury v. Madison.*[8] Although Congress and the president have often been at odds with the Court, its legal power to review acts of Congress has not been seriously questioned since 1803 (see Box 8.1). One reason is that judicial power has been accepted as natural, if not intended. Another reason is that the Supreme Court has rarely reviewed the constitutionality of the acts of Congress, especially in the past fifty

[7]C. Herman Pritchett, *The American Constitution* (New York: McGraw-Hill, 1959), p. 138.
[8]Marbury v. Madison, 1 Cr. 137 (1803).

years. When such acts do come up for review, the Court makes a self-conscious effort to give them an interpretation that will make them constitutional.

Judicial Review of State Actions

The power of the Supreme Court to review state legislation or other state action and to determine its constitutionality is neither granted by the Constitution nor inherent in the federal system. But the logic of the **supremacy clause** of Article VI of the Constitution, which declares it and laws made under its authority to be the supreme law of the land, is very strong. Furthermore, in the Judiciary Act of 1789, Congress conferred on the Supreme Court the power to reverse state constitutions and laws whenever they are clearly in conflict with the U.S. Constitution, federal laws, or treaties.[9] This power gives the Supreme Court jurisdiction over all of the millions of cases handled by American courts each year.

The supremacy clause of the Constitution not only established the federal Constitution, statutes, and treaties as the "supreme Law of the Land," but also provided that "the Judges in every State shall be bound thereby, any Thing in the Constitution or Laws of any State to the Contrary notwithstanding." Under this authority, the Supreme Court has frequently overturned state constitutional provisions or statutes and state court decisions it deems to contravene rights or privileges guaranteed under the federal Constitution or federal statutes.

The civil rights area abounds with examples of state laws that were overturned because the statutes violated guarantees of due process and equal protection contained in the Fourteenth Amendment to the Constitution. For example, in the 1954 case of *Brown v. Board of Education*, the Court overturned statutes from Kansas, South Carolina, Virginia, and Delaware that either required or permitted segregated public schools, on the basis that such statutes denied black school children equal protection of the law. In 1967, in *Loving v. Virginia*, the Court invalidated a Virginia statute prohibiting interracial marriages.[10]

State statutes in other subject matter areas are equally subject to challenge. In *Griswold v. Connecticut*, the Court invalidated a Connecticut statute prohibiting the general distribution of contraceptives to married couples on the basis that the statute violated the couples' rights to marital privacy.[11] In *Brandenburg v. Ohio*, the Court overturned an Ohio statute forbidding any person from urging criminal acts as a means of inducing political reform or from joining any association that advocated such activities on the grounds that the statute punished "mere advocacy" and therefore violated the free speech provisions of the Constitution.[12]

supremacy clause
Article VI of the Constitution, which states that all laws passed by the national government and all treaties are the supreme laws of the land and superior to all laws adopted by any state or any subdivision.

[9]This review power was affirmed by the Supreme Court in Martin v. Hunter's Lessee, 1 Wheaton 304 (1816).

[10]Brown v. Board of Education, 347 U.S. 483 (1954); Loving v. Virginia, 388 U.S. 1 (1967).

[11]Griswold v. Connecticut, 381 U.S. 479 (1965).

[12]Brandenburg v. Ohio, 395 U.S. 444 (1969).

Judicial Review and Lawmaking

Policy Principle

By interpreting existing statutes, as well as the Constitution, judges make law.

When courts of original jurisdiction apply existing statutes or past cases directly to citizens, the effect is the same as legislation. Lawyers study judicial decisions in order to discover underlying principles, and they advise their clients accordingly. Often the process is nothing more than reasoning by analogy; the facts in a particular case are so close to those in one or more previous cases that the same decision should be handed down. Such judge-made law is called common law.

The appellate courts are in another realm. Their rulings can be considered laws, but they are laws governing the behavior only of the judiciary. They influence citizens' conduct only because, in the words of Justice Oliver Wendell Holmes, who served on the Supreme Court from 1900–1932, lawyers make "prophecies of what the courts will do in fact."[13]

Institution Principle

Because the court system is hierarchical, decisions by higher courts constrain the discretion of judges in lower courts.

The written opinion of an appellate court is about halfway between common law and statutory law. It is judge-made and draws heavily on the precedents of previous cases. But it tries to articulate the rule of law controlling the case in question and future cases like it. In this respect, it is like a statute. But it differs from a statute in that a statute addresses itself to the future conduct of citizens, whereas a written opinion addresses itself mainly to the willingness or ability of courts in the future to take cases and render favorable opinions. Decisions by appellate courts affect citizens by giving them a cause of action or by taking it away from them. That is, they open or close access to the courts.

A specific case may help clarify the distinction. Before the Second World War, one of the most insidious forms of racial discrimination was the "restrictive covenant," a clause in a contract whereby the purchasers of a house agreed that if they later decided to sell it, they would sell only to a Caucasian. When a test case finally reached the Supreme Court in 1948, the Court ruled unanimously that citizens had a right to discriminate with restrictive covenants in their sales contracts but that the courts could not enforce these contracts. Its argument was that enforcement would constitute violation of the Fourteenth Amendment provision that no state shall "deny to any person within its jurisdiction equal protection under the law."[14] The Court was thereby predicting what it would and would not do in future cases of this sort. Most states have now forbidden homeowners to place such covenants in sales contracts.

Gideon v. Wainwright extends the point. When the Supreme Court ordered a new trial for Gideon because he had been denied the right to legal counsel, it said to all trial judges and prosecutors that henceforth they would be wasting their time if they cut corners in trials of indigent defendants.[15] It also invited thousands of prisoners to appeal their convictions.

Many areas of civil law have been constructed in the same way—by judicial messages to other judges, some of which are codified eventually into legislative

[13]Oliver Wendell Holmes, Jr., "The Path of the Law," *Harvard Law Review* 10 (1897), p. 457.
[14]Shelley v. Kraemer, 334 U.S. 1 (1948).
[15]Gideon v. Wainwright, 372 U.S. 335 (1963).

enactments. An example of great concern to employees and employers is that of liability for injuries sustained at work. Courts have sided with employees so often that it has become virtually useless for employers to fight injury cases. It has become "the law" that employers are liable for such injuries, without regard to negligence. But the law in this instance is simply a series of messages to lawyers that they should advise their corporate clients not to appeal injury decisions.

The appellate courts cannot decide what behavior will henceforth be a crime. They cannot directly prevent the police from forcing confessions or intimidating witnesses. In other words, they cannot directly change the behavior of citizens or eliminate abuses of power. What they can do, however, is make it easier for mistreated persons to gain redress.

In redressing wrongs, the appellate courts—and even the Supreme Court itself—often call for a radical change in legal principle. Changes in race relations, for example, would probably have taken a great deal longer if the Supreme Court had not rendered the 1954 *Brown* decision that redefined the rights of African Americans.

Similarly, the Supreme Court interpreted the separation of church and state doctrine so as to alter significantly the practice of religion in public institutions. For example, in a 1962 case, *Engel v. Vitale*, the Court declared that a once widely observed ritual—the recitation of a prayer by students in a public school—was unconstitutional under the establishment clause of the First Amendment. Almost all the dramatic changes in the treatment of criminals and of persons accused of crimes have been made by the appellate courts, especially the Supreme Court. The Supreme Court brought about a veritable revolution in the criminal process with three cases over less than five years: *Gideon v. Wainwright*, in 1963, was discussed on the previous page. *Escobedo v. Illinois*, in 1964, gave suspects the right to remain silent and the right to have counsel present during questioning. But the decision left confusions that allowed differing decisions to be made by lower courts. In *Miranda v. Arizona*, in 1966, the Supreme Court cleared up these confusions by setting forth what is known as the *Miranda rule:* arrested people have the right to remain silent, the right to be informed that anything they say can be held against them, and the right to counsel before and during police interrogation.[16]

One of the most significant changes brought about by the Supreme Court was the revolution in legislative representation unleashed by the 1962 case of *Baker v. Carr.*[17] In this landmark case, the Supreme Court held that it could no longer avoid reviewing complaints about the apportionment of seats in state legislatures. Following that decision, the federal courts went on to force reapportionment of all state, county, and local legislatures in the country.

Many experts on court history and constitutional law criticize the federal appellate courts for being too willing to introduce radical change, even when these

Miranda rule
Principles developed by the Supreme Court in the 1966 case of *Miranda v. Arizona* requiring that persons under arrest be informed of their legal rights, including their right to counsel, prior to police interrogation.

[16]Engel v. Vitale, 370 U.S. 421 (1962); Gideon v. Wainwright, 372 U.S. 335 (1963); Escobedo v. Illinois, 378 U.S. 478 (1964); and Miranda v. Arizona, 384 U.S. 436 (1966).
[17]Baker v. Carr, 369 U.S. 186 (1962).

experts agree with the general direction of the changes. Often they are troubled by the courts' (especially the Supreme Court's) willingness to jump into such cases prematurely—before the constitutional issues are fully clarified by many related cases through decisions by district and appeals courts in various parts of the country.[18] But from the perspective of the appellate judiciary, and especially the Supreme Court, the situation is probably one of choosing between the lesser of two evils: They must take the cases as they come and then weigh the risks of opening new options against the risks of embracing the status quo.

THE SUPREME COURT IN ACTION

How Cases Reach the Supreme Court

Given the millions of disputes that arise every year, the job of the Supreme Court would be impossible if it were not able to control the flow of cases and its own caseload. Its original jurisdiction is only a minor problem. The original jurisdiction includes (1) cases between the United States and one of the fifty states, (2) cases between two or more states, (3) cases involving foreign ambassadors or other ministers, and (4) cases brought by one state against citizens of another state or against a foreign country. The most important of these cases are disputes between states over land, water, or old debts. Generally, the Supreme Court deals with these cases by appointing a "special master," usually a retired judge, to actually hear the case and present a report. The Supreme Court then allows the states involved in the dispute to present arguments for or against the master's opinion.[19]

 Institution Principle

The courts have developed specific rules of access that govern which cases within their jurisdiction they will hear.

Rules of Access   Over the years, the courts have developed specific rules that govern which cases within their jurisdiction they will and will not hear. In order to have access to the courts, cases must meet certain criteria. These rules of access can be broken down into three major categories: case or controversy, standing, and mootness.

Article III of the Constitution and Supreme Court decisions define judicial power as extending only to "cases and controversies." This means that the case before a court must be an actual controversy, not a hypothetical one, with two truly adversarial parties. The courts have interpreted this language to mean that they do not have the power to render advisory opinions to legislatures or agencies about the constitutionality of proposed laws or regulations. Furthermore, even after a law is enacted, the courts will generally refuse to consider its constitutionality until it is actually applied.

---

[18]See Philip Kurland, *Politics, the Constitution and the Warren Court* (Chicago: University of Chicago Press, 1970).

[19]Walter F. Murphy, "The Supreme Court of the United States," in *Encyclopedia of the American Judicial System*, ed. Robert J. Janosik (New York: Scribner's, 1987).

Parties to a case must also have **standing**, that is, they must show that they have a substantial stake in the outcome of the case. The traditional requirement for standing has been to show injury to oneself; that injury can be personal, economic, or even aesthetic, for example. In order for a group or class of people to have standing (as in class action suits), each member must show specific injury. This means that a general interest in the environment, for instance, does not provide a group with sufficient basis for standing.

The Supreme Court also uses a third criterion in determining whether it will hear a case: that of **mootness.** In theory, this requirement disqualifies cases that are brought too late—after the relevant facts have changed or the problem has been resolved by other means. The criterion of mootness, however, is subject to the discretion of the courts, which have begun to relax the rules of mootness, particularly in cases where a situation that has been resolved is likely to come up again. In the abortion case *Roe v. Wade*, for example, the Supreme Court rejected the lower court's argument that because the pregnancy had already come to term, the case was moot. The Court agreed to hear the case because no pregnancy was likely to outlast the lengthy appeals process.

Putting aside the formal criteria, the Supreme Court is most likely to accept cases that involve conflicting decisions by the federal circuit courts, cases that present important questions of civil rights or civil liberties, and cases in which the federal government is the appellant.[20] Ultimately, however, the question of which cases to accept can come down to the preferences and priorities of the justices. If a group of justices believes that the Court should intervene in a particular area of policy or politics, they are likely to look for a case or cases that will serve as vehicles for judicial intervention. For many years, for example, the Court was not interested in considering challenges to affirmative action or other programs designed to provide particular benefits to minorities. In recent years, however, several of the Court's more conservative justices have been eager to push back the limits of affirmative action and racial preference, and have therefore accepted a number of cases that would allow them to do so. In 1995, the Court's decisions in *Adarand Constructors v. Pena*, *Missouri v. Jenkins*, and *Miller v. Johnson* placed new restrictions on federal affirmative action programs, school desegregation efforts, and attempts to increase minority representation in Congress through the creation of "minority districts" (see Chapter 10).[21] Similarly, because some justices have felt that the Court had gone too far in the past in restricting public support for religious ideas, the Court accepted the case of *Rosenberger v. University of Virginia*. This case was brought by a Christian student group against the University of Virginia, which had refused to provide student activities fund support for the group's magazine, *Wide Awake*. Other student publications received subsidies from the activities fund, but university

standing The right of an individual or organization to initiate a court case.

mootness A criterion used by courts to screen cases that no longer require resolution.

 Rationality Principle
The Supreme Court accepts cases based on the preferences and priorities of the justices.

[20]Gregory A. Caldeira and John R. Wright, "Organized Interests and Agenda Setting in the U.S. Supreme Court," *American Political Science Review* 82 (1988), pp. 1109–27.
[21]Adarand Constructors v. Pena, 115 S.Ct. 2038 (1995); Missouri v. Jenkins, 115 S.Ct. 2573 (1995); Miller v. Johnson, 115 S.Ct. 2475 (1995).

writ of *certiorari*
A decision concurred in by at least four of the nine Supreme Court justices to review a decision of a lower court; from the Latin "to make more certain."

writ of *habeas corpus* A court order demanding that an individual in custody be brought into court and shown the cause for detention. *Habeas corpus* is guaranteed by the Constitution and can be suspended only in cases of rebellion or invasion.

Collective Action Principle
Four of the nine Supreme Court justices need to agree to review a case.

policy prohibited grants to religious groups. Lower courts supported the university, finding that support for the magazine would violate the Constitution's prohibition against government support for religion. The Supreme Court, however, ruled in favor of the students' assertion that the university's policies amounted to support for some ideas but not others. The Court said this violated the students' First Amendment right of freedom of expression.[22]

Writs   Decisions handed down by lower courts can reach the Supreme Court in one of two ways: through a ***writ of certiorari***, or, in the case of convicted state prisoners, through a ***writ of habeas corpus***. A writ is a court document conveying an order of some sort. In recent years, an effort has been made to give the Court more discretion regarding the cases it chooses to hear. Before 1988, the Supreme Court was obligated to review cases on what was called a writ of appeal. This has since been eliminated, and the Court now has virtually complete discretion over what cases it will hear (see Process Box 8.1).

Most cases reach the Supreme Court through the writ of *certiorari*, which is granted whenever four of the nine justices agree to review a case. The Supreme Court was once so inundated with appeals that in 1925 Congress enacted laws giving it some control over its case load with the power to issue writs of *certiorari*. Rule 10 of the Supreme Court's own rules of procedure defines *certiorari* as "not a matter of right, but of sound judicial discretion . . . granted only where there are special and important reasons therefor." The reasons provided for in Rule 10 are

1. Where a state has made a decision that conflicts with previous Supreme Court decisions;
2. Where a state court has come up with an entirely new federal question;
3. Where one court of appeals has rendered a decision in conflict with another;
4. Where there are other inconsistent rulings between two or more courts or states; and
5. Where a single court of appeals has sanctioned too great a departure by a lower court from normal judicial proceedings (a reason rarely given).

The writ of *habeas corpus* is a fundamental safeguard of individual rights. Its historical purpose is to enable an accused person to challenge arbitrary detention and to force an open trial before a judge. But in 1867, Congress's distrust of Southern courts led it to confer on federal courts the authority to issue writs of *habeas corpus* to prisoners already tried or being tried in state courts of proper jurisdiction, where the constitutional rights of the prisoner were possibly being violated. This writ gives state prisoners a second channel toward Supreme Court review in case their direct appeal from the highest state court fails. The writ of *habeas corpus* is discretionary; that is, the Court can decide which cases to review.

[22]Rosenberger v. University of Virginia, 115 S.Ct. 2510 (1995).

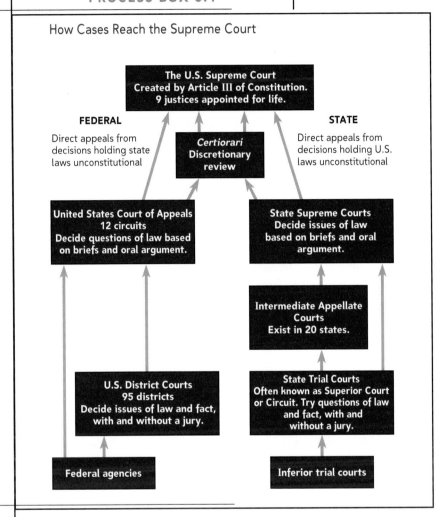

How Cases Reach the Supreme Court

The U.S. Supreme Court
Created by Article III of Constitution.
9 justices appointed for life.

FEDERAL

Direct appeals from decisions holding state laws unconstitutional

Certiorari
Discretionary review

STATE

Direct appeals from decisions holding U.S. laws unconstitutional

United States Court of Appeals
12 circuits
Decide questions of law based on briefs and oral argument.

State Supreme Courts
Decide issues of law based on briefs and oral argument.

Intermediate Appellate Courts
Exist in 20 states.

U.S. District Courts
95 districts
Decide issues of law and fact, with and without a jury.

State Trial Courts
Often known as Superior Court or Circuit. Try questions of law and fact, with and without a jury.

Federal agencies

Inferior trial courts

Controlling the Flow of Cases

In addition to the judges themselves, three other agencies or groups play an important role in shaping the flow of cases through the federal courts: the solicitor general, the Federal Bureau of Investigation and other federal agencies, and federal law clerks.

The Solicitor General If any single person has greater influence than the individual justices over the work of the Supreme Court, it is the solicitor general of the United States. The solicitor general is third in status in the Justice Department (below the attorney general and the deputy attorney general) but is the top government lawyer in virtually all cases before the appellate courts where the government is a party. Although others can regulate the flow of cases, the solicitor general has the greatest control, with no review of his or her actions by any higher authority in the executive branch. More than half the Supreme Court's total workload consists of cases under the direct charge of the solicitor general.

The solicitor general exercises especially strong influence by screening cases long before they approach the Supreme Court; indeed, the justices rely on the solicitor general to "screen out undeserving litigation and furnish them with an agenda to government cases that deserve serious consideration."[23] Typically, more requests for appeals are rejected than are accepted by the solicitor general. Agency heads may lobby the president or otherwise try to circumvent the solicitor general, and a few of the independent agencies have a statutory right to make direct appeals, but these are almost inevitably doomed to ***per curiam*** rejection—rejection through a brief, unsigned opinion by the whole Court—if the solicitor general refuses to participate.

The solicitor general can enter a case even when the federal government is not a direct litigant by writing an ***amicus curiae*** ("friend of the court") brief. A "friend of the court" is not a direct party to a case but has a vital interest in its outcome. Thus, when the government has such an interest, the solicitor general can file as *amicus curiae*, or the Court can invite such a brief because it wants an opinion in writing. The solicitor general also has the power to invite others to enter cases as *amici curiae*.

In addition to exercising substantial control over the flow of cases, the solicitor general can shape the arguments used before the Court. Indeed, the Court tends to give special attention to the way the solicitor general characterizes the issues. The solicitor general is the person appearing most frequently before the Court and, theoretically at least, the most disinterested. The credibility of the solicitor general is not hurt when several times each year he or she comes to the Court to withdraw a case with the admission that the government has made an error.

The FBI and Other Federal Agencies Another important influence on the flow of cases through the appellate judiciary comes from the Federal Bureau of Investigation (FBI), one of the bureaus of the Department of Justice. Its work provides data for numerous government cases against businesses, individual citizens, and state and local government officials. Its data are the most vital source of material for cases in the areas of national security and organized crime.

per curiam
Decision by an appellate court, without a written opinion, that refuses to review the decision of a lower court; amounts to a reaffirmation of the lower court's opinion.

amicus curiae
"Friend of the court"; individuals or groups who are not parties to a lawsuit but who seek to assist the court in reaching a decision by presenting additional briefs.

[23]Robert Scigliano, *The Supreme Court and the Presidency* (New York: Free Press, 1971), p. 162. For an interesting critique of the solicitor general's role during the Reagan administration, see Lincoln Caplan, "Annals of the Law," *The New Yorker*, 17 August 1987, pp. 30–62.

The FBI also has the important function of linking the Justice Department very closely to cases being brought by state and local government officials. Since the FBI has a long history of cooperation with state and local police forces, the solicitor general often joins (as *amicus curiae*) appeals involving state criminal cases.

In recent years, other federal agencies have expanded their own law enforcement activities. The Treasury Department is responsible for the Bureau of Alcohol, Tobacco, and Firearms as well as the Secret Service. The Immigration and Naturalization Service employs thousands of Border Patrol agents. All told, more than 41,000 criminal investigators now work for thirty-two federal agencies.[24] All these agencies now join the FBI in providing material for federal cases.

Law Clerks   Every federal judge employs law clerks to research legal issues and assist with the preparation of opinions. Each Supreme Court justice is assigned four clerks. The clerks are almost always honors graduates of the nation's most prestigious law schools. A clerkship with a Supreme Court justice is a great honor and generally indicates that the fortunate individual is likely to reach the very top of the legal profession. One of the most important roles performed by the clerks is to screen the thousands of petitions for writs of *certiorari* that come before the Court.[25] It is also likely that some justices rely heavily upon their clerks for advice in writing opinions and in deciding whether an individual case ought to be heard by the Court. It is often rumored that certain opinions were actually written by a clerk rather than a justice.[26] Although such rumors are difficult to substantiate, it is clear that at the end of long judicial careers, justices such as William O. Douglas and Thurgood Marshall had become so infirm that they were compelled to rely on the judgments of their law clerks.

The Case Pattern

The Supreme Court has discretion over which case will be reviewed. The solicitor general can influence the Court's choice by giving advice and by encouraging particular cases and discouraging or suppressing others. But, neither the court nor the solicitor general can suppress altogether the kinds of cases that individuals bring to court. Each new technology, such as computers and communications satellites, produces new disputes and the need for new principles of law. Newly awakened interest groups, such as the black community after World War II or the women's and the environmental movements in the 1970s, produce new legislation, new disputes, and new cases. Lawyers are professionally obligated to

---

[24]Jim McGee, "At the Justice Department, Big Government Keeps Getting Bigger," *Washington Post*, 5 April 1996, p. A17.

[25]H. W. Perry, Jr., *Deciding to Decide: Agenda Setting in the United States Supreme Court* (Cambridge, MA: Harvard University Press, 1991).

[26]Edward P. Lazarus, *Closed Chambers* (New York: Times Books, 1998).

appeal their clients' cases to the highest possible court if an issue of law or constitutionality is involved.

The litigation that breaks out with virtually every social change produces a pattern of cases that eventually is recognized by the state and federal appellate courts. Appellate judges may at first resist trying such cases by ordering them remanded (returned) to their court of original jurisdiction for further trial. They may reject some appeals without giving any reason at all (*certiorari* denied *per curiam*). But eventually, one or more of the cases from the pattern may be reviewed and may indeed make new law.

Although some patterns of cases emerge spontaneously as new problems produce new litigation, many interest groups try to set a pattern as a strategy for expediting their cases through the appeals process. Lawyers representing these groups have to choose the proper client and the proper case, so that the issues in question are most dramatically and appropriately portrayed. They also have to pick the right district or jurisdiction in which to bring the case. Sometimes they even have to wait for an appropriate political climate.

Rationality Principle

Groups will often file more than one suit in the hope that this will increase their chances of being heard in Court.

Group litigants have to plan carefully when to use and when to avoid publicity. They must also attempt to develop a proper record at the trial court level, one that includes some constitutional arguments and even, when possible, errors on the part of the trial court. One of the most effective litigation strategies used in getting cases accepted for review by the appellate courts is bringing the same type of suit in more than one circuit, in the hope that inconsistent treatment by two different courts will improve the chance of a Supreme Court review.

As we shall see more fully in Chapter 12, Congress will sometimes provide interest groups with legislation designed to facilitate their use of litigation. One important recent example is the 1990 Americans with Disabilities Act (ADA), enacted after intense lobbying by public interest and advocacy groups which, in conjunction with the 1991 Civil Rights Act, opened the way for disabled individuals to make extremely effective use of the courts to press their interests. As the sponsors of ADA had hoped, over time the courts have expanded the rights of the disabled as well as the definition of disability. In 1998, for example, the Supreme Court ruled that individuals with HIV were covered by the act.[27]

Analyzing American Politics

www.wwnorton.com/ lowi7/ch8

Analyze the impact of *amicus curiae* briefs on the Supreme Court.

The two most notable users of the pattern-of-cases strategy in recent years have been the National Association for the Advancement of Colored People (NAACP) and the American Civil Liberties Union (ACLU). For many years, the NAACP (and its Defense Fund organization—now a separate group) has worked through local chapters and with many individuals to encourage litigation on issues of racial discrimination and segregation. Sometimes it distributes petitions to be signed by parents and filed with local school boards and courts, deliberately sowing the seeds of future litigation. The NAACP and the ACLU often encourage private parties to bring suit and then join the suit as *amici curiae*.

One illustration of an interest group employing a carefully crafted litigation strategy to pursue its goals through the judiciary was the Texas-based effort to

[27]Bragdon v. Abbott, 118 S.Ct. 2186 (1998).

establish a right to free public school education for children of illegal aliens. The issue arose in 1977 when the Texas state legislature, responding to a sudden wave of fear about illegal immigration from Mexico, enacted a law permitting school districts to charge undocumented children a hefty tuition for the privilege of attending public school. A public interest law organization, the Mexican-American Legal Defense Fund, prepared to challenge the law in court after determining that public opposition precluded any chance of persuading the legislature to change its own law.

Part of the defense fund's litigation strategy was to bring a lawsuit in the northern section of Texas, far from the Mexican border, where illegal immigration would be at a minimum. Thus, in Tyler, Texas, where the complaint was initially filed, the trial court found only sixty undocumented alien students in a school district composed of 16,000. This strategy effectively contradicted the state's argument that the Texas law was necessary to reduce the burdens on educational resources created by masses of incoming aliens. Another useful litigation tactic was to select plaintiffs who, although illegal aliens, were nevertheless clearly planning to remain in Texas even without free public education for their children. Thus, all of the plaintiffs came from families that had already lived in Tyler for several years and included at least one child who was an American citizen by virtue of birth in the United States. By emphasizing the stability of such families, the defense fund argued convincingly that the Texas law would not motivate families to return to the poverty in Mexico from which they had fled, but would more likely result in the creation of a subclass of illiterate people who would add to the state's unemployment and crime rates. Five years after the lawsuit on behalf of the Tyler children began, the U.S. Supreme Court, in the case of *Plyler v. Doe*, held that the Texas law was unconstitutional under the equal protection clause of the Fourteenth Amendment.[28]

Thus, regardless of the wishes of the Justice Department or the Supreme Court, many pathbreaking cases are eventually granted *certiorari*, because continued refusal to review one or more of them would amount to a rule of law just as much as if the courts had handed down a written opinion. In this sense, the flow of cases, especially the pattern of significant cases, influences the behavior of the appellate judiciary.

The Supreme Court's Procedures

The Preparation The Supreme Court's decision to accept a case is the beginning of what can be a lengthy and complex process (see Figure 8.2). First, the attorneys on both sides must prepare *briefs*—written documents that may be several hundred pages long in which the attorneys explain why the Court should rule in favor of their client. Briefs are filled with referrals to precedents specifically chosen to show that other courts have frequently ruled in the same way that the Supreme Court is being asked to rule. The attorneys for both sides muster the most compelling precedents they can in support of their arguments.

briefs Written documents in which attorneys explain, with citations of case precedents, why the Court should rule in favor of their client.

[28]Plyler v. Doe, 457 U.S. 202 (1982).

FIGURE 8.2

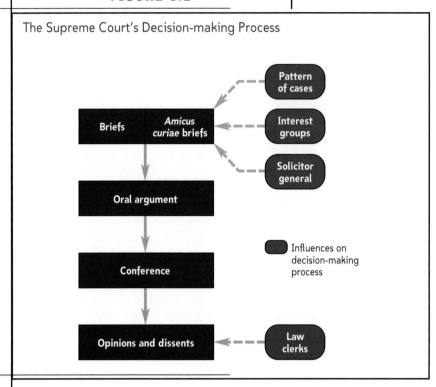

The Supreme Court's Decision-making Process

Pattern of cases

Briefs | *Amicus curiae* briefs

Interest groups

Solicitor general

Oral argument

Conference

Opinions and dissents

Law clerks

Influences on decision-making process

 Institution Principle

The Supreme Court's procedures allow for various individuals and groups to influence the decision-making process.

oral argument
Stage in Supreme Court proceedings in which attorneys for both sides appear before the Court to present their positions and answer questions posed by the justices.

As the attorneys prepare their briefs, they often ask sympathetic interest groups for their help. Groups are asked to file *amicus curiae* briefs that support the claims of one or the other litigant. In a case involving separation of church and state, for example, liberal groups such as the ACLU and Citizens for the American Way are likely to be asked to file *amicus* briefs in support of strict separation, whereas conservative religious groups are likely to file *amicus* briefs advocating increased public support for religious ideas. Often, dozens of briefs will be filed on each side of a major case. *Amicus* filings are one of the primary methods used by interest groups to lobby the Court. By filing these briefs, groups indicate to the Court where their group stands and signal to the justices that they believe the case to be an important one.

Oral Argument   The next stage of a case is ***oral argument,*** in which attorneys for both sides appear before the Court to present their positions and answer the justices' questions. Each attorney has only a half hour to present his or her case, and this time includes interruptions for questions. Certain members of the Court, such as Justice Antonin Scalia, are known to interrupt attorneys dozens of times. Others, such as Justice Clarence Thomas, seldom ask questions. For an attorney, the opportunity to argue a case before the Supreme Court is a singular honor and a mark of professional distinction. It can also be a harrowing experience, as justices interrupt a carefully prepared presentation. Nevertheless, oral argument can be very important to the outcome of a case. It allows justices to better understand the heart of the case and to raise questions that might not have been addressed in the opposing side's briefs. It is not uncommon for justices to go beyond the strictly legal issues and ask opposing counsel to discuss the implications of the case for the Court and the nation at large.

The Conference   Following oral argument, the Court discusses the case in its Wednesday or Friday conference. The chief justice presides over the conference and speaks first; the other justices follow in order of seniority. The Court's conference is secret, and no outsiders are permitted to attend. The justices discuss the case and eventually reach a decision on the basis of a majority vote. If the Court is divided, a number of votes may be taken before a final decision is reached. As the case is discussed, justices may try to influence or change one another's opinions. At times, this may result in compromise decisions. On the current Court, for example, several justices, including Rehnquist, Scalia, and Thomas, are known to favor overturning the 1973 *Roe v. Wade* decision that prohibited the states from outlawing abortions. Other justices, including Souter, Breyer, and Ginsburg, are known to oppose such a course of action. This division has resulted in several compromise decisions, in which the Court has allowed some state restriction of abortion but has not permitted states to outlaw abortion altogether.

Opinion Writing   After a decision has been reached, one of the members of the majority is assigned to write the *opinion.* This assignment is made by the chief justice, or by the most senior justice in the majority if the chief justice is on the losing side. The assignment of the opinion can make a significant difference to the interpretation of a decision. Every opinion of the Supreme Court sets a major precedent for future cases throughout the judicial system. Lawyers and judges in the lower courts will examine the opinion carefully to ascertain the Supreme Court's meaning. Differences in wording and emphasis can have important implications for future litigation. Once the majority opinion is drafted, it is circulated to the other justices. Some members of the majority may decide that they cannot accept all the language of the opinion and therefore write "concurring" opinions that support the decision but offer a somewhat different rationale or emphasis. In assigning an opinion, serious thought must be given to the impression the case will make on lawyers and on the public, as well as to the probability that one justice's opinion will be more widely accepted than another's.

One of the more dramatic instances of this tactical consideration occurred in 1944, when Chief Justice Harlan F. Stone chose Justice Felix Frankfurter to

opinion The written explanation of the Supreme Court's decision in a particular case.

write the opinion in the "white primary" case *Smith v. Allwright*. The chief justice believed that this sensitive case, which overturned the Southern practice of prohibiting black participation in nominating primaries, required the efforts of the most brilliant and scholarly jurist on the Court. But the day after Stone made the assignment, Justice Robert H. Jackson wrote a letter to Stone urging a change of assignment. In his letter, Jackson argued that Frankfurter, a foreign-born Jew from New England, would not win the South with his opinion, regardless of its brilliance. Stone accepted the advice and substituted Justice Stanley Reed, an American-born Protestant from Kentucky and a southern Democrat in good standing.[29]

dissenting opinion Decision written by a justice with the minority opinion in a particular case, in which the justice fully explains the reasoning behind his or her opinion.

Dissent   Justices who disagree with the majority decision of the Court may choose to publicize the character of their disagreement in the form of a ***dissenting opinion***. Dissents can be used to express irritation with an outcome or to signal to defeated political forces in the nation that their position is supported by at least some members of the Court. Ironically, the most dependable way an individual justice can exercise a direct and clear influence on the Court is to write a dissent. Because there is no need to please a majority, dissenting opinions can be more eloquent and less guarded than majority opinions. Some of the greatest writing in the history of the Court is found in the dissents of Oliver Wendell Holmes, Louis D. Brandeis, and William O. Douglas, the last of whom wrote thirty-five dissents in the Court's 1952–1953 term alone. Although there is no great dissenter in the current Court, Justice John Paul Stevens stands out with sixteen dissents in the 1996–1997 term and thirteen in the 1998–1999 term; the next highest numbers of dissents written during those terms were nine and eight, respectively.

Dissent plays a special role in the work and impact of the Court because it amounts to an appeal to lawyers all over the country to keep bringing cases of the sort at issue. Therefore, an effective dissent influences the flow of cases through the Court as well as the arguments that will be used by lawyers in later cases. Even more important, dissent emphasizes the fact that, although the Court speaks with a single opinion, it is the opinion only of the majority.

JUDICIAL DECISION MAKING

The judiciary is conservative in its procedures, but its impact on society can be radical. That impact depends on a variety of influences, two of which stand out above the rest. The first influence is the individual members of the Supreme Court, their attitudes and goals, and their relationships with each other. The second is the other branches of government, particularly Congress.

[29]*Smith v. Allwright*, 321 U.S. 649 (1944).

The Supreme Court Justices

The Supreme Court explains its decisions in terms of law and precedent. But although law and precedent do have an effect on the Court's deliberations and eventual decisions, it is the Supreme Court that decides what laws actually mean and what importance precedents will actually have. Throughout its history, the Court has shaped and reshaped the law. If any individual judges in the country influence the federal judiciary, they are the Supreme Court justices.

From the 1950s to the 1980s, the Supreme Court took an activist role in such areas as civil rights, civil liberties, abortion, voting rights, and police procedures. For example, the Supreme Court was more responsible than any other governmental institution for breaking down America's system of racial segregation. The Supreme Court virtually prohibited states from interfering with the right of a woman to seek an abortion and sharply curtailed state restrictions on voting rights. And it was the Supreme Court that placed restrictions on the behavior of local police and prosecutors in criminal cases.

But since the early 1980s, resignations, deaths, and new judicial appointments have led to many shifts in the mix of philosophies and ideologies represented on the Court. In a series of decisions between 1989 and 2001, however, the conservative justices appointed by Reagan and Bush were able to swing the Court to a more conservative position on civil rights, affirmative action, abortion rights, property rights, criminal procedure, voting rights, desegregation, and the power of the national government.

Although they are not the only relevant factor, shifts in judicial philosophy are the prime explanation for these Court tendencies. These shifts, in turn, result from changes in the Court's composition as justices retire and are replaced by new justices who tend to share the philosophical outlook and policy goals of the president who appointed them.

Activism and Restraint   One element of judicial philosophy is the issue of activism versus restraint. Over the years, some justices have believed that courts should interpret the Constitution according to the stated intentions of its framers and defer to the views of Congress when interpreting federal statutes. The late justice Felix Frankfurter, for example, advocated judicial deference to legislative bodies and avoidance of the "political thicket," in which the Court would entangle itself by deciding questions that were essentially political rather than legal in character. Advocates of *judicial restraint* are sometimes called "strict constructionists," because they look strictly to the words of the Constitution in interpreting its meaning.

The alternative to restraint is *judicial activism.* Activist judges such as the former chief justice Earl Warren and two of the leading members of his Court, Justices Hugo Black and William O. Douglas, believed that the Court should go beyond the words of the Constitution or a statute to consider the broader societal implications of its decisions. Activist judges sometimes strike out in new

judicial restraint
Judicial philosophy whose adherents refuse to go beyond the set text of the Constitution in interpreting its meaning.

judicial activism
Judicial philosophy that posits that the Court should see beyond the text of the Constitution or a statute in order to consider broader societal implications for decisions.

directions, promulgating new interpretations or inventing new legal and constitutional concepts when they believe these to be socially desirable. For example, Justice Harry Blackmun's decision in *Roe v. Wade* was based on a constitutional right to privacy that is not found in the words of the Constitution. Blackmun and the other members of the majority in the *Roe* case argued that the right to privacy was implied by other constitutional provisions. In this instance of judicial activism, the Court knew the result it wanted to achieve and was not afraid to make the law conform to the desired outcome.

Political Ideology   The second component of judicial philosophy is political ideology. The liberal or conservative attitudes of justices play an important role in their decisions.[30] Indeed, the philosophy of activism versus restraint is, to a large extent, a smokescreen for political ideology. For the most part, liberal judges have been activists, willing to use the law to achieve social and political change, whereas conservatives have been associated with judicial restraint. Interestingly, however, in recent years some conservative justices who have long called for restraint have actually become activists in seeking to undo some of the work of liberal jurists over the past three decades.

The importance of ideology was very clear during the Court's 2000–2001 term. In important decisions, the Court's most conservative justices—Scalia, Thomas, and Rehnquist, usually joined by Kennedy—generally voted as a bloc.[31] Indeed, Scalia and Thomas voted together in 99 percent of all cases. At the same time, the Court's most liberal justices—Breyer, Ginsburg, Souter, and Stevens—also generally formed a bloc with Ginsburg and Breyer and Ginsburg and Souter voting together 94 percent of the time.[32] Justice O'Connor, a moderate conservative, was the swing vote in many important cases. This ideological division led to a number of important 5-4 decisions. As we saw, in the main Florida election law case, *Bush v. Gore*, Justice O'Connor joined with the conservative bloc to give Bush a 5-4 victory.[33] On the other hand, in an important voting rights case, *Easley v. Cromwell*, Justice O'Connor joined with the four liberals to uphold the creation of a so-called majority–minority congressional district in South Carolina against charges of racial gerrymandering. More than 33 percent of all the cases heard by the court in its 2000–2001 term were decided 5 to 4.

In our discussion of congressional politics in Chapter 5, we described legislators as *policy oriented*. In conceiving of judges as legislators in robes, we are effectively claiming that judges, like other politicians, have policy preferences they seek to implement. For example, in recent years, Justice O'Connor has written a

[30]C. Herman Pritchett, *The Roosevelt Court* (New York: Macmillan, 1948); Jeffrey A. Segal and Harold J. Spaeth, *The Supreme Court and the Attitudinal Model* (New York: Cambridge University Press, 1993).

[31]Linda Greenhouse, "In Year of Florida Vote, Supreme Court Also Did Much Other Work," *New York Times*, 2 July 2001, p. A12.

[32]Charles E. Lane, "Laying Down the Law," *Washington Post*, 1 July 2001, p. A6.

[33]*Bush v. Gore*, 531 U.S. 98, 121 S.Ct. 525 (2000).

number of decisions that have furthered her goal that Congress return authority back to the states. The most recent of these decisions is the 2001 case of *Board of Trustees v. Garrett*, where the Court held that state employees could not sue the states for alleged violations of the Americans with Disabilities Act.[34]

Other Institutions of Government

Congress   At both the national and state level in the United States, courts and judges are "players" in the policy game because of the separation of powers. Essentially, this means that the legislative branch formulates policy (defined constitutionally and institutionally by a legislative process); that the executive branch implements policy (according to well-defined administrative procedures, and subject to initial approval by the president or the legislative override of his veto); and that the courts, when asked, rule on the faithfulness of the legislated and executed policy either to the substance of the statute or to the Constitution itself. The courts, that is, may strike down an administrative action either because it exceeds the authority granted in the relevant statute (statutory rationale) or because the statute itself exceeds the authority granted the legislature by the Constitution (constitutional rationale).

If the court declares the administrative agent's act as outside the permissible bounds prescribed by the legislation, we suppose the court's majority opinion can declare whatever policy it wishes. If the legislature is unhappy with this judicial action, then it may either recraft the legislation (if the rationale for striking it down were statutory) or initiate a constitutional amendment that would enable the stricken-down policy to pass constitutional muster (if the rationale for originally striking it down were constitutional).

Collective Action Principle
In reaching their decisions, Supreme Court judges must anticipate Congress's response.

In reaching their decisions, Supreme Court justices must anticipate Congress's response. As a result, judges will not always vote according to their true preferences, because doing so may provoke Congress to enact legislation that moves the policy further away from what the judges prefer. By voting for a lesser preference, the justices can get something they prefer to the status quo without provoking congressional action to overturn their decision. The most famous example of this phenomenon is the "switch in time that saved nine," when several justices voted in favor of New Deal legislation the constitutionality of which they doubted in order to diminish congressional support for President Roosevelt's plan to "pack" the Court by increasing the number of justices.

The President   The president's most direct influence on the Court is the power to nominate justices. Presidents typically nominate judges who they believe are close to their policy preferences and close enough to the preferences of a majority of senators, who must confirm the nomination.

Yet the efforts by presidents to reshape the federal judiciary are not always successful. Often in American history, judges have surprised and disappointed the

---

[34]*Board of Trustees of the University of Alabama v. Garrett*, 531 U.S. 356 (2001).

FIGURE 8.3

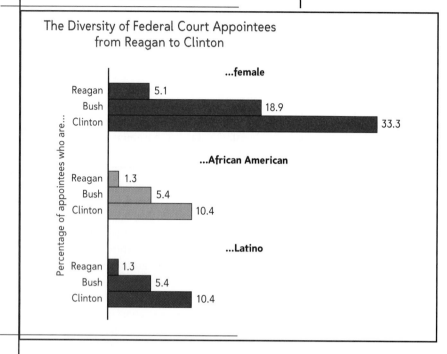

The Diversity of Federal Court Appointees
from Reagan to Clinton

...female

Reagan 5.1
Bush 18.9
Clinton 33.3

...African American

Reagan 1.3
Bush 5.4
Clinton 10.4

...Latino

Reagan 1.3
Bush 5.4
Clinton 10.4

Percentage of appointees who are...

presidents who named them to the bench. Justice Souter, for example, has been far less conservative than President George H. W. Bush and the Republicans who supported Souter's appointment in 1990 thought he would be. Likewise, Justices O'Connor and Kennedy have disappointed conservatives by opposing limitations on abortion.

Nevertheless, with a combined total of twelve years in office, both Reagan and Bush were able to exercise a good deal of influence on the composition of the federal district and appellate courts. By the end of Bush's term, he and Reagan together had appointed nearly half of all federal judges. Thus, whatever impact Reagan and Bush ultimately had on the Supreme Court, their federal appointments have certainly had a continuing influence on the temperament and behavior of the district and circuit courts.

President Clinton promised to appoint more liberal jurists to the district and appellate courts, as well as to increase the number of women and minorities serving on the federal bench. During his first two years in office, Clinton held to this promise (see Figure 8.3). More than 60 percent of his 128 judicial nominees were women or members of minority groups.[35] A large number of judicial vacancies remained unfilled, however, when the Republicans took control of Congress at the end of 1994. Soon after the election, Senator Orrin Hatch of Utah, the new chair of the Senate Judiciary Committee, which confirms judicial nominations, indicated his intention to oppose any nominee whom he deemed to be too liberal. This prompted the Clinton White House to withdraw some nominations and to search for district and appellate nominees who would be more acceptable to the Republicans.[36] It remains to be seen what impact President George W. Bush will have on the Court.

JUDICIAL POWER AND POLITICS

One of the most important institutional changes to occur in the United States during the past half-century has been the striking transformation of the role and power of the federal courts, those of the Supreme Court in particular. Understanding how this transformation came about is the key to understanding the contemporary role of the courts in America.

Traditional Limitations on the Federal Courts

For much of American history, the power of the federal courts was subject to five limitations.[37] First, courts were constrained by judicial rules of standing that limited access to the bench. Claimants who simply disagreed with governmental action or inaction could not obtain access. Access to the courts was limited to individuals who could show that they were particularly affected by the government's behavior in some area. This limitation on access to the courts diminished the judiciary's capacity to forge links with important political and social forces. Second, courts were traditionally limited in the character of the relief they could provide. In general, courts acted only to offer relief or assistance to individuals and not to broad social classes, again inhibiting the formation of alliances between the courts and important social forces. Third, courts lacked enforcement powers of their own and were compelled to rely upon executive or state agencies to ensure compliance with their edicts. If the executive or state agencies were unwilling to assist the courts, judicial enactments could go unheeded, as when President Andrew Jackson declined to enforce Chief Justice John Marshall's 1832 order to the state of Georgia to release two missionaries it had arrested on

[35]*Chicago Daily Law Bulletin*, 5 October 1994.

[36]R. W. Apple, Jr., "A Divided Government Remains, and with It the Prospect of Further Combat," *New York Times*, 7 November 1996, p. B6.

[37]For limits on judicial power, see Alexander Bickel, *The Least Dangerous Branch* (Indianapolis: Bobbs-Merrill, 1962).

Cherokee lands. Marshall asserted that the state had no right to enter the Cherokee's lands without their assent.[38] Jackson is reputed to have said, "John Marshall has made his decision, now let him enforce it."

Fourth, federal judges are, of course, appointed by the president (with the consent of the Senate). As a result, the president and Congress can shape the composition of the federal courts and ultimately, perhaps, the character of judicial decisions. Finally, Congress has the power to change both the size and jurisdiction of the Supreme Court and other federal courts. For example, Franklin Roosevelt's "court packing" plan encouraged the justices to drop their opposition to New Deal programs. In many areas, federal courts obtain their jurisdiction not from the Constitution but from congressional statutes. On a number of occasions, Congress has threatened to take matters out of the Court's hands when it was unhappy with the Court's policies.[39]

Institutional Reform
www.wwnorton.com/
lowi7/ch8
What are some of the institutional and political checks on judicial power?

In 1996, a Republican Congress succeeded in enacting new limits on the jurisdiction of the federal courts. The Immigration Reform Act limited the ability of the courts to hear class action suits brought on behalf of immigrants seeking to fight deportation proceedings. The Prison Litigation Reform Act limited the ability of federal judges to place state and local prison systems in the hands of special masters. Finally, a provision of the 1996 Budget Act limited the ability of the federal courts to listen to class action suits brought by legal services lawyers.[40] These restrictions were designed to curb what conservatives viewed as the excessive power of the judiciary.

As a result of these five limitations on judicial power, through much of their history the chief function of the federal courts was to provide judicial support for executive agencies and to legitimate acts of Congress by declaring them to be consistent with constitutional principles. Only on rare occasions did the federal courts actually dare to challenge Congress or the executive.[41]

Two Judicial Revolutions

Since the Second World War, however, the role of the federal judiciary has been strengthened and expanded. There have actually been two judicial revolutions in the United States since World War II. The first and most visible of these was the substantive revolution in judicial policy. As we saw in Chapter 4, in policy areas, including school desegregation, legislative apportionment, and criminal procedure, as well as obscenity, abortion, and voting rights, the Supreme Court was at

---

[38]Worcester v. Georgia, 6 Peters 515 (1832).

[39]See Walter Murphy, *Congress and the Court* (Chicago: University of Chicago Press, 1962).

[40]Linda Greenhouse, "How Congress Curtailed the Courts' Jurisdiction," *New York Times*, 22 October 1996, p. E5.

[41]Robert Dahl, "The Supreme Court and National Policy Making," *Journal of Public Law* 6 (1958), p. 279.

the forefront of a series of sweeping changes in the role of the U.S. government, and ultimately, in the character of American society.[42]

But at the same time that the courts were introducing important policy innovations, they were also bringing about a second, less visible revolution. During the 1960s and 1970s, the Supreme Court and other federal courts instituted a series of institutional changes in judicial procedures that had major consequences by fundamentally expanding the power of the courts in the United States. First, the federal courts liberalized the concept of standing to permit almost any group that seeks to challenge the actions of an administrative agency to bring its case before the federal bench. In 1971, for example, the Supreme Court ruled that public interest groups could use the National Environmental Policy Act to challenge the actions of federal agencies by claiming that the agencies' activities might have adverse environmental consequences.[43] Congress helped to make it even easier for groups dissatisfied with government policies to bring their cases to the courts by adopting Title 42, Section 1988, of the U.S. Code, which permits the practice of "fee shifting." Section 1988 allows citizens who successfully bring a suit against a public official for violating their constitutional rights to collect their attorneys' fees and costs from the government. Thus, Section 1988 encourages individuals and groups to bring their problems to the courts rather than to Congress or the executive branch. These changes have given the courts a far greater role in the administrative process than ever before. Many federal judges are concerned that federal legislation in areas such as health care reform would create new rights and entitlements that would give rise to a deluge of court cases. "Any time you create a new right, you create a host of disputes and claims," warned Barbara Rothstein, chief judge of the federal district court in Seattle, Washington.[44] Where issues of civil rights are in question, the 1976 Civil Rights Attorney's Fees Awards Act also provides for fee shifting. The act calls for the award of "reasonable attorney's fees" to a prevailing party in a civil rights law suit.

Second, the federal courts broadened the scope of relief to permit themselves to act on behalf of broad categories or classes of persons in "class action" cases, rather than just on behalf of individuals.[45] A ***class action suit*** is a procedural device that permits large numbers of persons with common interests to join together under a representative party to bring or defend a lawsuit. One example is the case of *In re Agent Orange Product Liability Litigation*, in which a federal judge in New York certified Vietnam War veterans as a class with standing to sue a manufacturer of herbicides for damages allegedly incurred from exposure to the defendant's product while in Vietnam.[46] The class potentially numbered in

Institution Principle

During the 1960s and 1970s, the courts liberalized the concept of standing.

class action suit
A lawsuit in which large numbers of persons with common interests join together under a representative party to bring or defend a lawsuit, such as hundreds of workers joining together to sue a company.

[42]Martin Shapiro, "The Supreme Court: From Warren to Burger," in *The New American Political System*, ed. Anthony King (Washington, DC: American Enterprise Institute, 1978).
[43]*Citizens to Preserve Overton Park v. Volpe*, 401 U.S. 402 (1971).
[44]Toni Locy, "Bracing for Health Care's Caseload," *Washington Post*, 22 August 1994, p. A15.
[45]See "Developments in the Law—Class Actions," *Harvard Law Review* 89 (1976), p. 1318.
[46]*In re Agent Orange Product Liability Litigation*, 100 F.R.D. 718 (D.C.N.Y. 1983).

the tens of thousands. In a similar vein, in 1999, a consortium of several dozen law firms prepared to file a class action suit against fire arms manufacturers on behalf of victims of gun violence. Claims could amount to billions of dollars. Some of the same law firms were involved earlier in the decade in a massive class action suit against cigarette manufacturers on behalf of the victims of tobacco-related illnesses. This suit eventually led to a settlement in which the tobacco companies agreed to pay out several billion dollars. The beneficiaries of the settlement included the treasuries of all fifty states, which received compensation for costs allegedly borne by the states in treating illnesses due to tobacco. Of course, the attorneys who brought the case also received an enormous settlement, splitting more than $1 billion.

Third, the federal courts began to employ so-called structural remedies, in effect retaining jurisdiction of cases until the court's mandate had actually been implemented to its satisfaction.[47] The best-known of these instances was Federal Judge W. Arthur Garrity's effort to operate the Boston school system from his bench in order to ensure its desegregation. Between 1974 and 1985, Judge Garrity issued fourteen decisions relating to different aspects of the Boston school desegregation plan that had been developed under his authority and put into effect under his supervision.[48] In another recent case, Federal Judge Leonard B. Sand imposed fines that would have forced the city of Yonkers, New York, into bankruptcy if it had refused to accept his plan to build public housing in white neighborhoods. After several days of fines, the city gave in to the judge's ruling.

Through these three judicial mechanisms, the federal courts paved the way for an unprecedented expansion of national judicial power. In essence, liberalization of the rules of standing and expansion of the scope of judicial relief drew the federal courts into linkages with important social interests and classes, while the introduction of structural remedies enhanced the courts' ability to serve these constituencies. Thus, during the 1960s and 1970s, the power of the federal courts expanded in the same way the power of the executive expanded during the 1930s—through links with constituencies, such as civil rights, consumer, environmental, and feminist groups, that staunchly defended the Supreme Court in its battles with Congress, the executive, or other interest groups.

During the 1980s and early 1990s, the Reagan and Bush administrations sought to end the relationship between the Court and liberal political forces. The conservative judges appointed by these Republican presidents modified the Court's position in areas such as abortion, affirmative action, and judicial procedure, though not as completely as some conservatives had hoped. Interestingly, however, the current Court has not been eager to surrender the expanded powers carved out by earlier, liberal Courts. In a number of decisions during the 1980s

History Principle

In the last fifty years, the power of the judiciary has been strengthened and expanded.

---

[47]See Donald Horowitz, *The Courts and Social Policy* (Washington, DC: Brookings Institution, 1977).
[48]Moran v. McDonough, 540 F. 2nd 527 (1 Cir., 1976; *cert denied* 429 U.S. 1042 [1977]).

and 1990s, the Court was willing to make use of its expanded powers on behalf of interests it favored.[49]

In the 1992 case of *Lujan v. Defenders of Wildlife*, the Court seemed to retreat to a conception of standing more restrictive than that affirmed by liberal activist jurists.[50] Rather than representing an example of judicial restraint, however, the *Lujan* case was actually a direct judicial challenge to congressional power. The case involved an effort by an environmental group, the Defenders of Wildlife, to make use of the 1973 Endangered Species Act to block the expenditure of federal funds being used by the governments of Egypt and Sri Lanka for public works projects. Environmentalists charged that the projects threatened the habitats of several endangered species of birds and, therefore, that the expenditure of federal funds to support the projects violated the 1973 act. The Interior Department claimed that the act affected only domestic projects.[51]

The Endangered Species Act, like a number of other pieces of liberal environmental and consumer legislation enacted by Congress, encourages citizen suits—suits by activist groups not directly harmed by the action in question—to challenge government policies they deem to be inconsistent with the act. Justice Scalia, however, writing for the Court's majority in the *Lujan* decision, reasserted a more traditional conception of standing, requiring those bringing suit against a government policy to show that the policy is likely to cause *them* direct and imminent injury.

Had Scalia stopped at this point, the case might have been seen as an example of judicial restraint. Scalia, however, went on to question the validity of any statutory provision for citizen suits. Such legislative provisions, according to Justice Scalia, violate Article III of the Constitution, which limits the federal courts to consideration of actual "Cases" and "Controversies." This interpretation would strip Congress of its capacity to promote the enforcement of regulatory statutes by encouraging activist groups not directly affected or injured to be on the lookout for violations that could provide the basis for lawsuits. This enforcement mechanism—which conservatives liken to bounty hunting—was an extremely important congressional instrument and played a prominent part in the enforcement of such pieces of legislation as the 1990 Americans with Disabilities Act. Thus, the *Lujan* case offers an example of judicial activism rather than of judicial restraint; even the most conservative justices are reluctant to surrender the powers now wielded by the Court.

There can be little doubt that the contemporary Supreme Court exercises considerably more power than the framers of the Constitution intended. Today, competing interests endeavor to make policy through the courts, and, as we have seen, Congress often enacts regulatory legislation—like the Endangered Species

[49]Mark Silverstein and Benjamin Ginsberg, "The Supreme Court and the New Politics of Judicial Power," *Political Science Quarterly* 102 (Fall 1987), pp. 371–88.

[50]Lujan v. Defenders of Wildlife, 112 S.Ct. 2130 (1992).

[51]Linda Greenhouse, "Court Limits Legal Standing in Suits," *New York Times*, 13 June 1992, p. 12.

Act—with the presumption that enforcement will be undertaken by the courts rather than the executive branch. Is this an ideal state of affairs? The answer is no. In an ideal world, public policies would be made through the democratically elected branches of our government while the courts would serve to deal with individual problems and injustices. Ours, however, is not always an ideal world. Democratic legislatures sometimes enact programs that violate constitutional rights. Congress and the president sometimes become locked in political struggles that blind them to the interests of certain citizens. On such occasions, we may be grateful that our "least dangerous branch" has some teeth.

SUMMARY

Millions of cases come to trial every year in the United States. The great majority—nearly 99 percent—are tried in state and local courts. The types of law are civil law, criminal law, and public law. There are three types of courts that hear cases: trial court, appellate court, and (state) supreme court.

There are three kinds of federal cases: (1) civil cases involving diversity of citizenship, (2) civil cases where a federal agency is seeking to enforce federal laws that provide for civil penalties, and (3) cases involving federal criminal statutes or where state criminal cases have been made issues of public law. Judicial power extends only to cases and controversies. Litigants must have standing to sue, and courts neither hand down opinions on hypothetical issues nor take the initiative. Sometimes appellate courts even return cases to the lower courts for further trial. They may also decline to decide cases by invoking the doctrine of political questions, although this is seldom done today.

The organization of the federal judiciary provides for original jurisdiction in the federal district courts, the U.S. Court of Claims, the U.S. Tax Court, the Customs Court, and federal regulatory agencies.

Each district court is in one of the twelve appellate districts, called circuits, presided over by a court of appeals. Appellate courts admit no new evidence; their rulings are based solely on the records of the court proceedings or agency hearings that led to the original decision. Appeals court rulings are final unless the Supreme Court chooses to review them.

The Supreme Court has some original jurisdiction, but its major job is to review lower court decisions involving substantial issues of public law. Supreme Court decisions can be reversed by Congress and the state legislatures, but this seldom happens. There is no explicit constitutional authority for the Supreme Court to review acts of Congress. Nonetheless, the 1803 case of *Marbury v. Madison* established the Court's right to review congressional acts. The supremacy clause of Article VI and the Judiciary Act of 1789 give the Court the power to review state constitutions and laws. Cases reach the Court mainly through the writ of *certiorari*. The Supreme Court controls its caseload by issuing few writs and by handing down clear leading opinions that enable lower courts to resolve future cases without further review.

Rationality Principle	Collective Action Principle	Institution Principle	Policy Principle	History Principle
Judges have political goals and policy preferences and act to achieve them.	Appointments to the federal bench involve informal bargaining (senatorial courtesy) as well as formal bargaining (Senate confirmation).	Because the court system is hierarchical, decisions by higher courts constrain the discretion of judges in lower courts.	A number of major policy issues have been fought and decided in the courts.	Since *Marbury v. Madison* (1803), the power of judicial review has not been in question.
The Supreme Court accepts cases based on the preferences and priorities of the justices.	The legal system coordinates private behavior by providing incentives and disincentives for specific actions.	The courts have developed specific rules of access that govern which cases within their jurisdiction they will hear.	By interpreting existing statutes, as well as the Constitution, judges make law.	In the last fifty years, the power of the judiciary has been strengthened and expanded.
Groups will often file more than one suit in the hope that this will increase their chances of being heard in Court.	Four of the nine Supreme Court justices need to agree to review a case.	The Supreme Court's procedures allow for various individuals and groups to influence the decision-making process.		
	In reaching their decisions, Supreme Court judges must anticipate Congress's response.	During the 1960s and 1970s, the courts liberalized the concept of standing.		

Both appellate and Supreme Court decisions, including the decision not to review a case, make law. The impact of such law usually favors the status quo. Yet, many revolutionary changes in the law have come about through appellate court and Supreme Court rulings—in the criminal process, in apportionment, and in civil rights.

The judiciary as a whole is subject to two major influences: (1) the individual members of the Supreme Court, who have lifetime tenure; and (2) the other branches of government, particularly Congress.

The influence of the individual member of the Supreme Court is limited when the Court is polarized, and close votes in a polarized Court impair the value of the decision rendered. Writing the majority opinion for a case is an opportunity for a justice to influence the judiciary. But the need to frame an opinion in such a way as to develop majority support on the Court may limit such opportunities. Dissenting opinions can have more impact than the majority opinion; they stimulate a continued flow of cases around that issue. The solicitor general is the most important single influence outside the Court itself because he or she controls the flow of cases brought by the Justice Department and also shapes the argument in those cases. But the flow of cases is a force in itself, which the Department of Justice cannot entirely control. Social problems give rise to similar cases that ultimately must be adjudicated and appealed. Some interest groups try to develop such case patterns as a means of gaining power through the courts.

In recent years, the importance of the federal judiciary—the Supreme Court in particular—has increased substantially as the courts have developed new tools of judicial power and forged alliances with important forces in American society.

FOR FURTHER READING

Abraham, Henry. *The Judicial Process*, 7th ed. New York: Oxford University Press, 1998.

Baum, Lawrence. *The Puzzle of Judicial Behavior*. Ann Arbor: University of Michigan Press, 1997.

Bickel, Alexander. *The Least Dangerous Branch*. Indianapolis: Bobbs-Merrill, 1962.

Epstein, Lee and Jack Knight. *The Choices Justices Make*. Washington, DC: Congressional Quarterly Press, 1998.

Kahn, Ronald. *The Supreme Court and Constitutional Theory, 1953–1993*. Lawrence: University Press of Kansas, 1994.

O'Brien, David M. *Storm Center: The Supreme Court in American Politics*, 5th ed. New York: W. W. Norton, 1999.

Perry, H. W. *Deciding to Decide: Agenda Setting in the United States Supreme Court*. Cambridge, MA: Harvard University Press, 1991.

Segal, Jeffrey A. and Harold J. Spaeth. *The Supreme Court and the Attitudinal Model*. New York: Cambridge University Press, 1993.

Silverstein, Mark. *Judicious Choices: The New Politics of Supreme Court Confirmations*. New York: W. W. Norton, 1994.

Tribe, Laurence. *Constitutional Choices*. Cambridge: Harvard University Press, 1985.

three

Politics

nine

Public Opinion

TIME LINE
ON PUBLIC OPINION

EVENTS	INSTITUTIONAL DEVELOPMENTS
Congressional investigation of Gen. St. Clair's conduct of war against Indians (1792)	George Washington begins policy of executive secrecy in regard to congressional investigations (1792)
Territorial expansion (1800s) — **1800**	
	Straw polls and other impressionistic means of measuring opinion (1830s–1890s)
Civil War (1861–1865)	Urban school systems—development of civic education programs (1880s)
	Birth of advertising industry—scientific manipulation of public opinion (1880s)
Democrats denounce polling as a Republican plot; they instruct their voters not to answer questions (1896)	
1900	
World War I (1914–1918)	Creel Committee tries to "sell" WWI to American public (1917)
Literary Digest poll predicts Hoover will defeat Roosevelt (1932)	Beginning of routine governmental efforts to manage opinion (1930s)
Media used to defeat Upton Sinclair in California campaign for governor (1934)	Media experts manipulate public opinion through negative campaign using newspapers, leaflets, and radio (1934)
Gallup and Roper use sample surveys in national political polls (1936)	Introduction of sample surveys to predict winners of national elections (1936)
Chicago Tribune poll shows Dewey victory over Truman (1948)	Growth of national polls (1930s–1950s)
1950	
Kennedy campaign uses computers to analyze polls and bellwether districts (1959–1960)	Emergence of computer analysis of polls and bellwether districts (1959–1960)
	Emergence of exit polls (1960s)
CBS uses computer bellwether system to correctly forecast winner of California Republican primary (1964)	Media attack government opinion manipulation (1960s and 1970s)
	Expansion of mass media; nationalization of public opinion (1960s–1980s)
1970	
CBS airs "Selling of the Pentagon" (1971)	
Exit polls used to predict presidential election outcome before polls close on West Coast (1976, 1980, 1984, 1988)	

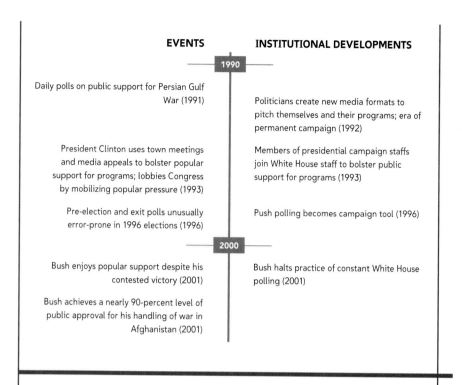

EVENTS	INSTITUTIONAL DEVELOPMENTS

1990

Daily polls on public support for Persian Gulf War (1991)

Politicians create new media formats to pitch themselves and their programs; era of permanent campaign (1992)

President Clinton uses town meetings and media appeals to bolster popular support for programs; lobbies Congress by mobilizing popular pressure (1993)

Members of presidential campaign staffs join White House staff to bolster public support for programs (1993)

Pre-election and exit polls unusually error-prone in 1996 elections (1996)

Push polling becomes campaign tool (1996)

2000

Bush enjoys popular support despite his contested victory (2001)

Bush halts practice of constant White House polling (2001)

Bush achieves a nearly 90-percent level of public approval for his handling of war in Afghanistan (2001)

After his 1992 election to the presidency, Bill Clinton found that public opinion could be quite fickle. By May 1993, Clinton's approval ratings had fallen sharply. For example, according to a May 4–6 *New York Times*/CBS News poll, 50 percent of Americans disapproved of the way President Clinton was handling the economy, while only 38 percent approved.[1] Only a month earlier, nearly half of all respondents to the same poll had said they approved of Clinton's economic performance, while only 37 percent had disapproved. Consistent with the pattern discussed in Chapter 6, Clinton's public approval rating briefly increased by 11 points in June 1993, after he ordered a cruise missile attack on Iraqi intelligence headquarters. The attack was in retaliation for an alleged Iraqi plot to assassinate former president Bush. Clinton himself

[1]Gwen Ifill, "As Ratings Stall, Clinton Tries Tune-Up," *New York Times*, 10 May 1993, p. A16; Richard Morin and Ann Devroy, "President's Popularity Continues to Weaken," *Washington Post*, 30 June 1993, p. 1.

- Opinions are shaped by individuals' characteristics and also by institutional, political, and governmental forces.

- Government shapes citizens' beliefs about the political system through the promotion of nationalism, property ownership, education, and political participation.

- Various methods of polling are used to measure public opinion.

- The government and political leaders use measures of public opinion to shape their policy initiatives, although the structure of American government insulates political decision making from direct popular pressure.

attributed his improved poll standing to what he termed better public understanding of his economic program. Within a few days, however, Clinton's approval rating had dropped back to 38 percent.

Clinton's approval rating continued to linger in this range during most of 1994. Despite the nation's strong economic performance during the first half of 1994, the majority of those polled disapproved of the president's handling of the economy.[2] By 1996, however, Clinton's popular standing seemed to have been fully restored. In the weeks prior to the 1996 presidential elections, Clinton's lead in the polls over his Republican challenger, Bob Dole, was as high as twenty-one points. Clinton continued to enjoy high levels of public approval throughout 1997 and 1998 despite his public acknowledgment of an extramarital relationship. Indeed, Clinton's poll standing remained high, even as he became only the second president in American history to be impeached by Congress! In October 2001, Clinton's successor George W. Bush achieved a nearly 90-percent approval rating from the American public when he ordered a massive military campaign against all terrorists. Earlier in the year, analysts had predicted that Bush's disputed presidential victory would make him an unpopular president.

Commentators and social scientists, of course, carefully plotted these massive changes in public opinion and pondered their causes. Significantly, no analyst charting these shifts in popular sentiment was so bold as to ask whether public opinion was right or wrong—whether it made sense or nonsense. Rather, opinion was viewed as some sort of natural force that, like the weather, affected everything but was itself impervious to intervention and immune to criticism.

Public opinion has become the ultimate standard against which the conduct of contemporary governments is measured. In the democracies, especially in the United States, both the value of government programs and the virtue of public officials are typically judged by the magnitude of their popularity. Most contemporary dictatorships, for their part, are careful at least to give lip service to the idea of popular sovereignty, if only to bolster public support at home and to maintain a favorable image abroad.

public opinion
Citizens' attitudes about political issues, leaders, institutions, and events.

Public opinion is the term used to denote the values and attitudes that people have about issues, events, and personalities. Although the terms are sometimes

[2]Richard Morin, "Clinton Ratings Decline Despite Rising Economy," *Washington Post*, 9 August 1994, p. 1

used interchangeably, it is useful to distinguish between values and beliefs on the one hand, and attitudes or opinions on the other. ***Values (or beliefs)*** are a person's basic orientations to politics. Values represent deep-rooted goals, aspirations, and ideals that shape an individual's perceptions of political issues and events. Liberty, equality, and democracy are basic political values that most Americans hold. The idea that governmental solutions to problems are inherently inferior to solutions offered by the private sector is a belief also held by many Americans. This general belief, in turn, may lead individuals to have negative views of specific government programs even before they know much about them. An ***attitude (or opinion)*** is a specific view about a particular issue, personality, or event. An individual may have an opinion about the impeachment of President Clinton or an attitude toward President Bush's tax and education programs. The attitude or opinion may have emerged from a broad belief about Democrats or tax and education policies, but an attitude itself is very specific. Some attitudes may be short-lived. Another useful term for understanding public opinion is *ideology*. ***Political ideology*** refers to a complex set of beliefs and values that, as a whole, form a general philosophy about government. As we shall see, liberalism and conservatism are important ideologies in America today.

In this chapter, we will examine the role of public opinion in American politics. First, we will look at the institutions and processes that shape public opinion in the United States, most notably the "marketplace of ideas" in which opinions compete for acceptance. Second, we will assess the government's role in shaping public opinion. Third, we will address the problem of measuring opinion. Finally, we will consider the question: "Is government responsive to public opinion?"

One reason that public policy and public opinion may not always coincide is, of course, that our's is a representative government, not a direct democracy. The framers of the Constitution thought that our nation would be best served by a system of government that allowed the elected representatives of the people an opportunity to reflect and consider their decisions rather than one that bowed immediately to shifts in popular sentiment. A century after the founding, however, the populist movement averred that government was

values (or beliefs) Basic principles that shape a person's opinions about political issues and events.

attitude (or opinions) A specific preference on a specific issue.

political ideology A cohesive set of beliefs that form a general philosophy about the role of government.

THE CENTRAL QUESTIONS

THE MARKETPLACE OF IDEAS

What is the government's role in promoting and maintaining the free exchange of ideas?

In what ways do Americans agree on fundamental values but disagree on political issues?

What do the differences between liberals and conservatives reveal about American political debate?

What influences the way we form political opinions?

SHAPING PUBLIC OPINION

How are political issues marketed and managed by the government, private groups, and the media?

MEASURING PUBLIC OPINION

How can public opinion be measured?

What problems can arise from public opinion polling?

PUBLIC OPINION AND GOVERNMENT POLICY

How responsive is the government to public opinion?

What explains the lack of consistency between government policy and public opinion?

Policy Principle

One reason why policy and opinion may not be consistent is that the United States is a representative government, not a direct democracy.

too far removed from the people and introduced procedures for direct popular legislation through the initiative and referendum. A number of states allow policy issues to be placed on the ballot where they are resolved by a popular vote. Some modern-day populists believe that initiative and referendum processes should be adopted at the national level, as well. Whether this would lead to greater responsiveness, however, is an open question to which we shall return.

THE MARKETPLACE OF IDEAS

Opinions are products of an individual's personality, social characteristics, and interests. But opinions are also shaped by institutional, political, and governmental forces that make it more likely that citizens will hold some beliefs and less likely that they will hold others. In the United States and the other Western democracies, opinions and beliefs compete for acceptance in what is sometimes called the ***marketplace of ideas.*** In America, it is mainly the "hidden hand" of the market that determines which opinions and beliefs will flourish and which will fall to the wayside. Thus, to understand public opinion in the United States, it is important to understand the origins and operations of this "idea market."

marketplace of ideas The public forum in which beliefs and ideas are exchanged and compete.

Origins of the Idea Market

Prior to the nineteenth century, each of the various regional, religious, ethnic, linguistic, and economic strata generally possessed their own ideas and beliefs based on their own experiences and life circumstances. The members of different primary groups generally had little contact with one another, and they knew remarkably little about the history, customs, or character—much less the opinions—of their nominal countrymen.

In every European nation and in America, city was separated from countryside and region from region by the lack of usable roads, the unavailability of effective communications media, and, in many nations in Europe, by the absence of even a common national language. Language barriers could be formidable. For example, before the nineteenth century, Parisians traveling just a few days from the capital often reported that it was impossible to understand the patois of the local populace and that outside of the larger towns it was difficult to find anyone who spoke even a few words of French.[3] Equally significant was the matter of class. The members of the different social classes, even when living near each other, existed in very different worlds. Often, each class spoke its own language, adhered to its own religious beliefs, maintained its own cultural orientations, and manifested distinct conceptions of the political and social universe.

The autonomy of the various regions, groups, and classes began to diminish in the nineteenth century. During this period, every European regime initiated

---

[3]Eugen Weber, *Peasants into Frenchmen* (Stanford: Stanford University Press, 1976).

the construction of what came to be called a "marketplace of ideas"—a national forum in which the views of all strata would be exchanged. Westerners often equate freedom of opinion and expression with the absence of state interference. Western freedom of opinion, however, is not unbridled freedom; rather, it is the structured freedom of a public forum constructed and maintained by the state. The creation and maintenance of this forum, this "marketplace of ideas," has required extensive governmental effort in the areas of education, communication, and jurisprudence.

First, in the nineteenth century, most Western nations engaged in intense efforts to impose a single national language on their citizens. In the United States, massive waves of immigrants during the nineteenth century meant that millions of residents spoke no English. In response, the American national government, as well as state and local governments, made vigorous efforts to impose the English language on these newcomers. Schools were established to provide adults with language skills. At the same time, English was the only language of instruction permitted in the public elementary and secondary schools. Knowledge of English became a prerequisite for American citizenship. With some exceptions, the efforts of the United States and other Western nations to achieve linguistic unification succeeded by the twentieth century.

Second, and closely related to the effort to achieve linguistic unity, was the matter of literacy. Prior to the nineteenth century, few ordinary people were able to read or write. Possession of these skills was, for the most part, limited to the upper strata. Widespread illiteracy in a pre-technological era meant that communication depended upon word of mouth, a situation hardly conducive to the spread of ideas across regional, class, or even village or neighborhood boundaries. During the nineteenth and twentieth centuries, however, all Western governments actively sought to expand popular literacy. With the advent of universal, compulsory education, children were taught to read and write their mother tongue. Together with literacy programs for adults, including extensive efforts by the various national military services to instruct uneducated recruits, this educational process led to the gradual reduction of illiteracy in the industrial West. Like the imposition of a common language, the elimination of illiteracy opened the way for the communication of ideas and information across primary group lines.[4]

A third facet of the construction of the marketplace of ideas was the development of various communications mechanisms. This process involved a number of elements. During the early nineteenth century, governments built hundreds of thousands of miles of roads, opening lines of communication among the various regions and between cities and the countryside. Road building was followed later in the century by governmental promotion of the construction of rail and telegraph lines, further facilitating the exchange of goods, persons, ideas, and information among previously disparate and often isolated areas. Such "internal

[4]See Richard Hoggart, *The Uses of Literacy* (Oxford, England: Oxford University Press, 1970).

improvements" constituted the most important activity undertaken by the American central government both before and after the Civil War. During the twentieth century, all Western regimes promoted the development of radio, telephone, television, and the complex satellite-based communications networks that link the world today.

The final key component of the construction of a free market of ideas was, and is, legal protection for free expression of ideas. This last factor is, of course, what most clearly distinguished the construction of the West's idea market from the efforts of authoritarian regimes. Obviously, the development of communications networks, linguistic unification, and universal literacy were goals pursued just as avidly by autocratic nation-builders as by the more liberal regimes.

In most Western nations, at the present time, there are few physical or legal impediments to the transmission of ideas and information across municipal, regional, class, ethnic, or other primary group boundaries. All groups are, to a greater or lesser extent, linked by a common language, mass communications media, and transportation networks. In the United States, for example, the newspapers, wire services, radio, television, Internet Web sites, and news magazines present a common core of ideas and information to virtually the entire citizenry. Every region of the country can be reached by mail, phone, and broadcast and electronic media; virtually no area is inaccessible by road, rail, or air transport; and persons, ideas, and information can move freely across regions and between economic strata and ethnic groups. Similarly, the lifting of travel restrictions has been a major element in efforts to bring about European unification in recent years.

The Idea Market Today

The operation of the idea market in the United States today has continually exposed individuals to concepts and information originating outside their own region, class, or ethnic community. It is this steady exposure that over time leads members of every social group to acquire at least some of the ideas and perspectives embraced by the others. Given continual exposure to the ideas of other strata, it is virtually impossible for any group to resist some modification of its own beliefs.

equality of opportunity
A universally shared American ideal that all have the freedom to use whatever talents and wealth they have to reach their fullest potential.

Common Fundamental Values   Today most Americans share a common set of political beliefs and opinions. First, Americans generally believe in ***equality of opportunity***: That is, they assume that all individuals should be allowed to seek personal and material success. Moreover, Americans generally believe that such success should be linked to personal effort and ability rather than family "connections" or other forms of special privilege. Second, Americans strongly believe in individual freedom. They typically support the notion that governmental interference with individuals' lives and property should be kept to the minimum consistent with the general welfare (although in recent years Americans have grown accustomed to greater levels of governmental intervention than would have been deemed appropriate by the founders of liberal theory). Third, most Americans

FIGURE 9.1

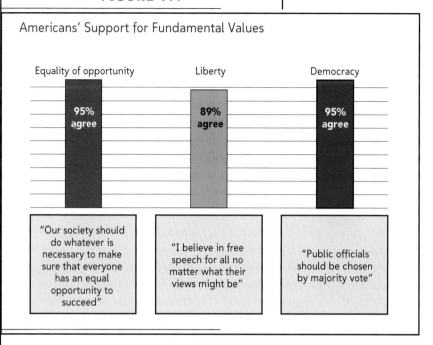

Americans' Support for Fundamental Values

Equality of opportunity — 95% agree — "Our society should do whatever is necessary to make sure that everyone has an equal opportunity to succeed"

Liberty — 89% agree — "I believe in free speech for all no matter what their views might be"

Democracy — 95% agree — "Public officials should be chosen by majority vote"

SOURCE: 1992 American National Election Studies; Herbert McCloskey and John Zaller, *The American Ethos: Public Attitudes toward Capitalism and Democracy* (Cambridge: Harvard University Press, 1984), p. 25; and Robert S. Erikson, Norman R. Luttbeg, and Kent L. Tedin, *American Public Opinion: Its Origins, Content, and Impact,* 4th ed. (New York: Macmillan, 1991), p. 108.

believe in *democracy*. They presume that everyone should have the opportunity to take part in the nation's governmental and policy-making processes and to have some "say" in determining how they are governed (see Figure 9.1).[5]

One indication that Americans of all political stripes share these fundamental political values is the content of the acceptance speeches delivered by Al Gore and George W. Bush upon receiving their parties' presidential nominations in 2000. Gore and Bush differed on many specific issues and policies. Yet the political visions they presented reveal an underlying similarity. A major emphasis of both candidates was equality of opportunity.

Gore referred frequently to opportunity in his speeches, as in this poignant story about his own parents' efforts to make better lives for themselves and their children:

[5]For a discussion of the political beliefs of Americans, see Harry Holloway and John George, *Public Opinion* (New York: St. Martin's, 1986). See also Paul R. Abramson, *Political Attitudes in America* (San Francisco: W. H. Freeman, 1983).

My father grew up in a small community named Possum Hollow in Middle Tennessee. When he was just eighteen he went to work as a teacher in a one-room school. . . . He entered public service to fight for the people. My mother grew up in a small farming community in northwest Tennessee. She went on to become one of the first women in history to graduate from Vanderbilt Law School. . . . Every hardworking family in America deserves to open the door to their dream.

Bush struck a similar note in his acceptance speech:

We will seize this moment of American promise. . . . And we will extend the promise of prosperity to every forgotten corner of this country. To every man and woman, a chance to succeed. To every child, a chance to learn. To every family, a chance to live with dignity and hope.

Thus, however much the two candidates differed on means and specifics, their understandings of the fundamental goals of government were quite similar.

Agreement on fundamental political values, though certainly not absolute, is probably more widespread in the United States than anywhere else in the Western world. During the course of Western political history, competing economic, social, and political groups put forward a variety of radically divergent views, opinions, and political philosophies. America was never socially or economically homogeneous. But two forces that were extremely powerful and important sources of ideas and beliefs elsewhere in the world were relatively weak or absent in the United States. First, the United States never had the feudal aristocracy that dominated so much of European history. Second, for reasons including America's prosperity and the early availability of political rights, no Socialist movements comparable to those that developed in nineteenth-century Europe were ever able to establish themselves in the United States. As a result, during the course of American history, there existed neither an aristocracy to assert the virtues of inequality, special privilege, and a rigid class structure, nor a powerful American Communist or Socialist party to seriously challenge the desirability of limited government and individualism.[6]

Agreement and Disagreement on Issues   Agreement on fundamental values, however, by no means implies that Americans do not differ with one another on a wide variety of issues. American political life is characterized by vigorous debate on economic, foreign policy, and social policy issues; race relations; environmental affairs; and a host of other matters.

Differences of political opinion are often associated with such variables as income, education, and occupation. Similarly, factors such as race, gender, ethnicity, age, religion, and region, which not only influence individuals' interests but

[6]See Louis Hartz, *The Liberal Tradition in America* (New York: Harcourt, Brace, 1955).

also shape their experiences and upbringing, have enormous influence on their beliefs and opinions. For example, individuals whose incomes differ substantially have rather different views on the desirability of a number of important economic and social programs. In general, the poor—who are the chief beneficiaries of these programs—support them more strongly than do those whose taxes pay for the programs. Similarly, blacks and whites have different views on questions of civil rights such as affirmative action—presumably reflecting differences of interest and historical experience. In recent years, many observers have begun to take note of a number of differences between the views expressed by men and those supported by women, especially on foreign policy questions, where women appear to be much more concerned with the dangers of war, and on social welfare issues, where women show more concern than men for the problems of the poor and unfortunate. Quite conceivably these differences—known collectively as the *"gender gap"*—reflect the results of differences in the childhood experiences and socialization of men and women in America. To say that individuals' opinions are related to their economic interests or social characteristics, however, is not to say that it is always easy or even possible to predict opinions from these factors. The views of "the rich," "women," or "young people" are hardly fixed and immutable attributes of these groups; instead, they often change as the interests and experiences of these groups interact with shifting economic, social, and political realities.

gender gap
A distinctive pattern of voting behavior reflecting the differences in views between men and women.

Liberalism and Conservatism   As we have seen, people's beliefs about government can vary widely. But for some individuals, this set of beliefs can fit together into a coherent philosophy about government. This set of underlying orientations, ideas, and beliefs through which we come to understand and interpret politics is called a political ideology. Ideologies take many different forms. Some people may view politics primarily in religious terms. During the course of European political history, for example, Protestantism and Catholicism were often political ideologies as much as they were religious creeds. Each set of beliefs not only included elements of religious practice but also involved ideas about secular authority and political action. Other people may see politics through racial lenses. Nazism was a political ideology that placed race at the center of political life and sought to interpret politics in terms of racial categories.

In America today, people often describe themselves as liberals or conservatives. Liberalism and conservatism are political ideologies that include beliefs about the role of the government, ideas about public policies, and notions about which groups in society should properly exercise power. Historically these terms were defined somewhat differently than they are today. As recently as the nineteenth century, a liberal was an individual who favored freedom from state control, while a conservative was someone who supported the use of governmental power and favored continuation of the influence of church and aristocracy in national life.

Today, the term *liberal* has come to imply support for political and social reform; support for extensive governmental intervention in the economy; the

liberal   A liberal today generally supports political and social reform; extensive governmental intervention in the economy; the expansion of federal social services; more vigorous efforts on behalf of the poor, minorities, and women; and greater concern for consumers and the environment.

expansion of federal social services; more vigorous efforts on behalf of the poor, minorities, and women; and greater concern for consumers and the environment. In social and cultural areas, liberals generally support abortion rights, are concerned with the rights of persons accused of crimes, support decriminalization of drug use, and oppose state involvement with religious institutions and religious expression. In international affairs, liberal positions are usually seen as including support for arms control, opposition to the development and testing of nuclear weapons, support for aid to poor nations, opposition to the use of American troops to influence the domestic affairs of developing nations, and support for international organizations such as the United Nations. Of course, liberalism is not monolithic. For example, among individuals who view themselves as liberal, many support American military intervention when it is tied to a humanitarian purpose, as in the case of America's military action in Kosovo in 1998–1999.

conservative
Today this term refers to those who generally support the social and economic status quo and are suspicious of efforts to introduce new political formulae and economic arrangements. Many conservatives also believe that a large and powerful government poses a threat to citizens' freedoms.

By contrast, the term *conservative* today is used to describe those who generally support the social and economic status quo and are suspicious of efforts to introduce new political formulae and economic arrangements. Conservatives believe strongly that a large and powerful government poses a threat to citizens' freedom. Thus, in the domestic arena, conservatives generally oppose the expansion of governmental activity, asserting that solutions to social and economic problems can be developed in the private sector. Conservatives particularly oppose efforts to impose government regulation on business, pointing out that such regulation is frequently economically inefficient and costly and can ultimately lower the entire nation's standard of living. As to social and cultural positions, many conservatives oppose abortion, support school prayer, are more concerned for the victims than the perpetrators of crimes, and support traditional family arrangements. In international affairs, conservatism has come to mean support for the maintenance of American military power. Like liberalism, conservatism is far from a monolithic ideology. Some conservatives support many government social programs. Republican George W. Bush calls himself a "compassionate conservative" to indicate that he favors programs that assist the poor and needy. Other conservatives oppose efforts to outlaw abortion, arguing that government intrusion in this area is as misguided as government intervention in the economy. Such a position is sometimes called "libertarian." The real political world is far too complex to be seen in terms of a simple struggle between liberals and conservatives.

Liberal and conservative differences manifest themselves in a variety of contexts. For example, the liberal approach to increasing airline safety in October 2001, was to create a work force of federal employees that would screen and inspect passenger luggage. The conservative approach was to call for better training of existing employees and supervision of private sector screeners. To some extent, contemporary liberalism and conservatism can be seen as differences of emphasis with regard to the fundamental American political values of liberty and equality. For liberals, equality is the most important of the core values. Liberals are willing to tolerate government intervention in such areas as college admissions and business decisions when these seem to result in high levels of race, class, or gender inequality. For conservatives, on the other hand, liberty is the core value. Conservatives oppose most efforts by the government, however well intentioned, to intrude into private life or the marketplace. This simple formula for distinguishing liberalism and conservatism, however, is not always accurate, because political ideologies seldom lend themselves to neat or logical characterizations.

Often political observers search for logical connections among the various positions identified with liberalism or with conservatism, and they are disappointed or puzzled when they are unable to find a set of coherent philosophical principles that define and unite the several elements of either of these sets of beliefs. On the liberal side, for example, what is the logical connection between opposition to U.S. government intervention in the affairs of foreign nations and calls for greater intervention in America's economy and society? On the conservative side, what is the logical relationship between opposition to governmental regulation of business and support for a ban on abortion? Indeed, the latter would seem to be just the sort of regulation of private conduct that conservatives claim to abhor.

Frequently, the relationships among the various elements of liberalism or the several aspects of conservatism are *political* rather than *logical*. One underlying basis of liberal views is that all or most represent criticisms of or attacks on the foreign and domestic policies and cultural values of the business and commercial strata that have been prominent in the United States for the past century. In some measure, the tenets of contemporary conservatism represent this elite's defense of its positions against its enemies, who include organized labor, minority groups, and some intellectuals and professionals. Thus, liberals attack business and commercial elites by advocating more governmental regulation, including consumer protection and environmental regulation, opposition to military weapons programs, and support for expensive social programs. Conservatives counterattack by asserting that governmental regulation of the economy is ruinous and that military weapons are needed in a changing world.

Of course, it is important to note that many people who call themselves liberals or conservatives accept only part of the liberal or conservative ideology. Although it appears that Americans have adopted more conservative outlooks on some issues, their views in other areas have remained largely unchanged or even have become more liberal in recent years (see Table 9.1). Thus, many individuals who are liberal on social issues are conservative on economic issues. There is certainly nothing illogical about these mixed positions. They simply indicate the relatively open and fluid character of American political debate.

The idea market thus has created a common ground for Americans in which discussion of issues is encouraged and based on common understandings. Despite the many and often sharp divisions that exist—between liberals and conservatives, different income groups, different regional groups—most Americans see the world through similar lenses.

TABLE 9.1

Have Americans Become More Conservative?

	1972	1978	1980	1982	1984	1986	1988	1992	1996	1998
Percentage responding "yes" to the following questions:										
Should the government help minority groups?	30%	25%	16%	21%	27%	26%	13%	27%	18%	26%
Should the government see to it that everyone has a job and a guaranteed standard of living?	27	17	22	25	28	25	24	30	24	30
Should abortion never be permitted?	9	10	8	13	13	13	12	12	13	12
Should the government provide fewer services and reduce spending?	NA	NA	27	32	28	24	25	33	31	26

NA = Not asked

SOURCE: Center for Political Studies of the Institute for Social Research, University of Michigan. Data were made available through the Inter-University Consortium for Political and Social Research.

How Are Political Opinions Formed?

An individual's opinions on particular issues, events, and personalities emerge as he or she evaluates these phenomena through the lenses of the beliefs and orientations that, taken together, comprise his or her political ideology. Thus, if a conservative is confronted with a plan to expand federal social programs, he or she is likely to express opposition to the endeavor without spending too much time pondering the specific plan. Similarly, if a liberal is asked to comment on former president Ronald Reagan, he or she is not likely to hesitate long before offering a negative view. Underlying beliefs and ideologies tend to automatically color people's perceptions and opinions about politics.

Opinions on particular issues, however, are seldom fully shaped by underlying ideologies. Few individuals possess ideologies so cohesive and intensely held that they will automatically shape all their opinions. Indeed, when we occasionally encounter individuals with rigid worldviews, who see everything through a particular political lens, we tend to dismiss them as "ideologues."

Although ideologies color our political perspectives, they seldom fully determine our views. This is true for a variety of reasons. First, as noted earlier, most individuals' ideologies contain internal contradictions. Take, for example, a conservative view of the issue of abortion. Should conservatives favor outlawing abortion as an appropriate means of preserving public morality, or should they oppose restrictions on abortion because these represent government intrusions into private life? In this instance, as in many others, ideology can point in different directions.

Second, individuals may have difficulty linking particular issues or personalities to their own underlying beliefs. Some issues defy ideological characterizations. Should conservatives support or oppose the proposed elimination of the Department of Commerce? What should liberals think about America's 1999 bombing of Serbia? Each of these policies combines a mix of issues and is too complex to be viewed through simple ideological lenses.

Finally, most people have at least some conflicting underlying attitudes. Most conservatives support *some* federal programs—defense, or tax deductions for businesses, for example—and wish to see them, and hence the government, expanded. Many liberals favor American military intervention in other nations for what they deem to be humanitarian purposes, but generally oppose American military intervention in the affairs of other nations.

Thus, most individuals' attitudes on particular issues do not spring automatically from their ideological predispositions. It is true that most people have underlying beliefs that help to shape their opinions on particular issues, but two other factors are also important: a person's knowledge of political issues and outside influences on that person's views.

Political Knowledge   As we have seen, general political beliefs can guide the formation of opinions on specific issues, but an individual's beliefs and opinions are not always consistent with one another. Studies of political opinion have shown that most people don't hold specific and clearly defined opinions on every political issue.[7] As a result, they are easily influenced by others. What best explains whether citizens are generally consistent in their political views or inconsistent and open to the influence of others? The key is knowledge and information about political issues. In general, knowledgeable citizens are better able to evaluate new information and determine whether it is relevant to and consistent with their beliefs and opinions. As a result, better-informed individuals can recognize their political interests and act consistently on behalf of them.

One of the most obvious and important examples of this proposition is voting. Despite the predisposition of voters to support their own party's candidates (see Chapter 11 for a discussion of party identification), millions of voters are affected by the information they receive about candidates during a campaign.

[7]John Zaller, *The Nature and Origins of Mass Opinion* (New York: Cambridge University Press, 1992).

During the 2000 presidential campaign, for instance, voters weighed the arguments of Al Gore against those of George W. Bush about who was better fit to run the U.S. economy based on what they (the voters) knew about the country's economic health. Many Republican voters actually supported Gore because they approved of his economic policies. Thus, citizens can use information and judgment to overcome their predispositions. Without some political knowledge, citizens would have a difficult time making sense of the complex political world in which they live.

This point brings up two questions, however. First, how much political knowledge is necessary to act as an effective citizen? And second, how is political knowledge distributed throughout the population? In a recent study of political knowledge in the United States, political scientists Michael X. Delli Carpini and Scott Keeter found that the average American exhibits little knowledge of political institutions, processes, leaders, and policy debates. For example, in a 1996 poll, only about half of all Americans could correctly identify Newt Gingrich, who was then the Speaker of the House of Representatives.[8] Does this ignorance of key political facts matter?

Another important concern is the character of those who possess and act upon the political information that they acquire. Political knowledge is not evenly distributed throughout the population. Those with higher education, income, and occupational status and who are members of social or political organizations are more likely to know about and be active in politics. An interest in politics reinforces an individual's sense of political efficacy and provides more incentive to acquire additional knowledge and information about politics. Those who don't think they can have an effect on government tend not to be interested in learning about or participating in politics. As a result, individuals with a disproportionate share of income and education also have a disproportionate share of knowledge and influence and are better able to get what they want from government.

The Influence of Political Leaders, Private Groups, and the Media   When individuals attempt to form opinions about particular political issues, events, and personalities, they seldom do so in isolation. Typically, they are confronted—sometimes bombarded—by the efforts of a host of individuals and groups seeking to persuade them to adopt a particular point of view. Someone trying to decide what to think about Bill Clinton, Al Gore, or George W. Bush could hardly avoid an avalanche of opinions expressed through the media, in meetings, or in conversations with friends. Given constant exposure to the ideas of others, it is virtually impossible for most individuals to resist some modification of their own beliefs. For example, African Americans and white Americans disagree on a number of matters. Yet, as political scientists Paul Sniderman and Edward Carmines have shown, considerable cross-racial agreement has evolved on fun-

[8]Michael X. Delli Carpini and Scott Keeter, *What Americans Know about Politics and Why It Matters* (New Haven: Yale University Press, 1996).

damental issues of race and civil rights.[9] Thus, to some extent, public opinion is subject to deliberate shaping and manipulation.

SHAPING PUBLIC OPINION

Public opinion is not some disembodied entity that stands alone and unalterable. Opinion can often be molded, shaped, or manipulated. In many areas of the world, governments determine which opinions their citizens may or may not express. People who assert views that their rulers do not approve of may be subject to imprisonment—or worse. Americans and the citizens of the other democracies are fortunate to live in nations where freedom of opinion and expression are generally taken for granted.

Even with freedom of opinion, however, not all ideas and opinions flourish. Both private groups and the government itself attempt to influence which opinions do take hold in the public imagination. We will first examine how government seeks to shape values that in turn influence public opinion. Then we will discuss the marketing of political issues by the government, by private groups, and by the media.

Enlisting Public Support for Government

All governments attempt to shape or structure citizens' underlying beliefs about the regime, the social and economic structure, and the political process. Governments seek to imbue their citizens with positive feelings toward the established order through the creation of a national ethos, the promotion of property ownership, education, and the opportunity to participate in national politics. Nationalism, property ownership, education, and political participation can be labeled "deadly virtues." These may be forces for good if they help to create a unified and public-spirited citizenry, or forces for evil if they are merely used as instruments of control.

Nationalism *Nationalism* is the belief that people who occupy the same territory have something important in common, making them separate from and superior to other people. It is based on myths about the origin and history of the people, their exploits and sufferings as a nation, their heroes, and their mission in the world. Such myths are not necessarily falsehoods. They are simply beliefs that are accepted whether they are true or false.

Nationalism takes root in family, community, and tribal loyalties, but it is strong enough to displace those local ties in favor of the nation. The great virtue of nationalism is precisely that it gives individuals something far larger than themselves with which to identify. It brings out nobility in people, calling on

nationalism
The widely held belief that the people who occupy the same territory have something in common, that the nation is a single community.

[9]Paul M. Sniderman and Edward G. Carmines, *Reaching Beyond Race* (Cambridge: Harvard University Press, 1997), Chapter 4.

them to sacrifice something—perhaps even their lives—for their society. Nationalism helps weave the social fabric together with a minimum of coercion. After September 11, many Americans clearly felt a new sense of nationalism as they flew flags from car windows and houses, volunteered to help in rescue efforts, and contributed hundreds of millions of dollars for relief efforts.

Nationalism also has a darker side, however. Since it encourages pride in one's own country, it can also produce distrust and hatred of others. This tendency is often encouraged by rulers as a means of whipping up support for a war or other international adventures. There will always be conflicts among nations, but these conflicts are much more likely to escalate toward full-scale war when each country is backed by strong national myths. The paramount example of the misuse of nationalism is the case of Nazi Germany, where nationalistic sentiment was perverted to justify aggression and murder on an unprecedented scale.

Private Property   Property ownership is probably a less universal factor in the manipulation of belief than nationalism, but that makes it no less important. Governments regard widespread property ownership to be a good, conservative force in society because it discourages disorder and revolution. The citizen who owns property has a stake in the existing order—a piece of the rock—which he or she will seek to protect.

Many important American leaders have dreamed of creating the ideal polity—political system—around property ownership. Thomas Jefferson, for example, believed that the American Republic ought to be composed of a population of farmers, each with enough property to appreciate social order and to oppose excessive wealth and power. Although the United States did not become a republic of farmers, this idea was certainly behind the federal government's nineteenth-century policy of giving millions of acres of land from the public treasury to persons who were willing to settle and improve it. ***Homesteading,*** or squatting, was the name for this method of gaining property ownership. It was justified—indeed encouraged—by the government in large part as a means of giving people a stake in their country.

Mass industrialization has expanded the meaning of property, but its value has not weakened. For most people, property is no longer a plot of land but instead is a mortgage on a house or a stock certificate that indicates ownership of a tiny proportion of some large corporation.

Education   In the United States, education is a multi-billion-dollar investment. Few people question the need for the investment because it promises to yield people with high-level skills, problem-solving capacity, and high productivity, along with a significant amount of social mobility. This is not to say that a formal education has helped every American child realize the ideal of success. But it does mean that education has made it possible for most children in America to join the workforce.

Formal schooling goes beyond skills and training, however. Schools shape values as well. Harry L. Gracey has described school as "academic boot camp."

homesteading
A national policy that permits people to gain ownership of property by occupying public or unclaimed lands, living on the land for a specified period of time, and making certain minimal improvements on that land. Also known as squatting.

He meant that beginning as early as kindergarten students learn "to go through the routines and to follow orders with unquestioning obedience, even when these make no sense to them. They learn to tolerate and even to prosper in the bureaucratized environment of school, and this is preparation for their later life."[10]

French sociologist Émile Durkheim (1858–1917) said essentially the same thing when he observed matter-of-factly that education "consists of a methodical socialization of the younger generation" and that the education process "is above all the means by which society perpetually recreates the conditions of its very existence."[11] This is usually done at the state and local government levels, where most educational policies in the United States are formulated. The schools themselves are capable of adjusting their curricula to the occupational needs of their region.

Participation and Co-optation   To participate means to share, or to take part in something. It is an association with others, usually for the purpose of taking joint action and is essential for any kind of democratic government. Even representation is not enough unless there is widespread participation in the choice of representatives. Virtually all political leaders endorse some types of participation, particularly voting.

Participation is an instrument of governance because it encourages people to give their consent to being governed. A broad and popularly based process of local consultation, discussion, town meetings, and secret ballots may actually produce a sense of the will of the people. But even when it does not produce a clear sense of that will, the purpose of participation is nonetheless fulfilled because the process itself produces consent. Deeply embedded in people's sense of fair play is the principle that those who play the game must accept the outcome. Those who participate in politics are similarly committed, even if they are consistently on the losing side. Why do politicians plead with everyone to get out and vote? Because voting is the simplest and easiest form of participation by masses of people. Even though it is minimal participation, it is sufficient to commit all voters to being governed, regardless of who wins. (Voting will be discussed in more detail in Chapter 10.)

There are many examples in recent American history of the use of participation to generate more favorable popular beliefs about the government. It is no coincidence, for example, that youths between the ages of eighteen and twenty-one were given the right to vote in the late 1960s just at a time when they were already participating at almost historic levels. Young people were politically active, but they were not participating in the conventional forms, and they were protesting against established authority. Congress and the state legislatures, therefore, ratified the Twenty-sixth Amendment in 1971, giving

[10]Harry L. Gracey, "Learning the Student Role: Kindergarten as Academic Boot Camp," in *The Quality of Life in America*, ed. A. David Hill (New York: Holt, 1973), p. 261.

[11]Émile Durkheim, *Education and Sociology*, trans. Sherwood D. Fox (Glencoe, IL: Free Press, 1956), p. 71.

eighteen-year-olds the right to vote. The vote was used to placate young Americans, to provide them with a conventional channel of participation, and to justify suppressing their disorderly activities. The following testimony by the late Senator Jacob Javits of New York is one example of the motivation behind the voting rights amendment:

> We all realize that only a tiny minority of college students on these campuses engaged in unlawful acts. But these deplorable incidents make a point. . . . I am convinced that self-styled student leaders who urged such acts of civil disobedience would find themselves with little or no support if students were given a more meaningful role in the political process. Passage of the [Twenty-sixth Amendment] . . . would give us the means, sort of the famous carrot and the stick, to channel this energy.[12]

The most familiar examples of co-optation through participation are the efforts of political leaders to balance their electoral tickets and their political appointments. Political party leaders in city, state, and national campaigns try their best to select candidates for public office who "represent" each of the important minorities in their constituency. This effort involves balancing ethnic, religious, and regional groups, as well as men and women and any other segments of the constituency. African American, Hispanic American, and women's movement leaders study presidential appointments with considerable interest. They do this not so much because an additional black or Hispanic or female representative would give them much more power but because such appointments are a measure of their current worth in national politics.

Nationalism, property ownership, education, and participation are used by all governments to bolster popular support for leaders and their policies. Through these four mechanisms, governments seek to give their citizens a more positive orientation toward the political and social order, regardless of their attitudes toward specific programs. Through these techniques, governments hope to convince their citizens voluntarily to obey laws, pay taxes, and serve in the armed forces. Many social scientists believe that if popular support falls below some minimum level, the result could be chaos or even some form of rebellion. This fear was especially manifest during the 1960s and 1970s when diminished levels of popular support did indeed coincide with increases in political violence and unrest. Trust in government edged up slightly during the 1980s, dropped again in the early 1990s, and rose during the mid- and late 1990s (see Figure 9.2). After September 11, trust in government rose sharply, but only time will tell whether this increase reflected *trust* or *hope*.

---

[12]U.S. Senate, Committee on the Judiciary, *Hearings before the Subcommittee on Constitutional Amendments on S.J. Res. 8, S.J. Res. 14, and S. J. Res. 78 Relating to Lowering the Voting Age to 18*, 14, 15, and 16 May 1968 (Washington, DC: Government Printing Office, 1968), p. 12.

FIGURE 9.2

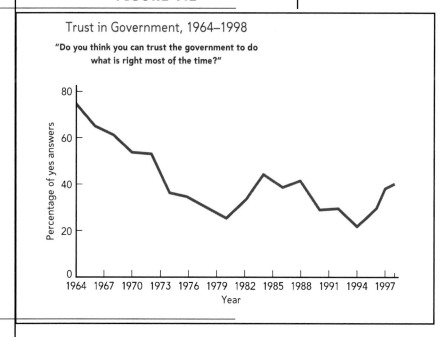

Trust in Government, 1964–1998

"Do you think you can trust the government to do
what is right most of the time?"

SOURCE: The National Election Studies, 13 September 1999, Graph 5A.1.2.

Marketing Political Issues

Beyond these broad efforts by the government to shape popular attachments to
the political regime, both the government and private groups attempt to muster
support for different political ideas and programs. Both use public relations to
enlist support and shape opinion.

Few ideas spread spontaneously. Usually, whether they are matters of fashion, science, or politics, ideas must be vigorously promoted to become widely
known and accepted. For example, the clothing, sports, and entertainment fads
that occasionally seem to appear from nowhere and sweep the country before
being replaced by some other new trend are almost always the product of careful
marketing campaigns by one or another commercial interest, rather than spontaneous phenomena. Even in the sciences, generally considered *the* bastions of
objectivity, new theories, procedures, and findings are not always accepted simply and immediately on their own merit. Often, the proponents of a new scientific principle or practice must campaign within the scientific community on
behalf of their views. Like their counterparts in fashion and science, successful—or at least widely held—political ideas are usually the products of carefully
orchestrated campaigns by government or by organized groups and interests,
rather than the results of spontaneous popular enthusiasm.

**Collective
Action
Principle**

Widely held political
ideas are usually the
products of orches-
trated campaigns
by government, orga-
nized groups, or
the media.

Government Management of Issues   All governments attempt, to a greater or lesser extent, to influence, manipulate, or manage their citizens' beliefs. In the United States, some efforts have been made by every administration since the nation's founding to influence public sentiment. But efforts to shape opinion did not become a routine and formal official function until World War I, when the Wilson administration created a censorship board, enacted sedition and espionage legislation, and attempted to suppress groups that opposed the war, like the International Workers of the World (IWW) and the Socialist party. Eugene Debs, a prominent Socialist and presidential candidate, was arrested and convicted of having violated the Espionage Law, and he was sentenced to ten years in prison for delivering a speech that defended the IWW.

At the same time, however, World War I was the first modern industrial war requiring a total mobilization of popular effort on the home front for military production. The war effort required the government to persuade the civilian population to bear the costs and make the sacrifices needed to achieve industrial and agricultural, as well as battlefield, success. The chief mechanism for eliciting the support of public opinion was the Committee on Public Information (CPI), chaired by journalist and publicist George Creel. The CPI organized a massive public relations and news management program to promote popular enthusiasm for the war effort. This program included the dissemination of favorable news, the publication of patriotic pamphlets, films, photos, cartoons, bulletins, and periodicals, and the organization of "war expositions" and speakers' tours. Special labor programs were aimed at maintaining the loyalty and productivity of the workforce. Many of the CPI's staff were drawn from the major public relations firms of the time.[13]

The extent to which public opinion is actually affected by governmental public relations efforts is probably limited. The government—despite its size and power—is only one source of information and evaluation in the United States. Very often, governmental claims are disputed by the media, by interest groups, and at times, by opposing forces within the government itself. Often, too, governmental efforts to manipulate public opinion backfire when the public is made aware of the government's tactics. Thus, in 1971, the United States government's efforts to build popular support for the Vietnam War were hurt when CBS News aired its documentary "The Selling of the Pentagon," which purported to reveal the extent and character of governmental efforts to sway popular sentiment. In this documentary, CBS demonstrated the techniques, including planted news stories and faked film footage, that the government had used to misrepresent its activities in Vietnam. These revelations, of course, had the effect of undermining popular trust in all governmental claims. During the 1991 Persian Gulf War, the U.S. military was much more careful about the accuracy of its assertions.

A hallmark of the Clinton administration was the steady use of techniques like those used in election campaigns to bolster popular enthusiasm for White

[13]See George Creel, *How We Advertised America* (New York: Harper and Brothers, 1920).

House initiatives. The president established a "political war room" in the Executive Office Building similar to the one that operated in his campaign headquarters. Representatives from all departments met in the war room every day to discuss and coordinate the president's public relations efforts. Many of the same consultants and pollsters who directed the successful Clinton campaign were employed in the selling of the president's programs.[14]

Indeed, the Clinton White House made more sustained and systematic use of public-opinion polling than any previous administration. For example, during his presidency Bill Clinton relied heavily on the polling firm of Penn & Schoen to help him decide which issues to emphasize and what strategies to adopt. During the 1995–1996 budget battle with Congress, the White House commissioned polls almost every night to chart changes in public perceptions about the struggle. Poll data suggested to Clinton that he should present himself as struggling to save Medicare from Republican cuts. Clinton responded by launching a media attack against what he claimed were GOP efforts to hurt the elderly. This proved to be a successful strategy and helped Clinton defeat the Republican budget.[15] The administration, however, asserted that it used polls only as a check on its communications strategy.[16]

Evidence exists to back up the assertions of the Clinton White House. The political scientists Robert Shapiro and Lawrence Jacobs studied how polls are used by politicians and discovered that the ideology of political leaders, not public opinion, was the decisive influence on the formulation of a policy. They also found that the primary use of polling was to choose the language, rhetoric, and arguments for policy proposals in order to build the public's support.[17] However, according to former Clinton adviser Dick Morris, the president met every week with key aides to examine poll data and devise strategies to bolster his popularity.[18] For example, in April 1996, the administration's polls showed that an initiative to crack down on "deadbeat dads" who failed to pay child support would be popular. Several weeks later, the president announced new regulations requiring states to take more aggressive action to compel payment. Similarly, in July 1996, Clinton signed the Republican-sponsored welfare reform bill which he had previously opposed, when polls indicated that he would gain 8 points in the polls if he signed the bill.[19]

Of course, at the same time that the Clinton administration worked diligently to mobilize popular support, its opponents struggled equally hard to mobilize popular opinion against the White House. A host of public and private interest

[14]Gerald F. Seib and Michael K. Frisby, "Selling Sacrifice," *Wall Street Journal*, 5 February 1993, p. 1.

[15]Michael K. Frisby, "Clinton Seeks Strategic Edge with Opinion Polls," *Wall Street Journal*, 24 June 1996, p. A16.

[16]James Carney, "Playing by the Numbers," *Time*, 11 April 1994, p. 40.

[17]Reported in Richard Morin, "Which Comes First, the Politician or the Poll?" *Washington Post National Weekly Edition*, 10 February 1997, p. 31.

[18]John F. Harris, "New Morris Book Portrays How Polls, Clinton, Intersected," *Washington Post*, 22 December 1998, p. A18.

[19]Dick Morris, *Behind the Oval Office* (New York: Renaissance, 1998).

groups opposed to President Clinton's programs crafted public relations campaigns designed to generate opposition to the president. For example, in 1994, while Clinton campaigned to bolster popular support for his health care reform proposals, groups representing small business and segments of the insurance industry, among others, developed their own publicity campaigns that ultimately convinced many Americans that Clinton's initiative posed a threat to their own health care. These opposition campaigns played an important role in the eventual defeat of the president's proposal. After he assumed office in 2001, President George W. Bush also began making some use of poll data to help shape his own policy agendas. The Bush White House's extensive public relations program was instrumental in coordinating efforts to maintain popular support for the war against terrorism.

Often, claims and counterclaims by the government and its opponents are aimed chiefly at elites and opinion makers rather than directly at the public. For example, many of the television ads about the health care debate were aired primarily in and around Washington and New York City, where they were more likely to be seen by persons influential in politics, business, and the media. The presumption behind this strategy is that such individuals are likely to be the key decision makers on most issues. Political, business, and media elites are also seen as "opinion leaders" who have the capacity to sway the views of larger segments of the public.

Private Groups and the Shaping of Public Opinion   Political issues and ideas seldom emerge spontaneously from the grass roots. We have already seen how the government tries to shape public opinion. But the ideas that become prominent in political life are also developed and spread by important economic and political groups searching for issues that will advance their causes. One example is the "right-to-life" issue that has inflamed American politics over the past twenty years.

The notion of right-to-life, whose proponents seek to outlaw abortion and overturn the Supreme Court's *Roe v. Wade* decision, was developed and heavily promoted by conservative politicians who saw the issue of abortion as a means of uniting Catholic and Protestant conservatives and linking both groups to the Republican coalition. These politicians convinced Catholic and evangelical Protestant leaders that they shared similar views on the question of abortion, and they worked with religious leaders to focus public attention on the negative issues in the abortion debate. To advance their cause, leaders of the movement sponsored well-publicized Senate hearings, where testimony, photographs, and other exhibits were presented to illustrate the violent effects of abortion procedures. At the same time, publicists for the movement produced leaflets, articles, books, and films such as *The Silent Scream*, to highlight the agony and pain ostensibly felt by the unborn when they were being aborted. All of this underscored the movement's claim that abortion was nothing more or less than the murder of millions of innocent human beings. Finally, Catholic and evangelical Protestant religious leaders were organized to denounce abortion from their church pulpits and increasingly, from their electronic pulpits on the Christian

Broadcasting Network (CBN) and the various other television forums available for religious programming. Religious leaders also organized demonstrations, pickets, and disruptions at abortion clinics throughout the nation.[20] Abortion rights remains a potent issue; it even influenced the health care reform debate.

Among President Clinton's most virulent critics were leaders of the religious Right who were outraged by his support for abortion and gay rights. Conservative religious leaders like the Rev. Jerry Falwell and Pat Robertson, leader of the Christian Coalition, used their television programs to attack the president's programs and to mount biting personal attacks on both Clinton and his wife, Hillary Rodham Clinton. Other conservative groups not associated with the religious Right also launched sharp assaults against Clinton. The nationally syndicated talk-show host Rush Limbaugh, for one, was a constant critic of the administration. All these leaders and groups strongly supported Clinton's impeachment in 1998 and 1999. Despite their efforts, however, they were unable to convince a majority of Americans that the president should be removed from office. President Bush, of course, was generally praised by conservatives for his opposition to abortion but castigated by liberal groups. Liberals declared Bush's election to be lacking in legitimacy and launched a strong, albeit unsuccessful, effort to prevent Bush from naming Senator John Ashcroft to the position of attorney general. Ashcroft was known for holding conservative views on many social issues and, especially, for his opposition to abortion.

Typically, ideas are marketed most effectively by groups with access to financial resources, public or private institutional support, and sufficient skill or education to select, develop, and draft ideas that will attract interest and support. Thus, the development and promotion of conservative themes and ideas in recent years has been greatly facilitated by the millions of dollars that conservative corporations and business organizations such as the Chamber of Commerce and the Public Affairs Council spend each year on public information and what is now called in corporate circles "issues management." In addition, conservative businessmen have contributed millions of dollars to such conservative institutions as the Heritage Foundation, the Hoover Institution, and the American Enterprise Institute.[21] Many of the ideas that helped those on the right influence political debate were first developed and articulated by scholars associated with institutions such as these. For example, in 1997, scholars associated with the conservative Hudson Institute developed the idea of organizing conservative Christians to protest the alleged mistreatment of Christians in the Third World, China, and the former Soviet Union. This issue, which gave rise to congressional legislation aimed at limiting American trade with nations deemed to mistreat Christians, provided a useful focus for political mobilization on the political Right.

---

[20]See Gillian Peele, *Revival and Reaction* (Oxford, England: Clarendon Press, 1985). Also see Connie Paige, *The Right to Lifers* (New York: Summit, 1983).

[21]See David Vogel, "The Power of Business in America: A Reappraisal," *British Journal of Political Science* 13 (January 1983), pp. 19–44.

Although they do not usually have access to financial assets that match those available to their conservative opponents, liberal intellectuals and professionals have ample organizational skills, access to the media, and practice in creating, communicating, and using ideas. During the past three decades, the chief vehicle through which liberal intellectuals and professionals have advanced their ideas has been the "public interest group," an institution that relies heavily upon voluntary contributions of time, effort, and interest on the part of its members. Through groups like Common Cause, the National Organization for Women, the Sierra Club, Friends of the Earth, and Physicians for Social Responsibility, intellectuals and professionals have been able to use their organizational skills and educational resources to develop and promote ideas.[22] Often, research conducted in universities and in liberal "think tanks" like the Brookings Institution provides the ideas upon which liberal politicians rely. For example, the welfare reform plan introduced by the Clinton administration in 1994 originated with the work of Harvard professor David Ellwood. Ellwood's academic research led him to the idea that the nation's welfare system would be improved if services to the poor were expanded in scope, but limited in duration. His idea was adopted by the 1992 Clinton campaign, which was searching for a position on welfare that would appeal to both liberal and conservative Democrats. The Ellwood plan seemed perfect: it promised liberals an immediate expansion of welfare benefits, yet it held out to conservatives the idea that welfare recipients would receive benefits only for a limited period of time. The Clinton welfare reform plan even borrowed phrases from Ellwood's book *Poor Support*.[23]

Journalist and author Joe Queenan has correctly observed that although political ideas can erupt spontaneously, they almost never do. Instead,

> issues are usually manufactured by tenured professors and obscure employees of think tanks. . . . It is inconceivable that the American people, all by themselves, could independently arrive at the conclusion that the depletion of the ozone layer poses a dire threat to our national well-being, or that an immediate, across-the-board cut in the capital-gains tax is the only thing that stands between us and the economic abyss. The American people do not have that kind of sophistication. *They have to have help.*[24]

Whatever their particular ideology or interest, those groups that can muster the most substantial financial, institutional, educational, and organizational resources—or, as we shall see later, access to government power—are also best able to promote their ideas in the marketplace. Obviously, these resources are most readily available to upper-middle- and upper-class groups. As a result,

[22]See David Vogel, "The Public Interest Movement and the American Reform Tradition," *Political Science Quarterly* 96 (Winter 1980), pp. 607–27.

[23]Jason DeParle, "The Clinton Welfare Bill Begins Trek in Congress," *New York Times*, 15 July 1994, p. 1.

[24]Joe Queenan, "Birth of a Notion," *Washington Post*, 20 September 1992, p. C1.

their ideas and concerns are most likely to be discussed and disseminated by books, films, newspapers, magazines, and the electronic media. As we shall see in Chapter 13, upper-income groups dominate the marketplace of ideas, not only as producers and promoters, but also as consumers of ideas. In general, and particularly in the political realm, the print and broadcast media and the publishing industry are most responsive to the tastes and views of the more "upscale" segments of the potential audience.

The Media and Public Opinion   The communications media are among the most powerful forces operating in the marketplace of ideas. The mass media are not simply neutral messengers for ideas developed by others. Instead, the media have an enormous impact on popular attitudes and opinions. Over time, the ways in which the mass media report political events help to shape the underlying attitudes and beliefs from which opinions emerge.[25] For example, for the past thirty years, the national news media have relentlessly investigated personal and official wrongdoing on the part of politicians and public officials. This continual media presentation of corruption in government and venality in politics has undoubtedly fostered the general attitude of cynicism and distrust that exists in the general public.

At the same time, the ways in which media coverage interprets or frames specific events can have a major impact on popular responses and opinions about these events.[26] As we shall see in Chapter 13, the media presented the 1996 budget battle between President Clinton and then-Speaker of the House Newt Gingrich in a way that served Clinton's interests. By forcing the closing of a number of government agencies, Gingrich hoped that the media would point out how smoothly life could proceed with less government involvement. Instead, the media focused on the hardships the closings inflicted on out-of-work government employees in the months before Christmas. The way in which the media framed the discussion helped turn opinion against Gingrich and handed Clinton an important victory.

MEASURING PUBLIC OPINION

As recently as fifty years ago, American political leaders gauged public opinion by people's applause or cheers and by the presence of crowds in meeting places. This direct exposure to the people's views did not necessarily produce accurate knowledge of public opinion. It did, however, give political leaders confidence in their public support—and therefore confidence in their ability to govern by consent.

[25]Zaller, *The Nature and Origins of Mass Opinion.*
[26]See Shanto Iyengar, *Is Anyone Responsible? How Television Frames Political Issues* (Chicago: University of Chicago Press, 1991); and Shanto Iyengar, *Do the Media Govern?* (Thousand Oaks, CA: Sage, 1997).

Abraham Lincoln and Stephen Douglas debated each other seven times in the summer and autumn of 1858, two years before they became presidential nominees. Their debates took place before audiences in parched cornfields and courthouse squares. A century later, the presidential debates, although seen by millions, take place before a few reporters and technicians in television studios that might as well be on the moon. The public's response cannot be experienced directly. This distance between leaders and followers is one of the agonizing problems of modern democracy. The communication media send information to millions of people, but they are not yet as efficient at getting information back to leaders. Is government by consent possible where the scale of communication is so large and impersonal? In order to compensate for the decline in their ability to experience public opinion for themselves, leaders have turned to science, in particular to the science of opinion polling.

It is no secret that politicians and public officials make extensive use of public opinion polls to help them decide whether to run for office, what policies to support, how to vote on important legislation, and what types of appeals to make in their campaigns. President Lyndon Johnson was famous for carrying the latest Gallup and Roper poll results in his hip pocket, and it is widely believed that he began to withdraw from politics because the polls reported losses in public support. All recent presidents and other major political figures have worked closely with polls and pollsters. Yet, even the most scientific measurements of public opinion do not necessarily lighten the burden of ignorance.

Getting Public Opinion Directly from People

American politicians want rapport with the people; they want to mingle, to shake hands, to get the feel of the crowd. And where crowds are too large to experience directly, the substitutes also have to be more direct than those described up to this point.

Approaches to the direct measurement of public opinion can be divided conveniently into two types—the impressionistic and the scientific. The impressionistic approach can be subdivided into at least three methods—person-to-person, selective polling, and the use of bellwether districts. The scientific approach may take on several different forms, but they all amount to an effort to use random sampling techniques and established and psychologically validated survey questions.

Person-to-Person   Politicians traditionally acquire knowledge about opinions through direct exposure to a few people's personal impressions—the person-to-person approach. They attempt to convert these impressions into reliable knowledge by intuition. When they are in doubt about first impressions, they seek further impressions from other people; but the individuals they rely on the most heavily are their friends and acquaintances. Presidents have usually relied on associates for political impressions. These few friends occupy an inner circle, and they give political advice after the experts and special leaders have finished.

The advantage of the person-to-person approach is that it is quick, efficient, and inexpensive. Its major disadvantage is that it can close off unpleasant information or limit the awareness of new issues. Franklin Roosevelt, for example, was one of the best-informed presidents, and yet, when he attempted to influence the Supreme Court by increasing the number of justices on it and when he attempted to punish some of the opposition leaders in Congress by opposing their renomination in local primaries, he was shocked by the degree of negative public reaction. His inner circle had simply lost touch with the post-1936 electorate.

President Nixon's downfall from the Watergate scandal has been attributed in part to the fact that he isolated himself in the White House and relied too heavily on a few close personal advisers. Consequently, it is argued, he was unaware first of the strength of his own position as he approached the 1972 re-election campaign and then to the extent to which his political position had deteriorated because of the scandal.

Selective Polling   When politicians lack confidence in their own intuition or that of their immediate associates, and especially when they distrust the reports they get from group advocates, they turn to rudimentary forms of polling. They may informally interview a few ordinary citizens from each of the major religious faiths or from different occupations in an effort to construct a meaningful distribution of opinions in a constituency. Many politicians have been successful with such impressionistic methods (although skeptics attribute their success to luck). Moreover, these politicians have used more systematic approaches as soon as they could afford to.

Newspapers have followed suit. Not too long ago, the top journalists on major newspapers, such as the *New York Times*, based many of their political articles on selective, impressionistic polling. But in recent years, their newspapers have, at great expense, become clients of Gallup, Roper, and other large scientific polling organizations. Some media organizations have even joined forces to produce their own polls. The *New York Times*/CBS News poll is one example.

Bellwether Districts   The bellwether originally was the lead sheep of a flock, on whose neck a bell was hung. The term now refers generally to something that is used as an indicator of where a group is heading. A *bellwether district* or town is assumed to be a good predictor of the attitudes of large segments of the national population. Maine was once an important bellwether state for forecasting national elections (and therefore for plotting national campaign strategies). The old saying "As Maine goes, so goes the nation" was based on two facts. First, the distribution of Maine's votes for presidential candidates was often like that of the national popular two-party votes. Second, for many years, the wintry state of Maine held its general election in September rather than November, which provided a meaningful opportunity for forecasting. (Because Maine now holds its election in November like the rest of the states, it is no longer a good bellwether.)

bellwether district A town or district that is a microcosm of the whole population or that has been found to be a good predictor of electoral outcomes.

The use of bellwether districts has been brought to greater and greater levels of precision in the past two decades because of advances in methods used by television networks. The three major networks have developed elaborate computerized techniques to predict the outcomes of elections within minutes after the polls close. The networks' news staffs spend months prior to election day selecting important districts—especially districts on the East Coast, where the polls close an hour to three hours earlier than in the rest of the country, thereby giving the forecasters a head start. They enter into a large computer the voting history of the selected districts, along with information about the opinions and the economic and social characteristics of the residents. As the voting results flow in from these districts on election night, the computer quickly compares them with prior elections and with other districts in the country in order to make fairly precise predictions about the outcome of the current election.

The commercial and political interests that rely on bellwether district methods closely guard the exact information they plug into the computer and the exact methods of weighing and comparing results in order to make their forecasts. It is nevertheless possible to evaluate the contributions this approach makes to political knowledge. First, the bellwether method is useful when there is an election involving a limited number of candidates. Second, it tends to work well only when the analysis takes place close to the actual day of the election. Third, the lasting knowledge to be gained from it is limited. No matter how accurately the bellwether district method forecasts elections, it is not particularly useful for stating what opinions people are holding, how consistently and with what intensity they hold opinions on various issues, why they hold these opinions, and how their opinions might be changing.

Constructing Public Opinion from Surveys

The population in which pollsters are interested is usually quite large. To conduct their polls they choose a sample from the total population. The selection of this sample is important. Above all, it must be representative; the views of those in the sample must accurately and proportionately reflect the views of the whole. To a large extent, the validity of the poll's results depends on the sampling procedure used, several of which are described below.

Quota sampling is the method used by most commercial polls. In this approach, respondents are selected whose characteristics closely match those of the general population along several significant dimensions, such as geographic region, sex, age, and race.

Probability sampling is the most accurate polling technique. By definition, this method requires that every individual in the population must have a known (usually equal) probability of being chosen as a respondent so that the researcher can give equal weight to all segments of society. A requirement, then, is a complete list of the population or a breakdown of the total population by cities

quota sampling A type of sampling of public opinion that is used by most commercial polls. Respondents are selected whose characteristics closely match those of the general population along several significant dimensions, such as geographic region, sex, age, and race.

probability sampling A method used by pollsters to select a sample in which every individual in the population has a known (usually equal) probability of being selected as a respondent so that the correct weight can be given to all segments of the population.

and counties. The simplest methods of obtaining a probability sample are **systematic sampling,** choosing every ninth name from a list, for instance, and **random sampling,** drawing from a container whose contents have been thoroughly mixed. This latter method, of course, can be simulated by computer-generated random numbers. Both quota sampling and probability sampling are best suited for polls of small populations.

For polls of large cities, states, or the whole nation, the method usually employed when a high level of accuracy is desired is **area sampling.** This technique breaks the population down into small, homogeneous units, such as counties. Several of these units are then randomly selected to serve as the sample. These units are, in turn, broken down into even smaller units. The process may extend even to individual dwellings on randomly selected blocks, for example. Area sampling is very costly and generally used only by academic survey researchers.

Some types of sampling do not yield representative samples and so have no scientific value. **Haphazard sampling,** for instance, is an unsystematic choice of respondents. A reporter who stands on a street corner and asks questions of convenient passersby is engaging in haphazard sampling. Systematically biased sampling occurs when an error in technique destroys the representative nature of the sample. A systematic error, for example, may cause a sample to include too many old people, too many college students, or too few minority group members.

Even with reliable sampling procedures, problems can occur. Validity can be adversely affected by poor question format, faulty ordering of questions, inappropriate vocabulary, ambiguity of questions, or questions with built-in biases. In some instances, bias may be intentional. Polls conducted on behalf of interest groups or political candidates are often designed to allow the sponsors of the poll to claim that they have the support of the American people.[27] Occasionally, respondents and pollsters may have very different conceptions of the meaning of the words used in a question. For example, an early Gallup poll that asked people if they owned any stock found that stock ownership in the Southwest was surprisingly high. It turned out that many of the respondents thought "stock" meant cows and horses rather than securities.[28] Often, apparently minor differences in the wording of a question can convey vastly different meanings to respondents and, thus, produce quite different response patterns. For example, for many years the University of Chicago's National Opinion Research Center has asked respondents whether they think the federal government is spending too much, too little, or about the right amount of money on "assistance for the poor." Answering the question posed this way, about two-thirds of all respondents seem to believe that the government is spending too little. However, the same survey also asks whether the government spends too much, too little, or about the right amount for "welfare." When the word "welfare" is substituted

systematic sampling A method used in probability sampling to ensure that every individual in the population has a known probability of being chosen as a respondent; for example, by choosing every ninth name from a list.

random sampling Polls in which respondents are chosen mathematically, at random, with every effort made to avoid bias in the construction of the sample.

area sampling A polling technique used for large cities, states, or the whole nation, when a high level of accuracy is desired. The population is broken down into small, homogeneous units, such as counties; then several units are randomly selected to serve as the sample.

haphazard sampling A type of sampling of public opinion that is an unsystematic choice of respondents.

---

[27]August Gribbin, "Two Key Questions in Assessing Polls: 'How?' and 'Why?'" *Washington Times*, 19 October 1998, p. A10.

[28]Charles W. Roll and Albert H. Cantril, *Polls* (New York: Basic Books, 1972), p. 106.

for "assistance for the poor," about half of all respondents indicate that too much is being spent by the government.[29]

In a similar vein, what seemed to be a minor difference in wording in two December 1998 *New York Times* survey questions on presidential impeachment produced vastly different results. The first question asked respondents, "If the full House votes to send impeachment articles to the Senate for a trial, then do you think it would be better for the country if Bill Clinton resigned from office, or not?" The second version of the question asked, "If the full House votes to impeach Bill Clinton, then do you think it would be better for the country if Bill Clinton resigned from office, or not?" Though the two questions seem almost identical, 43 percent of those responding to the first version said the president should resign, while 60 percent of those responding to the second version of the question said Clinton should resign.[30]

push polling
Polling technique that is designed to shape the respondent's opinion. For example, "If you knew that Candidate X was an adulterer, would you support his election?"

In recent years, a new form of bias has been introduced into surveys by the use of a technique called *push polling.* This technique involves asking a respondent a loaded question about a political candidate designed to elicit the response sought by the pollster and, simultaneously, to shape the respondent's perception of the candidate in question. For example, during the 1996 New Hampshire presidential primary, push pollsters employed by Lamar Alexander's rival campaign called thousands of voters to ask, "If you knew that Lamar Alexander had raised taxes six times in Tennessee, would you be less inclined or more inclined to support him?"[31] More than one hundred consulting firms across the nation now specialize in push polling.[32] Calling push polling the "political equivalent of a drive-by shooting," Representative Joe Barton (R-Tex.) launched a congressional investigation into the practice.[33] Push polls may be one reason that Americans are becoming increasingly skeptical about the practice of polling and increasingly unwilling to answer pollsters' questions.[34]

Sample Size The degree of precision in polling is a function of sample size, not population size. Just as large a sample is needed to represent a small population as to represent a large population. The typical size of a sample is from 450 to 1,500 respondents. This number, however, reflects a trade-off between cost and degree of precision desired. The degree of accuracy that can be achieved with a small sample can be seen from the polls' success in predicting election outcomes.

---

[29]Michael Kagay and Janet Elder, "Numbers Are No Problem for Pollsters. Words Are," *New York Times*, 9 August 1992, p. E6.

[30]Richard Morin, "Choice Words," *Washington Post*, 10 January 1999, p. C1.

[31]Donn Tibbetts, "Draft Bill Requires Notice of Push Polling," *Manchester Union Leader*, 3 October 1996, p. A6.

[32]"Dial S for Smear," *Memphis Commercial Appeal*, 22 September 1996, p. 6B.

[33]Amy Keller, "Subcommittee Launches Investigation of Push Polls," *Roll Call*, 3 October 1996, p. 1.

[34]For a discussion of the growing difficulty of persuading people to respond to surveys, see John Brehm, *Phantom Respondents* (Ann Arbor: University of Michigan Press, 1993).

Table 9.2 shows how accurate two of the major national polling organizations have been in predicting the outcomes of presidential elections. In only two instances between 1952 and 2000 did the final October poll of a major pollster predict the wrong outcome, and in both instances—Harris in 1968 and Gallup in 1976—the actual election was extremely close and the prediction was off by no more than two percentage points. In 2000, Gallup predicted a Bush victory, and so was technically correct, but Gore received more votes. Even in 1948, when the pollsters were deeply embarrassed by their almost uniform prediction of a Dewey victory over Truman, they were not off by much. For example, Gallup predicted 44.5 percent for Truman, who actually received 49.6 percent. Although Gallup's failure to predict the winner was embarrassing, its actual percentage error would not be considered large by most statisticians.

Since 1948, Gallup has averaged a difference of less than 1 percent between what it predicts and the actual election outcome—and all its predictions have been made on the basis of random samples of not more than 2,500 respondents. In light of a national voting population of more than 100 million, these estimates are impressive.

This ability to predict elections by projecting estimates from small samples to enormous populations validates the methods used in sample survey studies of public opinion: the principles of random sampling, the methods of interviewing, and the statistical tests and computer programming used in data analysis. It also validates the model of behavior by which social scientists attempt to predict voting behavior on the basis of respondents' characteristics rather than on the basis of only their stated intentions. This model of behavior is built on the respondent's voting intention and includes data on (1) the influence of the respondent's place in the social structure, (2) the influence of habit and previous party loyalty, (3) the influence of particular issues for each election, (4) the direction and strength of the respondent's general ideology, and (5) the respondent's occupational and educational background, income level, and so on. Each of these characteristics is treated as a variable in an equation leading to a choice among the major candidates in the election. The influence of the variables, or correlates, is far greater than most respondents realize.

Polling Errors   The polls are accurate but not infallible. In 1996, some major polls were quite wrong in their predictions of the popular vote divisions in both the presidential and congressional races. For example, the *New York Times*/CBS News poll taken two days before the election predicted that Clinton would defeat Dole by a 53 to 35 percent margin (the actual margin was 49 to 41 percent). Similarly, most polls predicted that Democratic House candidates would defeat their GOP rivals by a margin of ten points on a national basis. On Election Day, however, Republican candidates out-polled the Democrats. The most striking polling error made in 1996 occurred in New Hampshire, where exit polls showed Democratic senatorial candidate Dick Swett defeating Republican senator Bob Smith by a solid 52 to 47 percent. Smith assumed he had lost until early the next

TABLE 9.2

Two Pollsters and Their Records (1948–2000)

		HARRIS	GALLUP	ACTUAL OUTCOME
2000	Bush	47%	48%	48%
	Gore	47	46	49
	Nader	5	4	3
1996	Clinton	51%	52%	49%
	Dole	39	41	41
	Perot	9	7	8
1992	Clinton	44%	44%	43%
	Bush	38	37	38
	Perot	17	14	19
1988	Bush	51%	53%	54%
	Dukakis	47	42	46
1984	Reagan	56%	59%	59%
	Mondale	44	41	41
1980	Reagan	48%	47%	51%
	Carter	43	44	41
	Anderson		8	
1976	Carter	48%	48%	51%
	Ford	45	49	48
1972	Nixon	59%	62%	61%
	McGovern	35	38	38
1968	Nixon	40%	43%	43%
	Humphrey	43	42	43
	G. Wallace	13	15	14
1964	Johnson	62%	64%	61%
	Goldwater	33	36	39
1960	Kennedy	49%	51%	50%
	Nixon	41	49	49
1956	Eisenhower	NA	60%	58%
	Stevenson		41	42
1952	Eisenhower	47%	51%	55%
	Stevenson	42	49	44
1948	Truman	NA	44.5%	49.6%
	Dewey		49.5	45.1

All figures except those for 1948 are rounded. NA = Not asked

SOURCES: Data from the Gallup Poll and the Harris Survey (New York: Chicago Tribune-New York News Syndicate, various press releases, 1964–2000). Courtesy of the Gallup Organization and Louis Harris Associates.

morning when actual election results gave him a narrow victory. Some analysts believe that these poll errors are a subtle form of "liberal bias." Since voters often feel that the media have a liberal and Democratic slant, individuals who support the Republicans are slightly more reluctant to confess their true preferences to interviewers. Indications of this phenomenon have appeared in a number of Western democracies whose major media are deemed to be liberal in their political orientation.[35]

In 1998, Jesse Ventura's victory in the Minnesota gubernatorial election totally confounded the pollsters and revealed another weakness of pre-election polling. A poll conducted by the *Minneapolis Star Tribune* just six weeks before the election showed Ventura running a distant third to Democratic candidate Hubert Humphrey III, who seemed to have the support of 49 percent of the electorate, and the Republican Norm Coleman, whose support stood at 29 percent. Only 10 percent of those polled said they were planning to vote for Ventura. On Election Day, of course, Ventura out-polled both Humphrey and Coleman. Analysis of exit-poll data showed why the pre-election polls had been so wrong. In an effort to be more accurate, pre-election pollsters' predictions often take account of the likelihood that respondents will actually vote. This is accomplished by polling only people who have voted in the past or correcting for past frequency of voting. The *Star Tribune* poll was conducted only among individuals who had voted in the previous election. Ventura, however, brought to the polls not only individuals who had not voted in the last election but many people who had never voted before in their lives. Twelve percent of Minnesota's voters in 1998 said they came to the polls only because Ventura was on the ballot. This surge in turnout was facilitated by the fact that Minnesota permits same-day voter registration. Thus, the pollsters were wrong because Ventura changed the composition of the electorate.[36]

In 2000, the use of daily tracking polls by the major news organizations provided a picture of day-to-day shifts in the electorate's mood. The polls revealed that many voters—nearly 10 percent of the electorate—remained undecided until Election Day. This high level of indecision apparently resulted from voters' lack of enthusiasm for both major party candidates. In the end, the tracking polls proved misleading. Most polling organizations seemed to show a narrow lead for Bush up until Election Day, but when the actual votes were counted, Gore won a razor-thin popular plurality.

Interestingly, network exit polls also led to a major error on election night. After Florida polls closed, television networks declared Gore the winner in Florida on the basis of exit-poll results. Two hours later, the networks revised their estimates on the basis of actual vote counts and declared Florida too close to call. Furious Republicans asserted that the pollsters' errors might have

---

[35]Michael Barone, "Why Opinion Polls Are Worth Less," *U.S. News & World Report*, 9 December 1996, p. 52.

[36]Carl Cannon, "A Pox on Both Our Parties," in David C. Canon et. al., eds., *The Enduring Debate* (New York: Norton, 2000), p. 389.

persuaded GOP supporters that the race was hopeless and discouraged voting on the part of Republicans in western states where polls were still open. At 2 A.M., the networks proclaimed Bush the winner in Florida and, as a result, of the national election. Within one hour, however, they withdrew their projections and announced it was again too close to call. Ultimately, of course, the Florida results were not known until after a lengthy statewide recount and litigation by both presidential hopefuls.

Limits to Assessing Political Knowledge with Polls

The survey, or polling, approach to political knowledge has certain inherent problems. The most noted but least serious is the ***bandwagon effect,*** which occurs when polling results influence people to support the candidate marked as the probable victor. Some scholars argue that this bandwagon effect can be offset by an "underdog effect" in favor of the candidate trailing in the polls.[37]

Other problems with polling are more substantial. One, of course, is human error—bad decisions based on poor interpretations of the data. That in itself is a problem of the users of the polls, not of polling itself. But the two most serious problems inherent in polling are the source of most of the human error. They are the illusion of central tendency and the illusion of saliency.

The Illusion of Central Tendency   The assumption that attitudes tend toward the average or center is known as the ***illusion of central tendency.*** In any large statistical population, measurements tend to be distributed most heavily toward the middle, or average. Weights, heights, even aptitudes, tend so strongly toward the average that their graphic representation bulges high in the middle and low at each extreme, in the form of a bell-shaped curve. So many characteristics are distributed in the bell shape that it is called a "normal distribution." But are opinions normally distributed also? Some can be. Figure 9.3 shows the distribution for a hypothetical sample of individuals responding to the proposition that business in the United States has become too big. Respondents could agree or disagree, could agree strongly or disagree strongly, or could take a moderate to neutral position. The results shown by the figure indicate a bell-shaped curve.

But not all opinions in the United States are normally distributed. On at least a few issues, opinions are likely to be distributed bimodally, as shown in Figure 9.4. On a bimodal distribution of an issue, the population can be said to be polarized. For example, opinions about the right of women to have an abortion are highly polarized. Very few people are neutral; most are either strongly for or strongly against it.

bandwagon effect A situation wherein reports of voter or delegate opinion can influence the actual outcome of an election or a nominating convention.

illusion of central tendency The assumption that opinions are "normally distributed"— that responses to opinion questions are heavily distributed toward the center, as in a bell-shaped curve.

[37]See Michael Traugott in, "The Impact of Media Polls on the Public," in *Media Polls in American Politics,* ed. Thomas E. Mann and Gary R. Orren (Washington, DC: Brookings Institution, 1992), pp. 125–49.

FIGURE 9.3

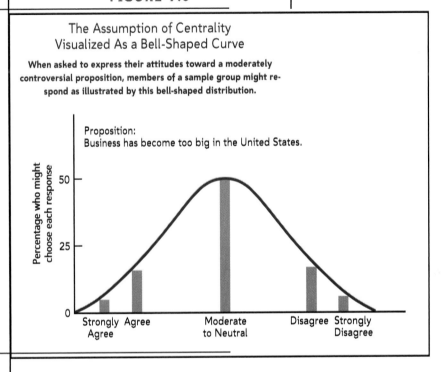

The Assumption of Centrality
Visualized As a Bell-Shaped Curve

When asked to express their attitudes toward a moderately
controversial proposition, members of a sample group might respond as illustrated by this bell-shaped distribution.

Proposition:
Business has become too big in the United States.

Percentage who might
choose each response

50

25

0

Strongly Agree
Agree

Moderate
to Neutral

Disagree Strongly
Disagree

Despite the variation in the actual distribution of opinions, politicians often assume that opinions are distributed more toward neutral and moderate than toward the extremes; and their assumption of (and wish for) a moderate electorate is reinforced by polling. A good poll can counteract this illusion. And, of course, people who come to the wrong conclusions on their own are not the responsibility of the pollsters. But the illusion of central tendency can be produced unintentionally by polls themselves. Respondents are usually required to express opinions in terms of five or six prescribed responses on a questionnaire. But this leaves out many of the issues' complexities. For example, during virtually the entire period of the Watergate affair between 1973 and 1974, the Gallup poll reported that most Americans were opposed when asked, "Should President Richard Nixon be impeached and compelled to leave the Presidency?" These findings strengthened the Nixon administration's view that the public supported the president. However, in mid-1974, the Gallup organization changed the wording of the question to ask if respondents "think there is enough evidence of possible wrongdoing in the case of President Nixon to bring him to trial before the Senate, or not?" With this new wording, as many as two-thirds of those surveyed answered that they favored impeachment. Apparently, most Americans

FIGURE 9.4

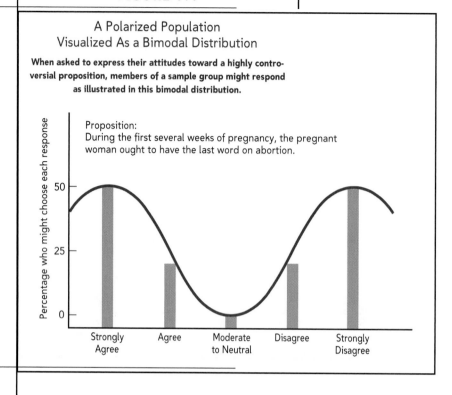

A Polarized Population
Visualized As a Bimodal Distribution

When asked to express their attitudes toward a highly controversial proposition, members of a sample group might respond
as illustrated in this bimodal distribution.

Proposition:
During the first several weeks of pregnancy, the pregnant
woman ought to have the last word on abortion.

Percentage who might choose each response

50

25

0

Strongly Agree Agree Moderate to Neutral Disagree Strongly Disagree

favored impeaching Nixon, as defined by the second question. However, they did
not want to convict him without a trial, as implied by the original question.
Thus, what had been seen by some as Americans' failure to respond to the serious charges made against the president, may have actually indicated that respondents' understanding of the impeachment process was more sophisticated
than that of the pollsters.[38]

In a similar vein, how does the intelligent person respond to such questions
as "Do you favor busing?" or "Should we spend more money on law and order?"
or "Has business become too big in America?" The more a respondent knows
about a given issue, the more subtleties and considerations have to be suppressed in order to report a position to the interviewer. Thus, many moderate
and neutral responses are actually the result of a balance among extreme but
conflicting views within the individual, called ambivalence.

In response to the proposition that business has become too big in America, a
respondent may disagree because he or she is a Socialist and feels bigger busi-

[38]Kagay and Elder, "Numbers Are No Problem."

ness can be nationalized more easily by the government, or a person may disagree because big businesses have too much power. The respondent may end up choosing a moderate or "it all depends" response to the question. Yet, the moderate attitude is a product of alternatives provided by the interviewer or questionnaire, not a weighing of real opinions.

Inasmuch as central tendency suggests moderation, and moderation around the center gives the appearance of consensus, then clearly the consensus reported in opinion polls is often artificial. This does not mean that the data or the findings are false. Nor does it mean that they have been deliberately distorted by the pollsters. Rather, an artificial consensus is the result of mixing different opinions through the mechanical limits of questionnaires and multiple-choice responses.

Opinion polls can produce an artificial central tendency in still another way. Each survey asks respondents a whole series of questions about a variety of specific issues. But since the polling agency's clients are usually interested in the general mood of the country, the agency summarizes the answers to these questions in such forms as "tending toward the right" or "generally holding to the Democratic line." These summaries can help campaigns and can help predict elections, but they can also betray the actual findings.

Some political advisers have used such summaries to bolster party morale. Kevin Phillips, for example, helped contribute to the rebuilding of the Republican party after it suffered its tremendous defeat in 1964. Phillips, a Republican conservative, wrote a book, *The Emerging Republican Majority*, in which he identified the political and social positions of the American middle class. He saw that in general they held positions different from those of higher- and lower-income groups and that in general they were angered by the "softness" and the extravagance of the Democrats.[39]

The Illusion of Saliency   Salient interests are interests that stand out beyond others, that are of more than ordinary concern to respondents in a survey or to voters in the electorate. Politicians, social scientists, journalists, or pollsters who assume something is important to the public when in fact it is not are creating an ***illusion of saliency***. This illusion can be created and fostered by polls despite careful controls over sampling, interviewing, and data analysis. In fact, the illusion is strengthened by the credibility that science gives survey results.

illusion of saliency
Impression conveyed by polls that something is important to the public when actually it is not.

Thus, if a survey includes questions on twenty subjects—because the pollsters or their clients feel they might be important issues—that survey can actually produce twenty salient issues. Although the responses may be sincere, the cumulative impression is artificial, since a high proportion of the respondents may not have concerned themselves with many of the issues until actually confronted with questions by an interviewer. For example, usually not more than 10 percent (rarely more than 20 percent) of the respondents will report that they have no attitude on an issue. Yet, equally seldom will more than 30 percent of a sample spontaneously cite one or more issues as the main reason for their choices. It is

[39]Kevin Phillips, *The Emerging Republican Majority* (New Rochelle, NY: Arlington House, 1969).

nearly impossible to discover how many respondents feel obliged to respond to questions for which they never had any particular concern before the interview.

In a similar vein, an issue may become salient to the public *because* it is receiving a great deal of attention from political leaders and the mass media rather than because of a groundswell of public interest in the issue. For example, the issue of health care was frequently cited by poll respondents as one of their major concerns *after* it was introduced by President Clinton in 1993 and after it had been given a great deal of media coverage. Prior to the president's September 1993 speech to the nation on health care reform, the issue was seldom, if ever, mentioned by members of the public asked to cite what they believed to be important issues. In this instance, as in many others, an issue became salient to the public only after it was introduced by a significant political figure. As the famous Austrian-American economist, Joseph Schumpeter, once observed, public opinion is usually the product rather than the motivator of the political process. In other words, the public's concerns are often shaped by powerful political forces, rather than the other way around.

Similarly, when asked in the early days of a political campaign which candidates they do, or do not, support, the answers voters give often have little significance because the choice is not yet salient to them. Their preference may change many times before the actual election. This is part of the explanation for the phenomenon of the post-convention "bounce" in the popularity of presidential candidates, which was observed after the 1996 and 2000 Democratic and Republican national conventions. In general, presidential candidates can expect about a five-percentage-point bounce in their poll standings immediately after a national convention, though the effects of the bounce tend to disappear rapidly. In 2000, Bush "bounced" to a solid lead over Gore following the Republican convention only to see Gore bounce back in front after the Democrats completed their own well-publicized conclave.

The problem of saliency has become especially acute as a result of the proliferation of media polls. The television networks and major national newspapers all make heavy use of opinion polls. Increasingly, polls are being commissioned by local television stations and local and regional newspapers as well.[40] On the positive side, polls allow journalists to make independent assessments of political realities—assessments not influenced by the partisan claims of politicians.

At the same time, however, media polls can allow journalists to make news when none really exists. Polling diminishes journalists' dependence upon news makers. A poll commissioned by a news agency can provide the basis for a good story even when the candidates, politicians, and other news makers refuse to cooperate by engaging in newsworthy activities. Thus, on days when little or nothing is actually taking place in a political campaign, poll results, especially apparent changes in candidate margins, can provide exciting news for voters.

Interestingly, because rapid and dramatic shifts in candidate margins tend to take place when voters' preferences are least fully formed, horse race news is

[40]See Mann and Orren, eds., *Media Polls in American Politics.*

most likely to make the headlines when it is actually least significant.[41] In other words, media interest in poll results is inversely related to the actual salience of voters' opinions and the significance of the polls' findings.

However, by influencing perceptions, especially those of major contributors, media polls can influence political realities. A candidate who demonstrates a lead in the polls usually finds it considerably easier to raise campaign funds than a candidate whose poll standing is poor. With additional funds, poll leaders can often afford to pay for television time and other campaign activities that will cement their advantage. For example, Bill Clinton's substantial lead in the polls during much of the summer of 1992 helped the Democrats raise far more money than in any previous campaign, primarily from interests hoping to buy access to a future President Clinton. For once, the Democrats were able to outspend the usually better-heeled Republicans. Thus, the appearance of a lead, according to the polls, helped make Clinton's lead a reality. Much the same effect was seen in 1996, when Clinton's lead in the polls caused many Republicans to write off the contest as hopeless weeks before the election.

The two illusions engendered by polling often put politicians on the horns of a dilemma in which they must choose between a politics of no issues (due to the illusion of central tendency) and a politics of too many trivial issues (due to the illusion of saliency). This has to be at least part of the explanation for why many members of Congress can praise themselves at the end of the year for the hundreds of things they worked on during the past session while not perceiving that they have neglected the one or two overriding issues of the day. Similarly, politicians preparing for major state or national campaigns compose position papers on virtually every conceivable issue—either because they will not make a judgment as to which are the truly salient issues or because they feel that stressing all issues is a way of avoiding a choice among the truly salient ones.

Public Opinion, Political Knowledge, and the Importance of Ignorance

Many people are distressed to find public opinion polls not only unable to discover public opinion, but unable to avoid producing unintentional distortions of their own. No matter how hard pollsters try, no matter how mature the science of opinion polling becomes, politicians forever may remain largely ignorant of public opinion.

Although knowledge is good for its own sake, and knowledge of public opinion may sometimes produce better government, ignorance also has its uses. It can, for example, operate as a restraint on the use of power. Leaders who think they know what the public wants are often autocratic rulers. Leaders who realize that they are always partially in the dark about the public are likely to be more modest in their claims, less intense in their demands, and more uncertain in

---

[41]For an excellent and reflective discussion by a journalist, see Richard Morin, "Clinton Slide in Survey Shows Perils of Polling," *Washington Post*, 29 August 1992, p. A6.

their uses of power. Their uncertainty may make them more accountable to their constituencies because they will be more likely to continue searching for consent.

One of the most valuable benefits of survey research is actually "negative knowledge"—knowledge that pierces through irresponsible claims about the breadth of opinion or the solidarity of group or mass support. Because this sort of knowledge reveals the complexity and uncertainty of public opinion, it can help make citizens less gullible, group leaders less strident, and politicians less deceitful. This alone gives public opinion research, despite its great limitations, an important place in the future of American politics.[42]

PUBLIC OPINION AND GOVERNMENT POLICY

One of the fundamental notions on which the U.S. government was founded is that "the public" should not be trusted when it comes to governing. The framers designed institutions that, although democratic, insulated government decision making from popular pressure. For example, the indirect elections of senators and presidents were supposed to prevent the government from being too dependent on the vagaries of public opinion.

Research from the 1950s and 1960s indicates that the framers' concerns were well founded. Individual-level survey analysis reveals that the respondents lacked fundamental political knowledge and had ill-formed opinions about government and public policy.[43] Their answers seemed nothing more than "doorstep opinions"—opinions given off the top of their heads. When an individual was asked the same questions at different times, he or she often gave different answers. The dramatic and unpredictable changes seemed to imply that the public was indeed unreliable as a guide for political decisions.

Benjamin Page and Robert Shapiro take issue with the notion that the public should not be trusted when it comes to policy making.[44] They contend that public opinion at the aggregate level is indeed "rational"—meaning that public opinion is coherent and stable, and that it moves in a predictable fashion in response to changing political, economic, and social circumstances.

How is this possible, given what previous studies have found? Page and Shapiro hypothesize that the individual-level responses are plagued with various types of errors that make the people's opinions seem incoherent and unstable. However, when a large number of individual-level responses to survey questions

Rationality Principle

Although individuals might not be cohesive in their political attitudes, aggregate public opinion is coherent and stable.

[42]For a fuller discussion of the uses of polling and the role of public opinion in American politics, see Benjamin Ginsberg, *The Captive Public* (New York: Basic Books, 1986).

[43]Angus Campbell, Philip E. Converse, Warren E. Miller, and Donald E. Stokes, *The American Voter* (New York: Wiley, 1960); Philip E. Converse, "The Nature of Belief Systems in Mass Publics" in *Ideology and Discontent*, ed. David E. Apter (New York: Free Press, 1964).

[44]Benjamin I. Page and Robert Y. Shapiro, *The Rational Public* (Chicago: University of Chicago Press, 1992).

are added up to produce an aggregate public opinion, the errors or "noise" in the individual responses, if more or less random, will cancel each other out, revealing a collective opinion that is stable, coherent, and meaningful. From their results, Page and Shapiro conclude that the general public can indeed be trusted when it comes to governing. But how closely should elected officials follow public opinion?

In democratic nations, leaders should pay heed to public opinion, and most evidence suggests that indeed they do. There are many instances in which public policy and public opinion do not coincide, but in general the government's actions are consistent with citizens' preferences. One study, for example, found that between 1935 and 1979, in about two-thirds of all cases, significant changes in public opinion were followed within one year by changes in government policy consistent with the shift in the popular mood.[45] Other studies have come to similar conclusions about public opinion and government policy at the state level.[46] Do these results imply that elected leaders merely pander to public opinion? The answer is no.

A recent study on the role that public opinion played during the failed attempt to enact health care reform during 1993–1994 found that public opinion polls had very little influence on individual members of Congress, who used these polls first to justify positions they had already adopted and then to shape public thinking on the issue. However, the study also found that congressional party leaders designed their health care legislation strategies based on their concerns about the effects of public opinion on the electoral fortunes of individual members. Leaders' concerns about public opinion thus help explain why the congressional policy-making process follows public opinion, even though individual members of Congress do not.[47]

In addition, there are always areas of disagreement between opinion and policy. For example, the majority of Americans favored stricter governmental control of handguns for years before Congress finally adopted the modest restrictions on firearms purchases embodied in the 1994 Brady Bill and the Omnibus Crime Control Act. Similarly, most Americans—blacks as well as whites—oppose school busing to achieve racial balance, yet such busing continues to be used in many parts of the nation. Most Americans are far less concerned with the rights of the accused than the federal courts seem to be. Most Americans oppose U.S. military intervention in other nations' affairs, yet such interventions continue to take place and often win public approval after the fact.

Several factors can contribute to a lack of consistency between opinion and governmental policy. First, the nominal majority on a particular issue may not

Analyzing American Politics
www.wwnorton.com/lowi7/ch9
Analyze how much and how often elected leaders pander to public opinion.

---

[45]Benjamin I. Page and Robert Y. Shapiro, "Effects of Public Opinion on Policy," *American Political Science Review* 77 (March 1983), pp. 175–90.

[46]Robert A. Erikson, Gerald Wright, and John McIver, *Statehouse Democracy: Public Opinion and Democracy in the American States* (New York: Cambridge University Press, 1994).

[47]Lawrence R. Jacobs, Eric D. Lawrence, Robert Y. Shapiro, and Steven S. Smith, "Congressional Leadership of Public Opinion," *Political Science Quarterly* 113 (1998), pp. 21–41.

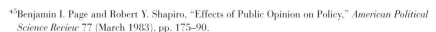

be as intensely committed to its preference as the adherents of the minority viewpoint. An intensely committed minority may often be more willing to commit its time, energy, efforts, and resources to the affirmation of its opinions than an apathetic, even if large, majority. In the case of firearms, for example, although the proponents of gun control are by a wide margin in the majority, most do not regard the issue as one of critical importance to themselves and are not willing to commit much effort to advancing their cause. The opponents of gun control, by contrast, are intensely committed, well organized, and well financed, and as a result are usually able to carry the day.

Institution Principle

Policy and opinion are not always consistent because the structure of American government insulates political decision making from direct popular pressure.

A second important reason that public policy and public opinion may not coincide has to do with the character and structure of the American system of government. The framers of the American Constitution, as we saw in Chapter 2, sought to create a system of government that was based upon popular consent but that did not invariably and automatically translate shifting popular sentiments into public policies. As a result, the American governmental process includes arrangements such as an appointed judiciary that can produce policy decisions that may run contrary to prevailing popular sentiment—at least for a time.

Perhaps the inconsistencies between opinion and policy could be resolved if we made broader use of a mechanism currently employed by a number of states—the ballot initiative. This procedure allows propositions to be placed on the ballot and voted into law by the electorate—bypassing most of the normal machinery of representative government. In recent years, several important propositions sponsored by business and conservative groups have been enacted.[48] For example, California's Proposition 209, approved by the state's voters in 1996, prohibited the state and local government agencies in California from using race or gender preferences in hiring, contracting, or university admissions decisions. Responding to conservatives' success, liberal groups launched a number of ballot initiatives in 2000. For example, in Washington State, voters were asked to consider propositions sponsored by teachers unions that would have required annual cost-of-living raises for teachers and more than $1.8 billion in additional state spending over the next six years.[49]

Institutional Reform

www.wwnorton.com/lowi7/ch9

Is government more responsive as a result of the initiative?

Initiatives such as these seem to provide the public with an opportunity to express its will. The major problem, however, is that government by initiative offers little opportunity for reflection and compromise. Voters are presented with a proposition, usually sponsored by a special interest group, and are asked to take it or leave it. Perhaps the true will of the people, not to mention their best interest, might lie somewhere between the positions taken by various interest groups. Perhaps, for example, California voters might have wanted affirmative action programs to be modified, but not scrapped altogether as Proposition 209 mandated. In a representative assembly, as opposed to a referendum campaign, a

[48]David S. Broder, *Democracy Derailed: Initiative Campaigns and the Power of Money* (New York: Harcourt, 2000).

[49]Robert Tomsho, "Liberals Take a Cue from Conservatives: This Election, the Left Tries to Make Policy with Ballot Initiatives," *Wall Street Journal*, 6 November 2000, p. A12.

compromise position might have been achieved that was more satisfactory to all the residents of the state. This is one reason the framers of the U.S. Constitution strongly favored representative government rather than direct democracy.

When all is said and done, however, there can be little doubt that in general the actions of the American government do not remain out of line with popular sentiment for very long. A major reason for this is, of course, the electoral process, to which we shall next turn. Lest we become too complacent, however, we should not forget that the close relationship between government and opinion in America may also partly be a result of the government's success in molding opinion.

SUMMARY

All governments claim to obey public opinion, and in the democracies politicians and political leaders actually try to do so.

The American government does not directly regulate opinions and beliefs in the sense that dictatorial regimes often do. Opinion is regulated by an institution that the government constructed and that it maintains—the marketplace of ideas. In this marketplace, opinions and ideas compete for support. In general, opinions supported by upper-class groups have a better chance of succeeding than those views that are mainly advanced by the lower classes.

Americans share a number of values and viewpoints but often classify themselves as liberal or conservative in their basic orientations. The meaning of these terms has changed greatly over the past century. Once liberalism meant opposition to big government. Today, liberals favor an expanded role for the government. Once conservatism meant support for state power and aristocratic rule. Today, conservatives oppose government regulation, at least of business affairs.

Although the United States relies mainly on market mechanisms to regulate opinion, even our government intervenes to some extent, seeking to influence both particular opinions and, more important, the general climate of political opinion. Political leaders' increased distance from the public makes it difficult for them to gauge public opinion. Until recently, public opinion on some issues could be gauged better by studying mass behavior than by studying polls. Population characteristics are also useful in estimating public opinion on some subjects. Another approach is to go directly to the people. Two techniques are used: the impressionistic and the scientific. The impressionistic method relies on person-to-person communication, selective polling, or the use of bellwether districts. A person-to-person approach is quick, efficient, and inexpensive; but because it often depends on an immediate circle of associates, it can also limit awareness of new issues or unpleasant information. Selective polling usually involves interviewing a few people from different walks of life. Although risky, it has been used successfully to gauge public opinion. Bellwether districts are a popular means of predicting election outcomes. They are used by the media as well as by some candidates.

Rationality Principle	Collective Action Principle	Institution Principle	Policy Principle	History Principle
Although individuals might not be cohesive in their political attitudes, aggregate public opinion is coherent and stable.	Widely held political ideas are usually the products of orchestrated campaigns by government, organized groups, or the media.	Policy and opinion are not always consistent because the structure of American government insulates political decision making from direct popular pressure.	One reason why policy and opinion may not be consistent is that the U.S. is a representative government, not a direct democracy.	The creation and maintenance of a marketplace of ideas required continued government involvement in the areas of education, communication, and jurisprudence.

The scientific approach to learning public opinion is random sample polling. One advantage of random sample polling is that elections can be very accurately predicted; using a model of behavior, pollsters are often able to predict how voters will mark their ballots better than the voters themselves can predict. A second advantage is that polls provide information on the bases and conditions of voting decisions. They make it possible to assess trends in attitudes and the influence of ideology on attitudes.

There are also problems with polling, however. An illusion of central tendency can encourage politicians not to confront issues. The illusion of saliency, on the other hand, can encourage politicians to confront too many trivial issues. Even with scientific polling, politicians cannot be certain that they understand public opinion. Their recognition of this limitation, however, may function as a valuable restraint.

FOR FURTHER READING

Erikson, Robert S. and Kent Tedin. *American Public Opinion: Its Origins, Content and Impact*, 6th ed. New York: Longman, 2001.

Gallup, George. *The Pulse of Democracy*. New York: Simon and Schuster, 1940.

Ginsberg, Benjamin. *The Captive Public: How Mass Opinion Promotes State Power.* New York: Basic Books, 1986.

Herbst, Susan. *Numbered Voices: How Opinion Polling Has Shaped American Politics.* Chicago: University of Chicago Press, 1993.

Key, V. O. *Public Opinion and American Democracy.* New York: Alfred A. Knopf, 1961.

Lippmann, Walter. *Public Opinion.* New York: Harcourt, Brace and Co., 1922.

Mueller, John. *Policy and Opinion in the Gulf War.* Chicago: University of Chicago Press, 1994.

Neuman, W. Russell. *The Paradox of Mass Politics: Knowledge and Opinion in the American Electorate.* Cambridge: Harvard University Press, 1986.

Page, Benjamin I., and Robert Y. Shapiro. *The Rational Public.* Chicago: University of Chicago Press, 1992.

Roll, Charles W., and Albert H. Cantril. *Polls: Their Use and Misuse in Politics.* New York: Basic Books, 1972.

Stimson, James. *Public Opinion in America: Moods, Cycles, and Swings.* Boulder, CO: Westview, 1991.

Sussman, Barry. *What Americans Really Think: And Why Our Politicians Pay No Attention.* New York: Pantheon, 1988.

Zaller, John. *The Nature and Origins of Mass Opinion.* New York: Cambridge University Press, 1992.

CHAPTER

ten

Elections

EVENTS		INSTITUTIONAL DEVELOPMENTS
George Washington elected president (1789)		Federalists in control of national government (1789–1800)
Thomas Jefferson elected president (1800)	**1800**	First electoral realignment—Jeffersonian Republicans defeat Federalists (1800)
Andrew Jackson elected president; beginning of party government (1828)		Second realignment—Jacksonian Democrats take control of White House and Congress (1828)
		Presidential nominating conventions introduced (1830s)
		Whig party forms (1830s)
Whigs win; William Henry Harrison elected president (1840)		
Lincoln elected president (1860); South secedes (1860–1861)		Civil War realignment—Republican party founded (1856); Whig party destroyed (1860)
Civil War (1861–1865)		
Reconstruction (1867–1877)		Under Reconstruction Acts, blacks enfranchised in South (1867)
	1870	Fifteenth Amendment forbids states to deny voting rights based on race (1870)
		Southern blacks lose voting rights through poll taxes, literacy tests, grandfather clause (1870s–1890s)
Contested presidential election—*Hayes v. Tilden* (1876); Republican Rutherford Hayes elected by electoral vote of 185–184 (1876)		Hayes's election leads to end of Reconstruction; voting rights of South restored (1877)
		Progressive reforms—direct primaries, civil service reform, Australian ballot, registration requirements; voter participation drops sharply (1890s–1910s)
Republican William McKinley elected president (1896)		Realignment of 1896; Republican hegemony (1896–1932)
	1900	
		Seventeenth Amendment authorizes direct election of senators (1913)
		Nineteenth Amendment gives women right to vote (1920)

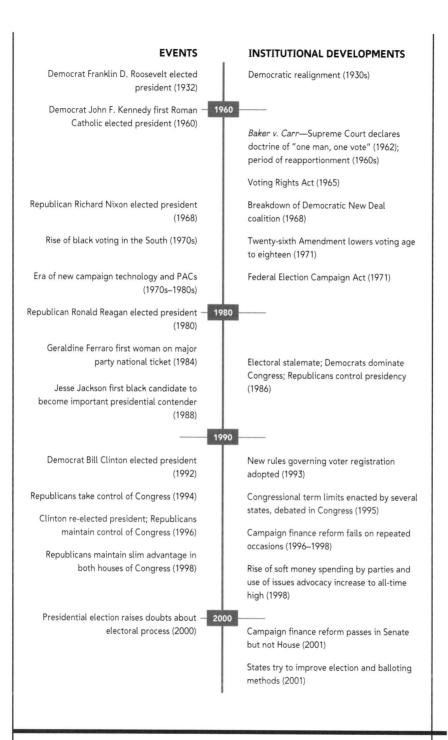

EVENTS	INSTITUTIONAL DEVELOPMENTS
Democrat Franklin D. Roosevelt elected president (1932)	Democratic realignment (1930s)
Democrat John F. Kennedy first Roman Catholic elected president (1960) — **1960**	
	Baker v. Carr—Supreme Court declares doctrine of "one man, one vote" (1962); period of reapportionment (1960s)
	Voting Rights Act (1965)
Republican Richard Nixon elected president (1968)	Breakdown of Democratic New Deal coalition (1968)
Rise of black voting in the South (1970s)	Twenty-sixth Amendment lowers voting age to eighteen (1971)
Era of new campaign technology and PACs (1970s–1980s)	Federal Election Campaign Act (1971)
Republican Ronald Reagan elected president (1980) — **1980**	
Geraldine Ferraro first woman on major party national ticket (1984)	Electoral stalemate; Democrats dominate Congress; Republicans control presidency (1986)
Jesse Jackson first black candidate to become important presidential contender (1988)	
1990	
Democrat Bill Clinton elected president (1992)	New rules governing voter registration adopted (1993)
Republicans take control of Congress (1994)	Congressional term limits enacted by several states, debated in Congress (1995)
Clinton re-elected president; Republicans maintain control of Congress (1996)	Campaign finance reform fails on repeated occasions (1996–1998)
Republicans maintain slim advantage in both houses of Congress (1998)	Rise of soft money spending by parties and use of issues advocacy increase to all-time high (1998)
Presidential election raises doubts about electoral process (2000) — **2000**	Campaign finance reform passes in Senate but not House (2001)
	States try to improve election and balloting methods (2001)

CORE OF THE ANALYSIS

• Elections are important because they promote accountability in elected officials, socialize political activity, expand citizen involvement, and prescribe conditions for acceptable participation in political life.

• The government exerts a measure of control over the electoral process by regulating the composition of the electorate, translating voters' choices into electoral decisions, and insulating day-to-day government from the impact of electoral decisions.

• The strongest influences on voters' decisions are partisan loyalty, issue and policy concerns, and candidate characteristics.

• The increasing importance of money in elections has profound consequences for American democracy.

• Ordinary voters have little influence on the political process today.

Rationality Principle

Elections allow multiple principals—citizens—to choose political agents to act on their behalf, but citizens usually have imperfect information about candidates and don't know how agents will act once in office.

adverse selection problem The problem of incomplete information—of choosing alternatives without knowing fully the details of available options.

O ver the past two centuries, elections have come to play a significant role in the political processes of most nations. The forms that elections take and the purposes they serve, however, vary greatly from nation to nation. The most important difference among national electoral systems is that some provide the opportunity for opposition while others do not. Democratic electoral systems, such as those that have evolved in the United States and western Europe, allow opposing forces to compete against and even to replace current office holders. Authoritarian electoral systems, by contrast, do not allow the defeat of those in power. In the authoritarian context, elections are used primarily to mobilize popular enthusiasm for the government, to provide an outlet for popular discontent and to persuade foreigners that the regime is legitimate—i.e., that it has the support of the people. In the former Soviet Union, for example, citizens were required to vote even though no opposition to Communist party candidates was allowed.

In democracies, elections can also serve as institutions of legitimation and as safety valves for social discontent. But beyond these functions, democratic elections facilitate popular influence, promote leadership accountability, and offer groups in society a measure of protection from the abuse of governmental power. Citizens exercise influence through elections by determining who should control the government. The chance to decide who will govern serves as an opportunity for ordinary citizens to make choices about the policies, programs, and directions of government action. In the United States, for example, recent Democratic and Republican candidates have differed significantly on issues of taxing, social spending, and governmental regulation. As American voters have chosen between the two parties' candidates, they have also made choices about these issues.

Nominally, of course, a democratic election is the collective selection of leaders and representatives. In terms now familiar to the reader, elections are occasions in which multiple *principals*—the citizens—choose political *agents* to act on their behalf. There are two kinds of problems that face even the most rational of citizen-principals in these circumstances. Electoral rules and arrangements may be characterized and ultimately assessed as mechanisms for coming to grips with these.

The first is known as the ***adverse selection problem.*** When choosing Candidate A over Candidate B, exactly what are we getting? To some degree, a candidate for office is a "pig in a poke." We may know some things about her and some other things about her opponent, but even in a world of investigative reporters, paparazzi, and Drudge reports on the Internet, we can't always know what we've selected. It may turn out badly, but then again it may not.[1] The reason for the possibility of adverse selection is incomplete information. The candidates themselves affect, in large measure, what we know about them, and it is often in their interest to hide or shroud in ambiguity items about themselves that, though possibly highly relevant to the choices of citizens, might harm their electoral prospects. The solution to this problem is openness and transparency—a wide-open and freewheeling electoral process, a well-heeled political opposition, and an activist press. The latter may at times be perceived as crossing the line between the public and the private—as many felt was the case in the intense scrutiny of former president Clinton's private life—but much better this than a press easily cowed and constrained, since the public depends on an independent press to counter the otherwise self-serving information that is offered up by the candidates themselves.

---

[1]A classic example of adverse selection is presidential selection of Supreme Court justices. Often a president finds that these men and women turn out much differently than expected. It is unlikely, for example, that President Eisenhower would have chosen Earl Warren, the former governor of California and 1948 Republican vice presidential candidate, to be chief justice of the Supreme Court, had he known of Warren's liberal leanings. Nor would he have appointed Justice Brennan, who turned out to be among the most liberal justices on the Court in the twentieth century. President Nixon, to give another example, appointed Harry Blackmun to the Court, the Justice who later crafted the famous pro-choice opinion Roe v. Wade. Finally, there was the near-fateful decision of the first President Bush in his elevation of Federal District Court Judge David Souter to the Supreme Court. Souter, in December 2000, joined the minority (only one vote short of a majority) that would have ordered the popular vote in Florida recounted—an action that might well have denied the second President Bush his presidency.

THE CENTRAL QUESTIONS

POLITICAL PARTICIPATION

How is political participation most commonly institutionalized as part of the political process?

REGULATING THE ELECTORAL PROCESS

What rules determine who can vote in elections?

What rules determine who wins elections?

How does the government determine the boundaries of electoral districts?

How is the ballot determined?

HOW VOTERS DECIDE

What are the primary influences on voters' decisions?

THE 2000 ELECTIONS

What is the significance of the 2000 elections?

CAMPAIGN FINANCE

How do candidates raise and spend campaign funds?

How does the government regulate campaign spending?

How does money affect how certain social groups achieve electoral success?

DO ELECTIONS MATTER?

Why has participation declined over time?

Why are elections important as institutions of democratic government?

moral hazard
Not knowing all aspects of the actions taken by an agent (nominally on behalf of the principal but potentially at the principal's expense).

The second problem is known as ***moral hazard.*** If adverse selection is a problem caused by hidden *information*, then moral hazard is a problem produced by hidden *action*. It is the problem of agents who, once selected, cannot easily be monitored in their behavior. A political leader does many things that are public, such as making speeches, attaching their names as sponsors of legislation, and voting on legislative motions. But behind their public records are many private acts that are imperfectly observed at best. These veiled encounters used to take place in the proverbial "smoke-filled rooms" of Washington, but today they take place in the private dining rooms of Capitol Hill where deals are struck between legislators and special interests, or in the "wink and nod" conversations between presidents and large donors (who may get to spend a night in the Lincoln bedroom of the White House or hitch a ride on Air Force One).[2] Political agents can also use their agenda power, their appointment power, and the bully pulpits that public office provides to advance these special interests. Moral hazard, the classic problem of delegation, makes principals vulnerable to abuses of the power just delegated to elected agents. As with the first problem, the solution to moral hazard is found in the way elections are conducted. If agents have strong incentives to want to renew their contracts—to be re-elected or to advance to a higher office—then they will take care not to abuse their delegated power, or at least not to take big risks that, if discovered, could damage their political reputations. Giving incumbents the incentive of possible re-election—indeed, tolerating small advantages that incumbency gives in electoral contests—will encourage them to moderate the inclination to strike private deals.

Thus, elections promote leadership accountability because the threat of defeat at the polls exerts pressure on those in power to conduct themselves in a responsible manner and to take account of popular interests and wishes when they make their decisions. As James Madison observed in *The Federalist Papers*, elected leaders are "compelled to anticipate the moment when their power is to cease, when their exercise of it is to be reviewed, and when they must descend to the level from which they were raised, there forever to remain unless a faithful discharge of their trust shall have established their title to a renewal of it."[3] It is because of this need to anticipate that elected officials constantly monitor public opinion polls as they decide what positions to take on policy issues.

suffrage The right to vote; see also **franchise.**

Finally, the right to vote, or ***suffrage,*** can serve as an important source of protection for groups in American society. The passage of the 1965 Voting Rights Act, for example, enfranchised millions of African Americans in the South, paving the way for the election of thousands of new black public officials at the local, state, and national levels and ensuring that white politicians could no longer ignore the views and needs of African Americans. The Voting Rights Act was one of

---

[2]Before his death in an airplane crash, Clinton's secretary of commerce, Ron Brown, a former head of the Democratic National Committee, used the frequent occasions of foreign travel required of his cabinet post to bring along many a Democratic fat cat. Republican office holders, of course, are no less vigilant in rewarding their fat-cat contributors.

[3]Clinton Rossiter, ed., *The Federalist Papers* (New York: New American Library, 1961), No. 57, p. 352.

the chief spurs for the elimination of many overt forms of racial discrimination as well as for the diminution of racist rhetoric in American public life.

The 2000 election highlighted a number of problems surrounding our current electoral process. First, despite the expenditure of $3 billion by the candidates and claims by both major parties that they planned major efforts to bring voters to the polls, voter turnout continued to hover at the 50 percent level, as it has in recent decades. Second, the election demonstrated that the ballots used in many parts of the United States, especially those cast using the now-infamous Votomatic machines, were prone to error. Third, the election outcome, as determined by the electoral college, produced a president who won 500,000 fewer popular votes than his opponent. Fourth, a variety of special interests pumped record amounts of money into political campaigns, renewing concerns that politicians are more accountable to wealthy donors than to mere voters. During the course of this chapter, we will examine these problems and possible solutions.

In this chapter, we will look first at what distinguishes voting from other forms of political activity. Second, we will examine the formal structure and setting of American elections. Third, we will see how—and what—voters decide when they take part in elections. Fourth, we will focus on recent national elections, including the 2000 presidential race. Fifth, we will discuss the role of money in the election process, particularly in recent elections. Finally, we will assess the place of elections in the American political process, raising the important question, "Do elections matter?"

POLITICAL PARTICIPATION

In the twenty-first century, voting is viewed as the normal form of mass political activity. Yet ordinary people took part in politics long before the introduction of the election or any other formal mechanism of popular involvement in political life. If there is any natural or spontaneous form of mass political participation, it is the riot rather than the election. Indeed, the urban riot and the rural uprising were a part of life in western Europe prior to the nineteenth century, and in eastern Europe until the twentieth. In eighteenth-century London, for example, one of the most notorious forms of popular political action was the "illumination." Mobs would march up and down the street demanding that householders express support for their cause by placing a candle or lantern in a front window. Those who refused to illuminate risked having their homes torched by the angry crowd. This eighteenth-century form of civil disorder may well be the origin of the expression "to shed light upon" an issue.

The fundamental difference between voting and rioting is that voting is a socialized and institutionalized form of mass political action.[4] When, where, how, and which individuals participate in elections are matters of public policy that

[4]For a fuller discussion, see Benjamin Ginsberg, *The Consequences of Consent* (New York: Random House, 1982).

Collective Action Principle

Elections are a mechanism to channel and limit political participation to actions within the system.

set the context for spontaneous individual choice. With the advent of the election, control over the agenda for political action passed at least in part from the citizen to the government.

In an important study of participation in the United States, Sidney Verba and Norman Nie define political participation as consisting of "activities 'within the system'—ways of influencing politics that are generally recognized as legal and legitimate."[5] This definition of participation is precisely in accord with most governments' desires. Governments try very hard to channel and limit political participation to actions "within the system." Even with that constraint, however, the right to political participation represents a tremendous advancement in the status of citizens on two levels. At one level, it improves the probability that they will regularly affect the decisions that governments make. On the other level, it reinforces the concept of the individual as independent from the state. It is on the basis of both dimensions that philosophers like John Stuart Mill argued that popular government was the ideal form of government.[6]

Those holding power are willing to concede the right to participate in the hope that it will encourage citizens to give their consent to being governed. This is a calculated risk for citizens. They give up their right to revolt in return for the right to participate regularly. They can participate, but only in ways prescribed by the government. Outside the established channels, their participation can be suppressed or disregarded. It is also a calculated risk for the politician, who may be forced into certain policy decisions or forced out of office altogether by citizens exercising their right to participate. This risk is usually worth taking, since in return, governments acquire consent, and through consent citizens become supporters of government action.[7]

In earlier chapters (see Chapter 1) we suggested the relationship between citizens and elected politicians is an instance of a principal-agent relationship. There are two basic approaches to this relationship—the consent approach and the agency approach. The consent approach and the agency approach are the flip sides of the same conceptual coin, but they place the emphasis differently, and it is worth spelling these differences out. The consent approach emphasizes the historical reality that the right of the citizen to participate in his or her own governance, mainly through the act of voting or other forms of consent, arises from an existing governmental order aimed at making it *easier* for the governors to govern by legitimizing their rule. The governors here are the active ones, and their nominal principals are seen mainly as nuisances that require soothing from time to time. The agency approach, on the other hand, treats *principals* as the active elements in the constitutional order. This approach takes the division and specialization of labor evident in everyday life as a metaphor for political relationships. The typical citizen would much rather devote scarce time and effort to

---

[5]Sidney Verba and Norman Nie, *Participation in America* (New York: Harper & Row, 1972), pp. 2–3.
[6]John Stuart Mill, *Considerations on Representative Government* (London: Basil Blackwell, 1948; orig. published 1859), pp. 141–42.
[7]See Ginsberg, *Consequences of Consent.*

his or her own private affairs instead of spending that time and effort on governance. Therefore, he or she chooses to delegate governance to agents—politicians—controlled through election. Here, the control of agents rather than the soothing of principals is emphasized. Although the emphases differ in these two approaches, they complement each other since, at the end of the day, citizen-principals do control the fate of their political leaders, and politician-agents do try to get away with whatever they can while satisfying their overseers at contract-renewal time.

Encouraging Electoral Participation

Americans are free to assert whatever demands, views, and grievances they might have through a variety of different means. Citizens may, if they wish, lobby, petition, demonstrate, or file suit in court. Although there are some legal impediments to many of these forms of participation, relatively few modes of political expression are directly barred by law.

Despite the availability of an array of alternatives, citizen participation in American politics, in practice, is generally limited to voting and a small number of other electoral activities (for example, campaigning). It is true that voter turnout in the United States is relatively low. But when, for one reason or another, Americans do seek to participate, their participation generally takes the form of voting.

The preeminent position of voting in the American political process is not surprising. The American legal and political environment is overwhelmingly weighted in favor of electoral participation. Probably the most influential forces helping to channel people into the voting booth are law, civic education, and the party system. The availability of suffrage is, of course, a question of law. But in addition to simply making the ballot available, state legislation in the United States prescribes the creation of an elaborate and costly public machinery that makes voting a rather simple task for individuals. Civic education, to a large extent mandated by law, encourages citizens to believe that electoral participation is the appropriate way to express opinions and grievances. The major parties are legally charged with staffing and operating the normal machinery of elections and in a number of vital ways help directly to induce citizens to participate.

Making It Easy to Vote   Despite complicating factors such as registration, the time, energy, and effort needed to vote are considerably less than are required for all but a few other political activities. The relatively low degree of individual effort required to vote, however, is somewhat deceptive. Voting is a simple way for large numbers of citizens to participate only because it is made simple by an elaborate and costly electoral system. The ease with which citizens can vote is a function of law and public policy. The costs of voting are paid mainly by the state.

In the United States, electoral contests are administered principally by states and localities. Although state law is sometimes conceived as only regulating and limiting suffrage, most states try to facilitate voting by as many citizens as possible. States and localities legally require themselves to invest considerable effort in the facilitation of voting. In every state, the steps needed to conduct an election fill hundreds of pages of statutes. At the state, county, and municipal levels, boards of elections must be established to supervise the electoral process. For every several hundred voters, in each state, special political units—precincts or election districts—are created and staffed exclusively for the administration of elections. During each electoral period, polling places must be set up, equipped with voting machines or ballots, and staffed by voting inspectors. Prior to an election, its date, the locations of polling places, and the names of candidates must be publicized. After each election, returns must be canvassed, tallied, reported, and often recounted.

Although every state makes voting relatively easy by providing for the creation and funding of election machinery, states obviously vary in the precise extent to which they encourage electoral participation. Indeed, until the 1970s, states varied enormously in their voter residence requirements, registration procedures, absentee voting rules, and the hours that polls remained open. Until recent years, literacy tests and poll taxes, often employed in a deliberately discriminatory manner, were also important in producing interstate differences in the ease of voting. One continuing problem involves the actual balloting methods used in many states, as we shall see later in the chapter.

Civic Education   Laws, of course, cannot completely explain why most people vote rather than riot or lobby. If public attitudes were completely unfavorable to elections, it is doubtful that *legal* remedies alone would have much impact.

Positive public attitudes about voting do not come into being in a completely spontaneous manner. Americans are taught to equate citizenship with electoral participation. Civic training, designed to give students an appreciation for the American system of government, is a legally required part of the curriculum in every elementary and secondary school. Although it is not as often required by law, civic education usually manages to find its way into college curricula as well.

In the elementary and secondary schools, through formal instruction and, more subtly, through the frequent administration of class and school elections, students are taught the importance of the electoral process. By contrast, little attention is given to lawsuits, direct action, organizing, parliamentary procedures, lobbying, or other possible modes of participation. For example, the techniques involved in organizing a sit-in or protest march are seldom part of an official school course of study.[8]

The New York State first-grade social studies curriculum offers a fairly typical case study of the training in political participation given very young children. The state Education Department provides the following guidelines to teachers:

---

[8]See Fred Greenstein, *Children and Politics* (New Haven: Yale University Press, 1969). See also Robert Weissberg, *Political Learning, Political Choice and Democratic Citizenship* (Englewood Cliffs, NJ: Prentice-Hall, 1974).

To illustrate the voting process, present a situation such as: Chuck and John would both like to be the captain of the kickball team. How will we decide which boy will be the captain? Help the children to understand that the fairest way to choose a captain is by voting.

Write both candidates' names on the chalk board. Pass out slips of paper. Explain to the children that they are to write the name of the boy they would like to have as their captain. Collect and tabulate the results on the chalk board.

Parallel this election to that of the election for the Presidency. Other situations which would illustrate the election procedure are voting for:

a game

an assignment choice

classroom helpers.[9]

Although secondary-school students elect student government representatives rather than classroom helpers and are given more sophisticated illustrations than kickball team elections, the same principle continues to be taught, in compliance with legal requirements. College students are also frequently given the opportunity to elect senators, representatives, and the like to serve on the largely ornamental representative bodies that are to be found at most institutions of higher learning. Obviously, civic education is not always completely successful. Rather than relying on the electoral process, people continue to demonstrate, sit in, and picket for various political causes.

Civic education, of course, does not end with formal schooling. Early training is supplemented by a variety of mechanisms, ranging from the official celebration of national holidays to the activities of private patriotic and political organizations. Election campaigns themselves are occasions for the reinforcement of training to vote. Campaigns and political conventions include a good deal of oratory designed to remind citizens of the importance of voting and the democratic significance of elections. Parties and candidates, even if for selfish reasons, emphasize the value of participation, of "being counted," and the virtues of elections as instruments of popular government. Exposure to such campaign stimuli appears generally to heighten citizens' interest in and awareness of the electoral process.

The Party System   Law and civic education do not directly stimulate voting as much as they create a favorable climate for electoral participation. Within the context of this climate, the major parties, until recent years at least, have been the principal agents responsible for giving citizens the motivation and incentive to vote. By law, in most American states, party workers staff the electoral machinery. Indeed, at one time, the parties even printed the ballots used by voters. Although the parties have played a role in both civic education and legal facilitation of voting, their principal efforts have been aimed at the direct mobilization of voters.

[9]The University of the State of New York, State Education Department, Bureau of Elementary Curriculum Development, *Social Studies—Grade 1, A Teaching System* (Albany, NY: 1971), p. 32.

One of the most interesting pieces of testimony to the lengths to which parties have been willing to go to induce citizens to vote is a list of Chicago precinct captains' activities in the 1920s and 1930s. Among other matters, these party workers helped constituents obtain food, coal, and money for rent; gave advice in dealing with juvenile and domestic problems; helped constituents obtain government and private jobs; adjusted taxes; aided with permits, zoning, and building-code problems; served as liaisons with social, relief, and medical agencies; provided legal assistance and help in dealing with government agencies; handed out Christmas baskets; and attended weddings and funerals.[10] Obviously, all these services were provided in the hope of winning voters' support at election time.

Rationality Principle

At least until recent years, political parties have been the primary agents for giving citizens the motivation and incentive to vote.

Party competition has long been known to be a key factor in stimulating voting. As political scientists Stanley Kelley, Richard Ayres, and William Bowen note, competition gives citizens an incentive to vote and politicians an incentive to get them to vote.[11] The origins of the American national electorate can be traced to the competitive organizing activities of the Jeffersonian Republicans and the Federalists. According to historian David Fischer,

> During the 1790s the Jeffersonians revolutionized electioneering. . . . Their opponents complained bitterly of endless "dinings," "drinkings," and celebrations; of handbills "industriously posted along every road"; of convoys of vehicles which brought voters to the polls by the carload; of candidates "in perpetual motion."[12]

The Federalists, although initially reluctant, soon learned the techniques of mobilizing voters: "mass meetings, barbecues, stump-speaking, festivals of many kinds, processions and parades, runners and riders, door-to-door canvassing, the distribution of tickets and ballots, electioneering tours by candidates, free transportation to the polls, outright bribery and corruption of other kinds."[13]

The result of this competition for votes was described by historian Henry Jones Ford in his classic *Rise and Growth of American Politics*.[14] Ford examined the pop-

---

[10]Harold Gosnell, *Machine Politics, Chicago Model*, rev. ed. (Chicago: University of Chicago Press, 1968), Chapter 4.

[11]Stanley Kelley, Jr., Richard E. Ayres, and William G. Bowen, "Registration and Voting: Putting First Things First," *American Political Science Review* 61 (June 1967), pp. 359–70.

[12]David H. Fischer, *The Revolution of American Conservatism* (New York: Harper & Row, 1965), p. 93. For a full account of parties as agents both of candidate selection and of mass mobilization, see John H. Aldrich, *Why Parties?* (Chicago: University of Chicago Press, 1995).

[13]Ibid., p. 109. With various forms of the secret ballot, it was often difficult to know exactly how a citizen voted—and thus chancy to bribe him if you couldn't know you were getting what you paid for. Because of this, it was often the case that buying votes was transformed into buying *non*participation—paying, that is, for those who opposed your candidates to "go fishing" on Election Day. For evidence of this in rural New York, see Gary Cox and Morgan Kousser, "Turnout and Rural Corruption in New York as a Test Case," *American Journal of Political Science* 25 (Nov. 1981), pp. 646–63.

[14]Henry Jones Ford, *The Rise and Growth of American Politics* (New York: Da Capo Press, 1967 reprint of 1898 edition), Chapter 9.

ular clamor against John Adams and Federalist policies in the 1790s that made government a "weak, shakey affair" and appeared to contemporary observers to mark the beginnings of a popular insurrection against the government.[15] Attempts by the Federalists initially to suppress mass discontent, Ford observed, might have "caused an explosion of force which would have blown up the government."[16] What intervened to prevent rebellion was Jefferson's "great unconscious achievement," the creation of an opposition party that served to "open constitutional channels of political agitation."[17] The creation of the Jeffersonian party diverted opposition to the administration into electoral channels. Party competition gave citizens a sense that their votes were valuable and that it was thus not necessary to take to the streets to have an impact upon political affairs. Whether or not Ford was correct in crediting party competition with an ability to curb civil unrest, it is clear that competition between the parties promoted voting.

The parties' competitive efforts to attract citizens to the polls are not their only influence on voting. Individual voters tend to form psychological ties with parties. Although the strength of partisan ties in the United States has declined in recent years, a majority of Americans continue to identify with either the Republican or Democratic party. Party loyalty gives citizens a stake in election outcomes that encourages them to take part with considerably greater regularity than those lacking partisan ties.[18] Even where both legal facilitation and competitiveness are weak, party loyalists vote with great regularity.

In recent decades, as we will see in Chapter 11, the importance of party as a political force in the United States has diminished considerably. The decline of party is undoubtedly one of the factors responsible for the relatively low rates of voter turnout that characterize American national elections. To an extent, the federal and state governments have directly assumed some of the burden of voter mobilization once assigned to the parties. Voter registration drives and public funding of electoral campaigns are two obvious ways in which government helps to induce citizens to go to the polls. Another more subtle public mechanism for voter mobilization is the primary election, which can increase voter interest and involvement in the electoral process. It remains to be seen, however, whether government mechanisms of voter mobilization can be as effective as party mechanisms. Of course, a number of private groups like the League of Women Voters, church groups, and civil rights groups have also actively participated in voter registration efforts, but none have been as effective as political parties.

Is It Rational to Vote?

Compared to other democracies, voter turnout in national elections is extremely low in the United States. It is usually around 50 percent for presidential

[15]Ibid., p. 125.
[16]Ibid.
[17]Ibid., p. 126.
[18]See Angus Campbell et al., *The American Voter* (New York: Wiley, 1960).

elections and between 30 percent and 40 percent for midterm elections. In other Western democracies, turnout regularly exceeds 80 percent. In defense of American citizens, it should be pointed out that occasions for voting as a form of civic activity occur more frequently in the United States than in other democracies. There are more offices filled by election in the United States than elsewhere—indeed, more offices per capita, which is somewhat startling given how large a democracy the United States is. Many of these are posts that are filled by appointment in other democracies. Especially unusual in this respect are elected judges in many jurisdictions and elected local "bureaucrats" (like the local sheriff and the proverbial town dog catcher). In addition, there are primaries as well as general elections, and, in many states, there are initiatives and referendums to vote on, too. It is a wonder that American citizens don't suffer from some form of democratic fatigue! Though many scholars have tried to answer the question, "Why is turnout so low?" others have argued that the real question should be, "Why is turnout so high?" That is, why does anyone turn out to vote at all?

If we think of voter turnout in terms of cost-benefit analysis, then it isn't obvious why people vote.[19] There are many costs to voting. People must take time out of their busy schedules, possibly incurring a loss of wages, in order to show up at the polls. In many states, voters have to overcome numerous hurdles just to register. If an individual wants to cast an informed vote, he or she must also spend time learning about the candidates and their positions.

Voters must bear these costs no matter what the outcome of the election, yet it is extremely unlikely that an individual's vote will actually affect the outcome, unless the vote makes or breaks a tie. Just making a close election one vote closer by voting for the loser, or the winner one vote more secure by voting for her, doesn't matter much. As the old saw has it, "Closeness only counts in horseshoes and dancing." It is almost certain that if an individual did not incur the costs of voting and stayed home instead, the election results would be the same. The probability of a single vote being decisive in a presidential election is about one in ten million.[20] Given the tiny probability that an individual's vote will determine whether or not the candidate he or she

[19]William H. Riker and Peter C. Ordeshook, "A Theory of the Calculus of Voting," *American Political Science Review* 62 (1968), pp. 25–42. Riker and Ordeshook conclude that someone caring only about the relative *benefits* from securing the victory of his or her favorite candidate over the opponent, net of the *costs* of voting, will want to weigh the likelihood that his or her vote is decisive. Since this probability is bound to be low—indeed, infinitesimal in a moderately large electorate (as we discuss in the text shortly)—the benefits will have to be extraordinary, relative to the costs to motivate participation. Hence, Riker and Ordeshook wonder why turnout is "so high" and look to reasons other than the simple (some say, "simplistic") cost-benefit analysis for the explanation.

[20]Andrew Gelman, Gary King, and John Boscardin, "Estimating the Probability of Events That Have Never Occurred: When Is Your Vote Decisive?" *Journal of the American Statistical Association* 93, 441 (March 1998), pp. 1–9.

prefers is elected, it seems as if those who turn out to vote are behaving irrationally.[21]

One possible solution to this puzzle is that people are motivated by more than just their preferences for electing a particular candidate—they are, in fact, satisfying their duty as citizens, and this benefit exceeds the costs of voting.[22] Yet this hypothesis still does not provide an adequate answer to the rationality of voting—it only speaks to the fact that people value the *act of voting* itself. That is, people have a "taste" for voting. But rational-choice approach cannot say where tastes come from[23] and therefore cannot say much about voter turnout.

John Aldrich offers another possible solution: he looks at the question from the politician's point of view.[24] Candidates calculate how much to invest in campaigns based on their probability of winning. In the unlikely event that an incumbent appears beatable, the challengers often invest heavily in their own campaigns because they believe the investment has a good chance of paying off. In response to these strong challenges, incumbents will not only work harder to raise campaign funds but also spend more of what they raise.[25] Parties seeking to maximize the number of positions in the government they control may also shift resources to help out the candidates in these close races.

More vigorous campaigns will generally lead to increased turnout. The increase is not necessarily due to citizens reacting to the closeness of the race (that is, the perception that their vote may affect the outcome) but to the greater effort and resources that candidates put into close races, which, in turn, reduce the costs of voting. Candidates share some of the costs of voting by helping citizens register and by getting them to the polls on election day. Heated advertising campaigns reduce the voters' costs of becoming informed (since candidates flood the public with information about themselves). This decrease in costs to individual voters in what strategic politicians perceive to be a close race at least partially explains why rational individuals would turn out to vote.

 Rationality Principle

Given the tiny probability that an individual's vote will determine the winner of an election, candidates need to reduce the cost of voting for citizens in order to mobilize them.

---

[21]A *strategic* cost-benefit analysis plays off the following reasonable argument: "If everyone determines that his or her vote doesn't matter, and no one votes, then *my* vote will determine the outcome!" This kind of strategic conjecturing has been analyzed in Thomas Palfrey and Howard Rosenthal, "Voter Participation and Strategic Uncertainty," *American Political Science Review* 79 (March 1985), pp. 62–79. They conclude that once all the back-and-forth conjecturing is done, the question of why anyone participates remains.

[22]This was Riker and Ordeshook's line of argument. They claim, in effect, that there is an *experiential* as well as an *instrumental* rationale for voting. In more economic terms, this is the view that voting is a form of consumption as much as it is a type of investment. For a brief and user-friendly development of this logic, see Kenneth A. Shepsle and Mark S. Bonchek, *Analyzing Politics: Rationality, Behavior, and Institutions* (New York: W. W. Norton, 1997) pp. 251–59.

[23]Brian Barry, *Sociologists, Economists, and Democracy* (London: Collier-Macmillan, 1970).

[24]John H. Aldrich, "Rational Choice and Turnout," *American Journal of Political Science* 37 (Feb. 1993), pp. 246–78.

[25]Gary C. Jacobson and Samuel Kernell, *Strategy and Choice in Congressional Elections*, 2nd ed. (New Haven: Yale University Press, 1983).

REGULATING THE ELECTORAL PROCESS

Institution Principle

The electoral process is governed by a variety of rules and procedures that allow those in power an opportunity to regulate the character and consequences of political participation.

Elections allow citizens to participate in political life on a routine and peaceful basis. Indeed, American voters have the opportunity to select and, if they so desire, depose some of their most important leaders. In this way, Americans have a chance to intervene in and to influence the government's programs and policies. Yet, it is important to recall that elections are not spontaneous affairs. Instead, they are formal government institutions. While elections allow citizens a chance to participate in politics, they also allow the government a chance to exert a good deal of control over when, where, how, and which of its citizens will participate. Electoral processes are governed by a variety of rules and procedures that allow those in power a significant opportunity to regulate the character—and perhaps also the consequences—of mass political participation.

Thus, elections provide governments with an excellent opportunity to regulate and control popular involvement. Three general forms of regulation have played especially important roles in the electoral history of the Western democracies. First, governments often attempt to regulate the composition of the electorate in order to diminish the electoral weight of groups they deem to be undesirable. Second, governments frequently seek to manipulate the translation of voters' choices into electoral outcomes. Third, virtually all governments attempt to insulate policy-making processes from electoral intervention through regulation of the relationship between electoral decisions and the composition or organization of the government.

Electoral Composition

Perhaps the oldest and most obvious device used to regulate voting and its consequences is manipulation of the electorate's composition. In the earliest elections in western Europe, for example, the suffrage was generally limited to property owners and others who could be trusted to vote in a manner acceptable to those in power. To cite just one illustration, property qualifications in France prior to 1848 limited the electorate to 240,000 of some 7 million men over the age of twenty-one.[26] Of course, no women were permitted to vote. During the same era, other nations manipulated the electorate's composition by assigning unequal electoral weights to different classes of voters. The 1831 Belgian constitution, for example, assigned individuals anywhere from one to three votes depending upon their property holdings, education, and position.[27] But even in the context of America's ostensibly universal and equal suffrage in the twentieth century, the composition of the electorate is still subject to manipulation. Until recent years, some states manipulated the vote by the discriminatory use of poll

[26]Stein Rokkan, *Citizens, Elections, Parties* (New York: David McKay, 1970), p. 149.
[27]John A. Hawgood, *Modern Constitutions Since 1787* (New York: D. Van Nostrand, 1939), p. 148.

FIGURE 10.1

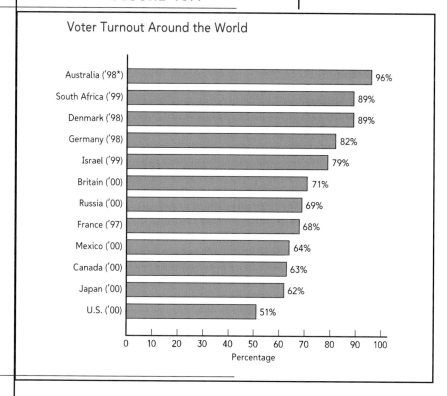

Voter Turnout Around the World

*NOTE: Year of the most recent national election.

SOURCES: www.agora.stm.it/elections and Center for Voting Democracy, www.fairvote.org/turnout

taxes and literacy tests or by such practices as the placement of polls and the scheduling of voting hours to depress participation by one or another group. Today the most important example of the regulation of the American electorate's composition is our unique personal registration requirements.

Levels of voter participation in twentieth-century American elections are quite low by comparison to those of the other Western democracies (see Figure 10.1).[28] Indeed, voter participation in presidential elections in the United States has barely averaged 50 percent recently (see Figure 10.2). Turnout in the 2000 presidential election was 51 percent. During the nineteenth century, by contrast, voter turnout in the United States was extremely high. Records, in fact, indicate that in some counties as many as 105 percent of those eligible voted in presidential elections. Some proportion of this total obviously was artificial—a result of the widespread

[28]See Walter Dean Burnham, "The Changing Shape of the American Political Universe," *American Political Science Review* 59 (1965), pp. 7–28.

FIGURE 10.2

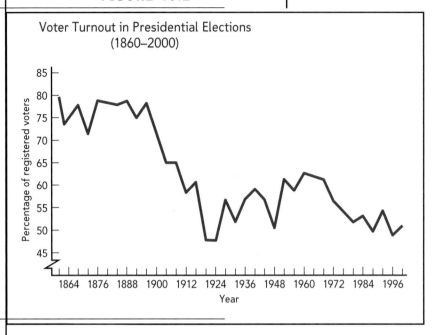

Voter Turnout in Presidential Elections (1860–2000)

SOURCES: For 1860–1928, U. S. Bureau of the Census, *Historical Statistics of the United States, Colonial Times to 1970*, Pt. 2, p. 1071. For 1932–1992, U.S. Bureau of the Census, *Statistical Abstract of the United States, 1993* (Washington, DC: Government Printing Office, 1993), p. 284. For 1996 and 2000, author's update.

corruption that characterized American voting practices during that period. Nevertheless, it seems clear that the proportion of eligible voters actually going to the polls was considerably larger in nineteenth-century America than it is today.

As Figure 10.2 indicates, the critical years during which voter turnout declined across the United States were between 1890 and 1910. These years coincide with the adoption of laws across much of the nation requiring eligible citizens to appear personally at a registrar's office to register to vote some time prior to the actual date of an election. Personal registration was one of several "Progressive" reforms of political practices initiated at the turn of the century. The ostensible purpose of registration was to discourage fraud and corruption. But to many Progressive reformers, "corruption" was a code word, referring to the type of politics practiced in the large cities where political parties had organized immigrant and ethnic populations. Reformers not only objected to the corruption that surely was a facet of party politics in this period, but they also opposed the growing political power of urban populations and their leaders.

Personal registration imposed a new burden upon potential voters and altered the format of American elections. Under the registration systems adopted after 1890, it became the duty of individual voters to secure their own eligibility.

History Principle

Between 1890 and 1910, voter turnout declined in the U.S. as a result of new registration requirements. Since that time, turnout has remained low in comparison with the nineteenth century.

This duty could prove to be a significant burden for potential voters. During a personal appearance before the registrar, individuals seeking to vote were (and are) required to furnish proof of identity, residence, and citizenship. While the inconvenience of registration varied from state to state, usually voters could register only during business hours on weekdays. Many potential voters could not afford to lose a day's pay in order to register. Second, voters were usually required to register well before the next election, in some states up to several months earlier. Third, since most personal registration laws required a periodic purge of the election rolls, ostensibly to keep them up-to-date, voters often had to re-register to maintain their eligibility. Thus, although personal registration requirements helped to diminish the widespread electoral corruption that accompanied a completely open voting process, they also made it much more difficult for citizens to participate in the electoral process.

Registration requirements particularly depress the participation of those with little education and low incomes because registration requires a greater degree of political involvement and interest than does the act of voting itself. To vote, a person need only be concerned with the particular election campaign at hand. Yet, requiring individuals to register before the next election forces them to make a decision to participate on the basis of an abstract interest in the electoral process rather than a simple concern with a specific campaign. Such an abstract interest in electoral politics is largely a product of education. Those with relatively little education may become interested in political events once the stimuli of a particular campaign become salient, but by that time it may be too late to register. As a result, personal registration requirements not only diminish the size of the electorate but also tend to create an electorate that is, in the aggregate, better educated, higher in income and social status, and composed of fewer African Americans and other minorities than the citizenry as a whole. Presumably this is why the elimination of personal registration requirements has not always been viewed favorably by some conservatives.[29]

Over the years, voter registration restrictions have been modified somewhat to make registration easier. In 1993, for example, Congress approved and President Clinton signed the "Motor Voter" bill to ease voter registration by allowing individuals to register when they applied for driver's licenses, as well as in public assistance and military recruitment offices.[30] In Europe, there is typically no registration burden on the individual voter; voter registration is handled automatically by the government. This is one reason that voter turnout rates in Europe are higher than those in the United States.

Another factor explaining low rates of voter turnout in the United States is the weakness of the American party system. During the nineteenth century, American political party machines employed hundreds of thousands of workers to organize and mobilize voters and bring them to the polls. The result was an

[29]See Kevin Phillips and Paul H. Blackman, *Electoral Reform and Voter Participation* (Washington, DC: American Enterprise Institute, 1975).
[30]Helen Dewar, "'Motor Voter' Agreement Is Reached," *Washington Post*, 28 April 1993, p. A6.

extremely high rate of turnout, typically more than 90 percent of eligible voters.[31] But political party machines began to decline in strength in the early twentieth century and by now have largely disappeared. Without party workers to encourage them to go to the polls and even to bring them there if necessary, many eligible voters will not participate. In the absence of strong parties, participation rates drop the most among poorer and less-educated citizens. Because of the absence of strong political parties, the American electorate is smaller and skewed more toward the middle class than toward the population of all those potentially eligible to vote.

Translating Voters' Choices into Electoral Outcomes

majority system
A type of electoral system in which, to win a seat in the parliament or other representative body, a candidate must receive a majority (50 percent plus 1) of all the votes cast in the relevant district.

plurality system
A type of electoral system in which victory goes to the individual who gets the most votes in an election, not necessarily a majority of votes cast.

proportional representation A multiple-member district system that allows each political party representation in proportion to its percentage of the vote.

With the exception of America's personal registration requirements, contemporary governments generally do not try to limit the composition of their electorates. Instead, they prefer to allow everyone to vote, and then to manipulate the outcome of the election. This is possible because there is more than one way to decide the relationship between individual votes and electoral outcomes. There are any number of possible rules that can be used to determine how individual votes will be translated. Two types of regulations are especially important: the rules that set the criteria for victory and the rules that define electoral districts.

The Criteria for Winning   In some nations, to win a seat in the parliament or other representative body, a candidate must receive a majority (50% + 1) of all the votes cast in the relevant district. This type of electoral system is called a *majority system* and was used in the primary elections of most Southern states until recent years. Generally, majority systems have a provision for a second or "runoff" election among the two top candidates if the initial contest drew so many contestants that none received an absolute majority of the votes cast.

In other nations, candidates for office need not receive an absolute majority of the votes cast to win an election. Instead, victory is awarded to the candidate who receives the greatest number of votes in a given election regardless of the actual percentage of votes this represents. Thus, a candidate who received 40 percent or 30 percent of the votes cast may win the contest so long as no rival receives more votes. This type of electoral process is called a *plurality system,* and it is the system used in almost all general elections in the United States.[32]

Most European nations employ still a third form of electoral system, called *proportional representation.* Under proportional rules, competing political par-

---

[31]Erik W. Austin and Jerome M. Clubb, *Political Facts of the United States since 1789* (New York: Columbia University Press, 1986), pp. 378–79.

[32]There are different types of plurality systems. The one currently utilized in the United States in congressional and presidential elections is single-member districts and first-past-the-post. For an accessible analysis of the different types of plurality systems and a model for analyzing electoral systems, see Shepsle and Bonchek, *Analyzing Politics*, pp. 178–87.

ties are awarded legislative seats roughly in proportion to the percentage of the popular vote that they receive. For example, a party that won 30 percent of the votes would receive roughly 30 percent of the seats in the parliament or other representative body. In the United States, proportional representation is used by many states in presidential primary elections. In these primaries, candidates for the Democratic and Republican nominations are awarded convention delegates in rough proportion to the percentage of the popular vote that they received in the primary. Early in the twentieth century, proportional representation systems were employed in many American cities, including New York, to elect city councils. Today these systems have nearly disappeared. Cambridge, Massachusetts, is one of the last cities to use such a system in city council elections. Elections to the New York City school board are also still conducted using a proportional representation system.

Generally, systems of proportional representation work to the electoral advantage of smaller or weaker social groups, while majority and plurality systems tend to help larger and more powerful forces. This is because in legislative elections, proportional representation reduces, while majority and plurality rules increase, the number of votes that political parties must receive to win legislative seats. For instance, in European parliamentary elections, a minor party that wins 10 percent of the national vote will also receive 10 percent of the parliamentary seats. In American congressional elections, by contrast, a party winning only 10 percent of the popular vote would probably receive no congressional seats at all.[33] Obviously, choices among types of electoral systems can have important political consequences. Competing forces often seek to establish an electoral system they believe will serve their political interests while undermining the fortunes of their opponents. For example, in 1937, New York City Council seats were awarded on the basis of proportional representation. This led to the selection of several Communist party council members. During the 1940s, to prevent the election of Communists, the city adopted a plurality system. Under the new rule, the tiny Communist party was unable to muster enough votes to secure a council seat. In a similar vein, the introduction of proportional representation for the selection of delegates to the Democratic party's 1972 national convention was designed in part to maximize the voting strength of minority groups and, not entirely coincidentally, to improve the electoral chances of the candidates they were most likely to favor.[34]

Institution Principle

The rules that set the criteria for winning an election have an effect on the outcome.

[33]For an argument that plurality systems are governance-oriented, whereas proportional systems are representation-oriented, see Shepsle and Bonchek, *Analyzing Politics*, pp. 188–91. This argument derives from the famous Duverger's Law—an argument that plurality systems encourage two-party competition (one party or the other secures a majority of seats in the legislature), whereas proportional systems encourage multiparty competition (many parties hold seats in the legislature, with the very frequent outcome that no party commands a majority on its own, and thus parties must build coalitions). The law was first described systematically by the French political scientist Maurice Duverger in *Political Parties* (New York: Wiley, 1954).

[34]See Nelson Polsby and Aaron Wildavsky, *Presidential Elections* (New York: Scribners, 1980).

Congressional Redistricting

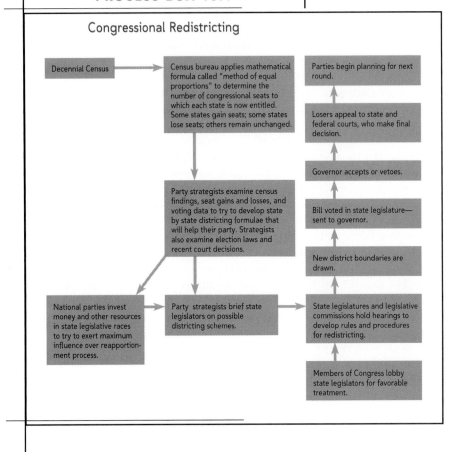

Decennial Census

Census bureau applies mathematical formula called "method of equal proportions" to determine the number of congressional seats to which each state is now entitled. Some states gain seats; some states lose seats; others remain unchanged.

Party strategists examine census findings, seat gains and losses, and voting data to try to develop state by state districting formulae that will help their party. Strategists also examine election laws and recent court decisions.

National parties invest money and other resources in state legislative races to try to exert maximum influence over reapportionment process.

Party strategists brief state legislators on possible districting schemes.

Parties begin planning for next round.

Losers appeal to state and federal courts, who make final decision.

Governor accepts or vetoes.

Bill voted in state legislature—sent to governor.

New district boundaries are drawn.

State legislatures and legislative commissions hold hearings to develop rules and procedures for redistricting.

Members of Congress lobby state legislators for favorable treatment.

gerrymandering
Apportionment of voters in districts in such ways as to give unfair advantage to one political party.

Electoral Districts   Despite the occasional use of proportional representation and majority voting systems, most electoral contests in the United States are decided on the basis of plurality rules. Rather than seeking to manipulate the criteria for victory, American politicians have usually sought to influence electoral outcomes by manipulating the organization of electoral districts. Congressional district boundaries in the United States are redrawn by governors and state legislatures every ten years, after the decennial census determines the number of House seats to which each state is entitled (see Process Box 10.1). The manipulation of electoral districts to increase the likelihood of one or another outcome is called *gerrymandering,* in honor of nineteenth-century Massachusetts governor Elbridge Gerry, who was alleged to have designed a district in the shape of a salamander to promote his party's interests. The principle is a simple one. Different distributions of voters among districts produce different electoral outcomes; those in a position to control the arrangements of districts are also in a position to manipulate the results. For example, until recent years, gerrymandering to dilute the voting strength of racial minorities was employed by many state legislatures. One of the more common strategies involved redrawing congressional boundary lines in such a way as to divide and disperse a black population that would have otherwise constituted a majority within the original district.

This form of racial gerrymandering, sometimes called "cracking," was used in Mississippi during the 1960s and 1970s to prevent the election of a black congressman. Historically, the black population in Mississippi was clustered in the western half of the state, along the Mississippi Delta. From 1882 until 1966, the delta was one congressional district. Although blacks constituted a clear majority within the district (66 percent in 1960), the continuing election of white congressmen was assured simply because blacks were denied the right to register and vote. With Congress's passage of the Voting Rights Act of 1965, however, the Mississippi state legislature moved swiftly to minimize the potential voting power of blacks by redrawing congressional district lines in such a way as to fragment the black population in the delta into four of the state's five congressional districts. Mississippi's gerrymandering scheme was preserved in the state's redistricting plans in 1972 and 1981 and helped to prevent the election of any black representative until 1986, when Mike Espy became the first African American since Reconstruction to represent Mississippi in Congress.

In recent years, the federal government has encouraged what is sometimes called "benign gerrymandering," designed to increase minority representation in Congress. The 1982 amendments to the Voting Rights Act of 1965 encourage the creation of legislative districts with predominantly African American or Hispanic American populations by requiring states, when possible, to draw district lines that take account of concentrations of African American and Hispanic American voters. These amendments were initially supported by Democrats who assumed that minority-controlled districts would guarantee the election of Democratic members of Congress. However, Republicans have championed these efforts, reasoning that if minority voters were concentrated in their own districts, Republican prospects in other districts would be enhanced.[35] Moreover, Republicans hoped some Democratic incumbents might be forced from office to make way for minority representatives. In some cases, the Republicans' theory has proved correct. As a result of the creation of a number of new minority districts in 1991, several long-term white Democrats lost their congressional seats. The 1993 Supreme Court decision in *Shaw v. Reno*, however, opened the way for challenges by white voters to the drawing of these districts. In the 5-to-4 majority opinion, Justice O'Connor wrote that if district boundaries were so "bizarre" as to be inexplicable on any grounds other than an effort to ensure the election of minority group members to office, white voters

---

[35]Roberto Suro, "In Redistricting, New Rules and New Prizes," *New York Times*, 6 May 1990, sec. 4, p. 5.

would have reason to assert that they had been the victims of unconstitutional racial gerrymandering.[36] In its 1995 decision in *Miller v. Johnson*, the Court questioned the entire concept of benign racial gerrymandering by asserting that the use of race as a "predominant factor" in the drawing of district lines was presumptively unconstitutional. However, the Court held open the possibility that race could be *one* of the factors taken into account in legislative redistricting. Similarly, in *Bush v. Vera*, the Court ruled that three Texas congressional districts with black or Hispanic majorities were unconstitutional because state officials put too much emphasis on race in drawing boundaries. "Voters," said the Court, "are more than mere racial statistics." In *Shaw v. Hunt*, the Court struck down a North Carolina black majority voting district for similar reasons. Most recently, in the 1997 case of *Abrams v. Johnson*, the Court upheld a new Georgia congressional district map that eliminated two of the state's three majority-black districts.[37]

Although governments do have the capacity to manipulate electoral outcomes, this capacity is not absolute. Electoral arrangements conceived to be illegitimate may prompt some segments of the electorate to seek other ways of participating in political life. Moreover, no electoral system that provides universal and equal suffrage can, by itself, long prevent an outcome favored by large popular majorities. Yet, faced with opposition short of an overwhelming majority, government's ability to manipulate the translation of individual choices into collective decisions can be an important factor in preserving the established distribution of power.

Insulating Decision-Making Processes

Virtually all governments attempt at least partially to insulate decision-making processes from electoral intervention. The most obvious forms of insulation are the confinement of popular election to only some governmental positions, various modes of indirect election, and lengthy tenure in office. In the United States, the framers of the Constitution intended that only members of the House of Representatives would be subject to direct popular selection. The president and members of the Senate were to be indirectly elected for rather long terms to allow them, as *The Federalist Papers* put it, to avoid "an unqualified complaisance to every sudden breeze of passion, or to every transient impulse which the people may receive."[38]

---

[36]Shaw v. Reno, 113 S.Ct. 2816 (1993); Linda Greenhouse, "Court Questions Districts Drawn to Aid Minorities," *New York Times*, 29 June 1993, p. 1. See also Joan Biskupic, "Court's Conservatism Unlikely to Be Shifted by a New Justice," *Washington Post*, 30 June 1993, p. 1.

[37]Bush v. Vera, 116 S.Ct. 1941 (1996); Shaw v. Hunt, 64 USLW 4437 (1996); Abrams v. Johnson, 95-1425 (1997).

[38]Rossiter, ed., *The Federalist Papers*, No. 71, p. 432.

The Electoral College In the early history of popular voting, nations often made use of indirect elections. In these elections, voters would choose the members of an intermediate body. These members would, in turn, select public officials. The assumption underlying such processes was that ordinary citizens were not really qualified to choose their leaders and could not be trusted to do so directly. The last vestige of this procedure in America is the *electoral college,* the group of electors who formally select the president and vice president of the United States.

When Americans go to the polls on election day, they are technically not voting directly for presidential candidates. Instead, voters within each state are choosing among slates of electors who have either been elected or appointed to their positions some months earlier. The electors who are chosen in the presidential race are pledged to support their own party's presidential candidate. In each state (except for Maine and Nebraska), the slate that wins casts all the state's electoral votes for its party's candidate.[39] Each state is entitled to a number of electoral votes equal to the number of the state's senators and representatives combined, for a total of 538 electoral votes for the fifty states and the District of Columbia. Occasionally, an elector breaks his or her pledge and votes for the other party's candidate. For example, in 1976, when the Republicans carried the state of Washington, one Republican elector from that state refused to vote for Gerald Ford, the Republican presidential nominee. Many states have now enacted statutes formally binding electors to their pledges, but some constitutional authorities doubt whether such statutes are enforceable.

In each state, the electors whose slate has won proceed to the state's capital on the Monday following the second Wednesday in December and formally cast their ballots. These are sent to Washington, tallied by the Congress in January, and the name of the winner is formally announced. If no candidate received a majority of all electoral votes, the names of the top three candidates would be submitted to the House, where each state would be able to cast one vote. Whether a state's vote would be decided by a majority, plurality, or some other fraction of the state's delegates would be determined under rules established by the House.

In 1800 and 1824, the electoral college failed to produce a majority for any candidate. In the election of 1800, Thomas Jefferson, the Jeffersonian Republican party's presidential candidate, and Aaron Burr, that party's vice presidential candidate, received an equal number of votes in the electoral college, throwing the election into the House of Representatives. (The Constitution at that time made no distinction between presidential and vice presidential candidates, specifying only that the individual receiving a majority of electoral votes

electoral college
The presidential electors from each state who meet in their respective state capitals after the popular election to cast ballots for president and vice president.

---

[39]State legislatures determine the system by which electors are selected and almost all states use this "winner-take-all" system. Maine and Nebraska, however, provide that one electoral vote goes to the winner in each congressional district and two electoral votes go to the winner statewide.

would be named president.) Some members of the Federalist party in Congress suggested that they should seize the opportunity to damage the Republican cause by supporting Burr and denying Jefferson the presidency. Federalist leader Alexander Hamilton put a stop to this mischievous notion, however, and made certain that his party supported Jefferson. Hamilton's actions enraged Burr and helped lead to the infamous duel between the two men, in which Hamilton was killed. The Twelfth Amendment, ratified in 1804, was designed to prevent a repetition of such a situation by providing for separate electoral college votes for president and vice president.

In the 1824 election, four candidates—John Quincy Adams, Andrew Jackson, Henry Clay, and William H. Crawford—divided the electoral vote; no one of them received a majority. The House of Representatives eventually chose Adams over the others, even though Jackson won more electoral and popular votes. This choice resulted from the famous "corrupt bargain" between Adams and Henry Clay. After 1824, the two major political parties had begun to dominate presidential politics to such an extent that by December of each election year, only two candidates remained for the electors to choose between, thus ensuring that one would receive a majority. This freed the parties and the candidates from having to plan their campaigns to culminate in Congress, and Congress very quickly ceased to dominate the presidential selection process.

On all but three occasions since 1824, the electoral vote has simply ratified the nationwide popular vote. Since electoral votes are won on a state-by-state basis, it is mathematically possible for a candidate who receives a nationwide popular plurality to fail to carry states whose electoral votes would add up to a majority. Thus, in 1876, Rutherford B. Hayes was the winner in the electoral college despite receiving fewer popular votes than his rival, Samuel Tilden. In 1888, Grover Cleveland received more popular votes than Benjamin Harrison, but received fewer electoral votes. And in 2000, Al Gore outpolled his opponent, George W. Bush, but lost the electoral college by a mere four electoral votes.

The outcome of the 2000 contest, in which the electoral college produced a result that was inconsistent with the popular vote, led to many calls for the abolition of this institution and the introduction of some form of direct popular election of the president. Within days of the election, several members of Congress promised to introduce a constitutional amendment that would bring an end to the electoral college, which one congressman called an "anachronism." Efforts to introduce such a reform, however, will likely be blocked by political forces that believe they benefit from the present system. For example, minority groups that are influential in large urban states with many electoral votes feel that their voting strength would be diminished in a direct, nationwide, popular election. At the same time, some Republicans believe that their party's usual presidential strength in the South and in parts of the Midwest and West gives them a distinct advantage in the electoral college. Some Democrats and Republicans also fear that the direct popular election of the president would give third parties more influence over the outcome. Thus, while political pressure will be great to abolish the current system, efforts toward that end will likely face the same fate as the over seven hundred previous attempts to reform it.

Frequency of Elections Somewhat less obvious are the insulating effects of electoral arrangements that permit direct, and even frequent, popular election of public officials, but tend to fragment the impact of elections upon the government's composition. In the United States, for example, the constitutional provision of staggered terms of service in the Senate was designed to diminish the impact of shifts in electoral sentiment upon the Senate as an institution. Since only one-third of its members were to be selected at any given point in time, the composition of the institution would be partially protected from changes in electoral preferences. This would prevent what *The Federalist Papers* called "mutability in the public councils arising from a rapid succession of new members."[40]

Size of Electoral Districts The division of the nation into relatively small, geographically based constituencies for the purpose of selecting members of the House of Representatives was, in part, designed to have a similar effect. Representatives were to be chosen frequently. And although not prescribed by the Constitution, the fact that each was to be selected by a discrete constituency was thought by Madison and others to diminish the government's vulnerability to mass popular movements.

In a sense, the House of Representatives was compartmentalized in the same way that a submarine is divided into watertight sections to confine the impact of any damage to the vessel. First, by dividing the national electorate into small districts, the importance of local issues would increase. Second, the salience of local issues would mean that a representative's electoral fortunes would be more closely tied to factors peculiar to his or her own district than to national responses to issues. Third, given a geographical principle of representation, national groups would be somewhat fragmented while the formation of local forces that might or might not share common underlying attitudes would be encouraged. No matter how well represented individual constituencies might be, the influence of voters on national policy questions would be fragmented. In Madison's terms, the influence of "faction" would thus become "less likely to pervade the whole body than some particular portion of it."[41]

The Ballot Another example of an American electoral arrangement that tends to fragment the impact of mass elections upon the government's composition is the Australian ballot (named for its country of origin). Prior to the introduction of this official ballot in the 1890s, voters cast ballots according to political parties. Each party printed its own ballots, listed only its own candidates for each office, and employed party workers to distribute its ballots at the polls. This ballot format had two important consequences. First, the party ballot precluded

[40]Rossiter, ed., *The Federalist Papers*, No. 62.
[41]Ibid., No. 10.

secrecy in voting. Because each party's ballot was distinctive in size and color, it was not difficult for party workers to determine how individuals intended to vote. This, of course, facilitated the intimidation and bribery of voters. Second, the format of the ballot prevented split-ticket voting. Because only one party's candidates appeared on any ballot, it was difficult for a voter to cast anything other than a straight party vote.

Australian ballot
An electoral format that presents the names of all the candidates for any given office on the same ballot. Introduced at the turn of the century, the Australian ballot replaced the partisan ballot and facilitated split-ticket voting.

The official *Australian ballot* represented a significant change in electoral procedure. The new ballot was prepared and administered by the state rather than the parties. Each ballot was identical and included the names of all candidates for office. This reform, of course, increased the secrecy of voting and reduced the possibility for voter intimidation and bribery. Because all ballots were identical in appearance, even the voter who had been threatened or bribed might still vote as he or she wished, without the knowledge of party workers. But perhaps even more important, the Australian ballot reform made it possible for voters to make their choices on the basis of the individual rather than the collective merits of a party's candidates. Because all candidates for the same office now appeared on the same ballot, voters were no longer forced to choose a straight party ticket. It was indeed the introduction of the Australian ballot that gave rise to the phenomenon of split-ticket voting in American elections.[42] Ticket splitting is especially prevalent in states that use the "office-block" ballot format, which does not group candidates by their partisan affiliations. By contrast, the "party-column" format places all the candidates affiliated with a given party in the same row or column. The former facilitates ticket splitting while the latter encourages straight-ticket voting.

It is this second consequence of the Australian ballot reform that tends to fragment the impact of American elections upon the government's composition. Prior to the reform of the ballot, it was not uncommon for an entire incumbent administration to be swept from office and replaced by an entirely new set of officials. In the absence of a real possibility of split-ticket voting, any desire on the part of the electorate for change could be expressed only as a vote against all candidates of the party in power. Because of this, there always existed the possibility, particularly at the state and local levels, that an insurgent slate committed to policy change could be swept into power. The party ballot thus increased the potential impact of elections upon the government's composition. Although this potential may not always have been realized, the party ballot at least increased the chance that electoral decisions could lead to policy changes. By contrast, because it permitted choice on the basis of candidates' individual appeals, the Australian ballot lessened the likelihood that the electorate would sweep an entirely new administration into power. Ticket splitting led to increasingly divided partisan control of government.

[42]Jerold G. Rusk, "The Effect of the Australian Ballot Reform on Split Ticket Voting: 1876–1908," *American Political Science Review* 64 (December 1970), pp. 1220–38.

The ballots used in the United States are a mix of forms developed as long ago as the 1890s when the states took over the printing of ballots from the political parties. These were modified during the 1940s and 1950s when voting machines and punch-card ballots were introduced, and ballots were further updated in some jurisdictions during the 1990s when more modern and accurate computerized voting methods were introduced. The choice of ballot format is a county decision and, within any state, various counties may use different formats depending on local resources and preferences. For example, the Palm Beach County butterfly ballot, which seemed to confuse many voters, was selected by Democratic election officials who thought its larger print would help elderly, predominantly Democratic voters read the names of the candidates. Not infrequently, as turned out to be the case in Florida, neighboring counties used completely different ballot systems. For example, the city of Baltimore, Maryland, introduced voting machines many years ago and continues to use them. Baltimore County, Maryland, uses more modern ballots that are optically scanned by computers. Neighboring Montgomery County, Maryland, employs a cumbersome punch-card system that requires voters to punch several different cards on both sides—a bewildering process that usually results in large numbers of spoiled ballots. In some states, including Florida, different precincts within the same county may use different voting methods, causing still more confusion.

As became only too evident during the struggle over Florida's votes, America's overall balloting process is awkward, confusing, riddled with likely sources of error and bias, and, in cases of close races, incapable of producing a result that will stand up to close scrutiny. Results can take several days to process and every recount appears to produce a slightly different result. Often, too, the process of counting and recounting is directed by state and county officials with political axes to grind. The Votomatic punch-card machines used in a number of Florida counties are notoriously unreliable. The Votomatics are popular with many county governments because they are inexpensive. About 37 percent of the precincts in America's 3,140 counties use Votomatics or similar machines.[43] However, voters often find it difficult to insert the punch cards properly, frequently punch the wrong hole, or do not sufficiently perforate one or more chads to allow the punch cards to be read by the counting machine. Votomatics and other punch-card voting devices generally yield a much higher rate of spoiled votes than other voting methods. Indeed, a 1988 Florida Senate race was won by Republican Connie Mack in part because of thousands of spoiled Votomatic ballots. To make matters worse, precinct-level election officials—often elderly volunteers—may not understand the rules themselves, and they are therefore unable to help voters with questions. These difficulties would not have been subject to public scrutiny so long as they affected only local races. In 2000, however, America's antiquated electoral machinery collapsed under the weight of a presidential election, revealing its flaws for all to see. Despite these problems, electoral officials are often reluctant to

---

[43]Chad Terhune and Joni James, "Presidential Race Brings Attention to Business of Voting Machines," *Wall Street Journal*, 16 November 2000, p. A16.

change voting methods because changes can affect the outcome of the next election perhaps in ways that run against officials' preferences.

Taken together, regulation of the electorate's composition, regulation of the translation of voters' choices into electoral decisions, and regulation of the impact of those decisions upon the government's composition allow those in power a measure of control over mass participation in political life. These techniques do not necessarily have the effect of diminishing citizens' capacity to influence their rulers' conduct. Rather in the democracies, at least, these techniques are generally used to *influence electoral influence.* They permit governments a measure of control over what citizens will decide that governments should do.

Institution Principle

The electoral college and the Australian ballot are two instances of how changes in electoral rules can affect the outcomes of elections.

HOW VOTERS DECIDE

Thus far, we have focused on the election as an institution. But, of course, the election is also a process in which millions of individuals make decisions and choices that are beyond the government's control. Whatever the capacity of those in power to organize and structure the electoral process, it is these millions of individual decisions that ultimately determine electoral outcomes. Sooner or later the choices of voters weigh more heavily than the schemes of electoral engineers.

The Bases of Electoral Choice

Three types of factors influence voters' decisions at the polls: partisan loyalty, issue and policy concerns, and candidate characteristics.

Partisan Loyalty   Many studies have shown that most Americans identify more or less strongly with one or the other of the two major political parties. Partisan loyalty was considerably stronger during the 1940s and 1950s than it is today. But even now most voters feel a certain sense of identification or kinship with the Democratic or Republican party. This sense of identification is often handed down from parents to children and is reinforced by social and cultural ties. Partisan identification predisposes voters in favor of their party's candidates and against those of the opposing party. Partisanship is most likely to assert itself in the less-visible races, where issues and the candidates are not very well known. State legislative races, for example, are often decided by voters' party ties. However, even at the level of the presidential contest, in which issues and candidate personalities become very important, many Americans supported George W. Bush or Al Gore only because of partisan loyalty. Once formed, partisan loyalties are resistant to change. But sufficiently strong events and experiences may have the effect of eroding or even reversing them. White males in the South, for example, have, over the latter part of the twentieth century, been transformed from strong partisans of the Democratic party to independents and even supporters of the Republican party. Voters tend to keep their party affiliations unless some crisis causes them to reexamine the bases of their loyalties and to conclude that they have not given their support to the appropriate party. During these relatively infrequent periods of electoral change, millions of voters can change their party ties. For example, at the beginning of the New Deal era between 1932 and 1936, millions of former Republicans transferred their allegiance to Franklin Roosevelt and the Democrats.

Partisan loyalty should be understood as more than a psychological attachment (though it certainly is that as well). It is also an informational shortcut—a way for voters to economize on information collection and processing. In many circumstances, it may be "enough" simply to know what party label a particular candidate wears. Any extra information—issue positions or personal attributes—may not influence the voter's choice once the partisan content has been taken on board. For example, once a particular voter learns that a candidate is a Democrat, he or she knows that this candidate is likely to be the preferred alternative; for another voter, however, that simple fact may be enough to cause him or her to vote for the other guy! In the last several decades, party label has begun to lose its capacity to signal likely candidate characteristics, and more and more voters have found their partisan attachments weakening, or disappearing altogether. The phenomenal rise in the proportion of the electorate who now identify only weakly with a party or who declare themselves independents is testimony to this fact.[44]

Issues   Issues and policy preferences are a second factor influencing voters' choices at the polls. Voters may cast their ballots for the candidate whose position on economic issues they believe to be closest to their own. Similarly, they may select the candidate who has what they believe to be the best record on foreign policy. Issues are more important in some races than others. If candidates actually "take issue" with one another, that is, articulate and publicize very different positions on important public questions, then voters are more likely to be able to identify and act upon whatever policy preferences they may have.

The ability of voters to make choices on the basis of issue or policy preferences is diminished, however, if competing candidates do not differ substantially or do not focus their campaigns on policy matters. Very often, candidates deliberately take the safe course and emphasize topics that will not be offensive to any voters. Thus, candidates often trumpet their opposition to corruption, crime, and inflation. Presumably, few voters favor these things. While it may be perfectly reasonable for candidates to take the safe course and remain as inoffensive as possible, this candidate strategy makes it extremely difficult for voters to make their issue or policy preferences the bases for their choices at the polls.

[44]For a detailed assessment of the political use of information-economizing devices like party labels, see Arthur Lupia and Mathew McCubbins, *The Democratic Dilemma* (New York: Cambridge University Press, 1998). For the classic argument that party loyalty is a *variable*, not a constant, and that the voter updates party loyalty on the basis of his or her experience with the parties and their candidates, see Morris P. Fiorina, *Retrospective Voting in American National Elections* (New Haven: Yale University Press, 1981).

prospective voting Voting based on the imagined future performance of a candidate.

restrospective voting Voting based on the past performance of a candidate.

Voters' issue choices usually involve a mix of their judgments about the past behavior of competing parties and candidates and their hopes and fears about candidates' future behavior. Political scientists call choices that focus on future behavior *prospective voting,* while those based on past performance are called *retrospective voting.* To some extent, whether prospective or retrospective evaluation is more important in a particular election depends on the strategies of competing candidates. Candidates always endeavor to define the issues of an election in terms that will serve their interests. Incumbents running during a period of prosperity will seek to take credit for the economy's happy state and define the election as revolving around their record of success. This strategy encourages voters to make retrospective judgments. By contrast, an insurgent running during a period of economic uncertainty will tell voters it is time for a change and ask them to make prospective judgments. Thus, Bill Clinton focused on change in 1992 and prosperity in 1996, and through well-crafted media campaigns was able to define voters' agenda of choices.

In 2000, the key issues at the presidential level were taxes, Social Security reform, health care, and education. Bush promised an across-the-board tax cut while Gore asserted that such a move would benefit wealthy Americans at the expense of the middle class. Both candidates proposed plans to strengthen the Social Security system, with Bush advocating partial privatization of the system; Gore, on the other hand, promised to more adequately fund the current system. In the realm of health care, both candidates promised prescription drug plans for seniors. Associated Press exit polls conducted on Election Day indicated that Bush voters saw taxes as the central issue of the campaign, while Gore voters focused on prescription drugs and Social Security.

 Rationality Principle
Issue voting motivates candidates to converge toward the median voter.

When voters engage in issue voting, competition between the two candidates has the effect of pushing the candidate issue positions toward the middle of the distribution of voter preferences. This is known as the *median voter theorem,* made famous by Duncan Black and Anthony Downs.[45] To see the logic of this claim, imagine a series of possible stances on a policy issue as points along a line, stretching from zero to one hundred. A voter whose ideal policy lies between, say, zero and twenty-five is said to be a liberal on this policy; one whose ideal lies between seventy-five and one hundred, a conservative; and one whose favorite policy is between twenty-five and seventy-five, a moderate. An issue voter cares only about issue positions, not partisan loyalty or candidate characteristics and would therefore vote for the candidate whose announced policy is closest to his or her own most-preferred policy.

Policy Principle
The median voter theorem predicts policy moderation on the part of candidates.

Consider now a candidate who announces as his policy the most-preferred alternative of the median voter. If his opponent picks any point to the right, then the median voter and all those with ideal policies to the left of the median voter's will

[45]See Duncan Black, *The Theory of Committees and Elections* (New York: Cambridge University Press, 1958), and Anthony Downs, *An Economic Theory of Democracy* (New York: Harper-Row, 1957). A general, accessible treatment of this subject is found in Shepsle and Bonchek, *Analyzing Politics,* Chapter 5.

support the first candidate. They constitute a majority, by definition of the median, so this candidate will win. Suppose instead that the opponent chose as her policy some point to the left of the median ideal policy. Then the median voter and all those with ideal policies to the right of the median voter's will support the first candidate—and he wins, again. In short, the median voter theorem says that the candidate whose policy position is closest to the ideal policy of the median voter will defeat the other candidate in a majority contest. We can conclude from this brief analysis that issue voting encourages two things—*candidate convergence* (both candidates rush toward the center in order to cozy up to the position of the median voter) and *policy moderation* (candidates adopt policies that are less extreme than they might otherwise prefer, in order to sway median voters). Even when voters are not exclusively issue voters, two-candidate competition still encourages a tendency toward convergence and moderation, although it will not fully run its course.

Candidate Characteristics Candidates' personal attributes always influence voters' decisions. Some analysts claim that voters prefer tall candidates to short ones, candidates with shorter names to candidates with longer names, and candidates with lighter hair to candidates with darker hair. Perhaps these rather frivolous criteria do play some role. But the more important candidate characteristics that affect voters' choices are race, ethnicity, religion, gender, geography, and social background. In general, voters prefer candidates who are closer to themselves in terms of these categories. Voters presume that such candidates are likely to have views and perspectives close to their own. Moreover, they may be proud to see someone of their ethnic, religious, or geographic background in a position of leadership. This is why, for many years, politicians sought to "balance the ticket," making certain that their party's ticket included members of as many important groups as possible.

Just as a candidate's personal characteristics may attract some voters, they may repel others. Many voters are prejudiced against candidates of certain ethnic, racial, or religious groups. And for many years voters were reluctant to support the political candidacies of women, although this appears to be changing.

Voters also pay attention to candidates' personality characteristics, such as their "decisiveness," "honesty," and "vigor." In recent years, integrity has become a key election issue. In the 2000 presidential race, Al Gore chose Joe Lieberman as his running mate in part because Lieberman had been sharply critical of Bill Clinton's moral lapses. The senator's presence on the Democratic ticket thus helped to defuse the GOP's efforts to link Gore to Clinton's questionable character. As the race progressed, Gore sought to portray Bush as lacking the intelligence and experience needed for the presidency. This effort met with some success, as a number of talk-show hosts began to caricature Bush as a simpleton who knew little about domestic or foreign policy. Exit polls indicated that many voters also had concerns about Bush's intelligence. For his part, Bush sought to portray Gore as dishonest and duplicitous—a man who would say anything to get elected, such as claiming credit for the development of the Internet. The Bush strategy was to suggest that Gore was morally on a par with his boss, Bill Clinton, an individual whose moral lapses were all too well known to the electorate. Bush's claim that Gore was a liar just like Clinton was designed to thwart Gore's efforts to distance himself from his boss. This effort, too, led to talk-show caricatures and raised concerns among voters. Ultimately, according to Associated Press exit polls, Bush won the votes of those who said they were concerned about "honesty," while Gore received the support of individuals who felt "experience" was an important presidential attribute.

All candidates seek, through polling and other mechanisms, to determine the best image to project to the electorate. At the same time, the communications media—television in particular—exercise a good deal of control over how voters perceive candidates. In recent years, the candidates have developed a number of techniques designed to wrest control of the image-making process away from the media. Among the chief instruments of this "spin control" are candidate talk-show appearances, used quite effectively by both Al Gore and George Bush. During one appearance, Bush gave Oprah Winfrey a big kiss to show that he was friendly and not "stiff" like his opponent Al Gore. (See Process Box 10.2 to find out how candidates conduct a presidential campaign.)

THE 2000 ELECTIONS

During periods of economic prosperity, Americans generally return the incumbent party to office. The 2000 national elections were held during a period of peace and one of the greatest periods of economic prosperity America has ever known. To further enhance the Democrats' prospects, Democratic partisans continued to outnumber Republican identifiers in the national electorate. Thus, all things considered, it seemed more than likely that Vice President Al Gore and his running mate, Connecticut senator Joe Lieberman, would lead the Democratic Party to victory against an inexperienced and little-known Republican presidential nominee—Texas governor George W. Bush. Bush is, of course, the eldest son of former president George H. W. Bush, who was driven from office by Bill Clinton and Al Gore in 1992. Indeed, most academic models of election outcomes predicted an easy Democratic victory, with some even forecasting a Gore landslide.

Nevertheless, when the results of the vote finally became known, George W. Bush and his running mate, former defense secretary Dick Cheney, appeared to have eked out the narrowest of electoral college victories—271 to 267—over Gore and Lieberman (see Figure 10.3). Indeed, in terms of popular vote totals, the Gore/Lieberman ticket actually outpolled the Republicans by slightly more than 500,000 votes, or about one-half of one percent of the approximately 103 million votes cast across the nation.

Election night produced unusual drama and confusion when it became clear that the election's outcome would hinge on voting results in Florida, a state with twenty-five electoral votes. Initially, the television networks declared Gore the winner in Florida on the basis of exit-poll results. This projection seemed to in-

How a Presidential Campaign Is Conducted

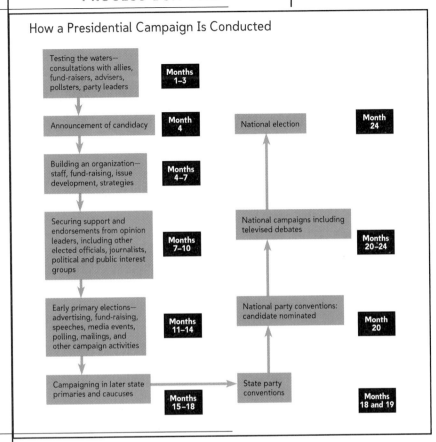

Testing the waters—consultations with allies, fund-raisers, advisers, pollsters, party leaders — **Months 1–3**

Announcement of candidacy — **Month 4**

Building an organization—staff, fund-raising, issue development, strategies — **Months 4–7**

Securing support and endorsements from opinion leaders, including other elected officials, journalists, political and public interest groups — **Months 7–10**

Early primary elections—advertising, fund-raising, speeches, media events, polling, mailings, and other campaign activities — **Months 11–14**

Campaigning in later state primaries and caucuses — **Months 15–18**

State party conventions — **Months 18 and 19**

National party conventions: candidate nominated — **Month 20**

National campaigns including televised debates — **Months 20–24**

National election — **Month 24**

dicate that Gore would likely win the presidency. Later that night, however, as votes were counted, it became clear that the exit polls were incorrect and that the Florida results were much in doubt. In the early hours of the next morning, all of the votes were tallied and Bush seemed to have won by fewer than 2,000 votes, out of nearly six million cast across the state. Vice President Gore called Governor Bush and conceded defeat.

Within an hour, however, Gore was on the phone to Bush again—this time to withdraw his concession. Under Florida law, the narrowness of Bush's victory—less than one-tenth of one percent—triggered an automatic recount. Moreover, reports of election irregularities had begun to surface. For example, nearly 20,000 votes in Palm Beach County had been invalidated because voters, apparently confused by the ballot, had indicated more than one presidential choice. Given

FIGURE 10.3

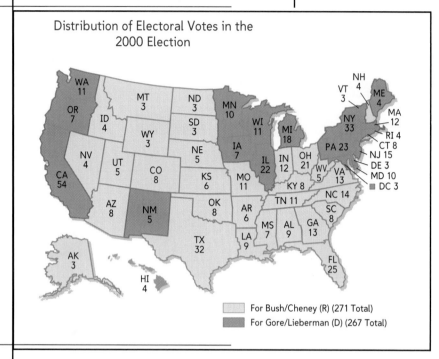

Distribution of Electoral Votes in the 2000 Election

For Bush/Cheney (R) (271 Total)

For Gore/Lieberman (D) (267 Total)

the closeness of the race and the various uncertainties, Democrats decided to await the results of a statewide recount of the vote.

While the recount of the counting of overseas absentee ballots narrowed Bush's margin of victory to a mere 980 votes, it did not change the result. In the meantime, Democrats filed a series of court challenges to the outcome, calling for a hand recount in at least three counties, Miami-Dade, Broward, and Palm Beach. Although Katherine Harris, Florida's top election official, announced that she would not accept the results of these hand recounts, Florida's supreme court ruled that the recounts must be included in the state's official election results. Under disputed circumstances, Miami-Dade County decided not to recount and Palm Beach County missed the deadline for recounted ballots. Gore gained several hundred votes in Broward County but not enough to change the results. These events led to further lawsuits in the Florida courts, the U.S. Court of Appeals, and the U.S. Supreme Court, as Gore refused to concede defeat until all possible legal appeals had been made. Florida's supreme court gave Gore a last-minute reprieve by ordering the manual recounting of approximately 43,000 ballots statewide. Bush appealed this hand recount to the U.S. Supreme Court. By a narrow 5-4 margin, the

Court blocked the further counting of Florida's disputed votes, effectively handing the presidency to Bush after a thirty-five-day struggle.

In Senate and House races, voting was also extremely close. Democrats gained some ground in both congressional chambers, but not enough to deprive the GOP of its control of either. Republicans held a narrow six-seat advantage in the House. The Senate was evenly divided 50-50 (although James Jeffords's defection from the GOP in May 2001 later gave the Democrats a slim advantage). Against all odds, Republicans appeared to have carried the day. Given an extremely buoyant economy, a nation at peace, and an edge in partisan attachments, how could the Democrats have lost? How could the race even have been close?

One key reason Al Gore and the Democrats were unable to capitalize on what seemed to be an ideal set of conditions was the tenor of Gore's national campaign. Early in the 2000 campaign, Gore made the fateful decision to distance himself from the person and political strategy of his boss, President Bill Clinton. Gore said repeatedly to interviewers, "I am my own man." Journalists correctly interpreted this declaration to mean that Gore wanted to distance himself from the scandals of the Clinton administration. Indeed, he sought to present a picture of moral rectitude and respect for family and religion that would prevent Republicans from linking him to the moral laxity associated with Bill Clinton. Gore made much of the strength of his marriage and religious beliefs. He refused to allow Clinton to participate in his campaign. He selected as his running mate Senator Joe Lieberman, not only the first Jew nominated for national office by either major party, but a man known for his strong religious beliefs and attention to moral values. Lieberman had been one of the first Democrats to criticize Bill Cinton's conduct in the Monica Lewinsky scandal. Gore thus used Lieberman's nomination to distinguish himself from Clinton on a moral level.

Gore's assertion that he wanted to be his own man, however, had another component that many journalists overlooked. Although Gore sought only to distinguish himself from Clinton's morals, he also distanced himself from his politics. In 1992 and 1996, Clinton adopted centrist positions on most domestic and foreign policy issues. In the 1992 election, the Arkansas governor aimed to present himself as a "new Democrat," i.e., one who differed sharply from the liberalism of George McGovern and Walter Mondale, which had brought the party defeat in 1972 and 1984. He adopted moderate positions on economic policy and even seemed to question the Democratic Party's stance on civil rights. He talked about middle-class concerns like crime, welfare reform, and fiscal restraint. His strategy of moderation helped bring victory in 1992 and again in 1996. In the later year's race, Clinton pursued a strategy of "triangulation," developed by his adviser, Dick Morris. This strategy called for the incumbent president to position himself midway between the liberalism of congressional Democrats and the conservatism of congressional Republicans. According to Morris, holding the center—in other words, locating his policy positions near the electorate's median voter—was the key to victory in the national election, and the strategy succeeded.

In choosing to be his own man, Gore abandoned Clinton's strategy. From his perspective, the problem with moderation and triangulation was that they failed to energize core Democratic constituencies, including liberal public interest groups, organized labor, and African Americans. Liberal groups had been furious with Clinton over his positions on welfare reform and education. Organized labor viewed Clinton as insufficiently committed to its cause; indeed, some unions considered backing Green Party candidate Ralph Nader and his message of opposition to global capitalism. African Americans felt a real rapport with Clinton and supported him as an individual, but expected more vigorous efforts from his successor with regard to civil rights causes.

Confronting a restive Democratic base, Gore chose to depart from "Clintonism" and move slightly to the left, *away* from the median. He attacked drug companies for charging too much. He promised African Americans stronger support for affirmative action. He pledged to expand Social Security and Medicare coverage for the elderly. He courted organized labor by promising to raise the minimum wage and appealed to the powerful teachers' unions by opposing school choice and voucher programs. Most importantly, Gore rejected the notion of using the projected government revenue surplus to cut federal income taxes. Thus, he promised tax cuts to selected Democratic constituencies but argued that an across-the-board cut would benefit only the wealthiest one-percent of Americans, at the expense of everyone else. In short, Gore became his own man by abandoning triangulation in favor of a more traditional Democratic populism; he diverged from the centrist location that Clinton believed was the key to his victory in 1996. By doing so, Gore gave the Bush campaign the opportunity to erode his initial advantage in the general campaign by allowing Bush to move closer to the median voter.

Gore's repositioning became evident to the public during the first presidential debate. Bush presented himself as a centrist who would "bring the country together." He eschewed appeals based on race, class, or gender. He promised a tax cut for all Americans and embraced such middle-class issues as education reform. Gore, on the other hand, pursued the rhetoric of Democratic populism. His mantra throughout the debate was that Bush would give a tax cut to the wealthiest one-percent while ignoring poorer Americans. Rather than wrap himself in the Clinton mantle of moderation—and unprecedented prosperity—Gore chose to appeal to the Democratic base with a message of populism and a hint of class warfare. Soon after the first debate, Gore's standing in the polls dropped while Bush's rose. By demanding to be his own man and distancing himself from Clinton, Gore made it difficult for himself to claim credit for the prosperity of the Clinton era.

In the closing days of the campaign, Gore abandoned his populist theme and focused instead on his opponent's qualifications for the presidency—Bush was said to be inexperienced and to lack the intelligence needed for the office; also, an old drunk-driving conviction surfaced to cast doubt on his character. This change of campaign tactics helped Gore to close the gap in the final week of the campaign. On Election Day, Gore actually outpolled Bush by a relatively small margin, leading to the first instance since 1888 of the popular-vote winner losing in the electoral college. Against the backdrop of peace and unprecedented prosperity, though, the election should not even have been close. Forced to suffer the indignity of being excluded from the campaign, Bill Clinton must have secretly savored Al Gore's fumbling efforts to be his own man.

When the 2000 election finally ended, one important question remained: Could the nation be governed effectively? The House and Senate were almost evenly divided. The presidency was decided by a few hundred votes and by a creaky institution last noticed in 1888. These results seemed tailor-made for a divided government and a divided nation. Consequently, the job of the next president and next Congress promised to be more difficult than at any other time in the nation's recent history.

CAMPAIGN FINANCE

Modern national political campaigns are fueled by enormous amounts of money. In a national race, millions of dollars are spent on media time, as well as on public opinion polls and media consultants. In 2000, political candidates and independent groups spent more than $3 billion on election campaigns. The average winning candidate in a campaign for a seat in the House of Representatives spent more than $500,000; the average winner in a senatorial campaign spent $4.5 million.[46] The 2000 Democratic and Republican presidential candidates were eligible to receive a total of $180 million in public funds to run their campaigns.[47] Each presidential candidate was also helped by tens of millions of dollars in so-called independent expenditures on the part of corporate and ideological "political action committees." As long as such political expenditures are not formally coordinated with a candidate's campaign, they are considered to be constitutionally protected free speech and are not subject to legal limitation or even reporting requirements. Likewise, independent soft money spending by political parties is also considered to be an expression of free speech.[48]

Analyzing American Politics
www.wwnorton.com/lowi7/ch10
Analyze how campaign spending affects the number of votes a candidate receives.

Sources of Campaign Funds

Federal Election Commission data suggest that approximately one-fourth of the private funds spent on political campaigns in the United States is raised through small, direct-mail contributions; about one-fourth is provided by large, individual gifts; and another fourth comes from contributions from PACs. The remaining fourth is drawn from the political parties and from candidates' personal or family resources.[49] Another source of campaign funds, which are not required to be reported to the Federal Election Commission, are independent expenditures by interest groups and parties.

[46]Jonathan Salant, "Million-Dollar Campaigns Proliferate in 105th," *Congressional Quarterly Weekly Report*, 21 December 1996, pp. 3448–51.

[47]U.S. Federal Election Commission, "Financing the 1996 Presidential Campaign," Internet Release, 28 April 1998.

[48]Buckley v. Valeo, 424 U.S. 1 (1976); Colorado Republican Party v. Federal Election Commission, 64 U.S.L.W. 4663 (1996).

[49]FEC reports.

Individual Donors   Direct mail serves both as a vehicle for communicating with voters and as a mechanism for raising funds. Direct-mail fund-raising efforts begin with the purchase or rental of computerized mailing lists of voters deemed likely to support the candidate because of their partisan ties, interests, or ideology. Candidates send out pamphlets, letters, and brochures describing their views and appealing for funds. Tens of millions of dollars are raised by national, state, and local candidates through direct mail each year, usually in $25 and $50 contributions, although in 2000, Bush and Gore collected about three-quarters of their donor contributions from individuals giving the $1,000 maximum amount.[50]

political action committees (PACs) Private groups that raise and distribute funds for use in election campaigns.

Political Action Committees   *Political action committees (PACs)* are organizations established by corporations, labor unions, or interest groups to channel the contributions of their members into political campaigns. Under the terms of the 1971 Federal Elections Campaign Act, which governs campaign finance in the United States, PACs are permitted to make larger contributions to any given candidate than individuals are allowed to make. Individuals may donate a maximum of $1,000 to any single candidate, but a PAC may donate as much as $5,000 to each candidate. Moreover, allied or related PACs often coordinate their campaign contributions, greatly increasing the amount of money a candidate actually receives from the same interest group. As a result, PACs have become central to campaign finance in the United States. Many critics assert that PACs corrupt the political process by allowing corporations and other interests to influence politicians with large contributions. It is by no means clear, however, that PACs corrupt the political process any more than large, individual contributions.

In recent years, candidates have learned to use several loopholes in the law governing PACs. For example, until a potential presidential candidate has actually declared his or her candidacy, expenditures by their political action committees generally do not count toward their presidential spending limits. A number of 2000 presidential hopefuls, including Dan Quayle, Jack Kemp, and John Kasich, began early to raise funds that were not subject to the nominal federal limits. In addition, candidates have discovered that federal regulations govern federal PACs, but not state PACs. Before 2000, a number of national candidates established state PACs, which then proceeded to engage in political activities at the national level. For example, Republican presidential hopeful Lamar Alexander established a national PAC and a Tennessee PAC in preparation for the 2000 presidential race. While his national PAC was subject to federal rules, Alexander's Tennessee PAC accepted unlimited contributions. Nothing prevented the Tennessee PAC from engaging in nationally helpful activities such as polling in Iowa or sponsoring a lobster-fest in New Hampshire.

[50]FEC reports.

The Candidates   On the basis of the Supreme Court's 1976 decision in *Buckley v. Valeo*, the right of individuals to spend their *own* money to campaign for office is a constitutionally protected matter of free speech and is not subject to limitation. Thus, extremely wealthy candidates often contribute millions of dollars to their own campaigns. Jon Corzine, for example, spent approximately $60 million of his own funds in a successful New Jersey Senate bid in 2000.

Independent Spending   As was noted above, "independent" spending is also free from regulation; private groups, political parties, and wealthy individuals, engaging in what is called ***issue advocacy***, may spend as much as they wish to help elect one candidate or defeat another, as long as these expenditures are not coordinated with any political campaign. Many business and ideological groups engage in such activities. Some estimates suggest that groups and individuals spent as much as $150 million on issue advocacy—generally through television advertising—during the 1996 elections.[51] Issue advocacy and independent expenditures increased even more during the 2000 election cycle, to an estimated $400 million or more. The National Rifle Association, for example, spent $3 million dollars reminding voters of the importance of the right to bear arms, while the National Abortion and Reproductive Rights League spent nearly $5 million to express its support for Al Gore.

issue advocacy
Independent spending by individuals or interest groups on a campaign issue but not directly tied to a particular candidate.

Some groups are careful not to mention particular candidates in their issues ads to avoid any suggestion that they might merely be fronts for a candidate's campaign committee. Most issues ads, however, are attacks on the opposing candidate's record or character. Organized labor spent more than $35 million in 1996 to attack a number of Republican candidates for the House of Representatives. Business groups launched their own multimillion-dollar issues campaign to defend the GOP House members targeted by labor.[52] In 2000, liberal groups ran ads bashing Bush's record on capital punishment, tax reform, and Social Security. Conservative groups attacked Gore's views on gun ownership, abortion, and environmental regulation.

Parties and Soft Money   State and local party organizations use soft money for get-out-the-vote drives and voter education and registration efforts. These are the party-building activities for which soft-money contributions are nominally made. Most soft-money dollars, however, are spent to assist candidates' reelection efforts in the form of "issue advocacy," campaigns on behalf of a particular candidate thinly disguised as mere advocacy of particular issues. For example, in 1996, issue advocacy commercials sponsored by state Democratic Party organizations looked just like commercials for Clinton. The issue commercials praised the president's stand on major issues and criticized the GOP's positions. The only difference was that the issue ads did not specifically call for the

---

[51]David Broder and Ruth Marcus, "Wielding Third Force in Politics," *Washington Post*, 20 September 1997, p. 1.
[52]Broder and Marcus, "Wielding Third Force in Politics."

reelection of President Clinton. In 2000, the Democratic Party raised and spent $371 million in support of its national, state, and local candidates. For its part, the GOP was able to raise more than $525 million. According to the Federal Election Commission, sources of Democratic funds included lawyers and lobbyists; the finance, insurance, and real estate industries; and organized labor. The GOP benefited from contributions by agribusiness, banks and financial interests, transportation concerns, healthcare corporations, and small business. Critics contend that soft money is less a vehicle for building parties than it is a mechanism for circumventing federal election laws.

In some instances, large donors to the Democratic and Republican parties do not want to be publicly identified. To accommodate these "stealth donors," both parties have created sham nonprofit groups to serve as the nominal recipients of the gifts. For example, in 1996 the Democratic Party established an organization called "Vote Now '96," which ostensibly worked to increase voter turnout. This organization received several million dollars in donations that were used on behalf of the Clinton/Gore re-election effort. For their part, Republicans created two nonprofit groups that took in more than $3 million.[53]

In these instances, issues campaigns seem to violate federal election law by actually being coordinated with candidate or party committees. Democrats, for example, have charged that a 1996 issues campaign nominally run by Americans for Tax Reform, a conservative nonprofit group, was actually controlled by the Republican National Committee. Americans for Tax Reform spent roughly $4 million in 1996 on an issues campaign supporting Republican candidates in 150 House districts. The campaign was directed by a former RNC official. The RNC admits that it donated $4.6 million to the group, but denies any further involvement with the antitax group's efforts.[54]

Public Funding   The Federal Elections Campaign Act also provides for public funding of presidential campaigns. As they seek a major party presidential nomination, candidates become eligible for public funds by raising at least $5,000 in individual contributions of $250 or less in each of twenty states. Candidates who reach this threshold may apply for federal funds to match, on a dollar-for-dollar basis, all individual contributions of $250 or less they receive. The funds are drawn from the Presidential Election Campaign Fund. Taxpayers can contribute $1 to this fund, at no additional cost to themselves, by checking a box on the first page of their federal income tax returns. Major party presidential candidates receive a lump sum (currently nearly $90 million) during the summer prior to the general election. They must meet all their general expenses from this money. Third-party candidates are eligible for public funding only if they received at least 5 percent of the vote in the previous presidential race. This

[53]Jill Abramson and Leslie Wayne, "Nonprofit Groups Were Partners to Both Parties in Last Election," *New York Times*, 24 October 1997, p. 1.
[54]Leslie Wayne, "Papers Detail GOP Ties to Tax Group," *New York Times*, 10 November 1997, p. A27.

stipulation effectively blocks pre-election funding for third-party or independent candidates, although a third party that wins more than 5 percent of the vote can receive public funding after the election. In 1980, John Anderson convinced banks to loan him money for an independent candidacy on the strength of poll data showing that he would receive more than 5 percent of the vote and thus would obtain public funds with which to repay the loans. Under current law, no candidate is required to accept public funding for either the nominating races or general presidential election. Candidates who do not accept public funding are not affected by any expenditure limits. Thus, in 1992 Ross Perot financed his own presidential bid and was not bound by the $55 million limit to which the Democratic and Republican candidates were held that year. Perot accepted public funding in 1996. In 2000, George W. Bush refused public funding and raised enough money to finance his own primary campaign. Eventually, Bush raised and spent nearly $200 million—twice the limit to which matching funds would have subjected him. Al Gore accepted federal funding and was nominally bound by the associated spending limitations. Soft money and independent spending, however, not limited by election law, allowed Gore to close the gap with his Republican opponent.

Campaign Finance Reform

The United States is one of the few advanced industrial nations that permit individual candidates to accept large private contributions from individual or corporate donors. Most mandate either public funding of campaigns or, as in the case of Britain, require that large private donations be made to political parties rather than to individual candidates. The logic of such a requirement is that a contribution that might seem very large to an individual candidate would weigh much less heavily if made to a national party. Thus, the chance that a donor could buy influence would be reduced.

Over the past several years, a number of pieces of legislation have proposed similar restrictions on the private funding of campaigns. Political reform has been blocked, however, because the two major parties disagree over the form it should take. The Republicans have developed a very efficient direct-mail apparatus and would be willing to place limits on the role of PACs. The Democrats, by contrast, depend more heavily on PACs and fear that limiting their role would hurt the party's electoral chances.

In the aftermath of the 1996 national elections, the role of soft money came under intense scrutiny. Both political parties raised and spent tens of millions of dollars in soft money to help their presidential candidates, congressional candidates, and candidates for state and local offices. Senators John McCain and Russell Feingold repeatedly initiated an effort to pass legislation to restrict both soft-money contributions and issues advocacy. A combination of partisan and constitutional concerns, however, repeatedly doomed the McCain-Feingold initiative to defeat.

Campaign finance reform efforts continued after the 2000 elections in 2001 when an amended form of the McCain-Feingold bill passed the Senate but was blocked in the House. A task force on campaign reform comprised of fourteen political scientists made the following recommendations:

1. Partial public funding should be offered to congressional candidates.
2. Contribution limits should be modestly increased and subsequently adjusted for inflation.
3. Reasonable limits should be imposed on soft money contributions and on total soft money spending by the parties.
4. Full disclosure of the sponsorship of all campaign-related issue advocacy should be required.
5. The administrative capacity and resources of the Federal Election Commission should be significantly increased.
6. Free air time providing direct access for candidates to communicate with citizens should be made available, either voluntarily by broadcasters or through specific mandates by Congress.[55]

If campaign finance reform were to occur sometime after 2001, it would likely take the form of one or more of these recommendations.

Implications for Democracy

The important role played by private funds in American politics affects the balance of power among contending social groups. Politicians need large amounts of money to campaign successfully for major offices. This fact inevitably ties their interests to the interests of the groups and forces that can provide this money. In a nation as large and diverse as the United States, to be sure, campaign contributors represent many different groups and often represent clashing interests. Business groups, labor groups, environmental groups, and pro-choice and right-to-life forces all contribute millions of dollars to political campaigns. Through such PACs as EMILY's List, women's groups contribute millions of dollars to women running for political office. One set of trade associations may contribute millions to win politicians' support for telecommunications reform, while another set may contribute just as much to block the same reform efforts. Insurance companies may contribute millions of dollars to Democrats to win their support for changes in the health care system, while physicians may contribute equal amounts to prevent the same changes from becoming law.

Despite this diversity of contributors, however, not all interests play a role in financing political campaigns. Only those interests that have a good deal of money to spend can make their interests known in this way. These interests are not monolithic, but they do not completely reflect the diversity of

---

[55]Task Force on Campaign Reform, "Campaign Reform: Insights and Evidence," Woodrow Wilson School of Public and International Affairs, Princeton University, 1998.

American society. The poor, the destitute, and the downtrodden also live in America and have an interest in the outcome of political campaigns. Who is to speak for them?

DO ELECTIONS MATTER?

What is the place of elections in the American political process? Unfortunately, recent political trends, such as the increasing importance of money, raise real questions about the continuing ability of ordinary Americans to influence their government through electoral politics.

Why Is There a Decline in Voter Turnout?

Despite the sound and fury of contemporary American politics, one very important fact stands out: participation in the American political process is abysmally low. Politicians in recent years have been locked in intense struggles. As we saw in Chapter 5, partisan division in Congress has reached its highest level of intensity since the nineteenth century. Nevertheless, millions of citizens have remained uninvolved. For every registered voter who voted in the 2000 elections, for example, one stayed home.

This lack of popular involvement is sometimes attributed to the shortcomings of American citizens—many millions do not go to the trouble of registering and voting. The 1993 Motor Voter bill was, at best, a very hesitant step in the direction of expanded voter participation. This act requires all states to allow voters to register by mail when they renew their driver's licenses (twenty-eight states already had similar mail-in procedures) and provides for the placement of voter registration forms in motor vehicle, public assistance, and military recruitment offices. Motor Voter did result in some increases in voter registration. Thus far, however, few of these newly registered individuals have actually gone to the polls to cast their ballots. After 1996, the percentage of newly registered voters who appeared at the polls actually dropped.[56]

A number of other simple institutional reforms could increase voter turnout. Same-day registration—currently used in several states, including Minnesota—could boost turnout by several percentage points. Weekend voting or, alternatively, making election day a federal holiday would make it easier for Americans to go to the polls. Weekend voting in a number of European nations has increased turnout by up to ten percentage points. One reform that has been suggested, but should not be adopted, is Internet voting. Computer use and Internet access remain highly correlated with income and education. This method of voting would reinforce the existing class bias in the voting process as well as introduce computer security problems.

Institution Principle
Instituting new election laws, such as same-day voter registration, could increase turnout.

---

[56]Peter Baker, "Motor Voter Apparently Didn't Drive Up Turnout," *Washington Post*, 6 November 1996, p. B7.

Even with America's current registration rules, higher levels of political participation could be achieved if competing political forces made a serious effort to mobilize voters. Unfortunately, however, contending political forces in the United States have found ways of attacking their opponents that do not require them to engage in voter mobilization, and many prefer to use these methods than to endeavor to bring more voters to the polls. The low levels of popular mobilization that are typical of contemporary American politics are very much a function of the way that politics is conducted in the United States today. The quasi-democratic character of American elections is underscored by the electoral college. This eighteenth-century device may have seemed reasonable to the Constitution's framers as a check on the judgment of a largely illiterate and uneducated electorate. Today, however, this institution undermines both the respect for and the legitimacy of electoral results. Abolition of the electoral college would have consequences for campaigning and for the party system. Candidates would be compelled to campaign throughout the nation rather than in the small number of states they see as the key "battlegrounds" for electoral college victory. This would be a welcome development. The abolition of the electoral college might also open the way for new parties that could either breathe new life into the political process or add to the confusion of presidential elections, or both. Time would tell.

There is another sense in which low turnout is the "fault" of the way politics is conducted in the United States. The median voter theorem suggests that there are centripetal forces at work in the first-past-the-post, winner-take-all American electoral system. Candidates—though occasionally they err as Al Gore did in 2000—head for the center and toward one another, much as Bill Clinton succeeded in doing in 1992 and 1996, and George W. Bush in 2000. This sometimes produces disillusionment, even disgust, in voters who find, in the immortal words of former third-party candidate George Wallace, that "there ain't a dime's worth of difference" between the candidates. According to the calculus of voting that we reviewed earlier, not only is the probability of a citizen's vote making a difference low, but with convergence of candidates, the relative benefit of electing one rather than the other has also declined. Many citizens conclude there is not much point to going to the polls. Turnout, according to this view, is a consequence not only of candidates failing to mobilize voters, but also of their failure, via the inexorable pull of the median voter, to differentiate themselves and thus inspire voters.

Why Do Elections Matter As Political Institutions?

Voting choices and electoral outcomes can be extremely important in the United States. Yet, observing the relationships between voters' choices, leadership composition, and policy output is only the first step toward understanding the significance of democratic elections. Important as they are, voters' choices and electoral results may still be less consequential for government and politics than the simple fact of voting itself. The impact of electoral decisions upon

Institutional Reform
www.wwnorton.com/
lowi7/ch10
What institutional
factors affect voter
turnout?

the governmental process is, in some respects, analogous to the impact made upon organized religion by individuals being able to worship at the church of their choice. The fact of worship can be more important than the particular choice. Similarly, the fact of mass electoral participation can be more significant than what or how citizens decide once they participate. Thus, electoral participation has important consequences in that it socializes and institutionalizes political action.

First, democratic elections socialize political activity. Voting is not a natural or spontaneous phenomenon. It is an institutionalized form of mass political involvement. That individuals vote rather than engage in some other form of political behavior is a result of national policies that create the opportunity to vote and discourage other political activities relative to voting. Elections transform what might otherwise consist of sporadic, citizen-initiated acts into a routine public function. This transformation expands and democratizes mass political involvement. At the same time, however, elections help to preserve the government's stability by containing and channeling away potentially more disruptive or dangerous forms of mass political activity. By establishing formal avenues for mass participation and accustoming citizens to their use, government reduces the threat that volatile, unorganized political involvement can pose to the established order.

Second, elections bolster the government's power and authority. Elections help to increase popular support for political leaders and for the regime itself. The formal opportunity to participate in elections serves to convince citizens that the government is responsive to their needs and wishes. Moreover, elections help to persuade citizens to obey. Electoral participation increases popular acceptance of taxes and military service upon which the government depends. Even if popular voting can influence the behavior of those in power, voting serves simultaneously as a form of co-optation. Elections—particularly democratic elections—substitute consent for coercion as the foundation of governmental power.

Finally, elections institutionalize mass influence in politics. Democratic elections permit citizens to select and depose public officials routinely, and elections can serve to promote popular influence over officials' conduct. But however effective this electoral sanction may be, it is hardly the only means through which citizens can reward or punish public officials for their actions. Spontaneous or privately organized forms of political activity, or even the threat of their occurrence, can also induce those in power to heed the public's wishes. The behavior of even the most rigid autocrat, for example, can be influenced by the possibility that his policies may provoke popular disobedience, clandestine movements, or riots and insurrection. The alternative to democratic elections is not clearly and simply the absence of popular influence; it can instead be unregulated and unconstrained popular intervention into governmental processes. It is, indeed, often precisely because spontaneous forms of mass political activity can have too great an impact upon the actions of government that elections are introduced. Walter Lippman, a journalist who

Institution Principle

Elections matter because they socialize and institutionalize political action.

helped to pioneer the idea of public opinion voicing itself through the press via the "opinion-editorial," or op-ed, page, once observed that "new numbers were enfranchised because they had power, and giving them the vote was the least disturbing way of letting them exercise their power."[57] The vote can provide the "least disturbing way" of allowing ordinary people to exercise power. If the people had been powerless to begin with, elections would never have been introduced.

Thus, although citizens can secure enormous benefits from their right to vote, governments secure equally significant benefits from allowing them to do so.

SUMMARY

Allowing citizens to vote represents a calculated risk on the part of power holders. On the one hand, popular participation can generate consent and support for the government. On the other hand, the right to vote may give ordinary citizens more influence in the governmental process than political elites would like.

Voting is only one of many possible types of political participation. The significance of voting is that it is an institutional and formal mode of political activity. Voting is organized and subsidized by the government. This makes voting both more limited and more democratic than other forms of participation.

All governments regulate voting in order to influence its effects. The most important forms of regulation include regulation of the electorate's composition, regulation of the translation of voters' choices into electoral outcomes, and insulation of policy-making processes from electoral intervention.

Voters' choices, themselves, are based on partisanship, issues, and candidates' personalities. Which of these criteria will be most important varies over time and depends upon the factors that opposing candidates choose to emphasize in their campaigns.

Campaign funds in the United States are provided by small, direct-mail contributions, large gifts, PACs, political parties, candidates' personal resources, and public funding. In 2000, some candidates also benefited from issues advocacy.

Campaign finance is regulated by the Federal Elections Campaign Act of 1971. Following the 1996 elections, the role of soft money was scrutinized. The McCain-Feingold bill, a bipartisan attempt to restrict soft money contributions and issues advocacy, failed in 2001 to gain passage in Congress.

Whatever voters decide, elections are important institutions because they socialize political activity, increase governmental authority, and institutionalize popular influence in political life.

[57]Walter Lippman, *The Essential Lippman*, ed. Clinton Rossiter and James Lare (New York: Random House, 1965), p. 12.

PRINCIPLES OF POLITICS IN REVIEW

Rationality Principle	Collective Action Principle	Institution Principle	Policy Principle	History Principle
Elections allow multiple principals—citizens—to choose political agents to act on their behalf, but citizens usually have imperfect information about candidates and don't know how agents will act once in office.	Elections are a mechanism to channel and limit political participation to actions within the system.	The electoral process is governed by a variety of rules and procedures that allow those in power an opportunity to regulate the character and consequences of political participation.	The median voter theorem predicts policy moderation on the part of candidates.	Between 1890 and 1910, voter turnout declined in the U.S. as a result of new registration requirements. Since that time, turnout has remained low in comparison with the nineteenth century.
At least until recent years, political parties have been the primary agents for giving citizens the motivation and incentive to vote.		The rules that set the criteria for winning an election have an effect on the outcome.		
Given the tiny probability that an individual's vote will determine the winner of an election, candidates need to reduce the cost of voting for citizens in order to mobilize them.		The electoral college and the Australian ballot are two instances of how changes in electoral rules can affect the outcomes of elections.		
Issue voting motivates candidates to converge toward the median voter.		Instituting new election laws, such as same-day voter registration, could increase turnout.		
		Elections matter because they socialize and institutionalize political action.		

FOR FURTHER READING

Black, Earl, and Merle Black. *The Vital South: How Presidents Are Elected.* Cambridge: Harvard University Press, 1992.

Brady, David. *Critical Elections and Congressional Policymaking.* Stanford: Stanford University Press, 1988.

Carmines, Edward G., and James Stimson. *Issue Evolution: The Racial Transformation of American Politics.* Princeton: Princeton University Press, 1988.

Conway, M. Margaret. *Political Participation in the United States.* Washington, DC: Congressional Quarterly Press, 1985.

Fowler, Linda. *Candidates, Congress, and the American Democracy.* Ann Arbor: University of Michigan Press, 1994.

Fowler, Linda, and Robert D. McClure. *Political Ambition: Who Decides to Run for Congress.* New Haven: Yale University Press, 1989.

Ginsberg, Benjamin, and Martin Shefter. *Politics by Other Means: Institutional Conflict and the Declining Significance of Elections in America*, 3rd ed. New York: W. W. Norton, 2002.

Jackson, Brooks. *Honest Graft: Big Money and the American Political Process.* New York: Alfred A. Knopf, 1988.

Piven, Frances Fox, and Richard A. Cloward. *Why Americans Don't Vote.* New York: Pantheon, 1988.

Reed, Adolph. *The Jesse Jackson Phenomenon.* New Haven: Yale University Press, 1987.

Reichley, A. James, ed. *Elections American Style.* Washington, DC: Brookings Institution, 1987.

Sorauf, Frank. *Inside Campaign Finance: Myths and Realities.* New Haven: Yale University Press, 1992.

Tate, Katherine. *From Protest to Politics: The New Black Voters in American Elections.* Cambridge: Harvard University Press, 1994.

Witt, Linda, Karen Paget, and Glenna Matthews. *Running as a Woman: Gender and Power in American Politics.* New York: Free Press, 1994.

eleven

Political Parties

EVENTS	INSTITUTIONAL DEVELOPMENTS
Parties form in Congress (1790s)	Washington peacefully assumes the presidency (1789)
	First party system: Federalists versus Democratic-Republicans (1790s)
Washington's farewell address warns against parties (1796)	
Thomas Jefferson elected president (1800) — **1800** —	Federalists try to retain power by Alien and Sedition Acts (1798) and by appointing "midnight judges" (1801)
Jefferson renominated by congressional caucus; re-elected by a landslide (1804)	Congressional caucuses nominate presidential candidates from each party (1804–1831)
James Monroe re-elected president; no Federalist candidate; no caucuses called (1820)	Destruction of Federalists; period of one partyism; "era of good feelings" (1810s–1820s)
	Democratic-Republican party splinters into National Republicans (Adams) and Democrats (Jackson) (1824)
Democrat Andrew Jackson elected president, ushering in "era of the common man" (1828)	Democrats use party rotation to replace National Republicans in government positions (1829)
— **1830** —	National nominating conventions replace caucuses as method of selecting presidential candidates from each party (1830s)
National nominating conventions held by Democrats and National Republicans (1831)	
Whig presidential candidates lose to Democratic candidate Martin Van Buren (1836)	Second party system: Whig party forms in opposition to Jackson—Democrats versus Whigs (1830s–1850s)
Whig William Henry Harrison elected president (1840)	Whigs gain presidency and majority in Congress; both parties organized down to the precinct level (1840)
— **1850** —	Third party system: destruction of Whigs; creation of Republicans—Democrats versus Republicans (1850s–1890s)
Republican Abraham Lincoln elected president (1860)	
Civil War (1861–1865)	Fourth party system: both the Democratic and Republican parties are rebuilt along new lines (1890s–1930s)
Reconstruction (1867–1877)	

EVENTS	INSTITUTIONAL DEVELOPMENTS
Republican William McKinley elected president; Democrats decimated (1896)	Shrinking electorate; enactment of Progressive reforms, including registration laws, primary elections, the Australian ballot, and civil service reform; decline of party machines; emergence of many one-party states (1890s)
Era of groups and movements; millions of southern and eastern European immigrants arrive in U.S. (1870s–1890s)	

1900

Republican Theodore Roosevelt becomes president (1901)	
Democrat Franklin D. Roosevelt elected president (1932)	Fifth party system: period of New Deal Democratic dominance (1930s–1960s)

1960

Democratic convention—party badly damaged; Republican Richard Nixon elected president (1968)	Disruption of New Deal coalition; decay of party organizations (1968)
Watergate scandal (1972–1974)	Federal Election Campaign Act regulates campaign finance (1972)
Nixon resigns (1974)	Introduction of new political techniques (1970s and 1980s)

1980

Republican Ronald Reagan elected president (1980)	Efforts by Republicans to build a national party structure (1980s)
Republican George H. W. Bush elected president; Democrats continue to control House and Senate (1988 and 1990)	Continuation of divided government, with Democrats controlling Congress and Republicans the White House (1980s–1992)

1990

Democrat Bill Clinton elected president; Democrats retain control of House and Senate (1992)	
Republicans win control of House and Senate (1994)	High levels of congressional party unity as Republicans seek to enact ambitious legislative program (1995)
Republicans retain control of Congress while Democrats hold White House (1996)	Divided government continues (1995–2000)

2000

Republicans win White House and maintain slim advantage in Congress (2000)	Unified government returns, momentarily (2000)
Senator James Jeffords leaves GOP, giving the Democrats control of the Senate (2001)	Divided government resumes (2001)

CORE OF THE ANALYSIS

- Today the Democratic and Republican parties dominate the American two-party political system.

- The most important functions of American political parties are facilitating mass electoral choice and providing the organization and leadership of Congress.

- The role of parties in electoral politics has declined in the United States over the last thirty years.

- New political technology has strengthened the advantage of wealthier political groups.

We often refer to the United States as a nation with a "two-party system." By this we mean that in the United States the Democratic and Republican parties compete for office and power. Most Americans believe that party competition contributes to the health of the democratic process. Certainly, we are more than just a bit suspicious of those nations that claim to be ruled by their people but do not tolerate the existence of opposing parties.

The idea of party competition was not always accepted in the United States. In the early years of the Republic, parties were seen as threats to the social order. In his 1796 "Farewell Address," President George Washington admonished his countrymen to shun partisan politics:

> Let me . . . warn you in the most solemn manner against the baneful effects of the spirit of party, generally. This spirit . . . exists under different shapes in all governments, more or less stifled, controlled, or repressed; but in those of the popular form it is seen in its greatest rankness and is truly their worst enemy.

Often, those in power viewed the formation of political parties by their opponents as acts of treason that merited severe punishment. Thus, in 1798, the Federalist party, which controlled the national government, in effect sought to outlaw its Democratic-Republican opponents through the infamous Alien and Sedition Acts, which, among other things, made it a crime to publish or say anything that might tend to defame or bring into disrepute either the president or the Congress. Under this law, twenty-five individuals—including several Republican newspaper editors—were arrested and convicted.[1]

These efforts to outlaw political parties obviously failed. By the mid-nineteenth century American politics was dominated by powerful "machines" that inspired enormous voter loyalty, controlled electoral politics, and, through elections, exercised enormous influence over government and policy in the United States. In recent years, these party machines have all but disappeared. Electoral politics has become a "candidate-centered" affair in which individual candidates for office build their own campaign organizations, while voters make choices based more on their reactions to the candidates than on loyalty to

---

[1]See Richard Hofstadter, *The Idea of a Party System* (Berkeley: University of California Press, 1969).

the parties. Party organization, as we saw in Chapter 5, continues to be an important factor in Congress. Even in Congress, however, the influence of party leaders is based more upon ideological affinity than any real power over party members. The weakness of the party system is an important factor in understanding contemporary American political patterns.[2]

In this chapter, we will examine the realities underlying the changing conceptions of political parties. As long as political parties have existed, they have been criticized for introducing selfish, "partisan" concerns into public debate and national policy. Yet political parties are extremely important to the proper functioning of a democracy. As we shall see, parties expand popular political participation, promote more effective choice in elections, and smooth the flow of public business in the Congress. Our problem in America today is not that political life is too partisan, but that our parties are not strong enough to function effectively. This is one reason that America has such low levels of popular political involvement. Unfortunately, some reforms currently being proposed, such as the elimination of so-called soft money, would further erode party strength in America. First, we will look at party organization and its place in the American political process. Second, we will consider why America has a two-party system, trace the history of each of the major parties, and look at some of the third parties that have come and gone over the past two centuries. Third, we will discuss the role of parties in election campaigns and the policy process. Finally, we will address the significance and changing role of parties in American politics today and answer the question, "Is the party over?"

THE CENTRAL QUESTIONS

WHAT ARE POLITICAL PARTIES?

Why do political parties form? What problems can they help solve?

How are political parties organized? At what levels are they organized?

THE TWO-PARTY SYSTEM IN AMERICA

How have political parties developed in the United States?

What are the historical origins of today's Democratic and Republican parties?

What is the history of party politics in America?

What has been the historical role of third parties in the United States?

FUNCTIONS OF THE PARTIES

What are the important electoral functions of parties?

How do the differences between Democrats and Republicans affect Congress, the president, and the policy-making process?

WEAKENING OF PARTY ORGANIZATION

What factors led to the diminishment of party strength in America? How has this development affected election campaigns?

How are parties important to contemporary politics?

---

[2]For an excellent discussion of the fluctuating role of political parties in the United States and the influence of government on that role, see John J. Coleman, *Party Decline in America: Policy, Politics, and the Fiscal State* (Princeton: Princeton University Press, 1996).

WHAT ARE POLITICAL PARTIES?

Political parties, like interest groups, are organizations seeking influence over government. Ordinarily, they can be distinguished from interest groups on the basis of their orientation. A party seeks to control the entire government by electing its members to office and thereby controlling the government's personnel. Interest groups, through campaign contributions and other forms of electoral assistance, are also concerned with electing politicians—in particular, those who are inclined in their policy direction. But interest groups ordinarily do not sponsor candidates directly, and, between elections, they usually accept government and its personnel as given and try to influence government policies through them. They are *benefit-seekers*, whereas parties are comprised mainly of *office-seekers*.[3]

Political parties organize because of three problems with which politicians and other political activists must cope. The first is the problem of collective action. This is chiefly an outgrowth of elections in which a candidate for office must attract campaign funds, assemble a group of activists and workers, and mobilize and persuade prospective voters to vote for him or her. Collective action is also a problem *inside* government, where kindred spirits in a legislature must arrange for, and then engage in, cooperation. The second problem for which parties are sometimes the solution is the problem of collective choice of policy.[4] The give-and-take within a legislature and between the legislature and the executive can make or break policy success and subsequent electoral success. The third problem follows from the fact that fellow politicians, like members of any organization, simultaneously seek success for the organization and success for themselves. This problem of ambition can undermine the collective aspirations of fellow partisans unless astutely managed. We briefly examine each of these three problems below.

Collective Action Principle

Parties facilitate collective action in the electoral process by helping candidates attract campaign funds, assemble campaign workers, and mobilize voters.

Policy Principle

Parties help resolve collective choice in the policy-making process by acting as permanent coalitions of individuals with similar policy goals.

Rationality Principle

Parties help deal with the threat to cooperation posed by ambitious individuals by regulating career advancement and resolving competition.

Facilitating Collective Action in the Electoral Process

Political parties as they are known today developed along with the expansion of suffrage and can be understood only in the context of elections. The two are so intertwined that American parties actually take their structure from the electoral process. The shape of party organization in the United States has followed a sim-

---

[3]This distinction is from John H. Aldrich, *Why Parties? The Origin and Transformation of Party Politics in America* (Chicago: University of Chicago Press, 1995).

[4]A slight variation on this theme is emphasized by Gary Cox and Mathew McCubbins in *Legislative Leviathan* (Berkeley: University of California Press, 1993). They suggest that parties in the legislature are electoral machines whose purpose is to preserve and enhance party reputation, thereby giving meaning to the party labels when elections are contested. By keeping order within their ranks, parties make certain that individual actions by members do not discredit the party label. This is an especially challenging task for party leaders when there is diversity within each party, as has often been the case in American political history.

ple rule: for every district where an election is held, there should be some kind of party unit. These units provide the brand name, the resources—both human and financial—the "buzz," and the link to the larger national organization, which all help the party's candidates to arouse interest in their candidacies, to stimulate commitment, and ultimately to overcome the free-riding that diminishes turnout in general elections. Republicans failed to maintain units in most of the Southern counties between 1900 and 1952; Democrats were similarly unsuccessful in many areas of New England. But for most of the history of the United States, two major parties have had enough of an organized presence to oppose each other in elections in most of the nation's towns, cities, and counties. This makes the American party system one of the oldest political institutions in the history of democracy.

Compared to political parties in Europe, parties in the United States have always seemed weak. They have no criteria for party membership—no cards for their members to carry, no dues to pay, no obligatory participation in any activity, no notion of exclusiveness. Today, they seem weaker than ever; they inspire less loyalty and are less able to control nominations. Some people are even talking about a "crisis of political parties," as though party politics were being abandoned. But there continues to be at least some substance to party organizations in the United States. It should not go unappreciated that third parties have regularly failed to make much headway in American national elections. Candidates lacking a major party label have almost always failed in their bids for election. If they achieve any measure of success, it is as a spoiler at best—like Ralph Nader's candidacy in the 2000 presidential election—and even then it is typically "one election and out."

Resolving Collective Choice in the Policy-making Process

Political parties are also essential elements in the process of making policy. Within the government, parties are coalitions of individuals with shared or overlapping interests who, as a rule, will support one another's programs and initiatives. Even though there may be areas of disagreement within each party, a common party label in and of itself gives party members a reason to cooperate. Because they are permanent coalitions, parties greatly facilitate the policy-making process. If alliances had to be formed from scratch for each legislative proposal, the business of government would slow to a crawl or would halt altogether. Parties create a basis for coalition and thus sharply reduce the time, energy, and effort needed to advance a legislative proposal. For example, in January 1998 when President Bill Clinton considered a series of new policy initiatives, he met first with the House and Senate leaders of the Democratic party. Although some congressional Democrats disagreed with the president's approach to a number of issues, all felt they had a stake in cooperating with Clinton to burnish the party's image in preparation for the next round of national elections. Without the support of a party, the president would be compelled to undertake the daunting and probably impossible task of forming a completely new coalition for each and every policy proposal—a virtually impossible task.

Dealing with the Problem of Ambition

To the extent that politicians share principles, causes, and constituencies, there is a basis for coordination, common cause, cooperation, and joint enterprise. But individual ambition, sometimes in the background but often in the foreground, constantly threatens to undermine any bases for cooperation. Political parties, by regulating career advancement, by providing for the orderly resolution of ambitious competition, and by attending to the post-career care of elected and appointed party officials, do much to rescue coordination and cooperation and permit fellow partisans to pursue common causes where feasible. Simple devices like primaries, for example, provide a context in which clashing electoral ambitions may be resolved. Representative partisan bodies, like the Democratic Committee on Committees in the House (with comparable bodies in the Senate and for the Republicans), resolve competing claims for power positions. In short, politics does not consist of foot soldiers walking in lockstep, but rather of ambitious and autonomous individuals seeking power. The unchecked and unregulated burnishing of individual careers is a formula for chaos and destructive competition in which the dividends of cooperation are rarely reaped. Political parties constitute organizations of relatively kindred spirits that try to capture some of those dividends by providing a structure in which ambition is not suppressed altogether, but is not so destructive either.

Party Organization: The Committees

In the United States, party organizations exist at virtually every level of government (see Figure 11.1). These organizations are usually committees made up of a number of active party members. State law and party rules prescribe how such committees are constituted. Usually, committee members are elected at local party meetings—called *caucuses*—or as part of the regular primary election. The best-known examples of these committees are at the national level—the Democratic National Committee and the Republican National Committee.

caucus A normally closed meeting of a political or legislative group to select candidates, plan strategy, or make decisions regarding legislative matters.

National Convention   At the national level, the party's most important institution is the quadrennial national convention. The convention is attended by delegates from each of the states; as a group, they nominate the party's presidential and vice presidential candidates, draft the party's campaign platform for the presidential race, and approve changes in the rules and regulations governing party procedures. Before World War II, presidential nominations occupied most of the time, energy, and effort expended at the national convention. The nomination process required days of negotiation and compromise among state party leaders and often required many ballots before a nominee was selected. In recent years, however, presidential candidates have essentially nominated themselves by winning enough delegate support in primary elections to win the official nomination on the first ballot. The actual convention has played little or no role in selecting the candidates.

FIGURE 11.1

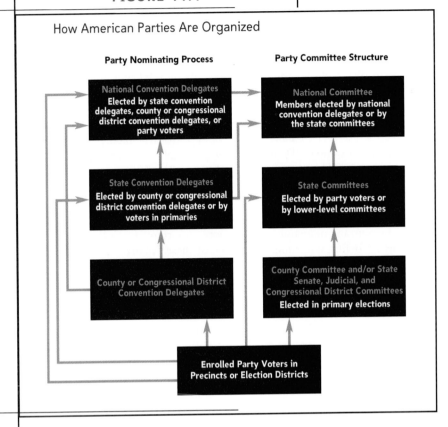

How American Parties Are Organized

Party Nominating Process

Party Committee Structure

National Convention Delegates
Elected by state convention delegates, county or congressional district convention delegates, or party voters

National Committee
Members elected by national convention delegates or by the state committees

State Convention Delegates
Elected by county or congressional district convention delegates or by voters in primaries

State Committees
Elected by party voters or by lower-level committees

County or Congressional District Convention Delegates

County Committee and/or State Senate, Judicial, and Congressional District Committees
Elected in primary elections

Enrolled Party Voters in Precincts or Election Districts

The convention's other two tasks, establishing the party's rules and its platform, remain important. Party rules can determine the relative influence of competing factions within the party and can also increase or decrease the party's chances for electoral success. In 1972, for example, the Democratic National Convention adopted a new set of rules favored by the party's liberal wing. Under these rules, state delegations to the Democratic convention were required to include women and members of minority groups in rough proportion to those groups' representation among the party's membership in that state. Liberals correctly calculated that women and African Americans would generally support liberal ideas and candidates. The rules also called for the use of proportional representation—a voting system liberals thought would give them an advantage by allowing the election of more women and minority delegates. (Although Republican rules do not require proportional representation for selecting delegates, some state legislatures have moved to compel both parties to use this system in all their presidential primaries.)

The convention also approves the party platform. Platforms are often dismissed as documents filled with platitudes that are seldom read by voters. To some extent this criticism is well founded. Not one voter in a thousand so much as glances at the party platform, and even the news media pay little attention to the documents. Furthermore, the parties' presidential candidates make little use of the platforms in their campaigns; usually they prefer to develop and promote their own themes. Occasionally, nominees even disavow their party's platform. In 1864, for example, Democratic presidential nominee General George McClellan repudiated his party's peace platform. Nonetheless, the platform can be an important document. The platform should be understood as a contract in which the various party factions attending the convention state their terms for supporting the ticket. For one faction, welfare reform may be a key issue. For another faction, tax reduction may be more important. For a third, the critical issue may be deficit reduction. When one of these "planks" is included in the platform, its promoters are asserting that this is what they want in exchange for their support of the ticket, while other party factions are agreeing that the position seems reasonable and appropriate.

Thus, party platforms should be seen more as internal party documents than as public pledges. In 1996, the Democratic platform devoted an entire paragraph to praising public school teachers and criticizing Republicans for "teacher bashing." Teachers unions are an important Democratic constituency, and were represented on the platform committee. The 1996 Republican platform strongly condemned same-sex marriage. This is not a topic that most Americans worry about on a daily basis. To the GOP's social conservatives, however, it is an important issue. The 2000 Democratic platform promised to protect the environment against the potentially damaging consequences of globalization. Again, this issue has little meaning to most voters but is of great concern to liberal environmentalists, an important Democratic constituency, who believe that American trade agreements contain provisions that essentially impose U.S. environmental standards on other nations. By including these planks in their platforms, each party was saying to these activists that they were welcome in the party coalition.

National Committee   Between conventions, each national political party is technically headed by its national committee. For the Democrats and Republicans, these are called the Democratic National Committee (DNC) and the Republican National Committee (RNC), respectively. These national committees raise campaign funds, head off factional disputes within the party, and endeavor to enhance the party's media image. The actual work of each national committee is overseen by its chairperson. Other committee members are generally major party contributors or fund raisers and serve in a largely ceremonial capacity.

For the party that controls the White House, the national committee chair is appointed by the president. Typically, this means that that party's national committee becomes little more than an adjunct to the White House staff. For a first-term president, the committee devotes the bulk of its energy to the re-election campaign. The national committee chair of the party not in control of the White House is selected by the committee itself and usually takes a broader view of the party's needs, raising money and performing other activities on behalf of the party's members in Congress and in the state legislatures. Governor Jim Gilmore of Virginia, chair of the Republican National Committee, is a political ally of President George W. Bush. The Democratic National Committee is chaired by real estate developer Terry McAuliffe, a close ally of former president Bill Clinton and one of the party's leading fund-raisers.

Congressional Campaign Committees   Each party forms House and Senate campaign committees to raise funds for House and Senate election campaigns. Their efforts may or may not be coordinated with the activities of the national committees. For the party that controls the White House, the national committee and the congressional campaign committees are often rivals, since both groups are seeking donations from the same people but for different candidates: the national committee seeks funds for the presidential race while the congressional campaign committees approach the same contributors for support for the congressional contests. In recent years, the Republican party has attempted to coordinate the fund-raising activities of all its committees. Republicans have sought to give the GOP's national institutions the capacity to invest funds in those close congressional, state, and local races where they can do the most good. The Democrats have been slower to coordinate their various committee activities, and this may have placed them at a disadvantage in recent congressional and local races. The efforts of the parties to centralize and coordinate fund-raising activities have helped bring about greater party unity in Congress. As members have come to rely upon the leadership for campaign funds, they have become more likely to vote with the leadership on major issues.

Collective Action Principle

The efforts of the parties to centralize and coordinate fund-raising activities have helped bring about greater party unity in Congress.

In recent years, the various party committees have raised prodigious amounts of money for national elections. Through October 2000, the Republican National Committee and the Republican congressional and senatorial campaign committees had, together, raised and spent more than $500 million to elect Republicans to national office. During the same period, the Democratic National Committee, along with the Democratic congressional and senatorial campaign committees, had raised nearly $400 million.[5] On the basis of the Supreme Court's decision in the 1996 case of the Colorado Republican Federal Campaign Committee against the Federal Election Commission, the government may not limit the amount of money a political party may spend on any given race so long as its expenditures are not coordinated with those of the candidate.[6] In practice, of course, some measure of coordination is almost inevitable.

[5]Federal Election Commission.
[6]Colorado Republican Federal Campaign Committee v. Jones, 95-489 (1996).

BOX 11.1

Boss Rule in Chicago

During the 1950s and 1960s, Mayor Richard J. Daley was the absolute ruler of the city of Chicago. Politicians, judges, the police and fire departments, and municipal agencies all were subservient to the Daley "machine." The source of machine power was its control of county and municipal elections. Those who supported Daley's political opponents often found that such heresy could be dangerous. Consider the case of one supporter of Republican Benjamin Adamowski, who opposed Daley in the 1957 mayoral election:

> The owner of a small restaurant at Division and Ashland, the heart of the city's Polish neighborhood, put up a big Adamowski sign. The day it went up the precinct captain came around and said, "How come the sign, Harry?""Ben's a friend of mine," the restaurant owner said. "Ben's a nice guy, Harry, but that's a pretty big sign. I'd appreciate it if you'd take it down.""No, it's staying up."
>
> The next day the captain came back, "Look, I'm the precinct captain. Is there anything wrong, any problem, anything I can help you with?" Harry said no. "Then why don't you take it down. You know how this looks in my job." Harry wouldn't budge. The sign stayed up.
>
> On the third day, the city building inspectors came. The plumbing improvement alone cost Harry $2,100.

SOURCE: Mike Royko, *Boss: Richard J. Daley of Chicago* (New York: E. P. Dutton, Inc., 1971). Copyright ©1971 by Mike Royko. Reprinted by permission of the publisher, E. P. Dutton, a division of Penguin Books, U.S.A. Inc.

State and Local Party Organizations Each of the two major parties has a central committee in each state. The parties traditionally also have county committees and, in some instances, state senate district committees, judicial district committees, and in the case of larger cities, city-wide party committees and local assembly district "ward" committees as well. Congressional districts also may have party committees.

Some cities also have precinct committees. Precincts are not districts from which any representative is elected but instead are legally defined subdivisions of wards that are used to register voters and set up ballot boxes or voting machines. A precinct is typically composed of three hundred to six hundred voters. Well-organized political parties—especially the famous old machines of New York, Chicago, and Boston—provide for "precinct captains" and a fairly tight group of party members around them (see Box 11.1). Precinct captains were usually members of long standing in neighborhood party clubhouses, which were important social centers as well as places for distributing favors to constituents.

In the nineteenth and early twentieth centuries, many cities and counties and even a few states upon occasion have had such well-organized parties that they were called machines and their leaders were called "bosses." Some of the great reform movements in American history were motivated by the excessive powers and abuses of these machines and their bosses. But few, if any, machines are left today. Traditional party machines depended heavily upon patronage, their power to control government jobs. With thousands of jobs to dispense, party bosses were able to recruit armies of political workers who, in turn, mobilized millions of voters. Today, because of civil service reform, party leaders no longer control many positions. Nevertheless, state and local party organizations are very active in recruiting candidates, conducting voter registration drives, and providing financial assistance to candidates. In many respects, federal election law has given state and local party organizations new life. Under current law, state and local party organizations can spend unlimited amounts of money on "party-building" activities such as voter registration and get-out-the-vote drives. As a result, the national party organizations, which have enormous fund-raising abilities but are limited by law in how much they can spend on candidates, each year transfer millions of dollars to the state and local organizations. The state and local parties, in turn, spend these funds, sometimes called soft money, to promote the candidacies of national, as well as state and local, candidates. In this process, as local organizations have become linked financially to the national parties, American political parties have become somewhat more integrated and nationalized than ever before. At the same time, the state and local party organizations have come to control large financial resources and play important roles in elections despite the collapse of the old patronage machines.[7]

THE TWO-PARTY SYSTEM IN AMERICA

Although George Washington, and in fact many leaders of the time, deplored partisan politics, the two-party system emerged early in the history of the new Republic. Beginning with the Federalists and the Democratic-Republicans in the late 1780s, two major parties would dominate national politics, although which particular two parties they were would change with the times and issues. This two-party system has culminated in today's Democrats and Republicans.

Historical Origins

Historically, parties form in one of two ways. The first, which could be called *internal mobilization*, occurs when political conflicts break out and government

[7]For a useful discussion, see John Bibby and Thomas Holbrook, "Parties and Elections," in *Politics in the American States*, ed. Virginia Gray and Herbert Jacob (Washington, DC: Congressional Quarterly Press, 1996), pp. 78–121.

officials and competing factions seek to mobilize popular support. This is precisely what happened during the early years of the American Republic. Competition in the Congress between northeastern mercantile and southern agrarian factions led Alexander Hamilton and the northeasterners to form a cohesive voting bloc within the Congress. The southerners responded by attempting to organize a popular following to change the balance of power within Congress. When the northeasterners replied to this southern strategy, the result was the birth of America's first national parties—the Democratic-Republicans, whose primary base was in the South, and the Federalists, whose strength was greatest in the New England states.

The second common mode of party organization, which could be called *external mobilization*, takes place when a group of ambitious politicians outside the established governmental framework develops and organizes popular support to win governmental power. For example, during the 1850s, politicians who opposed slavery and especially its expansion into the territories, many drawn from the ranks of the "Conscience" Whigs and "Free Soil" Democrats, built what became the Republican party by constructing party organizations and mobilizing popular support in the Northeast and West. The evolution of American political parties is shown in Process Box 11.1.

America's two major parties are now, of course, the Democrats and the Republicans. Each has had an important place in U.S. history.

The Democrats When the Democratic-Republican party splintered in 1824, Andrew Jackson emerged as the leader of one of its four factions. In 1830, Jackson's group became the Democratic party. This new party had the strongest national organization of its time and presented itself as the party of the common man.[8] Jacksonians supported reductions in the price of public lands and a policy of cheaper money and credit. Laborers, immigrants, and settlers west of the Alleghenies were quickly attracted to this new party.

From 1828, when Jackson was elected president, to 1860, the Democratic party was the dominant force in American politics. For all but eight of those years, the Democrats held the White House. In addition, a Democratic majority controlled the Senate for twenty-six years and the House for twenty-four years during the same time period. Nineteenth-century Democrats emphasized the importance of interpreting the Constitution literally, upholding states' rights, and limiting federal spending.

Between 1848 and 1860, the issue of slavery split the Democrats along geographic lines. In the South, many Democrats served in the Confederate government. In the North, one faction of the party (the Copperheads) opposed the war

---

[8]John Aldrich attributes the transformation of the Jacksonian faction into a mass electoral operation in 1828 to the genius of Martin Van Buren, a senator from New York (and subsequently Jackson's successor to the presidency). Van Buren appreciated the possibilities for mass mobilization and the necessity of a well-oiled national organization to enable free-riding and other collective-action difficulties to be overcome. See Aldrich, *Why Parties?*, Chapter 4.

How the Party System Evolved

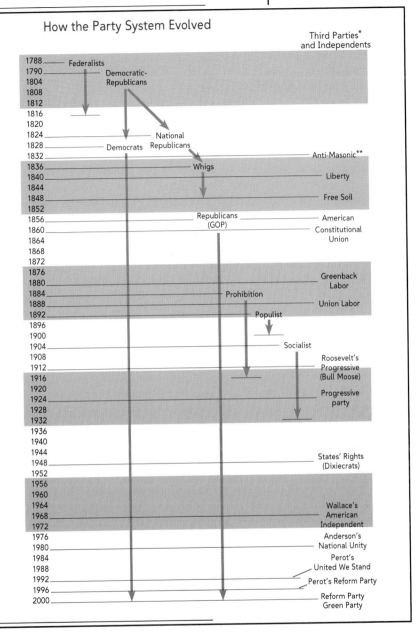

*Or in some cases, fourth party; most of these are one-term parties.

**The Anti-Masonics not only had the distinction of being the first third party, but they were also the first party to hold a national nominating convention, and the first to announce a party platform.

and advocated negotiating a peace with the South. Thus, for years after the war, Republicans denounced the Democrats as the "party of treason."

The Democratic party was not fully able to regain its political strength until the Great Depression. In 1933, Democrat Franklin D. Roosevelt entered the White House, and the Democrats won control of Congress as well. Roosevelt's New Deal coalition, composed of Catholics, Jews, Northern blacks, farmers, intellectuals, and members of organized labor, dominated American politics until the 1970s and served as the basis for the party's expansion of federal power and efforts to remedy social problems.

The Democrats were never fully united. In Congress, white southern Democrats often aligned with Republicans in the "conservative coalition" rather than with members of their own party. But the Democratic party remained America's majority party, usually controlling both Congress and the White House, for nearly four decades after 1932. By the 1980s, the Democratic coalition faced serious problems. The once-Solid South often voted for the Republicans, along with many blue-collar Northern voters. On the other hand, the Democrats increased their strength among African American voters and women.[9] The Democrats maintained a strong base in the bureaucracies of the federal government and the states, in labor unions, and in the not-for-profit sector of the economy. During the 1980s and 1990s, moderate Democrats were able to take control of the party nominating process and sought to broaden middle-class support for the party. This helped the Democrats elect a president in 1992. In 1994, however, the unpopularity of Democratic president Bill Clinton led to the loss of the Democrats' control over both houses of Congress for the first time since 1946. In 1996, Clinton was able to win re-election to a second term over the weak opposition of Republican candidate Robert Dole. Democrats were, however, unable to dislodge their GOP rivals from the leadership of either house of Congress in both 1996 and 1998.

After the 1998 elections, Clinton survived an effort by Republicans to impeach him after his admission of an inappropriate sexual relationship with White House intern Monica Lewinsky. Clinton was impeached in the House on a party-line vote but acquitted in the Senate (where a two-thirds majority is needed for conviction) on another party-line vote. As the two parties licked their wounds from this bruising struggle, they began preparations for the 2000 national presidential elections. Vice President Al Gore was the obvious front-runner, but he was seriously challenged by former senator Bill Bradley. Bradley's campaign appealed to the Democratic Party's most liberal constituencies, promising them renewed efforts in the realm of social spending. Gore, like Clinton, sought to keep his campaign and the Democratic Party firmly anchored

[9]A watershed event was the Voting Rights Act of 1965. This enabled African Americans in the South to register to vote, and, though once sympathetic to the "party of Lincoln," they moved their allegiance dramatically to the party of Roosevelt, Kennedy, and Johnson. This, in turn, accelerated the flow of white southerners out of the Democratic party. By the 1970s, the once-Solid South only occasionally could be depended upon by Democrats in presidential elections. A decade later, congressional and senatorial delegations from the South were increasingly Republican.

in the political center. Late in the presidential race, in which he was trailing in the polls, Gore shifted course and sought to appeal to the party's liberal, African American, and union-based wing. This strategy may have cost Gore some support among moderate Democrats and helped the GOP regain the presidency in 2000. Despite the lessons of Clinton's "triangulation," the Democratic Party has not yet found a way to firmly unite its liberal and more moderate wings.

The Republicans The 1854 Kansas-Nebraska Act overturned the Missouri Compromise of 1820 and the Compromise of 1850, which together had hindered the expansion of slavery in the American territories. The Kansas-Nebraska Act gave each territory the right to decide whether or not to permit slavery. Opposition to this policy galvanized antislavery groups and led them to create a new party, the Republicans. It drew its membership from existing political groups—former Whigs, Know-Nothings, Free Soilers, and antislavery Democrats. In 1856, the party's first presidential candidate, John C. Fremont, won one-third of the popular vote and carried eleven states.

The early Republican platforms appealed to commercial as well as antislavery interests. The Republicans favored homesteading, internal improvements, the construction of a transcontinental railroad, and protective tariffs, as well as the containment of slavery. In 1858, the Republican party won control of the House of Representatives; in 1860, the Republican presidential candidate, Abraham Lincoln, was victorious.

From the Civil War to the Great Depression, the Republicans were America's dominant political party, especially after 1896. In the seventy-two years between 1860 and 1932, Republicans occupied the White House for fifty-six years, controlled the Senate for sixty years, and the House for fifty. During these years, the Republicans came to be closely associated with business. The party of Lincoln became the party of Wall Street bankers and Main Street merchants.

The Great Depression, however, ended Republican hegemony. The voters held Republican president Herbert Hoover responsible for the economic catastrophe, and by 1936, the party's popularity was so low that Republicans won only eighty-nine seats in the House and seventeen in the Senate. The Republican presidential candidate, Governor Alfred M. Landon of Kansas, carried only two states. The Republicans won only four presidential elections between 1932 and 1980, and they controlled Congress for only four of those years (1947–1949 and 1953–1955).

The Republican party has widened its appeal over the last four decades. Groups previously associated with the Democratic party—particularly blue-collar workers and white southern Democrats—have been increasingly attracted to Republican presidential candidates (for example, Dwight D. Eisenhower, Richard Nixon, Ronald Reagan, George H. W. Bush, and George W. Bush). Yet, Republicans generally did not do as well at the state and local levels and, until recently, had little chance of capturing a majority in either the House or Senate. Yet in 1994, the Republican party finally won a majority in both houses of Congress, in large part because of the party's growing strength in the South.

During the 1990s, conservative religious groups, who had been attracted to the Republican camp by its opposition to abortion and support for school prayer, made a concerted effort to expand their influence within the party. This effort led to conflict between these members of the "religious Right" and more traditional "country-club" Republicans, whose major concerns were matters such as taxes and federal regulation of business. Despite these internal differences, the party swept the polls in 1994 and maintained its control of both houses of Congress in 1996. In 1998, however, severe strains began to show in the GOP coalition. After the GOP lost several House seats in the 1998 congressional elections, Speaker Newt Gingrich resigned and was eventually replaced by a relatively unknown Illinois congressman, Dennis Hastert. With their razor-thin majority and inexperienced leadership, congressional Republicans could do little more than fight the Democrats to a stalemate. In the meantime, like their Democratic rivals, Republicans prepared for the 2000 national elections. Texas governor George W. Bush, son of the former president, was the early front-runner. Bush raised an enormous amount of money and, like Bill Clinton, avoided taking positions that would upset any of his party's factions. At the same time, charging that Republicans had lost their ideological soul, commentator Pat Buchanan left the Republican Party to seek the Reform Party nomination. Republicans worried that Buchanan might draw conservative votes from the GOP ticket and help the Democrats win the election. In the end, Buchanan drew little support for his cause and was irrelevant to the outcome of the election. Bush sought to unite the party's centrist and right wings behind a program of tax cuts, education reform, military strength, and family values. Bush avoided issues that divided the GOP camp, like abortion. Most Republicans were very comfortable with Bush's message, but not with the messenger. Bush was seen, even by GOP stalwarts, as inexperienced and lacking some of the personal qualities needed for the presidency. Even so, Republicans enthusiastically supported his ticket. Bush's candidacy boded well for the future of the GOP insofar as Bush was able to find a political formula that could unite the party. Republicans hoped that future candidates might apply this formula to restore the GOP to its glory years.

Electoral Alignments and Realignments

electoral realignment The point in history when a new party supplants the ruling party, becoming in turn the dominant political force. In the United States, this has tended to occur roughly every thirty years.

In the United States, party politics has followed a fascinating pattern (see Figure 11.2). Typically, during the course of American political history, the national electoral arena has been dominated by one party for a period of roughly thirty years. At the conclusion of this period, the dominant party has been supplanted by a new party in what political scientists call an ***electoral realignment***. The realignment is typically followed by a long period in which the new party is the dominant political force in the United States—not necessarily winning every election but generally maintaining control of the Congress and usually of the White House as well.[10]

[10]See Walter Dean Burnham, *Critical Elections and the Mainsprings of American Electoral Politics* (New York: W. W. Norton, 1970). See also James L. Sundquist, *Dynamics of the Party System* (Washington, DC: Brookings Institution, 1983).

FIGURE 11.2

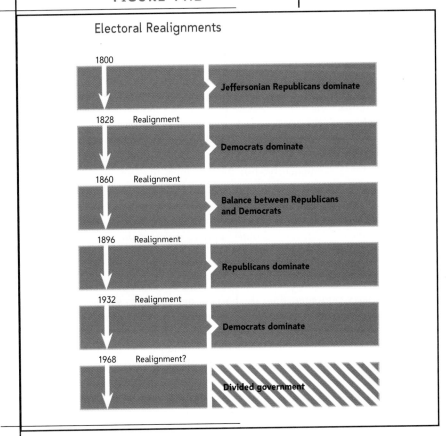

Electoral Realignments

1800
Jeffersonian Republicans dominate

1828 Realignment
Democrats dominate

1860 Realignment
Balance between Republicans and Democrats

1896 Realignment
Republicans dominate

1932 Realignment
Democrats dominate

1968 Realignment?
Divided government

History Principle

Typically, during the course of American political history, the national electoral arena has been dominated by one party for a period of roughly thirty years.

Although there are some disputes among scholars about the precise timing of these critical realignments, there is general agreement that at least five have occurred since the founding of the American Republic. The first took place around 1800 when the Democratic-Republicans defeated the Federalists and became the dominant force in American politics. The second realignment occurred in about 1828, when the Jacksonian Democrats took control of the White House and the Congress. The third period of realignment was centered around 1860. Struggles over slavery led to the collapse of the Whig party, which had been one of the nation's two major parties since the 1830s, and to divisions within the Democratic party. A number of new antislavery parties formed, with the Republicans emerging as the strongest of the new forces. During the fourth critical period, centered on the election of 1896, the Republicans reasserted their dominance of the national government, which had been weakening since the 1880s. The fifth realignment took place during the period 1932–1936 when the Democrats, led by Franklin Delano Roosevelt, took control of the White House and Congress and, despite sporadic interruptions, maintained control of both through the 1960s. Since that time, American party politics has been characterized primarily by *divided government*, wherein the presidency is controlled by one party while the other party controls one or both houses of Congress.

Historically, realignments occur when new issues combined with economic or political crises bring new, previously unaffiliated voters into the electorate and persuade large numbers of established voters to re-examine their traditional partisan loyalties and permanently shift their support from one party to another. The creation of new issues does not just *happen*. Rather, it is the fruit of political entrepreneurs, looking for opportunities to undermine the prevailing political orthodoxy and its political beneficiaries.[11] For example, during the 1850s, diverse regional, income, and business groups supported one of the two major parties, the Democrats or the Whigs, on the basis of their positions on various economic issues, such as internal improvements, the tariff, monetary policy, and banking. This economic alignment was shattered during the 1850s. The newly formed Republican party campaigned on the basis of opposition to slavery and, in particular, opposition to the expansion of slavery into the territories. The issues of slavery and sectionalism produced divisions within both the Democratic and the Whig parties, ultimately leading to the dissolution of the latter, and these issues compelled voters to re-examine their partisan allegiances. Many Northern voters who had supported the Whigs or the Democrats on the basis of their economic stands shifted their support to the Republicans as slavery, nativism, and prohibition replaced tariffs and economic concerns as the central items on the nation's political agenda. Many southern Whigs shifted their support to the Democrats. The new sectional alignment of forces that emerged was solidified by the trauma of the Civil War and persisted almost to the turn of the century.

In 1896, this sectional alignment was at least partially supplanted by an alignment of political forces based on economic and cultural factors. During the economic crises of the 1880s and 1890s, the Democrats forged a coalition consisting of economically hard-pressed Midwestern and Southern farmers, as well as small-town and rural economic interests. These groups tended to be descendants of British Isles, Dutch, and Hessian fundamentalist Protestants. The Republicans, on the other hand, put together a coalition comprising most of the business community, industrial workers, and city dwellers. In the election of 1896, Republican candidate William McKinley, emphasizing business, industry, and urban interests, decisively defeated Democrat William Jennings Bryan, who

divided government The condition in American government wherein the presidency is controlled by one party while the opposing party controls one or both houses of Congress.

 Rationality Principle

Electoral realignments are the results of the efforts of political entrepreneurs, who create new issues that bring new voters into the electorate or persuade established voters to shift their partisan loyalty.

---

[11]Such entrepreneurial efforts are not always successful. History tends mainly to remember the successful ones. For an intriguing development of this notion, see William H. Riker, *Liberalism Against Populism* (San Francisco: Freeman, 1982), especially Chapters 8 and 9. See also Andrew J. Polsky, "When Business Speaks: Political Entrepreneurship, Discourse, and Mobilization in American Partisan Regimes," *Journal of Theoretical Politics* 12 (2000), pp. 451–72.

spoke for sectional interests, farmers, and fundamentalism. Republican dominance lasted until 1932.

Such periods of critical realignment in American politics have had extremely important institutional and policy results. Realignments occur when new issue concerns coupled with economic or political crises weaken the established political elite and permit new groups of politicians to create coalitions of forces capable of capturing and holding the reins of governmental power. The construction of new governing coalitions during these realigning periods has effected major changes in American governmental institutions and policies. Each period of realignment represents a turning point in American politics. The choices made by the national electorate during these periods have helped shape the course of American political history for generations.[12]

Because, by definition, realignments require major shifts in the party identification of substantial portions of the electorate, many scholars have questioned whether or not realignments are possible today, given the weakness of political parties to mobilize the electorate. Although parties seem to play a significant role in elections, their connections to the electorate were weakened during the Progressive era and continued to wane throughout the twentieth century.[13]

American Third Parties

Although the United States is said to possess a two-party system, we have always had more than two parties. Typically, ***third parties*** in the United States have represented social and economic protests that, for one or another reason, were not given voice by the two major parties.[14] Such parties have had a good deal of influence on ideas and elections in the United States. The Populists, a party centered in the rural areas of the West and Midwest, and the Progressives, spokesmen for the urban middle classes in the late nineteenth and early twentieth centuries, are the most important examples in the past hundred years. More recently, Ross Perot, who ran in 1992 and 1996 as an independent, impressed some voters with his folksy style in the presidential debates and garnered almost 19 percent of the votes cast in the 1992 presidential election.

Table 11.1 shows a listing of all the parties that offered candidates in one or more states in the presidential election of 2000, as well as independent candidates who ran. With the exception of Ralph Nader, the third-party and independent candidates together polled only 1.02 million votes. They gained no electoral votes for president, and most of them disappeared immediately after the presidential election. The significance of Table 11.1 is that it demonstrates the large number of third parties running candidates and appealing to voters. Third-party candidacies also arise at the state and local levels. In New York, the Liberal and

third parties
Parties that organize to compete against the two major American political parties.

---

[12]Benjamin Ginsberg, *The Consequences of Consent* (New York: Random House, 1982), Chapter 4.
[13]Aldrich, *Why Parties?*
[14]For a discussion of third parties in the United States, see Daniel Mazmanian, *Third Parties in Presidential Elections* (Washington, DC: Brookings Institution, 1974).

TABLE 11.1

Parties and Candidates in 2000

CANDIDATE	PARTY	VOTE TOTAL	PERCENTAGE OF VOTE*
Al Gore	Democratic	50,996,116	48
George W. Bush	Republican	50,456,169	48
Ralph Nader	Green	2,831,066	3
Pat Buchanan	Reform	447,798	0
Harry Browne	Libertarian	385,515	0
Howard Phillips	Constitution	96,907	0
John Hagelin	Natural Law	83,134	0
James Harris	Socialist Workers	7,408	0
L. Neil Smith	Libertarian	5,775	0
Monica Moorehead	Workers World	5,335	0
David McReynolds	Socialist	4,233	0
Cathy Brown	Independent	1,606	0
Denny Lane	Grass Roots	1,044	0
Randall Venson	Independent	535	0
Earl Dodge	Prohibition	208	0
Louie Youngkeit	Independent	161	0
None of the above		3,315	0

*With 99 percent of votes tallied.

SOURCE: www.washingtonpost.com/wp-srv/onpolitics/elections/2000/results/whitehouse
Updated December 21, 2000.

Conservative parties have been on the ballot for decades. In 1998, Minnesota elected a third-party governor, former professional wrestler Jesse Ventura.

Although the Republican Party was only the third American political party ever to make itself permanent (by replacing the Whigs), other third parties have enjoyed an influence far beyond their electoral size. This was because large parts of their programs were adopted by one or both of the major parties, who sought to appeal to the voters mobilized by the new party, and so to expand their own electoral strength. The Democratic Party, for example, became a great deal more liberal when it adopted most of the Progressive program early in the twentieth century. Many Socialists felt that President Roosevelt's New Deal had adopted most of their party's program, including old-age pensions, unemployment compensation, an agricultural marketing program, and laws guaranteeing workers the right to organize into unions.

This kind of influence explains the short lives of third parties. Their causes are usually eliminated by the ability of the major parties to absorb their programs and to draw their supporters into the mainstream. There are, of course, additional reasons for the short duration of most third parties. One is the usual limitation of their electoral support to one or two regions. Populist support, for example, was primarily midwestern. The 1948 Progressive Party, with Henry Wallace as its candidate, drew nearly half its votes from the state of New York. The American Independent Party polled nearly 10 million popular votes and 45 electoral votes for George Wallace in 1968—the most electoral votes ever polled by a third-party candidate. But all of Wallace's electoral votes and the majority of his popular vote came from the states of the Deep South.

Americans usually assume that only the candidates nominated by one of the two major parties have any chance of winning an election. Thus, a vote cast for a third-party or independent candidate is often seen as a wasted vote. Voters who would prefer a third-party candidate may feel compelled to vote for the major-party candidate whom they regard as the "lesser of two evils" to avoid wasting their vote in a futile gesture. Third-party candidates must struggle—usually without success—to overcome the perception that they cannot win. Thus, in 1996, many voters who favored Ross Perot gave their votes to Bob Dole or Bill Clinton on the presumption that Perot was not really electable.

During the year prior to the 2000 national elections, Perot struggled with Minnesota governor Jesse Ventura for control of the Reform Party. Perot backed Pat Buchanan as the party's presidential nominee while Ventura promoted the candidacy of real-estate tycoon Donald Trump. Buchanan ultimately won the Reform Party's nomination, but only after a bitter convention battle that prompted many delegates to storm out of the convention hall. The winner of the nomination was not only guaranteed a spot on the ticket in most states, but also received approximately $12 million in federal campaign funds. Under federal election law, any minor party receiving more than 5 percent of the national presidential vote is entitled to federal funds, though considerably less than the major parties receive. The Reform Party qualified by winning 8.2 percent in 1996. Ralph Nader, the Green Party candidate in 2000, hoped to win the 5 percent of the vote that would entitle the Green Party to federal funds. Though Nader may have drawn enough liberal votes in New Hampshire and Florida to give those states—and the national election—to the GOP, hopes of achieving the 5 percent threshold were dashed.

As many scholars have pointed out, third-party prospects are also hampered by America's **single-member-district** plurality election system. In many other nations, several individuals can be elected to represent each legislative district. This is called a system of **multiple-member districts.** With this type of system,

single-member district An electorate that is allowed to elect only one representative from each district; the normal method of representation in the United States.

multiple-member district Electorate that selects all candidates at large from the whole district; each voter is given the number of votes equivalent to the number of seats to be filled.

the candidates of weaker parties have a better chance of winning at least some seats. For their part, voters are less concerned about wasting ballots and usually more willing to support minor-party candidates.

Reinforcing the effects of the single-member district, plurality voting rules (as was noted in Chapter 10) generally have the effect of setting what could be called a high threshold for victory. To win a plurality race, candidates usually must secure many more votes than they would need under most European systems of proportional representation. For example, to win an American plurality election in a single-member district where there are only two candidates, a politician must win more than 50 percent of the votes cast. To win a seat from a European multimember district under proportional rules, a candidate may need to win only 15 or 20 percent of the votes cast. This high American threshold discourages minor parties and encourages the various political factions that might otherwise form minor parties to minimize their differences and remain within the major-party coalitions.[15]

It would nevertheless be incorrect to assert (as some scholars have maintained) that America's single-member plurality election system guarantees that only two parties will compete for power in all regions of the country. All that can be said is that American election law depresses the number of parties likely to survive over long periods of time in the United States. There is nothing magical about two. Indeed, the single-member plurality system of election can also discourage second parties. After all, if one party consistently receives a large plurality of the vote, people may eventually come to see their vote *even for the second party* as a wasted effort. This happened to the Republican party in the Deep South before World War II.

FUNCTIONS OF THE PARTIES

Parties perform a wide variety of functions. They are mainly involved in nominations and elections—providing the candidates for office, getting out the vote, and facilitating mass electoral choice. That is, they help solve the problems of collective action and ambition to which we alluded earlier. They also influence the institutions of government—providing the leadership and organization of the various congressional committees. That is, they help solve the problem of collective choice concerning institutional arrangements and policy formulation that we also noted earlier.

Recruiting Candidates

One of the most important but least noticed party activities is the recruitment of candidates for local, state, and national office. Each election year, candidates must be found for thousands of state and local offices as well as for congressional

[15]See Maurice Duverger, *Political Parties* (New York: Wiley, 1954).

seats. Where they do not have an incumbent running for re-election, party leaders attempt to identify strong candidates and to interest them in entering the campaign.

An ideal candidate will have an unblemished record and the capacity to raise enough money to mount a serious campaign. Party leaders are usually not willing to provide financial backing to candidates who are unable to raise substantial funds on their own. For a House seat this can mean several hundred thousand dollars; for a Senate seat a serious candidate must be able to raise several million dollars. Often, party leaders have difficulty finding attractive candidates and persuading them to run. In 1998, for example, Democratic leaders in Kansas and Washington reported difficulties in recruiting congressional candidates. A number of potential candidates reportedly were reluctant to leave their homes and families for the hectic life of a member of Congress. GOP leaders in Washington and Massachusetts have had similar problems finding candidates to oppose popular Democratic incumbents.[16] Candidate recruitment has become particularly difficult in an era when political campaigns often involve mudslinging, and candidates must assume that their personal lives will be intensely scrutinized in the press.[17]

Nominations

Article I, Section 4, of the Constitution makes only a few provisions for elections. It delegates to the states the power to set the "Times, Places and Manner" of holding elections, even for U.S. senators and representatives. It does, however, reserve to Congress the power to make such laws if it chooses to do so. The Constitution has been amended from time to time to expand the right to participate in elections. Congress has also occasionally passed laws about elections, congressional districting, and campaign practices. But the Constitution and the laws are almost completely silent on nominations, setting only citizenship and age requirements for candidates. The president must be at least thirty-five years of age, a natural-born citizen, and a resident of the United States for fourteen years. A senator must be at least thirty, a U.S. citizen for at least nine years, and a resident of the state he or she represents. A member of the House must be at least twenty-five, a U.S. citizen for seven years, and a resident of the state he or she represents.

Nomination is the process by which a party selects a single candidate to run for each elective office. The nominating process can precede the election by many months, as it does when the many candidates for the presidency are eliminated from consideration through a grueling series of debates and state primaries until there is only one survivor in each party—the party's nominee.

Nomination is the parties' most serious and difficult business. When more than one person aspires to an office, the choice can divide friends and associates.

nomination The process through which political parties select their candidates for election to public office.

---

[16]Alan Greenblatt, "With Major Issues Fading, Capitol Life Lures Fewer," *Congressional Quarterly Weekly Report*, 25 October 1997, p. 2625.

[17]For an excellent analysis of the parties' role in recruitment, see Paul Herrnson, *Congressional Elections: Campaigning at Home and in Washington* (Washington, DC: Congressional Quarterly Press, 1995).

Types of Nominating Processes

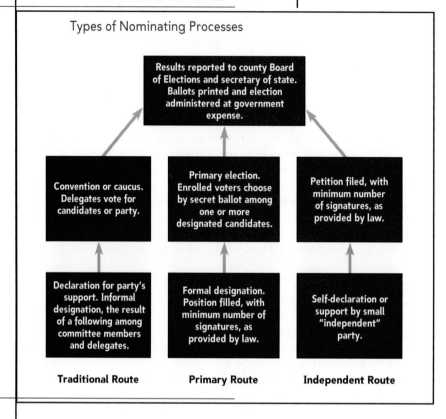

In comparison to such an internal dispute, the electoral campaign against the opposition is almost fun, because there the fight is against the declared adversaries. In the course of American political history, the parties have used three modes of nomination—the caucus, the convention, and the primary election (see Process Box 11.2).

The Caucus   In the eighteenth and early nineteenth centuries, nominations were informal, without rules or regulations. Local party leaders would simply gather all the party activists, and they would agree on the person, usually from among themselves, who would be the candidate. The meetings where candidates were nominated were generally called caucuses. Informal nomination by caucus sufficed for the parties until widespread complaints were made about cliques of local leaders or state legislators dominating all the nominations and leaving no place for the other party members who wanted to participate. Beginning in the

1830s, nominating conventions were proposed as a reform that would enable the mass membership of a party to express its will.

Nomination by Convention   A nominating convention is a formal caucus bound by a number of rules that govern participation and nominating procedures. Conventions are meetings of delegates elected by party members from the relevant county (county convention) or state (state convention). Delegates to each party's national convention (which nominates the party's presidential candidate) are chosen by party members on a state-by-state basis, for there is no single national delegate selection process.

Historically, the great significance of the convention mode of nomination was its effect on the presidential selection process and on the presidency itself. For about forty years after America's founding, the nomination of presidential candidates was dominated by meetings of each party's congressional delegations, meetings that critics called "King Caucus." In the early 1830s, when the major parties adopted the national nominating convention, they broke the power of King Caucus. This helped to give the presidency a mass popular base (see Chapter 6). Nevertheless, reformers in the early twentieth century regarded nominating conventions as instruments of "boss rule." They proposed replacing conventions with primaries, which provide for direct choice by the voters at an election some weeks or months before the general election.

Nomination by Primary Election   In primary elections, party members select the party's nominees directly rather than selecting convention delegates who then select the nominees. Primaries are far from perfect replacements for conventions, since it is rare that more than 25 percent of the enrolled voters participate in them. Nevertheless, they are replacing conventions as the dominant method of nomination.[18] At the present time, only a small number of states, including Connecticut, Delaware, and Utah, provide for state conventions to nominate candidates for statewide offices, and even these states also use primaries whenever a substantial minority of delegates vote for one of the defeated aspirants.

Primary elections are mainly of two types—closed and open. In a ***closed primary***, participation is limited to individuals who have previously declared their affiliation by registering with the party. In an ***open primary***, individuals declare their party affiliation on the actual day of the primary election. To do so, they simply go to the polling place and ask for the ballot of a particular party. The open primary allows each voter to consider candidates and issues before deciding whether to participate and in which party's contest to participate. Open primaries, therefore, are less conducive to strong political parties.

closed primary
A primary election in which voters can participate in the nomination of candidates, but only of the party in which they are enrolled for a period of time prior to primary day.

open primary
A primary election in which the voter can wait until the day of the primary to choose which party to enroll in to select candidates for the general election.

[18]For a discussion of some of the effects of primary elections see Peter F. Galderisi and Benjamin Ginsberg, "Primary Elections and the Evanescence of Third Party Activity in the United States," in *Do Elections Matter?* ed. Benjamin Ginsberg and Alan Stone (Armonk, NY: M. E. Sharpe Publishers, 1986), pp. 115–30.

But in either case, primaries are more open than conventions or caucuses to new issues and new types of candidates.

Independent Candidates   Process Box 11.2 indicated that the convention and primary methods are not the only ways that candidates can get on the ballot. State laws extend the right of independent candidacy to individuals who do not wish to be nominated by political parties or who are unable to secure a party nomination.

Although nomination by a political party is complicated, the independent route to the ballot is even more difficult. For almost all offices in all states, the law requires more signatures for independent nomination than for party designation. For example, the candidate for a party's nomination to Congress in New York must get 1,250 valid signatures within the congressional district, while the independent candidate must get 3,500 signatures.

Contested Nominations   Even though state laws favor party nomination, the task of the parties is not an easy one. Party organizations have grown weaker over the years, and the number of contested primaries—primaries where two or more designated candidates compete for the party's nomination—has increased. At the same time, the ability of the "regular" party leaders to win in such primaries has diminished. Regardless of who wins, a contested nomination is costly. Money that is spent on campaigning in the primaries is no longer available to spend in the general election against the opponent nominated by the other party. Moreover, contested primaries can be particularly bitter and the feud long-lasting because the candidates are members of the same party, and often consider opposition a personal affront.

But although contested nominations deplete party resources and interfere with party campaign strategy, they can be a sign of healthy politics because they expose parties to new or underrepresented interests. Indeed, parties have often been a channel for resolving important social conflicts. Contested nominations, especially contested primaries, can speed the resolution of such conflicts. Civil rights became a national issue in 1948 through a struggle within the Democratic party over the antidiscrimination commitment in its platform. In 1968, the Vietnam War was debated more by Democratic president Lyndon Johnson and antiwar Democratic senator Eugene McCarthy than by Hubert Humphrey (who ultimately became the Democratic presidential candidate) and Republican Richard Nixon. Any number of important local political issues have been re-solved between candidates fighting each other for the nomination for mayor or district attorney or governor.

Many important advances in the participation of ethnic and racial minorities have begun through victories in local primaries. Party leaders once considered the nominating process to be their own personal property. In fact, the Democratic party in many Southern states adopted rules excluding nonwhites from the primaries, on the grounds that political parties were the equivalent of private clubs. The Supreme Court did not invalidate all of these "white primaries" until 1944, when it held that primaries were an integral part of the electoral system and could not be left to private control.[19] The Court was recognizing a fact universally accepted well before 1944—that the nominating process is the first stage of the electoral process.

The Role of the Parties in Getting Out the Vote

The actual election period begins immediately after the nominations. Historically, this has been a time of glory for the political parties, whose popular base of support is fully displayed. All the paraphernalia of party committees and all the committee members are activated into local party work forces.

The first step in the electoral process involves voter registration. This aspect of the process takes place all year round. There was a time when party workers were responsible for virtually all of this kind of electoral activity, but they have been supplemented (and in many states virtually displaced) by civic groups such as the League of Women Voters, unions, and chambers of commerce.

Those who have registered have to decide on election day whether to go to the polling place, stand in line, and actually vote for the various candidates and referenda on the ballot. Political parties, candidates, and campaigning can make a big difference in convincing the voters to vote. Because it is costly for voters to participate in elections and because many of the benefits that winning parties bestow are public goods (i.e., parties cannot exclude any individual from enjoying them), people will try to free-ride by enjoying the benefits without incurring the costs of electing the party that provided the benefits. This is the *free-rider problem* (see Chapter 1) and parties are important because they help overcome this by mobilizing the voters to support the candidates.

On any general election ballot, there are likely to be only two or three candidacies where the nature of the office and the characteristics and positions of the candidates are well known to voters. But what about the choices for judges, the state comptroller, the state attorney general, and many other elective positions? Without partisan cues, voters are likely to find it extremely difficult to make informed choices about these candidates. And what about referenda? This method of making policy choices is being used more and more as a means of direct democracy. A referendum may ask: Should there be a new bond issue for financing the local schools? Should there be a constitutional amendment to increase the number of county judges? In 1996, Californians approved Proposition 201, a referendum that called for an end to most statewide affirmative action programs, including those employed for college admission. A proposition on the 1978 California ballot was a referendum to reduce local property taxes. It started a taxpayer revolt that spread to many other states and most voters knew where they stood on the issue. But the typical referendum question is one on which few voters have clear and knowledgeable positions. Parties and campaigns help most by giving information when voters must choose among obscure candidates and vote on unclear referenda.

Collective Action Principle

Parties can help mobilize voters who are potential free-riders.

[19]Smith v. Allwright, 321 U.S. 649 (1944).

Facilitation of Mass Electoral Choice

party identifica-tion An individual voter's psychological ties to one party or another.

Parties facilitate mass electoral choice. As the late Harvard political scientist V. O. Key pointed out long ago, the persistence over time of competition between groups possessing a measure of identity and continuity is virtually a necessary condition for electoral control.[20] *Party identification* increases the electorate's capacity to recognize its options. Continuity of party division facilitates organization of the electorate on the long-term basis necessary to sustain any popular influence in the governmental process. In the absence of such identity and continuity of party division, the voter is, in Key's words, confronted constantly by "new faces, new choices."[21] Parties lower information costs of participating by providing a kind of "brand name" recognizability; that is, voters know with a substantial degree of accuracy what positions a candidate will take just by identifying the candidate's party affiliation. In addition, parties give elections a kind of sporting-event atmosphere, with voters treating parties like teams that they can support and cheer on to victory. This enhances the entertainment value of participating in elections. Parties also direct the flow of government benefits, such as patronage jobs, to those who put the party in power. These and other activities encourage individuals to identify with and support one of the two parties.

 Rationality Principle

Parties can lower the cost of voting by facilitating a voter's choice.

Even more significant, however, is the fact that party organization is generally an essential ingredient for effective electoral competition by groups lacking substantial economic or institutional resources. Party building has typically been the strategy pursued by groups that must organize the collective energies of large numbers of individuals to counter their opponents' superior material means or institutional standing. Historically, disciplined and coherent party organizations were generally developed first by groups representing the political aspirations of the working classes. Parties, French political scientist Maurice Duverger notes, "are always more developed on the Left than on the Right because they are always more necessary on the Left than on the Right."[22] In the United States, the first political party was built by the Democratic-Republicans as a counterweight to the superior social, institutional, and economic resources that could be deployed by the incumbent Federalists. In a subsequent period of American history, the efforts of the Jacksonians to construct a coherent mass party organization were impelled by a similar set of circumstances. Only by organizing the power of numbers could the Jacksonian coalition hope to compete successfully against the superior resources that could be mobilized by its adversaries.

In the United States, the political success of party organizations forced their opponents to copy them in order to meet the challenge. It was, as Duverger points out, "contagion from the Left," that led politicians of the Center and Right to attempt to build strong party organizations.[23] These efforts were sometimes successful. In the United States during the 1830s, the Whig party, which was led

[20]V. O. Key, *Southern Politics* (New York: Random House, 1949), Chapter 14.
[21]Ibid.
[22]Duverger, *Political Parties*, p. 426.
[23]Ibid., Chapter 1.

by northeastern elites, carefully copied the effective organizational techniques devised by the Jacksonians. The Whigs won control of the national government in 1840. But even when groups nearer the top of the social scale responded in kind to organizational efforts by their inferiors, the net effect nonetheless was to give lower-class groups an opportunity to compete on a more equal footing. In the absence of coherent mass organization, middle- and upper-class factions almost inevitably have a substantial competitive edge over their lower-class rivals. Even when both sides organize, the net effect is still to erode the relative advantage of the well-off. Parties of the Right, moreover, were seldom actually able to equal the organizational coherence of the working-class opposition. As Duverger and others have observed, middle- and upper-class parties generally failed to construct organizations as effective as those built by their working-class foes, who typically commanded larger and more easily disciplined forces.

Although political parties continue to be significant in the United States, the role of party organizations in electoral politics has clearly declined over the past three decades. This decline, and the partial replacement of the party by new forms of electoral technology, is one of the most important developments in twentieth-century American politics.

The Parties' Influence on National Government

The ultimate test of the party system is its relationship to and influence on the institutions of government and the policy-making process. Thus, it is important to examine the party system in relation to Congress and the president.

Parties and Policy One of the most familiar observations about American politics is that the two major parties try to be all things to all people and are therefore indistinguishable from each other. Data and experience give some support to this observation. Parties in the United States are not programmatic or ideological, as they have sometimes been in Britain or other parts of Europe. But this does not mean there are no differences between them. During the Reagan era, important differences emerged between the positions of Democratic and Republican party leaders on a number of key issues, and these differences are still apparent today. For example, the national leadership of the Republican party supports maintaining high levels of military spending, cuts in social programs, tax relief for middle- and upper-income voters, tax incentives to businesses, and the "social agenda" backed by members of conservative religious denominations. The national Democratic leadership, on the other hand, supports expanded social welfare spending, cuts in military spending, increased regulation of business, and a variety of consumer and environmental programs.

Policy Principle
Policies typically reflect the goals of whichever party is in power.

These positions reflect differences in philosophy as well as differences in the core constituencies to which the parties seek to appeal. The Democratic party at the national level seeks to unite organized labor, the poor, members of racial minorities, and liberal upper-middle-class professionals. The Republicans, by contrast, appeal to business, upper-middle- and upper-class groups in the private sector, and social conservatives. Often, party leaders will seek to develop issues they hope will add new groups to their party's constituent base. During the 1980s, for example, under the leadership of Ronald Reagan, the Republicans devised a series of "social issues," including support for school prayer, opposition to abortion, and opposition to affirmative action, designed to cultivate the support of white Southerners. This effort was extremely successful in increasing Republican strength in the once solidly Democratic South. In the 1990s, under the leadership of Bill Clinton, who called himself a "new Democrat," the Democratic party sought to develop new social programs designed to solidify the party's base among working-class and poor voters, and new, somewhat more conservative economic programs aimed at attracting the votes of middle- and upper-middle-class voters.

As these examples suggest, parties do not always support policies because they are favored by their constituents. Instead, party leaders can play the role of policy entrepreneurs, seeking ideas and programs that will expand their party's base of support while eroding that of the opposition. It is one of the essential characteristics of party politics in America that a party's programs and policies often lead, rather than follow, public opinion. Like their counterparts in the business world, party leaders seek to identify and develop "products" (programs and policies) that will appeal to the public. The public, of course, has the ultimate voice. With its votes it decides whether or not to "buy" new policy offerings.

Through members elected to office, both parties have made efforts to translate their general goals into concrete policies. Republicans, for example, implemented tax cuts, increased defense spending, cut social spending, and enacted restrictions on abortion during the 1980s and 1990s. Democrats were able to defend consumer and environmental programs against GOP attacks and sought to expand domestic social programs in the late 1990s. In 2001, President Bush sought large cuts in federal taxes as well as shifts in the administration of federal social programs that would reduce the power of the federal bureaucracy and increase the role of faith-based organizations allied with the Republican party. Both parties, of course, have been hampered by internal divisions and the recurrent pattern of divided control of Congress and the executive branch that has characterized American politics for the past two decades.

Analyzing American Politics

www.wwnorton.com/
lowi7/ch11

Analyze the impact of party on congressional voting.

The Parties and Congress Congress, in particular, depends more on the party system than is generally recognized. First, the speakership of the House is essentially a party office. All the members of the House take part in the election of the Speaker. But the actual selection is made by the *majority party*. When the majority party caucus presents a nominee to the entire House, its choice is then invariably ratified in a straight party-line vote.

The committee system of both houses of Congress is also a product of the two-party system. Although the rules organizing committees and the rules defining the jurisdiction of each are adopted like ordinary legislation by the whole membership, all other features of the committees are shaped by parties. For example, each party is assigned a quota of members for each committee, depending upon the percentage of total seats held by the party. On the rare occasions when an independent or third-party candidate is elected, the leaders of the two

majority party
Party that holds the majority of legislative seats in either the House or the Senate.

Collective Action Principle

Cooperation in Congress is facilitated by the party system.

parties must agree against whose quota this member's committee assignments will count. Presumably the member will not be able to serve on any committee until the question of quota is settled.

As we saw in Chapter 5, the assignment of individual members to committees is a party decision. Each party has a "committee on committees" to make such decisions. Permission to transfer to another committee is also a party decision. Moreover, advancement up the committee ladder toward the chair is a party decision. Since the late nineteenth century, most advancements have been automatic—based upon the length of continuous service on the committee. This seniority system has existed only because of the support of the two parties, and each party can depart from it by a simple vote. During the 1970s, both parties reinstituted the practice of reviewing each chairmanship—voting anew every two years on whether each chair would be continued. In 2001, Republicans lived up to their 1995 pledge to limit House committee chairs to three terms. Existing chairmen were forced to step down, but were generally replaced by the next most senior Republican member of each committee.

President and Party   As we saw earlier, the party that wins the White House is always led, in title anyway, by the president. The president normally depends upon fellow party members in Congress to support legislative initiatives. At the same time, members of the party in Congress hope that the president's programs and personal prestige will help them raise campaign funds and secure re-election. During his two terms in office, President Bill Clinton had a mixed record as party leader. In the realm of trade policy, Clinton sometimes found more support among Republicans than among Democrats. In addition, although Clinton proved to be an extremely successful fund-raiser, congressional Democrats often complained that he failed to share his largesse with them. At the same time, however, a number of Clinton's policy initiatives seemed calculated to strengthen the Democratic party as a whole. Clinton's early health care initiative would have linked millions of voters to the Democrats for years to come, much as FDR's Social Security program had done in a previous era. But by the middle of Clinton's second term, the president's acknowledgement of his sexual affair with a White House intern threatened his position as party leader. Initially, Democratic candidates nationwide feared that the scandal would undermine their own chances for election, and many moved to distance themselves from the president. The Democrats' surprisingly good showing in the 1998 elections, however, strengthened Clinton's position and gave him another chance to shape the Democratic agenda.

Between the 1998 and 2000 elections, however, the president's initiatives on Social Security and nuclear disarmament failed to make much headway in a Republican-controlled Congress. The GOP was not prepared to give Clinton anything for which Democrats could claim credit in the 2000 elections. Lacking strong congressional leadership, however, the GOP did agree to many of Clinton's budgetary proposals in 1999 and dropped its own plan for large-scale cuts in federal taxes. Clinton's popular approval rating fell slightly after 1998 as some Americans apparently decided they had had enough of Bill Clinton. Some pundits called this "Clinton fatigue." In his 2000 presidential bid, Vice President Al Gore took great pains to distance himself from his old friend and boss. In an October 1999 debate with Bill Bradley, Gore said he had felt "anger and disappointment" toward President Clinton after the previous year's revelations of Clinton's sexual misconduct.[24]

When he assumed office in 2001, President George W. Bush called for a new era of bipartisan cooperation and the new president did receive the support of some Democratic conservatives. Generally, however, Bush depended on near-unanimous backing from his own party in Congress to implement his plans for cutting taxes as well as other elements of his program. After September 11, both parties united behind Bush's military response. Even then, however, the parties divided on other matters. One example was the airline safety bill, discussed in Chapter 5.

WEAKENING OF PARTY ORGANIZATION

George Washington's warning against the "baneful effects of the spirit of party" was echoed by the representatives of social, economic, and political elites in many nations who saw their right to rule challenged by groups able to organize the collective energies and resources of the mass public.

Opposition to party politics was the basis for a number of the institutional reforms of the American political process promulgated at the turn of the twentieth century during the so-called Progressive era. Many Progressive reformers were undoubtedly motivated by a sincere desire to rid politics of corruption and to improve the quality and efficiency of government in the United States. But simultaneously, from the perspective of middle- and upper-class Progressives and the financial, commercial, and industrial elites with which they were often associated, the weakening or elimination of party organization would also mean that power could more readily be acquired and retained by the "best men," that is, those with wealth, position, and education.

The list of anti-party reforms of the Progressive Era is a familiar one. The Australian ballot reform took away the parties' privilege of printing and distributing ballots and thus introduced the possibility of split-ticket voting. The introduction of nonpartisan local elections eroded grassroots party organization. The extension of "merit systems" for administrative appointments stripped party organizations of their vitally important access to patronage and thus reduced their ability to recruit workers. The development of the direct primary reduced party leaders' capacity to control candidate nominations. These reforms obviously did not destroy political parties as entities, but taken together they did substantially weaken party organizations in the United States. After the turn of the century, the strength of American political parties gradually diminished. Between the two world wars, organization remained the major tool available to contending electoral

---

[24]Ceci Connolly and Dan Baily, "Democrats Echo Themes in Face-Off," *Washington Post*, 28 October 1999, p.1.

forces, but in most areas of the country the "reformed" state and local parties that survived the Progressive era gradually lost their organizational vitality and coherence, and they became less effective campaign tools. While most areas of the nation continued to boast Democratic and Republican party groupings, reform did mean the elimination of the permanent mass organizations that had been the parties' principal campaign weapons.

High-Tech Politics

As a result of Progressive reform, American party organizations entered the twentieth century with rickety substructures. As the use of civil service, primary elections, and the other Progressive innovations spread during the period between the two world wars, the strength of party organizations continued to be eroded. By the end of World War II, political scientists were already bemoaning the absence of party discipline and "party responsibility" in the United States. This erosion of the parties' organizational strength set the stage for the introduction of new political techniques. These new methods represented radical departures from the campaign practices perfected during the nineteenth century. In place of manpower and organization, contending forces began to employ intricate electronic communications techniques to attract electoral support. This new political technology includes six basic elements.

> **History Principle**
> The erosion of the strength of party organizations set the stage for the introduction of new political campaign techniques and the rise of candidate-centered campaigns.

   1. *Polling.* Surveys of voter opinion provide the information that candidates and their staffs use to craft campaign strategies. Candidates employ polls to select issues, to assess their own strengths and weaknesses (as well as those of the opposition), to check voter response to the campaign, and to determine the degree to which various constituent groups are susceptible to campaign appeals. Virtually all contemporary campaigns for national and statewide office as well as many local campaigns make extensive use of opinion surveys. As we saw in Chapter 9, President Clinton made extensive use of polling data both during and after the 1996 presidential election to shape his rhetoric and guide his policy initiatives.

   2. *The broadcast media.* Extensive use of the electronic media, television in particular, has become the hallmark of the modern political campaign. One commonly used broadcast technique is the thirty- or sixty-second television spot advertisement—such as George H. W. Bush's "Willie Horton" ad in 1988 or Lyndon Johnson's famous "daisy girl" ad in 1964—which permits the candidate's message to be delivered to a target audience before uninterested or hostile viewers can psychologically, or physically, tune it out (see Box 11.2). Television spot ads and other media techniques are designed to establish candidate name recognition, to create a favorable image of the candidate and a negative image of the opponent, to link the candidate with desirable groups in the community, and to communicate the candidate's stands on selected issues.[25] These spot ads can have an important electoral

---

[25]For a discussion of the role of information in democratic politics in light of the cognitive limitations, restricted interest, and diminished attention spans of today's voters, see Arthur Lupia and Mathew D. McCubbins, *The Democratic Dilemma: Can Citizens Learn What They Need to Know?* (New York: Cambridge University Press, 1998).

The Daisy Girl

On September 7, 1964, NBC's *Monday Night at the Movies* was interrupted by what came to be one of the most famous and controversial political commercials ever shown on American television. In this ad, a little girl with long, light brown hair stood in a field picking daisy petals. As she pulled the petals, she counted, "1-2-3. . . . " At the same time, the voice of an announcer in the background counted backward, "10-9-8. . . ." As the counts continued, the announcer's voice became louder and the girl's voice more muted, until the girl reached 10 and the announcer counted down to 0. At that point, a blinding nuclear explosion destroyed everything, with President Johnson saying, "These are the stakes: To make a world in which all of God's children can live or go into the dark. We must either love each other or we must die." The announcer then urged viewers to vote for President Johnson on November 3. The ad was cut after one use, but the practice of short spots has continued.

impact. Generally, media campaigns attempt to follow the guidelines indicated by a candidate's polls, emphasizing issues and personal characteristics that appear important in the poll data. The broadcast media are now so central to modern campaigns that most candidates' activities are tied to their media strategies.[26] Candidate activities are designed expressly to stimulate television news coverage. For instance, members of Congress running for re-election or for president almost always sponsor committee or subcommittee hearings to generate publicity.

3. *Phone banks.* Through the broadcast media, candidates communicate with voters *en masse* and impersonally. Phone banks, on the other hand, allow campaign workers to make personal contact with hundreds of thousands of voters. Personal contacts of this sort are thought to be extremely effective. Again, poll data serve to identify the groups that will be targeted for phone calls. Computers select phone numbers from areas in which members of these groups are concentrated. Staffs of paid or volunteer callers, using computer-assisted dialing systems and prepared scripts, then place calls to deliver the candidate's message. The targeted groups are generally those identified by polls as either uncommitted or weakly committed, as well as strong supporters of the candidate who are contacted simply to encourage them to vote.

4. *Direct mail.* Direct mail serves both as a vehicle for communicating with voters and as a mechanism for raising funds. The first step in a direct mail

[26]Larry J. Sabato, *The Rise of Political Consultants* (New York: Basic Books, 1981).

campaign is the purchase or rental of a computerized mailing list of voters deemed to have some particular perspective or social characteristic. Often, sets of magazine subscription lists or lists of donors to various causes are employed. For example, a candidate interested in reaching conservative voters might rent subscription lists from the *National Review*; a candidate interested in appealing to liberals might rent subscription lists from the *New York Review of Books* or from the *New Republic*. Considerable fine-tuning is possible. After obtaining the appropriate mailing lists, candidates usually send pamphlets, letters, and brochures describing themselves and their views to voters believed to be sympathetic. Different types of mail appeals are made to different electoral subgroups. Often the letters sent to voters are personalized. The recipient is addressed by name in the text and the letter appears actually to have been signed by the candidate. Of course, these "personal" letters are written and even signed by a computer.

In addition to its use as a political advertising medium, direct mail has also become an important source of campaign funds. Computerized mailing lists permit campaign strategists to pinpoint individuals whose interests, background, and activities suggest that they may be potential donors to the campaign. Letters of solicitation are sent to these potential donors. Some of the money raised is then used to purchase additional mailing lists. Direct mail solicitation can be enormously effective.[27]

5. *Professional public relations.* Modern campaigns and the complex technology upon which they rely are typically directed by professional public relations consultants. Virtually all serious contenders for national and statewide office retain the services of professional campaign consultants. Increasingly, candidates for local office, too, have come to rely upon professional campaign managers. Consultants offer candidates the expertise necessary to conduct accurate opinion polls, produce television commercials, organize direct mail campaigns, and make use of sophisticated computer analyses.

6. *The Internet.* A more recent form of new technology has been the Internet. Most candidates for office set up a Web site as an inexpensive means to establish a public presence. The 1998 election saw increased use of the Internet by political candidates. Virtually all statewide candidates, as well as many candidates for Congress and local offices, developed Web sites providing contact information, press releases, speeches, photos, and information on how to volunteer, contact the candidate, or donate money to the campaign. During his campaign, Florida governor Jeb Bush sold "Jebware," articles of clothing emblazoned with his name, through his Web site. In the 2000 contest, the politician who made the most extensive use of the Internet was John McCain. McCain used his Web site to mobilize volunteers and to raise hundreds of thousands of dollars for his unsuccessful bid for the Republican presidential nomination. In the future, all politicians will use the Web to collect information about potential voters and supporters, which, in turn, will allow them to personalize mailings and calls as

[27]Ibid., p. 250.

well as E-mail advertising. One consultant now refers to politics on the Internet as "netwar," and asserts that "small, smart attackers" can defeat more powerful opponents in the new, information-age "battlespace."[28] Although the Internet has not yet become a dominant force in political campaigns, most politicians and consultants believe that its full potential for customizing political appeals is only now beginning to be realized.

Thus far, the political impact of the Internet has been limited by the fact that, unlike a TV commercial that comes to viewers without any action on their part, citizens must take the initiative to visit a Web site. In general, this means that only those already supporting a candidate are likely to visit the site, limiting its political utility. However, it may be possible to lure voters to Web sites through television advertising or, perhaps, through Internet links. California Republican gubernatorial hopeful Dan Lundgren, for example, linked his Web site to that of a burger chain. He still lost the race.

The number of technologically oriented campaigns increased greatly after 1971. The Federal Election Campaign Act of 1972 prompted the creation of large numbers of political action committees (PACs) by a host of corporate and ideological groups. This development increased the availability of funds to political candidates—conservative candidates in particular—which meant in turn that the new technology could be used more extensively. Initially, the new techniques were employed mainly by individual candidates who often made little or no effort to coordinate their campaigns with those of other political aspirants sharing the same party label. For this reason, campaigns employing new technology sometimes came to be called "candidate-centered" efforts, as distinguished from the traditional party-coordinated campaign. Nothing about the new technology, however, precluded its use by political party leaders seeking to coordinate a number of campaigns. In recent years, party leaders have learned to make good use of modern campaign technology. The difference between the old and new political methods is not that the latter is inherently candidate-centered while the former is strictly a party tool. The difference is, rather, a matter of the types of political resources upon which each method depends.

From Labor-Intensive to Capital-Intensive Politics

The displacement of organizational methods by the new political technology is, in essence, a shift from labor-intensive to capital-intensive competitive electoral practices. Campaign tasks were once performed by masses of party workers with some cash. These tasks now require fewer personnel but a great deal more money, for the new political style depends on polls, computers, and other electronic paraphernalia. Of course, even when workers and organ-

---

[28]Dana Milbanks, "Virtual Politics," *New Republic*, 5 July 1999, p. 22.

ization were the key electoral tools, money had considerable political significance. Nevertheless, during the nineteenth century, national political campaigns in the United States employed millions of people. Indeed, as many as 2.5 million individuals did political work during the 1880s.[29] The direct cost of the campaigns, therefore, was relatively low. For example, in 1860, Abraham Lincoln spent only $100,000 (about $2 million in today's dollars)—which was approximately twice the amount spent by his chief opponent, Stephen Douglas.

Modern campaigns depend heavily on money. Each element of the new political technology is enormously expensive. A sixty-second spot announcement on prime-time network television costs hundreds of thousands of dollars each time it is aired. Opinion surveys can be quite expensive; polling costs in a statewide race can easily reach or exceed the six-figure mark. Campaign consultants can charge substantial fees. A direct mail campaign can eventually become an important source of funds but is very expensive to initiate. The inauguration of a serious national direct mail effort requires at least $1 million in "front end cash" to pay for mailing lists, brochures, letters, envelopes, and postage.[30] While the cost of televised debates is covered by the sponsoring organizations and the television stations and is therefore free to the candidates, even debate preparation requires substantial staff work and research, and, of course, money. It is the expense of the new technology that accounts for the enormous cost of recent American national elections.

Certainly "people power" is not irrelevant to modern political campaigns. Candidates continue to utilize the political services of tens of thousands of volunteer workers. Nevertheless, in the contemporary era, even the recruitment of campaign workers has become a matter of electronic technology. Employing a technique called "instant organization," paid telephone callers use phone banks to contact individuals in areas targeted by a computer (which they do when contacting potential voters, as we discussed before). Volunteer workers are recruited from among these individuals. A number of campaigns—Richard Nixon's 1968 presidential campaign was the first—have successfully used this technique.

The displacement of organizational methods by the new political technology has the most far-reaching implications for the balance of power among contending political groups. Labor-intensive organizational tactics allowed parties whose chief support came from groups nearer the bottom of the social scale to use the numerical superiority of their forces as a partial counterweight to the institutional and economic resources more readily available to the opposition. The capital-intensive technological format, by contrast, has given a major boost to the political fortunes of those forces whose sympathizers are better able to

[29]M. Ostrogorski, *Democracy and the Organization of Political Parties* (New York: Macmillan, 1902).
[30]Timothy Clark, "The RNC Prospers, the DNC Struggles as They Face the 1980 Election," *National Journal*, 27 October 1980, p. 1619.

furnish the large sums now needed to compete effectively.[31] Indeed, the new technology permits financial resources to be more effectively harnessed and exploited than was ever before possible.

In a political process lacking strong party organizations, the likelihood that groups that do not possess substantial economic or institutional resources can acquire some measure of power is severely diminished. Dominated by the new technology, electoral politics becomes a contest in which the wealthy and powerful have a decided advantage.

The Role of the Parties in Contemporary Politics

Political parties make democratic government possible. We often do not appreciate that democratic government is a contradiction in terms. Government implies policies, programs, and decisive action. Democracy, on the other hand, implies an opportunity for all citizens to participate fully in the governmental process. The contradiction is that full participation by everyone is often inconsistent with getting anything done. At what point should participation stop and governance begin? How can we make certain that popular participation will result in a government capable of making decisions and developing needed policies? The problem of democratic government is especially acute in the United States because of the system of separated powers bequeathed to us by the Constitution's framers. Our system of separated powers means that it is very difficult to link popular participation and effective decision making. Often, after the citizens have spoken and the dust has settled, no single set of political forces has been able to win control of enough of the scattered levers of power to actually do anything. Instead of government, we have a continual political struggle.

Strong political parties are a partial antidote to the inherent contradiction between participation and government. Strong parties can both encourage popular involvement and convert participation into effective government. More than fifty years ago, a committee of the academic American Political Science Association (APSA) called for the development of a more "responsible" party government. By responsible party government, the committee meant political parties that mobilized voters and were sufficiently well organized to develop and implement coherent programs and policies after the election. Strong parties can link democratic participation and government.

Although they are significant factors in politics and government, American political parties today are not as strong as the "responsible parties" advocated by the APSA. Yet parties-as-organizations are more professional, better financed,

Institutional Reform

www.wwnorton.com/
lowi7/ch11

How much of a party's national platform gets adopted after the election?

---

[31]For discussions of the consequences, see Thomas Edsall, *The New Politics of Inequality* (New York: W. W. Norton, 1984). Also see Thomas Edsall, "Both Parties Get the Company's Money—But the Boss Backs the GOP," *Washington Post National Weekly Edition*, 16 September 1986, p. 14; and Benjamin Ginsberg, "Money and Power: The New Political Economy of American Elections," in *The Political Economy*; ed. Thomas Ferguson and Joel Rogers (Armonk, NY: M. E. Sharpe Publishers, 1984).

and more organized than ever before. Political scientists argue that parties have evolved into "service organizations," which, though they no longer hold a monopoly over campaigns, still provide services to candidates, without which it would be extremely difficult for candidates to win and hold office. Parties have not declined but have simply adapted to serve the interests of political actors.[32]

Many politicians, however, are able to raise funds, attract volunteers, and win office without much help from local party organizations. Once in office, these politicians often refuse to submit to party discipline; instead they steer independent courses. They are often supported by voters who see independence as a virtue and party discipline as "boss rule." As we just saw, analysts refer to this pattern as a "candidate-centered" politics to distinguish it from a political process in which parties are the dominant forces. The problem with a candidate-centered politics is that it tends to be associated with low turnout, high levels of special-interest influence, and a lack of effective decision making. In short, many of the problems that have plagued American politics in recent years can be traced directly to the independence of American voters and politicians and the candidate-centered nature of American national politics.

The health of America's parties should be a source of concern to all citizens. Can political parties be strengthened? The answer is, in principle, yes. For example, political parties could be strengthened if the rules governing campaign finance were revised to make candidates more dependent financially upon state and local party organizations rather than on personal resources or private contributors. Such a reform, to be sure, would require stricter regulation of party fund-raising practices to prevent soft money abuses. The potential benefit, however, of a greater party role in political finance could be substantial. If parties controlled the bulk of the campaign funds, they would become more coherent and disciplined, and might come to resemble the responsible parties envisioned by the APSA. Political parties have been such important features of American democratic politics that we need to think long and hard about how to preserve and strengthen them.

SUMMARY

Political parties seek to control government by controlling its personnel. Elections are one means to this end. Thus, parties take shape from the electoral process. The formal principle of party organization is this: for every district in which an election is held—from the entire nation to the local district, county, or precinct—there should be some kind of party unit.

The two-party system dominates U.S. politics. While the two parties agree on some major issues, the Democrats generally favor higher levels of social spending funded by higher levels of taxation than the GOP is willing to support. Republicans favor lower levels of domestic activity on the part of the federal

[32]See Paul Herrnson, *Party Campaigning in the 1980s* (Cambridge, MA: Harvard University Press, 1988).

Rationality Principle	Collective Action Principle	Institution Principle	Policy Principle	History Principle
Parties help deal with the threat to cooperation posed by ambitious individuals by regulating career advancement and resolving competition.	Parties facilitate collective action in the electoral process by helping candidates attract campaign funds, assemble campaign workers, and mobilize voters.	Third-party prospects for electoral success are hampered by America's single-member-district plurality election system.	Parties help resolve collective choice in the policy-making process by acting as permanent coalitions of individuals with similar policy goals.	Typically, during the course of American political history, the national electoral arena has been dominated by one party for a period of roughly thirty years.
Electoral realignments are the results of the efforts of political entrepreneurs, who create new issues that bring new voters into the electorate or persuade established voters to shift their partisan loyalty.	The efforts of the parties to centralize and coordinate fund-raising activities have helped bring about greater party unity in Congress.		Policies typically reflect the goals of whichever party is in power.	The construction of new governing coalitions during realigning periods has effected major changes.
Parties can lower the cost of voting by facilitating a voter's choice.	Parties can help mobilize voters who are potential free-riders.			The erosion of the strength of party organizations set the stage for the introduction of new political campaign techniques and the rise of candidate-centered campaigns.
	Cooperation in Congress is facilitated by the party system.			

government, but also support federal action on a number of social and moral issues such as abortion. Even though party affiliation means less to Americans than it once did, partisanship remains important. What ticket-splitting there is occurs mainly at the presidential level.

Voters' choices have had particularly significant consequences during periods of critical electoral realignment. During these periods, which have occurred roughly every thirty years, new electoral coalitions have formed, new groups have come to power, and important institutional and policy changes have occurred. The last such critical period was associated with Franklin Roosevelt's New Deal.

Third parties are short-lived for several reasons. They have limited electoral support, the tradition of the two-party system is strong, and a major party often adopts their platforms. Single-member districts with two competing parties also discourage third parties.

Nominating and electing are the basic functions of parties. Originally nominations were made in party caucuses, and individuals who ran as independents had a difficult time getting on the ballot. In the 1830s, dissatisfaction with the cliquish caucuses led to nominating conventions. Although these ended the "King Caucus" that controlled the nomination of presidential candidates, and thereby gave the presidency a popular base, they too proved unsatisfactory. Primaries have now more or less replaced the conventions. There are both closed and open primaries. The former are more supportive of strong political parties than the latter. Contested primaries sap party strength and financial resources, but they nonetheless serve to resolve important social conflicts and recognize new interest groups. Winning at the top of a party ticket usually depends on the party regulars at the bottom getting out the vote. At all levels, the mass communications media are important. Mass mailings, too, are vital in campaigning. Thus, campaign funds are crucial to success.

Congress is organized around the two-party system. The House speakership is a party office. Parties determine the makeup of congressional committees, including their chairs, which are no longer based entirely on seniority.

In recent years, the role of parties in political campaigns has been partially supplanted by the use of new political technologies. These include polling, the broadcast media, phone banks, direct mail fund-raising and advertising, professional public relations, and the Internet. These techniques are enormously expensive and have led to a shift from labor-intensive to capital-intensive politics. This shift works to the advantage of political forces representing the well-to-do.

FOR FURTHER READING

Aldrich, John H. *Why Parties?: The Origin and Transformation of Party Politics in America*. Chicago: University of Chicago Press, 1995.

Beck, Paul Allen, and Marjorie Randon Hershey. *Party Politics in America*, 9th ed. New York: Longman, 2001.

Chambers, William N., and Walter Dean Burnham. *The American Party Systems: Stages of Political Development*. New York: Oxford University Press, 1975.

Coleman, John J. *Party Decline in America: Policy, Politics, and the Fiscal State*. Princeton: Princeton University Press, 1996.

Grimshaw, William J. *Bitter Fruit: Black Politics and the Chicago Machine, 1931–1991*. Chicago: University of Chicago Press, 1992.

Hofstadter, Richard. *The Idea of a Party System: The Rise of Legitimate Opposition in the United States, 1780–1840*. Berkeley: University of California Press, 1970.

Kayden, Xandra, and Eddie Mahe, Jr. *The Party Goes On: The Persistence of the Two-Party System in the United States*. New York: Basic Books, 1985.

Lawson, Kay, and Peter Merkl. *When Parties Fail: Emerging Alternative Organizations*. Princeton: Princeton University Press, 1988.

Milkis, Sidney. *The President and the Parties: The Transformation of the American Party System since the New Deal*. New York: Oxford University Press, 1993.

Polsby, Nelson W. *Consequences of Party Reform.* New York: Oxford University Press, 1983.

Shafer, Byron, ed. *Beyond Realignment? Interpreting American Electoral Eras.* Madison: University of Wisconsin Press, 1991.

Smith, Eric R. A. N. *The Unchanging American Voter.* Berkeley: University of California Press, 1989.

Sundquist, James. *Dynamics of the Party System.* Washington, DC: Brookings Institution, 1983.

Wattenberg, Martin. *The Decline of American Political Parties, 1952–1996.* Cambridge: Harvard University Press, 1998.

EVENTS	INSTITUTIONAL DEVELOPMENTS
Early trade associations and unions formed (1820s and 1830s)	Term "lobbyist" is first used (1830)
Citizen groups and movements form— temperance (1820s), antislavery (1810–1830), women's (1848), abolition (1850s) **—1860—**	Local regulations restricting or forbidding manufacture and sale of alcohol (1830–1860); several states pass laws granting women control over their property (1839–1860s)
Civil War (1861–1865)	
Development of agricultural groups, including the Grange (1860s–1870s)	Lobbying is recognized in law and practice (1870s)

Grangers successfully lobby for passage of "Granger laws" to regulate rates charged by railroads and warehouses (1870s) |
Farmers' Alliances and Populists **—1880—** (1880s–1890s)	Beginnings of labor and unemployment laws (1880s)
American Federation of Labor (AFL) formed (1886)	Election of candidates pledged to farmers (1890s)
Growth of movement for women's suffrage (1890s)	Women's suffrage granted by Wyoming, Colorado, Utah, Idaho (1890s)
Middle-class Progressive movement and trade associations (1890s)	Laws for direct primary, voter registration, regulation of business (1890s–1910s)
—1900—	
Strengthening of women's movements— temperance (1890s) and suffrage (1914)	Prohibition (Eighteenth) Amendment ratified (1919)
World War I (1914–1918)	
Growth of trade associations (1920s)	Nineteenth Amendment gives women the vote (1920)
American Farm Bureau Federation (1920); farm bloc (1920s)	Corrupt practices legislation passed; lobbying registration legislation (1920s)
Teapot Dome scandal (1924)	Farm bloc lobbies for farmers (1921–1923)
CIO is formed (1938)	Wagner National Labor Relations Act (1935)
—1940—	
U.S. in World War II (1941–1945)	Federal Regulation of Lobbying Act (1946)
Postwar wave of strikes in key industries (1945–1946)	Taft-Hartley Act places limits on unions (1947)

	EVENTS		INSTITUTIONAL DEVELOPMENTS
Senate hearings into labor racketeering (1950s)	**1950**		
AFL and CIO merge (1955)			Landrum-Griffin Act to control union corruption (1959)
Civil rights movement—boycotts, sit-ins, vote drives (1957), March on Washington (1963)			Passage of Civil Rights acts (1957, 1960, 1964), Voting Rights Act (1965)
National Organization for Women (NOW) formed (1966)			
Vietnam War: antiwar movement (1965–1973)			
Public interest groups formed (1970s–1980s)	**1970**		Campaign spending legislation leads to PACs (1970s)
Watergate scandal (1972–1974)			Consumer, environmental, health, and safety legislation (1970s)
Pro-life and pro-choice groups emerge (post-1973)			*Roe v. Wade* (1973)
			Ethics in Government Act (1978)
Moral Majority formed (late 1970s)			PACs help to elect conservative candidates (1980s)
			Further regulation of lobbying (1980s)
	1990		
Interest groups influence Clinton health care and economic proposals (1993)			Proposals to restrict corporate lobbying activities (1993)
Expanded use of new technologies for grassroots lobby efforts (1993)			
Growth in power of conservative groups such as Christian Coalition and National Federation of Independent Business (1994)			Growth in influence of "soft money" in elections (1994–1998)
			Expanded use of litigation by interest groups (1990s–present)

CORE OF THE ANALYSIS

- Interest groups have proliferated over the last thirty years as a result of the expansion of the federal government and the "New Politics" movement.

- Interest groups use various strategies to promote their goals, including lobbying, gaining access to key decision makers, using the courts, going public, and influencing electoral politics.

- Though interest groups sometimes promote public concerns, they more often represent narrow interests.

In the spring of 1998, a seemingly unlikely meeting took place on Capitol Hill. Michael Eisner, chairman of the Walt Disney Company, stopped to visit Republican Senate majority leader Trent Lott to discuss issues of concern to the huge media and entertainment company. The meeting seemed unlikely because of Hollywood's well-known ties to the Democratic party. Yet with Republicans in control of Congress, Democrat Eisner had little choice but to turn to Republican Lott for help with a matter of great importance to his company—the extension of Disney's copyright on the corporation's greatest asset, Mickey Mouse. Without help from Congress, Disney's ownership of the famed rodent, worth billions of dollars, will expire in 2003, seventy-five years after it was issued. To make matters worse, Disney's ownership of Pluto expires in 2006, and its exclusive right to Goofy ends in 2008. Rights to other characters, including Bambi, Donald Duck, Snow White and all the dwarfs, expire soon thereafter. Eisner needed and eventually got congressional help to protect his company's most precious treasures, and working with the GOP was a small price to pay. After all, as a former Disney lobbyist put it, "Mickey Mouse is not a Republican or a Democrat."[1]

In actuality, despite the political liberalism of many well-known Hollywood personalities, the movie industry, like most of the nation's industries, is more concerned with the financial bottom line than with partisanship. The motion picture industry maintains an active lobbying arm in Washington, the Motion Picture Association of America, headed by Jack Valenti, once press secretary to President Lyndon Johnson. Under Valenti's leadership, the Hollywood studios have built strong ties to both parties and work vigorously to promote their political agenda, which includes strict protection for intellectual property, favorable tax treatment, and freedom from censorship. Valenti has encouraged the studios to adopt a bipartisan stance in dealing with lawmakers. Though most of the stars may be liberal Democrats, in recent years the film studios have contributed heavily to both political parties and have built bridges to members of Congress of all political stripes.

Though few other industries can boast a symbol as widely known as Mickey Mouse, the Hollywood studios are a fairly typical ***interest group***, that is, a group of individuals and organizations that share a common set of goals and have

interest group
A group of individuals and organizations that share a common set of goals and have joined together in an effort to persuade the government to adopt policies that will help them.

[1]Alan Ota, "Disney in Washington: The Mouse That Roars,"*Congressional Quarterly Weekly Report*, 8 August 1998, p. 2167.

joined together in an effort to persuade the government to adopt policies that will help them. There are thousands of interest groups in the United States. High-minded Americans have been complaining about the role of interest groups since the nation's founding. We should remember, however, that vigorous interest-group activity is a consequence and reflection of a free society. As James Madison put it so well in *The Federalist Papers*, No. 10, "liberty is to faction what air is to fire."[2]

As long as freedom exists, groups will organize and attempt to exert their influence over the political process. And groups will form wherever power exists. It should therefore be no surprise that even though interest groups have been part of the political landscape since the first days of the Republic, the most impressive growth in the number and scale of interest groups has been at the national level since the 1930s. But even as the growth of the national government leveled off in the 1970s and 1980s, and actually declined in the late 1980s and 1990s, the spread of interest groups continued. It is no longer just the expansion of the national government that spawns interest groups, but the *existence* of that government with all the power it possesses. As long as there is a powerful government in the United States, there will be a large network of interest groups around it.

The framers of the American Constitution feared the power that could be wielded by organized interests. Yet, they believed that interest groups thrived because of freedom— the freedom that all Americans enjoyed to organize and express their views. To the framers, this problem presented a dilemma. If the government were given the power to regulate or in any way to forbid efforts by organized interests to

THE CENTRAL QUESTIONS

THE GROUP BASIS OF POLITICS

Why do interest groups form?

Why is cooperation in groups difficult to achieve?
  How can the collective action problem be solved?

INTEREST GROUPS IN THE UNITED STATES

What interests are represented by organized groups?

What are the organizational components of interest groups?

What are the benefits of interest-group membership?

What are the characteristics of interest-group members?

THE PROLIFERATION OF GROUPS

Why has the number of interest groups grown in recent years?

What is the "New Politics" movement?

STRATEGIES: THE QUEST FOR POLITICAL POWER

What are some of the strategies interest groups use to gain influence?

What are the purposes of these strategies?

GROUPS AND INTERESTS: THE DILEMMA OF REFORM

What are the problems involved in curbing the influence of interest groups?

[2]Clinton Rossiter, ed., *The Federalist Papers* (New York: New American Library, 1961), No. 10, p.78.

interfere in the political process, the government would in effect have the power to suppress freedom. The solution to this dilemma was presented by James Madison:

> Take in a greater variety of parties and interest [and] you make it less probable that a majority of the whole will have a common motive to invade the rights of other citizens. . . . [Hence the advantage] enjoyed by a large over a small republic.[3]

According to the Madisonian theory, a good constitution encourages multitudes of interests so that no single interest can ever tyrannize the others. The basic assumption is that competition among interests will produce balance and compromise, with all the interests regulating each other.[4] Today, this Madisonian principle of regulation is called ***pluralism***. According to pluralist theory, all interests are and should be free to compete for influence in the United States. Moreover, according to pluralist doctrine, the outcome of this competition is compromise and moderation, since no group is likely to be able to achieve any of its goals without accommodating itself to some of the views of its many competitors.[5]

pluralism
The theory that all interests are and should be free to compete for influence in the government. The outcome of this competition is compromise and moderation.

There are tens of thousands of organized groups in the United States, ranging from civic associations to huge nationwide groups like the National Rifle Association, whose chief cause is opposition to restrictions on gun ownership, or Common Cause, a public interest group that advocates a variety of liberal political reforms. The huge number of *interest groups* competing for influence in the U.S., however, does not mean that all *interests* are fully and equally represented in the American political process. As we shall see, the political deck is heavily stacked in favor of those interests able to organize and to wield substantial economic, social, and institutional resources on behalf of their cause. This means that within the universe of interest-group politics it is political power—not some abstract conception of the public good—that is likely to prevail. Moreover, this means that interest-group politics, taken as a whole, is a political format that works more to the advantage of some types of interests than others. In general, a politics in which interest groups predominate is a politics with a distinctly upper-class bias.

In this chapter, we will examine some of the antecedents and consequences of interest-group politics in the United States. First, we will analyze the group basis of politics, the problems that result from collective action, and some solutions to these problems. Second, we will seek to understand the character of the interests promoted by interest groups. Third, we will assess the growth of interest-group activity in recent American political history, including the emergence of "public interest" groups. Fourth, we will review and evaluate the strategies that competing groups use in their struggle for influence. Finally, we will assess the question, "Are interest groups too influential in the political process?"

[3]Rossiter, ed., *The Federalist Papers*, No. 10, p. 83.
[4]Ibid.
[5]The best statement of the pluralist view is in David Truman, *The Governmental Process* (New York: Knopf, 1951), Chapter 2.

THE GROUP BASIS OF POLITICS

It is no accident that much political discourse is conducted in terms of groups. In any large society, it is simply impossible to think in highly disaggregated terms. Instead, we think about an issue in terms of the groups that take an interest in it, and a conflict in terms of the groups that line up on one side or the other of the divide. Farmers lobby both for price supports for their crops and for high tariffs to keep crops from other nations out of their domestic market; consumers, of course, are on the other side of these issues. Labor unions push for mandated wage increases and improvements in fringe benefits, which employer groups oppose. Minority groups urge passage of civil rights legislation, while those whose competitive advantage is eroded by it are in opposition. Economic producer organizations seek various protections from market competition, again at the expense of consumers. Professional groups want licensing authority, while those who use professional services want this authority regulated by public bodies. Associations of colleges and universities seek large student aid allocations and government research budgets, only to be opposed by those who want those limited budget allocations devoted to their own activities. The list is endless.

In a pluralistic political system these groups are known as "lobbies," "interest groups," or, more pejoratively, as "pressure groups." At the highest level of aggregation, these groups are actually collections of groups—so-called *peak associations* ranging from the AFL-CIO (whose members are unions), to the National Association of Manufacturers and the Business Roundtable (whose members are corporations), to the Farm Bureau Federation (whose members are local farm bureaus). At less august levels, groups simply represent aggregations of individuals sharing a common interest—the Possum Hollow Rod and Gun Club, the Harvard-MIT Apple User Group, the Boston Policemen's Benevolent Society, the Massachusetts Federation of High School Basketball Coaches, or the New England Political Science Association.

The very ubiquity of groups in pluralistic political systems explains why, for most of the first half of the twentieth century, the study of politics *was* the study of groups. Political outcomes were seen as the result of struggles among groups. Indeed, in its most famous representation, Arthur Bentley wrote almost like a physicist about the "parallelogram of forces" that constituted group interactions and infighting.[6] He thought of the status quo in any policy domain as something that gets "pushed around" by various forces. The net effect of this pushing and shoving—the resultant of the various group forces applied to the existing status quo—is a new policy status quo. Politics, in this view, becomes physics: each group is a "force vector," and the political outcome of a struggle is simply the mechanical resultant of the various forces at play.

---

[6]Arthur Bentley, *The Process of Government* (Evanston, Ill.: Principia Press, 1908). Its famous mid-century companions were V. O. Key, *Politics, Parties, and Pressure Groups*, 3rd ed. (New York: Crowell, 1952), and Truman, *The Governmental Process*.

The pull and tug of group infighting was, to nineteenth-century observers like Alexis de Tocqueville, the definitive feature of American political life. Indeed, they admired the voluntaristic political pluralism that was absent in less liberal societies. The group-based formulation of pluralistic politics took groups as fundamental and assumed their existence. The essential axiom was as follows: *Common interest, however defined and however arrived at, leads naturally to organizations coherently motivated to pursue that common interest; politics is all about how these coherently motivated organizations support and oppose one another.*

If this belief is correct, groups should form roughly in proportion to people's interests. We should find a greater number of organizations around interests shared by a greater number of people. The evidence for this pluralist hypothesis, however, is quite weak. Kay Schlozman and John Tierney examined interest groups that represent people's occupations and economic roles.[7] Using census data and listings of interest groups, they compared how many people in the United States have particular economic roles and how many organizations represent those roles in Washington. For example, they found that (in the mid-1980s) 4 percent of the population was looking for work, but only a handful of organizations actually represented the unemployed in Washington.[8]

There is a considerable disparity in Washington representation across categories of individuals in the population, as Table 12.1 suggests. Schlozman and Tierney note, for example, that there are at least a dozen groups representing senior citizens, but none for the middle-aged. Ducks Unlimited is an organization dedicated to the preservation of ducks and their habitats; turkeys, on the other hand, have no one working on their behalf. The pluralists' inability to explain why groups form around some interests and not others led some scholars to investigate the dynamics of collective action. Mancur Olson's work, already mentioned in Chapter 1 and discussed later in this chapter, is the most well-known challenge to the pluralists.

Cooperation in Groups

Groups of individuals pursuing some common interest or shared objective—maintenance of a hunting and fishing habitat, creation of a network for sharing computer software, lobbying for favorable legislation, playing a Beethoven symphony, etc.—consist of individuals who bear some cost or make some contribution on behalf of the joint goal. Each member of the Possum Hollow Rod and Gun Club, for example, pays annual dues and devotes one weekend a year to cleaning up the rivers and forests of the club-owned game preserve.

---

[7] Kay Lehman Schlozman and John T. Tierney, *Organized Interests and American Democracy* (New York: Harper and Row, 1986).

[8] Of course, the *number* of organizations is at best only a rough measure of the extent to which various categories of citizen are represented in the interest-group world of Washington.

TABLE 12.1

Who Is Represented by Organized Interests

ECONOMIC ROLE OF INDIVIDUAL	% OF U.S. ADULTS	% OF ORGS.	TYPE OF ORG. IN WASHINGTON, D.C.	RATIO OF ORGS./ ADULTS
Managerial/ Administrative	7	71.0	Business association	10.10
Professional/ Technical	9	17.0	Professional association	1.90
Student/ Teacher	4	4.0	Educational organization	1.00
Farm Workers	2	1.5	Agricultural organization	0.75
Unable to Work	2	0.6	Handicapped organization	0.30
Other Non-Farm Workers	41	4.0	Union	0.10
At Home	19	1.8	Women's organizations	0.09
Retired	12	0.8	Senior citizens organization	0.07
Looking for Work	4	0.1	Unemployment organization	0.03

We can think of this in an analytical fashion, somewhat removed from any of these specific examples, as an instance of two-person cooperation writ large. Accordingly, each of a very large number of individuals has, in the simplest situation, two options in his or her behavioral repertoire: "contribute" or "don't contribute." If the number of contributors to the group enterprise is sufficiently large, then a group goal is obtained. However, just as in the swamp-clearing example in Chapter 1, there is a twist. If the group goal is obtained, then *every member of the group enjoys its benefits, whether he or she contributed to its achievement or not.*

Collective Action Principle

The prisoners' dilemma, an example of a collective action problem, explains why cooperation in groups can be difficult to achieve.

Rationality Principle

In a group setting, rational individuals have an incentive to free-ride.

The Prisoners' Dilemma   Researchers often rely on the metaphor of the *prisoners' dilemma* when theorizing about social situations of collective action, like the swamp-clearing example of Chapter 1. According to this metaphor, two prisoners (A and B) who are accused of jointly committing a crime are kept in separate interview rooms. The arresting officers do not have enough evidence for a judge to give the prisoners the maximum sentence, so the officers hope that one of the prisoners will provide the additional evidence they require. The prisoners know that the officers have scant evidence against them and that they will probably receive a less severe sentence or escape punishment altogether if they remain silent. Each prisoner is offered the same plea bargain: "Testify against the other prisoner in exchange for freedom, provided that your accomplice does not also testify against you. Remain silent and you will possibly get the maximum sentence if your accomplice testifies against you."

If you assume that prisoners A and B are self-interested, rational actors (that given the choice between two alternatives, they will choose the one that offers the best deal) and that they prefer less jail time to more, they will face an unpleasant choice. Notice that in Table 12.2, prisoner A is better off choosing to "snitch," no matter what prisoner B does. If B also chooses to snitch, then A's choice to snitch gets A a three-year jail term, but a "don't snitch" choice would have resulted in six years for A—clearly worse. On the other hand, if B chooses not to snitch, then A gets no jail time instead of one year if he also chooses not to snitch. In short, A is always better off snitching. But this situation is symmetrical, so it follows that B is better off snitching too. If both prisoners snitch, the prosecutor is able to convict both of them, and they would each serve three years. If they had both been *irrational* and kept silent, they would only have gotten one year each! In game theory (from which the prisoners' dilemma is drawn), each player has a *dominant strategy*—snitching is best no matter what the other player does—and this leads paradoxically to an outcome in which each player is *worse* off.

The prisoners' dilemma provides the insight that rational individual behavior does not always lead to rational collective results. The logic of this situation is very compelling—if A appreciates the dilemma and realizes that B appreciates the dilemma, then A will still be drawn to the choice of snitching. The reasons for this are the temptation to get off scot-free (if he testifies and his accomplice doesn't) and the *fear* of being "suckered." The dilemma is brilliant because it applies to a wide range of circumstances.

Consider again the swamp-clearing example in which each person benefits from a drained swamp, even if he or she does not provide the required effort. So long as enough other people do so, any individual can "ride free" on the efforts of the others. This is a multiperson prisoners' dilemma because not providing effort, like snitching, is a dominant strategy, yet it is one that, if everyone avails him- or herself of it, leads to an unwanted outcome—a mosquito-infested swamp. The prospect of free-riding, as we shall see next, is the bane of collective action.

TABLE 12.2

The Prisoners' Dilemma

		PRISONER B	
		Snitch	Don't snitch
PRISONER A	Snitch	A gets three years B gets three years	A gains freedom B gets six years
	Don't snitch	A gets six years B gains freedom	A gets one year B gets one year

The Logic of Collective Action   Mancur Olson, writing in 1965, essentially took on the political science establishment by noting that the pluralist assumption of the time, that common interests among individuals are automatically transformed into group organization and collective action, was problematic. Individuals are tempted to "free-ride" on the efforts of others, have difficulty coordinating multiple objectives, and may even have differences of opinion about which common interest to pursue (conflicts of interest). In short, the group basis of politics is a foundation of jello: one cannot merely assume that groups arise and are maintained. Rather, formation and maintenance are the central *problems* of group life and politics generally.

Olson is at his most persuasive when talking about large groups and mass collective action, like many of the antiwar demonstrations and civil rights rallies of the 1960s. In these circumstances, the world of politics is a bit like the swamp-clearing example, where each individual has a rational strategy of not contributing. The logic of collective action makes it difficult to induce participation in and contribution to collective goals.

Olson claims that this difficulty is severest in large groups, for three reasons. First, large groups tend to be anonymous. Each household in a city is a taxpaying unit and may share the wish to see property taxes lowered. It is difficult, however, to forge a group identity or induce households to contribute effort or activity for the cause of lower taxes on such a basis. Second, in the anonymity of the large-group context, it is especially plausible to claim that no one individual's contribution makes much difference. Should the head of a household kill the better part of a morning writing a letter to his city council member in support of lower property taxes? Will it make much difference? If hardly anyone else writes, then the council member is unlikely to pay much heed to this one letter; on the other hand, if the council member is inundated with letters, would one more have a significant additional effect? Finally, there is the problem of enforcement. In a large group, are other group members going to punish a slacker? By definition, they cannot prevent the slacker from receiving the benefits of collective action, should those benefits materialize. (Every property owner's taxes will be lowered if anyone's is.) But more to the point, in a large, anonymous group it is often hard to know who has and who has not contributed, and, because there is only the most limited sort of group identity, it is hard for contributors to identify, much less take action against, slackers. As a consequence, many large groups that share common interests fail to mobilize at all—they remain *latent*.

This same problem plagues small groups, too, as the swamp-clearing problem in Chapter 1 reveals. But Olson argues that small groups manage to overcome the problem of collective action more frequently and to a greater extent than their larger counterparts. Small groups are more personal, and their members are therefore more vulnerable to interpersonal persuasion. In small groups, individual contributions may make a more noticeable difference so that individuals feel that their contributions are more essential. Contributors in small groups, moreover, often know who they are and who the slackers are. Thus, punishment, ranging from subtle judgmental pressure to social ostracism, is easier to effect.

In contrast to large groups that often remain latent, Olson calls these small groups *privileged* because of their advantage in overcoming the free-riding, co-ordination, and conflict-of-interest problems of collective action. It is for these perhaps counterintuitive reasons that small groups often prevail over, or enjoy greater privileges relative to, larger groups. These reasons, therefore, help explain why we so often see producers win out over consumers, owners of capital over owners of labor, and a party's elite over its mass members.

Why Join? A Solution to the Collective Action Problem

Despite the free-rider problem, interest groups offer numerous incentives to join. Most importantly, as Olson shrewdly noted in a most important theoretical insight, they make various "selective benefits" available only to group members (see Chapter 1). These benefits can be informational, material, solidary, or purposive. Table 12.3 gives some examples of the range of benefits in each of these categories.

informational benefits Special newsletters, periodicals, training programs, conferences, and other information provided to members of groups to entice others to join.

Informational benefits are the most widespread and important category of selective benefits offered to group members. Information is provided through conferences, training programs, and newsletters and other periodicals sent automatically to those who have paid membership dues.

material benefits Special goods, services, or money provided to members of groups to entice others to join.

Material benefits include anything that can be measured monetarily, such as special services, goods, and even money. A broad range of material benefits can be offered by groups to attract members. These benefits often include discount purchasing, shared advertising, and, perhaps most valuable of all, health and retirement insurance.

TABLE 12.3

Selective Benefits of Interest Group Membership

CATEGORY	BENEFITS
Informational benefits	Conferences
	Professional contacts
	Training programs
	Publications
	Coordination among organizations
	Research
	Legal help
	Professional codes
	Collective bargaining
Material benefits	Travel packages
	Insurance
	Discounts on consumer goods
Solidary benefits	Friendship
	Networking opportunities
Purposive benefits	Advocacy
	Representation before government
	Participation in public affairs

SOURCE: Adapted from Jack Walker, Jr., *Mobilizing Interest Groups in America: Patrons, Professions, and Social Movements* (Ann Arbor: University of Michigan Press, 1991), p. 86.

Another option identified on Table 12.3 is that of *solidary benefits.* The most notable of this class of benefits are the friendship and "networking" opportunities that membership provides. Another benefit that has become extremely important to many of the newer nonprofit and citizen groups is what has come to be called "consciousness-raising." One example of this can be seen in the claims of many women's organizations that active participation conveys to each member of the organization an enhanced sense of her own value and a stronger ability to advance individual as well as collective civil rights. A similar solidary or psychological benefit has been the mainstay of the appeal of group membership to discouraged and disillusioned African Americans since their emergence as a constitutionally free and equal people.

A fourth type of benefit involves the appeal of the purpose of an interest group. The benefits of religious interest groups provide us with the best examples

solidary benefits
Selective benefits of group membership that emphasize friendship, networking, and consciousness-raising.

 Collective Action Principle
Selective benefits are one solution to the collective action problem.

purposive benefits
Selective benefits of group membership that emphasize the purpose and accomplishments of the group.

of such *purposive benefits.* The Christian Right is a powerful movement made up of a number of interest groups that offer virtually no material benefits to their members. The growth and success of these groups depends upon the religious identifications and affirmations of their members. Many such religiously based interest groups have arisen, especially at state and local levels, throughout American history. For example, both the abolition and the prohibition movements were driven by religious interest groups whose main attractions were nonmaterial benefits.

Ideology itself, or the sharing of a commonly developed ideology, is another important nonmaterial benefit. Many of the most successful interest groups of the past twenty years have been citizen groups or public interest groups, whose members are brought together largely around shared ideological goals, including government reform, election and campaign reform, civil rights, economic equality, "family values," or even opposition to government itself.

The Role of Political Entrepreneurs

In a review of Olson's book,[9] Richard Wagner noticed that Olson's arguments about groups and politics in general, and his theory of selective incentives in particular, had very little to say about the internal workings of groups. In Wagner's experience, however, groups often came into being and then were maintained in good working order not only because of selective incentives, but also because of the extraordinary efforts of specific individuals—leaders, in ordinary language, or *political entrepreneurs* in Wagner's more colorful expression.

Wagner was motivated to raise the issue of group leaders because, in his view, Olson's theory was too pessimistic. Mass organizations in the real world—labor unions, consumer associations, senior-citizen groups, environmental organizations—all exist, some persisting and prospering over long periods. Contrary to Olson's suggestions, they seem to get jump-started somehow in the real world. Wagner suggests that a special kind of theory of selective incentives is called for. Specifically, he argues that certain selective benefits may accrue to *those who organize and maintain otherwise latent groups.*

Senator Robert Wagner (no relation) in the 1930s and Congressman Claude Pepper in the 1970s each had *private reasons*—electoral incentives—to try to organize laborers and the elderly, respectively. Wagner, a Democrat from New York, had a large constituency of working men and women who would reward him by re-electing him—a private, conditional payment—if he bore the cost of organizing (or at least of facilitating the organization of) workers. And this he did. The law that bears his name, the Wagner Act of 1935, made it much easier for unions to organize in the industrial north.[10] Likewise, Claude Pepper, a

[9]Richard Wagner, "Pressure Groups and Political Entrepreneurs," *Papers on Non-Market Decision Making I* (1966): 161–70.

[10]The Wagner Act made it possible for unions to organize by legalizing the so-called *closed shop*. If a worker took a job in a closed shop or plant, he or she was *required* to join the union there. "Do not contribute" was no longer an option, so that workers in closed shops could not free-ride on the efforts made by others to improve wages and working conditions.

Democratic congressman with a large number of elderly constituents in his South Miami district, saw it as serving his own electoral interests to provide the initial investment of effort for the organization of the elderly as a political force.

In general, a political entrepreneur is someone who sees a prospective cooperation dividend that is currently not being enjoyed. This is another way of saying that there is a latent group which, if it were to become manifest, would enjoy the fruits of collective action. For a price, whether in votes (as in the cases of Wagner and Pepper), a percentage of the dividend, nonmaterial glory, or other perks, the entrepreneur bears the costs of organizing, expends effort to monitor individuals for slacker behavior, and sometimes even imposes punishment on slackers (such as expelling them from the group and denying them any of its selective benefits).

Rationality Principle

Organizing collective action can provide private benefits to a political entrepreneur.

To illustrate this phenomenon, there is a story about a British tourist who visited China in the late nineteenth century. She was shocked and appalled to see teams of men pulling barges along the Yangtze River, overseen by whip-wielding masters. She remarked to her guide that such an uncivilized state of affairs would never be tolerated in modern societies like those in the West. The guide, anxious to please, but concerned that his employer had come to a wildly erroneous conclusion, hastily responded, "Madam, I think you misunderstand. The man carrying the whip is *employed* by those pulling the barge. He noticed that it is generally difficult, if you are pulling your weight along a tow path, to detect whether any of your team members are pulling theirs or, instead, whether they are 'free-riding' on your labors. He convinced the workers that his entrepreneurial services were required and that they should hire him. For an agreed-upon compensation, he monitors each team member's effort level, whipping those who shirk in their responsibilities. Notice, madam, that he rarely ever uses the whip. His mere presence is sufficient to get the group to accomplish the task."

Thus, political entrepreneurs, such as the whip-wielding driver, may be thought of as complements to Olsonian selective incentives in that both are ways of motivating groups to accomplish collective objectives. Indeed, if selective incentives *resolve* the paradox of collective action, then political entrepreneurs *dissolve* the paradox. Both are helpful, and sometimes both are needed in order to initiate and maintain collective action. Groups that manage, perhaps on their own, to get themselves organized at a low level of activity often take the next step of *creating* leaders and leadership institutions in order to increase the activity level and resulting cooperation dividends. Wagner, in other words, took Olson's theory of selective incentives and suggested an alternative explanation, one that made room for institutional solutions to the problem of collective action.

INTEREST GROUPS IN THE UNITED STATES

There are an enormous number of interest groups in the United States, and millions of Americans are members of one or more groups, at least to the extent of paying dues or attending an occasional meeting.

What Interests Are Represented?

Interest groups in the U.S. come in as many shapes and sizes as the interests they represent. When most people think about interest groups, they immediately think of groups with a direct economic interest in governmental actions. These groups are generally supported by groups of producers or manufacturers in a particular economic sector. Examples of this type of group include the National Petroleum Refiners Association, the American Farm Bureau Federation, and the National Federation of Independent Business, which represents small-business owners. At the same time that broadly representative groups like these are active in Washington, specific companies, like Disney, Shell Oil, IBM, and General Motors, may be active on certain issues that are of particular concern to them.

Labor organizations are equally active lobbyists. The AFL-CIO, the United Mine Workers, and the Teamsters are all groups that lobby on behalf of organized labor. In recent years, lobbies have arisen to further the interests of public employees, the most significant among these being the American Federation of State, County, and Municipal Employees.

Professional lobbies like the American Bar Association and the American Medical Association have been particularly successful in furthering their own interests in state and federal legislatures. Financial institutions, represented by organizations like the American Bankers Association and the National Savings & Loan League, although often less visible than other lobbies, also play an important role in shaping legislative policy.

Recent years have witnessed the growth of a powerful "public interest" lobby purporting to represent interests whose concerns are not addressed by traditional lobbies. These groups have been most visible in the consumer protection and environmental policy areas, although public interest groups cover a broad range of issues. The Natural Resources Defense Council, the Union of Concerned Scientists, and Common Cause are all examples of public interest groups.

The perceived need for representation on Capitol Hill has generated a public sector lobby in the past several years, including the National League of Cities and the "research" lobby. The latter group comprises think tanks and universities that have an interest in obtaining government funds for research and support, and it includes institutions such as Harvard University, the Brookings Institution, and the American Enterprise Institute. Indeed, universities have expanded their lobbying efforts even as they have reduced faculty positions and course offerings and increased tuition.[11]

Organizational Components

Although there are many interest groups, most share certain key organizational components. First, all groups must attract and keep members. Usually, groups

---

[11]Betsy Wagner and David Bowermaster, "B.S. Economics," *Washington Monthly* (November 1992), pp. 19–21.

appeal to members not only by promoting political goals or policies they favor but also by providing them with direct economic or social benefits. Thus, for example, the American Association of Retired Persons (AARP), which promotes the interests of senior citizens, at the same time offers members a variety of insurance benefits and commercial discounts. Similarly, many groups whose goals are chiefly economic or political also seek to attract members through social interaction and good fellowship. Thus, the local chapters of many national groups provide their members with a congenial social environment while collecting dues that finance the national office's political efforts.

Second, every group must build a financial structure capable of sustaining an organization and funding the group's activities. Most interest groups rely on yearly membership dues and voluntary contributions from sympathizers. Many also sell some ancillary services, such as insurance and vacation tours, to members. Third, every group must have a leadership and decision-making structure. For some groups, this structure is very simple. For others, it can be quite elaborate and involve hundreds of local chapters that are melded into a national apparatus. Finally, most groups include an agency that actually carries out the group's tasks. This may be a research organization, a public relations office, or a lobbying office in Washington or a state capital.

One example of a successful interest group is the National Rifle Association (NRA). Founded in 1871, the NRA claims a membership of over three million. It employs a staff of 350 and manages an operating budget of $5.5 million. Organized ostensibly to "promote rifle, pistol and shotgun shooting, hunting, gun collecting, home firearm safety and wildlife conservation," the organization has been highly effective in mobilizing its members to block attempts to enact gun-control measures, even though such measures are supported by 80 percent of the Americans who are asked about them in opinion polls. The NRA provides numerous benefits to its members, like sporting magazines and discounts on various types of equipment, and it is therefore adept in keeping its members enrolled and active. Though the general public may support gun control, this support is neither organized nor very intense. This allows the highly organized NRA to prevail even though its views are those of a minority. Although the enactment of the federal Brady Bill, requiring a waiting period for firearms purchases, and the 1994 crime control act, which banned the sale of several types of assault weapons, were defeats of the NRA's agenda, the organization remains one of the most effective lobbies in the nation. In 1994, for example, after a bitter struggle against environmental groups, the NRA was able to secure passage by the House of Representatives of legislation allowing hunting to continue in California's Mojave Desert. In this particular legislative battle, the NRA defeated environmental groups, animal-rights groups, and the White House, all of which had sought to put an end to the hunting.[12]

[12]Katherine Q. Seeyle, "In Victory for the NRA, House Backs Hunting in the Mojave," *New York Times*, 13 July 1994, p. D18.

The Characteristics of Members

As we saw earlier in the chapter, membership in interest groups is not randomly distributed in the population. People with higher incomes, higher levels of education, and management or professional occupations are much more likely to become members of groups than those who occupy the lower rungs on the socioeconomic ladder.[13] Well-educated, upper-income business and professional people are more likely to have the time and the money, and to have acquired through the educational process the concerns and skills needed to play a role in a group or association. Moreover, for business and professional people, group membership may provide personal contacts and access to information that can help advance their careers. At the same time, of course, corporate entities—businesses and the like—usually have ample resources to form or participate in groups that seek to advance their causes.

The result is that interest-group politics in the United States tends to have a very pronounced upper-class bias. Certainly, there are many interest groups and political associations that have a working-class or lower-class membership— labor organizations or welfare-rights organizations, for example—but the great majority of interest groups and their members are drawn from the middle and upper-middle classes. In general, the "interests" served by interest groups are the interests of society's "haves." Even when interest groups take opposing positions on issues and policies, the conflicting positions they espouse usually reflect divisions among upper-income strata rather than conflicts between the upper and lower classes.

In general, to obtain adequate political representation, forces from the bottom rungs of the socioeconomic ladder must be organized on the massive scale associated with political parties. Parties can organize and mobilize the collective energies of large numbers of people who, as individuals, may have very limited resources. Interest groups, on the other hand, generally organize smaller numbers of the better-to-do. Thus, the relative importance of political parties and interest groups in American politics has far-ranging implications for the distribution of political power in the United States. As we saw in Chapter 11, political parties have declined in influence in recent years. Interest groups, on the other hand, as we shall see shortly, have become much more numerous, more active, and more influential in American politics.

THE PROLIFERATION OF GROUPS

If interest groups and our concerns about them were a new phenomenon, we would not have begun this chapter with Madison in the eighteenth century. As long as there is government, as long as government makes policies that add value or impose costs, and as long as there is liberty to organize, interest groups

---

[13]Schlozman and Tierney, *Organized Interests and American Democracy*, p. 60.

will abound; and if government expands, so will interest groups. There was, for example, a spurt of growth in the national government during the 1880s and 1890s, arising largely from the first government efforts at economic intervention to fight large monopolies and to regulate some aspects of interstate commerce. In the latter decade, a parallel spurt of growth occurred in national interest groups, including the imposing National Association of Manufacturers (NAM) and numerous other trade associations. Many groups organized around specific agricultural commodities, as well. This period also marked the beginning of the expansion of trade unions as interest groups. Later, in the 1930s, interest groups with headquarters and representation in Washington began to grow significantly, concurrent with that decade's historic and sustained expansion of the national government (see Chapter 3).

Over the past thirty years, there has been an enormous increase both in the number of interest groups seeking to play a role in the American political process and in the extent of their opportunity to influence that process. This explosion of interest-group activity has three basic origins: first, the expansion of the role of government during this period; second, the coming of age of a new and dynamic set of political forces in the United States—a set of forces that have relied heavily on "public interest" groups to advance their causes; and third, a revival of grassroots conservatism in American politics.

History Principle

The explosion of interest-group activity has its origins in the expansion of the role of government since the 1960s.

The Expansion of Government

Modern governments' extensive economic and social programs have powerful politicizing effects, often sparking the organization of new groups and interests. The activities of organized groups are usually viewed in terms of their effects upon governmental action. But interest-group activity is often as much a consequence as an antecedent of governmental programs. Even when national policies are initially responses to the appeals of pressure groups, government involvement in any area can be a powerful stimulus for political organization and action by those whose interests are affected. A *New York Times* report, for example, noted that during the 1970s, expanded federal regulation of the automobile, oil, gas, education, and health care industries impelled each of these interests to increase substantially its efforts to influence the government's behavior. These efforts, in turn, had the effect of spurring the organization of other groups to augment or counter the activities of the first.[14] Similarly, federal social programs have occasionally sparked political organization and action on the part of clientele groups seeking to influence the distribution of benefits and, in turn, the organization of groups opposed to the programs or their cost. For example, federal programs and court decisions in such areas as abortion and school prayer were the stimuli for political action and organization by fundamentalist religious

[14]John Herbers, "Special Interests Gaining Power as Voter Disillusionment Grows," *New York Times*, 14 November 1978.

groups. Thus, the expansion of government in recent decades has also stimulated increased group activity and organization.

One contemporary example of a proposed government program that sparked intensive organization and political action by affected interests is the case of regulating the tobacco industry. In 1997, an enormous lobbying battle broke out in Washington, DC, over a proposed agreement regarding the liability of tobacco companies for tobacco-related illnesses. This agreement, reached between tobacco companies, state governments, trial lawyers (representing individuals and groups suing tobacco companies), and antismoking groups, called for the tobacco industry to pay the states and the trial lawyers nearly $400 billion over the next twenty-five years. In exchange, the industry would receive protection from much of the litigation with which it was plagued. The settlement as negotiated would have required congressional and presidential approval.

After the settlement was proposed in June 1997, both the White House and some members of Congress began raising objections. Because of the enormous amounts of money involved, all the interested parties began intensive lobbying efforts aimed at both Congress and the executive branch. The tobacco industry retained nearly thirty lobbying firms at an initial cost of nearly $10 million to press its claims. During the first six months of 1997, the tobacco industry also contributed more than $2.5 million to political parties and candidates whom the industry thought could be helpful to its cause. One Washington lobbying firm, Verner, Liipfert, Bernhard, McPherson, and Hand, alone received nearly $5 million in fees from the four leading cigarette makers. The firm assigned a number of well-connected lobbyists, including former Texas governor Ann Richards, to press its clients' cause. Verner, Liipfert also hired pollsters, public relations firms, and economists to convince the public and the Washington establishment that the tobacco settlement made good sense.[15] Eventually a compromise settlement was reached between the tobacco companies and the state governments.

The New Politics Movement and Public Interest Groups

The second factor accounting for the explosion of interest-group activity in recent years was the emergence of a new set of forces in American politics that can collectively be called the "New Politics" movement.

The New Politics movement is made up of upper-middle-class professionals and intellectuals for whom the civil rights and antiwar movements were formative experiences, just as the Great Depression and World War II had been for their parents. The crusade against racial discrimination and the Vietnam War led these young men and women to see themselves as a political force in opposition to the public policies and politicians associated with the nation's postwar

---

[15]Saundra Torry, "Army of Lobbyists Has Drawn $8 Million on Tobacco Fight," *Washington Post*, 11 September 1997, p. A4.

regime. In more recent years, the forces of New Politics have focused their attention on such issues as environmental protection, women's rights, and nuclear disarmament.

Members of the New Politics movement constructed or strengthened "public interest" groups such as Common Cause, the Sierra Club, the Environmental Defense Fund, Physicians for Social Responsibility, the National Organization for Women, and the various organizations formed by consumer activist Ralph Nader. Through these groups, New Politics forces were able to influence the media, Congress, and even the judiciary, and enjoyed a remarkable degree of success during the late 1960s and early 1970s in securing the enactment of policies they favored. New Politics activists also played a major role in securing the enactment of environmental, consumer, and occupational health and safety legislation.

New Politics groups sought to distinguish themselves from other interest groups—business groups, in particular—by styling themselves as "public interest" organizations to suggest that they served the general good rather than their own selfish interest. These groups' claims to represent *only* the public interest should be viewed with caution, however. Quite often, goals that are said to be in the general or public interest are also or indeed primarily in the particular interest of those who espouse them.

The term "public interest" has become so ubiquitous that it is not uncommon to find decidedly private interests seeking to hide under its cloak. For example, in 1996, the *Washington Post* looked into the finances of one public interest group, Contributions Watch. The group, presenting itself as an independent and nonpartisan organization working for campaign finance reform, released a study purporting to detail millions of dollars in political contributions to Democratic candidates by trial lawyers. The implication was that the lawyers' groups had made the contributions as part of their effort to defeat Republican tort law reform proposals. The *Post*'s investigation revealed that Contributions Watch was created by a professional lobbying firm, State Affairs Company. The lobbying firm had been retained by a major Washington law firm, Covington and Burling, on behalf of its client, Philip Morris Tobacco. The giant tobacco company had sought the cover of public interest to mask an attack on its enemies, the trial lawyers, who in 1997 brought billions of dollars in damage suits against the tobacco companies.[16] Contributions Watch insisted that its report was accurate.

Conservative Interest Groups

The third factor associated with the expansion of interest-group politics in contemporary America has been an explosion of grassroots conservative activity. For example, the Christian Coalition, whose major focus is opposition to abortion, has nearly two million active members organized in local chapters in every

[16]Ruth Marcus, "Tobacco Lobby Created Campaign 'Watchdog,'" *Washington Post*, 30 September 1996, p. 1.

state. Twenty of the state chapters have full-time staff and fifteen have annual budgets over $200,000.[17] The National Taxpayers Union has several hundred local chapters. The National Federation of Independent Business (NFIB) has hundreds of active local chapters throughout the nation, particularly in the Midwest and Southeast. Associations dedicated to defending "property rights" are organized at the local level throughout the West. Right-to-life groups are organized in virtually every U.S. congressional district. Even proponents of the rather exotic principle of "home schooling" are organized through the Home School Legal Defense Association (HSLDA), which has seventy-five regional chapters that, in turn, are linked to more than 3,000 local support groups.

These local conservative organizations were energized by the political struggles that marked Bill Clinton's two terms in office. For example, battles over the restrictions on gun ownership in the Clinton administration's 1993 crime bill helped the National Rifle Association (NRA) energize local gun owners' groups throughout the country. The struggle over a proposed amendment to the 1993 education bill, which would have placed additional restrictions on home schooling, helped the HSLDA enroll thousands of active new members in its regional and local chapters. After an intense campaign, HSLDA succeeded in both defeating the amendment and in enhancing the political awareness and activism of its formerly quiescent members. And, of course, the ongoing struggles over abortion and school prayer have helped the Christian Coalition, the Family Research Council, and other organizations comprising the Christian Right to expand the membership rolls of their state and local organizations. Anti-abortion forces, in particular, are organized at the local level throughout the United States and are prepared to participate in political campaigns and legislative battles. The importance of religious conservatives to the Republican party became quite evident in 2001. After his victory in the November 2000 presidential election, George W. Bush announced that his administration would seek to award federal grants and contracts to religious groups. By using so-called faith-based groups as federal contractors, Bush was seeking to reward religious conservatives for their past loyalty to the GOP and to ensure that these groups would have a continuing stake in Republican success.

Extensive, organized interest groups have allowed conservatives not only to bring pressure to bear upon the national government but also to become a real presence in the corridors of state capitols, county seats, and city halls. For example, spurred by conservative groups and conservative radio programs, legislators in all fifty states have introduced property rights legislation. Eighteen states have already enacted laws requiring a "takings impact analysis" before any new government regulation affecting property can go into effect.[18] Such legislation is designed to diminish the ability of state and local governments to enact land-use restrictions for environmental or planning purposes. In a similar vein, seventeen

[17]Rich Lowry, "How the Right Rose," *National Review* 66, 11 December 1995, pp. 64–76.
[18]Neil Peirce, "Second Thoughts About Taking Measures," *Baltimore Sun*, 18 December 1995, p. 13A.

states, pressed by local conservative groups, have recently enacted legislation protecting or expanding the rights of gun owners.[19]

STRATEGIES: THE QUEST FOR POLITICAL POWER

As we saw, people form interest groups in order to improve the probability that they and their policy interests will be heard and treated favorably by all branches and levels of the government. The quest for political influence or power takes many forms, but among the most frequently used strategies are lobbying, establishing access to key decision makers, using the courts, going public, and using electoral politics. These strategies do not exhaust all the possibilities, but they paint a broad picture of ways that groups utilize their resources in the fierce competition for power (see Process Box 12.1).

Lobbying

Lobbying is an attempt by an individual or a group to influence the passage of legislation by exerting direct pressure on members of the legislature. The First Amendment to the Constitution provides for the right to "petition the Government for a redress of grievances." But as early as the 1870s, "lobbying" became the common term for petitioning—and it is not an inaccurate one. Petitioning cannot take place on the floor of the House or Senate. Therefore, petitioners must confront members of Congress in the lobbies of the legislative chambers, giving rise to the term "lobbying."

The Federal Regulation of Lobbying Act defines a lobbyist as "any person who shall engage himself for pay or any consideration for the purpose of attempting to influence the passage or defeat of any legislation of the Congress of the United States." The Lobbying Disclosure Act requires all organizations employing lobbyists to register with Congress and to disclose whom they represent, whom they lobby, what they are lobbying for, and how much they are paid. More than 7,000 organizations, collectively employing many thousands of lobbyists, are currently registered.

Lobbying involves a great deal of activity on the part of someone speaking for an interest. Lobbyists badger and buttonhole legislators, administrators, and committee staff members with facts about pertinent issues and facts or claims about public support of them.[20] Lobbyists can serve a useful purpose in the legislative and administrative process by providing this kind of information. In 1978, during debate on a bill to expand the requirement for lobbying disclosures,

lobbying Strategy by which organized interests seek to influence the passage of legislation by exerting direct pressure on members of the legislature.

[19]Chris Warden, "A GOP Revolution That Wasn't," *Investor's Daily*, 2 January 1996, p. A1.

[20]For discussions of lobbying, see Jeffrey M. Berry, *Lobbying for the People* (Princeton: Princeton University Press, 1977) and John R. Wright, *Interest Groups and Congress: Lobbying, Contributions, and Influence* (Boston: Allyn & Bacon, 1996).

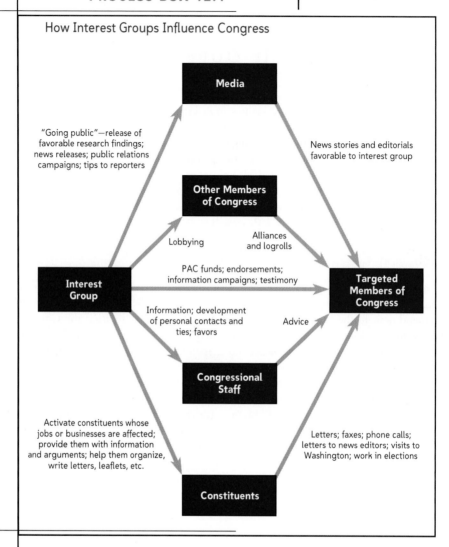

How Interest Groups Influence Congress

Media

"Going public"—release of favorable research findings; news releases; public relations campaigns; tips to reporters

News stories and editorials favorable to interest group

Other Members of Congress

Lobbying

Alliances and logrolls

Interest Group

PAC funds; endorsements; information campaigns; testimony

Targeted Members of Congress

Information; development of personal contacts and ties; favors

Advice

Congressional Staff

Activate constituents whose jobs or businesses are affected; provide them with information and arguments; help them organize, write letters, leaflets, etc.

Letters; faxes; phone calls; letters to news editors; visits to Washington; work in elections

Constituents

Democratic senators Edward Kennedy of Massachusetts and Dick Clark of Iowa joined with Republican senator Robert Stafford of Vermont to issue the following statement: "Government without lobbying could not function. The flow of information to Congress and to every federal agency is a vital part of our democratic system."[21] But they also added that there is a darker side to lobbying—one that requires regulation.

Types of Lobbyists   The business of lobbying is uneven and unstable. Some groups send their own loyal members to Washington to lobby for them. These representatives usually possess a lot of knowledge about a particular issue and the group's position on it, but they have little knowledge about or experience in Washington or national politics. They tend not to remain in Washington beyond the campaign for their issue.

Other groups select lobbyists with a considerable amount of Washington wisdom. During the battle over the 1996 federal budget, for example, medical specialists seeking favorable treatment under Medicare reimbursement rules retained a lobbying team that included former Minnesota Republican congressman Vin Weber, former New York Democratic congressman Tom Downey, and former Clinton chief legislative aide Patrick Griffin. Former Senate Finance Committee chair Robert Packwood was retained by lumber mills and other small businesses to secure a cut in the estate tax.

Because of the importance of good access to those in power, shifts in Washington's political winds often have major effects upon the lobbying industry. For example, soon after George W. Bush won the 2000 presidential election, the United States Telephone Association (USTA), a powerful Washington trade group, fired its president, Roy Neel, from his $600,000 per year position. Neel had been a longtime aide and chief of staff to former vice president Al Gore before assuming his position with the telephone group in 1994. The defeat of Gore's presidential bid, however, meant that Neel would no longer have the access to the White House that the USTA wanted. "It was pretty clear that the usefulness of a prominent Gore guy would be vastly diminished in the Bush administration," said one USTA board member. "These issues are too important to the health of our industry to gamble with."[22] For interest groups, politics is not about ideology or personal fulfillment. It is about business.

The Lobbying Industry   The lobbying industry in Washington is growing. New groups are moving in all the time, relocating from Los Angeles, Chicago, and other important cities. Local observers estimate that the actual number of people engaged in important lobbying (part-time or full-time) is closer to fifteen thousand. In addition to the various unions, commodity groups, and trade associations, the important business corporations keep their own representatives in Washington.

Many groups—even those with reputations for being powerful—are constantly forming and reforming lobby coalitions in order to improve their effectiveness

[21]"The Swarming Lobbyists," *Time*, 7 August 1978, p. 15.
[22]Quoted in Yochi J. Dreazen, "Former Gore Aide Discovers Loss of Influence Can Mean Lost Job," *Wall Street Journal*, 2 March 2001, p. A12.

with Congress and with government agencies.[23] The AFL and the CIO, for example, merged in 1955, largely for political advantage, despite many economic disagreements between them. In the 1970s, the venerable National Association of Manufacturers (NAM) tried vainly to work out a merger with the Chamber of Commerce of the United States. During that same period, more than two hundred top executives of some of America's most important business corporations—including AT&T, Boeing, Du Pont, General Motors, Mobil Oil, and General Electric—joined in Washington to form a business roundtable, hoping to coordinate their lobbying efforts on certain issues. In subsequent years, the roundtable worked effectively to promote business interests on labor law reform, tax policy, and consumer protection.

In 1993, Clinton proposed that companies employing lobbyists be prohibited from deducting lobbying costs as business expenses from their federal taxes. This would, in effect, make it more difficult and costly for firms to employ lobbyists on behalf of their concerns. Not surprisingly, this proposal was bitterly resented by the lobbying industry, which saw it as a mortal threat to its own business interests. How did lobbying firms respond? By lobbying, of course. The American League of Lobbyists, a trade group representing the lobbying industry, quickly mobilized its members to conduct a vigorous campaign to defeat the proposal. One worried Washington lobbyist, however, observed, "This seems so self-serving, you wonder who is going to listen to us anyway."[24]

Clinton's proposal would have potentially reduced the influence of business groups in the policy process. This would, of course, work to the advantage of liberal public interest groups linked to the Democratic party. For this reason, a variety of business groups joined forces with the lobbying industry to oppose the administration's efforts. In 1994, Congress first passed and then rejected legislation requiring disclosure of lobbying activities and prohibiting lobbyists from giving gifts worth more than twenty dollars to members.[25] Such lobbying-reform legislation could force interest groups to rely more heavily upon other "tactics of influence."

Gaining Access

Lobbying is an effort by outsiders to exert influence on Congress or government agencies by providing them with information about issues, support, and even threats of retaliation. Access is actual involvement in the decision-making process. It may be the outcome of long years of lobbying, but it should not be confused with lobbying. If lobbying has to do with "influence on" a government, access has to do with "influence within" it. Many interest groups resort to lobbying because they have insufficient access or insufficient time to develop it.

[23]See Robert H. Salisbury, *Interests and Institutions: Substance and Structure in American Politics* (Pittsburgh: University of Pittsburgh Press, 1992).

[24]Michael Weisskopf, "Lobbyists Rally Around Their Own Cause: Clinton Move to Eliminate Tax Break Sparks Intense Hill Campaign," *Washington Post*, 14 May 1993, p. A16.

[25]Phil Kuntz, "Ticket to a Better Image?" *Congressional Quarterly Weekly Report*, 7 May 1994, p. 1105.

One interesting example of a group that had access but lost it, turned to lobbying, and later used a strategy of "going public" (see page 534) is the dairy farmers. Through the 1960s, dairy farmers were part of the powerful coalition of agricultural interests that had full access to Congress and to the Department of Agriculture. During the 1960s, a series of disputes broke out between the dairy farmers and the producers of corn, grain, and other agricultural commodities over commodities prices. Dairy farmers, whose cows consume grain, prefer low commodities prices while grain producers obviously prefer to receive high prices. The commodities producers won the battle, and Congress raised commodities prices, in part at the expense of the dairy farmers. In the 1970s, the dairy farmers left the agriculture coalition, set up their own lobby and political action groups, and became heavily involved in public relations campaigns and both congressional and presidential elections. The dairy farmers encountered a number of difficulties in pursuing their new "outsider" strategies. Indeed, the political fortunes of the dairy operations were badly hurt when they were accused of making illegal contributions to President Nixon's re-election campaign in 1972.

Access is usually a result of time and effort spent cultivating a position within the inner councils of government. This method of gaining access often requires the sacrifice of short-run influence. For example, many of the most important organized interests in agriculture devote far more time and resources cultivating the staff and trustees of state agriculture schools and county agents back home than buttonholing members of Congress or bureaucrats in Washington.

Figure 12.1 is a sketch of one of the most important access patterns in recent American political history: the iron triangle. Each such pattern, like the defense example here, is almost literally a triangular shape, with one point in an executive branch program, another point in a Senate or House legislative committee or subcommittee, and a third point in some highly stable and well-organized interest group. The points in the triangular relationship are mutually supporting; they count as access only if they last over a long period of time. For example, access to a legislative committee or subcommittee requires that at least one member of it support the interest group in question. This member also must have built up considerable seniority in Congress. An interest cannot feel comfortable about its access to Congress until it has one or more of its "own" people with ten or more years of continuous service on the relevant committee or subcommittee.

A number of important policy domains, such as the environmental and welfare arenas, are controlled, not by highly structured and unified iron triangles, but by rival *issue networks.* These networks consist of like-minded politicians, consultants, public officials, political activists, and interest groups who have some concern with the issue in question. Activists and interest groups recognized as being involved in the area are sometimes called "stakeholders," and are customarily invited to testify before congressional committees or give their views to government agencies considering action in their domain.

Gaining Access to the Bureaucracy   A bureaucratic agency is one point in the iron triangle, and thus access to it is essential to the success of an interest group.

Policy Principle
Public policy can reveal the impact of lobbying and gaining access by groups affected by it.

Collective Action Principle
Gaining access requires coordination across the legislative and executive branches.

issue network
A loose network of elected leaders, public officials, activists, and interest groups drawn together by a specific policy issue.

FIGURE 12.1

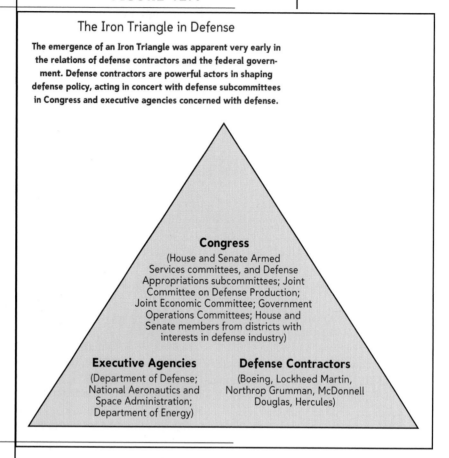

The Iron Triangle in Defense

The emergence of an Iron Triangle was apparent very early in the relations of defense contractors and the federal government. Defense contractors are powerful actors in shaping defense policy, acting in concert with defense subcommittees in Congress and executive agencies concerned with defense.

Congress

(House and Senate Armed Services committees, and Defense Appropriations subcommittees; Joint Committee on Defense Production; Joint Economic Committee; Government Operations Committees; House and Senate members from districts with interests in defense industry)

Executive Agencies

(Department of Defense; National Aeronautics and Space Administration; Department of Energy)

Defense Contractors

(Boeing, Lockheed Martin, Northrop Grumman, McDonnell Douglas, Hercules)

Working to gain influence in an executive agency is sometimes called corridoring—the equivalent of lobbying in the executive branch. Even when an interest group is very successful at getting its bill passed by Congress and signed by the president, the prospect of full and faithful implementation of that law is not guaranteed. Often, a group and its allies do not pack up and go home as soon as the president turns their lobbied-for new law over to the appropriate agency. Agencies, too, can fall under the influence or be captured by an interest group or a coalition of well-organized groups.[26] Granted, agencies are not passive and

[26]See especially Marver Bernstein, *Regulating Business by Independent Commission* (Princeton: Princeton University Press, 1955). See also George J. Stigler, "The Theory of Economic Regulation," *Bell Journal of Economics and Management Science* 2 (1971), pp. 3–21.

can do a good bit of capturing themselves. The point is that those groups that ignore the role of the agency in implementing legislation are simply not going to have any role in the outcome of agency decisions. On average, 40 percent of interest group representatives regularly contact both legislative and executive branch organizations, while 13 percent contact only the legislature and 16 percent only the executive branch.[27]

Using the Courts (Litigation)

Interest groups sometimes turn to litigation when they lack access or when they feel they have insufficient influence to change an unsatisfactory situation. They can use the courts to affect public policy in at least three ways: (1) by bringing suit directly on behalf of the group itself, (2) by financing suits brought by individuals, and (3) by filing a companion brief as *amicus curiae* (literally "friend of the court") to an existing court case.

Institution Principle

Groups can turn to the courts if they are not successful in the legislative and executive branches.

Among the most significant modern illustrations of the use of the courts as a strategy for political influence are those that accompanied the "sexual revolution" of the 1960s and the emergence of the movement for women's rights. Beginning in the mid-sixties, a series of cases was brought into the federal courts in an effort to force definition of a right to privacy in sexual matters. The effort began with a challenge to state restrictions on obtaining contraceptives for nonmedical purposes, a challenge that was effectively made in *Griswold v. Connecticut*, where the Supreme Court held that states could neither prohibit the dissemination of information about nor prohibit the actual use of contraceptives by married couples. That case was soon followed by *Eisenstadt v. Baird*, in which the Court held that the states could not prohibit the use of contraceptives by single persons any more than it could prohibit their use by married couples. One year later, the Court held, in the 1973 case of *Roe v. Wade*, that states could not impose an absolute ban on voluntary abortions. Each of these cases, as well as others, were part of the Court's enunciation of a constitutional doctrine of privacy.[28]

The 1973 abortion case sparked a controversy that brought conservatives to the fore on a national level. These conservative groups made extensive use of the courts to whittle away the scope of the privacy doctrine. They obtained rulings, for example, that prohibit the use of federal funds to pay for voluntary abortions. And in 1989, right-to-life groups were able to use a strategy of litigation that significantly undermined the *Roe v. Wade* decision, namely in the case of *Webster v. Reproductive Health Services*, which restored the right of states to place restrictions on abortion.[29]

---

[27]John P. Heinz, Edward O. Laumann, Robert L. Nelson, and Robert H. Salisbury, *The Hollow Core: Private Interests in National Policy Making* (Cambridge, MA: Harvard University Press, 1993).

[28]Griswold v. Connecticut, 381 U.S. 479 (1965); Eisenstadt v. Baird, 405 U.S. 438 (1972); Roe v. Wade, 410 U.S. 113 (1973).

[29]Webster v. Reproductive Health Services, 109 S.Ct. 3049 (1989).

Another extremely significant set of contemporary illustrations of the use of the courts as a strategy for political influence are those found in the history of the NAACP. The most important of these court cases was, of course, *Brown v. Board of Education*, in which the U.S. Supreme Court held that legal segregation of the schools was unconstitutional.[30]

Business groups are also frequent users of the courts because of the number of government programs applied to them. Litigation involving large businesses is most mountainous in such areas as taxation, antitrust, interstate transportation, patents, and product quality and standardization. Often a business is brought to litigation against its will by virtue of initiatives taken against it by other businesses or by government agencies. But many individual businesses bring suit themselves in order to influence government policy. Major corporations and their trade associations pay tremendous amounts of money each year in fees to the most prestigious Washington law firms. Some of this money is expended in gaining access. A great proportion of it, however, is used to keep the best and most experienced lawyers prepared to represent the corporations in court or before administrative agencies when necessary.

New Politics forces made significant use of the courts during the 1970s and 1980s, and judicial decisions were instrumental in advancing their goals. Facilitated by rules changes on access to the courts (the rules of standing are discussed in Chapter 8), the New Politics agenda was clearly visible in court decisions handed down in several key policy areas. In the environmental policy area, New Politics groups were able to force federal agencies to pay attention to environmental issues, even when the agency was not directly involved in activities related to environmental quality.

While the skirmishes continued on the environmental front, consumer activists were likewise realizing significant gains. Stung by harsh critiques in both the Nader Report and the Report of the American Bar Association in 1969, the Federal Trade Commission (FTC) became very responsive to the demands of New Politics activists. During the 1970s and 1980s, the FTC stepped up its activities considerably, litigating a series of claims arising under regulations prohibiting deceptive advertising in cases ranging from false claims for over-the-counter drugs to inflated claims about the nutritional value of children's cereal.

And while feminists and equal rights activists enjoyed enormous success in litigating discrimination claims under Title VII of the Civil Rights Act of 1964, anti-nuclear power activists succeeded in virtually shutting down the nuclear power industry. Despite significant defeats, most notably *Duke Power Company v. Carolina Environmental Study Group*, which upheld a federal statute limiting liability for damages accruing from nuclear power plant accidents, challenges to power plant siting and licensing regulations were instrumental in discouraging energy companies from pursuing nuclear projects over the long term.[31]

---

[30]Brown v. Board of Education, 347 U.S. 483 (1954).

[31]Duke Power Co. v. Carolina Environmental Study Group, 438 U.S. 59 (1978).

Groups will also sometimes seek legislation designed to help them secure their aims through litigation. During the 1970s, for example, Congress fashioned legislation meant to make it easier for environmental and consumer groups to use the courts. Several regulatory statutes, such as the 1973 Endangered Species Act, contained citizen-suit provisions that, in effect, gave environmental groups the right to bring suits challenging the decisions of executive agencies and the actions of business firms in environmental cases, even if the groups bringing suit were not being directly harmed by the governmental or private action in question. Such suits, moreover, could be financed by the expedient of "fee shifting"—that is, environmental or consumer groups could finance successful suits by collecting legal fees and expenses from their opponents.

In its decision in the 1992 case of *Lujan v. Defenders of Wildlife* (see Chapter 8), the Supreme Court seemed to question the constitutionality of citizen-suit provisions. Justice Scalia indicated that such provisions violated Article III of the U.S. Constitution, which limits the jurisdiction of the federal courts to actual cases and controversies.[32] This means that only persons directly affected by a case can bring it before the courts. If the Court were to continue to take this position, the capacity of public interest groups to employ a strategy of litigation would be diminished.

An important recent product of this relationship between legislation and litigation is the 1990 Americans with Disabilities Act (ADA), which took full effect in July 1992. The act resulted from the lobbying efforts of a host of public interest and advocacy groups and was aimed at allowing individuals with hearing, sight, or mobility impairments to participate fully in American life. Under the terms of this significant piece of legislation, businesses, private organizations, and local governmental agencies were required to make certain that their administrative procedures and physical plants did not needlessly deprive individuals with physical or emotional disabilities of access to the use of their facilities, or of employment and other opportunities.

Subsequently, the 1991 Civil Rights Act granted disabled individuals who believed that their rights under the ADA had been violated the right to sue for compensatory and punitive damages, as well as the right to demand a jury trial. In other words, this *legislation* encouraged individuals with disabilities to make use of *litigation* to secure their new rights and press their interests.

Hundreds of legal complaints were immediately filed. To make use of the opportunity for litigation, an advocacy group, the Disability Rights Litigation and Defense Fund, trained five thousand "barrier busters" to look for violators of the act and file lawsuits. Federal officials estimated that the ADA would generate approximately fifteen thousand discrimination cases every year—an estimate the act's critics consider much too low.[33]

---

[32]Lujan v. Defenders of Wildlife, 112 S.Ct. 2130 (1992); see also Linda Greenhouse, "Court Limits Legal Standing in Suits," *New York Times*, 13 June 1992, p. 12.

[33]See "Disabling America," *Wall Street Journal*, 24 July 1992, p.A10. See also Gary Becker, "How the Disabilities Act Will Cripple Business," *Business Week*, 14 September 1992, p. 14.

Going Public

Going public is a strategy that attempts to mobilize the widest and most favorable climate of opinion. Many groups consider it imperative to maintain this climate at all times, even when they have no issue to fight about. An increased use of this kind of strategy is usually associated with modern advertising. As early as the 1930s, political analysts were distinguishing between the "old lobby" of direct group representation before Congress and the "new lobby" of public relations professionals addressing the public at large to reach Congress.[34]

One of the best-known ways of going public is the use of institutional advertising. A casual scanning of important mass circulation magazines and newspapers will provide numerous examples of expensive and well-designed ads by the major oil companies, automobile and steel companies, other large corporations, and trade associations. The ads show how much these organizations are doing for the country, for the protection of the environment, or for the defense of the American way of life. Their purpose is to create and maintain a strongly positive association between the organization and the community at large in the hope that these favorable feelings can be drawn on as needed for specific political campaigns later on.

Collective Action Principle
Going public is a group strategy of mobilizing widespread support.

Going public is not limited to businesses or to upper-income professional groups. Many groups resort to it because they lack the resources, the contacts, or the experience to use other political strategies. The sponsorship of boycotts, sit-ins, mass rallies, and marches by Martin Luther King's Southern Christian Leadership Conference (SCLC) and related organizations in the 1950s and 1960s is one of the most significant and successful cases of going public to create a more favorable climate of opinion by calling attention to abuses. The success of these events inspired similar efforts on the part of women. Organizations such as the National Organization for Women (NOW) used public strategies in their drive for legislation and in their efforts to gain ratification of the Equal Rights Amendment. In 1993, gay rights groups organized a mass rally in their effort to eliminate restrictions on military service and other forms of discrimination against individuals based on their sexual preference.

Another form of going public is the grassroots lobbying campaign. In such a campaign, a lobby group mobilizes ordinary citizens throughout the country to write their representatives in support of the group's position. A grassroots campaign can cost anywhere from $40,000 to sway the votes of one or two crucial members of a committee or subcommittee, to millions of dollars to mount a national effort aimed at the Congress as a whole.

Among the most effective users of the grassroots lobby effort in contemporary American politics is the religious Right. Networks of evangelical churches have the capacity to generate hundreds of thousands of letters and phone calls to Congress and the White House. For example, the religious Right was outraged when President Clinton announced soon after taking office that he planned to

---

[34]E. Pendleton Herring, *Group Representation before Congress* (New York: McGraw-Hill, 1936).

end the military's ban on gay and lesbian soldiers. The Reverend Jerry Falwell, an evangelist leader, called upon viewers of his television program to dial a telephone number that would add their names to a petition urging Clinton to retain the ban on gays in the military. Within a few hours, 24,000 persons had called to support the petition.[35]

Grassroots lobbying campaigns have been so effective in recent years that a number of Washington consulting firms have begun to specialize in this area. Firms such as Bonner and Associates, for example, will work to generate grassroots telephone campaigns on behalf of or in opposition to important legislative proposals. Such efforts can be very expensive. Reportedly, one trade association recently paid the Bonner firm three million dollars to generate and sustain a grassroots effort to defeat a bill on the Senate floor.[36]

The annual tab for grassroots lobbying has been estimated at $1 billion, and the following case study illustrates why: the recent eight-year battle over the deregulation of electric power generation, transmission, and distribution—the nation's last regulated monopoly and our eighth-biggest industry—seemed to be finally coming to a head. Then it flopped. But not until "the K Street crowd"[37] had spent $50 million (over 1997, 1998, and 1999) on direct lobbying and another large but undetermined amount on grassroots appeals.[38] For example, between 1997 and 1999, the American Public Power Association, which represents municipal power utilities, spent $3.2 million on direct lobbying and $180,000 on grassroots campaigning. The Edison Electric Institute, the principal trade association of the private, investor-owned power companies, spent $41.2 million on direct lobbying and $1.5 million on grassroots campaigning. Five other major interest groups and trade associations, representing different slices of interest in electric power, spent varying amounts, some of which they were unwilling to report.[39]

Grassroots lobbying has become more prevalent in Washington over the last couple of decades because the adoption of congressional rules limiting gifts to members has made traditional lobbying more difficult. This circumstance makes all the more compelling the question of whether grassroots campaigning has reached an intolerable extreme. One case in particular may have tipped it over: in 1992, ten giant companies in the financial services, manufacturing, and high-tech industries began a grassroots campaign and spent millions of dollars to influence a decision in Congress to limit the ability of investors to sue for fraud.

---

[35]Michael Weisskopf, "Energized by Pulpit or Passion, the Public Is Calling," *Washington Post*, 1 February 1993, p. 1.

[36]Stephen Engelberg, "A New Breed of Hired Hands Cultivates Grass-Roots Anger," *New York Times*, 17 March 1993, p. A1.

[37]"The K Street crowd" is a reference to the street where most law firms that mainly engage in lobbying are located.

[38]Unlike spending on lobbying, these expenditures do not have to be reported; they therefore need to be reported voluntarily by each group, or estimated.

[39]James C. Benton, "Money and Power: The Fight Over Electricity Deregulation," *Congressional Quarterly Weekly Report*, 12 August 2000, pp.1964–69.

Retaining an expensive consulting firm, these corporations paid for the use of specialized computer software to persuade Congress that there was "an outpouring of popular support for the proposal." Thousands of letters from individuals flooded Capitol Hill. Many of those letters were written and sent by people who sincerely believed that investor lawsuits are often frivolous and should be curtailed. But much of the mail was phony, generated by the Washington-based campaign consultants; the letters came from people who had no strong feelings or even no opinion at all about the issue. More and more people, including leading members of Congress, are becoming quite skeptical of such methods, charging that these are not genuine grassroots campaigns but instead represent "Astroturf lobbying" (a play on the name of an artificial grass used on many sports fields). Such "Astroturf" campaigns have increased in frequency in recent years as members of Congress grow more and more skeptical of Washington lobbyists and far more concerned about demonstrations of support for a particular issue by their constituents. But after the firms mentioned above spent millions of dollars and generated thousands of letters to members of Congress, they came to the somber conclusion that "it's more effective to have 100 letters from your district where constituents took the time to write and understand the issue," because "Congress is sophisticated enough to know the difference."[40]

Using Electoral Politics

Many interest groups decide that it is far more effective to elect the right legislators than to try to influence the incumbents through lobbying or through a changed or mobilized mass opinion. Interest groups can influence elections by two means: financial support funded through political action committees, and campaign activism.

Political Action Committees   By far the most common electoral strategy employed by interest groups is that of giving financial support to the parties or to particular candidates. But such support can easily cross the threshold into outright bribery. Therefore, Congress has occasionally made an effort to regulate this strategy. Congress's most recent effort was the Federal Election Campaign Act of 1971 (amended in 1974), which we discussed in Chapter 10. This act limits campaign contributions and requires that each candidate or campaign committee itemize the full name and address, occupation, and principal business of each person who contributes more than $100. These provisions have been effective up to a point, considering the rather large number of embarrassments, indictments, resignations, and criminal convictions in the aftermath of the Watergate scandal.

   The Watergate scandal, itself, was triggered by the illegal entry of Republican workers into the office of the Democratic National Committee in the Watergate apartment building. But an investigation quickly revealed numerous

[40]Jane Fritsch, "The Grass Roots, Just a Free Phone Call Away," *New York Times*, 23 June 1995, pp. A1 and A22.

TABLE 12.4

PAC Spending, 1977–2000

YEARS	CONTRIBUTIONS
1977–1978 (est.)	$77,800,000
1979–1980	131,153,384
1981–1982	190,173,539
1983–1984	266,822,476
1985–1986	339,954,416
1987–1988	364,201,275
1989–1990	357,648,557
1991–1992	394,785,896
1993–1994	388,102,643
1995–1996	429,887,819
1997–1998	470,830,847
1999–2000	579,358,330

SOURCE: Federal Election Commission

violations of campaign finance laws, involving millions of dollars in unregistered cash from corporate executives to President Nixon's re-election committee. Many of these revelations were made by the famous Ervin Committee, whose official name and jurisdiction was the Senate Select Committee to Investigate the 1972 Presidential Campaign Activities.

Reaction to Watergate produced further legislation on campaign finance in 1974 and 1976, but the effect has been to restrict individual rather than interest-group campaign activity. Individuals may now contribute no more than $1,000 to any candidate for federal office in any primary or general election. A *political action committee (PAC)*, however, can contribute $5,000, provided it contributes to at least five different federal candidates each year. Beyond this, the laws permit corporations, unions, and other interest groups to form PACs and to pay the costs of soliciting funds from private citizens for the PACs.

Electoral spending by interest groups has been increasing steadily despite the flurry of reform following Watergate. Table 12.4 presents a dramatic picture of

political action committee A private group that raises and distributes funds for use in election campaigns.

FIGURE 12.2

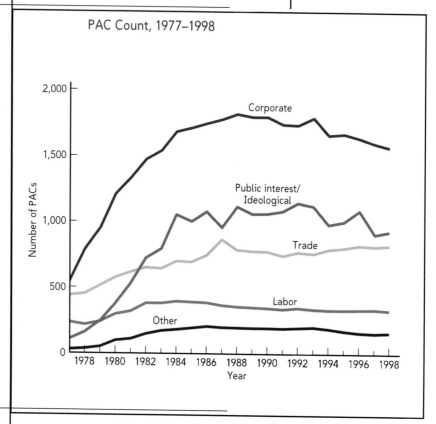

PAC Count, 1977–1998

SOURCE: Federal Election Commission, fecweb1.fec.gov/press/paccnt_grph.html

the growth of PACs as the source of campaign contributions. The dollar amounts for each year indicate the growth in electoral spending. The number of PACs has also increased significantly—from 608 in 1974 to more than 4,000 in 1999 (see Figure 12.2). Although the reform legislation of the early and mid-1970s attempted to reduce the influence of special interests over elections, the effect has been almost the exact opposite. Opportunities for legally influencing campaigns are now widespread.

Given the enormous costs of television commercials, polls, computers, and other elements of the new political technology (see Chapter 11), most politicians are eager to receive PAC contributions and are at least willing to give a friendly hearing to the needs and interests of contributors. It is probably not the case that most politicians simply sell their services to the interests that fund their campaigns. But there is considerable evidence to support the contention that interest groups' campaign contributions do influence the overall pattern of political behavior in Congress and in the state legislatures.

During the 2000 national election campaign, thousands of interest groups donated nearly $2 billion to political parties and candidates at the national, state, and local levels. PACs and individual donors gave $720 million to congressional candidates alone. One Senate candidate, Republican Rick Lazio of New York, raised $35 million from individuals and groups that hoped to thwart former first lady Hillary Rodham Clinton's Senate bid. For her part, Clinton received $24 million from backers of her ultimately successful effort to succeed retiring senator Daniel Patrick Moynihan.

Interests that donate large amounts of money to campaigns expect and often receive favorable treatment from the beneficiaries of their largesse. For example, in 2000 a number of major interests with specific policy goals made substantial donations to the Bush presidential campaign (Table 12.5). These interests included airlines, energy producers, banks, tobacco companies, and a number of others.

After Bush's election, these interests pressed the new president to promote their legislative and regulatory agendas. For example, MBNA America Bank was a major donor to the 2000 Bush campaign. The bank and its executives gave Bush $1.3 million. The bank's president helped raise millions more for Bush and personally gave $100,000 more to the president's inaugural committee after the election.[41] All told, MBNA and other banking companies donated $26 million to the GOP in 2000. Within weeks of his election, President Bush signed legislation providing MBNA and the others with something they had sought for years—bankruptcy laws making it more difficult for consumers to escape credit card debts. Such laws could potentially enhance the earnings of large credit card issuers like MBNA by tens of millions of dollars every year.

In a similar vein, a coalition of manufacturers led by the U.S. Chamber of Commerce and the National Association of Manufacturers also provided considerable support for Mr. Bush's 2000 campaign. This coalition sought, among other things, the repeal of new federal rules, promulgated in 2000 by the Occupational Health and Safety Administration (OSHA), designed to protect workers from repetitive motion injuries. Again, within weeks of his election, the president approved a resolution rejecting the rules. In March 2001, the House and Senate both voted to kill the ergonomic regulations.

During their years in the White House, Democrats also seemed to cater to the needs of well-heeled contributors. In 1997, for example, former vice president Gore helped win federal contracts for a Massachusetts hazardous-waste disposal firm whose officers contributed heavily to the Clinton-Gore re-election effort. After officers of Molten Metal Technology, Inc., contributed generously to the Clinton-Gore campaign, the firm received millions of dollars in Department of Energy contracts. The firm's chief Washington lobbyist, Peter Knight, is also

Analyzing American Politics

www.wwnorton.com/
lowi7/ch12

Analyze whether PAC contributions buy votes in Congress.

---

[41]Tom Hamburger, Laurie McGinley, and David S. Cloud, "Industries That Backed Bush Are Now Seeing Return on Investment," *Wall Street Journal*, 6 March 2001, p. 1.

TABLE 12.5

The GOP's Big 10 Investors

Contributions to the Bush campaign and the national and congressional campaign committees, by industry, for 1999–2000 election year.*

INDUSTRY	GEORGE W. BUSH	REPUBLICANS	% TO GOP	INAUGU-RATION	POLICY INTERESTS
Airlines	$0.18	$4.20	61	$0.17	Avoiding antitrust prosecution for proposed mergers and corporate practices; defeating consumer-protection legislation
Oil and Gas	1.84	25.40	78	1.39	Getting permission to drill in Alaska and other western states
Banks and Credit Cards	1.45	25.60	60	0.83	Passing bankruptcy-overhaul legislation requiring consumers to repay their debts when possible
Pharma-ceuticals	0.45	17.81	68	0.95	Avoiding price controls as Congress overhauls Medicare and adds drug benefits; defeating Clinton administration privacy rules
Tobacco	0.09	6.95	83	0.20	Getting rid of federal lawsuit accusing the industry of lying about health risks of smoking
Manufacturers/Distributors	1.38	19.87	70	1.84	Repealing the workplace ergonomics standard; curbing personal-injury lawsuits
Insurance	1.62	26.52	66	1.15	Rolling back individual marginal tax rates, estate tax; urging pension and retirement reform
Real Estate	4.30	41.72	55	1.62	Fighting newly proposed legislation that would allow banks to engage in real-estate activities
Securities and Investment	3.87	48.51	55	3.28	Expanding 401(k) and IRA contribution opportunities; will watch Social Security privatization especially closely
General Contractors	1.54	13.28	69	0.05	Repealing the estate tax; rolling back ergonomics rule and new mandates on hiring; promoting road funding, tax cuts

*Totals reflect campaign donations recorded at the Federal Election Commission, but not independent expenditures, such as the $60 million in issue advertising paid for by the pharmaceuticals industry. Monetary amounts are in millions of dollars.

SOURCE: *Wall Street Journal,* 6 March 2001, p. A8.

Gore's former chief of staff and a former chair of the Clinton-Gore re-election committee. Knight was able to arrange a visit by the vice president to Molten's plant to mark Earth Day. Gore, Knight, and Molten executives deny that there is any connection between the firm's campaign contributions and the contracts subsequently awarded to it by the federal government.[42]

PACs provide more than just the financial support that individual candidates receive. Under present federal law, there is no restriction on the amount that individuals and interests can contribute directly to the parties for voter registration, grassroots organizing, and other party activities not directly linked to a particular candidate's campaign. Such contributions, called **soft money**, allow individuals and interest groups to circumvent restrictions on campaign contributions. Critics argue that soft money contributions allow wealthy donors to have unfair influence in the political process. Perhaps this potential does exist. However, soft money also provides the national and state parties with the means to engage in voter registration and turnout drives. In 1996, the U.S. Supreme Court ruled in the case of *Colorado Republican Party v. Federal Election Commission* that the government could not restrict political parties' use of soft money.[43]

Indeed, PACs and campaign contributions provide organized interests with such a useful tool for gaining access to the political process that interests of all political stripes are now willing to suspend their conflicts and rally to the defense of political action committees when they come under attack. This support has helped to make the present campaign funding system highly resistant to reform. As we saw in Chapter 10, in May 1996, the Senate considered a bipartisan campaign finance bill sponsored by Senators John McCain (R-Ariz.), Russell Feingold (D-Wisc.), and Fred Thompson (R-Tenn.), which would have abolished political action committees. The bill was staunchly opposed by a coalition of business groups, labor unions, liberal groups like EMILY's List, and conservative groups like Americans for Tax Reform. Though these groups disagree on many substantive matters, they agreed on the principle that abolition of PACs would "diminish the ability of average citizens to join together to have their voices heard." A less positive interpretation was offered by Common Cause president Ann McBride, a proponent of abolishing PACs, who characterized the pro-PAC alliance as an example of "labor and business coming together and agreeing on the one thing that they can agree on, which is maintaining the status quo and their ability to use money to buy outcomes on Capitol Hill."[44]

An amended version of the McCain-Feingold bill was reintroduced in 2001. In this version, soft money contributions from interest groups would be banned. A number of interest groups opposed the new version of McCain-Feingold, fearing it would limit their influence, but, because of the sensitivity of the issue, few were willing to speak publicly against the bill. After receiving

soft money
Money contributed directly to political parties for voter registration and organization.

Institutional Reform
www.wwnorton.com/ lowi7/ch12
What if soft money contributions were banned?

[42] Guy Gugliotta and Edward Walsh, "House Fund-Raising Hearings Grow Stormy," *Washington Post*, 8 November 1997, p. A8.

[43] Filed as Colorado Republican Federal Campaign Committee v. Jones, 95-489 (1996).

[44] Ruth Marcus, "Campaign Finance Proposal Drawing Opposition from Diverse Groups," *Washington Post*, 1 May 1996, p. A12.

Senate approval, the bill died in the House of Representatives. Democrats and Republicans blamed one another for the bill's defeat but, in truth, many members on both sides of the aisle were relieved to see the defeat of a threat to their fund-raising abilities.

Often, the campaign spending of activist groups is carefully kept separate from party and candidate organizations in order to avoid the restrictions of federal campaign finance laws. So long as a group's campaign expenditures are not coordinated with those of a candidate's own campaign, the group is free to spend as much money as it wishes. Such expenditures are viewed as "issues advocacy" and are protected by the First Amendment and thus not subject to statutory limitation.[45]

During the 2000 election campaign, another source of PAC money surfaced—the "stealth PAC," so called because it "flew under the radar" of the Federal Election Commission's requirement that an independent expenditure by an individual or PAC be publicly disclosed. In that year's primaries, stealth PACs engaged in issues advocacy. However, because no reporting requirements were in place, no one knew exactly how much money they were spending, how many of them existed, where their money came from, or which candidates they supported. Nevertheless, the media and "watchdog" public interest groups were able to bring some details about them to the public's attention. For example, it was discovered that two prominent fundraisers for George W. Bush's presidential campaign spent $2.5 million on a series of "Republicans for Clean Air" ads that were critical of Senator John McCain, Bush's most formidable opponent in the Republican primaries. Later in 2000, campaign finance reformers in Congress won a small victory when they passed legislation that requires stealth PACs to fully disclose the names of their contributors and to detail where their money is spent. In support of this legislation, Maine senator Olympia Snowe said, "This is a good opportunity to bring sunshine to the political process." Still, other reformers wondered whether such a small success could translate into momentum for more substantive reforms.

Campaign Activism Financial support is not the only way that organized groups seek influence through electoral politics. Sometimes, activism can be even more important than campaign contributions. Campaign activism on the part of conservative groups played a very important role in bringing about the Republican capture of both houses of Congress in the 1994 congressional elections. For example, Christian Coalition activists played a role in many races, including ones in which Republican candidates were not overly identified with the religious Right. One post-election study suggested that more than 60 percent of the over 600 candidates supported by the Christian Right were successful in state, local, and congressional races in 1994.[46] The efforts of conservative

[45]Ruth Marcus, "Outside Groups Pushing Election Laws into Irrelevance," *Washington Post*, 8 August 1996, p. A9.

[46]Richard L. Burke, "Religious-Right Candidates Gain as GOP Turnout Rises," *New York Times*, 12 November 1994, p. 10.

Republican activists to bring voters to the polls is one major reason that turnout among Republicans exceeded Democratic turnout in a midterm election for the first time since 1970. This increased turnout was especially marked in the South, where the Christian Coalition was most active. In many Congressional districts, Christian Coalition efforts on behalf of the Republicans were augmented by grassroots campaigns launched by the National Rifle Association (NRA) and the National Federation of Independent Business (NFIB). The NRA had been outraged by Democratic support for gun control legislation, while NFIB had been energized by its campaign against employer mandates in the failed Clinton health care reform initiative. Both groups are well organized at the local level and were able to mobilize their members across the country to participate in congressional races.

In 1996, by contrast, it was the Democrats who benefited from campaign activism. Organized labor made a major effort to mobilize its members for the campaign. Conservative activists, on the other hand, were not enthusiastic about GOP presidential candidate Bob Dole or his running mate Jack Kemp and failed to mobilize their forces for a maximum campaign effort. Dole belatedly recognized his need for the support of these activists, but was never able to energize them in sufficient numbers to affect the outcome of the election.[47]

In 2000, civil rights groups and organized labor both made substantial efforts to mobilize their members for the Democrats. Indeed, it was the NAACP's voter registration drive that brought Al Gore close to victory in Florida, a state that had been considered safely in the Republican column. In Michigan, labor's efforts not only helped Gore carry the state but also brought about the defeat of incumbent Republican senator Spencer Abraham.

GROUPS AND INTERESTS: THE DILEMMA OF REFORM

James Madison wrote that "liberty is to faction what air is to fire."[48] By this he meant that the organization and proliferation of interests was inevitable in a free society. To seek to place limits on the organization of interests, in Madison's view, would be to limit liberty itself. Madison believed that interests should be permitted to regulate themselves by competing with one another. So long as competition among interests was free, open, and vigorous, there would be some balance of power among them and none would be able to dominate the political or governmental process.

There is considerable competition among organized groups in the United States. Nevertheless, interest-group politics is not as free of bias as Madisonian theory might suggest. Though the weak and poor do occasionally become

---

[47]John Harwood, "Dole Presses Hot-Button Issues to Try to Rouse GOP Activists Missing from Campaign So Far," *Wall Street Journal*, 16 October 1996, p. A22.

[48]*The Federalist Papers*, No. 10.

organized to assert their rights, interest-group politics is generally a form of political competition in which the wealthy and powerful are best able to engage.

Moreover, although groups sometimes organize to promote broad public concerns, interest groups more often represent relatively narrow, selfish interests. Small, self-interested groups can be organized much more easily than large and more diffuse collectives. For one thing, the members of a relatively small group—say, bankers or hunting enthusiasts—are usually able to recognize their shared interests and the need to pursue them in the political arena. Members of large and more diffuse groups—say, consumers or potential victims of firearms—often find it difficult to recognize their shared interests or the need to engage in collective action to achieve them.[49] This is why causes presented as public interests by their proponents often turn out, upon examination, to be private interests wrapped in a public mantle.

Thus, we have a dilemma to which there is no ideal answer. To regulate interest-group politics is, as Madison warned, to limit freedom and to expand governmental power. Not to regulate interest-group politics, on the other hand, may be to ignore justice. Those who believe that there are simple solutions to the issues of political life would do well to ponder this problem.

SUMMARY

Efforts by organized groups to influence government and policy are becoming an increasingly important part of American politics. Such interest groups use a number of strategies to gain power.

Lobbying is the act of petitioning legislators. Lobbyists—individuals who receive some form of compensation for lobbying—are required to register with the House and Senate. In spite of an undeserved reputation for corruption, lobbyists serve a useful function, providing members of Congress with a vital flow of information.

Access is participation in government. Groups with access have less need for lobbying. Most groups build up access over time through great effort. They work years to get their members into positions of influence on congressional committees.

Litigation sometimes serves interest groups when other strategies fail. Groups may bring suit on their own behalf, finance suits brought by individuals, or file *amicus curiae* briefs.

Going public is an effort to mobilize the widest and most favorable climate of opinion. Advertising is a common technique in this strategy. Others are boycotts, strikes, rallies, and marches.

Groups engage in electoral politics either by embracing one of the major parties, usually through financial support or through a nonpartisan strategy.

---

[49]Mancur Olson, *The Logic of Collective Action* (Cambridge: Harvard University Press, 1971).

PRINCIPLES OF POLITICS IN REVIEW

Rationality Principle	Collective Action Principle	Institution Principle	Policy Principle	History Principle
In a group setting, rational individuals have an incentive to free-ride.	The prisoners' dilemma, an example of a collective action problem, explains why cooperation in groups can be difficult to achieve.	Groups can turn to the courts if they are not successful in the legislative and executive branches.	Public policy can reveal the impact of lobbying and gaining access by groups affected by it.	The explosion of interest-group activity has its origins in the expansion of the role of government since the 1960s.
Organizing collective action can provide private benefits to a political entrepreneur.	Selective benefits are one solution to the collective action problem.			
	Gaining access requires coordination across the legislative and executive branches.			
	Going public is a group strategy of mobilizing widespread support.			

Interest groups' campaign contributions now seem to be flowing into the coffers of candidates at a faster rate than ever before.

The group basis of politics, present since the founding, is both a curse and a blessing. In overcoming the hurdles of collective action, groups are an important means by which Americans participate in the political process and influence its outcomes. But participation in group life does not draw representatively from the population, so while it increases citizen involvement, influence is not evenly distributed. Collective action thus remains a dilemma.

FOR FURTHER READING

Cigler, Allan J., and Burdett A. Loomis, eds. *Interest Group Politics*, 5th ed. Washington, DC: Congressional Quarterly Press, 1999.

Clawson, Dan, Alan Neustadtl, and Denise Scott. *Money Talks: Corporate PACs and Political Influence.* New York: Basic Books, 1992.

Hansen, John Mark. *Gaining Access: Congress and the Farm Lobby, 1919–1981.* Chicago: University of Chicago Press, 1991.

Heinz, John P., et al. *The Hollow Core: Private Interests in National Policy Making.* Cambridge: Harvard University Press, 1993.

Lowi, Theodore J. *The End of Liberalism.* New York: W. W. Norton, 1979.

Moe, Terry M. *The Organization of Interests.* Chicago: University of Chicago Press, 1980.

Olson, Mancur, Jr. *The Logic of Collective Action: Public Goods and the Theory of Groups.* Cambridge: Harvard University Press, 1971.

Petracca, Mark, ed. *The Politics of Interests: Interest Groups Transformed.* Boulder, CO: Westview, 1992.

Salisbury, Robert H. *Interests and Institutions: Substance and Structure in American Politics.* Pittsburgh: University of Pittsburgh Press, 1992.

Scholzman, Kay Lehman, and John T. Tierney. *Organized Interests and American Democracy.* New York: Harper & Row, 1986.

Truman, David. *The Governmental Process: Political Interests and Public Opinion.* New York: Knopf, 1951.

Vogel, David. *Fluctuating Fortunes.* New York: Basic Books, 1989.

Wright, John R. *Interest Groups and Congress: Lobbying, Contributions, and Influence.* Boston: Allyn & Bacon, 1996.

thirteen

The Media

TIME LINE ON THE MEDIA

EVENTS	INSTITUTIONAL DEVELOPMENTS
Alien and Sedition Acts attempt to silence opposition press (1798)	
1800	Newspapers and pamphlets serve leaders (early 1800s)
New printing presses introduced, allowing cheaper printing of more newspapers (1820s–1840s)	Expansion of popular press; circulation of more newspapers, magazines, and books (1840s)
First transmission of telegraph message, between Baltimore and Washington (1844)	Nation begins to be linked by telegraph communications network (1840s)
Creation of Associated Press (AP) (1848)	
1850	
Completion of telegraph connections across country to San Francisco (1861)	Advertising industry makes press financially free of parties; beginnings of an independent, nonpartisan press (1880s)
Rise of large corporations and municipal corruption spark Progressive reform efforts (1880s–1890s)	Beginning of "muckraking"—exposure of social evils by journalists (1890s)
Publisher William R. Hearst sparks Spanish-American War (1898)	Circulation war between Hearst's *N.Y. Journal* and Pulitzer's *N.Y. World* leads to "yellow journalism"—sensationalized reporting (1890s)
First news bulletins transmitted over radio; regular radio programs introduced (1920) — **1920**	Beginning of radio broadcasting (1920s)
NBC links radio stations into network (1926)	Regulation of broadcast industry begins with Federal Radio Commission (1927)
Great Depression (1929–1933)	*Near v. Minnesota*—Supreme Court holds that government cannot exercise prior restraint (1931)
Franklin D. Roosevelt uses radio "fireside chats" to reassure the nation and restore confidence (1930s)	Federal Communications Act creates Federal Communications Commission (FCC) (1934)
Televised Senate hearings (1950s) — **1950**	Television is introduced (late 1940s–1950s)
Televised Kennedy-Nixon debate (1960)	Fairness doctrine governing TV coverage (1960s)
Vietnam War; American officials in Vietnam leak information to the press (1960s–early 1970s)	Era of investigative reporting and critical journalistic coverage of government (1960s–1990s)

EVENTS	INSTITUTIONAL DEVELOPMENTS
	TV spot ads become candidates' major weapons (1960s–1990s)
John F. Kennedy uses televised news conference to mobilize public support for his policies (1961–1963)	Beginning of extended national television news coverage (1963)
"Daisy Girl" commercial helps defeat Goldwater and elect Lyndon Johnson president (1964)	*N.Y. Times v. Sullivan* asserts "actual malice" standard in libel cases involving public officials (1964)
	Vietnam War first war to receive extended television coverage, which contributes to expansion of opposition to the war (1965–1973)
	Red Lion Broadcasting v. U.S. establishes "right of rebuttal" (1969)

1970

Pentagon Papers on Vietnam War published by *N.Y. Times* and *Washington Post* (1971)	*N.Y. Times v. U.S.*—Supreme Court rules against prior restraint in *Pentagon Papers* case (1971)
Televised Watergate hearings (1973–1974)	

1980

Unsuccessful libel suits by Israeli general Ariel Sharon against *Time* magazine (1984) and by General William Westmoreland against CBS News (1985)	FCC stops enforcing fairness doctrine (1985)
Televised Iran-Contra hearings (1987)	
Live coverage of Persian Gulf War (1990)	**1990** Military controls media access throughout Persian Gulf conflict (1990–1991)
Talk show appearances, "infomercials," televised town meetings used by candidates during campaign (1992)	Politicians create new media formats to pitch themselves and their programs; era of permanent campaign (1992)
Talk radio programs help Republicans defeat Democrats in congressional elections (1994)	
Media frenzy during investigation of Clinton's affair with Monica Lewinsky (1998–1999)	
Early and incorrect election-night calls lead Gore to concede and then retract concession in 2000 presidential election	**2000** Growing use of Internet as source of political information and campaign tool (2000)
White House asks media for assistance in war against terrorism(2001)	

CORE OF THE ANALYSIS

- Nationalization of the news has contributed greatly to the nationalization of politics and of political perspectives in the United States.

- The three major influences on the media's coverage are the producers of the news, the sources of the news, and the audience for the news.

- The media have tremendous power to shape the political agenda, to shape our images of politicians and policies, and to influence our images of ourselves and our society.

- Freedom of the press is critical to the maintenance of a democratic society.

The American news media are among the world's most free. Newspapers, news magazines, the broadcast media, and news Web sites regularly present information that is at odds with the government's claims, as well as editorial opinions sharply critical of the highest-ranking public officials. For example, even though Bill Clinton appeared to gain considerable media support during his first two months in office, the media's overall stance on Clinton has been critical. In June 1994, long before the Monica Lewinsky affair led to a storm of media criticism, Clinton lashed out at the media, averring that no previous president had ever "been subject to more violent personal attacks than I have, at least in modern history." Clinton charged that talk radio programs presented "a constant, unremitting drumbeat of negativism and criticism," and he particularly castigated two of his strongest critics, conservative radio host Rush Limbaugh and fundamentalist television preacher Rev. Jerry Falwell. The president went on to denounce the press for unfair coverage of his administration.[1] Clinton's remarks were ironic because he had made such effective use of the media, particularly radio and television talk shows, during his 1992 presidential campaign. Andrea Mitchell of NBC News noted that Clinton had "had it so easy" on talk shows in 1992 that he was shocked by any criticism of his policies from that quarter.[2]

Other journalists declared that their attitude toward the White House had soured because of what they saw as the Clinton administration's repeated efforts to deceive the press and the public. One White House correspondent asserted that "nineteen months of repeated falsehoods and half-truths have corroded the relationship between this White House and the reporters who cover it,"[3] pointing particularly to deliberate administration efforts to deceive the press on aspects of the Whitewater affair, on First Lady Hillary Rodham Clinton's investments, and on the events surrounding the suicide of White House Deputy Counsel Vincent Foster.

[1]Douglas Jehl, "Clinton Calls Show to Assail Press, Falwell and Limbaugh," *New York Times*, 25 June 1994, p. 1.

[2]John H. Fund, "Why Clinton Shouldn't Be Steamed at Talk Radio," *Wall Street Journal*, 7 July 1994, p. A12.

[3]Ruth Marcus, "The White House Isn't Telling Us the Truth," *Washington Post*, 21 August 1994, p. C9.

By the end of August 1994, President Clinton and his advisers changed tactics and began to court rather than attack the news media. Clinton initiated a series of small, off-the-record gatherings with prominent journalists, including the correspondents for the major news networks; these events were designed to create a more positive image for the embattled president. According to some journalists who attended the gatherings, Clinton tried to flatter them by asking their advice on administration initiatives. Although Clinton's efforts appeared to have produced several sympathetic news stories, some journalists apparently were annoyed by the president's attempts to be nice to them. One responded to Clinton's request for advice by declaring that "advising presidents was not his province."[4] By 1996, editorial writers at least had forgiven Clinton for his earlier sins. Most of the leading daily newspapers, including the influential *New York Times* and *Washington Post*, endorsed the president for re-election. After Clinton left office in 2001, however, the national media launched a new set of offensives against him. The now former president was accused of improperly granting pardons to wealthy and well-connected criminals. He was also accused of appropriating for personal use furniture and other items that belonged to the government. Newly elected president George W. Bush suggested that the news media should turn its attention to his policy agenda rather than dwell on the misdeeds of the Clinton era. One conservative news magazine, the *Weekly Standard*, replied that attacking Clinton was much more fun.

The former president's comments to the contrary notwithstanding, the media actually handled Clinton with kid gloves during his first term, compared to their treatment of other recent presidents. Until the emergence of Monica Lewinsky, critical media coverage of the White House reached its apex during the Nixon administration, when the three television networks frequently presented hostile assessments of presidential claims, actions, and speeches. Typically, a presidential address to the nation was followed by a half hour of network commentary

THE CENTRAL QUESTIONS

THE MEDIA INDUSTRY AND GOVERNMENT

How has the nationalization of the news media contributed to the nationalization of American politics?

How is the media regulated by the government? How does this regulation differ between the broadcast media and the print media?

NEWS COVERAGE

How are media content, news coverage, and bias affected by the goals of the producers, subjects, and consumers of the news?

MEDIA POWER IN AMERICAN POLITICS

How do the media shape public perceptions of events, issues, and institutions?

What are the sources of media power?

MEDIA POWER AND RESPONSIBILITY

Are the media too powerful and thus in need of restriction, or are free media necessary for democracy?

[4]Howard Kurtz, "From Clinton, Schmooze Control," *Washington Post*, 26 August 1994, p. D1.

purporting to correct inaccuracies and errors in the president's statements. These critical analyses led Nixon's vice president, Spiro T. Agnew, to characterize television broadcasters as "nattering nabobs of negativism."

Adversarial or "attack" journalism has become commonplace in America and some critics have suggested that the media have contributed to popular cynicism and the low levels of citizen participation that characterize American political processes. But before we begin to think about means of compelling the media to adopt a more positive view of politicians and political issues, we should consider the possibility that media criticism is one of the major mechanisms of political accountability in the American political process. Without aggressive media coverage would we have known of Bill Clinton's misdeeds or, for that matter, those of Richard Nixon? Without aggressive media coverage would important questions be raised about the conduct of American foreign and domestic policy? It is easy to criticize the media for their aggressive tactics, but would our democracy function effectively without the critical role of the press?

We should also evaluate the sometimes adversarial relationship between the media and politicians in terms of the interests each has. Politicians want to sell their policy agenda to citizens and mobilize support for it, but they need the media to help communicate their message. Politicians would prefer to control the content of the news, but since the media have different goals and interests— market share, professional prestige, and, in some cases, political influence— news journalists and elected leaders often come into conflict with another. Finally, we should take into account the interests of citizens—the consumers of the news—and how their demands for certain types and amounts of political news influence the adversarial nature of media politics.[5]

In this chapter, we will examine the role and increasing power of the media in American politics. First, we will look at the media industry and government. Second, we will discuss the factors that help to determine "what's news," that is, the factors that shape media coverage of events and personalities. Third, we will examine the scope of media power in politics. Finally, we will address the question of responsibility: "In a democracy, to whom are the media accountable for the use of their formidable power?"

Rationality Principle

Media coverage can be analyzed in terms of the interests of members of the media, politicians, and consumers.

THE MEDIA INDUSTRY AND GOVERNMENT

The freedom to speak one's mind is one of the most cherished of American political values—one that is jealously safeguarded by the media. As we mentioned above, a wide variety of newspapers, news magazines, broadcast media, and Web sites regularly present information that is at odds with the government's claims,

[5]John Zaller, *A Theory of Media Politics: How the Interests of Politicians, Journalists, and Citizens Shape the News*, unpublished manuscript.

FIGURE 13.1

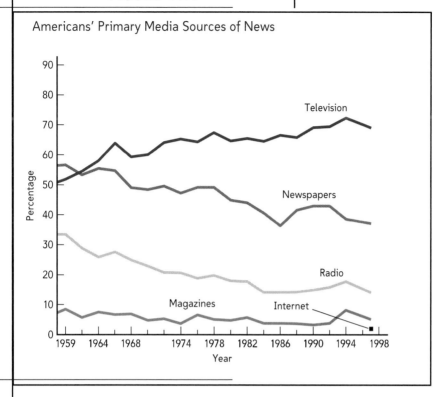

Americans' Primary Media Sources of News

Note: (Multiple responses permitted)

SOURCE: *America's Watching: Public Attitudes toward Television* (New York: Roper Starch Worldwide, 1995), p. 17, and 1997 Roper Starch Worldwide poll.

as well as editorial opinions that are sharply critical of high-ranking officials. Yet although thousands of media companies exist across the United States, surprisingly little variety appears in what is reported about national events and issues.

Types of Media

Americans obtain their news from broadcast media (radio, television), print media (newspapers and magazines), and, increasingly, from the Internet. Each of these sources has distinctive characteristics. Television news reaches more Americans than any other single news source (see Figure 13.1). Tens of millions of individuals watch national and local news programs every day. Television news, however, covers relatively few topics and provides little depth of coverage. Television news is more like a series of newspaper headlines connected to pictures. It serves the extremely important function of alerting viewers to issues and events, but provides little else.

Radio news is also essentially a headline service, but without pictures. In the short time—usually five minutes per hour—they devote to news, radio stations announce the day's major events without providing much detail. In major cities, all-news stations provide a bit more coverage of major stories, but for the most part these stations fill the day with repetition rather than detail. All-news stations like Washington, DC's WTOP or New York's WCBS assume that most listeners are in their cars and that, as a result, the people in the audience change markedly throughout the day as listeners reach their destinations. Thus, rather than use their time to flesh out a given set of stories, they repeat the same stories each hour to present them to new listeners. In recent years, radio talk shows have become important sources of commentary and opinion. A number of conservative radio hosts such as Rush Limbaugh have huge audiences and have helped to mobilize support for conservative political causes and candidates. Liberals have been somewhat slower to recognize the potential impact of talk radio.

The most important source of news is the old-fashioned newspaper. Newspapers remain critically important even though they are not the primary news sources for most Americans. The print media are important for two reasons. First, as we shall see later in this chapter, the broadcast media rely upon leading newspapers such as the *New York Times* and the *Washington Post* to set their news agenda. The broadcast media engage in very little actual reporting; they primarily cover stories that have been "broken," or initially reported, by the print media. For example, sensational charges that President Bill Clinton had an affair with a White House intern were reported first by the *Washington Post* and *Newsweek* before being trumpeted around the world by the broadcast media. It is only a slight exaggeration to observe that if an event is not covered in the *New York Times*, it is not likely to appear on the *CBS Evening News*. The print media are also important because they are the prime source of news for educated and influential individuals. The nation's economic, social, and political elites rely upon the detailed coverage provided by the print media to inform and influence their views about important public matters. The print media may have a smaller audience than their cousins in broadcasting, but they have an audience that matters.

A relatively new source of news is the Internet. Every day, several million Americans scan one of many news sites on the Internet for coverage of current events. For the most part, however, the Internet provides electronic versions of coverage offered by print sources. One great advantage of the Internet is that it allows frequent updating. It potentially can combine the depth of coverage of a newspaper with the timeliness of television and radio, and probably will become a major news source in the next decade. Already, most political candidates and many interest groups have created sites on the World Wide Web. Some of the more sensational aspects of President Clinton's relationship with Monica Lewinsky were first reported on a Web site maintained by Matt Drudge, an individual who specializes in posting sensational charges about public figures. Though many deny it, most reporters scan Drudge's site regularly hoping to pick up a bit of salacious gossip. In 2000, many Americans relied on Web sites such as CNN.com for up-to-the-minute election news during the campaign, the dramatic post-election battle in Florida, and in the aftermath of the terrorist attacks on New York City and Washington, D.C.[6] Acknowledging the growing importance of the Internet as a political communications medium, the U.S. Supreme Court posted its decisions in the Florida election cases as soon as they were issued. As on-line access becomes simpler and faster, the Internet could give Americans access to unprecedented quantities of information. If only computers could also give Americans the ability to make good use of that information!

Organization and Ownership of the Media

The United States boasts more than one thousand television stations, approximately eighteen hundred daily newspapers, and more than nine thousand radio stations. The great majority of these enterprises are locally owned and operated and present a good deal of news and many features with a distinctly local flavor. For many months, viewers of the Syracuse, New York, evening news were informed that the day's "top story" concerned the proposed construction of a local garbage-burning steam plant. Similarly, in Seattle, Washington, viewers were treated to years of discussion about the construction of a domed athletic stadium, and audiences in Baltimore, Maryland, watched and read about struggles over downtown redevelopment. In all these cases, the local media focused heavily on a matter of particular local concern, providing local viewers, readers, and listeners with considerable information and viewpoints.

Yet, however much variation the American news media offer in terms of local coverage, there is far less diversity in the reporting of national events and issues. Most of the national news that is published by local newspapers is provided by the one wire service, the Associated Press. More than five hundred of the nation's TV stations are affiliated with one of the four networks and carry its evening news reports. Dozens of others carry PBS (Public Broadcasting System) news. Several hundred local radio stations also carry network news or National Public Radio news broadcasts. At the same time, although there are only three truly national newspapers, the *Wall Street Journal*, the *Christian Science Monitor*, and *USA Today*, two other papers, the *New York Times* and the *Washington Post*, are read by political leaders and other influential Americans throughout the nation. Such is the influence of these two "elite" newspapers that their news coverage sets the standard for virtually all other news outlets. Stories carried in the *New York Times* or the *Washington Post* influence the content of many other papers as well as the network news. Note how often this text, like most others, relies upon *New York Times* and *Washington Post* stories as sources for contemporary events.

National news is also carried to millions of Americans by the three major news magazines—*Time*, *Newsweek*, and *U.S. News & World Report*. Thus, even though the number of TV and radio stations and daily newspapers

---

[6]For discussions of the growing role of the Internet, see Leslie Wayne, "On Web, Voters Reinvent Grass-Roots Activism," *New York Times*, 21 May 2000, p. 22. Also, James Fallows, "Internet Illusions," *New York Review of Books*, 16 November 2000, p. 28.

reporting news in the United States is enormous, and local coverage varies greatly from place to place, the number of sources of national news is actually quite small—one wire service, four broadcast networks, public radio and TV, two elite newspapers, three news magazines, and a scattering of other sources such as the national correspondents of a few large local papers, and the small independent radio networks. Beginning in the late 1980s, Cable News Network (CNN) became another major news source. The importance of CNN increased dramatically after its spectacular coverage of the Persian Gulf War. At one point, CNN was able to provide live coverage of American bombing raids on Baghdad, Iraq, after the major networks' correspondents had been forced to flee to bomb shelters. Even the availability of new electronic media on the Internet has failed to expand news sources. Most national news available on the World Wide Web, for example, consists of electronic versions of the conventional print media.

Since the enactment of the 1996 Telecommunications Act, which opened the way for further consolidation in the media industry, a wave of mergers and consolidations has further reduced the field of independent media across the country. Since that time, among the major news networks, ABC was bought by the Walt Disney Company; CBS was bought by Westinghouse Electric and later merged with Viacom, the owner of MTV and Paramount Studios; and CNN was bought by Time Warner. NBC has been owned by General Electric since 1986. Australian press baron Rupert Murdoch owns the Fox network plus a host of radio, television, and newspaper properties around the world. A small number of giant corporations now controls a wide swath of media holdings, including television networks, movie studios, record companies, cable channels and local cable providers, book publishers, magazines, and newspapers. These developments have prompted questions about whether enough competition exists among the media to produce a diverse set of views on political and corporate matters.[7]

Nationalization of the News

In general, the national news media cover more or less the same sets of events, present similar information, and emphasize similar issues and problems. Indeed, the national news services watch one another quite carefully. It is unlikely that a major story carried by one will not soon find its way into the pages or programming of the others. As a result, we have developed in the United States a rather centralized national news through which a relatively similar picture of events, issues, and problems is presented to the entire nation.[8] The nationalization of the news was accelerated by the development of radio networks in the 1920s and 1930s and was brought to a peak by the creation of the television networks after

[7]For a criticism of the increasing consolidation of the media, see the essays in Patricia Aufderheide et al., *Conglomerates and the Media* (New York: New Press, 1997).
[8]See Leo Bogart, "Newspapers in Transition," *Wilson Quarterly*, special issue, 1982; and Richard Harwood, "The Golden Age of Press Diversity," *Washington Post*, 22 July 1994, p. A23.

the 1950s. This nationalization of news content has very important consequences for American politics.

Nationalization of the news has contributed greatly to the nationalization of politics and of political perspectives in the United States. Prior to the development of the national media and the nationalization of news coverage, the news traveled very slowly. Every region and city saw national issues and problems mainly through its own local lens. Concerns and perspectives varied greatly from region to region, city to city, and village to village. Today, in large measure as a result of the nationalization of the media, residents of all parts of the country share similar ideas and perspectives.[9] They may not agree on everything, but they at least see the world in similar ways.

Regulation of the Broadcast and Electronic Media

In some countries, the government controls media content. In other countries, the government owns the broadcast media (e.g., the BBC in Britain), but it does not tell the media what to say. In the United States, the government neither owns nor controls the communications networks, but it does regulate the broadcast media.

American radio and television are regulated by the Federal Communications Commission (FCC), an independent regulatory agency established in 1934. Radio and TV stations must have FCC licenses that must be renewed every five years. The basic rationale for licensing is that there must be some mechanism to allocate radio and TV frequencies to prevent broadcasts from interfering with and garbling one another. License renewals are almost always granted automatically by the FCC. Indeed, renewal requests are now filed by postcard.

For more than sixty years, the broadcast media was subject to the control of the FCC, but in 1996 Congress passed the Telecommunications Act, a broad effort to do away with regulations in effect since 1934. The act loosened restrictions on media ownership and allowed for telephone companies, cable television providers, and broadcasters to compete with one another for telecommunication services. Following the passage of the act, several mergers occurred between telephone and cable companies and between different segments of the entertainment media, creating an even greater concentration of media ownership.

The Telecommunications Act of 1996 also included an attempt to regulate the content of material transmitted over the Internet. This law, known as the Communications Decency Act, made it illegal to make "indecent" sexual material on the Internet accessible to those under eighteen years of age. The act was immediately denounced by civil libertarians and brought to court as an infringement of free speech. The case reached the Supreme Court in 1997 and the act was ruled an unconstitutional infringement of the First Amendment's right to freedom of speech.

While the government's ability to regulate the content of the electronic media on the Internet has been questioned, the federal government has used its licensing

[9]See Benjamin Ginsberg, *The Captive Public* (New York: Basic Books, 1986).

equal time rule
A Federal Communications Commission requirement that broadcasters provide candidates for the same political office an equal opportunity to communicate their messages to the public.

power to impose several regulations that can affect the political content of radio and TV broadcasts. The first of these is the ***equal time rule.*** Under federal regulations, broadcasters must provide candidates for the same political office equal opportunities to communicate their messages to the public. If, for example, a television station sells commercial time to a state's Republican gubernatorial candidate, it may not refuse to sell time to the Democratic candidate for the same position.

right of rebuttal
A Federal Communications Commission regulation giving individuals the right to have the opportunity to respond to personal attacks made on a radio or TV broadcast.

The second FCC regulation affecting the content of broadcasts is the ***right of rebuttal.*** This means that individuals must be given the opportunity to respond to personal attacks. In the 1969 case of *Red Lion Broadcasting Company v. FCC,* for example, the U.S. Supreme Court upheld the FCC's determination that a television station was required to provide a liberal author with an opportunity to respond to an attack from a conservative commentator that the station had aired.[10]

fairness doctrine
A Federal Communications Commission requirement for broadcasters who air programs on controversial issues to provide time for opposing views.

For many years, a third important federal regulation was the ***fairness doctrine.*** Under this doctrine, broadcasters who aired programs on controversial issues were required to provide time for opposing views. In 1985, the FCC stopped enforcing the fairness doctrine on the grounds that there were so many radio and television stations—to say nothing of newspapers and news magazines—that in all likelihood many different viewpoints were already being presented without having to require each station to try to present all sides of an argument. Critics of this FCC decision charge that in many media markets the number of competing viewpoints is small. Nevertheless, a congressional effort to require the FCC to enforce the fairness doctrine was blocked by the Reagan administration in 1987.

Freedom of the Press

prior restraint
An effort by a governmental agency to block the publication of material it deems libelous or harmful in some other way; censorship. In the United States, the courts forbid prior restraint except under the most extraordinary circumstances.

Unlike the broadcast media, the print media are not subject to federal regulation. Indeed, the great principle underlying the federal government's relationship with the press is the doctrine against ***prior restraint.*** Beginning with the landmark 1931 case of *Near v. Minnesota,* the U.S. Supreme Court has held that, except under the most extraordinary circumstances, the First Amendment of the U.S. Constitution prohibits government agencies from seeking to prevent newspapers or magazines from publishing whatever they wish.[11] Indeed, in the case of *New York Times v. U.S.,* the so-called *Pentagon Papers* case, the Supreme Court ruled that the government could not even block publication of secret Defense Department documents furnished to the *New York Times* by a liberal opponent of the Vietnam War who had obtained the documents illegally.[12] In a 1990 case, however, the Supreme Court upheld a lower-court order restraining Cable Network News (CNN) from broadcasting tapes of conversations between former Panamanian leader Manuel Noriega and his lawyer, supposedly recorded by the

---

[10]Red Lion Broadcasting Company v. FCC, 395 U.S. 367 (1969).
[11]Near v. Minnesota, 283 U.S. 697 (1931).
[12]New York Times v. U.S., 403 U.S. 731 (1971).

U.S. government. By a vote of 7 to 2, the Court held that CNN could be restrained from broadcasting the tapes until the trial court in the Noriega case had listened to the tapes and had decided whether their broadcast would violate Noriega's right to a fair trial. This case would seem to weaken the "no prior restraint" doctrine. But whether the same standard will apply to the print media has yet to be tested in the courts. In 1994, the Supreme Court ruled that cable television systems were entitled to essentially the same First Amendment protections as the print media.[13]

Even though newspapers may not be restrained from publishing whatever they want, they may be subject to sanctions after the fact. Historically, newspapers were subject to the law of libel, which provided that newspapers that printed false and malicious stories could be compelled to pay damages to those they defamed. In recent years, however, American courts have greatly narrowed the meaning of libel and made it extremely difficult, particularly for politicians or other public figures, to win a libel case against a newspaper. The most important case on this topic is the 1964 U.S. Supreme Court case of *New York Times v. Sullivan*, in which the Court held that to be deemed libelous a story about a public official not only had to be untrue, but had to result from "actual malice" or "reckless disregard" for the truth.[14] In other words, the newspaper had to deliberately print false and malicious material. In practice, it is nearly impossible to prove that a paper deliberately printed false and damaging information and, as conservatives discovered in the 1980s, it is very difficult for a politician or other public figure to win a libel case. Libel suits against CBS News by General William Westmoreland and against *Time* magazine by General Ariel Sharon of Israel, both financed by conservative legal foundations who hoped to embarrass the media, were both defeated in court because they failed to show "actual malice." In the 1991 case of *Masson v. New Yorker Magazine*, this tradition was again affirmed when the Court held that fabricated quotations attributed to a public figure were libelous only if the fabricated account "materially changed" the meaning of what the person actually said.[15] For all intents and purposes, the print media can publish anything they want about a public figure.

NEWS COVERAGE

Because of the important role the media can play in national politics, it is essential to understand the factors that affect media coverage.[16] What accounts for the media's agenda of issues and topics? What explains the character of coverage—why does a politician receive good or bad press? What factors

[13]Cable News Network v. Noriega, 111 S.Ct. 451 (1990); Turner Broadcasting System, Inc. v. Federal Communications Commission, 93-44 (1994).

[14]New York Times v. Sullivan, 376 U.S. 254 (1964).

[15]Masson v. New Yorker Magazine, 111 S.Ct. 2419 (1991).

[16]See the discussions in Michael Parenti, *Inventing Reality* (New York: St. Martin's Press, 1986); Herbert Gans, *Deciding What's News* (New York: Vintage, 1980); and W. Lance Bennett, *News: The Politics of Illusion* (New York: Longman, 1986).

determine the interpretation or "spin" that a particular story will receive? Although a host of minor factors play a role, there are three major factors: (1) journalists or producers of the news; (2) politicians, who are usually the sources or topics of the news; and (3) citizens, the audience for the news.

Journalists

First, media content and news coverage are inevitably affected by the views, ideals, and interests of the individuals who seek out, write, and produce news and other stories. At one time, newspaper publishers exercised a great deal of influence over their papers' news content. Publishers such as William Randolph Hearst and Joseph Pulitzer became political powers through their manipulation of news coverage. Hearst, for example, almost singlehandedly pushed the United States into war with Spain in 1898 through his newspapers' relentless coverage of the alleged brutality employed by Spain in its efforts to suppress a rebellion in Cuba, then a Spanish colony. The sinking of the American battleship *Maine* in Havana Harbor under mysterious circumstances gave Hearst the ammunition he needed to force a reluctant President McKinley to lead the nation into war. Today, few publishers have that kind of power. Most publishers are more concerned with the business end of the paper than its editorial content, although a few continue to impose their interests and tastes on the news.

Rationality Principle

The goals and incentives of journalists—such as ratings, career success, and prestige—influence what is created and reported as news.

More important than publishers, for the most part, are the reporters. The goals and incentives of journalists are varied, but they often include considerations of ratings, career success and professional prestige, and political influence. For all of these reasons, journalists seek not only to *report* the news but also to *interpret* the news. Journalists' goals have a good deal of influence on what is created and reported as news.

Those who cover the news for the national media generally have a good deal of discretion or freedom to interpret stories and, as a result, have an opportunity to interject their own views and ideals into news stories. For example, the personal friendship and respect that some reporters felt for Franklin Roosevelt and John F. Kennedy helped to generate more favorable news coverage for these presidents. On the other hand, the dislike and distrust felt by many reporters for Richard Nixon was also communicated to the public. In the case of Ronald Reagan, the disdain that many journalists felt for the president was communicated in stories suggesting that he was often asleep or inattentive when important decisions were made.

Conservatives have long charged that the liberal biases of reporters and journalists result in distorted news coverage. A 1996 survey of Washington newspaper bureau chiefs and correspondents seems to support this charge.[17] The study, conducted by the Roper Center and the Freedom Forum, a conservative foundation, found that 61 percent of the bureau chiefs and correspondents polled called

[17]See Edith Efron, *The News Twisters* (Los Angeles: Nash Publishing, 1971).

themselves "liberal" or "liberal to moderate." Only 9 percent called themselves "conservative" or "conservative to moderate." In a similar vein, 89 percent said they had voted for Bill Clinton in 1992, while only 7 percent indicated that they had voted for George Bush. Fifty percent said they were Democrats, and only 4 percent claimed to be Republicans.[18] Another survey has indicated that even among the radio talk-show hosts lambasted by President Clinton, Democrats outnumber Republicans by a wide margin: of 112 hosts surveyed, 39 percent had voted for Clinton in 1992, and only 23 percent had supported George Bush.[19]

The linkage between substantial segments of the media and liberal interest groups is by no means absolute. Indeed, over the past several years a conservative media complex has emerged in opposition to the liberal media. This complex includes two major newspapers, the *Wall Street Journal* and the *Washington Times*, several magazines such as the *American Spectator*, and a host of conservative radio and television talk programs. The emergence of this conservative media complex has meant that liberal policies and politicians are virtually certain to come under attack even when the "liberal media" are sympathetic to them.

Probably more important than ideological bias is a selection bias in favor of news that the media view as having a great deal of audience appeal because of its dramatic or entertainment value. In practice, this bias often results in news coverage that focuses on crimes and scandals, especially those involving prominent individuals, despite the fact that the public obviously looks to the media for information about important political debates.[20] For example, even though most journalists may be Democrats, this partisan predisposition did not prevent an enormous media frenzy in January 1998 when reports surfaced that President Clinton may have had an affair with Lewinsky. Once a hint of blood appeared in the water, partisanship and ideology were swept away by the piranhalike instincts often manifested by journalists.

The Newsmakers: Politicians

News coverage is also influenced by politicians, who are subjects of the news and whose interests and activities are actual or potential news topics. In the almost never-ending battle over public opinion, politicians and journalists vie for control over how images of political leaders are presented to the public. In the last fifty years, the media has, for the most part, won this battle, although political leaders have fought back by developing new strategies. During the 1992 presidential campaign, candidates developed a number of techniques designed to

---

[18]Rowan Scarborough, "Leftist Press? Reporters Working in Washington Acknowledge Liberal Leanings in Poll," *Washington Times*, 18 April 1996, p. 1.

[19]Michael Kinsley, "Bias and Baloney," *Washington Post*, 26 November 1992, p. A29; and Fund, "Why Clinton Shouldn't Be Steamed at Talk Radio," p. A12.

[20]See Kathleen Hall Jamieson and Joseph N. Cappella, *The Spiral of Cynicism: The Press and the Public Good* (New York: Oxford University Press, 1997).

take the manipulation of the image-making process away from journalists and media executives. Among the most important of these techniques were the many town meetings and television talk and entertainment show appearances that all the major candidates made. Frequent exposure on such programs as *Larry King Live* and *Today* gave candidates an opportunity to shape and focus their own media images and to overwhelm any negative image that might be projected by the media. Politicians also seek to shape or manipulate their media images by cultivating good relations with reporters as well as through news leaks and staged news events. For example, during the lengthy investigation of President Clinton, which was conducted by Special Counsel Kenneth Starr, both the Office of the Special Counsel and the White House frequently leaked information designed to bolster their respective positions in the struggle. Starr admitted speaking to reporters on a not-for-attribution basis about aspects of his investigation of the president. One journalist, Steven Brill, accused a number of prominent reporters of serving as "lap dogs" for the Special Counsel, recording as fact the information fed to them by Starr.[21]

Rationality Principle
News coverage is influenced by the interests of politicians.

Some politicians become extremely adept image makers—or at least skilled at hiring publicists who are skillful image makers. Indeed, press releases drafted by skillful publicists often become the basis for reporters' stories. A substantial percentage of the news stories published every day were initially drafted by publicists and later rewritten only slightly, if at all, by busy reporters and editors. Furthermore, political candidates often endeavor to tailor their images for specific audiences. For example, to cultivate a favorable image among younger voters during his 1992 campaign, Bill Clinton made several appearances on MTV, and he continued to grant interviews to MTV after his election. His MTV forays came to an end, however, when he was severely criticized for discussing his preferred type of underwear with members of an MTV audience.

During his presidency, Bill Clinton was able to survive repeated revelations of sexual improprieties, financial irregularities, lying to the public, and illegal campaign fund-raising activities. Clinton and his advisers crafted what the *Washington Post* called a "toolkit" for dealing with potentially damaging media revelations. This toolkit included techniques such as chiding the press, browbeating reporters, referring inquiries quickly to lawyers who will not comment, and acting quickly to change the agenda. These techniques helped Clinton maintain a favorable public image despite the Monica Lewinsky scandal and even the humiliation of a formal impeachment and trial.

After he assumed office in 2001, George W. Bush sought to influence media coverage by introducing a new issue—education, taxes, the budget—every week. Bush hoped to attract media attention, control the headlines and demonstrate that his administration was vigorously undertaking the people's work. After the debut of the president's tax cut initiative in February 2001, Bush embarked on a multi-state speaking tour in support of his program. The president hoped to

---

[21]David Firestone, "Steven Brill Strikes a Nerve in News Media," *New York Times*, 20 June 1998, p. 4.

dominate local news coverage in a number of key states as a way of putting pressure on members of Congress to support his proposals.

Individual politicians are not the only ones trying to influence news coverage. As we saw in Chapter 10, by using media consultants and "issues managers," many social, economic, and political groups vigorously promote their ideas and interests through speeches, articles, books, news releases, research reports, and other mechanisms designed to attract favorable media coverage. Typically, competing forces seek to present—and to persuade the media to present—their own interests as more general or "public" interests. In recent years, for example, liberals have been very successful in inducing the media to present their environmental, consumer, and political reform proposals as matters of the public interest. Indeed, the advocates of these goals are organized in "public interest" groups. Seldom do the national media ever question a public interest group's equation of its goals with the general interest of all.

The capacity of politicians and groups to influence the news is hardly unlimited. Media consultants and issues managers may shape the news for a time, but it is generally not difficult for the media to penetrate the smoke screens thrown up by the news sources if they have a reason to do so. That reason is sometimes supplied by the third and most important factor influencing news content—the audience.

The Power of Consumers

The print and broadcast media are businesses that, in general, seek to show a profit. This means that like any other business, they must cater to the preferences of consumers. This has very important consequences for the content and character of the news media.

 Rationality Principle
Consumer preferences, such as those of the affluent or those of people who watch news for its entertainment value, influence news content.

Catering to the Upscale Audience In general, and especially in the political realm, the print and broadcast media and the publishing industry are not only responsive to the interests of consumers generally, but they are particularly responsive to the interests and views of the more "upscale" segments of the audience. The preferences of these audience segments have a profound effect upon the content and orientation of the press, of radio and television programming, and of books, especially in the areas of news and public affairs.[22]

Newspapers, magazines, and the broadcast media depend primarily upon advertising revenues for their profits. These revenues, in turn, depend upon the character and size of the audience that they are able to provide advertisers for their product displays and promotional efforts. From the perspective of most advertisers and especially those whose products are relatively expensive, the most desirable audiences for their ads and commercials consist of younger, upscale

[22]See Tom Burnes, "The Organization of Public Opinion," in *Mass Communication and Society*, ed. James Curran (Beverly Hills, CA: Sage, 1979), pp. 44–230. See also David Altheide, *Creating Reality* (Beverly Hills, CA: Sage, 1976).

consumers. What makes these individuals an especially desirable consumer audience is, of course, their affluence and their spending habits. Although they represent only a small percentage of the population, individuals under the age of fifty whose family income is in the 80th percentile or better account for nearly 50 percent of the retail dollars spent on consumer goods in the United States. To reach this audience, advertisers are particularly anxious to promote their products in the periodicals and newspapers and on the radio and television broadcasts that are known or believed to attract upscale patronage. Thus, advertisers flock to magazines like the *New Yorker, Fortune, Forbes, Architectural Digest,* and *Time.* Similarly, the pages of elite newspapers like the *New York Times* and the *Washington Post* are usually packed with advertisements for clothing, autos, computer equipment, stereo equipment, furs, jewelry, resorts and vacations, and the entire range of products and services that are such integral parts of the lifestyle of the well-to-do business and professional strata.

Although affluent consumers do watch television programs and read periodicals whose contents are designed simply to amuse or entertain, the one area that most directly appeals to the upscale audience is that of news and public affairs. The affluent—who are also typically well-educated—are the core audience of news magazines, journals of opinion, books dealing with public affairs, serious newspapers like the *New York Times* and the *Washington Post,* and broadcast news and weekend and evening public affairs programming. While other segments of the public also read newspapers and watch the television news, their level of interest in world events, national political issues, and the like is closely related to their level of education. As a result, upscale Americans are overrepresented in the news and public affairs audience. The concentration of these strata in the audience makes news, politics, and public affairs potentially very attractive topics to advertisers, publishers, radio broadcasters, and television executives.

Entire categories of events, issues, and phenomena of interest to lower-middle- and working-class Americans receive scant attention from the national print and broadcast media. For example, trade union news and events are discussed only in the context of major strikes or revelations of corruption. No network or national periodical routinely covers labor organizations. Religious and church affairs receive little coverage. The activities of veterans', fraternal, ethnic, and patriotic organizations are also generally ignored. Certainly, interpretations of economic events tend to reveal a class bias. For example, an increase in airline fares—a cost borne mainly by upper-income travelers—is usually presented as a negative development. Higher prices for commodities heavily used by the poor such as alcohol and cigarettes, on the other hand, are generally presented as morally justified.

The upscale character of the national media's coverage stands in sharp contrast to the topics discussed by radio and television talk shows and the small number of news tabloids and major daily newspapers that seek to reach a blue-collar audience. These periodicals and programs feature some of the same events described by the national media. But from the perspective of these outlets and their viewers and readers, "public affairs" includes healthy doses of celebrity gossip, crime news, discussions of the occult, and sightings of UFOs. Also featured are ethnic, fraternal, patriotic, and religious affairs, and even demolition derbies. Executives, intellectuals, and professionals, as well as the journalists and writers who serve them, may sneer at this blue-collar version of the news, but after all, are the stories of UFOs presented by the decidedly downscale *New York Post* any more peculiar than the stories of the UN told by the imperious *New York Times?*

The Media and Conflict   While the media respond most to the upscale audience, groups who cannot afford the services of media consultants and issues managers can publicize their views and interests through protest. Frequently, the media are accused of encouraging conflict and even violence as a result of the fact that the audience mostly watches news for the entertainment value that conflict can provide. Clearly, conflict can be an important vehicle for attracting the attention and interest of the media, and thus may provide an opportunity for media attention to groups otherwise lacking the financial or organizational resources to broadcast their views. But while conflict and protest can succeed in drawing media attention, these methods ultimately do not allow groups from the bottom of the social ladder to compete effectively in the media.

The chief problem with protest as a media technique is that, in general, the media upon which the protesters depend have considerable discretion in reporting and interpreting the events they cover. For example, should a particular group of protesters be identified as "freedom fighters" or "terrorists"? If a demonstration leads to violence, was this the fault of the protesters or the authorities? The answers to these questions are typically determined by the media, not by the protesters. This means that media interpretation of protest activities is more a reflection of the views of the groups and forces to which the media are responsive—as we have seen, usually segments of the upper-middle class—than it is a function of the wishes of the protesters themselves. It is worth noting that civil rights protesters received their most favorable media coverage when a segment of the white upper-middle class saw blacks as potential political allies in the Democratic party.

Typically, upper-class protesters—student demonstrators and the like—have little difficulty securing favorable publicity for themselves and their causes. Witness the sympathetic coverage given anti-apartheid protests and antiwar protests, and the benign treatment afforded even upper-middle-class fringe groups like the "animal liberationists." Upper-class protesters are often more skilled than their lower-class counterparts in the techniques of media manipulation. That is, they typically have a better sense—often as a result of formal courses on the subject—of how to package messages for media consumption. For example, it is important to know what time of day a protest should occur if it is to be carried on the evening news. Similarly, the setting, definition of the issues, and character of the rhetoric used, and so on, all help to determine whether a protest will receive favorable media coverage, unfavorable coverage, or no coverage at all. Moreover, upper-middle-class protesters can often produce their own media coverage through "underground" newspapers, college papers, student radio and television stations, and, now, the Internet. The same resources and skills that generally allow upper-middle-class people to publicize their ideas are usually not left behind when segments of this class choose to engage in disruptive forms of political action.

MEDIA POWER IN AMERICAN POLITICS

The content and character of news and public affairs programming—what the media choose to present and how they present it—can have far-reaching political consequences. Media disclosures can greatly enhance—or fatally damage— the careers of public officials. Media coverage can rally support for—or intensify opposition to—national policies. The media can shape and modify, if not fully form, public perceptions of events, issues, and institutions.

Shaping Events

In recent American political history, the media have played a central role in at least three major events. First, the media were critically important factors in the civil rights movement of the 1950s and 1960s. Television photos showing peaceful civil rights marchers attacked by club-swinging police helped to generate sympathy among Northern whites for the civil rights struggle and greatly increased the pressure on Congress to bring an end to segregation.[23] Second, the media were instrumental in compelling the government to negotiate an end to the Vietnam War. Beginning in 1967, the national media portrayed the war as misguided and unwinnable and, as a result, helped to turn popular sentiment against continued American involvement.[24] So strong was the effect of the media, in fact, that when Walter Cronkite told television news viewers that the war was unwinnable, President Lyndon B. Johnson was reported to have said, "If I've lost Walter, then it's over. I've lost Mr. Average Citizen."[25]

Finally, the media were central actors in the Watergate affair, which ultimately forced President Richard Nixon, landslide victor in the 1972 presidential election, to resign from office in disgrace. It was the relentless series of investigations launched by the *Washington Post*, the *New York Times*, and the television networks that led to the disclosures of the various abuses of which Nixon was guilty and ultimately forced Nixon to choose between resignation and almost certain impeachment.

[23]David Garrow, *Protest at Selma* (New Haven: Yale University Press, 1978).

[24]See Todd Gitlin, *The Whole World Is Watching* (Berkeley: University of California Press, 1980). See also William Hammond, *Reporting Vietnam: Media and Military at War* (Lawrence: University Press of Kansas, 1999).

[25]Quoted in George Brown Tindall, *America: A Narrative History*, 5th ed. (New York: W. W. Norton, 1996), p. 1541.

The Sources of Media Power

Agenda Setting The power of the media stems from several sources. The first is *agenda setting,* which means the media help to determine which political issues become part of the public debate. Groups and forces that wish to bring their ideas before the public in order to generate support for policy proposals or political candidacies must somehow secure media coverage. If the media are persuaded that an idea is newsworthy, then they may declare it an "issue" that must be resolved or a "problem" to be solved, thus clearing the first hurdle in the policy-making process. On the other hand, if an idea lacks or loses media appeal, its chance of resulting in new programs or policies is diminished. Some ideas seem to surface, gain media support for a time, lose media appeal, and then resurface.

agenda setting
Activities that help to determine which issues are taken up by political actors and institutions.

In most instances, the media serve as conduits for agenda-setting efforts by competing groups and forces. Occasionally, however, journalists themselves play an important role in setting the agenda of political discussion. For example, whereas many of the scandals and investigations surrounding President Clinton were initiated by his political opponents, the Watergate scandal that destroyed Nixon's presidency was in some measure initiated and driven by the *Washington Post* and the national television networks.

Framing A second source of the media's power, known as *framing,* is their power to decide how political events and results are interpreted by the American people. For example, during the 1995–1996 struggle between President Clinton and congressional Republicans over the nation's budget—a struggle that led to several partial shutdowns of the federal government—the media's interpretation of events forced the Republicans to back down and agree to a budget on Clinton's terms. At the beginning of the crisis, congressional Republicans, led by then-House Speaker Newt Gingrich, were confident that they could compel Clinton to accept their budget, which called for substantial cuts in domestic social programs. Republicans calculated that Clinton would fear being blamed for lengthy government shutdowns and would quickly accede to their demands, and that once Americans saw that life went on with government agencies closed, they would support the Republicans in asserting that the United States could get along with less government.

framing The power of the media to influence how events and issues are interpreted.

For the most part, however, the media did not cooperate with the GOP's plans. Media coverage of the several government shutdowns during this period emphasized the hardships imposed upon federal workers who were being furloughed in the weeks before Christmas. Indeed, Speaker Gingrich, who was generally portrayed as the villain who caused the crisis, came to be called the "Gin*grinch*" who stole Christmas from the children of hundreds of thousands of federal workers. Rather than suggest that the shutdown demonstrated that America could carry on with less government, media accounts focused on the difficulties encountered by Washington tourists unable to visit the capital's monuments, museums, and galleries. The woes of American travelers whose passports were delayed were given considerable attention. This sort of coverage

Analyzing American Politics
www.wwnorton.com/lowi7/ch13
Analyze the effects of media framing.

eventually convinced most Americans that the government shutdown was bad for the country. In the end, Gingrich and the congressional Republicans were forced to surrender and to accept a new budget reflecting many of Clinton's priorities. The Republicans' defeat in the budget showdown contributed to the unraveling of the GOP's legislative program and, ultimately, to the Republicans' poor showing in the 1996 presidential elections. The character of media coverage of an event thus had enormous repercussions of how Americans interpreted it.

In 2001, the Bush White House especially recognized the importance of framing when presidential aides held extensive discussions with television networks and Hollywood filmmakers about the portrayal of America's war on terriorism. The White House asked the media to sound a patriotic note and frame the war as a patriotic duty. By all accounts the media responded favorably, especially after several network news anchors became the targets of anthrax-laden letters that were possibly sent by terrorists.

Media Coverage of Elections and Government   The media's agenda-setting and framing powers may often determine how people perceive political candidates. In 1968, despite the growing strength of the opposition to his Vietnam War policies, the incumbent president, Lyndon Johnson, won two-thirds of the votes cast in New Hampshire's Democratic presidential primary. His rival, Senator Eugene McCarthy, received less than one-third. The broadcast media, however, declared the outcome to have been a great victory for McCarthy, who was said to have done much better than "expected" (or at least expected by the media). His "defeat" in New Hampshire was one of the factors that persuaded Johnson to withdraw from the 1968 presidential race.

The media also have a good deal of power to shape popular perceptions of politicians and political leaders. Most citizens will never meet Bill Clinton or Al Gore or George W. Bush. Popular perceptions and evaluations of these individuals are often based solely upon their media images. Obviously, through public relations and other techniques, politicians seek to cultivate favorable media images. But the media have a good deal of discretion over how individuals are portrayed or how they are allowed to portray themselves.

In the case of political candidates, the media have considerable influence over whether or not a particular individual will receive public attention, whether or not a particular individual will be taken seriously as a viable contender, and whether the public will perceive a candidate's performance favorably. Thus, if the media find a candidate interesting, they may treat him or her as a serious contender even though the facts of the matter seem to suggest otherwise. In a similar vein, the media may declare that a candidate has "momentum," a mythical property that the media confer upon candidates they admire. Momentum has no substantive meaning—it is simply a media prediction that a particular candidate will do even better in the future than in the past. Such media prophecies can become self-fulfilling as contributors and supporters jump on the bandwagon of the candidate possessing this "momentum." In 1992, when Bill Clinton's poll standings surged in the wake of the Democratic National Convention, the media determined that

Clinton had enormous momentum. In fact, nothing that happened during the remainder of the race led the media to change its collective judgment. In 1996, the national media portrayed Bob Dole's candidacy as hopeless almost from the very beginning. Coverage of the Republican convention and the presidential debates emphasized Clinton's "insurmountable" lead. The media's coverage of Dole's campaign became a self-fulfilling prophecy of his defeat.

During the 2000 presidential contest, the national media initially accepted Republican candidate George W. Bush's claim that his nomination was a foregone conclusion. At first, their consensus made it difficult for Bush's rivals to attract support or raise money, thus forcing other candidates, such as Elizabeth Dole, out of the race.[26] However, Senator John McCain of Arizona was able to use his Senate committee chairmanship to raise enough money to mount a challenge. In reality, McCain had little chance of defeating the front-runner, but seeing the possibility of a "horse race," the media gave McCain a great deal of generally positive coverage and helped him mount a noisy, if brief, challenge. McCain's hopes were dashed, though, when he was trounced by Bush in a series of primaries, including those in South Carolina and other GOP strongholds.

At the same time that the media were promoting McCain's candidacy, the networks and major newspapers were questioning Democratic Vice President Al Gore's status as a front-runner for the Democratic nomination even though Gore seemed to have as strong an early lead on the Democratic side as Bush did on the Republican side. When former New Jersey senator Bill Bradley announced his candidacy, the national media gave close attention to what was now deemed to be a horse race between the two men. Daily articles throughout 1999 declared one or the other to be gaining or losing momentum even though the race had barely begun. This horse-race coverage helped Bradley attract money and support and temporarily turned what had seemed a futile effort into a real contest, which Gore won handily.

The media's power to shape images is not absolute. Throughout the last decade, politicians implemented new techniques for communicating with the public and shaping their own images. For instance, Bill Clinton pioneered the use of town meetings and television entertainment programs as means for communicating directly with voters in the 1992 election. During the 2000 presidential race between Bush and Gore, both candidates made use of town meetings, as well as talk shows and entertainment programs like *The Oprah Winfrey Show*, *The Tonight Show with Jay Leno*, and *Saturday Night Live*, to reach mass audiences. During a town meeting, talk show, or entertainment program, politicians are free to craft their own images without interference from journalists.

In 2000, George W. Bush was also able to shape his image by effectively courting the press through informal interaction. Bush's "charm offensive" was successful. Journalists concluded that Bush was a nice fellow, if inexperienced, and refrained from subjecting him to harsh criticism and close scrutiny. Al Gore,

---

[26]William S. Klein, "Inside the Spin Machine: How Political News Is Made," *Washington Post*, 8 August 1999, p. B4.

on the other hand, seemed to offend journalists by remaining aloof and giving an impression of disdain for the press. Journalists responded by portraying Gore as "stiff." The result was unusually positive coverage for the Republican candidate and unusually negative coverage for the Democratic candidate.

During the Florida post-election battle in 2000, Bush and Gore fought to frame the story in very different ways. Gore forces asserted that the real story concerned a failure on the part of Florida authorities to make certain that every vote had been counted. Bush supporters, on the other hand, argued that the real story involved a Democratic effort to count the same votes again and again until Gore got the result he wanted. Thus, in their media appearances, Democrats continually reiterated the message that every vote must be counted while Republicans repeated the refrain that every vote had been counted many times. For emphasis, Republicans created placards that parodied the Democrats' Gore/Lieberman posters. In the GOP's version, the placards, frequently waved before the cameras, read Sore/Loserman.

In 2001, newly elected President Bush sought to present his plan for a large tax cut as an effort to give money back to the American people as well as to stimulate the lagging U.S. economy. Democrats, on the other hand, tried to portray Bush's initiative as threatening to produce deficits while serving the interests of wealthy Americans at the expense of the middle class. Each side mobilized evidence and experts in an effort to influence the way the media would frame the story. The result was a standoff. Liberal newspapers like the *New York Times* presented analyses suggesting that the major beneficiaries of Bush's proposals would be the richest 1 percent of Americans. Moderate and conservative papers, however, framed the story in a way more consistent with Bush's view of the tax plan.

In general, because politicians, interest groups, and others seeking positive news coverage know that the media look for drama and entertainment value, they will typically seek to package their message in a format that the media will deem interesting, controversial, or entertaining. The federal agency most adept at using the media to burnish its image and strengthen its claim on tax dollars is the National Aeronautics and Space Administration (NASA). In recent years, NASA has initiated a number of projects of dubious scientific value but high news appeal. For example, NASA sent former astronaut turned senator John Glenn on a space mission for no reason other than the enormous publicity that Glenn's dramatic return to space would produce. Of course, one NASA publicity effort, sending a teacher into space, ended in tragedy with the explosion of the *Challenger* spacecraft in 1986.

The Rise of Adversarial Journalism

The political power of the news media has increased greatly in recent years through the growing prominence of "adversarial journalism"—a form of journalism in which the media adopt a hostile posture toward the government and public officials.

During the nineteenth century, American newspapers were completely subordinate to the political parties. Newspapers depended on official patronage—legal notice and party subsidies—for their financial survival and were controlled by party leaders. (A vestige of that era survived into the twentieth century in such newspaper names as the *Springfield Republican* and the *St. Louis Globe-Democrat*.) At the turn of the century, with the development of commercial advertising, newspapers became financially independent. This made possible the emergence of a formally nonpartisan press.

Presidents were the first national officials to see the opportunities in this development. By communicating directly to the electorate through newspapers and magazines, Theodore Roosevelt and Woodrow Wilson established political constituencies independent of party organizations and strengthened their own power relative to Congress. President Franklin Roosevelt used the radio, most notably in his famous fireside chats, to reach out to voters and to make himself the center of American politics. FDR was also adept at developing close personal relationships with reporters, which enabled him to obtain favorable news coverage despite the fact that in his day a majority of newspaper owners and publishers were staunch conservatives. Following Roosevelt's example, subsequent presidents have sought to use the media to enhance their popularity and power. For example, through televised news conferences, President John F. Kennedy mobilized public support for his domestic and foreign policy initiatives.

During the 1950s and early 1960s, a few members of Congress also made successful use of the media—especially television—to mobilize national support for their causes. Senator Estes Kefauver of Tennessee became a major contender for the presidency and won a place on the 1956 Democratic national ticket as a result of his dramatic televised hearings on organized crime. Senator Joseph McCarthy of Wisconsin made himself a powerful national figure through his well-publicized investigations of alleged Communist infiltration of key American institutions. These senators, however, were more exceptional than typical. Through the mid-1960s, the executive branch continued to generate the bulk of news coverage, and the media served as a cornerstone of presidential power.

The Vietnam War shattered this relationship between the press and the presidency. During the early stages of U.S. involvement, American officials in Vietnam who disapproved of the way the war was being conducted leaked information critical of administrative policy to reporters. Publication of this material infuriated the White House, which pressured publishers to block its release; on one occasion, President Kennedy went so far as to ask the *New York Times* to reassign its Saigon correspondent. The national print and broadcast media discovered, however, that there was an audience for critical coverage among segments of the public skeptical of administration policy. As the Vietnam conflict dragged on, critical media coverage fanned antiwar sentiment. Moreover, growing opposition to the war among liberals encouraged some members of Congress, most notably Senator J. William Fulbright, chair of the Senate Foreign Relations Committee, to break with the president. In turn, these shifts in popular and congressional sentiment emboldened journalists and publishers to continue to present critical news reports. Through this process, journalists developed a commitment to adversarial journalism, while a constituency emerged that would rally to the defense of the media when it came under White House attack.

 History Principle

The Vietnam War shattered the favorable relationship that existed between the news media and elected leaders.

This pattern, established during the Vietnam War, endured through the 1970s and into the present. Political forces opposed to presidential policies, many members of Congress, and the national news media began to find that their interests often overlapped. Of course, in October 2001, this adversarial relationship was suspended temporarily when the media became more supportive of the government's efforts to combat global terrorism. However, the media did remain critical toward the government's handling of the anthrax scare.

For their part, aggressive use of the techniques of investigation, publicity, and exposure allowed the national media to enhance their autonomy and carve out a prominent place for themselves in American government and politics. The power derived by the press from adversarial journalism is one reason the media seem to relish opportunities to attack political institutions and to publish damaging information about important public officials. Increasingly, media coverage has come to influence politicians' careers, the mobilization of political constituencies, and the fate of issues and causes.

MEDIA POWER AND RESPONSIBILITY

The free media are absolutely essential to democratic government. We depend upon the media to investigate wrongdoing, to publicize and explain governmental actions, to evaluate programs and politicians, and to bring to light matters that might otherwise be known only to a handful of governmental insiders. In short, without free and active media, popular government would be virtually impossible. Citizens would have few means through which to know or assess the government's actions—other than the claims or pronouncements of the government itself. Moreover, without active—indeed, aggressive—media, citizens would be hard pressed to make informed choices among competing candidates at the polls. Often enough, the media reveal discrepancies between candidates' claims and their actual records, and between the images that candidates seek to project and the underlying realities.

At the same time, the increasing decay of party organizations (see Chapter 11) has made politicians ever more dependent upon favorable media coverage. National political leaders and journalists have had symbiotic relationships, at least since FDR's presidency, but initially politicians were the senior partners. They benefited from media publicity, but they were not totally dependent upon it so long as they could still rely upon party organizations to mobilize votes. Journalists, on the other hand, depended upon their relationships with politicians for access to information, and would hesitate to report stories that might antagonize valuable sources. Newsmen feared exclusion from the flow of information in retaliation. Thus, for example, reporters did not publicize potentially embarrassing information, widely known in Washington, about the personal lives of such figures as Franklin Roosevelt and John F. Kennedy.

With the decline of party, the balance of power between politicians and journalists has been reversed. Now that politicians have become heavily dependent

History Principle

The increasing decay of party organizations over the past fifty years has made politicians more dependent on the media.

Rationality Principle	Collective Action Principle	Institution Principle	Policy Principle	History Principle
Media coverage can be analyzed in terms of the interests of members of the media, politicians, and consumers.				The Vietnam War shattered the favorable relationship that existed between the news media and elected leaders.
The goals and incentives of journalists—such as ratings, career success, and prestige—influence what is created and reported as news.				The increasing decay of party organizations over the past fifty years has made politicians more dependent on the media.
News coverage is influenced by the interests of politicians.				
Consumer preferences, such as those of the affluent or those of people who watch news for its entertainment value, influence news content.				

upon the media to reach their constituents, journalists no longer need fear that their access to information can be restricted in retaliation for negative coverage.

Freedom gives the media enormous power. The media can make or break reputations, help to launch or to destroy political careers, and build support for or rally opposition against programs and institutions.[27] Wherever there is so much power, there exists at least the potential for its abuse or overly zealous use. All things considered, free media are so critically important to the maintenance of a democratic society that we must be prepared to take the risk that the media will occasionally abuse their power. The forms of governmental control that would prevent the media from misusing their power would also certainly destroy our freedom.

Institutional Reform
www.wwnorton.com/
lowi7/ch13
What forms of
media regulation
are permissible?

[27]See Martin Linsky, *Impact: How the Press Affects Federal Policymaking* (New York: W. W. Norton, 1986).

SUMMARY

The American news media are among the world's most free. The print and broadcast media regularly present information and opinions critical of the government, political leaders, and policies.

The media help to determine the agenda or focus of political debate in the United States, to shape popular understanding of political events and results, and to influence popular judgments of politicians and leaders.

Over the past century, the media have helped to nationalize American political perspectives. Media coverage is influenced by the perspectives of journalists, politicians, and upscale audiences. The attention that the media give to protest and conflict is also a function of audience factors.

Free media are an essential ingredient of popular government.

FOR FURTHER READING

Cook, Timothy. *Making Laws and Making News: Media Strategies in the House of Representatives.* Washington, DC: Brookings Institution, 1989.

Gans, Herbert. *Deciding What's News.* New York: Pantheon, 1979.

Graber, Doris. *Mass Media and American Politics*, 6th ed. Washington, DC: Congressional Quarterly Press, 2001.

Hallin, Daniel C. *The Uncensored War.* Berkeley and Los Angeles: University of California Press, 1986.

Hart, Roderick. *Seducing America: How Television Charms the Modern Voter.* New York: Oxford University Press, 1994.

Hess, Stephen. *Live From Capitol Hill: Studies of Congress and the Media.* Washington, DC: Brookings Institution, 1991.

Nacos, Brigitte L. *The Press, Presidents and Crises.* New York: Columbia University Press, 1990.

Owen, Diana. *Media Messages in American Presidential Elections.* Westport, CT: Greenwood, 1991.

Spitzer, Robert J., ed. *Media and Public Policy.* Westport, CT: Praeger, 1993.

West, Darrell. *Air Wars: Television Advertising in Election Campaigns, 1952–2000*, 3rd ed. Washington, DC: Congressional Quarterly Press, 2001.

Winfield, Betty Houchin. *FDR and the News Media.* Urbana: University of Illinois Press, 1990.

Appendix

The Declaration of Independence

In Congress, July 4, 1776

When in the course of human events, it becomes necessary for one people to dissolve the political bands which have connected them with another, and to assume among the Powers of the earth, the separate and equal station to which the Laws of Nature and of Nature's God entitle them, a decent respect to the opinions of mankind requires that they should declare the causes which impel them to the separation.

We hold these truths to be self-evident, that all men are created equal, that they are endowed by their Creator with certain unalienable rights, that among these are Life, Liberty, and the pursuit of Happiness. That to secure these rights, Governments are instituted among Men, deriving their just powers from the consent of the governed. That whenever any Form of Government becomes destructive of these ends, it is the Right of the People to alter or to abolish it, and to institute new Government, laying its foundation on such principles and organizing its powers in such form, as to them shall seem most likely to effect their Safety and Happiness. Prudence, indeed, will dictate that Governments long established should not be changed for light and transient causes; and accordingly all experience hath shown, that mankind are more disposed to suffer, while evils are sufferable, than to right themselves by abolishing the forms to which they are accustomed. But when a long train of abuses and usurpations, pursuing invariably the same Object evinces a design to reduce them under absolute Despotism, it is their right, it is their duty, to throw off such Government, and to provide new Guards for their future security.— Such has been the patient sufferance of these Colonies; and such is now the necessity which constrains them to alter their former Systems of Government. The history of the present King of Great Britain is a history of repeated injuries and usurpations, all having in direct object the establishment of an absolute Tyranny over these States. To prove this, let Facts be submitted to a candid world.

He has refused his Assent to Laws, the most wholesome and necessary for the public good.

He has forbidden his Governors to pass Laws of immediate and pressing importance, unless suspended in their operation till his Assent should be obtained; and when so suspended, he has utterly neglected to attend to them.

He has refused to pass other Laws for the accommodation of large districts of people, unless those people would relinquish the right of Representation in the Legislature, a right inestimable to them and formidable to tyrants only.

He has called together legislative bodies at places unusual, uncomfortable, and distant from the depository of their public Records, for the sole purpose of fatiguing them into compliance with his measures.

He has dissolved Representative Houses repeatedly, for opposing with manly firmness his invasions on the rights of the people.

He has refused for a long time, after such dissolutions, to cause others to be elected; whereby the Legislative powers, incapable of Annihilation, have returned to the People at large for their exercise; the State remaining in the mean time exposed to all dangers of invasion from without, and convulsions within.

He has endeavored to prevent the population of these States; for that purpose obstructing the Laws of Naturalization of Foreigners; refusing to pass others to encourage their migrations hither, and raising the conditions of new Appropriations of Lands.

He has obstructed the Administration of Justice, by refusing his Assent to Laws for establishing Judiciary powers.

He has made Judges dependent on his Will alone, for the tenure of their offices, and the amount and payment of their salaries.

He has erected a multitude of New Offices, and sent hither swarms of Officers to harass our People, and eat out their substance.

He has kept among us, in times of peace, Standing Armies without the Consent of our legislature.

He has affected to render the Military independent of and superior to the Civil Power.

He has combined with others to subject us to a jurisdiction foreign to our constitution, and unacknowledged by our laws; giving his Assent to their Acts of pretended Legislation:

For quartering large bodies of armed troops among us:

For protecting them, by a mock Trial, from Punishment for any Murders which they should commit on the Inhabitants of these States:

For cutting off our Trade with all parts of the world:

For imposing taxes on us without our Consent:

For depriving us in many cases, of the benefits of Trial by jury:

For transporting us beyond Seas to be tried for pretended offences:

For abolishing the free System of English Laws in a neighboring Province, establishing therein an Arbitrary government, and enlarging its Boundaries so as to render it at once an example and fit instrument for introducing the same absolute rule into these Colonies:

For taking away our Charters, abolishing our most valuable Laws, and altering fundamentally the Forms of our Governments:

For suspending our own Legislatures, and declaring themselves invested with Power to legislate for us in all cases whatsoever.

He has abdicated Government here, by declaring us out of his Protection and waging War against us.

He has plundered our seas, ravaged our Coasts, burnt our towns, and destroyed the lives of our people.

He is at this time transporting large armies of foreign mercenaries to compleat the works of death, desolation, and tyranny, already begun with circumstances of Cruelty & perfidy scarcely paralleled in the most barbarous ages, and totally unworthy the Head of a civilized nation.

He has constrained our fellow Citizens taken Captive on the high Seas to bear Arms against their Country, to become the executioners of their friends and Brethren, or to fall themselves by their Hands.

He has excited domestic insurrections amongst us, and has endeavored to bring on the inhabitants of our frontiers, the merciless Indian Savages, whose known rule of warfare, is an undistinguished destruction of all ages, sexes, and conditions.

In every stage of these Oppressions We have Petitioned for Redress in the most humble terms: Our repeated Petitions have been answered only by repeated injury. A Prince, whose character is thus marked by every act which may define a Tyrant, is unfit to be the ruler of a free people.

Nor have We been wanting in attention to our British brethren. We have warned them from time to time of attempts by their legislature to extend an unwarrantable jurisdiction over us. We have reminded them of the circumstances of our emigration and settlement here. We have appealed to their native justice and magnanimity, and we have conjured them by the ties of our common kindred to disavow these usurpations, which, would inevitably interrupt our connections and correspondence. They too must have been deaf to the voice of justice and of consanguinity. We must, therefore, acquiesce in the necessity, which denounces our Separation, and hold them, as we hold the rest of mankind, Enemies in War, in Peace Friends.

WE, THEREFORE, the Representatives of the UNITED STATES OF AMERICA, in General Congress, Assembled, appealing to the Supreme Judge of the world for the rectitude of our intentions, do, in the Name, and by Authority of the good People of these Colonies, solemnly publish and declare, That these United Colonies are, and of Right ought to be FREE AND INDEPENDENT STATES; that they are Absolved from all Allegiance to the British Crown, and that all political connection between them and the State of Great Britain, is and ought to be totally dissolved; and that as Free and Independent States, they have full Power to levy War, conclude Peace, contract Alliances, establish Commerce, and to do all other Acts and Things which Independent States may of right do. And for the support of this Declaration, with a firm reliance on the Protection of Divine Providence, we mutually pledge to each other our Lives, our Fortunes, and our sacred Honor.

The foregoing Declaration was, by order of Congress, engrossed, and signed by the following members:

John Hancock

NEW HAMPSHIRE	MASSACHUSETTS BAY	RHODE ISLAND
Josiah Bartlett	*Samuel Adams*	*Stephen Hopkins*
William Whipple	*John Adams*	*William Ellery*
Matthew Thornton	*Robert Treat Paine*	
	Elbridge Gerry	

CONNECTICUT
Roger Sherman
Samuel Huntington
William Williams
Oliver Wolcott

NEW YORK
William Floyd
Philip Livingston
Francis Lewis
Lewis Morris

NEW JERSEY
Richard Stockton
John Witherspoon
Francis Hopkinson
John Hart
Abraham Clark

PENNSYLVANIA
Robert Morris
Benjamin Rush
Benjamin Franklin
John Morton
George Clymer
James Smith
George Taylor
James Wilson
George Ross

DELAWARE
Caesar Rodney
George Read
Thomas M'Kean

MARYLAND
Samuel Chase
William Paca
Thomas Stone
Charles Carroll,
  of Carrollton

VIRGINIA
George Wythe
Richard Henry Lee
Thomas Jefferson
Benjamin Harrison
Thomas Nelson, Jr.
Francis Lightfoot Lee
Carter Braxton

NORTH CAROLINA
William Hooper
Joseph Hewes
John Penn

SOUTH CAROLINA
Edward Rutledge
Thomas Heyward, Jr.
Thomas Lynch, Jr.
Arthur Middleton

GEORGIA
Button Gwinnett
Lyman Hall
George Walton

Resolved, That copies of the Declaration be sent to the several assemblies, conventions, and committees, or councils of safety, and to the several commanding officers of the continental troops; that it be proclaimed in each of the United States, at the head of the army.

The Articles of Confederation

Agreed to by Congress November 15, 1777; ratified and in force
March 1, 1781

To all whom these Presents shall come, we the undersigned Delegates of the States affixed to our Names send greeting. Whereas the Delegates of the United States of America in Congress assembled did on the fifteenth day of November in the Year of our Lord One Thousand Seven Hundred and Seventy seven, and in the Second Year of the Independence of America agree to certain articles of Confederation and perpetual Union between the States of Newhampshire, Massachusetts-bay, Rhodeisland and Providence Plantations, Connecticut, New-York, New-Jersey, Pennsylvania, Delaware, Maryland, Virginia, North-Carolina, South-Carolina and Georgia in the Words following, viz. "Articles of Confederation and perpetual Union between the states of Newhampshire, Massachusetts-bay, Rhodeisland and Providence Plantations, Connecticut, New-York, New-Jersey, Pennsylvania, Delaware, Maryland, Virginia, North-Carolina, South-Carolina and Georgia.

Art. I. The Stile of this confederacy shall be "The United States of America."

Art. II. Each state retains its sovereignty, freedom and independence, and every Power, Jurisdiction and right, which is not by this confederation expressly delegated to the United States, in Congress assembled.

Art. III. The said states hereby severally enter into a firm league of friendship with each other, for their common defence, the security of their Liberties, and their mutual and general welfare, binding themselves to assist each other, against all force offered to, or attacks made upon them, or any of them, on account of religion, sovereignty, trade, or any other pretence whatever.

Art. IV. The better to secure and perpetuate mutual friendship and intercourse among the people of the different states in this union, the free inhabitants of each of these states, paupers, vagabonds and fugitives from Justice excepted, shall be entitled to all privileges and immunities of free citizens in the several states; and the people of each state shall have free ingress and regress to and from any other state, and shall enjoy therein all the privileges of trade and commerce, subject to the same duties, impositions and restrictions as the inhabitants thereof respectively, provided that such restriction shall not extend so far as to prevent the removal of property imported into any state, to any other state of which the Owner is an inhabitant; provided also that no imposition, duties or restriction shall be laid by any state, on the property of the united states, or either of them.

If any Person guilty of, or charged with treason, felony, or other high misdemeanor in any state, shall flee from Justice, and be found in any of the united states, he shall upon demand of the Governor or executive power, of the state from which he fled, be delivered up and removed to the state having jurisdiction of his offence.

Full faith and credit shall be given in each of these states to the records, acts and judicial proceedings of the courts and magistrates of every other state.

Art. V. For the more convenient management of the general interests of the united states, delegates shall be annually appointed in such manner as the legislature of each state shall direct, to meet in Congress on the first Monday in November, in every year, with a power reserved to each state, to recall its delegates, or any of them, at any time within the year, and to send others in their stead, for the remainder of the Year.

No state shall be represented in Congress by less than two, nor by more than seven Members; and no person shall be capable of being a delegate for more than three years in any term of six years; nor shall any person, being a delegate, be capable of holding any office under the united states, for which he, or another for his benefit receives any salary, fees or emolument of any kind.

Each state shall maintain its own delegates in a meeting of the states, and while they act as members of the committee of the states.

In determining questions in the united states, in Congress assembled, each state shall have one vote.

Freedom of speech and debate in Congress shall not be impeached or questioned in any Court, or place out of Congress, and the members of congress shall be protected in their persons from arrests and imprisonments, during the time of their going to and from, and attendance on congress, except for treason, felony, or breach of the peace.

Art. VI. No state without the Consent of the united states in congress assembled, shall send any embassy to, or receive any embassy from, or enter into any conference, agreement, or alliance or treaty with any King, prince or state; nor shall any person holding any office or profit or trust under the united states, or any of them, accept of any present, emolument, office or title of any kind whatever from any king, prince or foreign state; nor shall the united states in congress assembled, or any of them, grant any title of nobility.

No two or more states shall enter into any treaty, confederation or alliance whatever between them, without the consent of the united states in congress assembled, specifying accurately the purposes for which the same is to be entered into, and how long it shall continue.

No state shall lay any imposts or duties, which may interfere with any stipulations in treaties, entered into by the united states in congress assembled, with any king, prince or state, in pursuance of any treaties already proposed by congress, to the courts of France and Spain.

No vessels of war shall be kept up in time of peace by any state, except such number only, as shall be deemed necessary by the united states in congress assembled, for the defence of such state, or its trade; nor shall any body of forces be kept up by any state, in time of peace, except such number only, as in the judgment of the united states, in congress assembled, shall be deemed requisite to garrison the forts necessary for the defence of such state; but every state shall always keep up a well regulated and disciplined militia, sufficiently armed and accoutred, and shall provide and constantly have ready for use, in public stores, a due number of field pieces and tents, and a proper quantity of arms, ammunition and camp equipage.

No state shall engage in any war without the consent of the united states in congress assembled, unless such state be actually invaded by enemies, or shall have received certain advice of a resolution being formed by some nation of Indians to invade such state, and the danger is so imminent as not to admit of a delay, till the united states in congress asssembled can be consulted; nor shall any state grant commissions to any ships or vessels of war, nor letters of marque or reprisal, except it be after a declaration of war by the united states in congress assembled, and then only against the kingdom or state and the subjects thereof, against which war has been so declared, and under such regulations as shall be established by the united states in congress assembled, unless such state be infested by pirates; in which case vessels of war may be fitted out for that occasion, and kept so long as the danger shall continue, or until the united states in congress assembled shall determine otherwise.

Art. VII. When land-forces are raised by any state for the common defence, all officers of or under the rank of colonel, shall be appointed by the legislature of each state respectively by whom such forces shall be raised, or in such manner as such state shall direct, and all vacancies shall be filled up by the state which first made the appointment.

Art. VIII. All charges of war, and all other expences that shall be incurred for the common defence or general welfare, and allowed by the united states in congress assembled, shall be defrayed out of a common treasury, which shall be supplied by the several states, in proportion to the value of all land within each state, granted to or surveyed for any Person, as such land and the buildings and improvements thereon shall be estimated according to such mode as the united states in congress assembled, shall from time to time direct and appoint. The taxes for paying that proportion shall be laid and levied by the authority and direction of the legislatures of the several states within the time agreed upon by the united states in congress assembled.

Art. IX. The united states in congress assembled, shall have the sole and exclusive right and power of determining on peace and war, except in the cases mentioned in the sixth article—of sending and receiving ambassadors—entering into treaties and alliances, provided that no treaty of commerce shall be made whereby the legislative power of the respective states shall be restrained from imposing such imposts and duties on foreigners, as their own people are subjected to, or from prohibiting the exportation of any species of goods or commodities whatsoever—of establishing rules for deciding in all cases, what captures on land or water shall be legal, and in what manner prizes taken by land or naval forces in the service of the united states shall be divided or appropriated—of granting letters of marque and reprisal in times of peace—appointing courts for the trial of piracies and felonies committed on the high seas and establishing courts for receiving and determining finally appeals in all cases of captures, provided that no member of congress shall be appointed a judge of any of the said courts.

The united states in congress assembled shall also be the last resort on appeal in all disputes and differences now subsisting or that hereafter may arise between two or more states concerning boundary, jurisdiction or any other cause whatever; which authority shall always be exercised in the manner following. Whenever the legislative or executive authority or lawful agent of any state in controversy with another shall present a petition to congress stating the matter in question and praying for a hearing, notice thereof shall be given by order of congress to the legislative or executive authority of the other state in controversy, and a day assigned for the appearance of the parties by their lawful agents, who shall then be directed to appoint by joint consent, commissioners or judges to constitute a court for hearing and determining the matter in question: but if they cannot agree, congress shall name three persons out of each of the united states, and from the list of such persons each party shall alternately strike out one, the petitioners beginning, until the number shall be reduced to thirteen; and from that number not less than seven, nor more than nine names as congress shall direct, shall in the presence of congress be drawn out by lot, and the persons whose names shall be so drawn or any five of them, shall be commissioners or judges, to hear and finally determine the controversy, so always as a major part of the judges who shall hear the cause shall agree in the determination: and if either party shall neglect to attend at the day appointed, without shewing reasons, which congress shall judge sufficient, or being present shall refuse to strike, the congress shall proceed to nominate three persons out of each state, and the secretary of congress shall strike in behalf of such party absent or refusing; and the judgment and sentence of the court to be appointed, in the manner before prescribed, shall be final and conclusive; and if any of the parties shall refuse to submit to the authority of such court, or to appear to defend their claim or cause, the court shall nevertheless proceed to pronounce sentence, or judgment, which shall in like manner be final and decisive, the judgment or sentence and other proceedings being in either case transmitted to congress, and lodged among the acts of congress for the security of the parties concerned: provided that every commissioner, before he sits in judgment, shall take an oath to be administered by one of the judges of the supreme or superior court of the state, where the cause shall be tried, "well and truly to hear and determine the matter in question, according to the best of his judgment, without favour, affection or hope of reward:" provided also that no state shall be deprived of territory for the benefit of the united states.

All controversies concerning the private right of soil claimed under different grants of two or more states, whose jurisdictions as they may respect such lands, and the states which passed such grants are adjusted, the said grants or either of them being at the same time claimed to have originated antecedent to such settlement of jurisdiction, shall on the petition of either party to the congress of the united states, be finally determined as near as may be in the same manner as is before prescribed for deciding disputes respecting territorial jurisdiction between different states.

The united states in congress assembled shall also have the sole and exclusive right and power of regulating the alloy and value of coin struck by their own authority, or by that of the respective states—fixing the standard of weights and measures throughout the united states—regulating the trade and managing all affairs with the

Indians, not members of any of the states, provided that the legislative right of any state within its own limits be not infringed or violated—establishing and regulating post-offices from one state to another, throughout all the united states, and exacting such postage on the papers passing thro' the same as may be requisite to defray the expences of the said office—appointing all officers of the land forces, in the service of the united states, except regimental officers—appointing all the officers of the united states—making rules for the government and regulation of the said land and naval forces, and directing their operations.

The united states in congress assembled shall have the authority to appoint a committee, to sit in the recess of congress, to be denominated "A Committee of the States," and to consist of one delegate from each state; and to appoint such other committees and civil officers as may be necessary for managing the general affairs of the united states under their direction—to appoint one of their number to preside, provided that no person be allowed to serve in the office of president more than one year in any term of three years; to ascertain the necessary sums of Money to be raised for the service of the united states, and to appropriate and apply the same for defraying the public expences—to borrow money, or emit bills on the credit of the united states, transmitting every half year to the respective states an account of the sums of money so borrowed or emitted,—to build and equip a navy—to agree upon the number of land forces, and to make requisitions from each state for its quota, in proportion to the number of white inhabitants in such state; which requisition shall be binding, and thereupon the legislature of each state shall appoint the regimental officers, raise the men and cloath, arm and equip them in a soldier like manner, at the expence of the united states, and the officers and men so cloathed, armed and equipped shall march to the place appointed, and within the time agreed on by the united states in congress assembled: But if the united states in congress assembled shall, on consideration of circumstances judge proper that any state should not raise men, or should raise a smaller number than its quota, and that any other state should raise a greater number of men than the quota thereof, such extra number shall be raised, officered, cloathed, armed and equipped in the same manner as the quota of such state, unless the legislature of such state shall judge that such extra number cannot be safely spared out of the same, in which case they shall raise, officer, cloath, arm and equip as many of such extra number as they judge can be safely spared. And the officers and men so cloathed, armed and equipped, shall march to the place appointed, and within the time agreed on by the united states in congress assembled.

The united states in congress assembled shall never engage in a war, nor grant letters of marque and reprisal in time of peace, nor enter into any treaties or alliances, nor coin money, nor regulate the value thereof, nor ascertain the sums and expences necessary for the defence and welfare of the united states, or any of them, nor emit bills, nor borrow money on the credit of the united states, nor appropriate money, nor agree upon the number of vessels of war, to be built or purchased, or the number of land or sea forces to be raised, nor appoint a commander in chief of the army or navy, unless nine states assent to the same: nor shall a question on any other point, except for adjourning from day to day be determined, unless by the votes of a majority of the united states in congress assembled.

The congress of the united states shall have power to adjourn to any time within the year, and to any place within the united states, so that no period of adjournment be for a longer duration than the space of six Months, and shall publish the Journal of their proceedings monthly, except such parts thereof relating to treaties, alliances or military operations as in their judgment require secrecy; and the yeas and nays of the delegates of each state on any question shall be entered on the Journal, when it is desired by any delegate; and the delegates of a state, or any of them, at his or their request shall be furnished with a transcript of the said Journal, except such parts as are above excepted to lay before the legislatures of the several states.

Art. X. The committee of the states, or any nine of them, shall be authorised to execute, in the recess of congress, such of the powers of congress as the united states in congress assembled, by the consent of nine states, shall from time to time think expedient to vest them with; provided that no power be delegated to the said committee, for the exercise of which, by the articles of confederation, the voice of nine states in the congress of the united states assembled is requisite.

Art. XI. Canada acceding to this confederation, and joining in the measures of the united states, shall be admitted into, and entitled to all the advantages of this union: but no other colony shall be admitted into the same, unless such admission be agreed to by nine states.

Art. XII. All bills of credit emitted, monies borrowed and debts contracted by, or under the authority of congress, before the assembling of the united states, in pursuance of the present confederation, shall be deemed and considered as a charge against the united states, for payment and satisfaction whereof the said united states and the public faith are hereby solemnly pledged.

Art. XIII. Every state shall abide by the determinations of the united states in congress assembled, on all questions which by this confederation are submitted to them. And the Articles of this confederation shall be inviolably observed by every state, and the union shall be perpetual; nor shall any alteration at any time hereafter be made in any of them; unless such alteration be agreed to in a congress of the united states, and be afterwards confirmed by the legislatures of every state.

AND WHEREAS it hath pleased the Great Governor of the World to incline the hearts of the legislatures we respectively represent in congress, to approve of, and to authorize us to ratify the said articles of confederation and perpetual union. KNOW YE that we the undersigned delegates, by virtue of the power and authority to us given for that purpose, do by these presents, in the name and in behalf of our respective constituents, fully and entirely ratify and confirm each and every of the said articles of confederation and perpetual union, and all and singular the matters and things therein contained: And we do further solemnly plight and engage the faith of our respective constituents, that they shall abide by the determination of the united states in congress assembled, on all questions, which by the said confederation are submitted to them. And that the articles thereof shall be inviolably observed by the states we respectively represent, and that the union shall be perpetual. In Witness whereof we have hereunto set our hands in Congress. Done at Philadelphia in the state of Pennsylvania the ninth Day of July in the Year of our Lord one Thousand seven Hundred and Seventy-eight and in the third year of the independence of America.

The Constitution of the United States of America

Annotated with references to The Federalist Papers

[PREAMBLE]

We the People of the United States, in Order to form a more perfect Union, establish Justice, insure domestic Tranquility, provide for the common defence, promote the general Welfare, and secure the Blessings of Liberty to ourselves and our Posterity, do ordain and establish this Constitution for the United States of America.

84 (Hamilton)

ARTICLE I

Section 1
[LEGISLATIVE POWERS]

All legislative Powers herein granted shall be vested in a Congress of the United States, which shall consist of a Senate and House of Representatives.

10, 45
(Madison)

Section 2
[HOUSE OF REPRESENTATIVES, HOW CONSTITUTED, POWER OF IMPEACHMENT]

The House of Representatives shall be composed of Members chosen every second Year by the People of the several States, and the Electors in each State shall have the Qualifications requisite for Electors of the most numerous Branch of the State Legislature.

39, 45, 52–53, 57
(Madison)

No Person shall be a Representative who shall not have attained to the Age of twenty-five Years, and been seven Years a Citizen of the United States, and who shall not, when elected, be an inhabitant of that State in which he shall be chosen.

52 (Madison)

60 (Hamilton)

Representatives and *direct Taxes*[1] shall be apportioned among the several States which may be included within this Union, according to their respective Numbers, *which shall be determined by adding to the whole Number of free Persons, including those bound to Service for a Term of Years, and excluding Indians not taxed, three-fifths of all other Persons.*[2] The actual Enumeration shall be made within three Years after the first Meeting of the Congress of the United States, and within every subsequent Term of ten Years, in such Manner as they shall by Law direct. The Number of Representatives shall not exceed one for every thirty Thousand, but

54, 58 (Madison)

[1]Modified by Sixteenth Amendment.
[2]Modified by Fourteenth Amendment.

55–56
(Madison)

each State shall have at Least one Representative; *and until such enumeration shall be made, the State of New Hampshire shall be entitled to chuse three, Massachusetts eight, Rhode-Island and Providence Plantations one, Connecticut five, New-York six, New Jersey four, Pennsylvania eight, Delaware one, Maryland six, Virginia ten, North Carolina five, South Carolina five, and Georgia three.*[3]

When vacancies happen in the Representation from any State, the Executive Authority thereof shall issue Writs of Election to fill such Vacancies.

79 (Hamilton)

The House of Representatives shall chuse their Speaker and other Officers; and shall have the sole Power of Impeachment.

Section 3
[THE SENATE, HOW CONSTITUTED, IMPEACHMENT TRIALS]

39, 45
(Madison)
60 (Hamilton)

The Senate of the United States shall be composed of two Senators from each State, *chosen by the Legislature thereof,*[4] for six Years; and each Senator shall have one Vote.

62–63
(Madison)
59, 68
(Hamilton)

Immediately after they shall be assembled in Consequence of the first Election, they shall be divided as equally as may be into three Classes. The Seats of the Senators of the first Class shall be vacated at the Expiration of the second Year, of the second Class at the Expiration of the fourth Year, and of the third Class at the Expiration of the sixth Year, so that one third may be chosen every second Year: *and if vacancies happen by Resignation, or otherwise, during the Recess of the Legislature of any State, the Executive thereof may make temporary Appointments until the next Meeting of the Legislature, which shall then fill such Vacancies.*[5]

62 (Madison)
64 (Jay)

No person shall be a Senator who shall not have attained to the Age of thirty Years, and been nine Years a Citizen of the United States, and who shall not, when elected, be an Inhabitant of that State for which he shall be chosen.

The Vice-President of the United States shall be President of the Senate, but shall have no Vote, unless they be equally divided.

The Senate shall chuse their other Officers, and also a President pro tempore, in the Absence of the Vice-President, or when he shall exercise the Office of President of the United States.

39 (Madison)
65–67, 79
(Hamilton)

The Senate shall have the sole Power to try all Impeachments. When sitting for that Purpose, they shall be on Oath or Affirmation. When the President of the United States is tried, the Chief Justice shall preside: And no Person shall be convicted without the Concurrence of two-thirds of the Members present.

84 (Hamilton)

Judgment in Cases of Impeachment shall not extend further than to removal from Office, and disqualification to hold and enjoy any Office of honor, Trust or Profit under the United States: but the Party convicted shall nevertheless be liable and subject to Indictment, Trial, Judgment and Punishment, according to Law.

[3]Temporary provision.
[4]Modified by Seventeenth Amendment.
[5]Modified by Seventeenth Amendment.

Section 4
[ELECTION OF SENATORS AND REPRESENTATIVES]

 The Times, Places and Manner of holding Elections for Senators and Representatives, shall be prescribed in each State by the Legislature thereof; but the Congress may at any time by Law make or alter such Regulations, except as to the Places of chusing Senators.

59–61 (Hamilton)

 The Congress shall assemble at least once in every Year, and such Meeting shall be on the first Monday in December, unless they shall by Law appoint a different Day.[6]

Section 5
[QUORUM, JOURNALS, MEETINGS, ADJOURNMENTS]

 Each House shall be the Judge of the Elections, Returns and Qualifications of its own Members, and a Majority of each shall constitute a Quorum to do Business; but a smaller Number may adjourn from day to day, and may be authorized to compel the Attendance of absent Members, in such Manner, and under the Penalties as each House may provide.

 Each House may determine the Rules of its Proceedings, punish its Members for disorderly Behavior, and, with the Concurrence of two-thirds, expel a Member.

 Each House shall keep a Journal of its Proceedings, and from time to time publish the same, excepting such Parts as may in their Judgment require Secrecy; and the Yeas and Nays of the Members of either House on any questions shall, at the Desire of one-fifth of the present, be entered on the Journal.

 Neither House, during the Session of Congress, shall, without the Consent of the other, adjourn for more than three days, nor to any other Place than that in which the two Houses shall be sitting.

Section 6
[COMPENSATION, PRIVILEGES, DISABILITIES]

 The Senators and Representatives shall receive a Compensation for their Services, to be ascertained by Law, and paid out of the Treasury of the United States. They shall in all Cases, except Treason, Felony and Breach of the Peace, be privileged from Arrest during their Attendance at the Session of their respective Houses, and in going to and returning from the same; and for any Speech or Debate in either House, they shall not be questioned in any other Place.

 No Senator or Representative shall, during the time for which he was elected, be appointed to any civil Office under the authority of the United States, which shall have been created, or the Emoluments whereof shall have been encreased during such time; and no Person holding any Office under the United States, shall be a Member of either House during his Continuance in Office.

55 (Madison) 76 (Hamilton)

---

[6]Modified by Twentieth Amendment.

Section 7
[PROCEDURE IN PASSING BILLS AND RESOLUTIONS]

66
(Hamilton)

All Bills for raising Revenue shall originate in the House of Representatives; but the Senate may propose or concur with Amendments as on other Bills.

69, 73
(Hamilton)

Every Bill which shall have passed the House of Representatives and the Senate, shall, before it become a Law, be presented to the President of the United States; if he approve he shall sign it, but if not he shall return it, with his Objections to that House in which it shall have originated, who shall enter the Objections at large on their Journal, and proceed to reconsider it. If after such Reconsideration two-thirds of that House shall agree to pass the Bill, it shall be sent, together with the Objections, to the other House, by which it shall likewise be reconsidered, and if approved by two-thirds of that House it shall become a Law. But in all such Cases the Votes of both Houses shall be determined by Yeas and Nays, and the Names of the Persons voting for and against the Bill shall be entered on the Journal of each House respectively. If any Bill shall not be returned by the President within ten Days (Sundays excepted) after it shall have been presented to him, the Same shall be a Law, in like Manner as if he had signed it, unless the Congress by their Adjournment prevent its Return, in which Case it shall not be a Law.

69, 73
(Hamilton)

Every Order, Resolution, or Vote to which the Concurrence of the Senate and House of Representatives may be necessary (except on a question of Adjournment) shall be presented to the President of the United States; and before the Same shall take Effect, shall be approved by him, or being disapproved by him, shall be repassed by two-thirds of the Senate and House of Representatives, according to the Rules and Limitations prescribed in the Case of a Bill.

Section 8
[POWERS OF CONGRESS]

The Congress shall have Power

30–36
(Hamilton)
41 (Madison)

To lay and collect Taxes, Duties, Imposts and Excises, to pay the Debts and provide for the common Defence and general Welfare of the United States; but all Duties, Imposts and excises shall be uniform throughout the United States;

56 (Madison)

To borrow Money on the Credit of the United States;

42, 45, 56
(Madison)

To regulate Commerce with foreign Nations, and among the several States, and with the Indian Tribes;

32 (Hamilton)

To establish an uniform Rule of Naturalization, and uniform Laws on the subject of Bankruptcies throughout the United States;

42 (Madison)

To coin Money, regulate the Value thereof, and of foreign Coin, and fix the Standard of Weights and Measures;

42 (Madison)

To provide for the Punishment of counterfeiting the Securities and current Coin of the United States;

42 (Madison)

To establish Post Offices and post Roads;

42, 43
(Madison)

To promote the Progress of Science and useful Arts, by securing for limited Times to Authors and Inventors the exclusive Right to their respective Writings and Discoveries;

81 (Hamilton)

To constitute Tribunals inferior to the supreme Court;

To define and Punish Piracies and Felonies committed on the high Seas, and Offences against the Law of Nations;

To declare War, grant Letters of Marque and Reprisal, and make Rules concerning Captures on Land and Water;

To raise and support Armies, but no Appropriation of Money to that Use shall be for a longer Term than two Years;

To provide and maintain a Navy;

To make Rules for the Government and Regulation of the land and naval forces;

To provide for calling for the Militia to execute the Laws of the Union, suppress Insurrections and repel Invasions;

To provide for organizing, arming, and disciplining, the Militia, and for governing such Part of them as may be employed in the Service of the United States, reserving to the States respectively, the Appointment of the Officers, and the Authority of training the Militia according to the discipline prescribed by Congress;

To exercise exclusive Legislation in all Cases whatsoever, over such District (not exceeding ten Miles square) as may, by Cession of particular States, and the Acceptance of Congress, become the Seat of the Government of the United States, and to exercise like Authority over all Places purchased by the Consent of the Legislature of the State in which the Same shall be, for the Erection of Forts, Magazines, Arsenals, dock-Yards, and other needful Buildings;—And

To make all Laws which shall be necessary and proper for carrying into Execution the foregoing Powers, and all other Powers vested by this Constitution in the Government of the United States, or in any Department or Officer thereof.

42 (Madison)

41 (Madison)

23, 24, 26 (Hamilton)

41 (Madison)

29 (Hamilton)

29 (Hamilton)
56 (Madison)

32 (Hamilton)
43 (Madison)

29, 33 (Hamilton)
44 (Madison)

Section 9
[SOME RESTRICTIONS ON FEDERAL POWER]

The Migration or Importation of such Persons as any of the States now existing shall think proper to admit, shall not be prohibited by the Congress prior to the Year one thousand eight hundred and eight, but a Tax or Duty may be imposed on such Importation, not exceeding ten dollars for each Person.[7]

42 (Madison)

The privilege of the Writ of *Habeas Corpus* shall not be suspended, unless when in Cases of Rebellion or Invasion the public Safety may require it.

83, 84 (Hamilton)

No Bill of Attainder or ex post facto Law shall be passed.

84 (Hamilton)

No Capitation, or other direct, Tax shall be laid, unless in Proportion to the Census or Enumeration herein before directed to be taken.[8]

No Tax or Duty shall be laid on Articles exported from any State.

No Preference shall be given by any Regulation of Commerce or Revenue to the Ports of one State over those of another; nor shall vessels bound to, or from, one State, be obliged to enter, clear, or pay Duties in another.

32 (Hamilton)

No Money shall be drawn from the Treasury, but in Consequence of Appropriations made by Law; and a regular Statement and Account of the Receipts and Expenditures of all public Money shall be published from time to time.

---

[7]Temporary provision.
[8]Modified by Sixteenth Amendment.

No Title of Nobility shall be granted by the United States: And no Person holding any Office of Profit or Trust under them, shall, without the Consent of the Congress, accept of any present, Emolument, Office or Title, of any kind whatever, from any King, Prince, or foreign State.

Section 10
[RESTRICTIONS UPON POWERS OF STATES]

No State shall enter into any Treaty, Alliance, or Confederation; grant Letters of Marque and Reprisal; coin Money; emit Bills of Credit; make any Thing but gold and silver Coin a Tender in Payment of Debts; pass any Bill of Attainder, ex post facto Law, or Law impairing the Obligation of Contracts, or grant any Title of Nobility.

No State shall, without the Consent of the Congress, lay any Imposts or Duties on Imports or Exports, except what may be absolutely necessary for executing its inspection Laws: and the net Produce of all Duties and Imposts, laid by any State on Imports or Exports, shall be for the Use of the Treasury of the United States; and all such Laws shall be subject to the Revision and Control of the Congress.

No State shall, without the Consent of Congress, lay any Duty of Tonnage, keep Troops, or Ships of War in time of Peace, enter into any Agreement or Compact with another State, or with a foreign Power, or engage in War, unless actually invaded, or in such imminent Danger as will not admit of Delay.

ARTICLE II

Section 1
[EXECUTIVE POWER, ELECTION, QUALIFICATIONS OF THE PRESIDENT]

The executive Power shall be vested in a President of the United States of America. *He shall hold his Office during the Term of four years and, together with the Vice-President, chosen for the same Term, be elected, as follows:*[9]

Each State shall appoint, in such Manner as the Legislature thereof may direct, a Number of Electors, equal to the whole Number of Senators and Representatives to which the State may be entitled in the Congress: but no Senator or Representative, or Person holding an Office of Trust or Profit under the United States, shall be appointed an Elector.

The electors shall meet in their respective States, and vote by ballot for two Persons, of whom one at least shall not be an Inhabitant of the same State with themselves. And they shall make a List of all the Persons voted for, and of the Number of Votes for each; which List they shall sign and certify, and transmit sealed to the Seat of the Government of the United States, directed to the President of the Senate. The President of the Senate shall, in the Presence of the Senate and House of Representatives, open all the Certificates, and the Votes shall then be counted. The Person having the greatest Number of Votes shall be the President, if such Number be a

---

[9]Number of terms limited to two by Twenty-second Amendment.

Majority of the whole Number of Electors appointed; and if there be more than one who have such Majority and have an equal Number of Votes, then the House of Representatives shall immediately chuse by Ballot one of them for President; and if no person have a Majority, then from the five highest on the List the said House shall in like Manner chuse the President. But in chusing the President, the Votes shall be taken by States, the Representation from each State having one Vote; A quorum for this Purpose shall consist of a Member or Members from two-thirds of the States, and a Majority of all the States shall be necessary to a Choice. In every Case, after the Choice of the President, the person having the greatest Number of Votes of the Electors shall be the Vice-President. But if there should remain two or more who have equal vote, the Senate shall chuse from them by Ballot the Vice-President.[10]

The Congress may determine the Time of chusing the Electors, and the Day on which they shall give their Votes; which Day shall be the same throughout the United States.

No Person except a natural born Citizen, or a Citizen of the United States, at the time of the Adoption of this Constitution, shall be eligible to the Office of President; neither shall any Person be eligible to that Office who shall not have attained to the Age of thirty-five Years, and been fourteen Years a Resident within the United States.   64 (Jay)

In Case of the Removal of the President from Office, or his Death, Resignation, or Inability to discharge the Powers and Duties of the said Office, the same shall devolve on the Vice-President, and the Congress may by Law provide for the Case of Removal, Death, Resignation, or Inability, both of the President and Vice-President, declaring what Officer shall then act as President, and such Officer shall act accordingly, until the Disability be removed, or a President shall be elected.

The President shall, at stated Times, receive for his Services, a Compensation, which shall neither be encreased nor diminished during the Period for which he shall have been elected, and he shall not receive within that Period any other Emolument from the United States, or any of them.   73, 79 (Hamilton)

Before he enter on the Execution of his Office, he shall take the following Oath or Affirmation:—"I do solemnly swear (or affirm) that I will faithfully execute the Office of President of the United States, and will to the best of my Ability, preserve, protect and defend the Constitution of the United States."

Section 2
[POWERS OF THE PRESIDENT]

The President shall be Commander in Chief of the Army and Navy of the United States, and of the Militia of the several States, when called into the actual Service of the United States; he may require the Opinion, in writing, of the principal Officer in each of the executive Departments, upon any Subject relating to the Duties of their respective Offices, and he shall have Power to grant Reprieves and Pardons for Offences against the United States, except in Cases of Impeachment.   69, 74 (Hamilton)

---

[10]Modified by Twelfth and Twentieth Amendments.

42 (Madison)
64 (Jay)
66, 69, 76, 77
(Hamilton)
He shall have Power, by and with the Advice and Consent of the Senate, to make Treaties, provided two-thirds of the Senators present concur; and he shall nominate, and by and with the Advice and Consent of the Senate, shall appoint Ambassadors, other public Ministers and Consuls, Judges of the Supreme Court, and all other Officers of the United States, whose Appointments are not herein otherwise provided for, and which shall be established by Law: but the Congress may by Law vest the Appointment of such inferior Officers, as they think proper, in the President alone, in the Courts of Law, or in the Heads of Departments.

67, 76
(Hamilton)
The President shall have Power to fill up all Vacancies that may happen during the Recess of the Senate, by granting Commissions which shall expire at the End of their next Session.

Section 3
[POWERS AND DUTIES OF THE PRESIDENT]

69, 77, 78
(Hamilton)
42 (Madison)
He shall from time to time give to the Congress Information of the State of the Union, and recommend to their Consideration such Measures as he shall judge necessary and expedient; he may, on extraordinary Occasions, convene both Houses, or either of them, and in Case of Disagreement between them, with Respect to the Time of Adjournment, he may adjourn them to such Time as he shall think proper; he shall receive Ambassadors and other public Ministers; he shall take Care that the Laws be faithfully executed, and shall Commission all the Officers of the United States.

Section 4
[IMPEACHMENT]

39 (Madison)
69 (Hamilton)
The President, Vice-President and all civil Officers of the United States shall be removed from Office on Impeachment for, and Conviction of, Treason, Bribery, or other high Crimes and Misdemeanors.

ARTICLE III

Section 1
[JUDICIAL POWER, TENURE OF OFFICE]

65, 78, 79, 81, 82
(Hamilton)
The judicial Power of the United States, shall be vested in one supreme Court, and in such inferior Courts as the Congress may from time to time ordain and establish. The Judges, both of the supreme and inferior Courts, shall hold their Offices during good Behavior, and shall, at stated Times, receive for their Services, a Compensation, which shall not be diminished during their Continuance in Office.

Section 2
[JURISDICTION]

80 (Hamilton)
The judicial Power shall extend to all Cases, in Law and Equity, arising under this Constitution, the Laws of the United States, and Treaties made, or which shall be made, under their Authority;—to all Cases affecting Ambassadors, other public

Ministers and Consuls;—to all Cases of admiralty and maritime Jurisdiction;—to Controversies to which the United States shall be a party;—to Controversies between two or more States;—*between a State and Citizens of another State;*—between Citizens of different States,—between Citizens of the same State claiming Lands under Grants of different States, *and between a State,* or the Citizens thereof, *and foreign States, Citizens or Subjects.*[11]

In all Cases affecting Ambassadors, other public Ministers and Consuls, and those in which a State shall be Party, the supreme Court shall have original Jurisdiction. In all the other Cases before mentioned, the supreme Court shall have appellate Jurisdiction, both as to Law and Fact, with such Exceptions, and under such Regulations as Congress shall make.

81 (Hamilton)

The Trial of all Crimes, except in Cases of Impeachment, shall be by Jury; and such Trial shall be held in the State where the said Crimes shall have been committed; but when not committed within any State, the Trial shall be at such Place or Places as the Congress may by Law have directed.

83, 84 (Hamilton)

Section 3
[TREASON, PROOF, AND PUNISHMENT]

Treason against the United States, shall consist only in levying War against them, or in adhering to their Enemies, giving them Aid and Comfort. No Person shall be convicted of Treason unless on the Testimony of two Witnesses to the same overt Act, or on Confession in open Court.

43 (Madison)
84 (Hamilton)

The Congress shall have Power to declare the Punishment of Treason, but no Attainder of Treason shall work Corruption of Blood, or Forfeiture except during the Life of the Person attained.

43 (Madison)
84 (Hamilton)

ARTICLE IV

Section 1
[FAITH AND CREDIT AMONG STATES]

Full Faith and Credit shall be given in each State to the public Acts, Records, and judicial Proceedings of every other State. And the Congress may by general Laws prescribe the Manner in which such Acts, Records and Proceedings shall be proved, and the Effect thereof.

42 (Madison)

Section 2
[PRIVILEGES AND IMMUNITIES, FUGITIVES]

The Citizens of each State shall be entitled to all Privileges and Immunities of Citizens in the several States.

80 (Hamilton)

A person charged in any State with Treason, Felony or other Crime, who shall flee from Justice, and be found in another State, shall on Demand of the executive

---

[11]Modified by Eleventh Amendment.

Authority of the State from which he fled, be delivered up to be removed to the State having Jurisdiction of the Crime.

No person held to Service or Labour in one State, under the Laws thereof, escaping into another, shall, in Consequence of any Law or Regulation therein, be discharged from such Service or Labour, but shall be delivered up on Claim of the Party to whom such Service or Labour may be due.[12]

Section 3
[ADMISSION OF NEW STATES]

43 (Madison)

New States may be admitted by the Congress into this Union; but no new State shall be formed or erected within the Jurisdiction of any other State; nor any State be formed by the Junction of two or more States, or Parts of States, without the Consent of the Legislatures of the States concerned as well as of the Congress.

43 (Madison)

The Congress shall have Power to dispose of and make all needful Rules and Regulations respecting the Territory or other Property belonging to the United States; and nothing in this Constitution shall be so construed as to Prejudice any Claims of the United States, or of any particular State.

Section 4
[GUARANTEE OF REPUBLICAN GOVERNMENT]

39, 43
(Madison)

The United States shall guarantee to every State in this Union a Republican Form of Government, and shall protect each of them against Invasion; and on Application of the Legislature, or of the Executive (when the Legislature cannot be convened) against domestic Violence.

ARTICLE V

[AMENDMENT OF THE CONSTITUTION]

39, 43
(Madison)
85 (Hamilton)

The Congress, whenever two-thirds of both Houses shall deem it necessary, shall propose Amendments to this Constitution, or, on the Application of the Legislatures of two-thirds of the several States, shall call a Convention for proposing Amendments, which, in either Case, shall be valid to all Intents and Purposes, as Part of this Constitution, when ratified by the Legislatures of three-fourths of the several States, or by Conventions in three-fourths thereof, as the one or the other Mode of Ratification may be proposed by the Congress; *Provided that no Amendment which may be made prior to the Year One thousand eight hundred and eight shall in any Manner affect the first and fourth Clauses in the Ninth Section of the first Article;*[13] and that no State, without its Consent, shall be deprived of its equal Suffrage in the Senate.

[12]Repealed by Thirteenth Amendment.
[13]Temporary provision.

The Constitution of the United States of America

ARTICLE VI

All Debts contracted and Engagements entered into, before the Adoption of this Constitution, shall be as valid against the United States under this Constitution, as under the Confederation.

43 (Madison)

This Constitution, and the Laws of the United States which shall be made in Pursuance thereof; and all Treaties made, or which shall be made, under the Authority of the United States, shall be the supreme Law of the Land; and the Judges in every State shall be bound thereby, any Thing in the Constitution or Laws of any State to the Contrary notwithstanding.

27, 33 (Hamilton) 39, 44 (Madison)

The Senators and Representatives before mentioned, and the Members of the several State Legislatures, and all executive and judicial Officers, both of the United States and of the several States, shall be bound by Oath or Affirmation, to support this Constitution; but no religious Test shall be required as a Qualification to any Office or public Trust under the United States.

27 (Hamilton) 44 (Madison)

ARTICLE VII

[RATIFICATION AND ESTABLISHMENT]

The Ratification of the Conventions of nine States, shall be sufficient for the Establishment of this Constitution between the States so ratifying the Same.[14]

39, 40, 43 (Madison)

Done in Convention by the Unanimous Consent of the States present the Seventeenth Day of September in the Year of our Lord one thousand seven hundred and Eighty seven and of the Independence of the United States of America the Twelfth. *In Witness* whereof We have hereunto subscribed our Names,

G:⁰ WASHINGTON—
*Presidt, and Deputy
from Virginia*

New Hampshire	JOHN LANGDON	New York	ALEXANDER HAMILTON
	NICHOLAS GILMAN	New Jersey	WIL: LIVINGSTON
Massachusetts	NATHANIEL GORHAM		DAVID BREARLEY
	RUFUS KING		WM PATERSON
Connecticut	WM SAML JOHNSON		JONA: DAYTON
	ROGER SHERMAN		

[14]The Constitution was submitted on September 17, 1787, by the Constitutional Convention, was ratified by the conventions of several states at various dates up to May 29, 1790, and became effective on March 4, 1789.

Pennsylvania	B Franklin	Virginia	John Blair—
	Thomas Mifflin		James Madison Jr.
	Robt Morris		
	Geo. Clymer	North Carolina	Wm Blount
	Thos. FitzSimons		Richd Dobbs Spaight
	Jared Ingersoll		Hu Williamson
	James Wilson		
	Gouv Morris	South Carolina	J. Rutledge
			Charles Cotesworth Pinckney
Delaware	Geo Read		Charles Pinckney
	Gunning Bedfor Jun		Pierce Butler
	John Dickinson		
	Richard Bassett	Georgia	William Few
	Jaco: Broom		Abr Baldwin
Maryland	James McHenry		
	Dan of St Thos. Jenifer		
	Danl Carroll		

Amendments to the Constitution

*Proposed by Congress and Ratified by the Legislatures of the
Several States, Pursuant to Article V of the Original Constitution.*

Amendments I–X, known as the Bill of Rights, were proposed by Congress on September 25, 1789, and ratified on December 15, 1791. *The Federalist Papers* comments, mainly in opposition to a Bill of Rights, can be found in number 84 (Hamilton).

AMENDMENT I

[FREEDOM OF RELIGION, OF SPEECH, AND OF THE PRESS]

Congress shall make no law respecting an establishment of religion, or prohibiting the free exercise thereof; or abridging the freedom of speech, or of the press; or the right of the people peaceably to assemble, and to petition the Government for a redress of grievances.

AMENDMENT II

[RIGHT TO KEEP AND BEAR ARMS]

A well regulated Militia, being necessary to the security of a free State, the right of the people to keep and bear Arms, shall not be infringed.

AMENDMENT III

[QUARTERING OF SOLDIERS]

No Soldier shall, in time of peace be quartered in any house, without the consent of the Owner, nor in time of war, but in a manner to be prescribed by law.

AMENDMENT IV

[SECURITY FROM UNWARRANTABLE SEARCH AND SEIZURE]

The right of the people to be secure in their persons, houses, papers, and effects, against unreasonable searches and seizures, shall not be violated, and no Warrants shall issue, but upon probable cause, supported by Oath or affirmation, and particularly describing the place to be searched, and the persons or things to be seized.

AMENDMENT V

[RIGHTS OF ACCUSED PERSONS IN CRIMINAL PROCEEDINGS]

No person shall be held to answer for a capital, or otherwise infamous crime, unless on a presentment or indictment of a Grand Jury, except in cases arising in the land or naval forces, or in the Militia, when in actual service in time of War or in public danger; nor shall any person be subject for the same offence to be twice put in jeopardy of life or limb; nor shall be compelled in any Criminal Case to be a witness against himself, nor be deprived of life, liberty, or property, without due process of law; nor shall private property be taken for public use, without just compensation.

AMENDMENT VI
[RIGHT TO SPEEDY TRIAL, WITNESSES, ETC.]

In all criminal prosecutions, the accused shall enjoy the right to a speedy and public trial, by an impartial jury of the State and district wherein the crime shall have been committed, which district shall have been previously ascertained by law, and to be informed of the nature and cause of the accusation; to be confronted with the witnesses against him; to have compulsory process for obtaining Witnesses in his favor, and to have the Assistance of Counsel for his defence.

AMENDMENT VII
[TRIAL BY JURY IN CIVIL CASES]

In suits at common law, where the value in controversy shall exceed twenty dollars, the right of trial by jury shall be preserved, and no fact tried by a jury shall be otherwise re-examined in any Court of the United States, than according to the rules of the common law.

AMENDMENT VIII
[BAILS, FINES, PUNISHMENTS]

Excessive bail shall not be required, nor excessive fines imposed, nor cruel and unusual punishments inflicted.

AMENDMENT IX
[RESERVATION OF RIGHTS OF PEOPLE]

The enumeration in the Constitution, of certain rights, shall not be construed to deny or disparage others retained by the people.

AMENDMENT X
[POWERS RESERVED TO STATES OR PEOPLE]

The powers not delegated to the United States by the Constitution, nor prohibited by it to the States, are reserved to the States respectively, or to the people.

AMENDMENT XI
[Proposed by Congress on March 4, 1794; declared ratified on January 8, 1798.]

[RESTRICTION OF JUDICIAL POWER]

The Judicial power of the United States shall not be construed to extend to any suit in law or equity, commenced or prosecuted against one of the United States by Citizens of another State, or by Citizens or Subjects of any Foreign State.

AMENDMENT XII

[Proposed by Congress on December 9, 1803; declared ratified on September 25, 1804.]

[ELECTION OF PRESIDENT AND VICE-PRESIDENT]

The Electors shall meet in their respective states, and vote by ballot for President and Vice-President, one of whom, at least, shall not be an inhabitant of the same state with themselves; they shall name in their ballots the person voted for as President, and in distinct ballots the person voted for as Vice-President, and they shall make distinct lists of all persons voted for as President, and of all persons voted for as Vice-President, and of the number of votes for each, which lists they shall sign and certify, and transmit sealed to the seat of the government of the United States, directed to the President of the Senate;—The President of the Senate shall, in presence of the Senate and House of Representatives, open all the certificates and the votes shall then be counted;—The person having the greatest number of votes for President, shall be the President, if such number be a majority of the whole number of Electors appointed; and if no person have such majority, then from the persons having the highest numbers not exceeding three on the list of those voted for as President, the House of Representatives shall choose immediately, by ballot, the President. But in choosing the President, the votes shall be taken by states, the representation from each state having one vote; a quorum for this purpose shall consist of a member or members from two-thirds of the states, and a majority of all states shall be necessary to a choice. And if the House of Representatives shall not choose a President whenever the right of choice shall devolve upon them, before the fourth day of March next following, then the Vice-President, shall act as President, as in the case of the death or other constitutional disability of the President. The person having the greatest number of votes as Vice-President, shall be the Vice-President, if such a number be a majority of the whole number of Electors appointed, and if no person have a majority, then from the two highest numbers on the list, the Senate shall choose the Vice-President; a quorum for the purpose shall consist of two-thirds of the whole number of Senators, and a majority of the whole number shall be necessary to a choice. But no person constitutionally ineligible to the office of President shall be eligible to that of Vice-President of the United States.

AMENDMENT XIII

[Proposed by Congress on January 31, 1865; declared ratified on December 18, 1865.]

Section 1
[ABOLITION OF SLAVERY]

Neither slavery nor involuntary servitude, except as a punishment for crime whereof the party shall have been duly convicted, shall exist within the United States, or any place subject to their jurisdiction.

Section 2
[POWER TO ENFORCE THIS ARTICLE]

Congress shall have power to enforce this article by appropriate legislation.

AMENDMENT XIV
[Proposed by Congress on June 13, 1866; declared ratified on July 28, 1868.]

Section 1
[CITIZENSHIP RIGHTS NOT TO BE ABRIDGED BY STATES]

All persons born or naturalized in the United States, and subject to the jurisdiction thereof, are citizens of the United States and of the State wherein they reside. No state shall make or enforce any law which shall abridge the privileges or immunities of citizens of the United States; nor shall any State deprive any person of life, liberty, or property, without due process of law; nor deny to any person within its jurisdiction the equal protection of the laws.

Section 2
[APPORTIONMENT OF REPRESENTATIVES IN CONGRESS]

Representatives shall be apportioned among the several States according to their respective numbers, counting the whole number of persons in each State, excluding Indians not taxed. But when the right to vote at any election for the choice of electors for President and Vice-President of the United States, Representatives in Congress, the Executive and Judicial officers of a State, or the members of the Legislature thereof, is denied to any of the male inhabitants of such State, being twenty-one years of age, and citizens of the United States, or in any way abridged, except for participation in rebellion, or other crime, the basis of representation therein shall be reduced in the proportion which the number of such male citizens shall bear to the whole number of male citizens twenty-one years of age in such State.

Section 3
[PERSONS DISQUALIFIED FROM HOLDING OFFICE]

No person shall be a Senator or Representative in Congress, or elector of President and Vice-President, or hold any office, civil or military, under the United States, or under any State, who, having previously taken an oath, as a member of Congress, or as an officer of the United States, or as a member of any State legislature, or as an executive or judicial officer of any State, to support the Constitution of the United States, shall have engaged in insurrection or rebellion against the same, or given aid or comfort to the enemies thereof. But Congress may by a vote of two-thirds of each House, remove such disability.

Section 4
[WHAT PUBLIC DEBTS ARE VALID]

The validity of the public debt of the United States, authorized by law, including debts incurred for payment of pensions and bounties for services in suppressing insurrection or rebellion, shall not be questioned. But neither the United States nor any State shall assume or pay any debt or obligation incurred in aid of insurrection or rebellion against the United States, or any claim for the loss or emancipation of any slave; but all such debts, obligations and claims shall be held illegal and void.

Section 5
[POWER TO ENFORCE THIS ARTICLE]

The Congress shall have power to enforce, by appropriate legislation, the provisions of this article.

AMENDMENT XV

[Proposed by Congress on February 26, 1869; declared ratified on March 30, 1870.]

Section 1
[NEGRO SUFFRAGE]

The right of citizens of the United States to vote shall not be denied or abridged by the United States or by any State on account of race, color, or previous condition of servitude.

Section 2
[POWER TO ENFORCE THIS ARTICLE]

The Congress shall have power to enforce this article by appropriate legislation.

AMENDMENT XVI

[Proposed by Congress on July 12, 1909; declared ratified on February 25, 1913.]
[AUTHORIZING INCOME TAXES]

The Congress shall have power to lay and collect taxes on incomes, from whatever source derived, without apportionment among the several States, and without regard to any census or enumeration.

AMENDMENT XVII

[Proposed by Congress on May 13, 1912; declared ratified on May 31, 1913.]
[POPULAR ELECTION OF SENATORS]

The Senate of the United States shall be composed of two Senators from each State, elected by the people thereof, for six years; and each Senator shall have one vote. The electors in each State shall have the qualifications requisite for electors of the most numerous branch of the State Legislature.

When vacancies happen in the representation of any State in the Senate, the executive authority of such State shall issue writs of election to fill such vacancies:

Provided, That the Legislature of any State may empower the executive thereof to make temporary appointment until the people fill the vacancies by election as the Legislature may direct.

This amendment shall not be so construed as to affect the election or term of any Senator chosen before it becomes valid as part of the Constitution.

AMENDMENT XVIII

[Proposed by Congress December 18, 1917; declared ratified on January 29, 1919.]

Section 1
[NATIONAL LIQUOR PROHIBITION]

After one year from the ratification of this article the manufacture, sale, or transportation of intoxicating liquors within, the importation thereof into, or the ex-portation thereof from the United States and all territory subject to the jurisdiction thereof for beverage purposes is hereby prohibited.

Section 2
[POWER TO ENFORCE THIS ARTICLE]

The Congress and the several states shall have concurrent power to enforce this article by appropriate legislation.

Section 3
[RATIFICATION WITHIN SEVEN YEARS]

This article shall be inoperative unless it shall have been ratified as an amend-ment to the Constitution by the legislatures of the several states, as provided in the Constitution, within seven years from the date of the submission hereof to the states by the Congress.[15]

AMENDMENT XIX

[Proposed by Congress on June 4, 1919; declared ratified on August 26, 1920.]
[WOMAN SUFFRAGE]

The right of the citizens of the United States to vote shall not be denied or abridged by the United States or by any state on account of sex.

Congress shall have power to enforce this article by appropriate legislation.

AMENDMENT XX

[Proposed by Congress on March 2, 1932; declared ratified on February 6, 1933.]

Section 1
[TERMS OF OFFICE]

The terms of the President and Vice-President shall end at noon on the 20th day of January, and the terms of the Senators and Representatives at noon on the 3rd

[15]Repealed by Twenty-first Amendment.

day of January, of the years in which such terms would have ended if this article had not been ratified; and the terms of their successors shall then begin.

Section 2
[TIME OF CONVENING CONGRESS]

The Congress shall assemble at least once in every year, and such meeting shall begin at noon on the 3rd day of January, unless they shall by law appoint a different day.

Section 3
[DEATH OF PRESIDENT-ELECT]

If, at the time fixed for the beginning of the term of the President, the President-elect shall have died, the Vice-President-elect shall become President. If a President shall not have been chosen before the time fixed for the beginning of his term, or if the President-elect shall have failed to qualify, then the Vice-President-elect shall act as President until a President shall have qualified; and the Congress may by law provide for the case wherein neither a President-elect nor a Vice-President-elect shall have qualified, declaring who shall then act as President, or the manner in which one who is to act shall be selected, and such person shall act accordingly until a President or Vice President shall have qualified.

Section 4
[ELECTION OF THE PRESIDENT]

The Congress may by law provide for the case of the death of any of the persons from whom the House of Representatives may choose a President whenever the right of choice shall have devolved upon them, and for the case of the death of any of the persons from whom the Senate may choose a Vice-President whenever the right of choice shall have devolved upon them.

Section 5
[AMENDMENT TAKES EFFECT]

Sections 1 and 2 shall take effect on the 15th day of October following ratification of this article.

Section 6
[RATIFICATION WITHIN SEVEN YEARS]

This article shall be inoperative unless it shall have been ratified as an amendment to the Constitution by the legislatures of three-fourths of the several States within seven years from the date of its submission.

AMENDMENT XXI

[Proposed by Congress on February 20, 1933; declared ratified on December 5, 1933.]

Section 1
[NATIONAL LIQUOR PROHIBITION REPEALED]

The eighteenth article of amendment to the Constitution of the United States is hereby repealed.

Section 2
[TRANSPORTATION OF LIQUOR INTO "DRY" STATES]

The transportation or importation into any State, Territory, or Possession of the United States for delivery or use therein of intoxicating liquors, in violation of the laws thereof, is hereby prohibited.

Section 3
[RATIFICATION WITHIN SEVEN YEARS]

This article shall be inoperative unless it shall have been ratified as an amendment to the Constitution by conventions in the several States, as provided in the Constitution, within seven years from the date of the submission hereof to the States by the Congress.

AMENDMENT XXII
[Proposed by Congress on March 21, 1947; declared ratified on February 26, 1951.]

Section 1
[TENURE OF PRESIDENT LIMITED]

No person shall be elected to the office of President more than twice, and no person who has held the office of President or acted as President for more than two years of a term to which some other person was elected President shall be elected to the Office of the President more than once. But this Article shall not apply to any person holding the office of President when this Article was proposed by the Congress, and shall not prevent any person who may be holding the office of President, or acting as President, during the term within which this Article becomes operative from holding the office of President or acting as President during the remainder of such term.

Section 2
[RATIFICATION WITHIN SEVEN YEARS]

This Article shall be inoperative unless it shall have been ratified as an amendment to the Constitution by the legislatures of three-fourths of the several states within seven years from the date of its submission to the States by the Congress.

AMENDMENT XXIII
[Proposed by Congress on June 21, 1960; declared ratified on March 29, 1961.]

Section 1
[ELECTORAL COLLEGE VOTES FOR THE DISTRICT OF COLUMBIA]

The District constituting the seat of Government of the United States shall appoint in such manner as the Congress may direct:

A number of electors of President and Vice-President equal to the whole number of Senators and Representatives in Congress to which the District would be entitled if it were a State, but in no event more than the least populous State; they shall be in addition to those appointed by the States, but they shall be considered, for the purposes of the election of President and Vice-President, to be electors appointed by a State; and they shall meet in the District and perform such duties as provided by the twelfth article of amendment.

Section 2
[POWER TO ENFORCE THIS ARTICLE]
The Congress shall have power to enforce this article by appropriate legislation.

AMENDMENT XXIV

[Proposed by Congress on August 27, 1963; declared ratified on January 23, 1964.]

Section 1
[ANTI-POLL TAX]
The right of citizens of the United States to vote in any primary or other election for President or Vice-President, for electors for President or Vice-President, or for Senator or Representative of Congress, shall not be denied or abridged by the United States or any State by reasons of failure to pay any poll tax or other tax.

Section 2
[POWER TO ENFORCE THIS ARTICLE]
The Congress shall have power to enforce this article by appropriate legislation.

AMENDMENT XXV

[Proposed by Congress on July 7, 1965; declared ratified on February 10, 1967.]

Section 1
[VICE-PRESIDENT TO BECOME PRESIDENT]
In case of the removal of the President from office or his death or resignation, the Vice-President shall become President.

Section 2
[CHOICE OF A NEW VICE-PRESIDENT]
Whenever there is a vacancy in the office of the Vice-President, the President shall nominate a Vice-President who shall take the office upon confirmation by a majority vote of both houses of Congress.

Section 3
[PRESIDENT MAY DECLARE OWN DISABILITY]
Whenever the President transmits to the President pro tempore of the Senate and the Speaker of the House of Representatives his written declaration that he is unable to discharge the powers and duties of his office, and until he transmits to them a written declaration to the contrary, such powers and duties shall be discharged by the Vice-President as Acting President.

Section 4
[ALTERNATE PROCEDURES TO DECLARE AND TO END PRESIDENTIAL DISABILITY]

Whenever the Vice-President and a majority of either the principal officers of the executive departments, or of such other body as Congress may by law provide, transmit to the President pro tempore of the Senate and the Speaker of the House of Representatives their written declaration that the President is unable to discharge the powers and duties of his office, the Vice-President shall immediately assume the powers and duties of the office as Acting President.

Thereafter, when the President transmits to the President pro tempore of the Senate and the Speaker of the House of Representatives his written declaration that no inability exists, he shall resume the powers and duties of his office unless the Vice-President and a majority of either the principal officers of the executive departments, or of such other body as Congress may by law provide, transmit within four days to the President pro tempore of the Senate and the Speaker of the House of Representatives their written declaration that the President is unable to discharge the powers and duties of his office. Thereupon Congress shall decide the issue, assembling within 48 hours for that purpose if not in session. If the Congress, within 21 days after receipt of the latter written declaration, or, if Congress is not in session, within 21 days after Congress is required to assemble, determines by two-thirds vote of both houses that the President is unable to discharge the powers and duties of his office, the Vice-President shall continue to discharge the same as Acting President; otherwise, the President shall resume the powers and duties of his office.

AMENDMENT XXVI
[Proposed by Congress on March 23, 1971; declared ratified on June 30, 1971.]

Section 1
[EIGHTEEN-YEAR-OLD VOTE]

The right of citizens of the United States, who are eighteen years of age or older, to vote shall not be denied or abridged by the United States or by any State on account of age.

Section 2
[POWER TO ENFORCE THIS ARTICLE]

The Congress shall have power to enforce this article by appropriate legislation.

AMENDMENT XXVII
[Proposed by Congress on September 25, 1789; ratified on May 7, 1992.]

No law varying the compensation for the services of the Senators and Representatives shall take effect until an election of Representatives shall have intervened.

NO. 10: MADISON

Among the numerous advantages promised by a well-constructed Union, none deserves to be more accurately developed than its tendency to break and control the violence of faction. The friend of popular governments never finds himself so much alarmed for their character and fate as when he contemplates their propensity to this dangerous vice. He will not fail, therefore, to set a due value on any plan which, without violating the principles to which he is attached, provides a proper cure for it. The instability, injustice, and confusion introduced into the public councils have, in truth, been the mortal diseases under which popular governments have everywhere perished, as they continue to be the favorite and fruitful topics from which the adversaries to liberty derive their most specious declamations. The valuable improvements made by the American constitutions on the popular models, both ancient and modern, cannot certainly be too much admired; but it would be an unwarrantable partiality to contend that they have as effectually obviated the danger on this side, as was wished and expected. Complaints are everywhere heard from our most considerate and virtuous citizens, equally the friends of public and private faith and of public and personal liberty, that our governments are too unstable, that the public good is disregarded in the conflicts of rival parties, and that measures are too often decided, not according to the rules of justice and the rights of the minor party, but by the superior force of an interested and overbearing majority. However anxiously we may wish that these complaints had no foundation, the evidence of known facts will not permit us to deny that they are in some degree true. It will be found, indeed, on a candid review of our situation, that some of the distresses under which we labor have been erroneously charged on the operation of our governments; but it will be found, at the same time, that other causes will not alone account for many of our heaviest misfortunes; and, particularly, for that prevailing and increasing distrust of public engagements and alarm for private rights which are echoed from one end of the continent to the other. These must be chiefly, if not wholly, effects of the unsteadiness and injustice with which a factious spirit has tainted our public administration.

By a faction I understand a number of citizens, whether amounting to a majority or minority of the whole, who are united and actuated by some common impulse of passion, or of interest, adverse to the rights of other citizens, or to the permanent and aggregate interests of the community.

There are two methods of curing the mischiefs of faction: the one, by removing its causes; the other, by controlling its effects.

There are again two methods of removing the causes of faction: the one, by destroying the liberty which is essential to its existence; the other, by giving to every citizen the same opinions, the same passions, and the same interests.

It could never be more truly said than of the first remedy that it was worse than the disease. Liberty is to faction what air is to fire, an aliment without which it instantly expires. But it could not be a less folly to abolish liberty, which is essential to political life, because it nourishes faction than it would be to wish the annihilation of air, which is essential to animal life, because it imparts to fire its destructive agency.

The second expedient is as impracticable as the first would be unwise. As long as the reason of man continues fallible, and he is at liberty to exercise it, different opinions will be formed. As long as the connection subsists between his reason and his self-love, his opinions and his passions will have a reciprocal influence on each other; and the former will be objects to which the latter will attach themselves. The diversity in the faculties of men, from which the rights of property originate, is not less an insuperable obstacle to a uniformity of interests. The protection of these faculties is the first object of government. From the protection of different and unequal faculties of acquiring property, the possession of different degrees and kinds of property immediately results; and from the influence of these on the sentiments and views of the respective proprietors ensues a division of the society into different interests and parties.

The latent causes of faction are thus sown in the nature of man; and we see them everywhere brought into different degrees of activity, according to the different circumstances of civil society. A zeal for different opinions concerning religion, concerning government, and many other points, as well of speculation as of practice; an attachment to different leaders ambitiously contending for pre-eminence and power; or to persons of other descriptions whose fortunes have been interesting to the human passions, have, in turn, divided mankind into parties, inflamed them with mutual animosity, and rendered them much more disposed to vex and oppress each other than to co-operate for their common good. So strong is this propensity of mankind to fall into mutual animosities that where no substantial occasion presents itself the most frivolous and fanciful distinctions have been sufficient to kindle their unfriendly passions and excite their most violent conflicts. But the most common and durable source of factions has been the various and unequal distribution of property. Those who hold and those who are without property have ever formed distinct interests in society. Those who are creditors, and those who are debtors, fall under a like discrimination. A landed interest, a manufacturing interest, a mercantile interest, a moneyed interest, with many lesser interests, grow up of necessity in civilized nations, and divide them into different classes, actuated by different sentiments and views. The regulation of these various and interfering interests forms the principal task of modern legislation and involves the spirit of party and faction in the necessary and ordinary operations of government.

No man is allowed to be judge in his own cause, because his interest would certainly bias his judgment and, not improbably, corrupt his integrity. With equal, nay with greater reason, a body of men are unfit to be both judges and parties at the same time; yet what are many of the most important acts of legislation but so many judicial determinations, not indeed concerning the rights of single persons, but concerning the rights of large bodies of citizens? And what are the different classes of legislators but advocates and parties to the causes which they determine? Is a law proposed concerning private debts? It is a question to which the creditors are parties on one side and the debtors on the other. Justice ought to hold the balance between them. Yet the parties are, and must be, themselves the judges; and the most numerous party, or in other words, the most powerful faction must be expected to prevail. Shall domestic manufacturers be encouraged, and in what degree, by restrictions on foreign manufacturers? are questions which would be differently decided by the landed and the manufacturing classes, and probably by neither with a sole regard to justice and the public good. The apportionment of taxes on the various descriptions of property is an act which seems to require the most exact impartiality; yet there is, perhaps, no legislative act in which greater opportunity and temptation are given to a predominant party to trample on the rules of justice. Every shilling with which they overburden the inferior number is a shilling saved to their own pockets.

It is in vain to say that enlightened statesmen will be able to adjust these clashing interests and render them all subservient to the public good. Enlightened statesmen will not always be at the helm. Nor, in many cases, can such an adjustment be made at all without taking into view indirect and remote considerations, which will rarely prevail over the immediate interest which one party may find in disregarding the rights of another or the good of the whole.

The inference to which we are brought is that the *causes* of faction cannot be removed and that relief is only to be sought in the means of controlling its *effects*.

If a faction consists of less than a majority, relief is supplied by the republican principle, which enables the majority to defeat its sinister views by regular vote. It may clog the administration, it may convulse the society; but it will be unable to execute and mask its violence under the forms of the Constitution. When a majority is included in a faction, the form of popular government, on the other hand, enables it to sacrifice to its ruling passion or interest both the public good and the rights of other citizens. To secure the public good and private rights against the danger of such a faction, and at the same time to preserve the spirit and the form of popular government, is then the great object to which our inquiries are directed. Let me add that it is the great desideratum by which alone this form of government can be rescued from the opprobrium under which it has so long labored and be recommended to the esteem and adoption of mankind.

By what means is this object attainable? Evidently by one of two only. Either the existence of the same passion or interest in a majority at the same time must be prevented, or the majority, having such coexistent passion or interest, must be rendered, by their number and local situation, unable to concert and carry into effect schemes of oppression. If the impulse and the opportunity be suffered to coincide, we well know that neither moral nor religious motives can be relied on as an adequate control. They are not found to be such on the injustice and violence of individuals, and lose their efficacy in proportion to the number combined together, that is, in proportion as their efficacy becomes needful.

From this view of the subject it may be concluded that a pure democracy, by which I mean a society consisting of a small number of citizens, who assemble and administer the government in person, can admit of no cure for the mischiefs of faction. A common passion or interest will, in almost every case, be felt by a majority of the whole; a communication and concert results from the form of government itself; and there is nothing to check the inducements to sacrifice the weaker party or an obnoxious individual. Hence it is that such democracies have ever been spectacles of turbulence and contention; have ever been found incompatible with personal security or the rights of property; and have in general been as short in their lives as they have been violent in their deaths. Theoretic politicians, who have patronized this species of government, have erroneously supposed that by reducing mankind to a perfect equality in their political rights, they would at the same time be perfectly equalized and assimilated in their possessions, their opinions, and their passions.

A republic, by which I mean a government in which the scheme of representation takes place, opens a different prospect and promises the cure for which we are seeking. Let us examine the points in which it varies from pure democracy, and we shall comprehend both the nature of the cure and the efficacy which it must derive from the Union.

The two great points of difference between a democracy and a republic are: first, the delegation of the government, in the latter, to a small number of citizens elected by the rest; secondly, the greater number of citizens and greater sphere of country over which the latter may be extended.

The effect of the first difference is, on the one hand, to refine and enlarge the public views by passing them through the medium of a chosen body of citizens, whose wisdom may best discern the true interest of their country and whose patriotism and love of justice will be least likely to sacrifice it to temporary or partial considerations. Under such a regulation it may well happen that the public voice, pronounced by the representatives of the people, will be more consonant to the public good than if pronounced by the people themselves, convened for the purpose. On the other hand, the effect may be inverted. Men of factious tempers, of local prejudices, or of sinister designs, may, by intrigue, by corruption, or by other means, first obtain the suffrages, and then betray the interests of the people. The question resulting is, whether small or extensive republics are most favorable to the election of proper guardians of the public weal; and it is clearly decided in favor of the latter by two obvious considerations.

In the first place it is to be remarked that however small the republic may be the representatives must be raised to a certain number in order to guard against the cabals of a few; and that however large it may be they must be limited to a certain number in order to guard against the confusion of a multitude. Hence, the number of representatives in the two cases not being in proportion to that of the constituents, and being proportionally greatest in the small republic, it follows that if the proportion of fit characters be not less in the large than in the small republic, the former will present a greater option, and consequently a greater probability of a fit choice.

In the next place, as each representative will be chosen by a greater number of citizens in the large than in the small republic, it will be more difficult for unworthy candidates to practise with success the vicious arts by which elections are too often carried; and the suffrages of the people being more free, will be more likely to center on men who possess the most attractive merit and the most diffusive and established characters.

It must be confessed that in this, as in most other cases, there is a mean, on both sides of which inconveniencies will be found to lie. By enlarging too much the number of electors, you render the representative too little acquainted with all their local circumstances and lesser interests; as by reducing it too much, you render him unduly attached to these, and too little fit to comprehend and pursue great and national objects. The federal Constitution forms a happy combination in this respect; the great and aggregate interests being referred to the national, the local and particular to the State legislatures.

The other point of difference is the greater number of citizens and extent of territory which may be brought within the compass of republican than of democratic government; and it is this circumstance principally which renders factious combinations less to be dreaded in the former than in the latter. The smaller the society, the fewer probably will be the distinct parties and interests composing it; the fewer the distinct parties and interests, the more frequently will a majority be found of the same party; and the smaller the number of individuals composing a majority, and the smaller the compass within which they are placed, the more easily will they concert and execute their plans of oppression. Extend the sphere and you take in a greater variety of parties and interests; you make it less probable that a majority of the whole will have a common motive to invade the rights of other citizens; or if such a common motive exists, it will be more difficult for all who feel it to discover their own strength and to act in unison with each other. Besides other impediments, it may be remarked that, where there is a consciousness of unjust or dishonorable purposes, communication is always checked by distrust in proportion to the number whose concurrence is necessary.

Hence, it clearly appears that the same advantage which a republic has over a democracy in controlling the effects of faction is enjoyed by a large over a small republic—is enjoyed by the Union over the States composing it. Does this advantage consist in the substitution of representatives whose enlightened views and virtuous sentiments render them superior to local prejudices and to schemes of injustice? It will not be denied that the representation of the Union will be most likely to possess these requisite endowments. Does it consist in the greater security afforded by a greater variety of parties, against the event of any one party being able to outnumber and oppress the rest? In an equal degree does the increased variety of parties comprised within the Union increase this security? Does it, in fine, consist in the greater obstacles opposed to the concert and accomplishment of the secret wishes of an unjust and interested majority? Here again the extent of the Union gives it the most palpable advantage.

The influence of factious leaders may kindle a flame within their particular States but will be unable to spread a general conflagration through the other States. A religious sect may degenerate into a political faction in a part of the Confederacy; but the variety of sects dispersed over the entire face of it must secure the national councils against any danger from that source. A rage for paper money, for an abolition of debts, for an equal division of property, or for any other improper or wicked project, will be less apt to pervade the whole body of the Union than a particular member of it, in the same proportion as such a malady is more likely to taint a particular county or district than an entire State.

In the extent and proper structure of the Union, therefore, we behold a republican remedy for the diseases most incident to republican government. And according to the degree of pleasure and pride we feel in being republicans ought to be our zeal in cherishing the spirit and supporting the character of federalist.

PUBLIUS

NO. 51: MADISON

To what expedient, then, shall we finally resort, for maintaining in practice the necessary partition of power among the several departments as laid down in the Constitution? The only answer that can be given is that as all these exterior provisions are found to be inadequate the defect must be supplied, by so contriving the interior structure of the government as that its several constituent parts may, by their mutual relations, be the means of keeping each other in their proper places. Without presuming to undertake a full development of this important idea I will hazard a few general observations which may perhaps place it in a clearer light, and enable us to form a more correct judgment of the principles and structure of the government planned by the convention.

In order to lay a due foundation for that separate and distinct exercise of the different powers of government, which to a certain extent is admitted on all hands to be essential to the preservation of liberty, it is evident that each department should have a will of its own; and consequently should be so constituted that the members of each should have as little agency as possible in the appointment of the members of the others. Were this principle rigorously adhered to, it would require that all the appointments for the supreme executive, legislative, and judiciary magistracies should be drawn from the same fountain of authority, the people, through channels having no communication whatever with one another. Perhaps such a plan of constructing the several departments would be less difficult in practice than it may in contemplation appear. Some difficulties, however, and some additional expense would attend the execution of it. Some deviations, therefore, from the principle must be admitted. In the constitution of the judiciary department in particular, it might be inexpedient to insist rigorously on the principle: first, because peculiar qualifications being essential in the members, the primary consideration ought to be to select that mode of choice which best secures these qualifications; second, because the permanent tenure by which the appointments are held in that department must soon destroy all sense of dependence on the authority conferring them.

It is equally evident that the members of each department should be as little dependent as possible on those of the others for the emoluments annexed to their offices. Were the executive magistrate, or the judges, not independent of the legislature in this particular, their independence in every other would be merely nominal.

But the great security against a gradual concentration of the several powers in the same department consists in giving to those who administer each department the necessary constitutional means and personal motives to resist encroachments of the others. The provision for defense must in this, as in all other cases, be made commensurate to the danger of attack. Ambition must be made to counteract ambition. The interest of the man must be connected with the constitutional rights of the place. It may be a reflection on human nature that such devices should be necessary to control the abuses of government. But what is government itself but the greatest of all reflections on human nature? If men were angels, no government would be necessary. If angels were to govern men, neither external nor internal controls on government would be necessary. In framing a government which is to be administered by men over men, the great difficulty lies in this: you must first enable the government to control the governed; and in the next place oblige it to control itself. A dependence on the people is, no doubt, the primary control on the government; but experience has taught mankind the necessity of auxiliary precautions.

This policy of supplying, by opposite and rival interests, the defect of better motives, might be traced through the whole system of human affairs, private as well as public. We see it particularly displayed in all the subordinate distributions of power, where the constant aim is to divide and arrange the several offices in such a manner as that each may be a check on the other—that the private interest of every individual may be a sentinel over the public rights. These inventions of prudence cannot be less requisite in the distribution of the supreme powers of the State.

But it is not possible to give to each department an equal power of self-defense. In republican government, the legislative authority necessarily predominates. The remedy for this inconveniency is to divide the legislature into different branches; and to render them, by different modes of election and different principles of action, as little connected with each other as the nature of their common functions and their common dependence on the society will admit. It may even be necessary to guard against dangerous encroachments by still further precautions. As the weight of the legislative authority requires that it should be thus divided, the weakness of the executive may require, on the other hand, that it should be fortified. An absolute negative on the legislature appears, at first view, to be the natural defense with which the executive magistrate should be armed. But perhaps it would be neither altogether safe nor alone sufficient. On ordinary occasions it might not be exerted with the requisite firmness, and on extraordinary occasions it might be perfidiously abused. May not this defect of an absolute negative be supplied by some qualified connection between this weaker branch of the stronger department, by which the latter may be led to support the constitutional rights of the former, without being too much detached from the rights of its own department?

If the principles on which these observations are founded be just, as I persuade myself they are, and they be applied as a criterion to the several State constitutions, and to the federal Constitution, it will be found that if the latter does not perfectly correspond with them, the former are infinitely less able to bear such a test.

There are, moreover, two considerations particularly applicable to the federal system of America, which place that system in a very interesting point of view.

First. In a single republic, all the power surrendered by the people is submitted to the administration of a single government; and the usurpations are guarded against by a division of the government into distinct and separate departments. In the compound republic of America, the power surrendered by the people is first divided between two distinct governments, and then the portion allotted to each subdivided among distinct and separate departments. Hence a double security arises to the rights of the people. The different governments will control each other, at the same time that each will be controlled by itself.

Second. It is of great importance in a republic not only to guard the society against the oppression of its rulers, but to guard one part of the society against the injustice of the other part. Different interests necessarily exist in different classes of citizens. If a majority be united by a common interest, the rights of the minority will be insecure. There are but two methods of providing against this evil: the one by creating a will in the community independent of the majority—that is, of the society itself; the other, by comprehending in the society so many separate descriptions of citizens as will render an unjust combination of a majority of the whole very improbable, if not impracticable. The first method prevails in all governments possessing an hereditary or self-appointed authority. This, at best, is but a precarious security; because a power independent of the society may as well espouse the unjust views of the major as the rightful interests of the minor party, and may possibly be turned against both parties. The second method will be exemplified in the federal republic of the United States. Whilst all authority in it will be derived from and dependent on the society, the society itself will be broken into so many parts, interests and classes of citizens, that the rights of individuals, or of the minority, will be in little danger from interested combinations of the majority. In a free government the security for civil rights must be the same as that for religious rights. It consists in the one case in the multiplicity of interests, and in the other in the multiplicity of sects. The degree of security in both cases will depend on the number of interests and sects; and this may be presumed to depend on the extent of country and number of people comprehended under the same government. This view of the subject must particularly recommend a proper federal system to all the sincere and considerate friends of republican government, since it shows that in exact proportion as the territory of the Union may be formed into more circumscribed Confederacies, or States, oppressive combinations of a majority will be facilitated; the best security, under the republican forms, for the rights of every class of citizen, will be diminished; and consequently the stability and independence of some member of the government, the only other security, must be proportionally increased. Justice is the end of government. It is the end of civil society. It ever has been and ever will be pursued until it be obtained, or until liberty be lost in the pursuit. In a society under the forms of which the stronger faction can readily unite and oppress the weaker, anarchy may as truly be said to reign as in a state of nature, where the weaker individual is not secured against the violence of the stronger; and as, in the latter state, even the stronger individuals are prompted, by the uncertainty of their condition, to submit to a government which may protect the weak as well as themselves; so, in the former state, will the more powerful factions or parties be gradually induced, by a like motive, to wish for a government which will protect all parties, the weaker as well as the more powerful. It can be little doubted that if the State of Rhode Island was separated from the Confederacy and left to itself, the insecurity of rights under the popular form of government within such narrow limits would be displayed by such reiterated oppressions of factious majorities that some power altogether independent of the people would soon be called for by the voice of the very factions whose misrule had proved the necessity of it. In the extended republic of the United States, and among the great variety of interests, parties, and sects which it embraces, a coalition of a majority of the whole society could seldom take place on any other principles than those of justice and the general good; whilst there being thus less danger to a minor from the will of a major party, there must be less pretext, also, to provide for the security of the former, by introducing into the government a will not dependent on the latter, or, in other words, a will independent of the society itself. It is no less certain than it is important, notwithstanding the contrary opinions which have been entertained, that the larger the society, provided it lie within a practicable sphere, the more duly capable it will be of self-government. And happily for the *republican cause*, the practicable sphere may be carried to a very great extent by a judicious modification and mixture of the *federal principle*.

PUBLIUS

Glossary of Terms

administrative adjudication   Applying rules and precedents to specific cases to settle disputes with regulated parties.

administrative legislation   Rules made by **regulatory agencies** and commissions.

administrative regulation   Rules made by **regulatory agencies** and commissions.

adverse selection problem   The problem of incomplete information; of choosing alternatives without fully knowing the characteristics of the available options.

affirmative action   A policy or program designed to redress historic injustices committed against specified groups by making special efforts to provide members of these groups with access to educational and employment opportunities.

after-the-fact authority   The authority to follow up on the fate of a proposal once it has been approved by the full chamber.

agency loss   The difference between what a principal would like an agent to do and the agent's actual performance.

agency representation   The type of representation by which representatives are held accountable to their constituents if they fail to represent them properly; that is, constituents have the power to hire and fire their representatives. This is the incentive for good representation when the personal backgrounds, views, and interests of the representatives differ from their constituents'.

agenda power   The power to determine what will be considered within an institution. Agenda power allows a person or group to make proposals or to block proposals from being made. See also **veto power.**

agenda setting   The power of the media to bring public attention to particular issues and problems.

Aid to Families with Dependent Children (AFDC)   Federal funds, administered by the states, for children living with parents or relatives who fall below state standards of need. The largest federal cash transfer program (as distinguished from assistance in kind). In 1996, Congress abolished AFDC and replaced it with the **Temporary Assistance to Needy Families (TANF)** block grant.

amicus curiae   "Friend of the court"; individuals or groups who are not parties to a lawsuit but who seek to assist the court in reaching a decision by presenting additional briefs.

appellate court A court that hears the appeals of trial court decisions.

appropriations The amounts approved by Congress in statutes (bills) that each unit or agency of government can spend.

area sampling A polling technique used for large cities, states, or the whole nation, when a high level of accuracy is desired. The population is broken down into small, homogeneous units, such as counties; then several units are randomly selected to serve as the sample.

Articles of Confederation and Perpetual Union America's first written constitution. Adopted by the Continental Congress in 1777, the Articles of Confederation and Perpetual Union was the formal basis for America's national government until 1789, when it was supplanted by the Constitution.

attitude (or opinion) A specific preference on a specific issue.

Australian ballot An electoral format that presents the names of all the candidates for any given office on the same ballot. Introduced at the turn of the century, the Australian ballot replaced the partisan ballot and facilitated **split-ticket voting.**

authoritarian government A system of rule in which the government recognizes no formal limits but may nevertheless be restrained by the power of other social institutions.

autocracy A form of government in which a single individual—a king, queen, or dictator—rules.

automatic stabilizers A category of public policy, largely fiscal and monetary, that automatically works against inflationary and deflationary tendencies in the economy.

balance-of-power role The strategy whereby many countries form alliances with one or more other countries in order to counterbalance the behavior of other, usually more powerful, nation-states.

bandwagon effect A situation wherein reports of voter or delegate opinion can influence the actual outcome of an election or a nominating convention.

bellwether district A town or district that is a microcosm of the whole population or that has been found to be a good predictor of electoral outcomes.

bicameral legislature A legislative assembly composed of two chambers or houses; opposite of unicameral legislature.

bicameralism Having a legislative assembly composed of two chambers or houses; opposite of unicameralism.

bilateral treaty Treaty made between two nations; contrast with **multilateral treaty.**

Bill of Rights The first ten amendments to the U.S. Constitution, ratified in 1791. They ensure certain rights and liberties to the people.

bipartisanship Close cooperation between two parties; usually an effort by the two major parties in Congress to cooperate with the president in making foreign policy.

block grants Federal funds given to state governments to pay for goods, services, or programs, with relatively few restrictions on how the funds may be spent.

briefs Written documents in which attorneys explain—using case precedents—why the court should find in favor of their client.

bureaucracy The complex structure of offices, tasks, rules, and principles of organization that are employed by all large-scale institutions to coordinate the work of their personnel.

bureaucratic drift The common phenomenon of bureaucratic implementation that produces policy more to the liking of the bureaucracy than originally legislated, but without triggering a political reaction from elected officials.

by-product theory Mancur Olson's theory, which states that collective action can emerge as a consequence of providing group members private benefits. This access to **selective benefits** attracts membership.

cabinet The secretaries, or chief administrators, of the major departments of the federal government. Cabinet secretaries are appointed by the president with the consent of the Senate.

categorical grants-in-aid Funds given by Congress to states and localities, earmarked by law for specific categories such as education or crime prevention.

caucus A normally closed meeting of a political or legislative group to select candidates, plan strategy, or make decisions regarding legislative matters.

checks and balances Mechanisms through which each branch of government is able to participate in and influence the activities of the other branches. Major examples include the presidential veto power over congressional legislation, the power of the Senate to approve presidential appointments, and judicial review of congressional enactments.

chief justice Justice on the Supreme Court who presides over the Court's public sessions.

civil law A system of jurisprudence, including private law and governmental actions, to settle disputes that do not involve criminal penalties.

civil liberties Areas of personal freedom with which governments are constrained from interfering.

civil penalties Regulatory techniques in which fines or another form of material restitution is imposed for violating civil laws or common law principles, such as negligence.

civil rights Legal or moral claims that citizens are entitled to make upon the government.

class action suit A lawsuit in which large numbers of persons with common interests join together under a representative party to bring or defend a lawsuit, such as hundreds of workers joining together to sue a company.

clientele agencies Departments or bureaus of government whose mission is to promote, serve, or represent a particular interest.

client state   A **nation-state** whose foreign policy is subordinated to that of another nation.

closed primary   A primary election in which voters can participate in the nomination of candidates, but only of the party in which they are enrolled for a period of time prior to primary day. Contrast with **open primary.**

closed rule   Provision by the House Rules Committee limiting or prohibiting the introduction of amendments during debate.

cloture   Rule allowing a majority of two-thirds or three-fifths of the members in a legislative body to set a time limit on debate over a given bill.

coalitional drift   The possibility that a policy will change because the composition of the coalition that enacted the policy is so temporary and provisional.

coattail effect   Result of voters casting their ballot for president or governor and "automatically" voting for the remainder of the party's ticket.

collective action   The pooling of resources and the coordination of effort and activity by a group of people in order to achieve common goals.

commerce clause   Article I, Section 8, of the Constitution, which delegates to Congress the power "to regulate Commerce with foreign Nations, and among the several States, and with the Indian Tribes." This clause was interpreted by the Supreme Court in favor of national power over the economy.

conference   A gathering of House Republicans every two years to elect their House leaders. Democrats call their gathering the caucus.

conference committee   A joint committee created to work out a compromise on House and Senate versions of a piece of legislation.

conscription   Compulsory military service, usually for a prescribed period or for the duration of a war; "the draft."

conservative   Today this term refers to those who generally support the social and economic status quo and are suspicious of efforts to introduce new political formulae and economic arrangements. Many conservatives also believe that a large and powerful government poses a threat to citizens' freedoms.

constituency   The district comprising the area from which an official is elected.

constitutional government   A system of rule in which formal and effective limits are placed on the powers of the government.

constitutionalism   An approach to legitimacy in which the rulers give up a certain amount of power in return for their right to utilize the remaining powers.

containment   The primary cold war foreign policy of the United States during the 1950s and 1960s, whereby the U.S. used its political, economic, and military power to prevent the spread of communism to developing or unstable countries.

contracting power   The power of government to set conditions on companies seeking to sell goods or services to government agencies.

contributory programs Social programs financed in whole or in part by taxation or other mandatory contributions by their present or future recipients. The most important example is **Social Security,** which is financed by a payroll tax.

cooperative federalism A type of federalism existing since the New Deal era in which **grants-in-aid** have been used strategically to encourage states and localities (without commanding them) to pursue nationally defined goals. Also known as intergovernmental cooperation.

cost of living adjustments (COLAs) See **indexing.**

criminal law The branch of law that deals with disputes or actions involving criminal penalties (as opposed to civil law). It regulates the conduct of individuals, defines crimes, and provides punishment for criminal acts.

criminal penalties Regulatory techniques in which imprisonment or heavy fines and the loss of certain civil rights and liberties are imposed.

de facto segregation Racial segregation that is not a direct result of law or government policy but is, instead, a reflection of residential patterns, income distributions, or other social factors.

defendant The individual or organization charged with a complaint in court.

deficit An annual debt incurred when the government spends more than it collects. Each yearly deficit adds to the nation's total debt.

de jure segregation Racial segregation that is a direct result of law or official policy.

delegate The role of a representative who votes according to the preferences of his or her constituency.

delegated powers Constitutional powers assigned to one governmental agency that are exercised by another agency with the express permission of the first.

delegation The process of turning direct authority over to a representative who will make decisions on an individual's or group's behalf.

democracy A system of rule that permits citizens to play a significant part in the governmental process, usually through the selection of key public officials.

deregulation A policy of reducing or eliminating regulatory restraints on the conduct of individuals or private institutions.

deterrence The development and maintenance of military strength for the purpose of discouraging attack.

devolution A policy to remove a program from one level of government by deregulating it or passing it down to a lower level of government, such as from the national government to the state and local governments.

discount rate The interest rate charged by the **Federal Reserve** when commercial banks borrow in order to expand their lending operations. An effective tool of monetary policy.

dissenting opinion A decision written by a justice in the minority in a particular case in which the justice wishes to express his or her reasoning in the case.

distributive tendency The tendency of Congress to spread the benefits of a bill among many beneficiaries, a process which helps a bill's chances for becoming law.

divided government The condition in American government wherein the presidency is controlled by one party while the opposing party controls one or both houses of Congress.

double jeopardy Trial more than once for the same crime. The Constitution guarantees that no one shall be subjected to double jeopardy.

dual federalism The system of government that prevailed in the United States from 1789 to 1937 in which most fundamental governmental powers were shared between the federal and state governments. Compare with **cooperative federalism.**

due process The right of every citizen against arbitrary action by national or state governments.

economic expansionist role The strategy often pursued by capitalist countries to adopt foreign policies that will maximize the success of domestic corporations in their dealings with other countries.

elastic clause See **"necessary and proper" clause.**

electoral college The presidential electors from each state who meet in their respective state capitals after the popular election to cast ballots for president and vice president.

electoral realignment The point in history when a new party supplants the ruling party, becoming in turn the dominant political force. In the United States, this has tended to occur roughly every thirty years.

eminent domain The right of government to take private property for public use, with reasonable compensation awarded for the property.

entitlement Eligibility for benefits by virtue of a category of benefits defined by law. Category can only be changed by legislation. Deprivation of individual benefits can be determined only through **due process** in court.

equality of opportunity A universally shared American ideal that all have the freedom to use whatever talents and wealth they have to reach their fullest potential.

equal time rule A Federal Communications Commission requirement that broadcasters provide candidates for the same political office an equal opportunity to communicate their messages to the public.

executive agreement An agreement between the president and another country which has the force of a treaty but does not require the Senate's "advice and consent."

executive order A rule or regulation issued by the president that has the effect and formal status of legislation.

executive privilege The claim that confidential communications between a president and close advisers should not be revealed without the consent of the president.

ex post facto law "After the fact" law; law that is retroactive and that has an adverse effect on someone accused of a crime. Under Article I, Sections 9 and 10, of the Constitution, neither the state nor the national government can enact such laws; this provision does not apply, however, to civil laws.

expressed power The notion that the Constitution grants to the federal government only those powers specifically named in its text.

expropriation Confiscation of property with or without compensation.

faction Group of people with common interests, usually in opposition to the aims or principles of a larger group or the public.

fairness doctrine A Federal Communications Commission requirement for broadcasters who air programs on controversial issues to provide time for opposing views.

federalism System of government in which power is divided by a constitution between a central government and regional governments.

Federal Reserve Board Seven-member governing board of the **Federal Reserve System.**

Federal Reserve System (Fed) Consisting of twelve Federal Reserve Banks, the Fed facilitates exchanges of cash, checks, and credit; it regulates member banks; and it uses monetary policies to fight inflation and deflation.

filibuster A tactic used by members of the Senate to prevent action on legislation they oppose by continuously holding the floor and speaking until the majority backs down. Once given the floor, senators have unlimited time to speak, and it requires a **cloture** vote of three-fifths of the Senate to end the filibuster.

fiscal year The yearly accounting period, which for the national government is October 1–September 30. The actual fiscal year is designated by the year in which it ends.

food stamps The largest **in-kind benefits** program, administered by the Department of Agriculture, providing coupons to individuals and families who satisfy a "needs test"; the food stamps can be exchanged for food at most grocery stores.

formula grants **Grants-in-aid** in which a formula is used to determine the amount of federal funds a state or local government will receive.

framing The power of the media to influence how events and issues are interpreted.

franchise The right to vote; see **license, suffrage.**

free riding Enjoying the benefits of a good or action while permitting others to bear the costs of providing it. See also **public good.**

full faith and credit clause Article IV, Section 1, of the Constitution, which provides that each state must accord the same respect to the laws and judicial decisions of other states that it accords to its own.

gatekeeping authority   The right and power to decide if a change in policy will be considered.

gender gap   A distinctive pattern of voting behavior reflecting the differences in views between men and women.

gerrymandering   Apportionment of voters in districts in such a way as to give unfair advantage to one political party.

government   Institutions and procedures through which a territory and its people are ruled.

grants-in-aid   A general term for funds given by Congress to state and local governments. See also **categorical grants-in-aid.**

grass roots   Local communities and home-town political constituencies.

Great Compromise   Agreement reached at the Constitutional Convention of 1787 that gave each state an equal number of senators regardless of its population, but linked representation in the House of Representatives to population.

Gross Domestic Product (GDP)   An index of the total output of goods and services. A very imperfect measure of prosperity, productivity, inflation, deflation; its regular publication both reflects and influences business conditions.

haphazard sampling   A type of sampling of public opinion that is an unsystematic choice of respondents.

Holy Alliance role   A strategy pursued by a superpower to prevent any change in the existing distribution of power among nation-states, even if this requires intervention into the internal affairs of the country in order to keep an authoritarian ruler from being overturned.

homesteading   A national policy that permits people to gain ownership of property by occupying public or unclaimed lands, living on the land for a specified period of time, and making certain minimal improvements on that land. Also known as squatting.

home rule   Power delegated by the state to a local unit of government to manage its own affairs.

ideology   The combined doctrines, assertions, and intentions of a social or political group that justify its behavior.

illusion of central tendency   The assumption that opinions are "normally distributed"—that responses to opinion questions are heavily distributed toward the center, as in a bell-shaped curve.

illusion of saliency   Impression conveyed by polls that something is important to the public when actually it is not.

impeachment   To charge a governmental official (president or otherwise) with "Treason, Bribery, or other high Crimes and Misdemeanors" and bring him or her before Congress to determine guilt.

implementation The efforts of departments and agencies to translate laws into specific bureaucratic routines.

incumbency Holding a political office for which one is running.

independent agencies Agencies set up by Congress to be independent of direct presidential authority. Congress usually accomplishes this by providing the head or heads of the agency with a set term of office rather than allowing their removal at the pleasure of the president.

independent counsel An official appointed under the terms of the Ethics in Government Act to investigate criminal misconduct by members of the executive branch.

indexing Periodic adjustments of welfare payments, wages, or taxes, tied to the cost of living. Also known as **cost of living adjustments,** or **COLAs.**

informational benefits Special newsletters, periodicals, training programs, conferences, and other information provided to members of groups to entice others to join.

inherent powers Powers claimed by a president that are not expressed in the Constitution, but are inferred from it.

in-kind benefits Goods and services provided to needy individuals and families by the federal government, as contrasted with cash benefits. The largest in-kind federal welfare program is **food stamps.**

institutions Rules and procedures providing incentives for political behavior, thereby shaping politics.

instrumental behavior To do something in a purposeful manner, sometimes requiring forethought and even calculation.

interest group A group of individuals and organizations that share a common set of goals and have joined together in an effort to persuade the government to adopt policies that will help them.

interest-group liberalism The theory of governance that in principle all claims on government resources and action are equally valid, and that all interests are equally entitled to participation in and benefits from government.

iron triangle Name assigned by political scientists to the stable and cooperative relationship that often develops between a congressional committee or subcommittee, an administrative agency, and one or more supportive interest groups. Not all such relationships are triangular, but the iron triangle formulation is most typical.

issue advocacy Independent spending by individuals or interest groups on a campaign issue but not directly tied to a particular candidate.

issue network A loose network of elected leaders, public officials, activists, and interest groups drawn together by a specific policy issue.

judicial activism Judicial philosophy that posits that the Court should go beyond the words of the Constitution or a statute to consider the broader societal implications of its decisions.

judicial restraint Judicial philosophy whose adherents refuse to go beyond the clear words of the Constitution in interpreting its meaning.

judicial review Power of the courts to declare actions of the legislative and executive branches invalid or unconstitutional. The Supreme Court asserted this power in *Marbury v. Madison.*

jurisdiction The sphere of a court's power and authority.

Kitchen Cabinet An informal group of advisers to whom the president turns for counsel and guidance. Members of the official **cabinet** may or may not also be members of the Kitchen Cabinet.

laissez-faire An economic theory first advanced by Adam Smith, it calls for a "hands off" policy by government toward the economy, in an effort to leave business enterprises free to act in their own self-interest.

legislative clearance The power given to the president to require all agencies of the executive branch to submit through the budget director all requests for new legislation along with estimates of their budgetary needs.

legislative supremacy The preeminent position assigned to the Congress by the Constitution.

legislative veto A provision in a statute permitting Congress (or a congressional committee) to review and approve actions undertaken by the executive under authority of the statute. Although the U.S. Supreme Court held the legislative veto unconstitutional in the 1983 case of *Immigration and Naturalization Service v. Chadha,* Congress continues to enact legislation incorporating such a veto.

legitimacy Popular acceptance of a government and its decisions.

liberal A liberal today generally supports political and social reform; extensive governmental intervention in the economy; the expansion of federal social services; more vigorous efforts on behalf of the poor, minorities, and women; and greater concern for consumers and the environment.

license Permission to engage in some activity that is otherwise illegal, such as hunting or practicing medicine. Synonymous with franchise, permit, certificate of convenience and necessity.

line-item veto The power to veto specific provisions (lines) of a bill. Although most state governors possess this power to some degree, at this time the president of the United States does not, and must accept or veto a bill in its entirety. See also **veto.**

lobbying Strategy by which organized interests seek to influence the passage of legislation by exerting direct pressure on members of the legislature.

logrolling A legislative practice wherein reciprocal agreements are made between legislators, usually in voting for or against a bill. In contrast to bargaining, logrolling unites parties that have nothing in common but their desire to exchange support.

majority leader The elected leader of the party holding a majority of the seats in the House of Representatives or in the Senate. In the House, the majority leader is subordinate in the party hierarchy to the **Speaker of the House.**

majority party The party that holds the majority of legislative seats in either the House or the Senate.

majority rule Rule by at least one vote more than half (50 percent plus 1) of those voting.

majority system A type of electoral system in which, to win a seat in the parliament or other representative body, a candidate must receive a majority (50 percent plus 1) of all the votes cast in the relevant district.

mandate (electoral) A claim made by a victorious candidate that the electorate has given him or her special authority to carry out campaign promises.

market failure Instances when markets fail to produce efficient outcomes.

marketplace of ideas The public forum in which beliefs and ideas are exchanged and compete.

material benefits Special goods, services, or money provided to members of groups to entice others to join.

means testing Procedure by which a potential beneficiary of an assistance program must show a need for assistance and an inability to provide for it. Means testing determines eligibility for government public assistance programs.

Medicaid A federally financed, state-operated program for medical services to low-income people. Eligibility tied largely to **AFDC.**

Medicare National health insurance for the elderly and for the disabled.

minority leader The elected leader of the party holding less than a majority of the seats in the House or Senate.

Miranda rule Principles developed by the Supreme Court in the 1966 case of *Miranda v. Arizona* requiring that persons under arrest be informed of their legal rights, including their right to counsel, prior to police interrogation.

monetary techniques Efforts to regulate the economy through manipulation of the supply of money and credit. America's most powerful institution in the area of monetary policy is the **Federal Reserve Board.**

monopoly The existence of a single firm in a market that divides all the goods and services of that market. Absence of competition.

mootness A criterion used by courts to screen cases that no longer require resolution.

moral hazard The problem of not knowing all aspects of the actions taken by an agent, nominally on behalf of the principal but potentially at the principal's expense.

multilateral treaty A treaty among more than two nations.

multilateralism A foreign policy that seeks to encourage the involvement of several nation-states in coordinated action, usually in relation to a common adversary, with terms and conditions usually specified in a multicountry treaty, such as NATO.

multiple-member constituency Electorate that selects all candidates at large from the whole district; each voter is given the number of votes equivalent to the number of seats to be filled.

multiple-member district See **multiple-member constituency.**

Napoleonic role Strategy pursued by a powerful nation to prevent aggressive actions against themselves by improving the internal state of affairs of a particular country, even if this means encouraging revolution in that country. Based on the assumption that countries with comparable political systems will never go to war against each other.

nationalism The widely held belief that the people who occupy the same territory have something in common, that the nation is a single community.

nation-state A political entity consisting of a people with some common cultural experience (nation) who also share a common political authority (state) recognized by other sovereignties (nation-states).

"necessary and proper" clause Article I, Section 8, of the Constitution, which enumerates the powers of Congress and provides Congress with the authority to make all laws "necessary and proper" to carry them out; also referred to as the "elastic clause."

nomination The process through which political parties select their candidates for election to public office.

noncontributory programs Social programs that provide assistance to people based on demonstrated need rather than any contribution they have made.

oligarchy A form of government in which a small group of landowners, military officers, or wealthy merchants controls most of the governing decisions.

oligopoly The existence of two or more competing firms in a given market, where price competition is usually avoided because they know that they would all lose from such competition. Rather, competition is usually through other forms, such as advertising, innovation, and obsolescence.

open market operations Process whereby the Open Market Committee of the **Federal Reserve** buys and sells government securities, etc., to help finance government operations and to loosen or tighten the total amount of credit circulating in the economy.

open primary A primary election in which the voter can wait until the day of the primary to choose which party to enroll in to select candidates for the general election. Contrast with **closed primary.**

opinion The written explanation of the Supreme Court's decision in a particular case.

oral argument   Stage in Supreme Court procedure in which attorneys for both sides appear before the Court to present their positions and answer questions posed by the justices.

ordinance   The legislative act of a local legislature or municipal commission. Puts the force of law under city charter but is a lower order of law than a statute of the national or state legislature.

oversight   The effort by Congress, through hearings, investigations, and other techniques, to exercise control over the activities of executive agencies.

partisanship   Loyalty to a particular political party.

party identification   An individual voter's psychological ties to one party or another.

party vote   A **roll-call vote** in the House or Senate in which at least 50 percent of the members of one party take a particular position and are opposed by at least 50 percent of the members of the other party. Party votes are rare today, although they were fairly common in the nineteenth century.

path dependency   The idea that certain possibilities are made more or less likely because of the historical path taken.

patronage   The resources available to higher officials, usually opportunities to make partisan appointments to offices and to confer grants, licenses, or special favors to supporters.

per curiam   Decision by an appellate court, without a written opinion, that refuses to review the decision of a lower court; amounts to a reaffirmation of the lower court's opinion.

plaintiff   The individual or organization who brings a complaint in court.

plea bargains   Negotiated agreements in criminal cases in which a defendant agrees to plead guilty in return for the state's agreement to reduce the severity of the criminal charge the defendant is facing.

pluralism   The theory that all interests are and should be free to compete for influence in the government. The outcome of this competition is compromise and moderation.

plurality system   A type of electoral system in which victory goes to the individual who gets the most votes in an election, not necessarily a majority of votes cast.

pocket veto   Method by which the president vetoes a bill by taking no action on it when Congress has adjourned. See also **veto.**

police power   Power reserved to the state to regulate the health, safety, and morals of its citizens.

policy of redistribution   An objective of the graduated income tax—to raise revenue in such a way as to reduce the disparities of wealth between the lowest and the highest income brackets.

political action committee (PAC)   A private group that raises and distributes funds for use in election campaigns.

political ideology   A cohesive set of beliefs that form a general philosophy about the role of government.

poll tax   A state-imposed tax upon the voters as a prerequisite to registration. It was rendered unconstitutional in national elections by the Twenty-fourth Amendment and in state elections by the Supreme Court in 1966.

pork-barrel legislation   Appropriations made by legislative bodies for local projects that are often not needed but that are created so that local representatives can carry their home district in the next election.

power without diplomacy   Post–World War II foreign policy in which the goal was to use American power to create an international structure that could be run with a minimum of regular diplomatic involvement.

precedents   Prior cases whose principles are used by judges as the bases for their decisions in present cases.

principal-agent problems   The tensions that potentially arise when the self-interests of those who delegate power to an agent and the self-interests of the agent diverge. The principal must supervise the behavior of the agent in order to ensure that the agent does not abuse his or her position of power. See also **transaction costs.**

prior restraint   An effort by a governmental agency to block the publication of material it deems libelous or harmful in some way; censorship. In the United States, the courts forbid prior restraint except under the most extraordinary circumstances.

private bill   A proposal in Congress to provide a specific person with some kind of relief, such as a special exemption from immigration quotas.

privatization   Removing all or part of a program from the public sector to the private sector.

privileges and immunities clause   Article IV of the Constitution, which provides that the citizens of any one state are guaranteed the "privileges and immunities" of every other state, as though they were citizens of that state.

probability sampling   A method used by pollsters to select a sample in which every individual in the population has a known (usually equal) probability of being selected as a respondent so that the correct weight can be given to all segments of the population.

procedural due process   The Supreme Court's efforts to forbid any procedure that shocks the conscience or that makes impossible a fair judicial system. See also **due process.**

progressive/regressive taxes   A judgment made by students of taxation about whether a particular tax hits the upper brackets more heavily (progressive) or the lower brackets more heavily (regressive).

project grants   Grant programs in which state and local governments submit proposals to federal agencies and for which funding is provided on a competitive basis.

promotional techniques   A technique of control that encourages people to do something they might not otherwise do, or continue an action or behavior. There are three types: subsidies, contracts, and licenses.

proportional representation   A multiple-member district system that allows each political party representation in proportion to its percentage of the vote.

proposal power   The capacity to present a proposal to the full legislature.

prospective voting   Voting based on the imagined future performance of a candidate.

public assistance program   A noncontributory social program providing assistance for the aged, poor, or disabled. Major examples include **Aid to Families with Dependent Children (AFDC)** and **Supplemental Security Income (SSI).**

public good   Goods that are provided by the government because they are either not supplied by the market or are not supplied in sufficient quantities. See also **free riding.**

public law   Cases in private law, civil law, or criminal law in which one party to the dispute argues that a license is unfair, a law is inequitable or unconstitutional, or an agency has acted unfairly, violated a procedure, or gone beyond its jurisdiction.

public opinion   Citizens' attitudes about political issues, leaders, institutions, and events.

public policy   A governmental law, rule, statute, or edict that expresses the government's goals and provides for rewards and punishments to promote their attainment.

purposive benefits   **Selective benefits** of group membership that emphasize the purpose and accomplishments of the group.

push polling   Polling technique that is designed to shape the respondent's opinion. For example, "If you knew that Candidate X was an adulterer, would you support his election?"

quota sampling   A type of sampling of public opinion that is used by most commercial polls. Respondents are selected whose characteristics closely match those of the general population along several significant dimensions, such as geographic region, sex, age, and race.

rallying effect   The generally favorable reaction of the public to presidential actions taken in foreign policy, or more precisely, to decisions made during international crises.

random sampling   Polls in which respondents are chosen mathematically, at random, with every effort made to avoid bias in the construction of the sample.

reapportionment   The redrawing of election districts and the redistribution of legislative representatives due to shifts in population.

redistributive techniques   Economic policies designed to control the economy through taxing and spending (fiscal policy) and manipulation of the supply of money and credit (monetary policy).

referendum   The practice of referring a measure proposed or passed by a legislature to the vote of the electorate for approval or rejection.

regulation A particular use of government power, a "technique of control" in which the government adopts rules imposing restrictions on the conduct of private citizens.

regulatory agencies Departments, bureaus, or independent agencies whose primary mission is to eliminate or restrict certain behaviors defined as being evil in themselves or evil in their consequences.

regulatory tax A tax whose primary purpose is not to raise revenue but to influence conduct—e.g., a heavy tax on gasoline to discourage recreational driving.

regulatory techniques Techniques that government uses to control the conduct of the people.

representative democracy A system of government that provides the populace with the opportunity to make the government responsive to its views through the selection of representatives, who, in turn, play a significant role in governmental decision making.

reserve requirement The amount of liquid assets and ready cash that the Federal Reserve requires banks to hold to meet depositors' demands for their money. Ratio revolves above or below 20 percent of all deposits, with the rest being available for new loans.

retrospective voting Voting based on the past performance of a candidate.

revolutionary politics A form of politics that rejects the existing system of government entirely and attempts to replace it with a different organizational structure and a different ruling group.

right of rebuttal A Federal Communications Commission regulation giving individuals the right to have the opportunity to respond to personal attacks made on a radio or TV broadcast.

roll-call vote Vote in which each legislator's yes or no vote is recorded as the clerk calls the names of the members alphabetically.

rulemaking A quasi-legislative administrative process that produces regulations by government agencies.

selective benefits Special benefits available only to members of certain organizations or groups. By-product theory states that many people join for these selective benefits, not because of the group's main cause.

selective polling A sample drawn deliberately to reconstruct meaningful distributions of an entire constituency; not a random sample.

senatorial courtesy The practice whereby the president, before formally nominating a person for a federal judgeship, ensures that the senators from the candidate's state support the nomination.

seniority Priority or status ranking given to an individual on the basis of length of continuous service in an organization.

"separate but equal" rule   Doctrine that public accommodations could be segregated by race but still be equal.

separation of powers   The division of governmental power among several institutions that must cooperate in decision making.

single-member constituency   An electorate that is allowed to elect only one representative from each district; the normal method of representation in the United States.

single-member district   See **single-member constituency.**

Social Security   A contributory welfare program into which working Americans contribute a percentage of their wages, and from which they receive cash benefits after retirement.

soft money   Money contributed directly to political parties for voter registration and organization.

solidary benefits   Selective benefits of a group membership that emphasize friendship, networking, and consciousness-raising.

sovereignty   Supreme and independent political authority.

Speaker of the House   The chief presiding officer of the House of Representatives. The Speaker is elected at the beginning of every Congress on a straight **party vote.** The Speaker is the most important party and House leader and can influence the legislative agenda, the fate of individual pieces of legislation, and members' positions within the House.

split-ticket voting   The practice of casting ballots for the candidates of at least two different political parties in the same election. Voters who support only one party's candidates are said to vote a straight party ticket.

staff agency   An agency responsible for maintaining the bureaucracy, with responsibilities such as purchasing, budgeting, personnel management, planning.

standing   The right of an individual or organization to initiate a court case.

standing committee   A regular legislative committee that considers legislation within its designated subject area; the basic unit of deliberation in the House and Senate.

stare decisis   Literally "let the decision stand." A previous decision by a court applies as a precedent in similar cases until that decision is overruled.

state   A community that claims the monopoly of legitimate use of physical force within a given territory; the ultimate political authority; sovereign.

states' rights   The principle that states should oppose increasing authority of the national government; this was most popular before the Civil War.

statute   A law enacted by a state legislature or by Congress.

subsidies   Governmental grants of cash or other valuable commodities such as land to individuals or organizations. Subsidies can be used to promote activities desired by the government, to reward political support, or to buy off political opposition.

substantive due process A judicial doctrine used by the appellate courts, primarily before 1937, to strike down economic legislation the courts felt was arbitrary or unreasonable.

suffrage The right to vote; see also **franchise.**

Supplemental Security Income (SSI) A program providing a minimum monthly income to people who pass a "needs test" and who are sixty-five years or older, blind, or disabled. Financed from general revenues rather than from Social Security contributions.

supremacy clause Article VI of the Constitution, which states that all laws passed by the national government and all treaties are the supreme laws of the land and superior to all laws adopted by any state or any subdivision.

supreme court The highest court in a particular state or in the United States. This court primarily serves an appellate function.

systematic sampling A method used in probability sampling to ensure that every individual in the population has a known probability of being chosen as a respondent. For example, by choosing every ninth name from a list.

Temporary Assistance to Needy Families (TANF) See **Aid to Families with Dependent Children (AFDC).**

third parties Parties that organize to compete against the two major American political parties.

Three-fifths Compromise Agreement reached at the Constitutional Convention of 1787 which stipulated that for purposes of the apportionment of congressional seats, every slave would be counted as three-fifths of a person.

totalitarian government A system of rule in which the government recognizes no formal limits on its power and seeks to absorb or eliminate other social institutions that might challenge it.

transaction costs The anticipated costs involved in clarifying each aspect of a principal-agent relationship and then monitoring it to make sure arrangements are complied with.

treaty A formal agreement between sovereign nations to create or restrict rights and responsibilities. In the U.S. all treaties must be approved by a two-thirds vote in the Senate. See also **executive agreement.**

trial court The first court to hear a criminal or civil case.

trustee The role of a representative who votes based on what he or she thinks is best for his or her constituency.

turnout The percentage of eligible individuals who actually vote.

tyranny Oppressive and unjust government that employs cruel and unjust use of power and authority.

unfunded mandates Regulations or conditions for receiving grants that impose costs on state and local governments for which they are not reimbursed by the federal government.

unilateralism A foreign policy that seeks to avoid international alliances, entanglements, and permanent commitments in favor of independence, neutrality, and freedom of action.

values (or beliefs) Basic principles that shape a person's opinions about political issues and events.

veto The president's constitutional power to turn down acts of Congress. A presidential veto may be overridden by a two-thirds vote of each house of Congress. See also **line-item veto.**

veto power The power to defeat an item when it comes up for consideration or vote. See also **agenda power.**

whip system Primarily a communications network in each house of Congress, whips take polls of the membership in order to learn their intentions on specific legislative issues and to assist the majority and minority leaders in various tasks.

writ of *certiorari* A decision concurred in by at least four of the nine Supreme Court justices to review a decision of a lower court; from the Latin "to make more certain."

writ of *habeas corpus* A court order demanding that an individual in custody be brought into court and shown the cause for detention. *Habeas corpus* is guaranteed by the Constitution and can be suspended only in cases of rebellion or invasion.

Glossary of Court Cases

Abrams v. United States **(1919)** The Supreme Court upheld the convictions of five Bolshevik sympathizers under the Espionage Act, which made it an offense to intend interference in the war with Germany. Although the defendants actually opposed American intervention in the Russian Revolution, the Court imputed to them the knowledge that their actions would necessarily impede the war effort against Germany.

Adarand Constructors, Inc. v. Pena **(1995)** In this case, Adarand Constructors claimed that its equal protection rights had been violated when a firm with a federal Department of Transportation contract selected a minority-owned company for a subcontract, despite Adarand's submission of a lower bid for the project. With its decision in favor of Adarand, the Court prompted a review of federal affirmative action programs that classify people and organizations on the basis of race.

Agostini v. Felton **(1997)** By a 5-to-4 decision, the Court ordered a federal district court in New York to lift an injunction established in 1985 that forbade public school teachers from entering on parochial school grounds to provide remedial education.

Baker v. Carr **(1962)** The Court held that the issue of malapportionment of election districts raised a justiciable claim under the Equal Protection Clause of the Fourteenth Amendment. The effect of the case was to force the reapportionment of nearly all federal, state, and local election districts nationwide.

Barron v. Baltimore **(1833)** This was one of the most significant cases ever handed down by the Court. Chief Justice John Marshall confirmed the concept of "dual citizenship," wherein each American is separately a citizen of the national government and of the state government. This meant that the Bill of Rights applied only nationally, and not at the state or local level. The consequences of this ruling were felt well into the twentieth century.

Benton v. Maryland **(1969)** The Court ruled that double jeopardy was a right incorporated in the Fourteenth Amendment as a restriction on the states.

Board of Trustees of the University of Alabama v. Garrett **(2001)** This 5-to-4 decision held that state employees may not sue the state under the Americans with Disabilities Act.

Bolling v. Sharpe **(1954)** This case, which did not directly involve the Fourteenth Amendment because the District of Columbia is not a state, confronted the Court on the grounds that segregation is inherently unequal. Its victory in effect was "incorporation in reverse," with equal protection moving from the Fourteenth Amendment to become part of the Bill of Rights.

Bowsher v. Synar (1986)   This was the second of two cases since 1937 in which the Court invalidated an act of Congress on constitutional grounds. In this case, the Court struck down the Gramm-Rudman Act mandating a balanced federal budget, ruling that it was unconstitutional to grant the comptroller general "executive" powers.

Bragdon v. Abbott (1998)   The Court ruled that the Americans with Disabilities Act of 1990 applied to persons with human immunodeficiency virus (HIV).

Brandenburg v. Ohio (1969)   The Court overturned an Ohio statute forbidding any person from urging criminal acts as a means of inducing political reform or from joining any association that advocated such activities, on the grounds that the statute punished "mere advocacy" and therefore violated the free speech provisions of the federal Constitution.

Brown v. Board of Education (1954)   The Supreme Court struck down the "separate but equal" doctrine as fundamentally unequal. This case eliminated state power to use race as a criterion of discrimination in law and provided the national government with the power to intervene by exercising strict regulatory policies against discriminatory actions.

Brown v. Board of Education of Topeka, Kansas (Brown II) (1955)   One year after *Brown*, the Court issued a mandate for state and local school boards to proceed "with all deliberate speed" to desegregate schools.

Buckley v. American Constitutional Law Foundation (1999)   The Court ruled that Colorado's restrictions on the initiative-petition process was unconstitutional as an infringement of the First Amendment right to free speech.

Buckley v. Valeo (1976)   The Supreme Court limited congressional attempts to regulate campaign financing by declaring unconstitutional any absolute limits on the freedom of individuals to spend their own money on campaigns.

Bush v. Gore (2000)   This 5-to-4 decision prevented the recount of disputed ballots in several Florida counties during the 2000 presidential election; this decision ultimately gave Bush the victory in Florida and in the electoral college as a whole.

Cable News Network v. Noriega (1990)   The doctrine of "no prior restraint" was weakened when the Supreme Court held that Cable News Network (CNN) could be restrained from broadcasting supposedly illegally obtained tapes of conversations between former Panamanian leader Manuel Noriega and his lawyer until the trial court had listened to the tapes and had determined whether such a broadcast would violate Noriega's right to a fair trial.

Chicago, Burlington, and Quincy Railway Company v. Chicago (1897)   This case effectively overruled Barron by affirming that the due process clause of the Fourteenth Amendment did prohibit states from taking property for a public use without just compensation.

Citizens to Preserve Overton Park, Inc. v. Volpe (1971)   Beginning with the Supreme Court's decision in this case, the federal courts allowed countless challenges to federal agency actions, under the National Environmental Policy Act (NEPA), brought by public interest groups asserting that the agencies had failed to consider the adverse effects of their actions upon the environment as required by NEPA.

City of Boerne v. Flores (1997)   In this decision the Court supported a Texas federal district court's ruling that the Religious Freedom Restoration Act of 1993 is unconstitutional as a violation of the separation of powers.

The Civil Rights Cases (1883)   The Court struck down the Civil Rights Act of 1875, which attempted to protect blacks from discriminatory treatment by proprietors of public facilities. It ruled that the Fourteenth Amendment applied only to discriminatory actions by state officials and did not apply to discrimination against blacks by private individuals.

Clinton v. City of New York (1998)   The Court struck down the Line-Item Veto Act of 1996, ruling that the line-item veto power violated Article I of the Constitution.

Clinton v. Jones (1997)   The Court unanimously rejected President Clinton's claim of immunity from a civil suit while in office.

Colorado Republican Party v. Federal Election Committee (1996)   The Court held that the Federal Election Campaign Act of 1971 does not violate First Amendment rights by imposing spending limits on independent campaign expenditures by political parties.

Cooper v. Aaron (1958)   In this historic case, the Supreme Court required that Little Rock, Arkansas, desegregate its public schools by immediately complying with a lower court's order and warned that it is "emphatically the province and duty of the judicial department to say what the law is."

Craig v. Boren (1976)   In this decision, the Court made it easier for plaintiffs to file and win suits on the basis of gender discrimination.

Doe v. Bolton (1973)   This case extended the decision in *Roe* by striking down state requirements that abortions be performed in licensed hospitals; that abortions be approved beforehand by a hospital committee; and that two physicians concur in the abortion decision.

Dolan v. City of Tigard (1994)   This case overturned an Oregon building permit law that required a portion of property being developed to be set aside for public use. The Court established stricter guidelines to be followed in order for state and local governments to avoid violating the Fifth Amendment by taking property "without just compensation."

Dred Scott v. Sandford (1857)   The Court ruled against Scott, who was trying to establish that he was a free man because he lived for a time in free territory in the North, holding that he had no standing to sue because he was not and could not be a citizen since he was a Negro and a slave. The Court went on to declare the antislavery provision of the Missouri Compromise of 1820 unconstitutional.

Duke Power Company v. Carolina Environmental Study Group (1978) The Supreme Court dealt anti-nuclear power activists a significant blow by upholding a federal statute limiting liability for damages accruing from accidents at nuclear power plants.

Duncan v. Louisiana (1968) The Court established the right to trial by jury in state criminal cases where the accused faces a serious charge and sentencing.

Eisenstadt v. Baird (1972) The Court struck down state laws prohibiting the use of contraceptives by unmarried persons.

Engel v. Vitale (1962) In interpreting the separation of church and state doctrine, the Court ruled that organized prayer in the public schools was unconstitutional.

Escobedo v. Illinois (1964) The Supreme Court expanded the rights of the accused in this case by giving suspects the right to remain silent and the right to have counsel present during questioning.

Felker v. Turpin (1996) The Court unanimously upheld provisions of the Anti-Terrorism and Effective Death Penalty Act of 1996, which imposes tight time limits on appeals and restrictions on federal courts' review of death sentences, among other things.

Flast v. Cohen (1968) The Court ruled that a taxpayer has standing to file suit in federal court if alleging that Congress has breached restrictions placed on its taxing and spending powers by the Constitution.

Franklin v. Gwinnett County Public Schools (1992) This decision ruled that violators of Title IX of the 1972 Education Act could be sued for monetary damages. The result has been greatly increased enforcement of Title IX, which requires gender equality in education.

Freeman v. Pitts (1992) The Court unanimously overruled a decision of a court of appeals regarding judicial supervision of a school district's desegregation efforts. The Court held that federal courts have the authority to end their supervision and control of school districts in stages, even if full compliance has not been reached in every area of operations.

Frontiero v. Richardson (1973) The Court rendered an important decision relating to the economic status of women when it held that the armed services could not deny married women fringe benefits, such as housing allowances and health care, that were automatically granted to married men.

Garcia v. San Antonio Metropolitan Transit Authority (1985) The question of whether the national government had the right to regulate state and local businesses was again raised in this case. The Court ruled that the national government had the right to apply minimum-wage and overtime standards to state and local government employees. This case overturned *National League of Cities v. Usery* (1976).

Gibbons v. Ogden (1824) An early, major case establishing the supremacy of the national government in all matters affecting interstate commerce, in which John Marshall broadly defined what Article I, Section 8, meant by "commerce among the several states." He affirmed that the federal government alone could regulate trade, travel, and navigation between the states.

Gideon v. Wainwright (1963) The Warren Court overruled an earlier case (*Betts* [1942]) and established that "any person haled into court, who is too poor to hire a lawyer, cannot be assured a fair trial unless counsel is provided for him."

Gitlow v. New York (1925) The Court ruled that the freedom of speech is "among the fundamental personal rights and 'liberties' protected by the due process clause of the Fourteenth Amendment from impairment by the states."

Goldberg v. Kelly (1970) The Court ruled that recipients of Aid to Families with Dependent Children were entitled to a trial-type hearing prior to the termination of their benefits.

Griffin v. Prince Edward County School Board (1964) The Supreme Court forced all the schools in Prince Edward County, Virginia, to reopen after they had been closed for five years to avoid desegregation.

Griggs v. Duke Power Company (1971) The Court held that although the statistical evidence did not prove intentional discrimination, and although an employer's hiring requirements were race-neutral in appearance, their effects were sufficient to shift the burden of justification to the employer to show that the requirements were a "business necessity" that bore "a demonstrable relationship to successful performance."

Griswold v. Connecticut (1965) The Court ruled that the right to privacy included the right to marital privacy and struck down state laws restricting married persons' use of contraceptives and the circulation of birth control information.

Hague v. Committee for Industrial Organization (CIO) (1939) The Court extended the concept of a public forum to include public streets and meeting halls and incorporated the freedom of assembly into the list of rights held to be fundamental and therefore binding on the states as well as on the national government.

Hicklin v. Orbeck (1978) The Court overturned the "Alaska Hire" statute, which had stipulated that oil and gas companies with leases from the state of Alaska were required to hire qualified residents of Alaska over nonresidents. The Court held that the Alaska statute violated the "privileges and immunities" clause of the Constitution.

Hodgson v. Minnesota (1990) In this case the Supreme Court upheld a Minnesota statute requiring parental notification before an abortion could be performed on a woman under the age of eighteen.

Hopwood v. State of Texas (1996) The federal court of appeals decision—which applied only in Texas, Louisiana, and Mississippi—ruled that race could never be considered in granting admissions and scholarships at state colleges and universities.

Humphrey's Executor v. United States (1935) The Court in this case made a distinction between "purely executive" officials—whom the president could remove at his discretion—and officials with "quasi-judicial and quasi-legislative" duties—who could be removed only for reasons specified by Congress. This decision limited the president's removal powers.

Hustler *Magazine v. Falwell* (1988)   The Court ruled that televangelist Jerry Falwell was not libeled by a cartoon parody of him, which appeared in *Hustler*, and thus could not recover damages for emotional distress. This 9-to-0 vote was an indication of the Court's broad interpretation of freedom of speech.

***Immigration and Naturalization Service (INS) v. Chadha* (1983)**   This was the first of two cases since 1937 in which the Court invalidated an act of Congress on constitutional grounds. In this case the Court declared the legislative veto unconstitutional.

***In re Agent Orange Product Liability Litigation* (1983)**   In this case, a federal judge in New York certified Vietnam War veterans as a class with standing to sue a manufacturer of herbicides for damages allegedly incurred from exposure to the defendants' product while they were in Vietnam.

***In re Neagle* (1890)**   The Supreme Court held that the protection of a federal judge was a reasonable extension of the president's constitutional power to "take care that the laws be faithfully executed."

***In re Oliver* (1948)**   The Court incorporated the right to a public trial in the Fourteenth Amendment as a restriction on the states.

***Jacobellis v. Ohio* (1964)**   This case is famous for Justice Stewart's quip about how to determine if a form of speech is pornographic: "I know it when I see it."

***Katzenbach v. McClung* (1964)**   The Court gave an extremely broad definition to "interstate commerce" so as to allow Congress the constitutional authority to cover discrimination by virtually any local employer. Although the Court agreed that this case involved a strictly intrastate restaurant, they found a sufficient connection to interstate commerce resulting from the restaurant's acquisition of food and supplies so as to hold that racial discrimination at such an establishment would "impose commercial burdens of national magnitude upon interstate commerce."

***Korematsu v. United States* (1944)**   The Court held that it was not unconstitutional to impose legal restrictions on a single racial group, in this case wartime measures prohibiting persons of Japanese ancestry from living in certain areas.

***Lochner v. New York* (1905)**   Seeking to protect business from government regulation, the Court invalidated a New York state law regulating the sanitary conditions and hours of labor of bakers on the grounds that the law interfered with liberty of contract.

***Loving v. Virginia* (1967)**   The Court invalidated a Virginia statute prohibiting interracial marriages, on the grounds that the statute violated guarantees of due process and equal protection contained in the Fourteenth Amendment of the Constitution.

***Lujan v. Defenders of Wildlife* (1992)**   The Court restricted the concept of standing by requiring that a party bringing suit against a government policy show that the policy is likely to cause them direct and imminent injury.

Mack v. United States (1997) Filed with *Printz v. United States.*

Malloy v. Hogan (1964) The Court ruled that the right of a person to remain silent and avoid self-incrimination applied to the states as well as to the federal government. This decision incorporated the Fifth Amendment into the Fourteenth Amendment.

Mapp v. Ohio (1961) The Court held that evidence obtained in violation of the Fourth Amendment ban on unreasonable searches and seizures would be excluded from trial.

Marbury v. Madison (1803) This was the landmark case in which Chief Justice Marshall established that the Court had the right to rule on the constitutionality of federal and state laws, although judicial review was not explicitly granted by the Constitution.

Martin v. Hunter's Lessee (1816) In this case, the Supreme Court confirmed its congressionally conferred power to review and reverse state constitutions and laws whenever they are clearly in conflict with the U.S. Constitution, federal laws, or treaties.

Martin v. Wilks (1989) The Supreme Court further eased the way for employers to prefer white males when it held that any affirmative action program already approved by federal courts could be subsequently challenged by white males who alleged that the program discriminated against them.

Masson v. New Yorker Magazine (1991) The Supreme Court held that a successful libel claim must prove that an allegedly libelous author and/or publisher acted with requisite knowledge of falsity or reckless disregard as to truth or falsity in publishing the allegedly libelous material.

McCleskey v. Zant (1991) This ruling redefined the "abuse of writ" doctrine, thereby limiting the number of writs of *habeas corpus* appeals a death-row inmate can make.

McCulloch v. Maryland (1819) This was the first and most important case favoring national control of the economy over state control. In his ruling, John Marshall established the "implied powers" doctrine enabling Congress to use the "necessary and proper" clause of Article I, Section 8, to interpret its delegated powers. This case also concluded that, when state law and federal law were in conflict, national law took precedence.

Miller v. Johnson (1995) This decision struck down a congressional redistricting plan in the state of Georgia that had purposely created black-majority electoral districts. The Court found that the creation of electoral districts solely or predominantly on the basis of race violated the equal protection rights of non-black voters in those districts.

Milliken v. Bradley (1974) The Supreme Court severely restricted the *Swann* ruling when it determined in this case that only cities found guilty of deliberate and *de jure* segregation (segregation in law) would have to desegregate their schools. This ruling exempted most Northern states and cities from busing because school segregation in Northern cities is generally *de facto* segregation (segregation in fact) that follows from segregated housing and other forms of private discrimination.

Miranda v. Arizona (1966)   The Warren Court ruled that anyone placed under arrest must be informed of the right to remain silent and to have counsel present during interrogation.

Missouri ex rel. Gaines v. Canada (1938)   Rather than question the "separate but equal" doctrine, the Court in this case ruled that Missouri had violated the equal protection clause of the Fourteenth Amendment by not providing a law school for blacks. The ruling reiterated that states must furnish "equal facilities in separate schools."

Missouri v. Holland (1920)   The Court recognized that a treaty could enlarge federal power at the expense of the states, under the "supremacy clause" in Article VI.

Missouri v. Jenkins (1990)   The Court upheld the authority of a federal judge to order the Kansas City, Missouri, school board to raise taxes to pay for a school plan to achieve racial integration.

Missouri v. Jenkins (1995)   In this decision, part of an ongoing lower-court involvement in the desegregation efforts of the Kansas City, Missouri, school district, the Court found that a federal district court had exceeded its remedial powers in its efforts to eliminate the vestiges of past discrimination. While it did not overturn its previous decision in *Missouri v. Jenkins* (1990), the Court's opinion encouraged lower courts to withdraw from supervision of school districts when the requirements of the Constitution have been met.

Moran v. McDonough (1976)   In an effort to retain jurisdiction of the case until the court's mandated school-desegregation plan had been satisfactorily implemented, District Court Judge Arthur Garrity issued fourteen decisions relating to different aspects of the Boston school plan that had been developed under his authority and put into effect under his supervision.

Myers v. United States (1926)   The Court upheld a broad interpretation of the president's power to remove executive officers whom he had appointed, despite restrictions imposed by Congress. (Later limited by *Humphrey's*.)

NAACP v. Alabama (1958)   The Court recognized the right to "privacy in one's association" in its ruling protecting the NAACP from the state of Alabama using its membership list.

National Labor Relations Board v. Jones & Laughlin Steel Corporation (1937)   In a case involving New Deal legislation, the Court reversed its earlier rulings on "interstate commerce" and redefined it to permit the national government to regulate local economic and social conditions.

National League of Cities v. Usery (1976)   Although in this case the Court invalidated a congressional act applying wage and hour regulations to state and local governments, it reversed its decision nine years later in *Garcia v. San Antonio Metropolitan Transit Authority* (1985).

Near v. Minnesota **(1931)**   In this landmark case, which established the doctrine of "no prior restraint," the Court held that, except under extraordinary circumstances, the First Amendment prohibits government agencies from seeking to prevent newspapers or magazines from printing whatever they wish.

New State Ice Co. v. Liebmann **(1932)**   This case is most notable for Justice Brandeis's dictum that "one of the happy incidents of the federal system is that a single courageous state may, if its citizens choose, serve as a laboratory of democracy."

New York Times v. Sullivan **(1964)**   In this case, the Supreme Court held that to be deemed libelous, a story about a public official not only had to be untrue, but had to result from "actual malice" or "reckless disregard" for the truth. In practice, this standard of proof is nearly impossible to reach.

New York Times v. United States **(1971)**   In this case, the so-called *Pentagon Papers* case, the Supreme Court ruled that the government could not block publication of secret Defense Department documents that had been furnished to the *New York Times* by a liberal opponent of the Vietnam War who had obtained the documents illegally.

Palko v. Connecticut **(1937)**   The Court decided that double jeopardy was not a provision of the Bill of Rights protected at the state level. This was not reversed until 1969 in *Benton v. Maryland.*

Panama Refining Company v. Ryan **(1935)**   The Court ruled against a section of the National Industrial Recovery Act, a New Deal statute, as being an invalid delegation of legislative power to the executive branch.

Planned Parenthood of Southeastern Pennsylvania v. Casey **(1992)**   Abandoning *Roe*'s assertion of a woman's "fundamental right" to choose abortion, a bare majority of the Court redefined it as a "limited or qualified" right subject to regulation by the states, so long as the states do not impose an "undue burden" on women. Specifically, the Court upheld portions of Pennsylvania's strict abortion law that included the requirement of parental notification for minors and a twenty-four-hour waiting period.

Plessy v. Ferguson **(1896)**   The Court, in this famous case, held that the Fourteenth Amendment's "equal protection of the laws" was not violated by racial distinction as long as the "separate" facilities were "equal."

Plyler v. Doe **(1982)**   The Supreme Court invalidated on equal-protection grounds a Texas statute that withheld state funds from local school districts for the education of children who were illegal aliens and that further authorized the local school districts to deny enrollment to such children.

Pollock v. Farmers' Loan and Trust Company **(1895)**   In this case involving the unconstitutionality of an income tax of 2 percent on all incomes over $4,000, the Supreme Court declared that any direct tax as such must be apportioned in order to be valid.

Printz v. United States **(1997)**   With this ruling, the Court struck down the provision of the Brady Handgun Violence Prevention Act of 1993 that required state and local law enforcement officials to run background checks on gun purchasers. The Court found that it was unconstitutional for Congress to require state and local officials to enforce a federal law.

***Red Lion Broadcasting Co. v. FCC* (1969)** In upholding the fairness doctrine in this case, the Court differentiated between the broadcast media and the print media with regard to the First Amendment. The Court ruled that "a license permits broadcasting, but the licensee has no constitutional right to be the one who holds the license or to monopolize a radio frequency to the exclusion of his fellow citizens."

***Regents of the University of California v. Bakke* (1978)** This case addressed the issue of qualification versus minority preference. The Court held that universities could continue to take minority status into consideration because a "diverse student body" contributing to a "robust exchange of ideas" is a "constitutionally permissible goal" on which a race-conscious university admissions program may be predicated.

***Reno v. A.C.L.U.* (1997)** With this ruling, the Court repealed parts of the Communications Decency Act of 1996, extending First Amendment free speech principles to the Internet.

***Roe v. Wade* (1973)** This is the famous case that rendered unconstitutional all state laws making abortion a crime, ruling that the states could not interfere in a woman's "right to privacy" and her right to choose to terminate a pregnancy.

***Romer v. Evans* (1996)** The Court upheld the ruling of the Colorado State Supreme Court, which invalidated an amendment to the Colorado state constitution that forbade the enactment of ordinances outlawing discrimination against homosexuals.

***Rosenberger v. University of Virginia* (1995)** This case was brought by a group of students who published a Christian newspaper but who were refused funding for their publication by the University of Virginia's Student Activities Fund. The university argued that it excludes funding for religious activities because such funding would violate the principle of separation between church and state. A bare majority of the Court found that the university's policy violated the First Amendment guarantees of free speech and religious exercise and was not in itself a violation of the First Amendment's establishment clause.

***Roth v. United States* (1957)** An important obscenity case where a constitutional test for obscenity was proposed: "whether to the average person, applying contemporary community standards, the dominant theme of the material taken as a whole appeals to the prurient interests."

***St. Mary's Honor Center v. Hicks* (1993)** Hicks accused his former employer (St. Mary's Honor Center) of discharging him for racially motivated reasons, but ultimately failed to prove, as the law requires in such cases, that the adverse actions were racially motivated. A court of appeals then held that Hicks was entitled to judgment as a matter of law because he was able to prove that all of St. Mary's proffered reasons for firing him were pretextual. The Supreme Court reversed the decision, arguing that a court may not so rule in favor of judgment for the plaintiff just because it has rejected the employer's explanation of its actions.

Schechter Poultry Co. v. United States (1935) The Court declared the National Industrial Recovery Act of 1933 unconstitutional on the grounds that Congress had delegated legislative power to the executive branch without sufficient standards or guidelines for presidential discretion.

Seminole Tribe of Florida v. Florida (1996) This decision repealed a provision of the Indian Gaming Regulatory Act of 1988 that authorized Native American nations to bring suit in federal court against a state that does not in good faith negotiate a compact allowing the nation to conduct certain gaming activities. The Court found that this provision of the Act infringed on the states' sovereign immunity.

Shaw v. Hunt (1996) The Court reversed the ruling of the federal district court in North Carolina, finding that the creation of a majority black electoral district in the state was unconstitutional. Race was the primary factor considered in creating the district, which was not acceptable in this case under a proper reading of the Voting Rights Act.

Shaw v. Reno (1993) The Court ruled that a North Carolina congressional district was so irregular in its shape and clearly drawn to ensure the election of a minority representative that it violated the Fourteenth Amendment rights of white voters.

Shelley v. Kraemer (1948) In this case, the Supreme Court ruled against the widespread practice of "restrictive covenants," declaring that although private persons could sign such covenants, they could not be judicially enforced, since the Fourteenth Amendment prohibits any organ of the state, including the courts, from denying equal protection of its laws.

Shuttlesworth v. Birmingham Board of Education (1958) This decision upheld a "pupil placement" plan purporting to assign pupils on various bases, with no mention of race. This case interpreted *Brown v. Board of Education* to mean that school districts must stop explicit racial discrimination but were under no obligation to take positive steps to desegregate.

The Slaughter-House Cases (1873) The Court ruled that the federal government was under no obligation to protect the "privileges and immunities" of citizens of a particular state against arbitrary action by that state's government. This was similar to the *Barron* case, except it was thought that the Fourteenth Amendment would now incorporate the Bill of Rights, applying it to the states. The Court, however, ruled that the Fourteenth Amendment was meant to "protect Negroes as a class" and had nothing to do with individual liberties.

Smith v. Allwright (1944) The Supreme Court struck down the Southern practice of "white primaries," which legally excluded blacks from participation in the nominating process. The Court recognized that primaries could no longer be regarded as the private affairs of parties because parties were an integral aspect of the electoral process, and thus became an "agency of the State" prohibited from discriminating against blacks within the meaning of the Fifteenth Amendment.

Steel Seizure Case See *Youngstown Sheet and Tube Co. v. Sawyer.*

Swann v. Charlotte-Mecklenburg Board of Education (1971) This case involved the most important judicial extension of civil rights in education after 1954. The Court held that state-imposed desegregation could be brought about by busing, and under certain limited circumstances even racial quotas could be used as the "starting point in shaping a remedy to correct past constitutional violations."

Sweatt v. Painter (1950) The Court ruled in favor of a black student who refused to go to the Texas law school for blacks, arguing that it was inferior to the state school for whites. Although the Court still did not confront the "separate but equal" rule in this case, it did question whether any segregated facility could be equal.

Turner Broadcasting, Inc. v. FCC (1994) The Court upheld the 1992 Cable Television Act's "must carry" provision, which requires cable television systems to carry some local commercial and public broadcast stations, on the grounds that the act was not a violation of the First Amendment.

United States v. Curtiss-Wright Export Co. (1936) In this case the Court held that Congress may delegate a degree of discretion to the president in foreign affairs that might violate the separation of powers if it were in a domestic arena.

United States v. Darby Lumber Company (1941) This case upheld the constitutionality of the Fair Labor Standards Act of 1938, which made it unlawful to ship interstate commerce goods produced in violation of employment standards set by the law.

United States v. Lopez (1995) In this 5-to-4 decision, the Court struck down a federal law banning the possession of a gun near a school. This was the first limitation in almost sixty years on Congress's "interstate commerce" authority.

United States v. Morrison (2000) This 5-to-4 decision invalidated part of the 1994 Violence Against Women Act, calling it "an unconstitutional exercise" of congressional power to allow certain gender discrimination lawsuits. The decision limited federal power and shows the Court's tendency toward strict scrutiny.

United States v. Nixon (1974) The Court declared unconstitutional President Nixon's refusal to surrender subpoenaed tapes as evidence in a criminal prosecution. The Court argued that executive privilege did not extend to data in presidential files or tapes bearing upon criminal prosecution.

United States v. Pink (1942) The Court ruled that executive agreements have the same legal status as treaties, despite the fact that they do not require the "advice and consent" of the Senate.

United Steelworkers v. Weber (1979) In rejecting the claim of a white employee who had been denied a place in a training program in which half the spots were reserved for black employees, the Supreme Court claimed that Title VII of the Civil Rights Act of 1964 did not apply to affirmative action programs voluntarily established by private companies.

Wabash, St. Louis and Pacific Railway Company v. Illinois (1886) The Supreme Court struck down a state law prohibiting rate discrimination by a railroad, arguing that the route of an interstate railroad could not be subdivided into its separate state segments for purposes of regulation. In response to the need for some form of regulation, Congress passed the Interstate Commerce Act of 1887, creating the Interstate Commerce Commission (ICC), the first federal administrative agency.

Wards Cove Packing, Inc. v. Atonio (1989) The Court held that the burden of proof of unlawful discrimination should be shifted from the defendant (the employer) to the plaintiff (the person claiming to be the victim of discrimination).

Webster v. Reproductive Health Services (1989) In upholding a Missouri law that restricted the use of public medical facilities for abortion, the Court opened the way for states to again limit the availability of abortions.

Wickard v. Filburn (1942) In this case, the Supreme Court established the "cumulative effect" principle. The Court held that Congress could control a farmer's production of wheat for home consumption because the cumulative effect of home consumption of wheat by many farmers might reasonably be thought to alter the supply-and-demand relationships of the interstate commodity market.

Wiener v. United States (1958) Pursuant to *Humphrey's*, the Court ruled that the president did not have unrestrained power to remove an executive official from office.

Worcester v. Georgia (1832) The Court ruled that states could not pass laws affecting federally recognized Indian nations, and therefore, Georgia had no right to trespass on Cherokee lands without their assent. To which President Andrew Jackson is reported to have replied, "John Marshall has made his decision, now let him enforce it."

Youngstown Sheet and Tube Co. v. Sawyer (1952) This case is also known as the *Steel Seizure* case. During the Korean War, when the United Steelworkers threatened to go on strike, President Truman seized the mills and placed them under military operation. He argued he had inherent power to prevent a strike that would interfere with the war. The Court ruled against him, however, saying that presidential powers must be authorized by statute and did not come from anything inherent in the presidency.

Index

bureaus *(continued)*
   see also bureaucracy, federal
Burger Court, 127, 128
   on gender discrimination,
      142–43, 144
Burke, Richard L., 542*n*
Burlington Industries v. Ellerth,
   144*n*
Burnes, Tom, 563*n*
Burnham, Walter Dean, 425*n*,
      476*n*, 501
Burns, Nancy, 90*n*
Burr, Aaron, 433–34
Burrell, Barbara C., 169*n*, 173*n*
Bush, George H. W., 248, 252,
      258, 442, 475, 561
   administration of, 204, 245,
      301
   appointments of, 354
   assassination attempt on, 363
   cabinet of, 248
   on civil rights, 148
   congressional relations of, 215
   court appointments by, 347,
      350, 354, 413*n*
   foreign policy of, 224–25, 226
   grants-in-aid reduced by, 97
   judicial appointments of,
      325–26
   new federalism and, 97
   news conferences held by, 253
   1988 election of, *see* elections
      of 1988
   1992 campaign of, *see*
      elections of 1992
   Persian Gulf War and, 26,
      224, 226
   presidency under, 224–25
   vetoes by, 199, 230*n*
Bush, George W., 84, 182, 204,
      251, 258, 351, 376,
      413*n*, 469, 475
   administration of, 182, 204,
      301
   approval ratings of, 364, 384
   bureaucratic reform and, 302
   as "compassionate
      conservative," 372
   Congress and, 226
   in elections of 2000, 203,
      316–17, 327–28, 348,
      369–70, 376, 396–98,
      441–47, 448, 454, 476,
      527, 542
   interest groups and, 539
   judicial appointments of,
      326–27
   media and, 562–63, 568,
      569–70
   as president, 492, 539, 551,
      570
   public opinion and, 259–60
   religious groups and, 524

   tax program of, 492, 562–63,
      570
   and war against terrorism,
      226, 259, 302, 322, 364,
      384, 492, 568
Bush, Jeb, 495
Bush v. Gore, 327, 348
Bush v. Vera, 432
business interests, judiciary used
      by, 532
Business Roundtable, 509
busing, desegregation and,
      139–41, 403
Butler, David, 174*n*
Butler, Pierce, 44
by-product theory, 18–19
Byrd, Robert, 196, 207*n*
Byrnes, James F., 133

CAB (Civil Aeronautics Board),
      295
cabinet, U.S., 227, 244, 265
   distrust of, 244
   government by, 244
   "inner," 244
cabinet government, 244
   parliamentary, 262–63
   reshuffling of, 264
Cable News Network (CNN),
      554–55, 556, 558–59
Cable News Network v. Noriega,
      559*n*
Cain, Bruce, 174*n*
Caldeira, Gregory A., 337*n*
California, 170, 174, 487
   "Proposition 209" of, 149, 404
California, University of, 146
Calvert, Randall, 205*n*
Cambridge, Mass., 429
Cameron, Charles, 232*n*, 235,
      251*n*
campaign contributions, 447–48,
      501
   from candidates' personal
      resources, 447, 449, 456
   corporate, 447, 450
   democracy and, 452–53
   independent, 447, 448, 449,
      450
   "issue advocacy" and, 449,
      452, 456
   nonprofit groups and, 450
   public, 450–51, 456
   reform of, 451–53, 456, 499,
      523, 537–38, 541–43
   sources of, 447–51, 456
   stealth donors and, 450
campaigns, political, *see* political
      campaigns
Campbell, Angus, 166*n*, 402*n*,
      421*n*
Cannon, Carl, 395*n*
Cannon, Daniel C., 395*n*

Cannon, Joe, 25
Cantril, Albert H., 391*n*, 407
capital punishment, 84
Caplan, Lincoln, 340*n*
Capone, Al, 289
Cappella, Joseph N., 561*n*
Caraley, Demetrios, 109
Cardozo, Benjamin, 122
career administrators, at State
      Department, 292
Carmines, Edward G., 376–77,
      458
Carney, Eliza Newlin, 107*n*
Carney, James, 383*n*
Carter, Jimmy:
   administration of, 225
   on bureaucracy, 272, 286,
      287, 301
   draft evaders granted amnesty
      by, 224
   media and, 253
   1976 election of, 249, 301
   vetoes of, 230*n*
Case Act (1972), 209
"case" or "controversy," 336
cash benefits, 298
Casper, Jonathan D., 135*n*, 136*n*
categoric grants-in-aid, 92–93
Catholics, 371
caucuses:
   congressional, 179–80,
      193–94, 205*n*, 213
   nominating, 238–39, 250,
      466, 484–85, 501
causes of action, 65, 154
CBN (Christian Broadcasting
      Network), 384–85
CBO (Congressional Budget
      Office), 96, 193, 305
CBS, 382, 389, 554, 556, 559
CEA (Council of Economic
      Advisers), 244, 246
censorship, 368
Census:
   of 1980, 174
   of 2000, 174
Central Intelligence Agency (CIA),
      224, 247, 285, 302, 303
CEQ (Council on Environmental
      Quality), 246
certiorari, 140, 338, 341, 342,
      343, 356
Chafee, John, 196–97
Challenger, 570
Chamber of Commerce, 385,
      487, 528, 539
Chambers, William N., 501
charity, *see* welfare state
Charlotte, N.C., integration in,
      140
charter schools, 90
checks and balances, 44, 50–51,
      58, 66, 99–100, 107

see also separation of powers
Cheney, Dick, 181, 248–49, 442
Chicago, Burlington and Quincy Railroad Company v. Chicago, 120n
Chicago, Ill., boss rule in, 470
Chicago, University of, 391
child labor laws, 82
child support, 383
China, People's Republic of, 75n, 225, 385
  local government in, 88n
  student uprising in, 88n
Chong, Dennis, 153n
Christian Broadcasting Network (CBN), 384–85
Christian Coalition, 257, 385, 523–24, 542–43
Christian Science Monitor, 555
Chubb, Jerome, 428n
CIA, see Central Intelligence Agency
Cigler, Allan J., 545
CIO (Congress of Industrial Organizations), 256
Citadel, 143–44
Citizens for the American Way, 344
citizenship:
  dual, 118–19, 153–54
  single national, 119
Citizens to Preserve Overton Park, Inc. v. Volpe, 353n
City of Boerne v. Flores, 83, 103n
Civil Aeronautics Board (CAB), 295
civil law, 318, 319–20, 328, 334–35
civil liberties, 66, 117–29, 337, 347
  civil rights vs., 115–17, 153
  as criterion of exclusion, 134
  defined, 115, 153
  nationalization of, 120–22
  police and, 124
  time line on, 110–11
  see also Bill of Rights
civil rights, 66, 84, 98, 125, 129–55, 333, 337, 347, 354, 509, 513
  civil liberties vs., 115–17, 153
  conditions of grants for, 95
  defined, 116, 153, 155
  demonstrations for, 134–35
  legislative guarantees of, see *specific acts*
  opinions on, 151, 376–77
  purpose of, 129
  state laws and, 82–83, 333
  time line on, 110–11
  treaty power and, 131
  universalization of, 142–56

see also African Americans; civil rights movement; discrimination; racial discrimination; racial integration; school desegregation; segregation
Civil Rights Act (1875), 82, 83, 120, 130
Civil Rights Act (1964), 135, 139
  1982 Amendment to, 174
  Title II, 141n
  Title VI, 140
  Title VII, 141–42, 144, 532
Civil Rights Act (1965), 135
Civil Rights Act (1991), 147, 342, 533
Civil Rights Attorney Fees Act (1976), 353
Civil Rights Cases, 120n, 129
Civil Rights Commission, 139
civil rights movement, 82–83, 149, 291–92, 354, 522
  as collective action, 152–53
  government and political action in, 137
  media's shaping of, 566
  motivation in, 152–53
  polarization of, 150
  Supreme Court as producer of, 135–36
civil service, 493
  affirmative action in, 146
  reform of, 471
Civil Service Reform Act (1978), 301
Civil War, U.S., 9, 59, 65, 79, 81, 82, 105, 119, 211, 239, 368, 472–74, 475, 478
Clark, Dick, 526
Clark, Timothy, 497n
class action suits, 142, 352, 353–54
class system, U.S., 256
Clawson, Dan, 545
Clay, Henry, 25, 434
Cleveland, Grover, 434
Clinton, Bill, 249, 252, 261, 469, 476, 568
  acceptance speech of, 7
  administrative reforms of, 276, 301–2, 310
  appointments of, 128, 244, 245, 325–26, 350–51
  approval rating of, 220–21, 260–61, 363–64, 382–83, 491–92
  budgets proposed by, 212–13, 383, 384, 491
  "bully pulpit" strategy of, 261
  bureaucracy and, 276, 310
  cabinet and staff of, 244

  campaign finance reform of, 258
  centrist strategy of, 249, 255–56, 445–46, 475
  Congress and, 199, 204, 207, 209, 212–13, 215, 254–56, 301–2, 490, 491
  conservative assaults on, 199, 211–13, 550–51, 561
  "Contract with America" and, 66
  as Democratic party leader, 490, 491
  economic program of, 244, 255–56
  education policies of, 286–87
  foreign policy of, 234
  fund raising efforts of, 220
  Gore chosen by, 249
  health care reform and, 202, 207, 255, 257, 384, 400, 491, 543
  homosexual rights and, 145, 234, 534–35
  impeachment of, 103, 168, 210, 212, 220, 234, 256, 261, 364, 385, 392, 474, 562
  judiciary and, 128, 147–48, 325–26
  legislative initiatives of, 233–34
  media and, 253, 413, 440, 551, 561, 562, 569
  military and, 294
  motor voter bill and, 427
  new federalism and, 97
  1992 election of, see elections of 1992
  1996 re-election of, see elections of 1996
  policy successes of, 255–56, 257, 276, 465, 493
  political difficulties of, 220, 255–56, 260–61, 385, 474, 491, 528, 551, 554, 561, 562
  public opinion and, 220–21, 257–58, 260–61, 363–64, 376, 382–83, 392, 474, 476, 491–92, 493
  staff cuts of, 245
  tobacco industry and, 522
  trade policy of, 491
  2000 election and, 235, 441–42, 445–47, 492
  veto power and, 230n, 232
  welfare reform and, 384
Clinton, Bill, administration of, 215, 524
  on affirmative action, 147–49
  university research and, 386

Index

Gallup Polls, 388, 389, 391, 393, 394, 397
gambling, 83
Gamm, Gerald, 184n
Gans, Herbert, 559n, 574
Garcia v. San Antonio Metropolitan Transit Authority, 240n
Garrity, W. Arthur, 140, 354
Garrow, David, 126n, 156, 566n
gatekeeping, 21, 203
gay and lesbian movement, 145
  see also homosexuals
Gelman, Andrew, 422n
gender discrimination, 84, 142–44
  see also feminism; women
gender gap, 371
General Accounting Office, 193, 305, 306
General Electric, 528, 556
General Motors, 86, 528
Genêt, Edmond, 224
George, John, 369n
Georgia, 41, 42, 351–52, 432
Gephardt, Richard, 180, 192, 208
Gephardt health care reform bill, 192
Germany, Nazi, 8, 378
Germany, reunified, 261
Gerry, Elbridge, 430
gerrymandering, 174, 348, 430–31
  benign, 431–32
Gibbons, Thomas, 80
Gibbons v. Ogden, 80–82
Gideon v. Wainwright, 124, 334, 335
Gilmore, Jim, 469
Gilmour, John, 199n
Gingrich, Newt, 183, 309, 376, 387, 567–68
  fall of, 476, 567–68
Ginsberg, Benjamin, 355n, 402n, 407, 416n, 458, 479n, 485n, 498n, 557n
  fall of, 476
Ginsburg, Douglas, 209
Ginsburg, Ruth Bader, 128, 316, 345, 348
Gitlin, Todd, 566n
Gitlow v. New York, 121n
Glaser, Comstock, 279n
Glendon, Mary Ann, 156
Glenn, John, 570
globalization:
  economics and, 296
  of media, 368
Goals 2000, 286–87
Goldberg, Arthur, 124
Goldwater, Barry, 205n
Goosetree, Robert E., 230n

GOP, *see* Republican party
Gore, Albert, Jr., 248, 302, 376, 449, 541, 568
  in elections of 2000, 248, 316, 327, 348, 369–70, 376, 396–97, 434, 438, 441–47, 448, 449, 454, 474–75, 492, 527, 568
  enhanced status of, 249
  as vice-president, 249
Gosnell, Harold, 420n
government:
  agencies, 13–14
  aristocratic, 55–56
  authoritarian, 8–9
  cabinet, 244
  changing role of, 79–91
  coalition, 262–63
  coercion and, 9–10
  complexity of, 7–8
  control and, 8–13
  defined, 8
  divided, 251, 261, 264–65
  foundations of, 9–10
  freedom and, 6–7, 8–12
  growth of, 6–7, 27
  local, *see* local governments
  of multiparty majority, 264–65
  necessity for, 8–12
  parliamentary, *see* parliamentary systems
  politics and, 12–13, 137
  popular, 416
  presidential, *see* presidential government
  republican, 56
  of single-party minority, 264–65
  state, *see* state governments
  unified, 263–64
government, U.S.:
  citizens' relationship with, 54–56, 74, 115–17
  as commercial republic, 77–82
  divided, 103, 104, 106, 261, 264–65, 478, 490
  domestic policies of, 77–79
  downsizing of, 309–12
  economy and, *see* economy, U.S.
  enlisting public support for, 54, 55, 377–81
  expansion of, 64, 82–83, 521–22
  federalism and, 76–78
  founding of, 29–66
  growth of, 299–305
  as legislative government, 235–40, 241–42
  limitations on, 49–52, 56–58, 64, 74, 77–82, 105–7, 120–21

media and, 552–59, 568–70, 572–73, 574
mythology of, 31–32, 42
New Deal expansion of, 239–40
police power of, 239
political parties and, 489–91
as presidential, 221–22, 238–42, 300
private sector vs., 364
public ignorance about, 376, 401, 402–3
reinvention of, 301–2
shutdown of, 567–68
spending cuts in, 272
state vs., 76–79, 82–87, 106, 118–19
time line on, 30
trust in, 380–81
Graber, Doris, 574
Gracey, Harry L., 378–79
Gramm-Rudman-Hollings Act (1985), 102n, 240n
grand juries, 122
grants-in-aid, 91–93, 109
  categoric, 92–93
grass-roots lobbying, 202, 524, 534–36, 542–43
grass-roots populism, 384, 536
Gray, Virginia, 471n
Great Britain, 263, 557
Great Compromise (Connecticut Compromise) (1787), 41–42, 44
Great Depression, 6, 239, 242, 474, 475
Great Society, 211
Green, Donald P., 153n
Greenberg, Jack, 156
Greenblatt, Alan, 483n
Greenhouse, Linda, 84n, 86n, 149n, 316n, 348n, 352n, 355n, 432n, 533n
Green party, 446, 481
Greenstein, Fred I., 418n
Gregory, Charles O., 142n
Grenke, Janet M., 203n
Gribbin, August, 391n
Griffin, Patrick, 527
Griffin v. Prince Edward County School Board, 138n
Griggs v. Duke Power Company, 142n, 147n
Grimshaw, William J., 501
Griswold v. Connecticut, 124n, 333, 531n
Grodzins, Morton, 94, 109
Groseclose, Timothy, 233n
group rights, as alien to American tradition, 150
groups, *see* interest groups
Grover, William F., 230n
Grunwald, Michael, 6n

power of, 567–70, 572–74
presidential use of, 252–54, 265, 568–69
print, *see* magazines, news; newspapers; press
protest and, 565–66
public opinion and, 382, 387, 388, 389, 574
regulation of, 557–58
responsibility and, 552, 572–74
sources and, 561–62
time line on, 548–49
types of, 553–55
upper class favored by, 563–64, 574
median voter theorem, 440–41
Medicaid, 297, 298
Medicare, 7, 297, 383, 446, 527
Meltsner, Arnold, 287*n*
Merida, Kevin, 173*n*
merit system, for administrative appointments, 492
Merkl, Peter, 501
Mexican-American Legal Defense Fund, 342
Meyer, Michael J., 117*n*
Meyerson, Allen R., 207*n*
Michigan, 86, 150, 543
Milbanks, Dana, 496*n*
military, court system of, 321–22
military, U.S., 37
    cuts in, 276, 292–94, 309
    growth of, 276–78
    hierarchy in, 292–93
    homosexuals in, 145, 234, 534–35
    industry relationship with, 294
    pork-barrel politics and, 294, 309
    president and, 223–24, 227, 228
    women in, 143–44
militias, survivalist, 292
Milkis, Sidney M., 267, 501
Mill, John Stuart, 416
Miller, Dan, 172–73
Miller, Gary J., 280*n*
Miller, Warren, 166*n*, 402*n*
Miller v. Johnson, 174, 337, 432
Milliken v. Bradley, 139–40
minimum wage, 96, 240*n*
ministerial portfolios, 262
Minnesota, 127*n*, 395, 453
Minnesota Star Tribune, 395
minorities:
    congressional representation of, 337, 431–32
    see also civil rights; *specific minority groups*
minority leaders, 213
    in House, 180–81, 206
    in Senate, 181, 204, 206

Minow, Martha, 117*n*, 156
Miranda rule, 124, 335
Miranda v. Arizona, 124, 335
Mississippi, 148, 431
Missouri, 85, 86, 89, 127*n*
Missouri Compromise (1820), 475
Missouri ex rel. Gaines v. Canada, 131*n*
Missouri v. Holland, 131*n*
Missouri v. Jenkins, 141, 337
Mitchell, Andrea, 550
mixed regimes, 50
Mobil Oil, 528
Moe, Terry M., 243*n*, 280*n*, 546
Molten Metal Technology, Inc., 539–41
Mondale, Walter, 253, 445
Monroe, James, 221
Montana, 89, 176
Montesquieu, 49, 98
Moore, W. John, 83*n*
moral hazard, 414
Moran v. McDonough, 354*n*
Morin, Richard, 363*n*, 364*n*, 383*n*, 392*n*, 401*n*
Morris, Dick, 257, 383, 445
Morris, Dwight, 172*n*
Morrison, Samuel E., 39*n*
Morrison v. Olson, 227*n*
Motion Picture Association of America, 506
Motor-Voter Act (1993), 427, 453
Moynihan, Daniel Patrick, 539
MTV, 556, 562
Mueller, John, 407
multilateral collective security treaties, *see* treaties
Murdoch, Rupert, 556
Murphy, Walter F., 336*n*, 352*n*
Mushroom Caucus, 193
Music, Kimberley, 197*n*
Myers v. U.S., 227*n*

NAACP, *see* National Association for the Advancement of Colored People
NAACP v. Alabama ex rel. Patterson, 124*n*
Nacos, Brigitte L., 574
Nader, Ralph, 446, 465, 479, 481, 523
Nader Report, 532
Nagel, Jack H., 232*n*
Nakamura, David, 143*n*
NAM (National Association of Manufacturers), 509, 521, 528, 539
Nathan, Richard, 301*n*
National Abortion and Reproductive Rights League, 449

National Aeronautics and Space Administration (NASA), 285, 570
National Assembly, French, 175
National Association for the Advancement of Colored People (NAACP), 124, 132, 133, 136, 342, 532, 543
    Legal Defense Fund of, 132, 136, 342
National Association of Manufacturers (NAM), 509, 521, 528, 539
National Economic Council, 244
National Education Association (NEA), 272, 287
National Endowment for the Arts, 207
National Environmental Policy Act, 353
National Federation of Independent Business (NFIB), 524, 543
National Guard, 138, 228
National Industrial Recovery Act (1933), 102*n*, 225*n*, 242*n*
nationalism, 54, 377–80
National Labor Relations Act (Wagner Act) (1935), 240
National Labor Relations Board (NLRB), 240
National Labor Relations Board v. Jones & Laughlin Steel Corporation, 123*n*, 240
National League of Cities v. Usery, 240*n*
National Opinion Research Center (NORC), 391
National Organization for Women (NOW), 385, 523, 534
National Partnership for Reinventing Government, 302
National Performance Review (NPR), 276, 301–2, 310
National Public Radio (NPR), 555
National Review, 495
National Rifle Association (NRA), 196, 449, 508, 519, 524, 543
National Security Agency (NSA), 224
National Security Council (NSC), 224, 244, 246–47, 303
national standards, setting of, 95–96
national supremacy, 48, 68, 80–82
National Taxpayers Union, 524
Native Americans, 37, 83
Nava, Michael, 156

police patrol method of,
307–8
Owen, Diana, 574

Packwood, Robert, 527
PACs, *see* political action
committees
Page, Benjamin I., 402–3, 402*n*,
403*n*, 407
Paget, Karen, 458
Paige, Connie, 385*n*
Palfrey, Thomas, 423*n*
Palko v. Connecticut, 122, 123,
124
Palley, Marian Lief, 109
Palmer, John L., 301*n*
Palmer, Kenneth T., 92*n*
Palmer, R. R., 69
Panama, U.S. invasion of, 226
Panama Refining Co. v. Ryan,
102*n*, 242*n*
Paraguay, 225*n*
Paramount Studios, 556
pardons, granting of, 224
Parent, William A., 117*n*
Parenti, Michael, 559*n*
parliamentary systems, 107, 162,
237
coalition government and,
262–63
divided government and, 261,
264–65
government formation process
in, 262–65
principal-agent relationship
in, 262
specialization of labor in,
261–62
participation, political, 415–21
decline of, 453–56
education and, 417–21, 427,
564
elections as limit on, 415–16,
455–56
encouragement of, 416–21
party system and, 419–21,
453–56, 487
see also elections; suffrage;
voting
parties, political, *see* political
parties
party committees, 466, 468–70
party conventions, nomination
by, 433–34, 435, 484,
485, 501
party discipline, congressional,
203–8, 205*n*, 213–15,
254–55
and access to floor, 205, 206,
213
leadership resources and,
203–8
party votes, 204

patents, government policy on,
77, 532
Paterson, William, 41
path dependency, principle of,
26–27
patronage policy:
direct, 170–71
as tool of management, 243
see also public policy
peak associations, 509
Pear, Robert, 192*n*
Peele, Gillian, 385*n*
Peirce, Neal, 524*n*
Penn & Schoen, 383
Pennsylvania, 41, 127
Revolutionary radicalism in,
38
Pentagon, *see* Defense
Department, U.S.
Pentagon Papers case, 558
Pepper, Claude, 516–17
per curiam, 340, 342
Perot, H. Ross, 479, 481
Perry, H. W., Jr., 341*n*, 358
Persian Gulf War, 26, 224, 226,
278, 382
media coverage of, 556
Personal Responsibility and
Work Opportunity
Reconciliation Act
(1996), 84, 97, 299, 383
personnel interchange, access
gained through, 544
Peterson, Paul E., 110
petitioning, *see* lobbying
Petracca, Mark P., 546
Pfiffner, James P., 267
Philip Morris Tobacco, 523
Phillips, Kevin, 399, 427*n*
phone banks, 494, 497, 501
Physicians for Social
Responsibility, 385, 523
Pianin, Eric, 7*n*, 168*n*
Pink, United States v., 209*n*, 225
Piven, Frances Fox, 458
*Planned Parenthood of
Southeastern
Pennsylvania v. Casey*,
127
plea bargains, 321
Plessy, Homer, 130
Plessy v. Ferguson, 123, 130,
131, 133
Plunkitt, George Washington, 23
pluralistic politics, 508,
543–44
Plyler v. Doe, 343*n*
pocket veto, 230
police power, 81, 289
civil liberties and, 124
policy making, 245
political change and, 144
policy moderation, 441

political action committees
(PACs), 169, 183, 203,
448, 496
campaign contributions made
by, 447, 451–53, 456,
536–42
debate on, 541–42
defined, 15*n*
proposed abolition of, 541–42
soft money and, 541–42
spending by, 537
"stealth," 542
women candidates and, 169
see also interest groups
political campaigns:
activism and, 542–43
candidates and, 168–69,
482–83, 496–97, 499
candidate selection process
and, 250, 482–83
federal regulation of financing
of, 220, 258, 449,
451–53, 498–99
high-tech, 493–96, 501
"instant organization" of, 497
"issues campaigns" and, 449
media scrutiny and, 483
money spent on, 415, 483,
496–97
as "permanent," 258, 261
soft money and, 449–50,
451–53, 456
volunteers and, 497
see also campaign
contributions; elections;
specific elections
political entrepreneurs, 19*n*,
516–17
political ideology, 365, 371–73,
374–76, 383
political machines, 462, 470–71
political participation, *see*
participation, political
political parties, 459–502
as agencies of State, 131
as basis of political
organization, 498–99
changing significance of, 463,
488
coalitions in, 465, 478–79
collective action and, 464–65
committees of, 466, 468–70
conflicts within, 490
Congress and, 203–8,
489–91, 501
congressional campaign
committees and, 469
congressional leadership and,
179–84
consultants and, 536
contemporary politics and,
498–99
contributions to, 469, 471, 522

bureaucracy and, 306–7
Congress and, 66, 107,
    197–99, 207, 209,
    210–13, 222–23,
    225–26, 228–34,
    236–44, 249–52, 294,
    295, 300, 433–35
constitutional provisions for,
    46–47, 66, 68, 222–34,
    265
deception and, 261
and delegation of power,
    242–43
Democratic dominance of,
    476–78
democratized, 249–50
dual nature of, 220–21
early weakness of, 101,
    237–38, 265
enhancement of, 241–42
executive appointments and,
    227–28
executive orders power of,
    234
in foreign policy, *see* foreign
    policy, U.S.
formal resources of, 223–25,
    243–49
as imperial, 225–26
independence of, 46–47,
    238–39
informal resources of, 249–61
institutional, *see* Executive
    Office of the President
judicial power of, 223, 224
judiciary and, 147–48,
    325–28, 349–52
in legislative process, 212,
    215, 227–34, 300
managerial, 228–34, 250–52,
    300–303
"mandate" and, 249–50
military policy and, 223–24,
    227, 228, 265
New Deal and, 239–40, 256,
    300
as permanent campaign, 261
political parties and, 101–2,
    254–56, 265, 432–35,
    489, 491–92
popular base of, 220–21, 233,
    235, 238, 250, 257–61,
    265, 300, 501
press and, 252–54, 571–72
Republican dominance of,
    475
rise of, 235–42
strength of, 44
success and failure of, 235–36
supremacy of, 211
time line on, 218–19
veto power of, 197–99,
    232–33, 253

see also executive branch;
    Executive Office of the
    President
president:
    as chief clerk, 221
    as chief executive, 221,
        226–28, 300–303
    as commander-in-chief,
        223–24
    as head of government, 223,
        226–34, 265
    as head of state, 223–26, 265
    indirect election of, 99, 223
    as legislator, *see* legislative
        process
    see also executive branch
presidential approval ratings,
    258–61
    domestic issues and, 259–61
    international events and,
        259–60
Presidential Election Campaign
    Fund, 450
presidential government,
    226–34, 241–42
    cabinet in, 244, 265
    EOP in, 245–48, 265
    patronage in, 243
    rise of, 300
    vice presidency in, 248–49
    White House staff in, 244–45,
        265
President's Committee on
    Administrative
    Management, 300
President's Committee on Civil
    Rights, 130–31
press, 553, 554
    freedom of, 121–22, 558–59
    libel suits and, 558–59
    presidency and, 571–72
    public opinion in, 455–56
    see also magazines, news;
        media; newspapers
pressure groups, *see* interest
    groups; lobbying
primary elections, 421, 429, 484,
    485–86, 492, 501, 568
    campaigning costs of, 486
    closed, 485
    direct, 492
    open, 485
    see also elections
prime ministers, 262
principles:
    interests vs., 32–33, 74
    wielding of, 53–54
Printz, United States v., 83, 103n
prisoners' dilemma game, 512–13
Prison Litigation Reform Act
    (1996), 352
prisons, 278
    for-profit, 90

Pritchett, C. Herman, 332n,
    348n
privacy, right to, 124–25, 333,
    348
    marital, 124–25
    women and, 124, 531
private bills, 171
private sector vs. government,
    364
privatization, 90
    downsizing and, 310
privileges and immunities,
    86–87, 120–22
probability sampling, 390–91
procedural controls, 307
procedural limits, 8, 116
product liability, 199
product quality and
    standardization, 532
professional lobbies, 523
Progressive era, 479, 492–93
Progressive party, 479, 481
Prohibition, 60, 64
project grants, 92
property interests, 65, 68, 77,
    117
    Constitution and, 40
    Fourteenth Amendment and,
        120
    governmental support and,
        377, 378, 380
    protection of, 11–12, 53, 128,
        524
property-rights movement, 5
"Proposition 201," 487
"Proposition 209," 149, 404
protectionism, 53
protective tariffs, *see* tariffs
Protestantism, 371
public accommodations,
    discrimination in, 141n
Public Affairs Council, 385
Public Broadcasting System
    (PBS), 555
public goods, providing of, 12
public hearings, 304
public interest groups, 151, 296,
    341–43, 385, 508,
    522–23, 563
    see also interest groups
public law, 318, 320, 329
public opinion, 361–407
    attitude and, 365
    debate on, 402–3
    definition of, 364–65
    education and, 376, 377,
        378–79, 380
    elites and, 384
    formation of, 374–76
    gender differences and, 371
    governmental manipulation of,
        382–84
    government policy and, 401–5

public opinion *(continued)*
  importance of, 364–65
  income differences and, 376,
    386–87, 405
  marketplace of, *see*
    marketplace of ideas
  measurement of, 387–96
  media and, 376–77, 382, 387,
    388, 389
  nationalism and, 377–80
  participation and co-optation
    in, 379–80
  political ideology and, 365,
    371–73, 374–75, 383
  political leaders and,
    376–77
  politics vs. logic in, 373,
    374–75
  presidency and, 220–21
  as presidential resource,
    257–61
  in press, 455–56
  private groups and, 384–87
  private property and, 377,
    378, 380
  rallying effect and, 259–60
  regional variations and, 557
  shaping of, 377–87
  socioeconomic differences
    and, 370–71
  time line on, 362–63
public policy, 77, 85, 86
  on civil rights, *see* civil rights
  implementation of, 299
  lobbying and, 525–31
  political parties and, 465,
    489–90, 498
  state control over, 96–98
  welfare, *see* welfare state
  see also specific policies
public relations:
  cost of, 497–98
  professional, 384, 495, 501
  public opinion and, 381, 382
public services, 89–90
public trial, right to, 123*n*
public works, 85, 89–90
Publius, *see* Hamilton, Alexander
Pulitzer, Joseph, 560
"pupil placement" laws, 138
  see also education
purposive benefits, 515–16
push polling, 392

Quayle, J. Danforth, 448
Queenan, Joe, 386
quotas, 155
  racial, 139, 146–51
  see also affirmative action
quota sampling, 390

race, as criterion of exclusion,
  130, 134

racial discrimination, 82–83, 85,
  130–51, 152, 333, 335
  347, 348, 376–77
  electoral redistricting and, 174
  gender discrimination vs.,
    142–44
  after World War II, 130–51,
    334
  see also African Americans;
    civil rights; civil rights
    movement, discrimination
racial integration:
  Southern resistance to,
    132–41, 228
  in World War II, 130–31
  see also school desegregation
radio, 368, 566
  news coverage on, 554, 556
  see also broadcast media;
    media
rallies, 534
rallying effect, 259–60
Randolph, Edmund, 41, 44
Randolph, John, 25
random sampling, in polling,
  391, 406
Ratcliffe, R. G., 148*n*
Rayburn, Sam, 205*n*
Reagan, Ronald, 183, 234, 245,
  252, 258, 374, 475
  administration of, 204, 215,
    303, 340*n*, 354, 558
  on bureaucracy, 272, 286,
    301, 303
  cabinet and staff of, 245
  campaign promises fulfilled
    by, 7
  Congress and, 215
  court appointments by, 209,
    347, 350, 354
  education policies of, 286
  grants-in-aid reduced by, 93,
    97
  judicial appointments of,
    325–26, 350
  media and, 253, 558, 560
  new federalism and, 97
  1980 election of, 6–7, 183,
    249
  1984 election of, 7
  vetoes of, 230*n*
  War Powers Resolution
    violated by, 226
Reagan Revolution, 272
  critical electoral realignment
    in, 490
realists, political, 74
reapportionment, 335
rebuttal, right of, 558
recognition, power of, 206
Reconstituted Right, *see* Reagan
  Revolution; Republican
  party

Reconstruction, 210
redistricting, 174
  racial minorities and, 337
Red Lion Broadcasting Company
  v. FCC, 558
Reed, Adolph, 458
Reed, Stanley, 346
Reed, Thomas B., 25
Reform Party, 476, 481
Regents of the University of
  California v. Bakke,
  146–47
regulated federalism, 95–96
regulatory agencies, 285,
  294–96, 355, 356
regulatory policy, 95–96,
  239–40, 295–96
  public attitudes towards,
    370–71
  shrinkage of, *see* deregulation
  as technique of control, 299
  see also public policy
Rehnquist, William H., 126–28,
  141, 147*n*, 322, 326,
  345, 348
Rehnquist Court, 126–29
Reichley, A. James, 458
religion:
  extreme cults and, 292
  freedom of, 103*n*, 117, 127,
    337–38
  in public institutions, 127, 335
  Republican party and, 476,
    542–43
Religious Freedom Restoration
  Act, 103*n*
religious right, 385, 516, 524,
  534–35, 542–43
removal power, 227–28
Reno v. American Civil Liberties
  Union, 128
Report of the American Bar
  Association, 532
Report on Manufactures
  (Hamilton), 79*n*, 237
Report on Public Credit
  (Hamilton), 236–37
representation, 41–44, 53,
  163–75
  agency, 165–66
  concept of, 163–64, 201
  elections and, 168–75
  Federalists vs. Anti-
    Federalists on, 54–56
  House vs. Senate differences
    in, 166–68
  power and, 164–75, 210–13
  principle of, 75
  types of, 164–65
representatives:
  constituencies and, 55
  as delegates, 164
  as trustees, 164